Middle Egyptian

This book is a thorough introduction to the writing system of ancient Egypt and the language of hieroglyphic texts. It contains 26 lessons, exercises (with answers), a list of hieroglyphic signs, and a dictionary. It also includes a series of 25 essays on the most important aspects of ancient Egyptian history, society, religion, and literature. The combination of grammar lessons and cultural essays allows users not only to read hieroglyphic texts but also to understand them. The book gives readers the foundation they need to understand the texts on monuments and to read the great works of ancient Egyptian literature in the original. It can also serve as a complete grammatical description of the classical language of ancient Egypt for specialists in linguistics and other related fields.

James P. Allen is Curator of Egyptian Art at the Metropolitan Museum of Art in New York, and has also been a Research Associate and Lecturer in Egyptology at Yale University since 1986. He has published numerous articles on Egyptian language, religion, and history, and is the author of *The Inflection of the Verb in the Pyramid Texts* (1984) and *Genesis in Egypt: The Philosophy of Ancient Egyptian Creation Accounts* (1989).

Middle Egyptian

An Introduction to the Language and Culture of Hieroglyphs

James P. Allen

CAMBRIDGE
UNIVERSITY PRESS

PUBLISHED BY THE PRESS SYNDICATE OF THE UNIVERSITY OF CAMBRIDGE
The Pitt Building, Trumpington Street, Cambridge, United Kingdom

CAMBRIDGE UNIVERSITY PRESS
The Edinburgh Building, Cambridge CB2 2RU, UK
40 West 20th Street, New York, NY 10011–4211, USA
10 Stamford Road, Oakleigh, VIC 3166, Australia
Ruiz de Alarcón 13, 28014 Madrid, Spain
Dock House, The Waterfront, Cape Town 8001, South Africa

http://www.cambridge.org

First published 2000
Reprinted 2000 (twice)

Printed in the United Kingdom at the University Press, Cambridge

Typeset in Bembo [AU]

A catalogue record for this book is available from the British Library

Library of Congress Cataloguing in Publication data
Allen, James P., 1945–
Middle Egyptian: an introduction to the language and culture of hieroglyphs / by James P. Allen
p. cm.
Includes bibliographical references and index.
ISBN 0 521 65312 6 (hardback)
1. Egyptian language – Grammar. I. Title.
PJ1135.A45 1999
493′.15 – dc21 99–24295
CIP

ISBN 0 521 65312 6 hardback
ISBN 0 521 77483 7 paperback

Contents

Preface

The decipherment of ancient Egyptian hieroglyphic writing is one of the great success stories of modern archeology. Before 1822, the civilization of ancient Egypt was mute and mysterious, its images bizarre and incomprehensible to a world convinced that all thought of any worth began with the ancient Greeks. Today we are able to read the ancient Egyptian texts and, more importantly, to understand a great deal of what they meant to the people who wrote them. In the process we have discovered a world of rich imagination, sophisticated thought, and profoundly moving emotion.

Despite the remarkable achievement behind this discovery, however, the language of the ancient texts remains inaccessible to all but a handful of scholars. There are any number of good and widely available translations of ancient Egyptian texts, but the same cannot be said for studies of the Egyptian language itself. Those who want to be able to read the texts for themselves, to understand the inscriptions on monuments in Egypt or in museums, or simply to learn a fascinating ancient language for its own sake soon discover that this is no easy task. Though grammars of ancient Egyptian do exist, they are usually intended as reference works for specialists and are difficult for anyone but the most dedicated student to learn from. Most of them are also obsolete in some respects, reflecting an understanding of Egyptian grammar that is outdated or incomplete. A number of excellent grammars for the beginning student have appeared in recent years, but these are generally in languages other than English or are not easily accessible.

The present book has been written to address this shortcoming. It is designed to be usable by interested nonspecialists who want to learn Egyptian on their own as well as by students following a course of professional instruction. Its lessons and exercises offer a solid foundation in Middle Egyptian, the language of most hieroglyphic inscriptions and the classical speech of ancient Egyptian literature.

Learning Egyptian presents a number of problems not encountered in studying most other languages. The culture of ancient Egypt differs from our own in more than just its language. Its texts are full of terms and concepts that have no direct counterpart in the modern world. To help you understand these, each grammatical lesson in this book is also complemented by a short essay on some aspect of Egyptian society and thought. This foundation will make it possible for you not only to translate the hieroglyphic texts but also to understand what they have to say.

Ancient Egyptian is a dead language, and our knowledge of it is restricted to the limited number of its texts that have managed to survive. We learn Egyptian, therefore, not as a means of communication but as a tool for reading those texts. The purpose of this book is to enable you to understand the grammar and content of Middle Egyptian texts and not — or only accidentally — to teach you how to write your own Egyptian sentences. The exercises in each lesson and the accompanying dictionary in the back of the book therefore go in one direction only, from Egyptian to English.

As you will discover in the course of the first few lessons, the hieroglyphic writing system does not represent very well what Middle Egyptian was like as a spoken language. For that reason, we cannot usefully approach ancient Egyptian as we might other languages, learning the grammar through phrases and sentences designed around the scenarios of everyday life. Because hieroglyphs usually do not reveal the actual form of a word, we cannot rely just on the written form to tell us what a word means. We also have to pay close attention to syntax: how words are put together into the phrases and sentences of Egyptian texts.

In learning Middle Egyptian, therefore, we also need to learn the mechanics of syntax — concepts such as predicates, adverbial modifiers, and subordinate clauses. Experience has shown that beginning students often find these concepts a major hurdle to learning Egyptian — and conversely, once they are understood, a significant aid to reading Egyptian texts. For that reason, the lessons in this book devote a good deal of time to the discussion of syntax. Grammatical terms are defined when they are first introduced, and syntactic constructions are illustrated with examples from English as well as Egyptian. This approach should make it possible for you to perceive syntax as less of a barrier and more of a tool in your efforts to learn Middle Egyptian.

Studies of Egyptian syntax have been dominated historically by two major schools of grammatical theory. The present book subscribes to neither of these exclusively. The emphasis in these lessons is on a practical approach to recognizing Egyptian forms and constructions, using terms and analyses from both schools of thought together with more recent advances in our understanding of how the language works. Discussions of the different grammatical theories are relegated to the final lesson, where you can evaluate their usefulness on the basis of what you have learned.

This book is the result of more than two decades of thinking about the most effective way to present Middle Egyptian grammar to beginning students, coupled with practical application in the classroom. I am grateful especially to the faithful corps of students who have patiently endured six years of instruction and reading Egyptian texts with me in the Metropolitan Museum of Art: Beatrice Cooper (who laboriously proofread the lessons and checked every cross-reference in them, thereby saving me from innumerable errors), Charles Herzer, Anne and David Mininberg, Howard Schlossman, and Elinor Smith. Their dedicated efforts have shown me the benefits of some approaches as well as the impracticality of others, and this book in its present form is in large part a tribute to their continued interest and comments.

I owe a special debt of gratitude to those who have supported and encouraged my interest in Egyptian grammar, in particular Dr. Dorothea Arnold, Curator-in-charge of the Metropolitan Museum's Department of Egyptian Art, and Prof. William Kelly Simpson, of Yale University. Above all, I am grateful to the unwavering commitment and support of my wife, Susan J. Allen. Without her, this book could not have been written.

Map of Egypt

showing major sites mentioned in this book

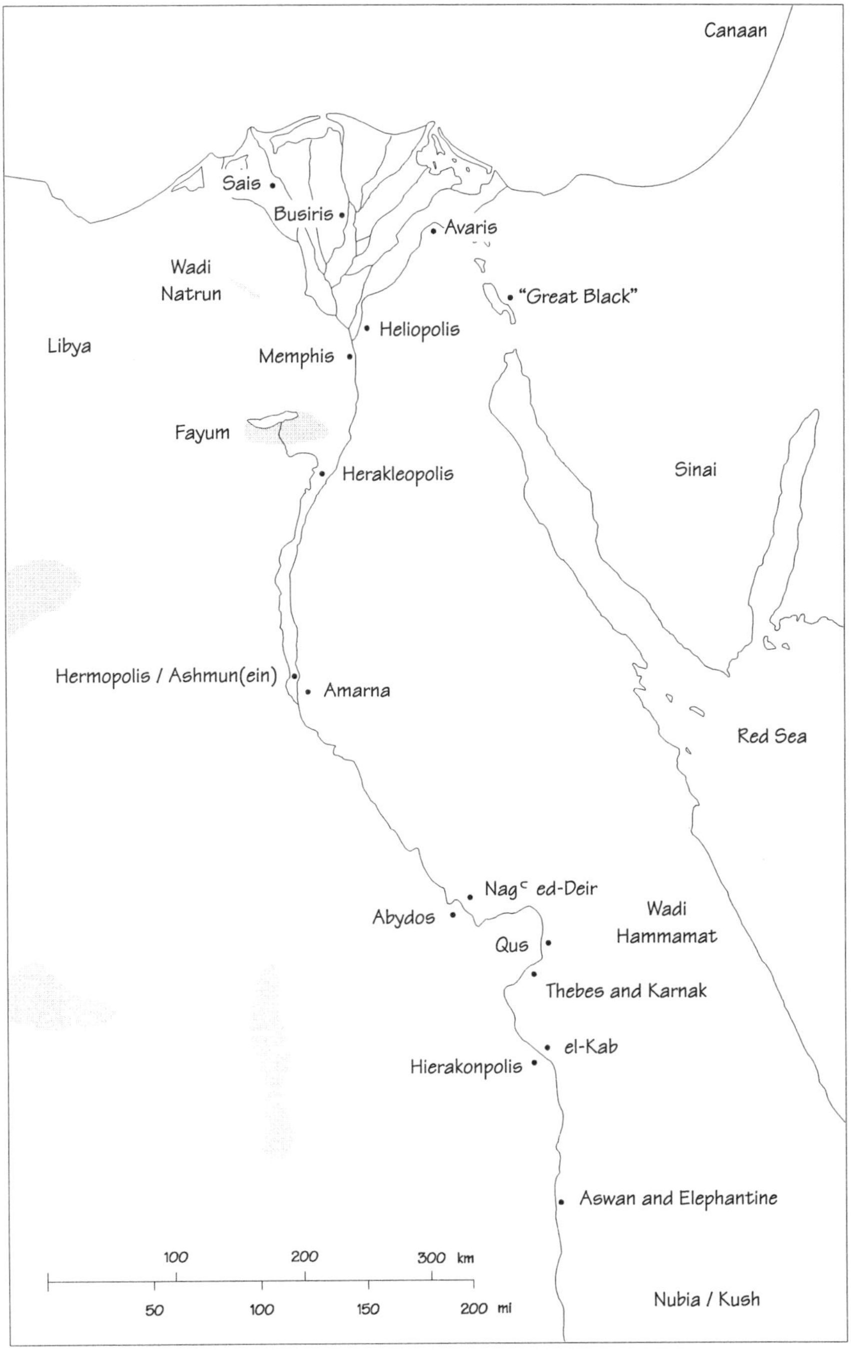

1. Egyptian Language and Writing

Language

1.1 Family

Egyptian is the ancient and original language of Egypt. It belongs to the Afro-Asiatic language family, and is related both to Asiatic (or "Semitic") languages such as Arabic, Ethiopic, and Hebrew, and to North African (or "Hamitic") languages such as Berber and Cushitic.

1.2 History

Egyptian first appeared in writing shortly before 3000 BC and remained in active use until the eleventh century AD. This lifespan of more than four thousand years makes it the longest continually attested language in the world. Beginning with the Muslim conquest of Egypt in AD 641, Arabic gradually replaced Egyptian as the dominant language in Egypt. Today, the language of Egypt is Arabic. Egyptian is a dead language, like Latin, which can only be studied in writing, though it is still spoken in the rituals of the Coptic (Egyptian Christian) Church.

Throughout its long lifetime, Egyptian underwent tremendous changes. Scholars classify its history into five major phases:

1. **Old Egyptian** is the name given to the oldest known phase of the language. Although Egyptian writing is first attested before 3000 BC, these early inscriptions consist only of names and labels. Old Egyptian proper is dated from approximately 2600 BC, when the first connected texts appeared, until about 2100 BC.

2. **Middle Egyptian**, sometimes called Classical Egyptian, is closely related to Old Egyptian. It first appeared in writing around 2100 BC and survived as a spoken language for some 500 years, but it remained the standard hieroglyphic language for the rest of ancient Egyptian history. Middle Egyptian is the phase of the language discussed in this book.

3. **Late Egyptian** began to replace Middle Egyptian as the spoken language after 1600 BC, and it remained in use until about 600 BC. Though descended from Old and Middle Egyptian, Late Egyptian differed substantially from the earlier phases, particularly in grammar. Traces of Late Egyptian can be found in texts earlier than 1600 BC, but it did not appear as a full written language until after 1300 BC.

4. **Demotic** developed out of Late Egyptian. It first appeared around 650 BC and survived until the fifth century AD.

5. **Coptic** is the name given to the final phase of Egyptian, which is closely related to Demotic. It appeared at the end of the first century AD and was spoken for nearly a thousand years thereafter. The last known texts written by native speakers of Coptic date to the eleventh century AD.

1.3 Dialects

Besides these chronological changes, Egyptian also had several dialects. These regional differences in speech and writing are best attested in Coptic, which had five major dialects. They cannot be detected in the writing of earlier phases of Egyptian, but they undoubtedly existed then as well: a letter from about 1200 BC complains that a correspondent's language is as incomprehensible as that of a northern Egyptian speaking with an Egyptian from the south. The southern dialect, known as Saidic, was the classical form of Coptic; the northern one, called Bohairic, is the dialect used in Coptic Church services today.

WRITING

1.4 Hieroglyphs

The basic writing system of ancient Egyptian consisted of about five hundred common signs, known as hieroglyphs. The term "hieroglyph" comes from two Greek words meaning "sacred carvings," which are a translation, in turn, of the Egyptians' own name for their writing system, "divine speech." Each sign in this system is a hieroglyph, and the system as a whole is called hieroglyphic (*not* "hieroglyphics").

Unlike Mesopotamian cuneiform or Chinese, whose beginnings can be traced over several hundred years, hieroglyphic writing seems to appear in Egypt suddenly, shortly before 3000 BC, as a complete system. Scholars are divided in their opinions about its origins. Some suggest that the earlier, developmental stages of hieroglyphic were written on perishable materials, such as wood, and simply have not survived. Others argue that the system could have been invented all at once by an unknown genius — possibly influenced by the idea of Mesopotamian cuneiform, which is somewhat earlier.

Although people since the ancient Greeks have tried to understand this system as a mystical encoding of secret wisdom, hieroglyphic is no more mysterious than any other system that has been used to record language. Basically, *hieroglyphic is nothing more than the way the ancient Egyptians wrote their language*. To read hieroglyphic, therefore, you have to learn the Egyptian language.

1.5 Hieroglyphic spelling

Each hieroglyph is a picture of a real thing that existed in the world of the ancient Egyptians: for instance, the ground plan of a simple house (𓉐), a human mouth (𓂋), or a pair of legs in motion (𓂻). These could be used to write the words that they depicted, or related words: for example, 𓉐 "house"; 𓂻 "come." When a hieroglyph is used in this manner, it is called an **ideogram** ("idea writing"). We still use ideograms, even in English: "I ♥ my dog."

Ideographic writing is simple and direct, but it is pretty much limited to things that can be pictured. All languages, however, also contain many words for concepts that cannot be conveyed by a simple picture. Successful writing systems must find a way to express those ideas as well. Most written languages do so by a system of signs that represent not things but the **sounds** of the language. This allows their writers to "spell out" words. A sign used in this way is called a **phonogram** ("sound writing"). English writing uses phonograms almost exclusively: each letter in our alphabet is a symbol that represents a sound rather than an object of the real world.

The idea that symbols could be used to represent the sounds of a language rather than real objects is one of the most important, and ancient, of all human discoveries. It is often called "the rebus principle." A rebus is a message spelled out in pictures that represent sounds rather than the things they are pictures of: for example, the pictures of an eye (𓁹), a bee (𓆤), and a leaf (𓇋) can be put together as the English rebus 𓁹𓆤𓇋, meaning "I believe" ("eye-bee-leaf") — which has nothing to do with eyes, bees, or leaves. The hieroglyphic system of writing used this principle too. Many Egyptian hieroglyphs could be used not only as ideograms, but also as phonograms. For example, the signs for "house" (𓉐) and "mouth" (𓂋) were also used as phonograms in the word 𓉐𓂋 "ascend," which has nothing to do with houses or mouths.

In Middle Egyptian, words spelled with phonograms usually have an ideogram added at the end. This extra sign, called a **determinative**, has two functions: it shows that the signs preceding it are to be read as phonograms rather than ideograms, and it indicates the general idea of the word. Thus, the word meaning "ascend" is usually written 𓉐𓂋𓂻: the "walking legs" sign indicates that this is a word having to do with motion.

To summarize: the individual pictures of the Egyptian hieroglyphic writing system are used in three different ways:

1. as **ideograms**, to represent the things they actually depict: for example, 𓂋 "mouth."
2. as **phonograms**, to represent the sounds that "spell out" individual words: for example, 𓉐𓂋 "ascend." Used in this way, the hieroglyphs stand for sounds rather than for pictures of things.
3. as **determinatives**, to show that the signs preceding are meant as phonograms, and to indicate the general idea of the word: for example, the "walking legs" in 𓉐𓂋𓂻 "ascend."

All hieroglyphs have the potential to be used in each of these ways. In practice, however, their use was generally more restricted. Some occur mostly as ideograms or determinatives, others almost exclusively as phonograms. The "house" sign (𓉐) is one of the few hieroglyphs that was regularly used in all three functions: as an ideogram, meaning "house"; as a phonogram, with the value *pr*; and as a determinative, after words denoting buildings.

1.6 Direction

Unlike English, which is always written from left to right, and normally in horizontal rows, hieroglyphs could be written in four different directions:

in a horizontal row, left to right (𓉐𓂋𓂻) or right to left (𓂻𓉐𓂋)

in a vertical column, left to right (𓉐𓂋𓂻) or right to left (𓉐𓂋𓂻)

This flexibility is a useful feature of hieroglyphic writing. The Egyptians often took advantage of it to produce pleasingly symmetrical inscriptions. For example, on the offering-table pictured below, one inscription begins at the top and runs down the right side (A), while a similar one faces it on the left (B); at the bottom, two shorter inscriptions (C and D) face each other the same way:

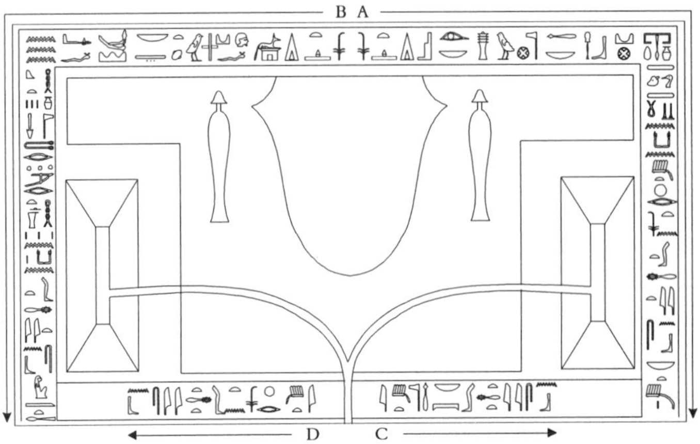

When hieroglyphs accompany pictures of human beings or the gods, they normally face in the same direction as the individual they refer to. In the scene reproduced below, the man on the left, facing right, is a sculptor; on the right, facing left, is the seated statue he is working on. Above the sculptor's head are two rows of hieroglyphs, also facing right, which identify him as "Overseer of sculpting, Itjau"; the three rows of hieroglyphs above the statue read "Statue of the courtier, overseer of priests, Henenit the Black," and they face left, like the statue itself.

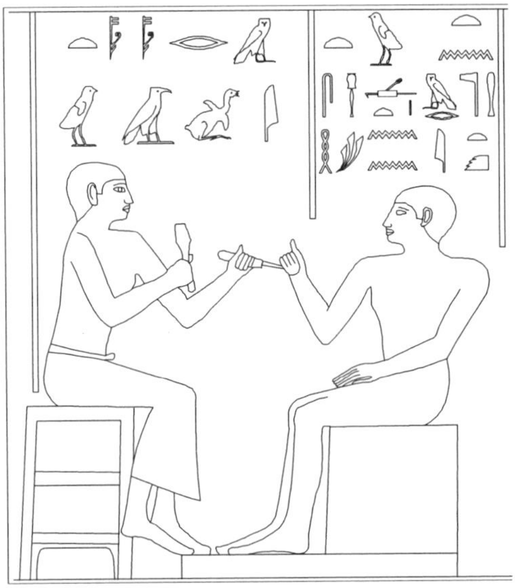

Usually, signs with an obvious front and back (like [hieroglyph]) face the **beginning** of their inscription, as they do in the illustrations above. The normal rule is to read "into" the signs: the lefthand inscriptions in these figures are read from right to left, and the righthand ones from left to right. Once in a while, however, this rule is reversed, and the signs face the *end* of the inscription; such inscriptions are called "retrograde," and are found almost exclusively in religious texts.

1.7 Groups

The words of hieroglyphic texts follow one after the other: in the scene reproduced above, for example, the three rows on the right contain, in order, the words "Statue of" (row 1), "courtier, overseer (of) priests" (row 2), and "Henenit (the) Black" (row 3) (the words in parentheses do not appear in the hieroglyphs). The signs that spell out these words, however, are arranged in groups, rather than one after the other like the letters of an English word.

This kind of organization is a fundamental principle of all hieroglyphic writing. The arrangement of the groups depends on the shape of the individual signs. In general, every hieroglyph has one of three basic shapes:

1. tall signs: for example,  and .
2. flat signs: for example, and .
3. small signs: for example, and .

Tall signs tend to stand by themselves, but the other signs are usually arranged into square or rectangular groups. In the name "Henenit the Black," for instance, the first two tall signs stand alone, one after the other (); the next two, which are flat, are arranged in a square (); the tall sign following stands alone (); and the last two small signs are grouped in a rectangle with one above the other (). Sometimes a tall sign can be made smaller and grouped with a flat one, as in  "overseer" in the scene above. When signs of dissimilar shapes are grouped, they are usually centered, like the hieroglyphs  in the same scene. If a flat or small sign has to stand alone it is centered in the row, like and in the lefthand inscription of the scene.

The groups of a hieroglyphic inscription are meant to be read from beginning to end and from top to bottom. In the word  "courtier," for example, the order is . Direction and grouping are the only organizing methods used in hieroglyphic writing. Hieroglyphic texts do not separate the words by spaces, and there are no punctuation marks. This makes hieroglyphic inscriptions difficult to read at first, but with practice it becomes easier to see words rather than strings of signs, justasyoucanreadthisstringoflettersbecauseyouknowenglish.

1.8 The uses of hieroglyphs

Hieroglyphic was used to write Old and Middle Egyptian. Although Middle Egyptian ceased to be a spoken language by about 1600 BC, hieroglyphic texts continued to use it until the end of ancient Egyptian history. Most hieroglyphic inscriptions are found on the walls of ancient Egyptian temples and tombs, or on objects such as statues, offering tables, coffins, sarcophagi (stone coffins), and stelae (large slabs of stone or wood). In these places the texts can serve as labels (as in the scene above) or dedications (as on the offering-table above); they can also record the speech of the participants in a scene. Longer hieroglyphic inscriptions are usually historical or autobiographical texts, or religious texts such as hymns and funerary spells.

Hieroglyphs were normally carved into stone, wood, or ivory, or painted on plaster. Because all hieroglyphic signs are individual pictures, the ancient sculptors and painters took as much care in making them as they did with the other elements of a scene, such as the figures of animals, people, or gods. Sometimes, however, the artists carved or painted only the outline of each sign; this is particularly true in long hieroglyphic texts.

1.9 Cursive hieroglyphs and hieratic

Besides carving or painting inscriptions, the ancient Egyptians also wrote texts with a reed brush and ink on papyrus, leather, or wood. In these handwritten texts it is very rare to find hieroglyphs made with the same detail as those in hieroglyphic inscriptions. Such documents employed a much simpler form of each sign, called **cursive hieroglyphic**. Here is a sample of cursive writing, with the same text reproduced in regular hieroglyphs next to it:

Cursive hieroglyphic inscriptions are usually written from right to left in columns, like the sample above, and are found almost exclusively in religious texts such as the "Book of the Dead."

For most handwritten texts, the Egyptians used an even more cursive style of writing, which the ancient Greeks called **hieratic** ("priestly"). Hieratic is almost as old as hieroglyphic itself. The relationship between hieratic and hieroglyphic is the same as that between our handwriting and printing. Like cursive hieroglyphs, each hieratic sign has a hieroglyphic counterpart, although these are not always as self-evident in hieratic as they are in cursive hieroglyphs. Here is a sample hieratic text, with the corresponding hieroglyphs transcribed below it:

Hieratic was written with a reed brush and ink, usually on papyrus, and always written from right to left. Originally, it could be written in either rows or columns; after about 1800 BC, however, columns were used only in religious texts, and all other hieratic texts were written in rows. Hieratic occasionally has a kind of punctuation: some copies of literary texts use a small dot to separate units of thought, such as the lines of a poem.

Hieratic was used to write Old, Middle, and Late Egyptian. For Old and Middle Egyptian it served as an alternative means of writing alongside hieroglyphic. The two scripts were used for different kinds of documents: hieroglyphic for formal texts meant to be permanent, such as tomb and temple inscriptions, and hieratic usually for more temporary texts, such as letters and accounts. Hieratic texts often reflect the contemporary colloquial language more closely than hieroglyphic, particularly after about 1600 BC; Late Egyptian is written almost exclusively in hieratic.

1.10 Demotic

Late Egyptian hieratic writing became more cursive and abbreviated as time went on, particularly in administrative documents. Eventually, it developed into the script we call **demotic** (from the Greek for "popular"). Here is an example of demotic writing:

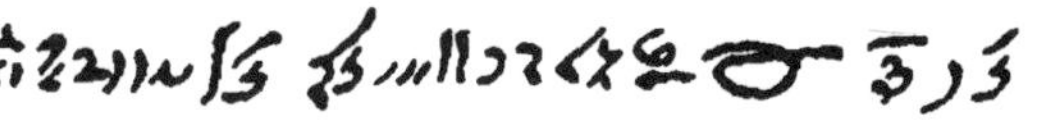

The term "demotic" is used to refer to both writing and language: the phase of Egyptian known as Demotic (capitalized) is written only in the demotic script. Since demotic developed out of hieratic, it is even farther removed from hieroglyphic, and it is almost impossible to recognize the hieroglyphic ancestors of demotic signs. For this reason, scholars do not usually transcribe demotic writing into hieroglyphs; instead, they **transliterate** it into the letters of our alphabet (see Lesson 2): the transliteration of the text above reads *ḏd.f n.w m-jr ẖsf t3 ntj jw.j ḏd.s ḏd.w p3y.n nb ꜥ3.*

The first Demotic texts appeared around 650 BC. From then on, demotic was the normal means of writing Egyptian; hieratic, like cursive hieroglyphic, was kept only for religious manuscripts (hence its name "priestly"); and hieroglyphic was used in monumental inscriptions. Like hieratic, demotic was mostly written with a brush and ink on papyrus. Toward the end of Egyptian civilization, however, only priests were still able to read hieroglyphic writing; inscriptions that were meant to have a larger audience were sometimes carved in demotic instead. The Rosetta Stone, which records a decree issued in 196 BC to honor the pharaoh Ptolemy V, is inscribed in hieroglyphic (the sacred script of the priesthood that issued the decree), demotic (the normal Egyptian script), and Greek (the native language of the Ptolemaic pharaohs).

1.11 Coptic

The Egyptians who adopted Christianity, after the first century AD, began to translate the sacred scriptures of this new religion into their own language, but they were reluctant to use the demotic script for this purpose because of its association with the older, "pagan" religion. Instead, they wrote their sacred texts in the letters of the Greek alphabet. This script is called **Coptic**, the same term used for the Egyptian branch of Christianity. The Coptic alphabet has thirty-two letters: twenty-four taken from Greek, seven for sounds that Egyptian had but Greek did not, and one monogram (one letter standing for two). Here is a sample of Coptic writing (with the words separated), and its equivalent in the letters of our alphabet:

ⲡⲉⲛⲉⲓⲱⲧ	ⲉⲧϩⲛ̄ⲙ̄ⲡⲏⲩⲉ	ⲙⲁⲣⲉⲡⲉⲕⲣⲁⲛ	ⲟⲩⲟⲡ
peneiôt	eth'n'mpêue	marepekran	ouop

These are the first words of the Christian "Lord's Prayer" ("Our-father, who-is-in-heaven, may-your-name-be hallowed"). For more on the Coptic alphabet, see § 2.5.

Like "Demotic," the term "Coptic" refers to a phase of the Egyptian language as well as a writing system. As Egypt became Christian, the older writing systems were relegated to the texts and temples of the old religion. By the end of the fifth century AD, Coptic had become the only means of writing Egyptian, for secular and religious (Christian) texts alike. It remained in use until the death of the language itself, some six centuries later.

1.12 Decipherment

After the introduction of Coptic, the four ancient Egyptian scripts — hieroglyphic, hieratic, demotic, and Coptic — existed side by side for about two hundred years. Hieratic died out sometime in the third century AD, the last hieroglyphic inscription was carved in AD 394, and the last known Demotic text dates to AD 452. Thereafter, even though Egyptian continued to be spoken and written (as Coptic), the knowledge of the earlier writing systems was lost.

The earliest major attempt to recover this lost knowledge probably dates from the fourth century AD, slightly before the last ancient texts were inscribed. This was a work called *Hieroglyphica* ("Hieroglyphics"), supposedly written by an Egyptian named Horapollo and later translated into Greek (the earliest copy of it dates to the fifteenth century AD). There is reason to believe that the author had some knowledge of hieroglyphic writing, but his explanation of the system is purely allegorical — perhaps because it was intended for a Greek audience, who had long believed in the mystical symbolism of hieroglyphic signs. He explains, for example, that the word for "son" is written with a goose because geese love their offspring more than any other animal does. The picture of a goose () is in fact used to write the word "son," but only as a phonogram (because one word for "goose" had the same sound as the word for "son"); it is also used as a phonogram in other words that have nothing to do with either geese or offspring.

Horapollo's allegorical explanations were highly influential, and his system dominated attempts at decipherment for the next fourteen centuries. Only with the work of Athanasius Kircher, in the mid-seventeenth century, did scholars begin to think that hieroglyphs could represent sounds as well as ideas. Kircher knew Coptic, and he also had the inspired notion that this last phase of Egyptian might be somehow related to the language of the hieroglyphs. But Kircher also believed in the mystical nature of the ancient script, and this eventually doomed to failure all his attempts at decipherment.

It was not until the discovery of the Rosetta Stone, in 1799, that scholars were able to make practical use of Kircher's ideas. For the first time they were presented with a hieroglyphic text (on the top third of the stone) that had an undisputed translation into a known language (Greek, on the stone's bottom third). Scholars in several countries worked on the new text and succeeded in identifying many of the hieroglyphic groups with words in the Greek translation. But the final breakthrough eluded all of them except one, a young French schoolteacher named Jean-François Champollion.

From the work of two of his contemporaries, the Swede Johan Åkerblad and the Englishman Thomas Young, Champollion suspected that some hieroglyphic signs might be read phonetically. He began compiling a list of such signs by studying royal names, which could easily be identified by the "cartouche" (name-ring) surrounding them. The cartouches on the Rosetta Stone all corresponded to the name of the pharaoh Ptolemy V in the Greek text:

 = ΠΤΟΛΕΜΑΙΟΣ (Ptolemaios).

Using this as a starting point, Champollion next looked at the cartouches on an obelisk whose base had been inscribed with Greek texts honoring another Ptolemy and two queens named Cleopatra. Here he found the same cartouche along with another, which he identified as the name Cleopatra:

 = ΚΛΕΟΠΑΤΡΑ (Kleopatra).

Both cartouches had some of the same signs, and by their position in the two names he was able to identify them as *p* (𓊪), *t* (𓏏), *o* (𓍯), and *l* (𓃭). With these he was able to assign values to most of the other signs as well: *m* (𓐝), *i* (𓇌), *s* (𓋴), *e* (𓇋), *a* (𓄿), *t* (𓂧), and *r* (𓂋).

This convinced Champollion that hieroglyphs could be used alphabetically, at least for foreign names, though he still believed that they could also be read symbolically. The next step, and the real breakthrough, came when he began working on a cartouche with the signs 𓇳𓄟𓋴𓋴. From his previous work, Champollion was able to recognize the last two signs as *s*. Seeking a value for the first symbol, he thought of the sun and the Coptic word for "sun," *re*. This gave him *re–...–s–s* and immediately reminded him of the name Ramesses, which was known from a list of pharaonic names in a Greek history of Egypt written around 300 BC. Champollion then noticed the sign 𓄟 in a hieroglyphic group on the Rosetta Stone corresponding to the word for "birth" in the Greek text. Since the Coptic word for "birth" is *mise*, this confirmed his reading of the name Ramesses (*re–mes–s–s*, meaning "The sun is the one who gave him birth").

Champollion's discovery proved three things about hieroglyphs: they could be used both as phonograms (𓋴 = *s*) and as ideograms (𓇳 = *re* "sun"), and the language of hieroglyphic inscriptions was the same as that of Coptic (𓇳 = *re* "sun," 𓄟𓋴 = *mise* "birth"). With this foundation he was able to make rapid progress in reading not only the Rosetta Stone but other hieroglyphic texts as well. The announcement of his discovery, on September 29th, 1822, marks the beginning of the modern science of Egyptology.

Since Champollion's time, Egyptologists have continually refined our knowledge of ancient Egyptian writing, words, and grammar. Except for the most obscure words, hieroglyphic texts can be read today almost as easily as those of any other known language.

ESSAY 1. ANCIENT EGYPTIAN HISTORY

Scholars divide the long history of ancient Egypt into periods and dynasties. A dynasty is a series of kings related by family, geographic origin, or some other feature. Our current system of dynasties dates to the work of an Egyptian priest named Manetho, who wrote a history of Egypt about 300 BC. Using older Egyptian archives as his source, Manetho divided Egypt's pharaohs into thirty dynasties. These divisions are still used for the most part, though scholars have been able to revise them on the basis of more ancient historical material.

The dynastic history of Egypt begins around 3000 BC, when the country was unified under a single government. Before that time, Egypt was divided into a number of local centers of power; this is known as the Predynastic Period. Manetho began his Dynasty 1 with the legendary king Menes, who united the south and north and built a new capital at Memphis (just south of modern Cairo). Scholars have not been able to identify Menes with any of the known historical pharaohs. Today, the first king of Dynasty 1 is generally assumed to be either Aha or his predecessor, Narmer. In fact, there is evidence that a number of kings even before Narmer had control of most if not all of Egypt; to preserve the traditional dynastic numbering, scholars group these earlier pharaohs into a "Dynasty 0."

Dynasties 1 and 2 are known as the Archaic Period (ca. 3000–2650 BC). During this time we can trace the development of most traditional aspects of Egyptian civilization: government, religion, art, and writing. The first full bloom of Egyptian culture came during the Old Kingdom, Dynasties 3–6 (ca. 2650–2150 BC). This was the time when the great pyramids were built and the first full hieroglyphic texts appeared.

After Dynasty 6 the central government weakened, and Egypt entered a phase of its history known as the First Intermediate Period (Dynasties 8–11, ca. 2150–2040 BC; Manetho's Dynasty 7 does not correspond to any known historical kings). Toward the end of this period, Egypt was ruled by two competing local dynasties: Dynasty 10, with its capital at Herakleopolis in the north; and Dynasty 11, based at Thebes in the south.

Around 2040 BC, a king of Dynasty 11, known as Mentuhotep II, managed to gain control of the entire country; this event marks the beginning of the Middle Kingdom (Dynasties 11-12, ca. 2040–1780 BC). Dynasty 12, ruling from a new capital at Lisht (about 30 miles south of modern Cairo), inaugurated the second flowering of Egyptian culture. During its rule the first great works of Egyptian literature were written, in the phase of the language known as Middle Egyptian.

After Dynasty 12 central authority over the entire country weakened once again, and Egypt entered its Second Intermediate Period (Dynasties 13–17, ca. 1780–1550 BC). This era began during Dynasty 13, when a series of local rulers took control of the Delta (Dynasty 14). Around 1650 BC the rulers of an Asiatic settlement in the Delta gained control of most of the country. The Egyptians called these kings Hyksos, meaning "foreign rulers"; they are traditionally assigned to Dynasty 15. Meanwhile, the area around Thebes, in the south of Egypt, was governed by a succession of native dynasties (the 16th and 17th).

After a series of battles lasting some two decades, the last kings of Dynasty 17 were able to conquer the Hyksos and reestablish a unified government. Their success marks the beginning of Dynasty 18 and the period of Egyptian history known as the New Kingdom (Dynasty 18, ca. 1550–1295 BC). Once again Egyptian culture flourished, as the pharaohs of Dynasty 18 extended Egyptian influence over much of the Near East and inaugurated great building projects in Egypt itself. The end of Dynasty 18 saw the rule of the heretic pharaoh Akhenaten (who tried to establish the worship of a single god) and his successors, including Tutankhamun — a series of reigns known as the Amarna Period (ca. 1350–1323 BC).

The last pharaoh of Dynasty 18, Haremhab (ca. 1323–1295 BC), managed to quell the internal disruption that resulted from Akhenaten's experiment, and his successors once again presided over a strong and stable Egypt. Most of the kings of the next two dynasties were named Ramesses, and their rule is known as the Ramesside Period (Dynasties 19–20, ca. 1295–1070 BC). The reign of Ramesses II (ca. 1279–1213 BC) was the high point of this time, marked by a peace treaty with the Hittites (the second great power in the Near East), impressive advances in Egyptian theology and philosophy, and the greatest building projects since the time of the pyramids, 1300 years earlier.

Though most of them bore the same name, the successors of Ramesses II were hard pressed to live up to his legacy. After the death of the last Ramesside pharaoh, Ramesses XI, Egypt once more fell into a time of disunity. For the next four hundred years, a time known as the Third Intermediate Period (ca. 1070–650 BC), the country was torn between competing dynasties of native rulers (Dynasties 21 and 24) and pharaohs originating from Libya (Dynasties 22–23) and Nubia (Dynasty 25). Not until 650 BC was Egypt able to prosper under a period of stable, unified rule by a single dynasty of native kings. The rulers of this dynasty, the 26th (672–525 BC), governed from the city of Sais, in the north, and their reign is known as the Saite Period. It was marked by a resurgence in the arts, based on the classical forms of the Old and Middle Kingdom.

The Saite Period ended brutally, with the conquest of Egypt by a Persian army in 525 BC. For the first time in its dynastic history, Egypt was governed not as an independent country but as the province of a foreign empire. During the next two hundred years, known as the Late Period (Dynasties 27–30, 525–332 BC), Egypt tottered between Persian rule (Dynasty 27) and brief periods when native pharaohs managed to regain control (Dynasties 28–30). In 343 BC the Persians conquered Egypt for the final time, ending the reign of Nectanebo II, the last native Egyptian to rule his country until the Egyptian revolution in AD 1952.

When Alexander the Great destroyed the Persian Empire in 332 BC, he gained control of Egypt as well. After Alexander's death in 323 BC, the rule of Egypt passed to one of his generals, named Ptolemy. Though they were of Macedonian origin, Ptolemy and his descendants governed Egypt as pharaohs. The country prospered during the three hundred years of their reign, known as the Ptolemaic Period (323–30 BC), with a strong central government and an ongoing program of rebuilding and renewing the older monuments.

Ptolemaic rule ended in 30 BC, when the coalition of Mark Antony and the Ptolemaic ruler Cleopatra VII was defeated by Octavian, the future Caesar Augustus. Egypt became a province of the Roman Empire. Although its ancient customs continued under Roman rule for the next four hundred years, Egypt gradually lost its old identity, first to Christianity and then, beginning in AD 641, to Islam. The Roman conquest of 30 BC is generally considered as the end of ancient Egyptian civilization.

Exercise 1

1. Below are four different hieroglyphic texts from real inscriptions. Write numbers next to the hieroglyphs in each one showing the order in which the signs are supposed to be read.

a. 

"The sun's rays are protection over you, their hands holding health and life" (from one of the shrines of Tutankhamun)

b. 

"I was his servant, his true confidant" (from an autobiographical inscription)

c. 

"You shall reveal to him your secrets" (from the tomb of Seti I)

d. 

"I have followed him by night and day to all his places" (from an autobiography)

2. Try to arrange the following strings of hieroglyphs into groups, preserving the same order (you can adjust the size of individual signs where necessary).

a. 

"I have made my tomb by the king's blessing."

b. 

"A royal offering of Anubis on His Mountain, he who is in the mummy-wrappings, lord of the Sacred Land."

c. 

"Then he laughed at me because of that which I said."

d. 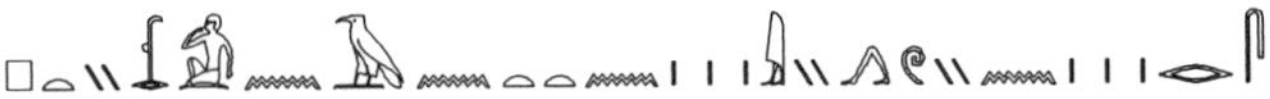

"What is the reason we have returned?"

e. 

"Look, your name will exist forever in the temple."

2. The Sounds of Middle Egyptian

2.1 Spelling

Hieroglyphic writing represents ancient Egyptian words. When ancient Egyptian was still a living language, those words were spoken as well as written. Hieroglyphs used as phonograms ("sound writing": see § 1.5) represent the sounds of those words, just as the letters of the English alphabet represent the sounds of the English language. Unlike the English alphabet, however, hieroglyphic writing usually shows only the consonants of Egyptian words. Not until Coptic did the ancient Egyptians use a writing system that regularly indicated the vowels as well. For earlier stages of the language — including Middle Egyptian — we are left with only the "skeleton" of Egyptian words. This approach to writing is not peculiar to hieroglyphic: among modern languages, Hebrew and Arabic regularly omit the vowels in writing.

As far as can be determined, Middle Egyptian had some 25 consonants. Each consonant could be represented in hieroglyphic writing by a single sign; such signs are called **uniliteral** ("one-letter") hieroglyphs. In effect, these uniliteral hieroglyphs constituted an Egyptian "alphabet"; but they were never used as such by the Egyptians, only in combination with other hieroglyphs.

Like English, Middle Egyptian used a conservative system of spelling. Words sometimes showed the consonants they had had in Old Egyptian, even when some of those were no longer pronounced in Middle Egyptian — just as English retains, for example, the *b* in *debt* and the *gh* in *night*, even though the consonants these letters represent ceased to be pronounced hundreds of years ago. Middle Egyptian had probably also developed some new sounds that were not represented by uniliteral signs of their own. Here too, Egyptian is similar to English: we use two letters, for example, to represent the sound *sh* (as in *shot*), because the Greek and Latin languages, from which our alphabet comes, did not have that sound. Finally, Egyptian spelling was not always consistent. Most words could be spelled in several different ways: with ideograms alone, with a combination of phonograms and ideograms, and with one or more determinatives (or none at all). English spelling itself only became standardized in the last two hundred years.

2.2 Transliteration

These features make it impossible to know exactly how any one word was pronounced in Middle Egyptian. Nonetheless, Egyptologists need to be able to write about Egyptian words and to compile dictionaries of them. To do so, Egyptologists use a system of **transliteration**: that is, a set of alphabetical symbols that represent each of the uniliteral hieroglyphs. Egyptology has used several systems of transliteration since the time of Champollion. Two are commonly in use today: the traditional and the European systems. This book uses European transliteration, because it requires fewer special signs than the traditional system. A third system, found mostly in the publications of E.A.W. Budge, is now outdated, but is useful to know because many of Budge's books are still in print. A fourth system, without special signs, is used for computerized texts.

2.3 Uniliteral signs

The table below shows the uniliteral hieroglyphs of Middle Egyptian, along with their transliteration in the European system and the names by which Egyptologists commonly refer to them. The table is arranged in the order used in dictionaries of ancient Egyptian. To be able to use the dictionaries (including the one in the back of this book), you will need to memorize this order.

SYMBOL	TRANSL.	NAME
(vulture)	ꜣ	aleph ("AL-if")
(reed-leaf); also (dual strokes)	j	j
(double reed-leaf)	y	y
(arm)	ꜥ	ayin ("EYE-in")
(quail-chick); also (curl of rope)	w	w
(foot)	b	b
(stool)	p	p
(horned viper)	f	f
(owl); also (unknown object)	m	m
(water) ; also (red crown)	n	n
(mouth)	r	r
(enclosure)	h	h
(rope)	ḥ	"dotted h"
(unknown object)	ḫ	"third h"
(belly and udder)	ẖ	"fourth h"
(doorbolt)	z	z
(bolt of cloth)	s	s
(pool)	š	shin
(hill)	q	q
(basket) (also)	k	k
(jar-stand); also (bag)	g	g
(bread-loaf)	t	t
(hobble)	ṯ	"second t"
(hand)	d	d
(cobra)	ḏ	"second d"

These signs are among the most common of all Egyptian hieroglyphs; every text contains some of them, and most words were written with one or more of them — some words, only with them. Your first exercise should be to study this table until you can reproduce it and can give the transliteration of each sign from memory.

The next table shows the differences between the European system of transliteration and the other three systems mentioned above. It is given here only for reference; but you will find it useful to know the others, particularly the traditional system, in reading other books about Middle Egyptian language and writing.

	TRADITIONAL	BUDGE	COMPUTER		TRADITIONAL	BUDGE	COMPUTER
ꜣ	ꜣ	a	A	*ḫ*	ḫ	χ, kh	x
j	i͗	ȧ	i	*ẖ*	ẖ	χ, kh	X
y	y	ȧ, y	ii	*z*	s	s	z, s
ꜥ	ꜥ	ā	a	*s*	ś	s	s
w	w	u	w	*š*	š	ś, sh	S
b	b	b	b	*q*	ḳ	q	q
p	p	p	p	*k*	k	k	k
f	f	f	f	*g*	g	ḳ	g
m	m	m	m	*t*	t	t	t
n	n	n	n	*ṯ*	ṯ	θ, th	T
r	r	r	r	*d*	d	ṭ	d
h	h	h	h	*ḏ*	ḏ	t′, tch	D
ḥ	ḥ	ḥ	H				

2.4 **Sounds**

It is important to remember that the transliteration symbols are only a convention that Egyptologists use to represent the consonants of Middle Egyptian: they are *not* an accurate guide to the way those consonants actually sounded. We cannot know exactly how the consonants were pronounced, though we can make some educated guesses based on their Coptic descendants and on how Egyptian words were written in other ancient languages (and vice-versa). The following list shows the sounds that most Egyptologists now think the consonants may actually have had in Middle Egyptian:

ꜣ Uncertain, probably a kind of *l* or *r*. This sound began to disappear from the spoken language during the Middle Kingdom. Most words simply lost the consonant, but in some cases, it was replaced by *y* or by a "glottal stop" (the sound at the beginning of the two vowels of "uh-oh").

j In most cases, *j* probably had no sound of its own, but only served to indicate that a syllable began or ended with a vowel. In some words, however, *j* seems to have had the same sound as *y*.

y Like English *y* as in "yet."

ꜥ A sound made deep in the throat, somewhat like the *r* of modern French and German. It exists in Hebrew and Arabic as the consonant named "ayin." Originally ꜥ probably sounded like English *d* as in *deed*, and in Middle Egyptian it may still have had that sound in some words in some dialects.

w Mostly like English *w* as in *wet*. In some cases, however, it may have been pronounced like the English vowel *u* in *glue*.

b Probably like English *b* as in *bet*. In some words (or dialects), it may have had a softer sound, like that of Spanish *cabo* (to approximate it in English, try pronouncing the word *hobo* without putting your lips completely together).

p Probably like English *p* as in *pet*.

f Probably like English *f* as in *fat*. In some words, perhaps like the sound of German *Pferd* (an *f* sound that starts out as a *p*).

m Like English *m* as in *met*.

n In most cases like English *n* as in *net*. In some words, however, this consonant seems to have been pronounced like English *l* as in *let*.

r Probably a "flapped" *r* as in Spanish *pero*, made with a single tap of the tongue against the roof of the mouth. To English speakers, this often sounds like *d*. In some words, *r* seems to have been pronounced like English *l* as in *let*. Some dialects may have pronounced every *r* this way, as that of the Fayum did later in Coptic.

h Probably like English *h* as in *hot*.

ḥ A sound like English *h*, but deeper in the throat. It exists in Arabic and Hebrew, and is similar to the sound made by someone breathing on their glasses before cleaning them.

ḫ Probably a sound like the *ch* in German *ach*. To approximate it in English, try saying *lock* without closing your throat completely. Some Egyptologists think it may have been closer to the Arabic and Hebrew consonant called "ghayin" (try saying *log* without completely closing your throat).

ẖ Probably like the preceding sound followed by *y* (try saying *cue* without closing your throat, or *hue* with a very strong *h*). Egyptologists who believe *ḫ* sounded like "ghayin" think *ẖ* sounded like the *ch* in German *ach*.

z/s In Middle Egyptian, these two consonants were pronounced the same, probably like English *s* as in *set*. Originally, *z* was different, perhaps like English *th* as in *think*. Although *z* and *s* were essentially one consonant in Middle Egyptian, and could often be written interchangeably, it is important to learn the original spelling of words with these consonants, because they are often arranged separately in dictionaries, like the one in the back of this book (*z* comes before *s*).

š Like English *sh* as in *shot*.

q A kind of *k*, probably either like Arabic and Hebrew *q* (as deep in the throat as possible), or with some kind of "emphasis," like *q* in some Ethiopic languages (a sound difficult to describe in English).

k Like English *k* as in *kick*. In some words, probably also *k* followed by *y*, as in English *Kew* or (spelled with *c* instead of *k*) *cue*.

g Uncertain, probably like English *g* as in *get* or, if *q* was like Arabic and Hebrew *q*, then perhaps *k* with some kind of "emphasis."

t Like English *t* as in *toe*.

ṯ Like English *t* followed by *y*, as in the British pronunciation of *tune*. To many English speakers, this sounds the same as the *ch* in *chew*. To approximate it, try saying *chew* with the tip of the tongue instead of the flat part.

d Probably *t* with some kind of "emphasis," though some Egyptologists think it was more like English *d* as in *sadder*.

ḏ The preceding sound followed by *y*. If *d* was like English *d*, then *ḏ* was like the *d* in the British pronunciation of *dune*. To many English speakers, this sounds the same as the *j* in *June*. To approximate it, try saying *June* with the tip of the tongue instead of the flat part.

Before the introduction of the Coptic alphabet, Egyptian had no signs for the vowels. From Coptic, however, Egyptologists have been able to determine that Middle Egyptian probably had three vowels: *a* (as in *father* and *ah*), *i* (as in *bit* or *elite*), and *u* (as in *put* or *gnu*).

2.5 Coptic

The sounds described in the previous section existed throughout most of the lifetime of ancient Egyptian. By the time the Coptic alphabet was introduced, however, some of them had disappeared while others, particularly the vowels, had changed. The table below shows the Coptic alphabet and the sounds that its letters probably represented in most dialects.

ⲁ	*a* as in *father*	ⲡ	*p*
ⲃ	Egyptian *b*	ⲣ	*r*
ⲅ	*k* or *g*	ⲥ	*s*
ⲇ	*t* or *d*	ⲧ	Egyptian *t* and *d*
ⲉ	*e* as in *met*	ⲩ	*w* (ⲟⲩ = *u* as in *gnu*)
ⲍ	*s*	ⲫ	= ⲡϩ
ⲏ	*e* as in *great*	ⲭ	= ⲕϩ
ⲑ	= ⲧϩ	ⲯ	= ⲡⲥ
ⲓ	*i* as in *bit*, also *y*	ⲱ	*o* as in *note*
	(ⲉⲓ = *i* as in *elite*)	ϣ	Egyptian *š*
ⲕ	*k*	ϥ	*f*
ⲗ	*l*	ϩ	Egyptian *h* or *ḥ*
ⲙ	*m*	ϧ, ⳉ	Egyptian *ẖ*
ⲛ	*n*	ϫ	Egyptian *ṯ* and *ḏ*
ⲝ	= ⲕⲥ	ϭ	*ky* as in *cue*
ⲟ	*o* as in *hot*	ϯ	= ⲧⲓ

2.6 Pronunciation

As you can see from the preceding sections, Egyptian and Coptic had many sounds that do not occur in English. Egyptologists normally pronounce the consonants with their closest English equivalents (only the most fastidious actually try to pronounce them as they think the ancients might have). Many consonants (*b*, *p*, *f*, *m*, *n*, *r*, *h*, *s*, *k*, *g*, *t*, *d*) are pronounced as they would be in English. The following table shows the way that most American Egyptologists pronounce the rest of the Egyptian consonants:

- *ꜣ* *a* as in *ah* — example: *mꜣꜣ* "see," pronounced "mah-ah"
- *j* *ee* as in *meet* — example: *bjt* "bee," pronounced "beet"
- *y* usually like *ee* as in *meet* — example: *ky* "other," pronounced "kee"
- *ꜥ* *a* as in *ah* — example: *mꜣꜥt* "order," pronounced "mah-aht"
- *w* at the beginning of a word, like English *w*; otherwise, usually like *oo* as in *too* — examples: *wj* "me," pronounced "wee"; *tw* "you," pronounced "too"
- *ḥ* like English *h* — example: *ḥwj* "hit," pronounced "hoo-ee"
- *ḫ* if possible, like the *kh* sound in German *ach* (most English speakers can make this sound with a little practice); otherwise, like English *k* — example: *ḫꜥw* "appearance," pronounced "khah-oo" or "kah-oo"
- *ẖ* the preceding sound followed by *y* — example: *ẖꜣy* "thwart," pronounced "khyah-ee" or "kyah-ee"
- *z* like English *z* or *s* — example: *zj* "man," pronounced "zee" or "see"
- *š* like English *sh* — example: *šj* "lake," pronounced "shee"
- *q* like English *k* — example: *qꜣꜣw* "hill," pronounced "kah-ah-oo"
- *ṯ* like English *ch* — example: *ṯꜣw* "wind," pronounced "chah-oo"
- *ḏ* like English *j* — example: *ḏꜣj* "cross," pronounced "jah-ee."

Because hieroglyphs do not preserve the original vowels of Egyptian words, Egyptologists normally put a short *e* (as in *met*) where necessary between consonants other than *ꜣ*, *j*, *y*, and *w*. Here is a short sentence in transliteration, showing how most Egyptologists would pronounce it:

jnk sḏmw r wn mꜣꜥ tm dj nmꜥ n nb ḏbꜣw

ee-nek sej-em-oo er wen mah-ah tem dee nem-ah en neb jeb-ah-oo.

(The sentence, from a Middle Egyptian autobiographical inscription, means "I am a proper judge, who does not give preference to the one who can pay.")

2.7 Transcription

To write Egyptian names or other words in English, Egyptologists do not normally use the transliteration alphabet. Instead, they use a system of transcription based on the way Egyptian consonants are normally pronounced by English speakers. In this system, most of the consonants that are transliterated with regular English letters (*b*, *p*, *f*, *m*, *n*, *r*, *h*, *z/s*, *q*, *k*, *g*, *t*, *d*) are transcribed the same way, with an *e* inserted where needed: for example, "Men-nefer" for Egyptian *mn-nfr* (the ancient name of Memphis). The other consonants are represented as follows:

3 and *ʿ*	*a* — example: "Maat" (Egyptian *m3ʿt*, the name of a goddess)
j	*i* — example: "Isesi" (Egyptian *jzzj*, a 5th-Dynasty pharaoh)
y	*y* or *i* — example: "Pepy" or "Pepi" (Egyptian *ppy*, a 6th-Dynasty pharaoh)
w	*w* or *u* — example: "Wenis" or "Unis" (Egyptian *wnjs*, a 6th-Dynasty pharaoh)
ḥ	*h* — example: "Heh" (Egyptian *ḥḥ*, the name of a god)
ḫ and *ẖ*	*kh* — example: "Sekhem-khet" (Egyptian *sḫm-ẖt*, a 3rd-Dynasty pharaoh)
š	*sh* — example: "Hatshepsut" (Egyptian *ḥ3t-špswt*, an 18th-Dynasty female pharaoh)
ṯ	*tj* — example: "Tjenenet" (Egyptian *ṯnnt*, a place-name). Some Egyptologists use the older transcription *th* ("Thenenet").
ḏ	*dj* — example: "Djeser-djeseru" (Egyptian *ḏsr-ḏsrw*, the name of Hatshepsut's mortuary temple at Thebes). Some Egyptologists use the older transcription *z* ("Zeser-zeseru").

Besides these conventions, many transcriptions of Egyptian proper names use forms based on the ancient Greek pronunciation of those names, or on Coptic. This is particularly true for the names of pharaohs and gods. For example, most Egyptologists transcribe the name of the goddess *nbt-ḥwt* (sister of Isis and Osiris) as "Nephthys," from the Greek pronunciation, rather than as "Nebet-hut," and the name of the god *jmn* as "Amun" instead of "Imen," based on its Coptic pronunciation. These transcriptions are not always consistent: the 12th-Dynasty pharaonic name *z-n-wsrt*, for example, has been transcribed as "Sesostris" (Greek) and "Senwosret" (based on Coptic), as well as "Senusret" (and even, in older books, "Usertesen," based on a misreading of the hieroglyphs as *wsrt-z-n*). This can be confusing for the beginner going from one publication to another. Unfortunately, there is no solution to the problem other than trying to remember the different transcriptions.

2.8 Writing conventions and sound changes

Hieroglyphic writing normally showed all the consonants of a word. Sometimes, however, the consonants that appear in hieroglyphs do not always reflect the true consonants of a Middle Egyptian word. There are three main reasons why this could be the case:

1. **Abbreviated spellings**

A uniliteral sign is sometimes omitted to make a more compact grouping of signs. The most common example of this is the word *rmṯ* "people," which is written as  (the group of three signs at the end is a determinative meaning "group of people"). The sign for *m* was apparently left out so that those for *r* and *t* could be nicely grouped together instead of strung out one after another (as in ). Despite its abbreviated spelling, we know that this word had an *m* because it is sometimes written with one and because its Coptic descendant, ⲣⲱⲙⲉ, also has one.

2. **"Weak" consonants**

The consonants *3*, *j*, *y*, and *w* were often omitted in writing, and for that reason are known as "weak" consonants. This happens sometimes in the middle of words and often at the end: some examples are *h3b* "send" ( or ), *jrj* "pertaining to" ( or ), *šndyt* "kilt" (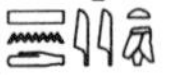 or ), and *hrw* "day" (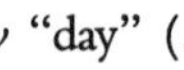 or ). Egyptologists are divided about how to represent the shorter spellings. Some transliterate the full spelling whether or not the weak consonants are shown, while others use only the consonants actually shown in hieroglyphs (e.g., in the shorter examples above: *hb*, *jr*, *šndt*, and *hr*). This book uses the full transliteration, with any omitted consonants shown in parentheses: thus, for the examples above, *h3b* and *h(3)b*, *jrj* and *jr(j)*, *šndyt* and *šnd(y)t*, *hrw* and *hr(w)*.

3. **Sound changes**

Because hieroglyphic spelling was conservative, Middle Egyptian words were often written as they had been in Old Egyptian, even when one or more of the consonants had changed over time. Sometimes, however, a scribe would use a spelling that reflected more closely how the word was actually pronounced in Middle Egyptian. These differences in spelling affect mostly the following consonants:

r This consonant tended to disappear at the end of words. More conservative spellings still show the *r* sign, but others can omit it: for example, *ḫnr* "confine," which is written  or . Sometimes a reed-leaf was used in place of the original *r* (), and once in a while the scribe combined the "traditional" and "modern" spellings by showing both the *r* and a reed-leaf ().

l Hieroglyphic had no special sign for this sound, though it probably existed in many dialects of Middle Egyptian. To write it, scribes normally used  or . Words with the consonant *l* sometimes alternate between these two signs: for example, *dlg* "dwarf," which could be written  (*d3g*),  (*dng*), or even  (*d3ng*). (Because we cannot know for certain how  or were pronounced in each word, Egyptologists usually transliterate these signs as *3* and *n*, rather than *l*.)

t In Egyptian, feminine words usually ended in *t* (see Lesson 4). By the time of Middle Egyptian, this consonant had probably disappeared at the end of words. Conservative spellings still show it, but it can also be left out: for example,  *nbdt* "braid," also spelled  *nbd(t)*.

ṯ In some words, this sound had changed to *t* by Middle Egyptian. Spellings can show either the original consonant, or the Middle Egyptian one: for example,  *ṯw* or  *tw* "you." Because of this sound change, Middle Egyptian scribes sometimes used the sign to write *t*: for example,  for  *tn* "this."

ḏ In some words, this sound had changed to *d* by Middle Egyptian. Spellings can show either the original consonant or the Middle Egyptian one: for example, 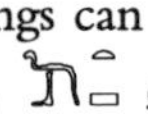 *ḏbt* or  *dbt* "brick."

ESSAY 2. ANCIENT EGYPTIAN GEOGRAPHY

Hieroglyphic texts reflect the ancient Egyptian view of the world. Understanding these texts is not just a matter of translation: it also requires an appreciation of ancient Egyptian geography.

In the ancient Egyptian mind, the world existed inside a kind of "bubble" surrounded by an infinite ocean. Life was possible because the atmosphere (Egyptian *šw*, the god Shu) kept the waters of the ocean (Egyptian *nw* or *nnw*, the god Nu or Nun) from falling on the earth, just like the air inside a balloon keeps it inflated. At the top of this world "bubble" was the sky (Egyptian *pt*; also *nwt*, the goddess Nut), which was seen as the surface of the infinite ocean where it met the atmosphere. In the middle was the earth itself (Egyptian *t3*; also *gbb*, the god Geb), which was thought of as a flat plate of land. The Egyptians also imagined that a similar space existed below the earth. This region was known as the Duat (Egyptian *dw3t*); the sky at its bottom was the feminine counterpart of Nun, called Naunet (Egyptian *nnwt*). Religious documents such as the "Book of the Dead" show the Egyptian concept of the world in pictures of Geb reclining on his side, with Shu standing over him and holding up the body of Nut, who arches above both of them, touching the earth with her hands and feet.

Because the sky was water, the Egyptians imagined that it contained marshes around its edge, like those of northern Egypt itself. In the middle was open water, dotted here and there by islands, including the great string of the Milky Way, which the Egyptians called the "Path of Sailing Stars" (*msqt-sqdw*).

Life inside the world was possible not only because of the atmosphere but also because of the sun (Egyptian *r*ᶜ, the god Re or Ra). During the day, the sun sailed in his "day-boat" across the waters of the sky. At night he transferred to the "night-boat" and sailed through the Duat, across the waters of the under-sky (Naunet), while the stars emerged to sail across the sky above the earth. Each journey lasted twelve hours, making a full day twenty-four hours long — the ancestor of our 24-hour day.

Between the day and night skies was a region known as the Akhet (Egyptian *3ḫt*), into which the sun set before descending into the Duat, and into which he rose before appearing in the morning sky. The concept of the Akhet was a practical explanation of why light fades gradually after sunset and appears gradually before sunrise, instead of disappearing and reappearing with the sun all at once.

Egypt itself was the center of the ancient Egyptian world; the countries around it were called simply *ḫ3swt* "deserts." Egypt's southern border was at Aswan (Egyptian *3bw*), about 400 miles south of modern Cairo; beyond was the land of Nubia (from the ancient Egyptian word *nbw* "gold"). To the north lay the Mediterranean Ocean, known to the Egyptians as the "Great Blue-Green" (*w3ḏ-wr*). For most of ancient Egyptian history Egypt was largely a desert, as it is today: life is only possible in this land because of the Nile (known in Egyptian only as *jtrw* "the river"). Because the Nile flows from south to north, the southern part of Egypt is known as Upper Egypt, and the northern part as Lower Egypt. This reflects the Egyptians' own view, in which south was "up": in Egyptian, the words for "left" and "east" are the same (*j3bt*), and the word for "west" (*jmnt*) can also mean "right."

The Egyptians had several names for their own country, including *tꜣ-mrj* "land of the hoe" and *kmt*, "black" (in contrast to *dšrt*, the "red" of the desert). The most common name, however, was simply *tꜣwj* "Two Lands." This reflects the geographical division between Upper and Lower Egypt. To the south is the narrow Nile Valley (Egyptian *šmꜥw* "Thin" or *rsw* "South"); just north of modern Cairo (and ancient Memphis) the Nile branches out — nowadays into two branches, east and west, but in ancient times into seven. This region is known as the Delta; in ancient times it was largely marshland, and the Egyptians called it *mḥw* "Marsh."

For most of Egyptian history the political capital of the country was at Memphis (the Greek pronunciation of the Egyptian name *mn-nfr*), just south of modern Cairo. Egypt itself was divided administratively into districts, called "nomes" (Egyptian *spꜣt*), each of which had its own capital and local government. At most, there were 22 nomes in Upper Egypt and 20 in Lower Egypt, but their number varied throughout history; there were probably fewer nomes in the Middle Kingdom than later. Egypt also had, as it still does, several large oases in its western desert (our word "oasis" comes from the Greek pronunciation of the Egyptian word *wḥꜣt* "oasis"), administered from the nomes closest to them. The most important of these is the Fayum (the Arabic pronunciation of Egyptian *pꜣ-ym* "the lake"); it lies some 40 miles southwest of modern Cairo and less than ten miles west of the Nile Valley, around a large lake fed by a tributary of the Nile.

EXERCISE 2

1. Pronounce the following transliterations of Egyptian (from texts of Senwosret III inscribed at the Egyptian fort of Semna, in Nubia; the dots in (f) separate parts of words: see § 3.7).
   a. *jnk nswt ḏdw jrrw* ("I am a king whose words command action")
   b. *jr gr m ḫt pḥ, ssḫm jb pw n ḫrwy* ("To do nothing after an attack is to strengthen the heart of the enemy")
   c. *qnt pw ꜣd, ẖzt pw ḥm-ḫt* ("Aggression is brave, retreat is contemptible")
   d. *nj rmṯ js nt šft st, ḥwrw pw sḏw jbw* ("They are not a people to respect: they are wretches with broken spirits")
   e. *srwd tꜣš n wtt sw* ("who makes firm the border of the one who begot him")
   f. *n mrwt ꜥḥꜣ.ṯn ḥr.f* ("in order that you may fight for it")
   g. *r tm rdj zn sw nḥsj nb m ḫd m ḥrt* ("to not allow any Nubian to pass it going downstream or overland")

2. Give an English transcription for the following proper names: (a) *j-m-ḥtp*, (b) *mnṯw-wsr*, (c) *nj-mꜣꜥt-rꜥ*, (d) *ḫꜥ-m-wꜣst*, (e) *qn-m-ḫpš*, (f) *ḏḥwtj-m-ḥꜣt*.

3. Give the Egyptian transliteration for the following proper names: (a) User-hat, (b) Meret-mut, (c) Amen-em-hat, (d) Amen-hotep, (e) Senedjem-ib, (f) Tjenti.

4. Put the following words in alphabetical order: *sqr, jnm, wjꜣ, zḥ, ḏd, sk, jrj, ꜥꜣ, sw, šw, nḥḥ, šft, dpt, ḫd, ẖzj, nẖ, tꜣ, jꜥj, ꜥb, nḫt, ꜣw, fdt, pn, mrj, bꜣk, rn, qꜣj, ṯꜣ, gr, hrw, fsj, sgr, jz, ṯzj, dšr, rw, bꜣq, mnmnt, nḫꜣ, wꜣḫ, ḥḏ, kꜣ.*

3. Multiliteral Signs

3.1 Biliteral signs

Most of the uniliteral signs introduced in Lesson 2 seem to have been chosen on the basis of the "rebus principle" (see § 1.5). For example, the picture of a mouth (𓂋) was apparently chosen to represent the consonant *r* from the word for "mouth," which was something like **ra* (the asterisk shows that this is a hypothetical reconstruction; the pronunciation is deduced from the Coptic word **ⲣⲟ** "mouth"). The inventors of hieroglyphic writing ignored the vowels and concentrated only on the consonants. The sign for *r* could therefore be used not just for the sound *ra* but for the consonant *r* in any word, regardless of the vowels around it. By the same principle, we might choose to represent the consonant *b* in English words with the picture of a "bee" (), and so write the words "be," "by," "bay," and "ebb" as , ignoring the vowels.

The rebus principle is not limited to single consonants. In an English rebus we might use the picture of a leaf () to write not only the word "leaf" but also the second syllable of the word "belief" (). If we ignored the vowels, we could use the same sign  to write the words "life," "laugh," "loaf," and "elf" as well. In doing so, we would be using  to represent *two* consonants, *l* plus *f*. In the hieroglyphic system such signs are known as **biliteral** ("two-letter") signs. An example is the picture of a tree branch (𓆱), which was used as a biliteral sign for *ḫt*, from the Egyptian word **ḫit* or **ḫut* "wood."

Biliteral signs are among the most frequent of all hieroglyphs. There were nearly a hundred in common use. The table spread over the following two pages shows these signs, arranged in the order of their first consonant, reading down the table, and their second consonant, reading across. To find the biliteral sign *ḫt*, for example, scan down the first column to the *ḫ* row, then across to the *t* column.

As you can see from the table, not every possible combination of two consonants has a corresponding biliteral sign: there are none with the consonant *f* as the first or second consonant, and none with the consonants *h*, *ẖ*, *š*, or *g* as the second consonant. Conversely, some two-consonant combinations have more than one sign.[1] When this is the case, the different signs are generally used in different words. Some biliterals are very common, and are used in the writing of many different words. Others are less frequent, and are used to spell only one word or family of words. For example, the biliteral 𓆼 is used for *ḫ3* in many words that have this two-consonant combination, while the sign 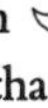 is used for *ḫ3* only in the word *ḫ3wt* "offering table." Some signs can also be used for more than one two-consonant combination: for example, the hieroglyph 𓍋 has the value *3b* in some words and *mr* in others.

1 In the table, commas separate different biliterals with the same value; slashes separate different forms of a single sign. You can find more information about these signs and how they are used in the sign list at the back of this book.

Biliteral Signs (ending in *3–r*)

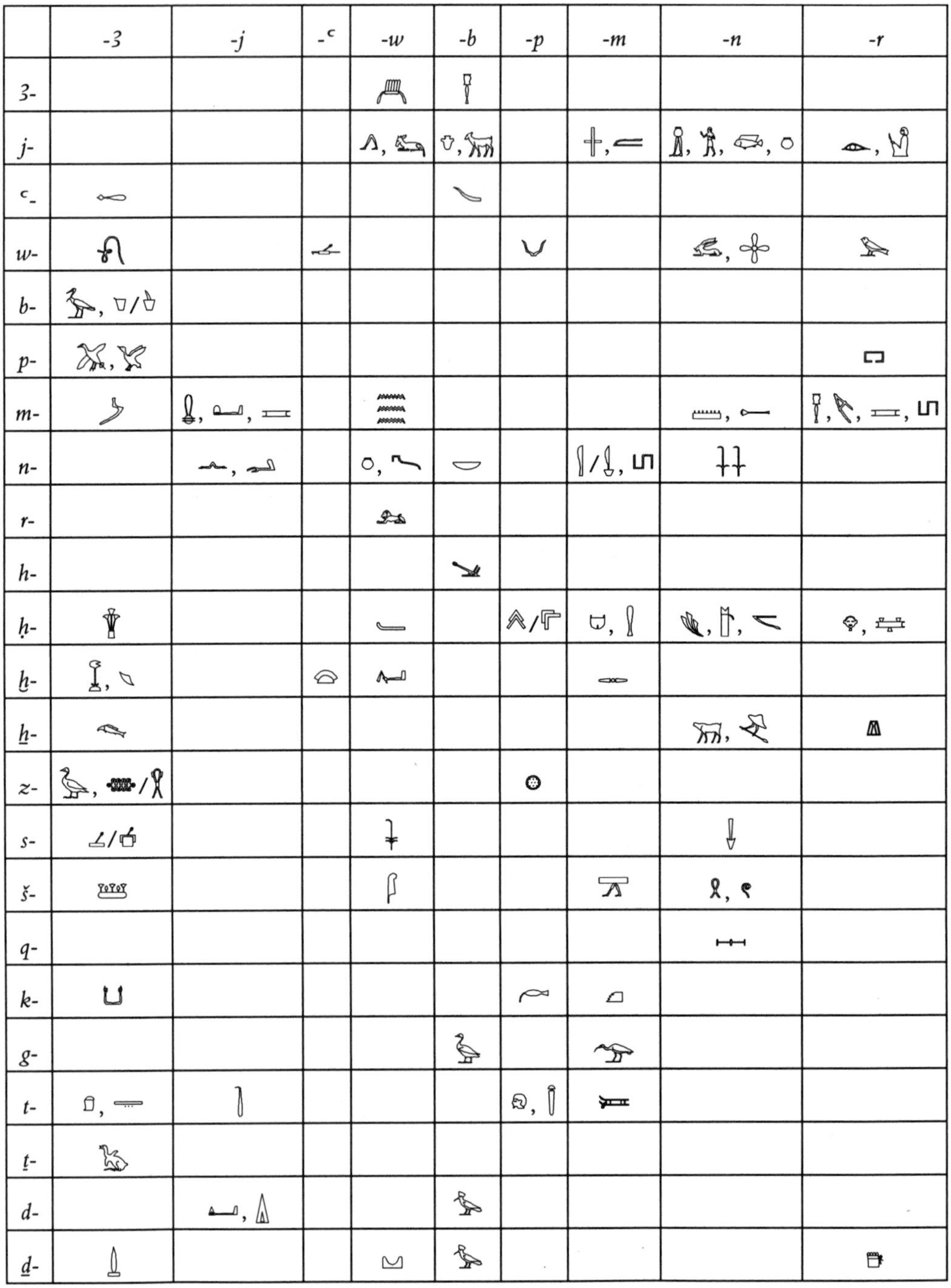
-3
-j
-ᶜ
-w
-b
-p
-m
-n
-r
3-
j-
ᶜ-
w-
b-
p-
m-
n-
r-
h-
ḥ-
ḫ-
ẖ-
z-
s-
š-
q-
k-
g-
t-
ṯ-
d-
ḏ-

Biliteral Signs (ending in *ḥ*–*ḏ*)

	-*ḥ*	-*ḫ*	-*z*	-*s*	-*q*	-*k*	-*t*	-*ṯ*	-*d*	-*ḏ*
ꜣ-										
j-										
ꜥ-										
w-										
b-										
p-										
m-										
n-										
r-										
h-										
ḥ-										
ḫ-										
ẖ-										
z-										
s-										×
š-										
q-										
k-										
g-				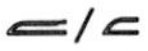						
t-										
ṯ-										
d-										
ḏ-										

3.2 Phonetic complements

For the beginner the sheer number of biliteral signs can be overwhelming. Because they are used so frequently, however, they must be learned in order to read hieroglyphic texts. (A good method for doing so is to prepare a set of "flash cards" with which you can drill yourself.) Fortunately, the hieroglyphic writing system itself offers some help in reading biliteral signs — once you have memorized the uniliteral signs.

Although the biliterals could be, and often were, used by themselves to write two-consonant words or two consonants of larger words, very often scribes wrote them together with uniliteral signs that "spell out" the biliterals. When used in this way, the uniliteral signs are called "phonetic complements." In Middle Egyptian, phonetic complements are used mostly to "spell out" the **second** consonant of a biliteral. The "house" hieroglyph 𓉐, for example, is regularly complemented by the uniliteral 𓂋 when it is used as the biliteral phonogram *pr*. The group 𓉐𓂋 is to be read *pr*, not *prr*: the 𓂋 sign isn't supposed to be read in addition to 𓉐 but together with it. This is an important rule to remember: **a uniliteral sign following a biliteral sign is almost always a phonetic complement and not an additional letter**. To write *prr*, a scribe would use two 𓂋 signs (𓉐𓂋𓂋). The only common exception to this rule is the sign 𓁹: when used as a biliteral (*jr*) it normally has no phonetic complement (𓁹); the group 𓁹𓂋 is normally read *jrr*.

Most biliterals in Middle Egyptian (except 𓁹) are written with a phonetic complement for their second consonant. A few also can have one for their first consonant: in those cases, the biliteral sign normally occurs between the two complements (for example, 𓂝𓄋𓃀 *ꜥb*), though sometimes it can precede both of them (for example, 𓍑𓅓𓂋 *mr*). Here again, the complements are meant to be read **with** the biliteral, not in addition to it: thus, the group 𓂝𓄋𓃀, for example, is to be read *ꜥb*, not *ꜥꜥbb*, and 𓍑𓅓𓂋 is to be read *mr*, not *mrmr*.

Phonetic complements are a handy aid to reading hieroglyphs, since they offer a clue to the consonants that the biliteral stands for. In the few cases where a sign can have more than one biliteral value, the complements also indicate which value is meant: thus, 𓍑𓂋 is to be read *mr*, but 𓍑𓃀 stands for *ꜣb*. The table on the preceding two pages has been arranged to help you look up the value of a biliteral sign based on its phonetic complements. To find the value of 𓈍𓂝, for example, look down the ꜥ column (answer: *ḫꜥ*); to find the value of 𓏏𓍃𓅓, look across the *t* row (answer: *tm*).

3.3 Phonograms as ideograms

Since the biliteral signs are all pictures of real objects, they can also be used as ideograms to write the words for those objects. When used this way in Middle Egyptian, the biliterals normally have **no** phonetic complements, and usually are written with a stroke: for example, 𓉐𓏤 "house" or 𓍑𓏤 "mace." The stroke is a signal meaning "read the sign for what it represents, not for how it sounds." The same convention is used with the uniliteral signs: for instance, 𓂋𓏤 "mouth."

As you might expect, the ideograms normally have the same consonants as the uniliteral or biliteral signs (which is how the signs got to be used as phonograms in the first place). Thus, the word for "house" is *pr*, "mace" is *ḥḏ*, and "mouth" is *r*. Since this is so, we can say that the signs are still used as phonograms even when they are also used as ideograms. The difference is one of range: ideograms refer to one and only one word, while phonograms can normally be used in many words, which have nothing at all to do with the object that the sign represents. When used as an ideogram, the sign Ⲓ, for example, refers **only** to the word "mace," which happens to have the consonants *ḥḏ*; as a phonogram, however, it can occur in many words, such as ⲒⲈⲰ *ḥḏw* "onions" (with the determinative of a plant) and ⲒⲒⲞ *sḥḏ* "brighten" (with the determinative of the sun), which happen to have the same two consonants *ḥḏ*.

3.4 Triliteral signs

In addition to uniliteral and biliteral phonograms, hieroglyphic also had signs representing three consonants; these are called **triliteral** ("three-letter") signs. Like biliterals, triliteral signs were often written with phonetic complements to "spell out" all or part of their value. An example is the familiar hieroglyph ⲫ, which represents a sandal-strap. This sign could be used as an ideogram to write the word "sandal-strap" (ⲫⲓ). In Egyptian, this word has three consonants, *ꜥnḫ*. The same three consonants, however, also appear in the verb "live" (*ꜥnḫ*). For that reason (and not because living has anything to do with sandal-straps), the ⲫ sign was also used as a phonogram in writing this verb and words related to it: for example, ⲫ or ⲫⲞ "live" and "life" (*ꜥnḫ*), ⲒⲫⲞ "cause to live, nourish" (*sꜥnḫ*), and ⲫⲞⲢⲘ "the living" (*ꜥnḫw*, with the determinative for a group of people). This use of the ⲫ hieroglyph is actually much more common than its use as an ideogram, for obvious reasons: people tend to talk about life more than they do about sandal-straps, even in ancient Egypt.

Triliteral signs are just about as frequent as the uniliteral and biliteral hieroglyphs. The following list shows these signs, arranged alphabetically:

jwn	*jm3*	*jsw*	*jdn*		
ꜥwt	*ꜥb3*	*ꜥpr*	*ꜥnḫ*	*ꜥḥꜥ*	*ꜥš3*
w3ḥ	*w3s/w3b*	*w3ḏ*	*wbn*	*wḥ3*	*wḥꜥ*	*wḥm*	*wsr*	*wsḫ*	*wḏꜥ*	*wḏb*
b3s		*p3q*	*psḏ*		
m3ꜥ	*mwt*	*msn*	*mdḥ*		
nfr	*nnj*	*nḥb*	*nṯr*	*nḏm*	*rwḏ/rwd*
ḥnw	*ḥq3*	*ḥtp*	*ḥtm*		
ḫpr	*ḫnt*	*ḫnt*	*ḫrw*	*ḫsf*	*ẖnm*
zw3	*zwn*	*zm3*			

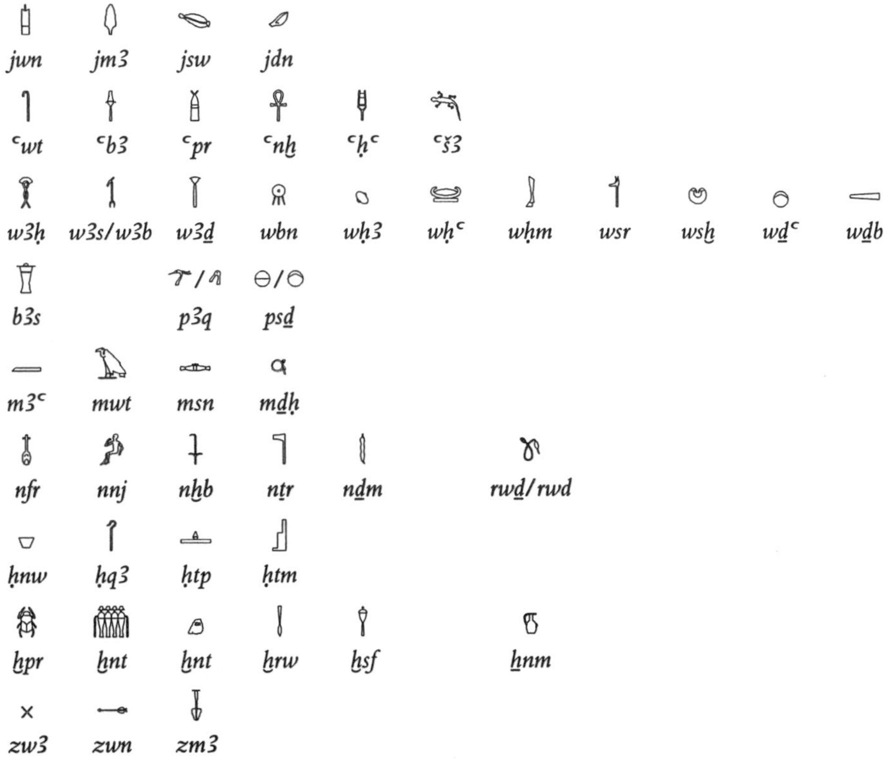

s3b	*s3ṯ*	*sj3*	*sw3*	*sb3*	*spr*	*snḏ/snd*	*sḫm*	*sšm*	*stp*	*sḏm*
šmꜥ	*šms*	*šnꜥ*	*šzp*	*šsr*						
k3p		*grg*		*tjw*		*ṯ3z*				
dw3	*db3*	*dmḏ/dmd*	*dšr*		*ḏꜥm*	*ḏb3*				

As you can see from this list, some triliteral signs can have more than one value, just like some biliterals. Unlike the biliterals, however, most triliteral phonograms were limited to spellings of only one word and its relatives. Most of the Egyptian words with the consonants *ꜥnḫ*, for instance, have something to do with "life" (except for *ꜥnḫ* "sandal-strap"), even if the connection is not immediately obvious: the word *ꜥnḫ* "oath" (with the determinative of a speaking man), for example, comes from the fact that, in Egyptian, oaths began with a form of the verb *ꜥnḫ* "live." For this reason it is not as important to memorize the triliteral signs: you can learn them as you learn the words they are used to write.

3.5 Summary

In this lesson and the two preceding ones, you have learned about the three different ways in which hieroglyphs can be used to write Egyptian words:

1. as **ideograms** ("idea writing") — using the signs to write the word for the object they depict: for example, *pr* "house." In Middle Egyptian, ideograms are usually written with just the one hieroglyph and a stroke.

2. as **phonograms** ("sound writing") — using the signs to represent the consonants of words rather than pictures of objects. Phonograms can represent one (uniliteral), two (biliteral), or three (triliteral) consonants, and are used in writing many words that have nothing at all to do with the objects that are pictured in the hieroglyphs themselves. Biliteral and triliteral signs are usually "complemented" by one or more uniliteral signs, usually representing the last one or two consonants of the multiliteral phonograms. In most cases, the phonetic complements are meant to be read **with** the sign they complement, not in addition to it: for example, *ꜥb* (not *ꜥꜥbb*), *ꜥnḫ* (not *ꜥnḫnḫ*).

3. as **determinatives** — using one or more signs added at the end of a word to indicate the general idea of the word: for example, *pr* "ascend," where the "walking legs" determinative indicates that this is a word having to do with motion; and *ꜥnḫ* "oath," where the determinative of a man with his hand to his mouth shows that this is a word having to do with the use of the mouth. Determinatives also serve to indicate that the signs preceding them are to be read as phonograms rather than ideograms. Since hieroglyphic does not separate words by spaces, determinatives are also a useful guide to knowing where one word ends and the next one begins.

These three uses of hieroglyphs mean that an Egyptian word could only be written in two ways: either as an ideogram, or with phonograms. Writing with ideograms, of course, was only possible for words that could actually be pictured (such as "house"). Since there were about 500 hieroglyphs in common use, only about the same number of words could theoretically be written this way; in practice, however, the number was much less, since not all hieroglyphs seem to have been actually used as ideograms. The rest of the 17,000 or so known Egyptian words had to be written with phonograms.

Contrary to popular belief (and the general opinion of scholars before hieroglyphs were deciphered), writing with ideograms was therefore the exception in hieroglyphic, rather than the rule. Even words that we might imagine could have been written with an ideogram often used phonograms instead. The verb "speak," for example, theoretically could have been written 𓀁𓏤, using the hieroglyph of a man with his hand to his mouth. But this hieroglyph seems to have been used in Middle Egyptian only as a determinative; the verb "speak" was always written with the phonograms 𓆓𓂧 (*ḏd*) — sometimes with the determinative 𓀁, but more often without it. This is why it is so important to memorize the uniliteral and biliteral phonograms: they are the backbone of the hieroglyphic system.

Determinatives were used only for words written with phonograms, for obvious reasons (there is no need to add the determinative 𓉐 to the word 𓉐𓏤 *pr* "house," for example). Besides their practical value, determinatives can add a nuance to the hieroglyphic writing of a word that is often impossible to capture with a single word in translation. The word *mwt* "mother," for example, is normally written as 𓅐𓏏𓁐, with the determinative of a woman (the first sign, representing a vulture, is a triliteral phonogram *mwt*, followed by the phonetic complement *t*). When the "mother" in question is a goddess, however, the word can be written as 𓅐𓏏𓅆, with the "divine" determinative of a falcon on a standard: even though the hieroglyphs still represent only the single Egyptian word *mwt*, the nuance added by this determinative requires two words in translation, "divine mother."

Despite their usefulness, however, determinatives were not added to every word spelled with phonograms. Some "small" words, such as prepositions ("in," "to"), never have determinatives; and a few of the more common words, such as "speak" and "live," are often written without these signs as well. Texts written in cursive hieroglyphs or hieratic tend to have more determinatives than do carved or painted hieroglyphic inscriptions, since the effort required to make an additional sign is much less in handwriting than in carving or painting. By the same token, handwritten texts also tend to use more phonetic complements.

3.6 Nonstandard spelling

Even though it was often "written in stone," hieroglyphic spelling was not fixed. Scribes could add or omit phonetic complements and determinatives, and some words could be written either with ideograms or phonograms. You should not expect to find the same word spelled the same way in every text, or even in the same text. No matter how they were spelled, however, the Egyptian words themselves remained the same, just as the English spellings "love," "luv," and even "♥" all represent the same word. This is one reason why Egyptologists use transliteration: to show the words represented by the hieroglyphs, regardless of their hieroglyphic spelling.

Whatever their use, hieroglyphs themselves were still pictures, and because of that characteristic scribes could sometimes play with the hieroglyphic writing of words. For example, the name of the goddess Hathor, which means "Enclosure of Horus," is usually written as , with the falcon representing the god Horus () actually shown inside an enlarged version of the hieroglyph for "enclosure" (). Some spellings of hieroglyphic words can be even more playful. The preposition *m-ḫnw* "inside" (literally, "in the interior") is usually written in straightforward fashion as (with the "house" determinative), but scribes sometimes wrote it with the signs instead; this derives from an ancient Egyptian pun: the signs are to be read "water" (*mw*) "under" (*ẖr*) "pot" (*nw*), and this obviously sounded similar to the word for "inside" (*mw-ẖr-nw* = *m-ḫnw*).

Although it tended to be conservative in spelling, hieroglyphic wasn't a frozen system. Scribes seem to have been aware of its underlying principles, and from time to time they used these to invent new spellings. These could involve new uses of older hieroglyphs, like the pun for *m-ḫnw*, or completely new ideograms or determinatives: the word *mry* "beloved," for instance, is normally written with phonograms (), but in one text the scribe replaced it with a new ideogram, the picture of a man touching a woman. In Ptolemaic and Roman times the fad for new and clever spellings was so popular that the hieroglyphic system itself was practically reinvented; one text even consists mostly of crocodile signs, each of which is to be read differently. These later texts are much more difficult to read than most hieroglyphic inscriptions, even for specialists.

3.7 Transliteration

Besides the letters introduced in Lesson 2, Egyptologists also use a number of symbols in transliterating hieroglyphic texts:

( ) Parentheses are used to add words or parts of words that aren't represented in hieroglyphs but were part of the word nonetheless. They are mostly used to show the "weak" consonants, which are often omitted in hieroglyphs. Examples: *h(3)b*, *r(m)ṯ* (see § 2.8).

[ ] Square brackets show words or parts of words missing in hieroglyphs. Unlike parentheses, square brackets are used for parts of a hieroglyphic inscription that were originally present but have become damaged or broken away. If Egyptologists can be fairly certain what the missing words were, they restore them between square brackets; if not, they use three dots (called an "ellipsis") between the brackets. Examples: *sw ẖr t3 [n] ꜥ3mw*, *t3[…] n3 n ꜥ3mw*.

⌜ ⌝ Half brackets enclose words or parts of words for which Egyptologists think the original scribe used the wrong hieroglyphs; example: *⌜s⌝w*. They can also be used to indicate restorations of missing text that are considered likely but uncertain.

⟨ ⟩ Pointed brackets are used to add words or parts of words that aren't represented in the hieroglyphs and which Egyptologists think were left out by mistake; example: *jn⟨ḥ⟩wj*.

This book uses small capitals to transliterate and translate names that the hieroglyphic writes in cartouches; example: *JMN-M-Ḥ3T* "AMENEMHAT." A dash is sometimes used to link compound words, such as the three parts of this name (which means "Amun-in-front").

Most Egyptologists also use a dot in transliteration. Many words that the Egyptians probably pronounced as a single word actually consist of several elements, and the dot is used to separate these elements to make them easier for us to recognize. For example, the word *ḏd.n.f* "he has spoken," consists of three elements: the verb *ḏd* "speak"; the consonant *n*, a mark of the past tense; and *f*, the pronoun "he." The dot is usually pronounced like "e" as in *met*: i.e., "jed-en-ef" (rather than "jed-nef"). You will learn more about the use of the dot in subsequent lessons.

ESSAY 3. ANCIENT EGYPTIAN SOCIETY

Ancient Egypt was a layered society, with a thin veneer of bureaucracy on top of a vast underlayer of peasants and craftsmen. With few exceptions we know very little about the "common people" of this society. Most of the art and inscriptions we have were produced for royal monuments, temples, and the tombs of pharaohs and their officials. The other members of Egyptian society have left us very little of their lives. They probably were not taught to read and write, and could not afford to be buried in inscribed tombs or coffins. The houses and villages in which they lived — built for the most part of mud-brick — are largely buried under the towns and fields of modern Egypt, and so have not been excavated. The picture we have of ancient Egypt therefore reflects the lives of perhaps only ten percent of its population. Nonetheless, we can be fairly certain that the outlook and values of this elite are fairly representative of Egyptian society as a whole. The texts themselves often tell us as much, and Egyptian history is full of examples of people who rose from humble beginnings to become important members of the bureaucracy.

The ancient Egyptians divided their world into three classes of sentient beings: the gods (𓊹𓊹𓊹 *nṯrw*), the akhs (𓅜𓏤𓏤𓏤 *3ḫjw*), and the living (𓋹𓈖𓐍𓅱 *ꜥnḫw*). The gods were the original forces and elements of nature, whose wills and actions governed all life (see Essay 4). The akhs were the spirits of those who had died and made the successful transition to life after death (see Essay 5). They did not live in some heavenly paradise, but in this world, among the living. After spending the night asleep in their tombs, the akhs would wake each morning at sunrise and "come forth from the necropolis" to enjoy an ideal life, free from the cares of physical existence. Because they were spirits, they existed on the same level as the gods, and shared many of the gods' powers.

At the apex of the living stood the pharaoh. It was his responsibility to maintain order within Egypt and to keep Egypt's enemies at bay, so that all Egyptians could enjoy a peaceful life. It is a common misperception that the Egyptians considered their pharaoh a god. This is only partly true. The Egyptians knew that the pharaoh was a human being, who had been born and would one day die. But unlike the rest of humanity, the pharaoh also possessed a divine power, because his will and actions could cause enormous changes in society, just like those of the gods.

This dual nature of the king is reflected in two Egyptian words. When referring to the king's divine power, texts use the word *nswt* (𓇓𓏏 — for the spelling, see § 4.15), usually translated "king." It is the *nswt*, for example, who issues decrees, appoints officials, and represents Egypt before the gods. When referring to the individual who happened to hold this divine power, texts use the word *ḥm* (𓍛). It is usually translated "Majesty," but it really means something like "incarnation": the *ḥm* is the individual in whom the divine power of kingship is incarnated. This term is used not only in referring to the king (*ḥm.f* "His Incarnation"), but also in addressing the king (*ḥm.k* "Your Incarnation "), and even by the king in referring to himself (*ḥm.j* "My Incarnation"). The two terms are sometimes combined in one phrase: for example, *ḥm n nswt NB-K3* "the Incarnation of King NEB-KA" — which actually means "the incarnation of kingship (in the person called) NEB-KA." The Egyptians also referred to the king as "pharaoh." This is the Hebrew pronunciation of the Egyptian term *pr-ᶜ3*, meaning "Big House." It originally referred to the royal estate, but came to be used of the king himself, in the same way that "the White House" can refer to the President of the United States.

Egyptian pharaohs normally had several wives, only one of whom (at a time) was the "Chief Queen" (*ḥmt-nswt wrt*, literally, "chief king's-wife"). These women often came from powerful families of the elite, and their marriage to the king was a way for the pharaoh to ensure the support of his aristocracy. For similar reasons, pharaohs sometimes accepted the daughters of foreign kings as secondary wives. Once a dynasty had been established, a pharaoh often married his half-sister (daughter of the previous pharaoh by a different mother) — rarely his full sister — in order to keep the succession to the throne within the immediate royal family.

Below the pharaoh, Egypt was organized into a large, complex bureaucracy of officials who governed all aspects of Egyptian society on the national and local level. The national administration was headed by the vizier ( *ṯ3tj*). Local government was usually organized by nomes (see Essay 2), and during the early Middle Kingdom these areas were headed by local rulers known as nomarchs. Egyptian officials viewed their rank and official responsibilities as signs of success in life, and their inscriptions record their accumulated titles in great detail. There were two kinds of Egyptian titles, defining an official's status in the nobility (often in terms of his closeness to the king) and his actual bureaucratic responsibilities. The most common examples of the former are  *(j)r(j)-pᶜ(t)* "member of the elite"; 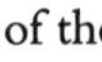 *ḥ3t(j)-ᶜ*, meaning something like "high official" (literally, "whose arm is in front");  *smr-wᶜt(j)* "courtier" (literally, "unique friend"); and  *ḫtmt(j)-bjt(j)* "royal sealer." Relatively few Egyptians rose high enough in the bureaucracy to gain such indications of rank. Titles of responsibility were much more common. Many of them used the word *jmj-r* "overseer" (written  or ) followed by the domain of responsibility; these ranged from the greatest general (*jmj-r mšᶜ wr* "chief overseer of the army") to the humblest *jmj-r š3w* "overseer of pigs."

The great mass of untitled Egyptians was known as the  *rḫyt* "subjects." Most of them were farmers, laborers, and craftsmen. Egyptian society included not only native Egyptians but people of all origins. Like modern America, ancient Egypt was a melting-pot of people from many different lands, including Nubians (*nḥsjw*) and Asiatics (*ᶜ3mw*). The open nature of Egyptian society could include such immigrants as long as they offered allegiance to the pharaoh and became useful members of society. Many foreigners who were first brought to Egypt as the spoils of war, to serve in the households of high officials, later became members of Egyptian families through adoption or marriage. Egyptians were conscious of differences in skin color and other physical characteristics — images of Egyptian men were painted red; those of women, yellow, presumably to indicate less frequent exposure to the sun — but as far as we can tell, they did not base any of their social relations on physical characteristics alone.

Women in ancient Egypt were legally equal to men, but they confined their activies to their households and household industries, such as weaving. Women did not serve as high officials. With few exceptions, the only woman's title was *nbt-pr* "mistress of the house"; this did not mean merely "housewife," but "manager of the household estate." Except for the pharaoh, Egyptian men normally did not marry within their immediate families, and had only one wife at a time. A wife was often called the "sister" (*snt*) of her husband, but not because they had the same parents: instead, the term was one of affection, indicating that the relationship between husband and wife by marriage was as close as that between real brother and sister.

EXERCISE 3

Transliterate the following words (determinatives are explained in parentheses).

1. "Amun" (god)
2. "blessing" (speak, think)
3. "head, above"
4. "secret" (abstract)
5. "build" (effort)
6. "go"
7. "he, him"
8. "under"
9. "appear"
10. "face, over"
11. "the above" (sky)
12. "feed" (use the mouth)
13. "all"
14. "companion" (man)
15. "likeness"
16. "great"
17. "exist"
18. "enter" (motion)
19. "big"
20. "come"
21. "stop" (motion)
22. "pyramid" (pyramid)
23. "Orion" (star)
24. "fetch"
25. "beloved"
26. "new" (abstract)
27. "who gives birth"
28. "witness" (accuracy and speak)
29. "interior" (house)
30. "victorious"
31. "wipe" (effort)
32. "place" (place)
33. "hair" (hair)
34. "take" (force)
35. "give"
36. "fluid" (effluent)
37. "ear" (ear)
38. "stable, steady" (abstract)
39. "staff" (wood)
40. "plow" (plow)
41. "arrow" (arrow)
42. "wild"
43. "brighten" (sun)
44. "bring to mind" (think)

45.  "take away" (force)
46.  "fear" (emotion)
47.  "gate" (house)
48.  "seed" (seed)
49.  "water"
50.  "ball" (ball)
51.  "eye"
52.  "heart"
53.  "ferry" (boat)
54.  "naked" (cloth)
55.  "conceive" (pregnant woman)
56.  "narrow" (bad)
57.  "son" (man)
58.  "daughter" (woman)
59.  "snake" (snake)
60.  "tomb" (house)
61.  "tongue" (flesh)
62.  "swim" (water)
63.  "skin" (skin)
64.  "widow" (woman)
65.  "give"
66.  "pass" (path and motion)
67.  "bow"
68.  "form" (mummy)
69.  "perish" (bad)
70.  "black" (hair)
71.  "empty" (bad)
72.  "protection" (abstract)
73.  "pound" (pounding)
74.  "eternity" (time)
75.  "stela" (stela)
76.  "hack up" (hoe, effort)
77.  "strength" (force)
78.  "what is done"

4. Nouns

4.1 Definitions

Nouns are words that languages use to designate things. The things can be real or imaginary objects, concepts, and actions, and even words themselves: *cat, dragon*; *happiness, telekinesis*; *talking, mind-reading*; *the word "this."* Nouns that refer to objects can be general enough to apply to many different things (*country, goddess*) or specific enough to refer to only one thing (*Egypt, Isis*); the latter are called "proper nouns," and in English are regularly capitalized.

4.2 Parts of nouns

The English nouns *member, members, membership*, and *nonmember* all have in common the word *member*. This word is called the "root" of these five nouns. The noun *member* itself consists only of the root; the others are formed by adding things to this root: the ending *–s* for the plural, the ending *–ship* to give the meaning "group of members" or "quality of being a member," and the prefix *non–* to indicate the opposite of *member*.

Egyptian nouns are built up in the same way, of roots and additions. Some consist only of the root, while others have one or more prefixes, endings, or suffixes. In this lesson we will learn about noun roots and the endings used to indicate gender and number.

4.3 Roots

As in English, the root of an Egyptian noun is simply the part that all related nouns have in common. In the words *nṯr* "god," *nṯrw* "gods," *nṯrt* "goddess," and *nṯrj* "divine," for example, the root is *nṯr* and the others parts are endings added to the root. Most Egyptian roots consist of two or three consonants, but some have as many as five.

4.4 Gender

English divides nouns into three genders: masculine (which can be replaced by *he* or *him*), feminine (which can be replaced by *she* or *her*), and neuter (which can be replaced by *it* or *its*). In English, some nouns are naturally masculine, feminine, or neuter: *father, mother, rock*. Others have no natural gender, and can be used for any of the three: *The speaker gave his report, The speaker expressed her opinion, Attach the speaker to its base*.

Egyptian has only two genders, masculine and feminine, and all Egyptian nouns must be one or the other. It is usually easy to tell which gender a noun is: with very few exceptions, all feminine nouns have the ending *t* added to the root: for example, *snt* "sister" (root *sn* "sibling"). Masculine nouns often have no special ending, though some have the ending *j* or *w* added to the root: examples are *sn* "brother," *ḫftj* "enemy," and *ḥfȝw* "snake."

It is important to keep in mind that the feminine *t* is an added ending, not an original part of the noun itself. (To mark this difference, some Egyptologists separate the feminine ending from the root by a dot in transliteration: *sn.t*). In a few masculine nouns the last consonant is *t*, but this is a part of the root, not the feminine ending; the most common example is  *ḫt* "wood."

As in English, some Egyptian nouns are naturally masculine or feminine; these follow the same rule as other nouns: examples are *jtj* "father" and *mwt* "mother." Like English too, Egyptian had many pairs of masculine and feminine nouns. The feminine counterpart of a masculine noun is made by adding the feminine ending *t* to the root, not to the masculine noun (even though this often appears to be the case, since many masculine nouns have the same form as the root). Here are some examples of such pairs:

 *sn* "brother"	 *snt* "sister"	(root *sn*)
 *ḥq(ꜣ)* "(male) ruler"	 *ḥq(ꜣ)t* "female ruler"	(root *ḥqꜣ*)
 *nṯr* "god"	 *nṯrt* "goddess"	(root *nṯr*)
 *ḫftj* "(male) enemy"	 *ḫftt* "female enemy"	(root *ḫft*)
 *ḥfꜣw* "(male) snake"	 *ḥfꜣt* "female snake"	(root *ḥfꜣ*).

There are very few exceptions to this general pattern of masculine and feminine nouns. The most important has to do with the very common feminine noun  *ḫt* "thing" (originally *jḫt*, not the same as masculine  *ḫt* "wood"). When this noun refers to an actual thing, it has the meaning "thing" or "property," and is feminine. But it can also be used with the more general meaning "something, anything," without referring to anything specific, and in that case it tends to be masculine. Another exception has to do with proper names of places, such as countries and towns: these are often treated as feminine, regardless of their ending.

4.5 Number

Besides gender, nouns can also indicate whether they refer to one thing or more than one. This property is called "number." Modern English nouns have two numbers, singular and plural. Middle Egyptian nouns can also be singular or plural.

In English, nouns normally refer to only one thing (singular) unless they are specially marked to show that they refer to more than one (plural). Plural marking is fairly complicated in English: most nouns simply add *s* (*ruler, rulers*), but some add *es* (*wish, wishes*), others add *en* (*ox, oxen*), still others change their form (*mouse, mice*), and some don't change at all (*one sheep, forty sheep*).

As in English, Egyptian nouns normally are singular unless they are marked otherwise. Unlike English, Egyptian has a very simple rule for marking the plural: masculine nouns add *w* to the **noun**, feminine nouns add *wt* to the **root** (i.e., in place of the feminine singular ending *t*). To illustrate this rule, here are the plural forms of the noun pairs from the preceding section:

sn "brother": *snw* "brothers"	*snt* "sister": *snwt* "sisters"
ḥqꜣ "ruler": *ḥqꜣw* "rulers"	*ḥqꜣt* "female ruler": *ḥqꜣwt* "female rulers"
nṯr "god": *nṯrw* "gods"	*nṯrt* "goddess": *nṯrwt* "goddesses"
ḫftj "enemy": *ḫftjw* "enemies"	*ḫftt* "female enemy": *ḫftwt* "female enemies"
ḥfꜣw "snake": *ḥfꜣww* "snakes"	*ḥfꜣt* "female snake": *ḥfꜣwt* "female snakes."

This rule is absolutely consistent in Egyptian: all nouns form their plurals by it, without exception. The rule can also be stated as follows: All Egyptian nouns mark the plural by means of *w*; masculine nouns add *w* to the **end** of the noun, feminine nouns add *w* **before** the feminine ending *t*.

4.6 Writing the plural

Although the Egyptian rule for forming plural nouns is consistent, the way in which plurals are shown in hieroglyphs is not so rigid. The *w* that distinguishes the plural from the singular is a "weak" consonant (see § 2.8), and is often omitted in writing. Middle Egyptian texts almost never indicate the plural just by writing this ending. The most frequent means of marking the plural is by adding three short strokes to the singular as an extra determinative. These "plural strokes" can be written horizontally (ı ı ı or ııı), vertically (or ), or grouped ( or ), depending on the scribe's preference and the shape of the surrounding signs; sometimes dots were used instead of strokes (∘∘∘, , , etc.). Masculine nouns sometimes write the plural ending in addition to this determinative; feminine nouns almost always use just the determinative. Here are hieroglyphic writings of the plurals from the preceding section:

 *snw* "brothers"	 *snwt* "sisters"
 *ḥq(3)w* "rulers"	 *ḥq(3)wt* "female rulers"
 *nṯrw* "gods"	 *nṯrwt* "goddesses"
 *ḫftjw* "enemies"	 *ḫftwt* "female enemies"
 *ḥf3ww* "snakes"	 *ḥf3wt* "female snakes."

The plural determinative actually replaces an older way of showing the plural, which was to write the determinative of the singular noun three times, and sometimes even the entire word itself three times: for example,  *ḥq3w* "rulers,"  *snwt* "sisters,"  *nṯrw* "gods." In Middle Egyptian this archaic system is hardly ever used, except in religious texts. The plural *nṯrw* "gods," however, is normally written  rather than with the plural determinative.

The plural determinative has two qualities. On the one hand, it indicates that the preceding noun refers to more than one thing; on the other, it shows that the preceding noun has an ending *w* (masculine) or *wt* (feminine). For this reason, plural strokes are sometimes used with words that aren't real plurals. In the word  *rḫyt* "population," for example, plural strokes are used because the word refers to a group of people, even though the noun itself is singular (as it is in English); such nouns are known as "collectives." The abstract noun  *nfrw* "perfection," on the other hand, is written with plural strokes because it ends in *w*, even though the *w* is a masculine singular ending here (as it is in *ḥf3w* "snake") and not a plural: the noun is singular (as it is in English). Such writings are often called "false plurals."

4.7 The dual

Although hieroglyphic writing used three strokes to mark the plural, plural nouns can refer to any number of things, not only three. To indicate just two things, however, ancient Egyptian had a special form of the noun, called the "dual." Like the plural, the dual is marked by special endings: *wj* for masculine nouns, and *j* for feminine nouns. For both genders, the ending is added to the singular form of the noun; examples:

sn "brother": *snwj* "two brothers"	*snt* "sister": *sntj* "two sisters"
ḥq3 "ruler": *ḥq3wj* "two rulers"	*ḥq3t* "female ruler": *ḥq3tj* "two female rulers"
nṯr "god": *nṯrwj* "two gods"	*nṯrt* "goddess": *nṯrtj* "two goddesses"

ḫftj "enemy": *ḫftjwj* "two enemies" *ḫftt* "female enemy": *ḫfttj* "two female enemies"
ḥfꜣw "snake": *ḥfꜣwwj* "two snakes" *ḥfꜣt* "female snake": *ḥfꜣtj* "two female snakes."

The normal way of writing the dual in Middle Egyptian was to show the ending; the "weak" consonant *j* was often omitted, but when it was shown it was usually written with the sign :

masculine *–wj*: , , or  feminine *–tj*:  or , sometimes  or .

Dual nouns could also be indicated by the older system of doubling the determinative or by writing the singular twice. In Middle Egyptian this archaic practice was more common for duals than for plurals. Representative hieroglyphic spellings of the duals above are:

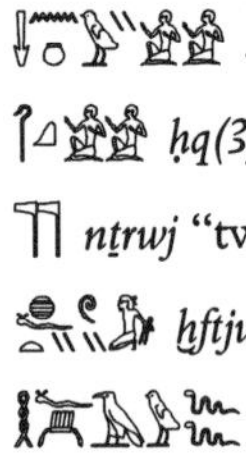
snwj "two brothers"
ḥq(ꜣ)wj "two rulers"
nṯrwj "two gods"
ḫftjwj "two enemies"
ḥfꜣwwj "two snakes"

sntj "two sisters"
ḥq(ꜣ)tj "two female rulers"
nṯrtj "two goddesses"
ḫfttj "two female enemies"
ḥfꜣtj "two female snakes."

As with writings of the plural, hieroglyphic also has some examples of "false duals." The most common example occurs for the word *nwtj* "local" (from *nwt* "town"): since this word had the same consonantal form (though perhaps not the same pronunciation) as *nwtj* "two towns," it was often written as a dual ().

4.8 Summary of gender and number

All Egyptian nouns indicate both gender (masculine or feminine) and number (singular, plural, or dual). The markings for these features are:

MASCULINE

singular	ROOT	example: *sn* "brother" (root *sn*)
	ROOT + *j*	example: *ḫftj* "enemy" (root *ḫft*)
	ROOT + *w*	example: *ḥfꜣw* "snake" (root *ḥfꜣ*)
plural	SINGULAR + *w*	examples: *snw*, *ḫftjw*, *ḥfꜣww*
dual	SINGULAR + *wj*	examples: *snwj*, *ḫftjwj*, *ḥfꜣwwj*

FEMININE

singular	ROOT + *t*	examples: *snt*, *ḫftt*, *ḥfꜣt*
plural	ROOT + *wt*	examples: *snwt*, *ḫftwt*, *ḥfꜣwt*
dual	SINGULAR + *j*	examples: *sntj*, *ḫfttj*, *ḥfꜣtj*

As with the feminine ending, some Egyptologists separate the plural and dual endings by a dot in transliteration: for example, *ḥqꜣ* "ruler," *ḥqꜣ.w* "rulers," *ḥqꜣ.wj* "two rulers," *ḥqꜣ.t* "female ruler," *ḥqꜣ.wt* "female rulers," *ḥqꜣ.tj* "two female rulers." In this book, the dot is used only to separate prefixes and suffixes (which we will learn about later), not endings. You may want to use the dot before the gender and number endings in your own transliterations, however, to help you remember the endings and how they are attached to nouns.

4.9 Defined and undefined nouns

By themselves, all nouns except proper nouns refer to classes of things rather than to specific individuals: the noun *snake*, for instance, can be applied to any serpent. When they are used in sentences, however, nouns are usually **defined** or **undefined**.

Defined nouns can refer to only one specific thing or (if they are plural) one specific group of things. Proper names, by definition (§ 4.1), are always defined. Other nouns can be defined in a number of different ways: in English, for example, by a possessive pronoun ("her snake") or a demonstrative ("those snakes"). Undefined nouns can refer to any number of things from the same class. The following sentences illustrate the difference between defined and undefined nouns:

Jack won't eat snake means that Jack won't eat any snake (undefined).

Jack won't eat her snake means only that Jack isn't interested in consuming one particular snake (defined): he might eat someone else's, however.

Jill doesn't like snakes means that Jill dislikes all snakes (undefined).

Jill doesn't like those snakes means only that Jill is averse to a particular group of snakes (defined): she might actually like other snakes, or snakes in general.

In English, the most common way to indicate whether a noun is defined or undefined is by the definite article *the* or the indefinite article *a* (also *an*, plural *some* or *any*): *Jack won't eat the snake*, *Jill doesn't like any snakes.*

Egyptian nouns are also usually defined or undefined when they are used in sentences. Egyptian uses many of the same methods as English to mark these uses, such as possessive pronouns and demonstratives for defined nouns, and words like *any* for undefined nouns; we will meet these in Lessons 5 and 6. Unlike English, however, standard Middle Egyptian had no definite or indefinite articles. A noun such as *ḥfȝw* can mean "the snake" or "a snake." The absence of words for "the" and "a" may seem confusing at first, but you will soon find that it presents no problem in reading most Egyptian sentences. Many modern languages, such as Russian, also have no definite or indefinite articles, and do quite well without them.

Although standard Middle Egyptian had no articles, there is some evidence that the spoken language did. They turn up from time to time in nonstandard texts, and by the time of Late Egyptian had become a regular part of the written language as well. We will come back to them in the next lesson.

4.10 Noun phrases

Nouns are always single words, whether those words themselves are singular or not. Most languages, including English, have ways to put two nouns together in order to refer to a thing that has both nouns in common. Examples in English are *milkman*, which is formed from the nouns *milk* and *man* and refers to a man who delivers milk; and *milk bottle*, which refers to a container for milk. The result of joining nouns in this way is called a "compound noun" or a "noun phrase" (a **phrase** is two or more words).

Middle Egyptian also has noun phrases. These are used to express three different relationships between the two nouns: apposition, connection, and possession.

4.11 Apposition

The word "apposition" means simply "side by side." Nouns are said to be "in apposition" when both are used together to refer to the same thing. An English example is *our friend the dog*. In many cases of apposition, one of the nouns is general and the other is a proper noun (see § 4.1): *Queen Anne, the pharaoh Ramesses II, God the father*. As in English, two Egyptian nouns can be in apposition: *z3.k ḥrw* "your son, Horus." Many cases of Egyptian apposition involve titles followed by a proper name: for example, *zẖ3w rꜥ-ms* "scribe Ra-mose."

4.12 Connection

In English, two nouns can be connected in a phrase by the word *and*: *salt and pepper, Jack and Jill*. They can also be linked by the word *or*: *coffee or tea*. In these kinds of phrases, known as **conjunction** or **coordination** (*and*) and **disjunction** (*or*), the two nouns do not refer to the same thing (unlike apposition).

Middle Egyptian had no word for "and." Conjunction is normally expressed just by one noun following the other: *t ḥnqt* "bread and beer" (literally, "bread, beer"). Sometimes, however, the words  *ḥnꜥ* "together with" or  *ḥr* "upon" can be used to link the two nouns: *ḥ3tj ḥnꜥ zm3* "the heart and the lungs" (literally, "heart together with lungs"), *ḏꜥ ḥr ḥyt* "stormwind and rain" (literally, "stormwind upon rain").

Disjunction, too, is expressed usually just by putting one noun after the other: *ḏbꜥ s3ḥ* "a finger or a toe" (literally, "finger, toe"). Occasionally, however, it is marked more clearly by putting the phrase  *r-pw* (meaning something like "whichever") *after* the second noun: *z zt r-pw* "a man or a woman" (literally, "man, woman, whichever").

4.13 Possession

Noun phrases can also indicate that one noun belongs to another. In English we can express this relationship in two ways: (1) by making the first noun possessive: *the girl's toys, the girls' mother*, or (2) by putting the word *of* between the two nouns: *the toys of the girl, the mother of the girls*. Egyptian also had two ways of expressing a relationship of possession between two nouns.

1. The **direct genitive** is similar to the English possessive construction. In Egyptian, however, the possessor noun is always **second**, and there is no change to either noun (at least, none is visible in writing). In other words, the direct genitive is expressed just by juxtaposing two nouns (putting one after the other), with the possessor noun second. Such noun phrases can usually be translated by an English possessive construction, though sometimes a translation with "of" sounds better. Here are some examples of the direct genitive:

r jz "the tomb's door" or "the door of the tomb" (*r* "mouth, door," *jz* "tomb")
ḥmt wꜥb "a priest's wife" or "the wife of a priest" (*ḥmt* "woman, wife," *wꜥb* "priest")
z3 zj "a man's son" or "son of a man" (*z3* "son," *zj* "man")
ẖrwj stẖ "Seth's testicles" or "the testicles of Seth" (*ẖrwj* "two testicles," *stẖ* "Seth")
nswt t3wj "Egypt's king" or "the king of Egypt" (*nswt* "king," *t3wj* "Two Lands" = Egypt)
nswt nṯrw "the gods' king" or "king of the gods" (*nswt* "king," *nṯr* "god")
ḏdwt tpjw-ꜥ "the ancestors' sayings" or "the sayings of the ancestors" (*ḏdt* "saying," *tpj-ꜥ* "ancestor").

As these examples illustrate, either the first noun (A) or the second (B) may be masculine or feminine; singular, plural, or dual; and defined or undefined. In every case, however, the direct genitive indicates that A belongs to B. This is a very common construction in Egyptian.

2. The **indirect genitive** is similar to the English construction with *of*, with two nouns linked by a special word that indicates possession. Like the direct genitive, this construction could be used to link nouns of any gender or number, defined and undefined. The linking word, which is called the "genitival adjective," originally had the same gender and number as the first noun (A), but by Middle Egyptian there were only three forms in common use:

𓈖 *n* used when A is masculine singular
𓈖𓏌𓏤 *nw* used when A is masculine plural or dual
𓈖𓏏 *nt* used when A is feminine (regardless of number).

The genitival adjective actually means "belonging to," but it can usually be translated by "of." Here are some examples of the indirect genitive:

z3 n zj "the son of a man" (*z3* = masculine singular)
smrw nw stp-z3 "courtiers of the palace" (*smrw* = masculine plural)
ẖrwj nw stẖ "the testicles of Seth" (*ẖrwj* = masculine dual)
swḥt nt njw "the egg of an ostrich" (*swḥt* = feminine singular)
ḥmwt nt wrw "the wives of the chiefs" (*ḥmwt* = feminine plural)
jzwtj nt j.ḫmw-sk "the two crews of Imperishable Stars" (*jzwtj* = feminine dual).

By the time Middle Egyptian was no longer a spoken language, the three forms of the genitival adjective had been reduced to just one, 𓈖 *n*. Already in good Middle Egyptian, however, we can find examples of *n* used after masculine plurals or duals (instead of *nw*) and feminine nouns (instead of *nt*): *ꜥ3w n sẖtj* "the donkeys of the peasant," *ẖrwj n stẖ* "the testicles of Seth," *jwꜥwt n tpj-t3* "the inheritance of a survivor."

4.14 Summary of noun phrases

The preceding sections show that a phrase of two juxtaposed nouns A B can express several different relationships in Middle Egyptian: apposition ("A, B"), connection ("A and B," "A or B"), and possession ("B's A," "A of B"). In two of these, the relationship can also be expressed by specific words added to the noun phrase: A *ḥnꜥ* B or A *ḥr* B ("A and B") and A B *r-pw* ("A or B") for connection, and A *n/nw/nt* B "A of B" for possession.

When the phrase consists only of the nouns, without additional words, it may seem difficult to decide which of the three different relationships is meant. In most cases, however, the context (surrounding words) and even the nouns themselves make only one meaning likely. The phrase *ḥmt wꜥb* in § 4.13, for example, is most likely to mean "priest's wife" (possession), unless the context is about two people "the woman and the priest" (connection); apposition ("the woman, a priest") is unlikely because the two nouns are different genders. As you will see when you begin reading sentences and longer texts, the nouns and their context almost always rule out all but one relationship — which is presumably why Egyptian usually did not feel the need to add additional words.

4.15 Honorific transposition

In the direct genitive, the possessing noun is **always** second. Although this rule seems to have been inflexible in the spoken language, however, hieroglyphic writing sometimes reverses the order of the two nouns. This happens most often when the possessing noun is *nṯr* "god" or *nswt* "king" (often abbreviated ; for the spelling, see below): in that case, the possessing noun is often written first, out of respect, even though it was spoken second. This practice is known as "honorific transposition." The transliteration of honorific transposition follows the order of speaking, not writing; a dash is often used to connect the two words.

The phrase "temple," for instance, is to be read *ḥwt-nṯr* (literally, "god's enclosure" or "enclosure of god"), not *nṯr ḥwt* (which would mean "the god of the enclosure"). Here are some other common examples of honorific transposition:

- *mdw-nṯr* "god's words" (the Egyptian term for "hieroglyphs": see § 1.4)
- *ḥm-nṯr* "priest" (literally, "god's servant")
- *ḥtpw-nṯr* "god's offerings"
- *z3-nswt* "prince" (literally, "king's son")
- *z3t-nswt* "princess" (literally, "king's daughter")
- *mwt-nswt* "king's mother"
- *ḥmt-nswt* "queen" (literally, "king's wife")
- *zẖ3w-nswt* "king's scribe."

The noun *nswt* "king" itself may involve honorific transposition. This word is actually an archaic noun phrase consisting of the words *n* "of" and *swt* "sedge" (the emblematic plant of Upper Egypt). The exact sense of the phrase "of the sedge" is uncertain. It could mean "he who belongs to the sedge," with honorific transposition of the word ; but it could also mean "he to whom the sedge belongs," in which case the unusual order of the hieroglyphs may just reflect the desire to make a compact group (instead of).

Transposition is very common in personal names. Many Egyptian names honored a particular god or goddess, and in writing the deity's name was often put first. Sometimes this reflects the actual order of the spoken words, as in *ptḥ-wr* "Ptah-wer" (meaning "Ptah is great"). Other cases, however, involve honorific transposition, as in *z3-ptḥ* "Siptah" (meaning "Ptah's son"). Royal names, in particular, follow this pattern: examples are *z-n-wsrt* "Senwosret" (meaning "Man of the goddess Wosret") and *mry-rᶜ* "Meri-re" (meaning "Re's beloved"). A similar practice involves the noun *mry* "beloved"; when the king is called the "beloved" of a god, the god's name is often put first: *mry-jmn* "beloved of Amun."

Middle Egyptian also used honorific transposition in filiations (appositions involving two personal names and the word *z3* "son" or *z3t* "daughter"). In texts from the Middle Kingdom, the father's name was normally written first out of respect: , for example, is to be read *z3-mrw rnsj* "Meru's son, Rensi" (the egg is an ideogram for *z3* "son"), not *mrw z3 rnsj* "Meru, son of Rensi." This practice is found in documents from the Middle Kingdom; later Middle Egyptian texts use the normal order A *z3* B "A, son of B."

ESSAY 4. THE GODS

The ancient Greek historian Herodotus, who supposedly visited Egypt in the fifth century BC, described the Egyptians as "religious to excess, far beyond any other race of men" (*History* II, 37). Modern observers often have the same impression. Apart from tombs, the greatest surviving representatives of Egypt's architecture are its temples; Egyptian art is dominated by figures of the gods; the names of most Egyptians honored the gods; and there is hardly any Egyptian text or inscription that does not at least mention one or more of the gods.

Herodotus's statement that the Egyptians were religious "to excess," however, reflects a particularly Western notion of religion, one which (beginning with the Greeks) has separated religion from other spheres of daily human existence, such as government, social behavior, intellectual pursuits, and science. In ancient Egypt there was no such separation. What we call Egyptian "religion" is nothing less than the way in which the ancient Egyptians understood their world and related to it.

Whether or not they believe in the existence of a god (or gods), most modern societies view the world objectively, as a collection of impersonal elements and forces. We understand, for example, that the wind arises from the pressure differential between areas of low and high pressure; that people get sick because of germs or viruses; and that things grow and change because of chemical and biological processes. This knowledge is the inheritance of centuries of scientific experimentation and thought. It has given us today a detailed understanding of how the world works and how we can deal with it for our own well-being and happiness.

The ancient Egyptians faced the same physical universe we do, and like us they attempted to understand and deal with it. But, without the benefit of our accumulated knowledge, they had to find their own explanations for natural phenomena and their own methods of dealing with them. The answers they came up with are what we call Egyptian "religion."

Where we see impersonal elements and forces at work in the world, the Egyptians saw the wills and actions of beings greater than themselves: the gods. Not knowing the scientific origin of disease, for example, they could only imagine that some malevolent force was behind it. Though they might — and did — develop practical remedies to combat disease, they also believed it was necessary to drive off or appease the forces that had caused the illness in the first place. Egyptian medical texts, therefore, contain not only detailed descriptions of physical maladies and pharmaceutical prescriptions for them but also "magical" spells to be used in combating malevolent forces. What we distinguish as the "science" of medicine and the "religion" of magic were to the Egyptians one and the same thing.

Egyptian gods and goddesses are nothing more or less than the elements and forces of the universe. The gods did not just "control" these phenomena, like the Greek god Zeus with his lightning bolts: they *were* the elements and forces of the world. We recognize this quality by saying that the Egyptian gods were "immanent" in the phenomena of nature. The wind, for example, was the god Shu; in one text, Shu describes himself as follows: "I am Shu ... my clothing is the air ... my skin is the pressure of the wind." When an Egyptian felt the wind on his face, he felt that Shu had brushed against him.

Just as there are hundreds of recognizable elements and forces in nature, so too there were hundreds of Egyptian gods. The most important, of course, are the greatest natural phenomena. They included Atum, the original source of all matter, and his descendants: Geb and Nut, the earth and sky; Shu, the atmosphere (see Essay 2); Re, the sun; Osiris, the male power of generation; and Isis, the female principle of motherhood. What we would consider abstract principles of human behavior were also gods and goddesses: for example, order and harmony (Maat), disorder and chaos (Seth), creativity (Ptah), reasoning (Thoth), rage (Sekhmet), and love (Hathor).

The power of kingship, too, was a god (Horus), embodied not only in the sun as the dominant force of nature but also in the person of the pharaoh as the dominant force in human society (see Essay 3). Our separation of "religion" from "government" would have been incomprehensible to an ancient Egyptian, to whom kingship itself was a divine force. Although the ancient Egyptians could, and did, rebel against individual kings and even assassinate them, they never replaced the pharaonic system with another method of government. To do so would have been as unthinkable as replacing the sun with something else.

The Egyptians saw the wills and actions of their gods at work in the phenomena of everyday life: Re, in the daily return of light and warmth; Osiris and Isis, in the miracle of birth; Maat or Seth, in the harmony or discord of human relations; Ptah and Thoth, in the creation of buildings, art, and literature; and Horus, in the king whose rule made life itself possible. In many cases, they also saw the presence of their gods in certain species of animals: Horus, for example, in the falcon, who soars over all other living creatures; or Sekhmet, in the ferocity of the lion. This association is the key to the many images of animal-headed gods in Egyptian art. To an Egyptian, the image of a lion-headed woman, for example, conveyed two things at once: first, that it was not the image of a human female, and was therefore a goddess; and second, that the goddess in question was Sekhmet. Such images were not an attempt to portray what the gods might look like if they could be seen; instead, they are nothing more than large-scale *ideograms*.

Since the Egyptians saw the gods at work in all natural and human behavior, their attempts to explain and deal with that behavior naturally focused on the gods. Egyptian myths are the counterpart of our scientific textbooks: both explain what the world is like and why it behaves the way it does. Egyptian hymns, prayers, and offering rituals had the same purpose as our genetic engineering and nuclear power plants: both are attempts to mediate the effects of natural forces and to turn them to human advantage.

Although the Egyptians recognized most natural and social phenomena as separate divine forces, they also realized that many of these were interrelated and could also be understood as different aspects of a single divine force. That realization is expressed in the practice known as "syncretism," the combining of several gods into one. The sun, for example, can be seen not only as the physical source of heat and light (Re) but also as the governing force of nature (Horus), whose appearance at dawn from the Akhet (see Essay 2) makes all life possible — a perception embodied in the combined god Re-Harakhti (Re, Horus of the Akhet). The tendency to syncretism is visible in all periods of Egyptian history. It explains not only the combination of various Egyptian gods but also the ease with which the Egyptians accepted foreign deities, such as Baal and Astarte, into their pantheon, as different forms of their own familiar gods.

By the 18th Dynasty, Egyptian theologians had even begun to recognize that *all* divine forces could be understood as aspects of a single great god, Amun, "king of the gods." The name Amun means "hidden." Although his will and actions could be seen in the individual phenomena of nature, Amun himself was above them all: "farther than the sky, deeper than the Duat ... too secret to uncover his awesomeness ... too powerful to know." Of all the Egyptian gods, Amun alone existed apart from nature, yet his presence was perceptible in all the phenomena of daily life. The Egyptians expressed this dual character in the combined form Amun-Re: a god who was "hidden," yet manifest in the greatest of all natural forces.

Despite this discovery, however, the ancient Egyptians never abandoned their belief in many gods. In this respect, the Egyptian understanding of divinity was similar to the later Christian concept of the Trinity: a belief that one god can have more than one person. As bizarre as the gods of the Egyptians may seem to modern observers, the religion of ancient Egypt itself was not all that different from religions that are more familiar to us. Far from being an isolated phenomenon of human history, Egyptian religion actually stands at the beginning of modern intellectual inquiry and development.

EXERCISE 4

1. Give the plural and dual of the following nouns (in transliteration):

a. *z3* "son"	e. *mjw* "cat"	i. *šmᶜyt* "singer"	m. *ḥwt-nṯr* "temple"
b. *ḥmt* "woman"	f. *zḫ3w* "scribe"	j. *st* "place"	n. *z3-nswt* "prince"
c. *jtj* "father"	g. *mnjw* "herder"	k. *pr* "house"	o. *sḫtj* "peasant"
d. *mwt* "mother"	h. *nbt* "mistress"	l. *nwt* "town"	p. *ḏrt* "hand"

2. Transliterate and translate the following nouns (the singular is given in parentheses):

a.  — *rd* "foot"

b.  — *ẖt* "belly"

c.  — *msḏr* "ear"

d.  — *sprw* "petitioner"

e.  — *ḫt* "thing"

f.  — *jᶜrt* "uraeus" (a protective serpent)

g.  — *ms* "child"

h.  — ᶜ "arm, hand"

i.  — *z3t* "daughter"

j.  — *msyt* "waterfowl"

3. Transliterate and translate the following noun phrases (NB: some may be capable of more than one translation):

a.  — *nbt* "mistress," *pt* "sky"

b.  — *nṯr* "god," *ḥwt* "enclosure"

c.  — *st* "place," *ᶜnḫ* "living"

d.  — *rm* "fish," *3pd* "bird"

e.  — *t3* "land"

f.  — *jtrw* "river"

g.  — *sb3* "star"

h. 

i. 

j. 

k. 

l.  — *r* "speech," *kmt* "Egypt"

m.  — *t* "bread," *mw* "water"

n.  — *ṯ3w* "air, breath," *ꜥnḫ* "life"

4. Below are some damaged texts with missing signs or words marked by square brackets. Fill in the missing hieroglyphs and the gaps in transliteration.

   a. 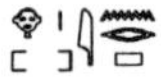 *ḥr […] jnr* "surface (face) of the stone"

   b.  *ḥwt-nṯr […] jmn* "temple of Amun"

   c.  *snw[…] snwt* "brothers and sisters"

   d.  *sn[…] wsjr* "Osiris's two sisters"

   e. 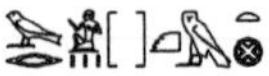 *wrw […] kmt* "great ones of Egypt"

   f.  *ḫt […] ꜥnḫ* "wood of life" (idiom for "food")

5. Pronouns

5.1 Definitions

Pronouns are words that languages use to stand in for nouns (the word "pronoun" means "for a noun"). In the English sentence *As for Jack, he applies himself to his lessons*, for example, the pronouns *he, himself,* and *his* all refer to the same thing as the noun *Jack*; they are used so that the speaker doesn't have to repeat the same noun (*As for Jack, Jack applies Jack to Jack's lessons*). Although all three pronouns refer to the same thing, they have different forms (and different grammatical names) because they do different jobs in the sentence: *he* is a subject pronoun, used here to indicate the actor of the verb *applies*; *himself* is a reflexive pronoun, serving as object of the verb; and *his* is a possessive pronoun, the owner here of the noun *lessons*.

Besides the various forms they may take, pronouns also belong to several different categories. *He, himself,* and *his* are all **personal** pronouns. "Person" is a term grammarians use to describe the participants in a conversation. The **first person** is the speaker or speakers: English first-person pronouns are *I, me, my, mine, myself* (singular); and *we, us, our, ours, ourselves* (plural). The **second person** is the person or persons spoken to: second-person pronouns in English are *you, your, yours* (singular or plural); *yourself* (singular) and *yourselves* (plural). The **third person** refers to people or things spoken about; in English, third-person pronouns also indicate the gender and number of their referent (the person or thing they refer to): masculine singular *he, him, his, himself*; feminine singular *she, her, hers, herself*; neuter singular *it, its, itself*; and plural *they, them, their, theirs, themselves.*

A second category consists of **demonstrative** pronouns, words that "point" to their referent. English examples are *this, that, these,* and *those.* **Interrogative** pronouns belong to a third category. These are "question" words, such as English *who* (*Who did it?*), *what* (*What did they do?*), and *which* (*Which was it?*).

The different kinds and categories of pronouns are not peculiar to English. All languages have them in one form or another. They also existed in ancient Egyptian.

5.2 Personal pronouns

English has four kinds of personal pronouns: subject (*he*), object (*him*), possessive (*his*), and reflexive (*himself*). Middle Egyptian also had four kinds. Three of these are called **suffix**, **dependent**, and **independent** pronouns; we will meet the fourth kind later. As in English, these pronouns indicated the person, gender, and number of their referent. The distribution of these features was a bit different in Egyptian than it is in English:

- first-person pronouns indicated only number: singular (abbreviated 1s), plural (1pl), or dual (1du). This is true for the spoken language and for most hieroglyphic texts. But hieroglyphic *writing* was able to indicate whether the speaker was male or female, and it occasionally did so, as we will see. This is a feature of writing only, and cannot be reflected either in transliteration or in translation.

- second-person pronouns indicated both gender and number, producing probably six such pronouns in all: masculine singular (2ms) and feminine singular (2fs), masculine plural (2mpl) and feminine plural (2fpl), masculine dual (2mdu) and feminine dual (2fdu). The distinction between masculine and feminine in the plural and dual was indicated only by vowels (if it existed at all), and cannot be seen in writing. As a result, we need to talk about only four second-person pronouns: masculine singular (2ms), feminine singular (2fs), plural (2pl), and dual (2du).
- third-person pronouns also indicated gender and number. As in the second person, there may have been as many as six third-person pronouns, but only four can be distinguished in writing: masculine singular (3ms), feminine singular (3fs), plural (3pl), and dual (3du).

Altogether, Middle Egyptian theoretically had as many as eighteen forms of these three personal pronouns. In texts, however, there are far fewer forms. Some of the differences cannot be seen in writing, and the dual forms were rarely used and seem to have been disappearing from the language. For the most part, therefore, we need to learn only eight forms — the same number as in English.

5.3 Personal pronouns: suffix

The suffix pronouns are the most common of all Egyptian pronouns. They are called suffixes because they were added to the end of words. They are always part of the word they are added to, and could not stand by themselves as separate words. Of all the various things that could be added to the end of an Egyptian word (which we will meet in subsequent lessons), the suffix pronouns were always the last. Most Egyptologists separate them from the rest of the word by a dot (.). The suffix pronouns that appear in Middle Egyptian texts are the following.

1S	*.j*	𓀀, 𓇋, 𓇋𓀀, 𓏤; **often not written** This suffix was probably just the vowel *i* (pronounced "ee"). As a result, it was often omitted in writing, like other vowels. The sign 𓀀 is an ideogram, and could be replaced by other ideograms for specific speakers: 𓁐 (woman), 𓀭 (god), 𓅆 (god or king), 𓀮 or 𓀯 (king), 𓁁 (deceased).
2MS	*.k*	𓎡
2FS	*.ṯ*	𓍿; also 𓏏 *.t* (see § 2.8.3)
3MS	*.f*	𓆑
3FS	*.s*	𓋴, 𓊃
1PL	*.n*	𓈖𓏥, 𓈖
2PL	*.ṯn*	𓍿𓈖𓏥, 𓍿𓈖; also 𓏏𓈖𓏥, 𓏏𓈖 *.tn* (see § 2.8.3)
3PL	*.sn*	𓋴𓈖𓏥, 𓊃𓈖𓏥, 𓋴𓈖, 𓊃𓈖 The 3pl suffix *.sn* was eventually replaced by a suffix *.w*, written 𓅱𓏥 or 𓏲𓏥. The latter became the standard 3pl suffix pronoun in Late Egyptian. It occasionally appears in nonstandard Middle Egyptian texts, beginning in Dynasty 18.

The dual suffix pronouns have the forms *.nj* (1du), *.ṯnj* or *.tnj* (2du), and *.snj* (3du). Writings are the same as the plural forms without plural strokes or with \\ in place of the plural strokes: or ; or , or . These forms are found mostly in older religious texts; normally the plural forms are used for both plural and dual.

5.4 **Personal pronouns: dependent**

Unlike the suffix pronouns, the dependent pronouns were separate words, but they are called "dependent" because they are always used after some other word. The forms of the dependent pronoun in Middle Egyptian are the following:

1S	*wj*	, , , , etc. The essential part of this pronoun is the first consonant *w* (or), which is always written. The second consonant *j* is written like the 1s suffix pronoun: it is often omitted in writing; when shown it can be written with any of the ideograms used for the suffix pronoun (for example, for a god, for the king, and so forth).
2MS	*ṯw*	; also , *tw* (see § 2.8.3)
2FS	*ṯn*	; also *tn* (see § 2.8.3)
3MS	*sw*	,
3FS	*sj*	, , ,
1PL	*n*	,
2PL	*ṯn*	, ; also , *.tn* (see § 2.8.3)
3PL	*sn*	, , ,
3N	*st*	,

Note that the plural forms look the same as the plural forms of the suffix pronouns.

The third-person pronoun *st* is neutral in gender and number: it can be used for both the singular and plural. For the most part, the 3ms form *sw* "he, him," the 3fs form *sj* "she, her," and the 3pl form *sn* "they, them" are used to refer to living beings (people or gods), and *st* is used in place of other nouns or plurals ("it," "they, them"). When these are plural, *st* sometimes is written with plural strokes (,).

5.5 **Personal pronouns: independent**

The independent pronouns were separate words, and did not have to depend on some other word in a sentence. The independent pronouns have the following forms in Middle Egyptian:

1S	*jnk*	, , , , , , The signs and are determinatives, and can be replaced by the other signs that are used as ideograms in writings of the 1s suffix and dependent pronouns: for example, or when the speaker is the king.
2MS	*ntk*	

2FS	*nt<u>t</u>*	; also  *ntt* (see § 2.8.3)
3MS	*ntf*	
3FS	*nts*	
1PL	*jnn*	 These are later spellings. This pronoun has not been found in any texts earlier than the New Kingdom, but it certainly existed in Middle Egyptian.
2PL	*nt<u>t</u>n*	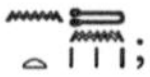; also  *nttn* (see § 2.8.3)
3PL	*ntsn*	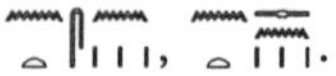.

If you examine the second- and third-person forms, you will see that they actually consist of the element *nt* followed by the appropriate suffix pronoun. The first-person forms are built of the element *jn* followed by a suffix; for the plural, this suffix is the regular suffix pronoun.

Originally the second- and third-person forms consisted of the dependent pronoun plus an ending *t*, at least in the singular. Two holdovers of this older system are still used occasionally in Middle Egyptian, particularly in religious texts:

2S	*<u>t</u>wt*	; also  (from *twt* "image") *twt* (see § 2.8.3)
3S	*swt*	.

These were originally the masculine forms, but in Middle Egyptian they are used for the feminine as well: thus, *<u>t</u>wt* is equivalent to *ntk* and *nt<u>t</u>*, and *swt* is used like *ntf* and *nts*.

5.6 Personal pronouns: summary

The following table summarizes the three different forms of the personal pronouns that are normally used in Middle Egyptian:

	SUFFIX	DEPENDENT	INDEPENDENT	TRANSLATIONS
1S	*.j*	*wj*	*jnk*	"I, me, my"
2MS	*.k*	*<u>t</u>w, tw*	*ntk*	"you, your"
2FS	*.<u>t</u>, .t*	*<u>t</u>n, tn*	*nt<u>t</u>, ntt*	"you, your"
3MS	*.f*	*sw*	*ntf*	"he, him, his, it, its"
3FS	*.s*	*sj, st*	*nts*	"she, her, it, its"
1PL	*.n*	*n*	*jnn*	"we, us, our"
2PL	*.<u>t</u>n, tn*	*<u>t</u>n, tn*	*nt<u>t</u>n, nttn*	"you, your"
3PL	*.sn*	*sn, st*	*ntsn*	"they, them, their."

The translations given here apply for the most part to *each* of the three forms: for example, all three forms of the 3ms suffix pronoun have to be translated "he" or "it" in some cases, "him" in other cases, and "his" or "its" in still others. There is not a simple one-to-one correspondence between the Egyptian and English personal pronouns. For this reason, you should learn to think of the pronouns as representing a particular person, gender, and number and not as words corresponding to the English pronouns: memorize *.f* (for example) as "the 3ms suffix pronoun" and not as "he," "him," or "his."

5.7 Suffix pronouns with nouns

The English translation of the Egyptian personal pronouns depends on how the pronouns are used. Each of the three forms had more than one function in Egyptian. Most of these uses we will meet in future lessons, but here we will consider how the suffix pronouns are used with nouns.

When added to the end of a noun, the suffix pronouns are the equivalent of the English possessive pronouns; for example, with the noun 𓉐𓏤 *pr* "house":

1S	𓉐𓏤𓀀	*pr.j*	"my house"
2MS	𓉐𓏤𓎡	*pr.k*	"your house" (spoken to a man)
2FS	𓉐𓏤𓍿 or 𓉐𓏤𓏏	*pr.ṯ* or *pr.t*	"your house" (spoken to a woman)
3MS	𓉐𓏤𓆑	*pr.f*	"his house," "its house"
3FS	𓉐𓏤𓋴	*pr.s*	"her house," "its house"
1PL	𓉐𓈖𓏥	*pr.n*	"our house"
2PL	𓉐𓏤𓍿𓈖𓏥 or 𓉐𓏤𓏏𓈖𓏥	*pr.ṯn* or *pr.tn*	"your house" (spoken to more than one person)
3PL	𓉐𓏤𓋴𓈖𓏥	*pr.sn*	"their house."

The suffix pronoun is always added at the very end of the noun, after any endings or determinatives: for example, 𓋴𓈖𓏏𓏭𓁐𓁐𓆑 *sntj.f* "his two sisters," 𓋴𓈖𓏌𓅱𓀀𓏥𓍿 *snw.ṯ* "your brothers." Note that the gender and number of the noun have nothing to do with the gender and number of the suffix pronoun, just as in English: *his sister, his sisters*; *our mother, our mothers*. When added to a dual noun, however, the suffix pronouns themselves sometimes have an extra ending 𓏭 *j*, copied from that of the dual: for example, 𓂾𓂾𓆑𓏭 *rdwj.fj* "his two feet," 𓂝𓏤𓅱𓏭𓋴𓏭 *ꜥwj.sj* "her two arms" (but also 𓂾𓂾𓆑 *rdwj.f* and 𓂝𓏤𓅱𓏭𓋴 *ꜥwj.s*).

It is important to remember that the first-person singular suffix pronoun is often omitted in writing. The signs 𓉐𓏤, therefore, can be a writing of *pr.(j)* "my house" as well as *pr* "house." It is also important to remember that the seated man 𓀀 can be both a determinative of nouns and an ideogram for the first-person singular suffix pronoun. In some cases, it is not always clear which function it is supposed to have. The signs 𓅭𓀀, for example, can be read in three different ways:

> *z3* "son" (𓀀 as determinative),
> *z3.j* "my son" (𓀀 as 1s suffix, *z3* without determinative), and
> *z3.(j)* "my son" (𓀀 as determinative, 1s suffix not written).

In the same way, the signs 𓅭𓀀𓀀 can also be read three ways:

> *z3wj* "two sons" (both 𓀀 as determinatives of the dual),
> *z3wj.(j)* "my two sons" (both 𓀀 as determinatives of the dual, 1s suffix not written), and
> *z3.j* "my son" (first 𓀀 as determinative, second 𓀀 as 1s suffix).

This may seem confusing at first, but you will eventually find that it creates little or no problem in reading most texts. Usually, the context will tell you whether or not a singular or dual is being referred to, and whether a 1s suffix should be read or not.

5.8 Demonstrative pronouns: forms and meanings

English has basically two demonstrative pronouns: *this* (plural *these*) and *that* (plural *those*). Middle Egyptian has four. Each of the four appears in three different forms:

MASCULINE SINGULAR	FEMININE SINGULAR	NEUTRAL
pn	*tn*	*nn*
pf ; also *pf3*	*tf* ; also *tf3*	*nf* ; also *nf3*
pw	*tw*	*nw*
p3	*t3*	*n3*

As you can see from this chart, the masculine singular forms all begin with *p*–; the feminine singular, with *t*–; and the neutral forms, with *n*–. The four different demonstratives are formed by adding another consonant to these beginnings: –*n*, –*w*, –*3*, and –*f* (or –*f3*).

The –*n* demonstratives are the most common in Middle Egyptian, and can mean either "this, these" or "that, "those." The translation depends on context: i.e., on whether the reference is to something nearby ("this, these") or more distant ("that, those"). The –*f* demonstratives are normally used to contrast with the –*n* series, in which case they are translated by "that, "those" and the –*n* series by "this, "these." The –*w* demonstratives are an older equivalent of the –*n* series, and have the same meanings; they are still used in Middle Egyptian, though usually in religious texts or in special functions. The –*3* demonstratives seem to be a colloquial (spoken-language) counterpart of the –*n* series, but they also occur in good literary Middle Egyptian texts.

5.9 Demonstrative pronouns: uses

As in English, the demonstrative pronouns of Middle Egyptian can be used either by themselves ("this, that, these, those") or with nouns ("this house, that house, these houses, those houses").

Although all the demonstratives can be used by themselves, Middle Egyptian normally prefers the neutral forms (*nn*, *nf*/*nf3*, *nw*, *n3*) for that function. In that case the demonstrative usually means "this" or "that": for example, *ḏd.n.f nn* "He said this," *ptr n3* "What is that?"

When they are used with nouns, the masculine singular demonstratives are coupled with masculine singular nouns; the feminine singular forms, with feminine singular nouns; and the neutral forms, with plural or dual nouns. The following examples illustrate how the demonstratives and nouns are used together in Middle Egyptian:

MASCULINE SINGULAR	FEMININE SINGULAR
nṯr pn "this god, that god"	*nṯrt tn* "this goddess, that goddess"
nṯr pw "this god, that god"	*nṯrt tw* "this goddess, that goddess"
nṯr pf or *pf nṯr* "that god"	*nṯrt tf* or *tf nṯrt* "that goddess"
p3 nṯr "this god, that god"	*t3 nṯrt* "this goddess, that goddess"
PLURAL	
nn n nṯrw "these gods, those gods"	*nn n nṯrwt* "these goddesses, those goddesses"
nw n nṯrw "these gods, those gods"	*nw n nṯrwt* "these goddesses, those goddesses"
nf3 n nṯrw "those gods"	*nf3 n nṯrwt* "those goddesses"
n3 n nṯrw "these gods, those gods"	*n3 n nṯrwt* "these goddesses, those goddesses."

The singular forms *pn/tn* and *pw/tw* always **follow** the noun (literally, "god this," etc.); *p3* and *t3* always **precede** the noun (like *this* and *that* in English); and *pf/tf* (or *pf3/tf3*) can follow or precede the noun.

With plurals, the demonstratives always **precede** the noun and are joined to it by *n*, which is the "genitival adjective" (§ 4.13.2). The form *n* shows that the demonstrative pronoun is actually singular: *nn n nṯrw* means literally "this of gods." Note that the same form is used for masculine and feminine plurals. Because the neutral forms are actually singular, the noun following *n* is sometimes singular rather than plural in form, though the meaning is still plural: for example, *nn n sḫtj* "these peasants" (literally, "this of peasant") instead of *nn n sḫtjw*.

When the singular demonstratives are used with the first noun of a noun phrase of possession (§ 4.13), they follow the entire phrase if it is a direct genitive and the first noun if it is an indirect genitive: *ḥwt-nṯr tn* "this temple (god's enclosure)," *jrt tn nt ḥrw* "this Eye of Horus." This conforms to a general rule that **nothing can stand between the two nouns of a direct genitive**. The demonstratives can also be used with nouns that have a suffix pronoun: *ḏrt.j tn* "this my hand."

5.10 Demonstrative pronouns: peculiarities

The forms, uses, and meanings we looked at in the preceding section apply to the demonstrative pronouns in general. Certain of the demonstratives, however, have more specialized features.

1. When gods or human beings are invoked, the singular demonstratives *pw* and *tw* are sometimes used after their names. In this use (called the vocative), there is no good English translation for the demonstratives: *h3 nḫt pw* "Oh, Nakht!"— literally, "Oh, this Nakht!" The same construction can be used when the vocative is a regular noun: *jrt tw nt ḥrw* "O Eye of Horus!" When *pw* and *tw* are used with nouns (vocative or otherwise), they sometimes have the forms ,  *pwy* and ,  *twy*.

2. The demonstratives *nn* and *nw* were originally used only by themselves, and a separate set of demonstratives was used with plural nouns:

MASCULINE PLURAL		*jpn*		*jpw*	"these, those"
FEMININE PLURAL		*jptn*		*jptw*	"these, those."

   These older plurals are occasionally found in Middle Egyptian, mostly in texts of a religious nature. They are used **after** nouns, like the singular forms: *nṯrw jpn* "these gods, those gods"; *nṯrwt jptn* "these goddesses, those goddesses." The *–w* forms are used with plural vocatives: *nṯrw jpw* "O gods!," *nṯrwt jptw* "O goddesses!"

3. The demonstratives *p3*, *t3*, and *n3* usually have the meanings "this, that, these, those." In some cases, however, the demonstrative sense is very weak, and the pronouns are equivalent to the English definite article *the* (see § 4.9): for example, *p3 mḫr* "the warehouse." By Late Egyptian, *p3*, *t3*, and *n3* had actually become the definite article, and were no longer used as demonstratives. This is a development that is paralleled in many languages: the definite articles in modern English, German, French, Spanish, and Italian, for example, all come from words that were once — and in some cases, still are — demonstratives. In Egyptian, the use of *p3*, *t3*, and *n3* as the definite article began in the spoken language probably before the Middle Kingdom.

At one time this usage was apparently considered a mark of lower-class or "street" language: in his autobiography, one early Middle Kingdom official claims "I am one who talks according to the style of officials, whose speech is free of *p3*'s."

4. All the demonstratives except the *–3* series seem to have disappeared from spoken Egyptian by the end of the Middle Kingdom, though they are still used in writing. As the spoken language weakened the *–3* series to definite articles, it developed a new set of demonstratives to replace them. These were formed by adding an ending *y* to the old demonstratives, producing masculine singular  (etc.) *p3y*, feminine singular  *t3y*, and neutral  *n3y*. Like the use of *p3*, *t3*, and *n3* as the definite article, these forms occasionally appear in Middle Egyptian texts, particularly after the Middle Kingdom. When used with a noun, they stand first, like *p3*, *t3*, and *n3*: for example, *p3y zp* "this occasion."

5. Along with the definite article and the *–3y* demonstratives, the spoken language also developed a new way of expressing possession, by adding the suffix pronouns to the demonstratives instead of the noun:

MASCULINE SINGULAR	*p3y* + suffix + masculine noun: *p3y.sn pr* "their house"
FEMININE SINGULAR	*t3y* + suffix + feminine noun: *t3y.j ḥmt* "my wife"
PLURAL	*n3y* + suffix + *n* + plural noun: *n3y.s n ẖrdw* "her children."

This created a new set of possessive pronouns, which are the equivalent of the English possessives: for example,  *p3y.j t3 ḥnᶜ p3y.k* "my land and yours." These new forms occasionally appear in Middle Egyptian texts from the Second Intermediate Period and later. Note that the demonstrative part (*p3y*, *t3y*, *n3y*) always corresponds to the gender and number of the noun (*p3y* with masculine singular nouns, *t3y* with feminine singular nouns, and *n3y* with plurals), and has nothing to do with gender and number of the suffix pronoun, just as in the more usual possessive construction in which the suffix pronoun is added to the end of the noun (§ 5.7): for example, *pr.sn* and *p3y.sn pr* "their house," *ḥmt.k* and *t3y.k ḥmt* "your wife," *ẖrdw.s* and *n3y.s n ẖrdw* "her children."

5.11 Interrogative pronouns

The interrogative pronouns are always used in questions. Unlike the other pronouns, they have only one form. There are five common interrogative pronouns in Middle Egyptian:

mj , ,  "who?," "what?"

This is the most common Middle Egyptian interrogative. It corresponds to the dependent pronouns, and like them is used mostly after other words, as we will see in Lessons 7, 15, and 23.

ptr  "who?," "what?"; also *ptj* (see § 2.8.3) , 

This interrogative corresponds to the independent pronouns; it usually stands first in the sentence. The word *ptr* is actually a contraction of two words, the demonstrative ,  *pw* and  *tr*, a kind of word called a "particle," which is often found in questions. In some texts the two words are spelled out more fully:  *pw-tr*. Very rarely, *pw* is used as an interrogative by itself, without *tr*.

jḫ "what?"

This word is occasionally used instead of *mj*, and only when the question is about things ("what?") rather than people or gods ("who?").

jšst "what?"

This is a more common form of *jḫ*, and actually consists of two words: *jš* (a variant form of *jḫ*) and the third-person dependent pronoun *st*. Like *jḫ*, it is used only when the question is about things; but like *ptr*, it can stand at the beginning of a sentence.

zy, *zj* , , "which?," "which one?," "which ones?"

Like the English interrogative *which*, this pronoun can be used by itself or with a noun. In the latter case, *zy* always stands first, and is actually the first noun of a direct genitive: for instance, *zy w3t* "which path?" (literally, "which of path?").

As you can see, the five interrogative pronouns correspond to the English question words *who*, *what*, and *which*. Egyptian has five such pronouns, rather than the three of English, partly because they are used in different ways and in different kinds of sentences. We will meet some of these uses in Lessons 7 and 10, and the rest later in this book.

ESSAY 5. THE GODS ON EARTH

The Egyptian gods were cosmic beings, the elements and forces of nature. As such, they existed on a scale far removed from that of ordinary human beings. Yet their actions often touched individual human lives. The god Shu, for example, existed not only in the atmosphere and the wind but also in individual human breaths; the god Osiris not only brought the sun back to life each morning but also transmitted life from parent to child in each mother's womb.

Because they saw such connections between cosmic phenomena and human experience, the Egyptians believed that their gods were not just distant objects of worship but living beings who could be approached and prayed to. For that reason, the Egyptians built shrines and temples to their gods. These were viewed as places in which the god could — and did — dwell, usually in the form of a statue or other sacred image. The Egyptians saw no contradiction between such images and the cosmic scale of the gods themselves. Each image was viewed as a means by which the god could interact with people, in the same way that Shu was present in each human breath.

Most Egyptian temples have a common plan, with an open-air courtyard in front, a columned hall in the middle, and a sanctuary at the back that housed the god's image. To go from the courtyard to the sanctuary was to journey from the human sphere to the divine — from the familiar sunlit and tangible world to a place of darkness and mystery. The sanctuary itself was normally a small, windowless room, with a pedestal in its middle. The pedestal held a miniature bark in the form of a papyrus skiff, carrying a closed shrine (represented by the hieroglyph). The god's image was housed in this shrine, usually in the form of a gold statue.

The Egyptians thought of these temples, and their sacred images, in much the same way as they viewed the houses of their high officials and the palace of the king. The temple of Luxor, for instance, was known as the "Southern Private Apartment" of the god Amun, his wife Mut, and their son Khonsu. In human society, the royal palace and official residences were off-limits to all but the immediate family and their servants. Normal Egyptians could approach the pharaoh or high officials to seek their assistance only when they appeared in public audience. Often, requests had to be relayed through underlings, rather than directly to the king or officials themselves. Only on special occasions such as public processions did most Egyptians even get to see their rulers.

In the same way, the temples of the gods and goddesses were viewed as their private domains. Like the palace or the houses of high officials, they were accessible only to a limited number of outsiders, including the pharaoh and the god's own immediate servants: the Egyptian word for "priest,"  *ḥm-nṯr*, means literally "god's servant." Priests tended the divine image like servants ministering to a master. In the temple ritual, held several times a day, the priests would open the shrine, remove the statue, bathe it, anoint it with oils, and clothe it in fine linen before reinstalling it in the shrine. A meal of real food was then presented to the image. At the end of the ritual, the priests would close the doors of the shrine and depart, sweeping away their footprints as they left.

Priestly service of this kind was ideally performed by the king, as the high priest of every god. Normally, however, the duty was delegated to the temple's own priests, acting in the king's stead. During the Old and Middle Kingdoms, priestly service was largely undertaken by civil officials as part of their social responsibilities. Ordinary functions such as cleaning the temple and preparing the god's food offerings were tended to by local residents, who served in tours of duty lasting several weeks. Men performing these mundane duties were called  *wꜥb*, literally, "cleaner." Women also served the god, usually by singing and playing the sistrum (a kind of rattle) in processions. Only in the New Kingdom did the priesthood begin to become a permanent profession. Eventually each temple had its own hierarchy, with a high priest ( *ḥm-nṯr tpj* "first god's-servant"); several subordinates (called "second," "third," and "fourth god's-servant"); specialists for linen, oils, and so forth; and a host of *wꜥb*-priests.

Temples also served as the focal point of Egyptian intellectual life. Their libraries held not only the scrolls of liturgies, hymns, and other sacred texts, but also collections of literature. Several Egyptian texts describe how the king had these libraries searched, or searched them himself, to find the proper rituals for a particular ancient ceremony. Schooling also seems to have been a temple function, where young men — and perhaps also some women — were taught to read and write in the  *ꜥt sb3(w)* "room of teaching."

Apart from the daily temple ritual, the high point of temple life was the periodic festivals in which the bark with the god's shrine would be brought out in procession on carrying poles shouldered by the priests. In Thebes, for example, there were several such occasions during the course of the year, including the "Beautiful Feast of the Valley," in which the image of Amun would be transported from his temple at Karnak, in northeastern Thebes, to visit the royal mortuary temples on the West Bank; and the Feast of Opet, in which the barks of Amun, Mut, and Khonsu were transported from Karnak to Luxor.

For most Egyptians these public holidays were the only opportunity they had to see their gods. Even then they saw only the closed shrines; the images themselves remained hidden inside. In the New Kingdom these processions became an opportunity to ask the gods for special interventions, called "oracles." Questions could be delivered in writing, through the priests, for judgment in the course of the procession. Often these oracles were the court of last resort for legal opinions, when local officials were unable to decide between two litigants. A man might ask, for example, "Should the place be given to Menna?" and the god would respond: favorably, by causing the bark to advance or dip on the priest's shoulders; or unfavorably, by retreating or remaining still. The pharaoh Thutmose III even records how he was selected to be king through such a manifestation, when the god's bark singled him out during a procession in Karnak.

These practices can give the impression that there was a significant distance between ordinary people and the temples and images of the gods. Nonetheless, all Egyptians seem to have felt that their gods were accessible to ordinary people through private prayer. The extent to which this was true in the Old and Middle Kingdoms is uncertain, but from the New Kingdom onward there is abundant evidence of individual prayer and devotion, particularly to Amun, whom we might consider the most "unreachable" of all the gods (see Essay 4). Even in earlier times, however, there seems to have been a sense that the gods, as distant as they might be, were concerned for the well-being and interests of all people, even the most humble. In a text from the early Middle Kingdom, a king instructs his successor:

> "Take care of people, the flock of the god. It is for their heart that he has made the sky and the earth. It is for them that he has driven back the darkness of the waters. He has made air for the heart just so that their noses might live. They are his likenesses, that came from his body. It is for their hearts that he rises in the sky. It is to nourish them that he has made the plants, animals, birds, and fish … It is for them that he has built his shrine around them. When they weep, he is listening. It is for them that he has made rulers … to lift up the back of the needy … For the god knows every name."

EXERCISE 5

1. Transliterate and translate:
   a.  — *ms* "offspring," *sn* "sibling"
   b.  — *3ḫt* "field"
   c.  — *ḥmt* "woman, wife," *pr* "house"
   d. 
   e.  — *ḫnw* "property" (singular), *sḫtj* "peasant"
   f.  — *ꜥ3* "donkey"
   g.  — *nb* "lord," *sp3t* "estate"
   h.  — *ẖrd* "child"
   i.  — *ḥknw* "oil" (singular)
   j.  — *nhw* "loss," *mšꜥ* "expeditionary force, army"
   k.  — *st* "place," *snḏm* "residence"

l.  — *smr* "courtier"

m.  — *dpt* "boat"

n.  — *h3w* "vicinity" (singular)

o. 

p.  — *ḥr* "face"

q.  — *mwt* "mother"

r.  — *qnyt* "braves" (collective noun: see § 4.6)

s.  t.  — *qnbt* "council," *ḫt* "thing"

2. From Exercise 5.1, above, convert the following into the plural (transliterate, write in hieroglyphs, and translate):

d.  m.  o. 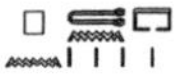 q. 

3. From Exercise 5.1, above, convert the following into the singular (transliterate, write in hieroglyphs, and translate):

f. 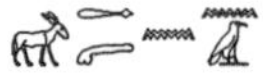 l.  t. 

4. From Exercise 5.1, above, convert the following into the colloquial (spoken-language) form (see § 5.10.5; transliterate, write in hieroglyphs, and translate):

b.  c. 

6. Adjectives

6.1 Definitions

Adjectives are words that describe qualities, such as size ("big," "narrow"), color ("black, red"), and value ("good," "cheap"). In English, adjectives are mostly used to modify nouns — that is, in a noun phrase (§ 4.10) that specifies what kind of noun is meant: *a big house, red ink, the cheap hats.* Less often, English adjectives can be used without a noun: *land of the free, home of the brave.* When an adjective is used without an accompanying noun, English usually requires the addition of the word *one* or *ones* in place of the noun: *a big one* (not **a big*), *the cheap ones* (not **the cheap*).

There are three kinds of adjectives in Middle Egyptian: primary, secondary, and derived. Secondary and derived adjectives come from verbs, nouns, or prepositions; primary adjectives do not. Egyptian had only one primary adjective: *nb* meaning "all," "every." Most Egyptian adjectives fall into the secondary category. These adjectives are actually a verb-form, called a participle, which we will meet later: for example, the adjective *nfr*, meaning "good, beautiful, perfect," which comes from the verb *nfr*, meaning "to be (or become) good, beautiful, perfect." Derived adjectives are made from a noun or a preposition. An example from a noun is the word *nwtj* "local" (often written as a "false dual" : see § 4.7), formed from *nwt* "town." The "genitival adjective" (§ 4.13.2) is another derived adjective, from the preposition *n* "to, for" (which we will meet in Lesson 8). Egyptologists use the word *nisbe* (pronounced "NISS-bee" or "NIZZ-beh"), taken from Arabic grammar, as a term for derived adjectives.

6.2 Adjectives as modifiers

Egyptian adjectives were often used to modify nouns. When they are used in this way, adjectives generally have the same gender and number as the noun; this feature is known as "agreement." In Middle Egyptian, modifying adjectives have three basic forms: masculine singular, masculine plural, and feminine. The masculine singular is the basic form: primary and secondary adjectives have no ending in this form, and nisbes have the ending *–j*:

nb "all" *nfr* "good" *nwtj* "local."

Masculine plural adjectives add the ending *–w* to the singular form. This is the same ending used for masculine plural nouns (§ 4.5), and is written in the same ways (§ 4.6): for example,

nbw *nfrw* *nwtjw.*[1]

Feminine adjectives add the ending *–t* to the masculine singular form of primary and secondary adjectives, and *in place of* the ending *–j* of nisbes:

nbt *nfrt* *nwtt.*

1 The hieroglyph is not the uniliteral *3*, but a triliteral sign with the value *tjw*: see the Sign List, G4 (vs. G1).

When they modify a plural noun, feminine adjectives occasionally are written with plural strokes (e.g., ), but otherwise they have the same form as the singular. Originally there was a separate feminine plural adjective, formed like the feminine plural noun: for example, *ḥmwt nfrwt* "good women" (see the next section). But since feminine adjectives that modify nouns often have no plural strokes in Middle Egyptian, it seems that the original plural form had disappeared, leaving only one form of the feminine adjective. During its lifetime as a spoken language, Middle Egyptian gradually lost all but the masculine singular form of modifying adjectives. As a result, you will occasionally see the masculine singular form used to modify plural or feminine nouns.

When they are used to modify a noun, adjectives always **follow** the noun. Here are some examples of noun phrases with modifying adjectives:

	SINGULAR	PLURAL
MASCULINE	*sḫtj nb* "every peasant"	*sḫtjw nbw* "all peasants"
FEMININE	*ḥmt nfrt* "good woman"	*ḥmwt nfrt* "good women."

The rule that adjectives must follow their noun is invariable. This helps to distinguish the adjective *nb* "all, every" from the noun *nb* "lord, master, owner" (feminine *nbt* "lady, mistress"): thus,  *pr nb* "every house" but  *nb pr* "lord of the house, owner of the house";  *prw nbw* "all the houses" but  *nbw prw* "lords of the houses";  *ḥwt nbt* "every enclosure" but  *nbt ḥwt* "mistress of the enclosure."

6.3 Adjective order

Like English, Egyptian could use several adjectives as modifiers, not just one. In this case all the adjectives should have the same form: for example,  *ḫt nbt nfrt wꜥbt* "every good and clean thing." As this example shows, when *nb* "all" is used with other adjectives, it is always put first. The same is true of demonstratives: 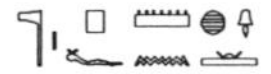 *nṯr pf mnḫ* "that beneficent god." Naturally, since suffix pronouns are part of the noun they are used with, they also precede any adjectives:  *sḫrw.j jqrw* "my excellent plans."

In the preceding lesson, we learned about the general rule that nothing can stand between the two nouns of a direct genitive (see § 5.9). When one or more adjectives modify the second noun of a direct genitive, this is not a problem: for example, *ḥmt wꜥb nb* "every priest's wife, the wife of every priest" (*nb* modifies *wꜥb* "priest"). When adjectives modify the **first** noun of a direct genitive, however, they must also follow the entire noun phrase, or else the noun phrase must be converted to an indirect genitive: for example, *ḥmt wꜥb nbt* or *ḥmt nbt nt wꜥb* "every wife of a priest" (*nbt* modifies *ḥmt* "wife"). When adjectives follow a direct genitive, it is important to pay attention to their endings, because these can show which noun of the direct genitive the adjective is meant to modify.

6.4 Adjectives as nouns

Most Egyptian adjectives can also be used by themselves, as nouns. The only exception is the primary adjective *nb*, which can only be used as a modifier, never as a noun by itself. When you encounter the word *nb* without a preceding noun, it must therefore be the noun *nb* "lord, master" and not the adjective *nb* "all, each, every": thus,  *nb pn* "this lord" and  *nbt tn* "this mistress," not "all this."

In fact, all Egyptian adjectives (except *nb*) *are* nouns. A noun followed by one or more adjectives is actually a noun phrase of apposition (§ 4.11), in which the adjectives are used in apposition to the noun: *sḫrw.j jqrw* "my excellent plans," for example, actually means "my plans, the good ones." Because Egyptian adjectives indicate gender and number, Egyptian often does not need to use another noun with the adjective, unlike English. The feminine singular adjective *nfrt*, for instance, can be used by itself to refer to any "good," "beautiful," or "perfect" person or thing: for example, *nfrt* "the beautiful woman," or *nfrt* "a good thing." Sometimes the scribe will add a determinative to indicate what more specifically kind of person or thing is meant: for example,  *nfrt* "the beautiful woman,"  *nfrt* "a pretty cow,"  "a good thing, something good."

When they are used as nouns, adjectives behave like other nouns. They can have the same plural and dual forms as other nouns (§§ 4.5–4.8): for example, masculine *nfr* "a good one," *nfrw* "good ones," *nfrwj* "two good ones"; feminine *nfrt* "a good one," *nfrwt* "good ones," *nfrtj* "two good ones." Like other nouns, they can also have suffix pronouns, and can even be modified by demonstratives or other adjectives: for example, *nfrt.sn* "their good one," *nfr pn* "this good one," *nfrw nbw* "all the good ones."

6.5 The *nfr ḥr* construction

Like other nouns, adjectives used as nouns can also be part of a noun phrase. One very common example of this is a phrase in which the adjective is the first noun of a direct or indirect genitive (§ 4.13): for example,  *nfr ḥr* "good of face" — literally, "a good one of face." Egyptologists often refer to this kind of phrase as "the *nfr ḥr* construction." Sometimes it can be translated more or less directly into English, as in this example (which is actually an Egyptian expression for "kindly"). In most cases, however, a direct translation sounds odd in English, and the construction has to be paraphrased instead of translated word for word. For example, a man might describe himself as  *ꜥš3 zrw* "one who has many sheep" — literally, "many of sheep" (the plural strokes after *ꜥš3* are a determinative for "many"). Similarly, young women might be called  *nfrwt nt ḥꜥw.sn* "those who have beautiful bodies" — literally, "beautiful ones of their bodies." This construction can even occur when the adjective is used to modify another noun, as in  *zẖ3w jqr n ḏbꜥw.f* "a scribe skilled with his fingers" — literally, "a scribe, a skilled one of his fingers."

The *nfr ḥr* construction is typically used to describe the characteristics of someone or something. The *nfr* part refers to the person or thing being described, and the *ḥr* part refers to something that the person or thing owns or has. Egyptian assigns the adjectival quality to the owner rather than the thing owned, whereas English normally does the reverse: thus, a man is described as *ꜥš3 zrw* "many of sheep" in Egyptian but as "one who has many sheep" in English. We will consider this difference further in § 6.9, below.

6.6 The interrogative adjective

In Lesson 5 we met the Egyptian interrogative pronouns (§ 5.11). Egyptian has one interrogative adjective:  *wr* "how much?, how great?" This is actually the adjective *wr* "great" used as a noun (see § 6.4). Like the interrogative pronouns, it is used only in questions, as we will see in the next lesson.

6.7 Apparent adjectives

Some Egyptian words that are translated by English adjectives are not adjectives in Egyptian. The most common of these is the word for "other," which has the following forms:

MASCULINE SINGULAR	 *ky*
FEMININE SINGULAR	 *kt*,  *kty*
PLURAL	, , ,  *kjwj*

This is actually an old dual noun; the plural looks like a dual dual! When it is used with a noun, *ky* always **precedes** the noun:  *ky sb(3)* "another gate, the other gate";  *kt ḫt* "the other thing, another thing";  *kjw(j) bjtjw* "other Lower Egyptian kings" (for *bjtj*, see the Essay at the end of this lesson). When used in this way, *ky* does not actually modify the noun: instead, it is the first noun of a noun phrase of apposition (see § 4.11). Thus, *ky sb3* really means "another, a gate" or "the other, the gate." Since it is a noun, *ky* can also be used by itself: for example, *ky* "another one, the other one." It can also take a suffix pronoun, as other nouns do:  *kty.f w3t* "its other path" — literally, "its other one, the path." When the plural is used by itself to mean "others" or "the others," it has a different form from that used to modify plural nouns:  *kt-ḫt* or  *kt-ḫj* — actually, a compound noun formed from *kt* "other" and *ḫt* "thing."

Other apparent adjectives have only one form. Like *ky*, they are nouns that can be used by themselves or in a noun phrase with other nouns. They include:

ṯnw	; also  *tnw* (see § 2.8.3) "each, each one"
nhj	 "some, a little, a few."

These words are always the first noun of a genitival noun phrase; *ṯnw* is used in the direct genitive, and *nhj* in the indirect genitive:  *ṯnw rnpt* "each year" (literally, "each one of year");  *nhj n r(m)ṯ* "a few people" (literally, "some of people"),  *nh(j) n ḥm3t* "a little salt, some salt" (literally, "some of salt").

Middle Egyptian also uses a few prepositional phrases (consisting of a preposition followed by a noun) that are best translated by the English adjectives "whole, complete, entire." The most common are:

r ḏr	literally, "to the limit"
r 3w	literally, "according to the length"
mj qd	literally, "like the shape" (the  sign is a determinative in this word)
mj qj	literally, "like the character."

These phrases are used to modify a noun. They always stand after the noun and any other modifiers the noun may have, and usually have a third-person suffix pronoun that agrees in gender and number with the noun: for example,  *t3 pn r ḏr.f* "this entire land" (literally, "this land to its limit"),  *ḥwt-nṯr mj qd.s* "the whole temple" (literally, "the god's enclosure like its shape").

6.8 Comparative and superlative

Adjectives can be used not only to describe a quality but also to compare that quality to something else. Most adjectives in English have three forms for this purpose. The regular form simply describes a quality: for example, *a cheap hat.* A second form, called the "comparative," is used to compare a quality to some other standard. In English, the comparative of many adjectives is made by adding the ending *–er* to the adjective: *a cheaper hat.* For other adjectives, the comparative has to be formed by using the word *more* with the regular adjective: *a more expensive hat.* A third form, called the "superlative," is used to indicate that the quality is the highest of all. This is formed by adding the ending *–est* to some adjectives and by using the word *most* with others: *the cheapest hat, the most expensive hat.* A few English adjectives have special forms for the comparative and superlative: for example, *good, better, best.*

Egyptian is simpler than English because its adjectives have **no** comparative or superlative forms. The adjective *nfr*, for example, can mean not only "good," or "beautiful" but also "better" or "more beautiful" and "best" or "most beautiful." In some cases, only the context will tell which of these three senses the adjective is meant to have. Often, however, Egyptian uses special constructions with the adjective to indicate that it has comparative or superlative meaning rather than its regular sense.

The **comparative** is indicated by adding a phrase with the preposition *r* "with respect to" after the adjective. The preposition points to the thing that the adjective is being compared to, almost always another noun or noun phrase: for example, *nṯr mnḫ r nṯr nb* "a god more beneficent than any god" — literally, "a god beneficent with respect to every god." This comparative phrase can be added not only to adjectives that modify a noun, as in the preceding example, but also to those that are used by themselves: for example, *nfrt r ḫt nbt* "something better than anything" — literally, "a good one with respect to everything."

The **superlative** can be shown in several ways. Egyptian normally uses the superlative for adjectives that stand by themselves and do not modify a noun. Most often, it is indicated by a direct or indirect genitive: for example, *wr wrw* or *wr n wrw* "the greatest of the great" or "the greatest of all" — literally, "the great one of the great ones." Sometimes the word *jm(j)* "among" is used after the adjective instead of a genitive: *wr jm(j) sꜥḥw* "greatest of the dignitaries" or "the greatest dignitary" — literally, "the great one among the dignitaries."

6.9 Egyptian expressions for "have"

To indicate possession, English can say that the owner "has" something, using a form of the verb of possession, *have.* Not all languages, however, show possession in this way. Arabic and Russian, for example, do not. Like these languages, Egyptian too has no exact counterpart for English *have* or its synonyms (*possess, own*). In place of such words, Egyptian uses other kinds of expressions. One of the most common involves the noun *nb* as the first noun of a direct genitive. In many cases, such phrases can be translated by "lord of," as in *nb pt* "lord of the sky." In others, however, *nb* is used to indicate possession, not mastery. Thus, a man might describe himself as *nb ꜥ3w*, meaning that he is an "owner of donkeys" or that he "has donkeys," not that he rules as "lord of donkeys."

Other Egyptian expressions of ownership use adjectival phrases. The *nfr ḥr* construction usually has this connotation, and can normally be translated by an English "have" expression. This is true of all the examples cited in § 6.5, above:

nfr ḥr "one good of face" = "one who has a good face"
ʿš3 zrw "one many of sheep" = "one who has many sheep"
nfrwt nt ḥʿw.sn "ones beautiful of their bodies" = "women who have beautiful bodies"
zḫ3w jqr n ḏbʿw.f "a scribe skilled of his fingers" = "a scribe who has skilled fingers."

In each case, Egyptian assigns the adjectival quality to the owner rather than the thing owned, whereas English normally does the reverse.

Another means of indicating possession involves the genitival adjective *n* (§ 4.13.2). This is actually a nisbe, meaning "belonging"; it therefore has the masculine singular ending *–j*, like other nisbes (*nj*), although the ending is hardly ever shown in the writing of this word. Because it is an adjective, *n(j)* is not limited to expressing just the genitive. One example of its adjectival use is the noun *nswt* "king" (§ 4.15): this is actually a compound word *n(j)-swt*, which probably means "he who has the sedge" (the emblematic plant of Upper Egypt) — literally, "the belonging one of the sedge." We will meet more examples of this use of *n(j)* in the next lesson.

ESSAY 6. THE KING'S NAMES

The king was not only the pinnacle of Egyptian society but also the link between human beings and the gods, since he was human himself yet embodied a divine power (see Essay 3). This dual nature is reflected in many of the king's attributes, particularly in his official titulary, which also reflects his rule over both parts of Egypt, Upper and Lower (see Essay 2).

From the Fifth Dynasty onward, every Egyptian king had five official names, though not all of these are known for every king. Here is the fivefold titulary of the pharaoh Amenemhat III of Dynasty 12:

The first part of the titulary is known as the **Horus** name. It is the oldest of the five names, and consists of three elements: (1) a falcon perched on (2) a schematic rendering of the archaic palace, within which is (3) the king's name. The falcon is emblematic of Horus, the god of kingship. The schematic palace is known as a *serekh* (Egyptian *srḫ*, from the word *srḫ* "make known"). Its lower part represents the niched façade of early mudbrick palaces, and its upper part is a rudimentary ground plan of the palace. Together, the three elements are a hieroglyph meaning "The divine power of kingship (Horus) is incarnated in the individual who resides in the palace." The Horus name of Amenemhat III is *ʿ3 b3w*, a *nfr ḥr* construction (§ 6.5) meaning "He whose impressiveness is great" — literally, "great of impressiveness."

The second name is known as the **Two Ladies**. It first appears in Dynasty 1. The "Two Ladies" (*nbtj*) are the vulture-goddess Nekhbet (*nẖbt*), protector of Upper Egypt, and the cobra-goddess Wadjet (*w3ḏt*), protective deity of Lower Egypt. Amenemhat III's Two Ladies name is *jṯ jwᶜt t3wj* "He who takes possession of the inheritance of the Two Lands."

The third part of the titulary is the **Gold Falcon** name, also known as the Horus of Gold. In Egyptian it is called *rn n nbw* "the name of gold," and is first attested in Dynasty 4. Gold was the traditional material of the gods' skins. With the falcon perched on top of the hieroglyph for "gold," this name indicates that the king was the human incarnation of the god of kingship, Horus. The same idea is reflected in occasional statues of the king as a falcon; in one text the pharaoh Thutmose III of Dynasty 18 even calls himself *bjk n nbw* "a falcon of gold." The Gold Falcon name of Amenemhat III, *w3ḥ ᶜnẖ*, is another *nfr ḥr* construction meaning "He whose life is permanent" — literally, "permanent of life."

The last two names of the titulary are almost always written inside a ring of rope called a "cartouche." The Egyptian word for "cartouche," *šnw* "circle," refers to the circle of the world (see Essay 2), and the combination of the cartouche with the king's name inside it originally indicated that the king has dominion over the whole world. Eventually, however, it became merely a device for marking a royal name; after the Middle Kingdom, the names of queens and royal children could also be written inside cartouches.

The fourth name is the king's **throne name**, also called the prenomen. This is the youngest of the five names, first appearing in Dynasty 5. Eventually it became the most important of all the king's names, and from the Middle Kingdom onward it is often the only name by which the king is mentioned in texts. The throne name usually honors the sun-god Re (whose hieroglyph is always written first, in honorific transposition). It seems to have been a kind of motto by which the king indicated what he intended to be the major theme of his reign; in some cases, pharaohs even adopted the throne name of an illustrious predecessor to show that their reign would be a revival of past glory. Amenemhat III's throne name, *n(j)-m3ᶜt-rᶜ*, means "He to whom the world-order (Maat) of Re belongs" (for the construction, see § 6.9, above).

The throne name is preceded by the title *(n)swt bjt(j)*, which combines two words for "king." The first of these, more fully *n(j)-swt*, is both the general word for "king" (see Essay 3) and more specifically the designation of the king as ruler of Upper Egypt. The second is a nisbe (§ 6.1) from the noun *bjt* "bee"; it was used both as a general term for ancestral kings and a specific designation of the king as ruler of Lower Egypt. The title as a whole thus identifies the pharaoh both as "King of Upper and Lower Egypt" and as the current incarnation of a line of royal ancestors.

The fifth part of the titulary is the **Son of Re** name, also called the nomen. First attested with a cartouche in Dynasty 4, the title *z3 rᶜ* "Son of Re" establishes a direct connection between the earthly king and Re, the ruling force in nature. The name in the cartouche following this title is the king's own personal name, given to him at birth. In the case of Amenemhat III, his name, *jmn-m-ḥ3t*, means "Amun in Front" and honors the god Amun of Thebes, ancestral home of Dynasty 12. Although Egyptian texts usually referred to the king, during his life and after his death, by the throne name, Egyptologists use the Son of Re name instead. Since many kings were named after their fathers or grandfathers, a dynasty often had several kings with the same Son of

Re name. To distinguish these, Egyptologists number the kings (e.g., Amenemhat III). These numbers are a modern convention: they were not used by the Egyptians themselves.

Besides the king's official titulary, Egyptian also used a number of other titles and epithets to refer to the king. The terms  *nswt* "king" and  *ḥm* "incarnation" were discussed in Essay 3. These words were used only for Egyptian kings; foreign rulers were called  *ḥq3* "ruler" (also used for the Egyptian king) or  *wr* "great one." The term  *pr-ꜥ3* "Big House" is also discussed in Essay 3; it is first used to refer to the pharaoh, rather than the royal estate, at the end of Dynasty 18. The king was also called 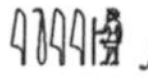 *jty* "sovereign" (also spelled , a "false dual"); this word may be a nisbe from *jtj* "father" (if so, it should be transliterated *jtjj* rather than *jty*). Some common epithets of the king are  *nṯr nfr* "good god,"  *nb t3wj* "lord of the Two Lands," and  *nb ḫꜥw* "lord of appearances." These are often used before the king's cartouches, after the titles *nswt bjtj* and *z3 rꜥ*.

Exercise 6

Transliterate and translate:

1.  — *sḫr* "plan"
2.  — *jnw* "product," *sḫt-ḥm3t* "Field of Salt" (Wadi Natrun Oasis)
3.  — *ꜥt* "room"
4.  — *ḫnw* "interior," *ꜥḥ* "palace"
5.  — *3ḫt* "Akhet" (see Essay 2), *j3btj* nisbe from *j3bt* "east"
6. 
7. 
8.  — *ꜥ3* "big, great," *pḥtj* "strength"
9.  — *mnḏ* "breast"
10.  — *ḫt* "thing"
11.  — *wr* "great," *mnw* "monument"
12. 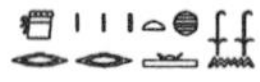
13.  — *zp* "time, occasion"
14.  — *ḫnyt* "crew" (collective: see § 4.6)
15. 
16.  — *pḫrt* "prescription" (collective: see § 4.6), *3ḫ* "effective"
17.  — *rnpt* "year," *ꜥš3* "many"
18.  — *mrwt* "serfs" (collective: see § 4.6)

7. Adjectival and Nominal Sentences

7.1 Definitions

In the preceding lessons we have discussed three kinds of Egyptian words — nouns, pronouns, and adjectives — and some combinations of these words in phrases. Words are the basic building blocks of any language, and the most general way of referring to something. Phrases have a narrower focus: they make it possible to talk about something more specifically than single words do. Thus, the phrase *sḫr pn jqr* "this excellent plan" — which contains a noun (*sḫr* "plan"), a pronoun (*pn* "this"), and an adjective (*jqr* "excellent") — is much more specific than the individual words themselves: *sḫr* alone could refer to any kind of plan, *pn* by itself does not indicate which "this" is meant, and *jqr* used separately just means "an excellent one" or "the excellent one."

By themselves, words and phrases are just ways of referring to something. They don't actually say anything about what they're referring to. The Egyptian phrase *sḫr pn jqr* or the English phrase *this excellent plan*, for example, refers to a specific kind of plan, but doesn't say anything about that plan. In order to say something about words or phrases, languages combine them into **sentences**.

Every sentence contains two parts: a **subject** and a **predicate**. The subject is what is being talked about, and the predicate is what is said about it. In the English sentence *This plan is excellent*, for example, *This plan* is the subject and *is excellent* is the predicate.

In English, every sentence must contain a verb, such as the word *is* in the example just given. Verbs are the most complicated part of a language. This is as true for Egyptian as it is for English; we will begin to consider Egyptian verbs in Lesson 13. The most common verb in English is *be*, and every English sentence must at least contain a form of this verb (such as *is*), unless some other verb is used instead. Thus, we can say *This plan seems excellent*, using a form of the verb *seem*; but we cannot say (in good, grammatical English) **This plan excellent*, without any verb at all.

Although Egyptian has verbs, like English, it is different from English in one important respect: Egyptian has no verb corresponding to the simple English verb *is*. Egyptian is not unusual in this: many languages do not have such a verb, including modern Arabic and Russian. In such languages it is possible to make a sentence without any verb at all: a sentence like *This plan excellent* is perfectly grammatical in them. These are called **nonverbal sentences**. Egyptian has several kinds of nonverbal sentences. In this lesson, we will look at nonverbal sentences that combine nouns, pronouns, and adjectives.

ADJECTIVAL SENTENCES

7.2 Adjectival predicates

Although an Egyptian sentence might not contain a verb, it still must contain a subject and a predicate in order to be a sentence. In the English sentence *This plan is excellent*, the predicate consists of two words: the verb *is* and the adjective *excellent*. The verb *is* itself doesn't really add any information to the sentence: what is really important is the adjectival part of the predicate, *excellent*. For that reason, grammarians call a predicate such as *is excellent* an **adjectival predicate**. Egyptian also has adjectival predicates: unlike English, they consist only of the adjective itself, without a verb. Egyptologists normally call sentences with such predicates "adjectival sentences," which is short for the more accurate designation "sentences with adjectival predicates."

All adjectival sentences follow the pattern PREDICATE–SUBJECT, with the predicate first and the subject second. This is the reverse of English, where the predicate is second: for example,

 *jqr sẖr pn* "This plan is excellent,"

literally, "excellent this plan," where *jqr* is the predicate and *sẖr pn* is the subject. When it is used as an adjectival predicate, the adjective always has the simplest form, which is normally that of the masculine singular (§ 6.2). This is true regardless of whether it has a masculine, feminine, or plural subject: for example,

 *jqr nn n sẖrw* "These plans are excellent," and

 *nfr ḥmt tn* "This woman is beautiful."

By definition, adjectival predicates must contain an adjective. Normally, only secondary adjectives (§ 6.1) are used as adjectival predicates. Examples with nisbes as adjectival predicate are limited (see § 7.5 below), and the primary adjective *nb* can only be used to modify a noun (§ 6.4).

The rule that adjectival predicates are masculine singular in form has one exception. Egyptian uses the old masculine dual form of the adjective (with the ending *–wj*: see § 4.7) in exclamatory adjectival sentences. These are almost always translated in English with the word *How* as the first word of the sentence: for example,

 *nfrwj ḥmt tn* "How beautiful this woman is!,"

literally, "This woman is doubly beautiful." The ending is written in the same way as other dual endings: i.e., , , , or . Because the "weak" consonant *j* is often omitted in writing, it is important to remember that this is the only time an adjectival predicate can have an ending: thus, a sentence like  must be read *jqrw(j) sẖrw* "How excellent are the plans!" and not **jqrw sẖrw* "The plans are excellent."

7.3 The subject in adjectival sentences

The subject of an adjectival sentence is often a noun; this includes anything that can function like a noun, including noun phrases (like those in the examples above), as well as adjectives themselves (§ 6.4): for example,

 *nfr dšrwt* "The red ones are beautiful."

The subject of an adjectival sentence can also be a pronoun. Only demonstrative pronouns and personal pronouns seem to have been used as subjects (§§ 5.2 and 5.8). Like nominal subjects, they always **follow** the adjectival predicate: for instance,

 *nfrwj nn* "How beautiful this is!"

When the subject is a personal pronoun, the **dependent** pronouns are used (§ 5.4). In Middle Egyptian normally **only the second and third-person pronouns** were used as the subject of an

adjectival sentence; for first-person subjects Egyptian normally used a different kind of sentence, which we will meet later in this lesson. The pattern is the same as that for other kinds of subjects:

2MS	*nfr ṯw* "You are good" (also *nfr tw*)
2FS	*nfr ṯn* "You are good" (also *nfr tn*)
3MS	*nfr sw* "He is good"
3FS	*nfr sj* "She is good"
2PL	*nfr ṯn* "You are good" (also *nfr tn*)
3PL	*nfr sn* "They are good"
3N	*nfr st* "It is good"; "They are good" (also).

Personal pronouns are common as subjects in adjectival sentences. Like other subjects, the personal pronouns can also be used with "exclamatory" adjectival predicates ending in *–wj*: for example, *nfrwj st* "How good it is!"

7.4 Additions to adjectival sentences

The combination of an adjectival predicate and its subject is the bare minimum needed for an adjectival sentence. Occasionally, however, other elements can be added to these:

1. The word *wrt* "very" is sometimes added between the adjectival predicate and its subject: for example, *št3 wrt w3t* "The path is very inaccessible."

2. Adjectival predicates, like adjectives themselves, can have comparative meaning (see § 6.8). The comparative phrase introduced by *r* comes after the subject: for instance, *nfr st r ḫt nbt* "It is better than anything" (literally, "It is good with respect to every thing").

3. Instead of using a noun or noun phrase as subject, Egyptian sometimes prefers to use a personal pronoun as subject and to put the noun after it, in apposition to the pronoun: for example, *r(w)dwj sw jb.j* "How firm is my heart!" (literally, "It, my heart, is doubly firm"). Note that the pronoun *sw* and the noun *jb.j* agree in gender (masculine) and number (singular).

7.5 Adjectival sentences of possession

As we saw in § 6.9, the genitival adjective *n* is actually a nisbe *n(j)*, meaning "belonging." Nisbes are rarely used as adjectival predicates, but *n(j)* is an exception. It appears in a fairly common adjectival sentence that has the pattern *n(j)* A B. Like other adjectival predicates, *n(j)* always has the simplest form in this use, which is that of the masculine singular (written). The adjectival sentence *n(j)* A B means either "A belongs to B" *or* "B belongs to A," depending on what A is:

1. When A is a **dependent** pronoun (§ 5.4), the possessive sentence means "A belongs to B." Although the first-person dependent pronouns are not used in normal adjectival sentences, they are used here: for example,

n(j) wj rᶜ "I belong to Re."

In the spoken language, the adjectival predicate *n(j)* and the dependent pronoun were apparently pronounced together as one word. For that reason, they are sometimes written as one word in hieroglyphs, especially in the following combinations:

1S *n(j) wj* ; but also or *nw(j)* = *n(j)-w(j)* "I belong"

3MS *n(j) sw* ; but also *nsw* = *n(j)-sw* "he belongs"

3FS *n(j) sj* or ; but also or *ns(j)* = *n(j)-s(j)* "she belongs."

This construction is very common in personal names of the pattern *n(j)-sw*-B or *n(j)-s(j)*-B, where B is the name of a god. The god's name is sometimes written first, in honorific transposition: for example, *n(j)-sw-mnṯw* "He belongs to Montu."

2. When A is an **independent** pronoun (§ 5.5), the possessive sentence means "B belongs to A": for example,

n(j) ntk hrw "The day belongs to you" or "The day is yours."

As with the dependent pronouns, the combination of the adjectival predicate *n(j)* and the independent pronoun was apparently pronounced as a single word. As a result, the of *n(j)* and the initial of the independent pronouns is often written only once, so that the combination *n(j)-ntk*, for example, looks just like the independent pronoun *ntk*: i.e., *ntk nbw* "Gold belongs to you." The combination *n(j)-jnk*, with the first-person singular pronoun, is often contracted to *nnk*: for example, *nnk pt nnk t3* "The sky is mine, the earth is mine."

3. Normally, only the dependent or independent pronouns are used as A in the *n(j)* A B type of adjectival sentence. In personal names, however, both A and B can be nouns. In this case, B is usually the name of a god or the king, and the sentence means "A belongs to B": for example, *n(j)-ꜥnḫ-ptḥ* "Life belongs to Ptah" (with the god's name in honorific transposition). Such names are very common in the Old Kingdom, but rare thereafter.

4. In all three types of *n(j)* A B adjectival sentence, B is usually a noun, but it can also be a pronoun: for example, *nnk sw* "He belongs to me." B can also be the interrogative adjective (§ 6.6): *n(j)-sw wr* "How much is it?" (literally, "It belongs to how much?").

NOMINAL SENTENCES

7.6 Nominal predicates

In the English sentence *This plan is a disaster*, the predicate consists of three words: the verb *is* and the noun phrase *a disaster*. As with adjectival predicates, the verb *is* doesn't really add any information to the sentence: what is important is the nominal part of the predicate, *a disaster*. For that reason, grammarians call a predicate such as *is a disaster* a **nominal predicate**. Pronouns can also be part of a predicate: for example, *The plan is that one*. Since pronouns "stand for" nouns, they are normally considered together with nominal predicates.

Egyptian also has nominal predicates: unlike English, they consist only of the noun or noun phrase itself, without a verb. Egyptologists normally call sentences with such predicates "nominal sentences," which is short for the more accurate designation "sentences with nominal predicates." Egyptian nominal sentences are more varied than those that have an adjectival predicate. There are three types in Middle Egyptian, with the following patterns: A B, A *pw*, and A *pw* B.

7.7 A B nominal sentences

In Middle Egyptian, the A B pattern is mostly used when A or B is a pronoun. In such sentences, A is normally an **independent** pronoun (§ 5.5), and B is a noun or noun phrase: for example,

 *jnk wḥmw jqr* "I am an excellent herald,"

where A is the independent pronoun *jnk* and B is the noun phrase *wḥmw jqr* (literally, "I an excellent herald"). A can be a noun or noun phrase if B is the neutral form of a demonstrative pronoun such as *nn* "this" (§§ 5.8–5.9): for example,

 *dpt m(w)t nn* "This is the taste of death."

Note that the independent pronouns are always **first** (*jnk* B "I am B") and the demonstratives are always **second** (A *nn* "This is A"). Under normal circumstances, the demonstrative stands as close to the beginning of the sentence as possible. In the example given above, it is last because the two elements of the direct genitive *dpt m(w)t* canot be separated (see §§ 5.9 and 6.3). With an indirect genitive, however, the demonstrative can move farther forward:

 *st nf3 nt ḫnt* "That is a place of landing"

(i.e., a place one can land in). This is possible because the indirect genitive is actually an adjective, and like other adjectives that modify nouns it actually stands in apposition to the noun it follows (see § 6.4): thus, the sentence just cited literally means "That is a place, one belonging to landing."

7.8 A B nominal sentences with nouns

The A B pattern was originally the normal one for all nominal sentences, and could be used when A and B were both nouns or noun phrases. In Middle Egyptian, however, its use with two nouns or noun phrases is mostly limited to the following circumstances:

1. A or B contains a noun of kinship or the noun *rn* "name"; for example,

 *mwt.j nwt* "My mother is Nut,"

where A is the noun phrase *mwt.j* and B is the proper name *nwt* (see Essay 2); and

 *rn n (j)t(j).s*[1] *ywj3* "The name of her father is Yuia,"

where A is the noun phrase *rn n (j)t(j).s* and B is the proper name *ywj3*. Nouns such as *mwt* "mother" and *rn* "name" are known as "inalienables," because they designate relationships that are normally unbreakable: one cannot choose to have a different biological mother, for example.

2. A and B contain the same noun in two different noun phrases: for example,

 *mkt.t mkt rᶜ* "Your (2fs) protection is the protection of Re,"

where A is the noun phrase *mkt.t* and B is the noun phrase *mkt rᶜ*.[2] Such constructions are known as "balanced sentences." They are fairly common in Egyptian, and can be found in other languages as well: for example, modern colloquial Arabic *beiti beitak* "My house (*beit*) is your house."

1 The word *jtj* "father" is often written or , without either of the "weak" consonants and with the sign as a determinative.

2 The in *mkt* is taken from the word  or  *m.k* "behold!," originally *mj.k*.

7.9 **A *pw* nominal sentences**

The A *pw* pattern consists of two parts. The first part, A, can be any noun or noun phrase, or a pronoun; B is the demonstrative pronoun or *pw* (§ 5.8): for example,

z3.j pw "He is my son."

When it is used to modify a noun (§ 5.9), *pw* is always masculine singular, but in the A *pw* sentence it is neutral, and can have a masculine singular, feminine singular, or plural referent. Depending on the context, A *pw* can mean "He is A," "She is A," "They are A," "It is A," "This is A," "That is A," "These are A," or "Those are A": for example,

rʿ pw "It is Re"

ḥmt wʿb pw "She is a priest's wife"

ḥwrw[3] *pw* "They are miserable ones."

These are examples of the A *pw* sentence where A is a noun or noun phrase. A can also be an independent or demonstrative pronoun: for example,

ntf pw "It is he" *p3 pw* "It is this."

Like demonstratives in the A B nominal sentence, *pw* stands as close to the beginning of the sentence as possible. In the examples cited above, *pw* is last because A is either a noun (*z3.j*, *rʿ*, *ḥwrw*) or a direct genitive (*ḥmt wʿb*), which cannot be separated. If the noun phrase in A has an indirect genitive or a modifying adjective, however, *pw* comes after the noun and before any modifiers (including the indirect genitive):

sẖtj pw n sẖt-ḥm3t "He is a peasant of the Wadi Natrun"

t3 pw nfr "It is a good land,"

ḥw pw ḥnʿ sj3 "They are (the gods) Hu and Sia,"

literally, "He is a peasant, one belonging to the Wadi Natrun" (for *sẖt-ḥm3t*, literally "Field of Salt," see Exercise 6, no. 2, and the map on page xiii); "It is a land, a good one"; and "It is Hu, together with Sia" (§ 4.12).

7.10 **A *pw* B nominal sentences**

As we saw in § 7.8, there are only a few instances in which the A B nominal sentence can be used if both A and B are nouns or noun phrases. Middle Egyptian normally uses a different nominal-sentence pattern, A *pw* B, if both A and B are nouns or noun phrases: for example,

pẖrt pw ʿnḫ "Life is a cycle."

As this example shows, A *pw* B often has to be translated "B is A" (more on this in § 7.12). This pattern can also be used even if A or B is a noun of kinship: for instance, *snt.f pw tfnt* "His sister is (the goddess) Tefnut."

3 Note the difference between the two birds and : the first, with a forked tail, is the biliteral sign *wr*, the second, with a rounded tail, is a determinative meaning "bad" or "small."

In the A *pw* B sentence, *pw* always comes before B; but, as in the A *pw* sentence, it also comes as close to the front of the sentence as possible. This means that, in some cases, *pw* can stand "inside" A if A is a noun phrase with parts that can be separated: for example,

 *mnw pw n z(j) nfrw.f* "The monument of a man is his goodness"

instead of **mnw n z(j) pw nfrw.f* (for *nfrw*, see § 4.6). If A is a direct genitive, of course, it cannot be separated:  *ẖzrw ḏwt pw sr(j)w* "Officials are dispellers of evil."

7.11 Summary of nominal sentences

The three nominal-sentence patterns are normally used with the following parts:

1. A B ("A is B" or "B is A")
   - A is an independent pronoun: *jnk wḥmw jqr* "I am an excellent herald."
   - B is a demonstrative pronoun: *dpt mwt nn* "This is the taste of death."
   - Both A and B can be nouns or noun phrases if:
     - one includes a term of kinship or the noun *rn* "name": *mwt.j nwt* "My mother is Nut"; *rn n jtj.s ywj3* "The name of her father is Yuia."
     - the sentence is a "balanced" sentence with the same noun in A and B: *mkt.t mkt rʿ* "Your protection is the protection of Re."

2. A *pw* ("It is A")
   - A is a noun or noun phrase: *z3.j pw* "He is my son."
   - A is an independent pronoun: *ntf pw* "It is he."
   - A is a demonstrative pronoun: *p3 pw* "It is this."

3. A *pw* B ("B is A" or "A is B")
   - A and B are both nouns or noun phrases: *pẖrt pw ʿnḫ* "Life is a cycle."

If you examine the three nominal-sentence patterns closely, you can see that A *pw* is actually a form of the A B pattern, in which B is always *pw*. In fact, then, there are only two nominal-sentence patterns in Middle Egyptian: A B and A *pw* B. Egyptologists call these the bipartite pattern (A B) and the tripartite pattern (A *pw* B). With a few exceptions, they actually complement each other: A *pw* B is normally used when both A and B are nouns or noun phrases, and A B is normally used when one element is a pronoun.

7.12 Subject and predicate in nominal sentences

In the adjectival sentence it is obvious which element is the subject and which is the predicate. The adjective is always the predicate, since it says something about the noun or pronoun that follows, and not vice-versa: thus, *nfr ḥmt tn* says something about "this woman" (namely, that she "is beautiful") and not something about "beautiful." Also, the adjectival predicate always comes before its subject in the sentence.

It is not always so easy to pick out the subject and predicate in nominal sentences. In both nominal-sentence patterns, A B and A *pw* B, either A or B can be the predicate or subject, depending on what the sentence says and the context in which it is used. The A *pw* B sentence *pẖrt pw ʿnḫ* "Life is a cycle," for example, says something about *ʿnḫ* "life" — namely, that it is *pẖrt* "a cycle" — so A is the predicate and B is the subject. In the A *pw* B sentence *mnw pw n zj nfrw.f*

"The monument of a man is his goodness," however, the positions are reversed: this sentence says something about A (*mnw n zj* "the monument of a man") — namely, that it is *nfrw.f* "his goodness" — so B is the predicate and A is the subject.

One way to figure out which element is the subject and which is the predicate is to ask yourself what the sentence is about, as we did for the two sentences in the preceding paragraph: this will help identify the subject. Another way is to think of the sentence as the answer to a question: this will help identify the predicate, since questions always ask for the predicate. Thus, *pẖrt pw ꜥnḫ* answers the question "What is life?" ("Life is a cycle"), so *pẖrt* is the predicate; while *mnw pw n zj nfrw.f* answers the question "What is the monument of a man?" ("The monument of a man is his goodness"), so *nfrw.f* is the predicate here.

In spoken English we normally put stress on the nominal predicate. This cannot be seen in normal written sentences, but it can be indicated by putting the stressed part in boldface: "Life is **a cycle**," "The monument of a man is **his goodness**." We know from Coptic that spoken Egyptian also stressed the predicate (stressed and unstressed words are pronounced differently in Coptic). Thus, the A B pattern was pronounced "A **B**" (with stress on B) when B was the predicate and "**A** B" (with stress on A) when A was the predicate, and the same thing is true for the A *pw* B pattern.

Of course, we cannot see the stress in hieroglyphic texts, just as we cannot see it in normal written English sentences. Nevertheless, in most cases the subject and predicate will be clear from the actual sentence itself.

1. In A B sentences where at least one element is a pronoun,
   - *pw* or a demonstrative pronoun in B is always the subject: for example, *rꜥ pw* "He is **Re**" (answers the question "Who is he?"); *dpt mwt nn* "This is **the taste of death**" (answers the question "What is this?").
   - a third-person independent pronoun in A is always the predicate: for example, *ntf rꜥ* "**He** is Re" (answers the question "Who is Re?").
   - a first-person or second-person independent pronoun in A can be the subject or the predicate: for example, *jnk z3.k* can mean "I am **your son**" (answers the question "Who are you?") or "**I** am your son" (answers the question "Who is my son?"). In these cases, only the context can indicate which meaning is meant.

2. In A B sentences where both elements are nouns or noun phrases,
   - kinship terms in A are normally the subject: for example, *mwt.j nwt* "My mother is **Nut**" (answers the question "Who is your mother?"). Egyptian regularly puts the kinship term in A and the predicate in B (*mwt.j nwt*, not **nwt mwt.j*).
   - a noun phrase with *rn* is always the subject: for example, *rn n jtj.s ywj3* "The name of her father is **Yuia**" (answers the question "What is the name of her father?"). Unlike kinship terms, a noun phrase with *rn* can stand either in the A position, as in the example just given, or in the B position: an example of the latter is *b3b3 z3 r-jnt rn.f* "His name is Baba, son of Re-inet" (answers the question "What is his name?"). In either case, the noun phrase with *rn* is the subject.
   - B is usually the predicate in balanced sentences: for example, *mkt.t mkt rꜥ* "Your protection is **the protection of Re**" (answers the question "What is your protection?").

3. In A *pw* B sentences,
   - when A and B are both nouns or noun phrases, either can be the predicate. This is the normal use of the A *pw* B pattern (§ 7.11). In most cases, the subject and predicate will be obvious from the content of the sentence itself, as we saw above; if not, the context will usually indicate which is which.
   - an independent pronoun in A is normally the predicate. Normally, Egyptian uses the A B pattern when A is an independent pronoun. Because the A B pattern can be ambivalent when the pronoun is the first or second person, however, Egyptian sometimes uses the A *pw* B pattern to make it clear that the pronoun is supposed to be the predicate: for example, *jnk pw šw* "**I** am Shu" (answers the question "Who is Shu?"). This is not a very common construction.

As you can see from this list, there are really very few cases where the identity of the subject and predicate in the nominal sentence are not obvious from the sentence itself. The list probably seems complicated when you read it through for the first time, but after a bit of practice you will find that identifying the subject and predicate comes almost naturally — as, of course, it did for the Egyptians themselves.

It is important to remember that independent pronouns can have two different functions in nominal sentences: as subject or as predicate:

- Independent pronouns as SUBJECT (answers the question "Who are you?"):

1S	*jnk ḥq3*	"I am **the ruler**" (*ḥq3t* if feminine)
2MS	*ntk ḥq3*	"You are **the ruler**"
2FS	*ntṯ ḥq3t*	"You are **the ruler**"
3MS	*ḥq3 pw*	"He is **the ruler**"
3FS	*ḥq3t pw*	"She is **the ruler**"
1PL	*jnn ḥq3w*	"We are **the rulers**" (*ḥq3wt* if feminine)
2PL	*nttn ḥq3w*	"You are **the rulers**" (*ḥq3wt* if feminine)
3PL	*ḥq3w pw*	"They are **the rulers**" (*ḥq3wt* if feminine)

- Independent pronouns as PREDICATE (answers the question "Who is the ruler?"):

1S	*jnk ḥq3*	"**I** am the ruler" (*ḥq3t* if feminine; also *jnk pw ḥq3*: see § 7.12.3)
2MS	*ntk ḥq3*	"**You** are the ruler"
2FS	*ntṯ ḥq3t*	"**You** are the ruler"
3MS	*ntf ḥq3*	"**He** is the ruler"
3FS	*nts ḥq3t*	"**She** is the ruler"
1PL	*jnn ḥq3w*	"**We** are the rulers" (*ḥq3wt* if feminine)
2PL	*nttn ḥq3w*	"**You** are the rulers" (*ḥq3wt* if feminine)
3PL	*ntsn ḥq3w*	"**They** are the rulers" (*ḥq3wt* if feminine)

The two tables look the same except in the third person, where A *pw* is used for third-person subject pronouns but *ntf* B (etc.) when the pronoun is the predicate. Each of these tables, listing the different forms needed to say the same thing for different persons and numbers, is known as a "paradigm." Paradigms exist in every language. In English, for example, the present tense of the verb *be* has the following paradigm: *I am, you are, he/she/it is, we are, you are, they are.* Paradigms are an important part of every language, and must be memorized in order to understand the language. We will meet another paradigm in § 7.14, and many more in future lessons.

7.13 Interrogatives in nominal sentences

In § 5.11 we met a number of interrogative pronouns. Most of these pronouns can be used in nominal sentences; when they are, they are always the predicate. The most common nominal-sentence patterns used with interrogative pronouns in Middle Egyptian are the following:

1. *mj* "who?" "what?"
   This pronoun is mostly used in sentences that we will consider in Lessons 15 and 23. Occasionally, however, it can also be used with a personal pronoun as subject. Two patterns are found in Middle Egyptian:
   - INDEPENDENT PRONOUN + *mj*: *ṯwt mj* "Who are you?"
     For *ṯwt*, see § 5.5. This pattern, where the independent pronoun precedes *mj*, is found mostly in archaic religious texts.
   - *jn mj* + DEPENDENT PRONOUN: *(j)n mj tr ṯw* "Who are you?"
     The words *jn* and *tr* are both particles (see § 5.11 *ptr*), and are not translated. The pronoun *mj* in nominal sentences is almost always used after *jn*. The combination *jn mj* was evidently pronounced as one word, which became ⲚⲒⲘ in Coptic. The same pronunciation may have existed already in Middle Egyptian, since we occasionally find the spellings (as above) and *(j)n-mj*.

2. *ptr* "who?" "what?"
   The pronoun *ptr* is the most common interrogative in nominal sentences. It always stands first in the sentence, and can be followed by a noun (or noun phrase) or a **dependent** pronoun as subject: for example, *ptr rn.k* "What is your name?," *ptj sj t3 r(w)d-ḏdt* "Who is she, this (woman named) Rud-djedet?"

3. *jšst* "what?"
   This interrogative is occasionally used in the A *pw* nominal sentence *jšst pw* "What is it?" (literally, "It is what?").

4. *zy* "which?"
   The pronoun *zy* can be found in two nominal-sentence patterns in Middle Egyptian:
   - INDEPENDENT PRONOUN + *zy*: *ntk zy* "Which one are you?"
   - *zy pw* B: *zy tj pw mjw pw ʿ3* "Which is that great cat?"
     The word *tj* here is a writing of the particle *tr* (see § 5.11 *ptr*), and is not translated.

As you can see from these examples, Egyptian normally prefers to put the interrogative pronoun first in the nominal sentence, except when an independent pronoun is the subject.

The interrogative adjective *wr* (§§ 6.6, 7.5.4) is also used in nominal sentences, as the predicate: *wr pw* "How much is it?" (literally, "It is how much?").

Uses of Adjectival and Nominal Sentences

7.14 The first person in adjectival sentences

We saw above (§ 7.3) that sentences with an adjectival predicate are regularly limited to second and third-person subjects, except for *n(j) wj* B "I belong to B" (§ 7.5.1). In place of *nfr wj* "I am good," Egyptian normally uses the nominal-sentence construction *jnk nfr*, literally, "I am a good one." The usual paradigm for adjectival sentences with a pronominal subject is therefore:

1MS	*jnk nfr* "I am (a) good (one)"
2MS	*nfr ṯw* "You are good"
2FS	*nfr ṯn* "You are good"
3MS	*nfr sw* "He is good"
3FS	*nfr sj* "She is good"
1PL	*jnn nfrw* "We are good (ones)"
2PL	*nfr ṯn* "You are good"
3PL	*nfr sn* "They are good"
3N	*nfr st* "It is good," "They are good."

It is important to remember that even though *jnk nfr* is used as the first-person counterpart of *nfr ṯw* and *nfr sw*, it is still a nominal sentence and not an adjectival one. The adjective in *jnk nfr* is (usually) the predicate, but it is a nominal predicate, not an adjectival one.

7.15 Nominal vs. adjectival sentences

Sometimes Egyptian uses a nominal sentence where we might expect an adjectival one. In one text where a path is described, for example, the text says  *ḥns pw* "It is narrow." The pronoun *pw* here shows that this is a nominal sentence (A *pw*). Even though *ḥꜣns* "narrow" is an adjective, it is used here like a noun (see § 6.4), and not as an adjectival predicate: the sentence therefore actually means "It is a narrow one." To say "It is narrow," Egyptian would use the adjectival sentence  *ḥns st*. Of course, there is not much difference in meaning between "It is a narrow one" and "It is narrow"; but the difference does exist, in Egyptian as in English, and you should be aware of it.

7.16 Tense in nominal and adjectival sentences

All the adjectival and nominal sentences in this lesson were translated with the English verb *is* (or *am* and *are* for the first and second persons). As we saw at the beginning of the lesson (§ 7.1), this verb is required in English but does not actually exist in Egyptian, since Egyptian nominal and adjectival sentences have no word corresponding to *is* (or to *am* or *are*). By adding these words in our English translations, however, we also introduce into the translations a feature called **tense**, which exists in every English verb form.

Tense refers to time. The verb *is* in an English sentence such as *The path is very inaccessible* indicates that the path has the quality of inaccessibility at the time the sentence is spoken: this is called the **present tense**. If we say *The path was very inaccessible*, we indicate that it had the quality of inaccessibility before the time of speaking — it may still be inaccessible, but the important thing is that it was inaccessible before: this is known as the **past tense**. And if we say *The path will* *be very inaccessible*, we mean that this will be true after the sentence is spoken (whether or not it is true now): this is called the **future tense**.

Since Egyptian nominal and adjectival sentences have no verbs, **they have no inherent tense**. An Egyptian adjectival sentence such as *št3 wrt w3t* (cited in § 7.4.1) simply connects the quality *št3 wrt* "very inaccessible" with the subject *w3t* "path" without limiting that connection to the past, present, or future. The same is true for a nominal sentence such as *pẖrt pw ʿnẖ* (discussed in §§ 7.10 and 7.12): this simply connects the notion of *pẖrt* "a cycle" with that of *ʿnẖ* "life," without indicating whether the connection is supposed to be true in the past, present, or future.

Because they have no tense, Egyptian nominal and adjectival sentences are much more flexible in meaning than their English translations. Egyptian uses such sentences in two ways:

1. **without reference to tense**. Such statements are known as "**generic**." They are meant to indicate relationships that are always true. In English, generic statements normally use the present tense. For example, the sentence *pẖrt pw ʿnẖ* "Life is a cycle" says something about life that has always been true, is true when the statement is made, and will be true in the future.

2. **with the tense of their context**. Many nominal and adjectival sentences are not generic statements but are instead simply not specific about time. The sentence *št3 wrt w3t*, for example, is not intended as the statement of a universal truth: instead, it is only meant to connect the quality of *št3 wrt* "very inaccessible" with *w3t* "the path." The context in which this statement is made indicates when the connection is meant to be valid. If it occurs in a story, for example, it will normally have past tense: in fact, the text from which this sentence is taken is an autobiography in which an official describes how he made it possible for a colossal statue to be moved from its quarry even though *št3 wrt w3t* "the path was very inaccessible." The same sentence could have been used, however, by a scout reporting to the official that *št3 wrt w3t* "the path is very inaccessible" or even that *št3 wrt w3t* "the path will be very inaccessible."

These uses mean that Egyptian nominal and adjectival sentences can be translated not only with the present tense (*is, am, are*) but also as past (*was, were*) or future (*will be*). Although this seems hazy compared to English, when you read actual texts you will find that it is not a problem, since either the sentence itself (e.g., *pẖrt pw ʿnẖ*) or its context will indicate the tense automatically.

7.17 Phrases and sentences

You may have noticed that some of the sentences we have considered in this lesson look the same as the noun and adjective phrases we met in previous lessons: for example,

 *nfr ḥr* "good of face" (§ 6.5) or "The face is good" (§ 7.2)

 *mwt.j nwt* "my mother, Nut" (§ 4.11) or "My mother is Nut" (§ 7.8)

 *z3.j pw* "this my son" (§§ 5.8–5.9) or "He is my son" (§ 7.9).

For such short groups of words, taken out of context, it is in fact impossible to decide whether a phrase or a nonverbal sentence is meant. In actual texts, however, the context almost always indicates how the words are to be read. Most adjectival and nominal sentences, moreover, are clear enough in themselves that they can only be read as sentences, not as phrases.

ESSAY 7. HUMAN NATURE

The ancient Egyptians had very specific ideas about human nature. In order for every human being (including the king) to exist, five different elements were thought to be necessary. References to these elements occur in Egyptian texts of all kinds. To understand what many of the texts are talking about, we need to appreciate what the Egyptians thought about the five elements and their function in human life.

The easiest element for us to understand is the physical one: the **body** ( *ḥꜥ*). The body is the physical shell within which every human being exists. The Egyptians recognized that the body derived from an individual's parents, from the father's seed planted in the mother's womb. They also realized that it consisted of parts; for this reason, the plural  *ḥꜥw*, meaning something like "body parts," was often used instead of the singular as the word for "body."

The most important part of the body was the heart ( *jb*). To the Egyptians, this was not only the center of physical activity but also the seat of thought and emotion (the Egyptians do not seem to have understood the function of the brain). This is a common human belief; we still have remnants of it in such English phrases as "broken-hearted" and "heartfelt wishes." In Egyptian texts where the word *jb* is used, the translation "mind" sometimes makes better sense than the literal "heart." To refer to the heart as a physical organ, Egyptian also used the word  *ḥ3tj* (a nisbe from *ḥ3t* "front": i.e., the "frontal" organ) rather than *jb*; often, however, the two terms seem to be interchangeable.

Along with each body came a **shadow** ( *šwt*).[4] The shadow is an essential adjunct to the body, since every body casts one. Because the shadow derives from the body, the Egyptians believed it had something of the body — and, therefore, of the body's owner — in it. The representations of gods are sometimes called their "shadows" for the same reason.

Every individual also had a **ba** ( *b3*). This is perhaps the most difficult of the Egyptian ideas about human beings to understand. Essentially, the ba is everything that makes a person an individual except for the body. The ba also refers to the impression that an individual makes on others, somewhat like our concept of an individual's "personality"; this notion underlies the abstract noun *b3w* (usually written , a "false plural"), which means something like "impressiveness." Like the Western notion of "soul" (with which *b3* is sometimes translated), the ba is spiritual rather than physical, and is the part of a person that lives on after the body dies. The Egyptians imagined it as being able to move freely from the mummified body out of the tomb and into the world of the living; for this reason, it is sometimes shown, and written, as a human-headed bird (). The concept of the ba is mostly associated with human beings and the gods, but other things, such as a door, can have a ba as well. This is presumably because such things can have a distinct "personality" or make a distinct impression, even though they are not alive in the same way that human beings and the gods are.

4 In this spelling, the sign is "tucked into" the belly of the quail-chick, even though it is to be read after the bird (i.e., as *šwt*, not *šwtw*). This arrangement is fairly common for and a bird sign, especially when it represents the feminine ending *t*; another example is *mwt* "mother."

Along with a body, shadow, and ba, every living individual also had a **ka** (*k3*). This concept means something like "life force." The ka is what makes the difference between a living person and a dead one: death occurs when it leaves the body. The Egyptians believed that the life force of the ka originated with the creator, was transmitted to mankind in general through the king, and was passed on to individual human beings from their fathers. The notion of this transmission was sometimes represented metaphorically as an embrace; this seems to be the origin of the "extended arms" sign with which the word *k3* is written in hieroglyphs.

The Egyptians also thought that the ka was sustained through food and drink — understandably, since without these substances, human beings die. This notion underlies the abstract noun *k3w* (written as a "false plural"), which means something like "energy" — specifically, the energy available from food and drink. It also lies behind the custom of presenting offerings of food and liquids to the dead. The Egyptians were aware that such offerings were never physically consumed by the deceased; what was being presented, however, was not the food itself, but the energy (*k3w*) within the food, which the deceased's spirit could make use of. During life, when a person was given something to eat or drink, it was often with the words *n k3.k* "for your ka."

Only human beings and the gods seem to have had a ka; even though animals were considered to be living beings, it is not known whether the Egyptians thought they had a ka as well. Like the ba, the ka was a spiritual entity. As such, it could not actually be depicted. To represent the ka, however, the Egyptians occasionally used a second image of the individual himself; for this reason, the word *k3* is sometimes translated as "double."

The fifth essential element of every person was the **name** (*rn*). Names were much more important to the Egyptians than they are in our society. They were thought to be essential parts of their owners, as necessary for existence as the four other elements. This is why Egyptians who could afford to do so expended a great deal of effort and resources ensuring that their names would continue to survive in their tombs and on their monuments — and conversely, why the names of some individuals were hacked out of their monuments by their enemies after death. Even during life, people could be essentially deprived of existence by banning their names: for example, a man named Dedu-Amun, who had been banished from society, could be referred to only as "he who is separate from the name Dedu-Amun."

The Egyptians considered each of these five elements an integral part of every individual, and they thought that no human being could exist without them. This explains, in part, why mummification of the body was considered necessary for the afterlife (see Essay 8 for more information on this subject). Each element was also thought to contain something of its owner. This was particularly true for the name; the mention of an individual's name can bring to mind a picture of that person, even if he or she is no longer living. Writing a person's name on a statue or next to a carved image could identify the image with that individual and thereby give the person an alternative physical form other than the body. This is why Egyptian tombs contained statues and reliefs of the tomb owner; for the same reason, pious Egyptians often had statues of themselves carved to be placed in the temples, so that they themselves could always be in the presence of the god. By the same token, writing the name of a person on a small clay statue and then smashing the statue was considered an effective means of destroying the name's owner.

The identification of a name with its owner was so strong that names themselves were treated as persons. In fact, it often makes more sense to translate the word *rn* as "identity" rather than "name." Knowing a person's name was the same as knowing the person himself. For this reason, the gods — who are ultimately "too great to investigate, too powerful to know" — are often said to have "inaccessible" or "secret" names that no one can know, even the other gods.

EXERCISE 7

Transliterate and translate the following sentences; underline the predicate in each.

1.  — *wr* "great"
2. 
3.  — *mnḫ* "beneficent"
4. 
5.  — *ḫt* "property"
6.  — from a story: *wsḫ* "broad," *st* "place"
7.  — see n. 4 in the Essay
8. 
9.  — *ꜥ3* "great," *pḥtj* "strength" (false dual)
10.  — *ḥn* "attack"
11. 
12. 
13.  — *qsn* "difficult"
14.  — *dmj* "harbor," *jmnt* "the West"
15.  — *sḏm* "listening," *n* "for," *rmṯ* "people" (see § 2.8.1)
16.  — *šw* "free, devoid," *ḥ3w* "excess"
17.  — *mjk3* "brave," *m3* "lion" (spelling taken from *m33* "see")
18.  — *w3w* "wave," *w3ḏ-wr* "sea" (literally, "great blue-green")
19.  — from a story: *ḥf3w* "snake"
20.  — from a story: *mḥ* "cubit" (20⅔ inches), 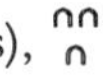 "30"
21.  — from a story: *ḫbzwt* "beard," ıı "2"
22.  — from a story: *ꜥrq* "bent"
23. 
24.  — *bw* "thing, product," *wr* "chief, main," *jw* "island"

25.  — *wsjr* "Osiris"

26.  — *wꜥb* "clean," *ꜥ* "hand, arm"

27.  — *jtj* "father"

28. 

29.  — *ḏt* "self"

30.  — from a story

31.  — *mjtn* "way, path"

32.  — *mdw* "speaker"

33.  — *nḫ* "pitiful," *m3r* "poor" (see § 2.8.3)

34. 

35.  — *ḥmw* "rudder"

36.  — *ḏ3rw* "need"

37.  — *bw-nfr* "goodness"

38.  — *ḥmwtj* "craftsman," nisbe from *ḥmwt* "craft"

39.  — *w3ḥ* "lasting"

40.  — *mḫ3t* "scale, measure of worth," *ns* "tongue"

41.  — *wnḏwt* "tenants" (collective noun)

42.  — *grḥ* "end"

8. Prepositions and Adverbs

Prepositions

8.1 Definitions

Prepositions are words that languages use to relate one thing to another. In the English sentence *Jill's cat is inside the house*, for example, the preposition *inside* relates the noun phrase *Jill's cat* to the noun phrase *the house*, and indicates that the second object contains the first. Prepositions are often followed by nouns or noun phrases, as in this example, but they can also be used with pronouns or by themselves. Thus, it is also possible in English to say *Jill's cat is inside it*, substituting the personal pronoun *it* for the noun phrase *the house*, or simply *Jill's cat is inside*, with the preposition used by itself. When a preposition is used with a noun, noun phrase, or pronoun, it is said to **govern** them. A preposition that is used by itself is said to function as an **adverb**, or adverbially; we will consider adverbs and adverbial function in more detail later in this lesson.

Prepositions are among the most idiosyncratic words of any language. Often it is impossible to translate the prepositions of one language exactly into those of another. The French preposition *à*, for example, must be translated with the English prepositions *to, at, into, on, by, for, from*, or *with*, depending on how it is used; conversely, the single English preposition *by* corresponds to the French prepositions *par, à, sur*, or *en*, also depending on the way it is used. In fact, it is rare to find a preposition in one language that corresponds exactly to one and only one preposition in another language.

8.2 Primary prepositions

Egyptian also has prepositions, and it uses them in much the same ways that English does. Unlike English, however, Egyptian can have as many as three different forms of its prepositions, depending on how they are used. The following list shows the primary prepositions of Middle Egyptian (in alphabetical order), the different forms they can have, and the English prepositions or prepositional phrases that correspond to them.

1. *jmjtw* (also , , etc.); adverbially *jmjtw-nj*
   "between, among"; adverbially "between them, among them"

   This preposition means "between" when it is used with a dual: *jmjtw b3tj* "between two bushes"; when it is used with two different nouns (or noun phrases), the second is introduced by the preposition *r* (see § 8.2.7): *jmjtw ẖ3st tn r nhrn* "between this country and Naharina" (literally, "between this country with respect to Naharina"). When *jmjtw* is used with a plural, it means "among, amidst, in the midst of": *jmjtw šzpw* "among the sacred images." In texts from Dynasty 18, the preposition is often spelled *r-jmjtw* (, etc.): *r-jmjtw srw* "amidst the nobles." The adverbial form *jmjtw-nj* is actually a compound of *jmjtw* and the adverbial form *nj* (see § 8.2.6).

2. 𓇋𓈖 *jn*
"by"

The word *jn* is not really a preposition, but it is used like the English preposition *by* to indicate the agent with a passive verb form (as in "I was blessed by the king"). In this use, *jn* is always followed by a noun or noun phrase, never a personal pronoun. We will consider this and other uses of *jn* in future lessons.

3. 𓅓 *m* (also 𓐝); with personal pronouns or adverbially 𓇋𓅓 *jm* (also 𓇋𓐝)
"in"; adverbially "therein," "there," or "in it," "of them," etc.

This is the most common of all Egyptian prepositions. Basically, *m* means "in," but English often requires other translations, depending on how *m* is used:

- "in" or "into" space: *m pr* "in the house"; *ᶜq m pr* "enter into the house"
- "in," "by," "for," or "during" time: *m grḥ* "in the night, by night"; *m rnpwt 3* "for three years, during three years"
- "in" a state: *m ḥtp* "in peace"
- "in" or "of" a material or contents: *m jnr* "in stone, of stone," *ᶜḥᶜw m rnpwt* "a period of years," *wᶜ jm* "one thereof, one of them"
- "from" or "of" a place or state (i.e., starting from "in"): *prj m nwt* "emerge from (in) the town," *šw m ᶜbᶜ* "free from boasting, free of boasting"
- "as" something or someone (i.e., "in" the capacity of): *ḫᶜj m nswt* "appear as king"
- "with," "through," or "by" something (i.e., "in" the use of): *wrḥ m mrḥt* "anoint with oil"; *jnj m zš3* "get through prayer, by prayer"; *njs m rn* "call by name."

4. 𓏇𓇋 *mj* (also 𓏇); adverbially 𓏇𓇌 *my*
"like"; adverbially "likewise"

The preposition *mj* always indicates that one thing is like another. It can usually be translated as "like," but English sometimes requires another translation:

- "like" something: *mj sḫr nṯr* "like the plan of a god"
- "in accordance with, according to" something: *mj nt-ᶜ.f nt rᶜ nb* "according to his daily custom" (literally, "like his custom of every day")
- "as well as" something: *hrw mj grḥ* "day as well as night" (literally, "day like night").

5. 𓅓𓅓 *mm* (also 𓅓𓏥, 𓅓𓏥𓂝, 𓅓𓅓𓏤, etc.)
"among"; adverbially "among them"

This preposition is used with a plural noun or a noun with plural sense: *mm ᶜnḫw* "among the living," *mm mw* "among the waters." The difference between *mm* and *jmjtw* (§ 8.2.1) is that *jmjtw* indicates a specific physical position while *mm* is used in a more general sense, without specifying an actual position.

6. 𓈖 *n* (also 𓂜 *nj*, only before a noun); adverbially 𓈖𓏭 *nj* (also 𓈖)
"to, for"; adverbially "thereto, therefor" or "for it," etc.

The preposition *n* is used to indicate the goal of something. It is normally translated in English with the prepositions *for* and *to*, but some uses require a different translation:

- "to" or "for" something: *rdj j3w n wsjr* "giving praise to Osiris"; *nfr sḏm n rmṯ* "Listening is good for people" (Exercise 7, no. 15). The preposition *n* normally indicates the goal of motion when the goal is a person: e.g., *šmj n ky* "go to another person"
- "at" in the sense of "to, toward": *dg3 n qꜥḥwj.k* "look at your elbows"
- "in, for" time: *n 3bd 2* "in two months," *n ḏt* "for ever"
- "for, at, because of" something: *rmj n mr* "weep for/at/because of pain."

7. 𓂋 *r*; at the beginning of a sentence 𓇋𓂋 *jr*, sometimes also 𓇋𓂋 with personal pronouns (usually 𓂋); adverbially 𓇋𓂋𓏭 *jrj* (often 𓇋𓂋)
"with respect to"; adverbially "thereto" or "with respect to it, pertaining to it," etc.

The preposition *r* has the basic meaning "with respect to." Depending on how it is used, many different translations are required in English:

- "to," "toward," "at" a place: *prj r pt* "go to/toward the sky," *r rdwj ḥm.f* "at the feet of His Incarnation," *spr r ẖnw* "arrive at the royal residence"; *r* normally indicates the goal of motion when the goal is a place: e.g., *šmj r nn-nswt* "go to Herakleopolis"
- "at" a time: *r tr pn* "at this season"
- "to, in order to, for" a purpose: *r jnt ꜥqw* "in order to get food," *h3b r msw-nswt* "send for the king's children"
- "against" something: *jrj r* "act against" someone or something (vs. *jrj n* "act for, on behalf of" someone or something)
- "from" something, indicating separation or distinction: *rḫ wḫ3 r rḫ* "to know the foolish man from the knowledgeable" (i.e., "to know the difference between a foolish and a knowledgeable man": literally, "to know the foolish one with respect to the knowledgeable one"), *fḫ r kpnj* "depart from Byblos" (literally, "depart with respect to Byblos"). This is also the sense of *r* when it is used with a comparative adjective (§§ 6.8, 7.4.2): *nfr r ḫt nbt* "better than everything" (literally, "good with respect to everything").
- "concerning, about, according to" something: *ḏd r* "speak about" something (compare English "speak to the subject"); *r hp* "according to the law."
- "as for" at the beginning of a sentence: *jr sf wsjr pw* "As for yesterday, it is Osiris."

8. 𓇉𓄿 *ḥ3* (also 𓇉𓄿𓁶)
"behind, around"

The preposition *ḥ3* is related to the noun 𓇉𓄿𓁶 "back of the head." Its basic sense is "behind and around": *pẖr ḥ3 jnbw* "going around the walls," *z3 ḥ3 ẖrd* "protection around a child."

9. 𓎛𓈖𓂝 *ḥnꜥ*; adverbially 𓎛𓈖𓂝𓏥 *ḥnꜥw* (usually 𓎛𓈖𓂝)
"together with"; adverbially "with them," etc.

The preposition *ḥnꜥ* indicates that one thing accompanies another: *ḥnꜥ snw.j* "together with my siblings." The same meaning underlies the use of *ḥnꜥ* in coordination (§ 4.12), where it is usually translated "and": *ḥ3tj ḥnꜥ zm3* "the heart and the lungs." Note that the English preposition *with* has two different meanings, indicating accompaniment and means. The former corresponds to Egyptian *ḥnꜥ*; the latter, to the Egyptian preposition *m* (§ 8.2.3).

10. *ḥr* (also); with personal pronouns often *ḥr*
"on"; not used adverbially

The preposition *ḥr* is related to the noun *ḥr* "face, surface" (spelled the same way). It has the basic meaning "on" but its uses require many different translations in English:

- "on, upon, in, at, by" something, indicating placement or position: *ḥr w3t* "on the path," *ḥr ḫt q3* "upon a high tree," *ḥr rdwj* "on foot," *ḥr wnmj.f* "on his right, at his right," *ḥr kmt* "in Egypt" ("on the Blackland"), *ḥr jb.f* "in his heart, on his mind"; *prj ḥr ḫrw* "come forth at the sound" of something; *sw3 ḥr jz* "pass by the tomb"
- "than, with, and" indicating addition: *jrj ḥ3w ḥr nfr* "do more than well" (literally, "do excess on good"), *psj ḥr bjt* "cook with honey." This meaning underlies the use of *ḥr* in coordination (§ 4.12), where it is usually translated "and": *ḏᶜ ḥr ḥyt* "stormwind and rain."
- "for, per," indicating distribution: *t-ḥḏ ḥr wᶜb nb* "a loaf of white bread for each priest"
- "from, of" indicating physical origin (literally, "from on"): *nbw ḥr ḫ3st* "gold from the desert," *prrt nbt ḥr ḫ3t* "everything that comes from the altar," *ᶜwn ḥwrw ḥr ḫt.f* "rob a poor man of his property"
- "at, with, concerning, about, because of, for," indicating cause (nonphysical origin): *ḥtp ḥr* "content at/with" something, *ḥzj ḥr* "bless because of, on account of" something, *rs-tp ḥr* "watchful concerning" something, *jj ḥr* "come about," "come for" something; *mhj ḥr* "forget about" something; *ᶜḥ3 ḥr* "fight for, on behalf of" someone.

11. *ḫft* (not **ḫtf*; also); adverbially *ḫftw* (also)
"opposite, in accordance with"; adverbially "accordingly"

The preposition *ḫft* indicates that something is opposed to something else. It is normally used in the spatial sense, of two things facing each other: *ᶜḥᶜ ḫft* "stand opposite, before" someone, *ḏd ḫft* "speak in front of, before" someone. This sense underlies the nisbe *ḫftj* "opponent, enemy." When *ḫft* governs a noun or pronoun referring to a thing, it usually means "in accordance with": *ḫft zẖ3 pn* "in accordance with this writing," *ḫft ḫ3y* "according to measure."

12. *ḫnt* (also); adverbially *ḫntw* (also)
"at the head of"; adverbially "before, previously"

The preposition *ḫnt* indicates that something is in front of something else: *ḥmsj ḫnt nṯrw* "sit in front of the gods." It normally carries the connotation of superiority: *ḫnt ᶜnḫw* "at the head of the living." The difference between *ḫft* and *ḫnt* is one of position: *ḫft* implies that two things are facing each other, while *ḫnt* indicates that something is first in line or priority. When used adverbially, *ḫnt* refers to time: *ḫpr ḫntw* "happen before, previously."

13. *ḫr*
"near"; not used adverbially

The preposition *ḫr* indicates the proximity of one thing to another. It is regularly used when the noun, noun phrase, or pronoun governed by the preposition is someone of higher status: *ḏd ḫr ḥm.f* "speak to His Incarnation," *ḫr nṯrw* "in the presence of the gods." This preposition is especially common in two phrases: *ḫr ḥm n* "during the incarnation of" followed by a king's name (i.e., "during the reign of"); and *jm3ḫy ḫr* "honored by," followed by the name of a god. Often *ḫr* is used to relate one person to another when the nature of the relationship cannot be specified because social customs prohibit a direct relationship. Thus, an Egyptian speaks *n* "to" an equal or an underling, but normally *ḫr* "near" the king or the gods.

14.  *ḫt*
"throughout"; not used adverbially

The meaning of this preposition is essentially the same as that of its English counterpart: *ḫpr ḫt t3* "happen throughout the land."

15.  *ẖr*, adverbially 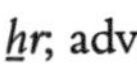 *ẖrj*
"under"; adverbially "under it, under them," etc.

The basic sense of *ẖr* is "under": *ḥmsj ẖr ḥt3w* "sit under an awning," *ẖr mw* "under water." To be "under" something is also to carry or have it: hence, *jw ẖr jnw* "come with tribute." Egyptian often uses the preposition *ẖr* literally where English uses more general prepositions: *3tp ẖr jtj* "loaded with grain" (literally, "loaded under grain"), *t3 ẖr ršwt* "the land in joy," *wrḏ ẖr šmt* "tired from walking."

16.  *tp*; with personal pronouns often  *tp*
"atop"; not used adverbially

This preposition is related to the word *tpj* "head" (spelled the same way). It indicates position above something: *tp jnb* "on top of the wall." Like *ḥr* (§ 8.2.10), *tp* often implies contact with a surface, but *ḥr* indicates closer proximity to the surface than *tp*: thus, *ᶜnḫ tp t3* "live on earth" but *sḏr ḥr t3* "lie on the ground"; both prepositions can also mean simply "above." When *tp* has to be translated in a way that does not imply position above something, this is usually because English views a relationship differently than Egyptian does: for example, English normally thinks of speech as lying "in the mouth," while Egyptian puts it *tp r* "atop the mouth."

17.  *ḏr*
"since"; adverbially "over, finished"

The preposition *ḏr* is related to the noun *ḏr* "limit, end." In Middle Egyptian, it is used mostly in expressions of time: *ḏr rk ḥrw* "since the age of Horus."

8.3 Compound prepositions

The seventeen words listed in the preceding section are all primary prepositions, each consisting of a single word. Besides these Egyptian has a large number of compound prepositions, formed from several words. Such prepositions are common in most languages. The English compound preposition *alongside*, for example, is derived from the preposition *along* and the noun *side*.

Egyptian compound prepositions always contain at least one of the primary prepositions. They are formed in three ways:

1. preposition plus noun or noun phrase: for example,  *m ḥ3t* "in front of,"  *r ḥ3ṯ* "to the front of," and  *ẖr ḥ3t* "at the front of," all of which use the noun  *ḥ3t* "front." This is the most common way of forming compound prepositions; compare English *alongside*, *inside*.

2. preposition plus infinitive or infinitival phrase (the infinitive is discussed in Lesson 14): for example,  *r ḏb3* "in exchange for, instead of," from the preposition *r* and the infinitive *ḏb3* "replace" (literally, "to replace"). Compare English *together with* (originally, *to gather with*).
3. adverb or adverbial phrase plus preposition: for example,  *ḥrw r* "apart from, in addition to, as well as," from the adverb *ḥrw* "apart" and the preposition *r* (literally, "apart with respect to"). Compare English *apart from*.

The meaning of most Egyptian compound prepositions is clear from their components, and we do not need to consider them individually here. In dictionaries (such as the one at the back of this book), you will find the meaning of a compound preposition listed under its major component. Thus, to find the meaning of *ẖr ḥ3t*, you would look under *ḥ3t*, while that of *ḥrw r* would be found under *ḥrw*.

8.4 The object of prepositions

The noun, noun phrase, or pronoun that the preposition governs is called the **object** of the preposition. In many languages, nouns and pronouns have a special form when they are used as the object of a preposition. In English this is true only for personal pronouns; nouns, noun phrases, and other kinds of pronouns have no special form after prepositions in English: e.g., *boys* and *for boys*, *the big boat* and *in the big boat*, *this* and *under this*; but *they* and *with them*, not **with they*.

Egyptian is the same as English in this respect: nouns, noun phrases, and other kinds of pronouns have no special form after prepositions: e.g., *ẖrdw* "boys," *n ẖrdw* "for boys"; *dpt ʿ3t* "the big boat," *m dpt ʿ3t* "in the big boat"; *nn* "this," *ẖr nn* "under this." For personal pronouns, Egyptian uses the *suffix* form (§ 5.3) as the object of prepositions: for example,

1S 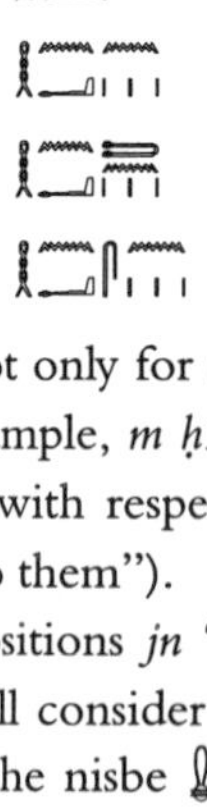	*ḥnʿ.j*	"with me"
2MS	*ḥnʿ.k*	"with you"
2FS	*ḥnʿ.ṯ*	"with you"
3MS	*ḥnʿ.f*	"with him, with it"
3FS	*ḥnʿ.s*	"with her, with it"
1PL	*ḥnʿ.n*	"with us"
2PL	*ḥnʿ.ṯn*	"with you"
3PL	*ḥnʿ.sn*	"with them."

This is true not only for the primary prepositions, such as *ḥnʿ*, but also for the compound prepositions: for example, *m ḥ3t.k* "in front of you" (literally, "in your front"), *r ḏb3.s* "in exchange for it" (literally, "with respect to its replacement"), and *ḥrw r.sn* "as well as them" (literally, "apart with respect to them").

The prepositions *jn* "by" (§ 8.2.2) and *mj* "like" (§ 8.2.4) are not used with personal pronouns. We will consider *jn* when we discuss the passive in later lessons. Egyptian uses the noun *mjtw* or the nisbe *mjtj* (see § 8.6), both of which mean "likeness," instead of *mj* with a personal pronoun: for example, *sẖtj mjtw.j* "a peasant like me" (literally, "a peasant, my likeness").

8.5 The preposition *n* with adjectival predicates

The preposition *n* "to, for" is often used in a special kind of adjectival sentence in which the predicate has no subject. This usually corresponds to English sentences in which the pronoun *it* is used as a "dummy subject": for example, *nfr n.tn* "It is good for you," *bjnwj n.j* "How bad it is for me!" Although English requires a subject, the pronoun *it* in such sentences really doesn't refer to anything; for that reason, Egyptian simply omits the subject.

8.6 Prepositional nisbes

As we saw in Lesson 6, Egyptian is able to make an adjective out of a noun by adding an ending (masculine *–j*, feminine *–t*) to the noun: for example, *nwtj* and *nwtt* "local," from *nwt* "town." Such derived adjectives are known as nisbes (§§ 6.1–6.2). The same procedure is used to make adjectives out of prepositions. Most of the primary prepositions have a nisbe form:

1. *jmj* "inherent in," from *m* "in" (also , , , , etc.)
2. *mjtj* "similar," from *mj* "like" (also , , etc.); not always distinguishable from the noun (also) *mjtw* "likeness" (see § 8.4). Both words are formed from an abstract noun *mjt* "similarity," which is itself a feminine nisbe ("that which is like") formed from *mj*.
3. *nj* "belonging to," from *n* "to, for" (usually); also known as the "genitival adjective." We have seen its use in the indirect genitive (§ 4.13.2) and as an adjectival predicate (§ 7.5).
4. *jrj* "pertaining to," from *r* "with respect to" (also , ,)
5. *ḥ3(j)* "surrounding," from *ḥ3* "behind, around"
6. *ḥnᶜ(j)* "accompanying," from *ḥnᶜ* "with"
7. *ḥrj* "upper, lying on" from *ḥr* "on" (also , ,)
8. *ḫftj* "opposing," from *ḫft* "opposite" (often)
9. *ḫntj* "foremost," from *ḫnt* "at the head of" (often)
10. *ḫr(j)* "adjacent," from *ḫr* "near"
11. *ẖrj* "lower, lying under" from *ẖr* "under" (often)
12. *tpj* "standing atop," from *tp* "atop" (also , ,).

8.7 Uses of the prepositional nisbes

Like other nisbes, those formed from prepositions can be used both to modify nouns and as nouns in their own right: for example, *ᶜt ḥrt* "an upper room," *ḥrt nbt* "every upper one." In both uses, prepositional nisbes often govern a following noun, noun phrase, or pronoun, just as prepositions themselves do. This kind of construction is usually impossible to translate directly into good English; instead, English has to use the words "who is, who are, which is, which are" followed by the relevant preposition, or the preposition alone: for example, *nṯrw jmjw pt* "the gods who are in the sky" or "the gods in the sky" (literally, "the gods, the inherent ones of the sky"); *jmjw.s* "those who are in it" or "those in it" (literally, "its inherent ones").

Prepositional nisbes are often used as nouns in their own right. Two very common examples of this are words designating a person's office or function and phrases referring to gods or kings (the latter are called "epithets"): for example,  *jr(j)-ʿt* "roomkeeper" (literally, "one pertaining to a room"),  *ẖr(j)-ḥ(3)b* (also written  and ) "lector priest" (literally, "he who is under the festival-scroll": the priest who carries the scroll with the liturgy for festival rites); 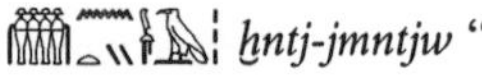 *ḫntj-jmntjw* "Foremost of the westerners" (literally, "he who is at the head of the westerners," an epithet of Osiris),  *tpj-ḏw.f* "He who is atop his mountain" (an epithet of Anubis).

Like other nouns, prepositional nisbes can be modified by adjectives, and can have suffix pronouns. Adjectives that modify prepositional nisbes always agree with the nisbe itself, and not with the noun or pronoun that the nisbe governs: i.e., *jrj-ʿt nb* "every roomkeeper" (not *jrj ʿt nbt*, which would mean "one pertaining to every room"). Such adjectives normally follow the entire nisbe phrase, as in the example just given; to avoid confusion about which element the adjective modifies, however, they can come between the nisbe and whatever the nisbe governs: for example, *jrj nb sšm* "every functionary" (literally, "every one pertaining to a function"), as opposed to *jrj sšm nb* "one pertaining to every function." Similar considerations govern the placement of suffix pronouns: thus, *jmt ḥ3t.sn* "that which is in front of them" (literally, "the inherent one of their front") but *jmt.sn ḥ3t* "their predecessor" (literally, "their inherent one of the front").

8.8 Special uses of the nisbe 

The nisbe ,  *ẖrj* "lower, lying under" is often used to denote the possession of something: thus, the *ẖrj-ḥ3b* "lector-priest" is the one who has ("who is under") the festival-scroll. If the nisbe modifies or refers to a place, it can indicate location: for example,  (with honorific transposition; abbreviated , ) *ẖrt-nṯr* "the place where the god is" ("that which is under the god"), the Egyptian term for "cemetery" or "necropolis." This use is particularly common with the word  *bw* "place": for instance,  *bw ẖr(j).f* "the place where he is" (literally, "the place lying under him").

8.9 "Reverse" nisbes

Although a prepositional nisbe such as *jmt* often has to be translated into English as "who is in" or "which is in," it is important to remember that such translations are only an approximation of the nisbe's meaning: the nisbe itself is an adjective (in this case, meaning something like "inherent"). Like other adjectives, prepositional nisbes can also be used in the *nfr ḥr* construction. As we saw in §§ 6.5 and 6.9, a phrase such as *ʿš3 zrw* "many of sheep" can be used to refer to someone who has many sheep: the adjective *ʿš3* actually refers to the sheep's owner, even though it is the sheep themselves that are "many," not the owner. Prepositional nisbes can be used in the same way.

Normally, a phrase such as  *mḏ3t jmt pr* means "the scroll that is in the house," where *jmt pr* is an adjectival phrase indicating where *mḏ3t* "the scroll" is. But since *jmt* is an adjective, the phrase *jmt pr* can also be understood as a *nfr ḥr* construction. In that case, although *jmt* still refers to *mḏ3t*, it is actually *pr* "the house" that is "in" something, and not *mḏ3t* "the scroll": *mḏ3t jmt pr* then means "the scroll that the house is in." The phrase *jmt pr* (used by itself, without *mḏ3t*) is actually an Egyptian idiom for "will" (as in "last will and testament"): it refers to a papyrus scroll in which the contents of a person's estate (*pr* "house") are listed.

Such uses are known as "reverse nisbes." The relationship between *jmt* and *pr* in the reverse nisbe *mḏ3t jmt pr* "the scroll that the house is in" is exactly the same as that between *ʿš3* and *zrw* in the *nfr ḥr* construction *zj ʿš3 zrw* "a man many of sheep": Egyptian makes the adjective refer to the noun it modifies (*mḏꜣt* and *zj*), even though what the adjective describes (*ꜥšꜣ* "many" and *jmt* "inherent, being in") is actually a quality of the noun that follows it (*zrw* and *pr*). This is true even when the adjectival phrases are used by themselves, without a preceding noun: *ꜥšꜣ zrw* "he who has many sheep," *jmt pr* "that which the house is in."

Since a phrase such as *jmt pr* can mean both "that which is in the house" and "that which the house is in," usually only the context will indicate which meaning is intended. For some phrases, however, the reverse meaning is normal. One very common example is the title *jmj-r* "overseer" (usually spelled or). This seems to mean "the one in whom (*jmj*) the mouth (*r*) is" — i.e., the person who gives commands. It normally precedes another noun or noun phrase, indicating what the person is overseer of: for example, *jmj-r pr* "steward" ("overseer of the house"), *jmj-r mšꜥ* "general" ("overseer of the army"). As a prepositional nisbe, however, *jmj-r* can also mean "the one who is in the mouth": for this reason, it is often spelled (e.g., *jmj-r pr*), with the sign of a tongue (i.e., "that which is in the mouth"), even though its normal meaning is apparently the reverse.

8.10 Prepositional phrases as modifiers

English can use a prepositional phrase as a modifier: for example, *the gods in the sky*. In Egyptian, however, a prepositional phrase normally has to be converted to the corresponding nisbe in order to modify a noun: thus, *nṯrw jmjw pt* "the gods in the sky," and not **nṯrw m pt*. In a few cases, however, Egyptian does seem to use a prepositional phrase rather than the corresponding nisbe as a modifier. The most frequent examples of this involve the preposition *m* used adverbially in the expressions *bꜣk jm* "the worker therein" (an idiom meaning "yours truly" or "your humble servant") and *wꜥ jm nb* "every one of them."

Another common instance of a prepositional phrase used as modifier involves the preposition *n* "to, for." The genitival adjective *n(j)* "belonging to," which is the nisbe of the preposition *n* "to, for," is normally used as a modifier only when it is followed by a noun or noun phrase. This is the construction known as the "indirect genitive," which we have already met (§ 4.13.2): *zꜣ n(j) zj* "the son of a man" (literally, "the son belonging to a man"). When the possessor is a personal pronoun, Egyptian normally uses the suffix pronouns: *zꜣ.f* "his son." Occasionally, however, it can use a special construction consisting of the preposition *n* (not the nisbe), a suffix pronoun, and the nisbe *jm* (also spelled *jmy*). This corresponds to the English construction "of him, of his," and so forth: for example,

ms n.f jmy "a child of his, a child belonging to him"

tꜣ ḥꜣt n.n jmy "that front of ours"

hdmw n.sn jm "the footstool belonging to them."

As these examples show, the gender and number of the preceding noun have no effect on the possessive phrase that follows: since *n* is a preposition rather than a nisbe, it does not have to agree in gender and number with the noun it modifies. In older texts, however, the nisbe sometimes agrees in gender with the noun: *prt-ḫrw n.k jmyt* "the invocation-offering of yours" (modifying the feminine noun phrase *prt-ḫrw*, literally, "the sending-forth of the voice").

ADVERBS

8.11 Definitions

Adverbs are words or phrases that languages use to indicate *where, when, why*, or *how* something happens or is true. The primary use of adverbs is to modify verbs (the word "adverb" means "attached to a verb"): for example, in the sentence *The treaty was signed here*, the adverb *here* tells where the treaty was signed (*was signed* is a verb form). Prepositional phrases can be used as adverbs: thus, we can also say *The treaty was signed in this room*, with the prepositional phrase *in this room* indicating where the treaty was signed.

Adverbs can modify adjectives, prepositions, or other adverbs, as well as verbs. We have already seen an example of an adverb used to modify a preposition: in the English compound preposition *apart from* (§ 8.3.3), the adverb *apart* specifies the meaning of the preposition *from*. Adverbs have the same function when they are used to modify adjectives or other adverbs: in the phrase *a moderately heavy rain*, for instance, the adverb *moderately* specifies how heavy the rain is; similarly, in the phrase *almost always* the adverb *almost* narrows the meaning of the adverb *always*. Adverbs are thus similar to adjectives: just as adjectives or adjectival phrases modify nouns (§ 6.1), adverbs or adverbial phrases are used to modify verbs, adjectives, prepositions, and other adverbs.

Adverbs can be single words, such as *here, apart*, and *moderately*. They can also consist of several words, such as *almost always*; this is called an adverbial phrase. Most adverbial phrases are actually prepositional phrases used as adverbs, as in the example *in this room*, given above. Although prepositions themselves are not adverbs, prepositional phrases normally are, since such phrases usually indicate where, when, why, or how something happens or is true. Prepositions themselves can also be used as adverbs, as we saw in § 8.1.

8.12 Primary adverbs

Primary adverbs are single words that are not derived from another word and are used exclusively as adverbs. Egyptian has perhaps three such adverbs: *ꜥꜣ* "here"; *rsj* "entirely, at all" (also *rssj*); and *grw* "also, further, any more" (usually *gr*).

8.13 The interrogative adverb

We have already met the interrogative pronouns (§ 5.11) and adjective (§6.6). Middle Egyptian has one interrogative adverb: *ṯn(j)* "where?" (also *ṯnj*, etc.; and *ṯnw*, a spelling taken from the word for "each," § 6.7). Like the other interrogatives, *ṯnj* is used only in questions — mostly in sentences with an adverbial or verbal predicate, which we will treat in later lessons. For other interrogative adverbs, Egyptian uses a preposition plus an interrogative pronoun (§ 5.11): for example, *mj mj, mj jḫ* "how?" (literally, "like what?"); *ḥr mj, r mj* "why?" (literally, "because of what?, with respect to what?"). Interrogative "when?" is expressed by the pronoun *zy* plus a noun of time: for instance, *zy nw* "when?" (literally, "which moment?").

8.14 Other adverbs

In English, many adverbs are formed from adjectives by adding the ending *–ly*: for example, *badly* (from *bad*) and *moderately* (from *moderate*). Egyptian also formed adverbs from adjectives. Sometimes the adverb looks the same as the adjective: for example, *nfr* "well" (from the adjective *nfr* "good"), *ꜥšꜣ* "often" (from *ꜥšꜣ* "many"), *wr* "much" (from *wr* "great"). Often, an ending *–w* is added to the adjective, as in *ꜥꜣw* "greatly" (from *ꜥꜣ* "big"). Since *w* is a "weak" consonant, however, it can be omitted in writing (§ 2.8.2), and these adverbs, too, often look like the adjectives they come from. In a few cases Egyptian forms an adverb from an adjective by adding a final *–t*: the most common example is *wrt* "very" (from *wr* "great"), which we met in § 7.4.1. Adverbs can also be made from adjectives by using a preposition with the adjective: for example, *r ꜥꜣt* "greatly" (literally, "with respect to a big one"), *m mꜣ(w)t* "anew" (literally, "in what is new"). These are regular prepositional phrases, in which the adjective is used as a noun.

Egyptian, like English, uses many nouns of time as adverbs. In English, the noun *today*, for example, can be used as a noun (*That's enough for today*) and adverbially (*Jill will sing today*). Some common Egyptian nouns used in this way are *mjn* "today," *sf* "yesterday," and *ḏt* "forever." Noun phrases can be used in the same way: for example, *hrw pn* "this day, today," and *rꜥ nb* "every day." Egyptian also uses prepositions with such nouns to form adverbs: *m mjn* "today," *n ḏt* "forever."

English can use its reflexive pronouns as adverbs, as in *Jack did it himself*. The Egyptian counterpart to this is the noun (or) *ḏs* "self" plus a suffix pronoun, which is also used adverbially: for example, *ḫft ḥr (n)swt ḏs.f* "in front of the face of the king himself." When *ḏs* plus a suffix pronoun modifies another suffix pronoun, it often has to be translated by the English adjective "own": for instance, *m hꜣw.k ḏs.k* "in your own day and age" (literally, "in your time yourself").

8.15 Prepositional adverbs

As in English, a prepositional adverb is simply the preposition used without an object: *rdj ḫt jm.s* "put something in it," *rdj ḫt jm* "put something in." Most of the primary prepositions can have this function, as we saw in § 8.2; and for those that apparently cannot, adverbial use may simply not be attested in surviving texts. In most cases the primary preposition has a special form in adverbial use, usually made by adding the ending *–j* or *–w* to the preposition: *my* (= *mjj*), *nj*, *jrj*, *ḥrj*; *ḥnꜥw*, *ḫftw*, *ḫntw*. Some prepositions can also be used adverbially by adding the prepositional adverb *jrj* to the regular form of the preposition: *ḫft jrj* "accordingly" (instead of *ḫftw*), *mm jrj* "among them" (instead of *mm*). Compound prepositions formed of a preposition plus a noun or infinitive can be used adverbially just by omitting the object: *jj m ḥꜣt* "come in front," *rdj r ḏbꜣ* "give in exchange." Compounds in which the preposition is preceded by an adverb use the adverbial form of the preposition: *ḥrw jrj* "additionally."

Egyptian is much freer than English in using prepositions adverbially. English often uses a different word in place of the prepositional adverb, or requires a pronominal object: for example, *Jack spoke about Jill* or *Jack spoke about her*, but not **Jack spoke about*. English prepositional adverbs were originally formed by adding the prefix *there–* to the preposition: *thereabout, therein, thereby, therewith, therefrom*, etc. This procedure is now considered archaic for all but a few prepositions, though it is still used in formal or legal English. Because of this difference between the two languages, English translations of Egyptian prepositional adverbs often have to add a pronominal object that does not appear in Egyptian: for example, *gs zj jm* "anoint a man with it," or, more archaically, "anoint a man therewith."

8.16 Uses of adverbs

When adverbs modify prepositions, they normally precede the preposition. This use is common in compound prepositions such as *ḥrw r* "apart from" (§ 8.3.3); similarly, *š3ʿ m* "beginning from," *nfryt r* "down to." Adverbs that modify adjectives or other adverbs normally follow the word they modify: for example, *jqr wrt* "very excellent," *r ʿ3t wrt* "very greatly."

Adverbs do not normally modify nouns, either in Egyptian or in English. An exception in Egyptian, involving the prepositional adverb *jm*, has already been noted in § 8.10 above. Other uses of adverbs will be discussed in Lesson 10.

8.17 Comparative and superlative adverbs

English adverbs that are formed from adjectives can have comparative or superlative meaning, indicated by using the adverbs *more* and *most* in front of the adverb: for example, *greatly*, *more greatly*, *most greatly*. Egyptian adverbs derived from adjectives can also have comparative or superlative sense. Like adjectives (§ 6.8), they have no special form to indicate this meaning, and the sense is usually obvious from the context in which they are used. In some cases, however, comparative meaning is indicated by a phrase introduced by the preposition *r*, as it is for adjectives: for example, *wr r ḫt nbt* "more greatly than anything" (literally, "greatly with respect to everything").

ESSAY 8. DEATH AND THE AFTERLIFE

The ancient Egyptians believed that death occurred when the ka (see Essay 7) left the body. After death the body was mummified by packing it in natron, a kind of salt, in order to remove all moisture from it. The embalmers also removed the major internal organs, leaving only the heart in place. The brain was pulled out through the nose in pieces, by means of a metal hook, and discarded. The liver, lungs, stomach, and intestines were surgically removed, mummified separately, and placed in four vases, called Canopic jars, each topped by a lid representing one of the four gods known as the "sons of Horus": Imseti (*jmstj*, human-headed) for the liver; Hapi (*ḥpy*, baboon-headed) for the lungs; Dua-mutef (*dw3-mwt.f*, jackal-headed) for the stomach; and Qebeh-senuef (*qbḥ-snw.f*, falcon-headed) for the intestines. After drying out, the body was wrapped in linen bandages (to keep it from falling apart) and anointed with oils. The bodies of poor people who could not afford mummification were wrapped in a reed mat and buried in a grave dug in the sand; ironically, this practice often dried and preserved them better than those which had been mummified artificially.

The entire process of mummification took 70 days. At the end of this time the body was escorted to its tomb in the necropolis, normally located in the desert cliffs on the west side of the Nile. At the tomb priests performed a ceremony on the mummy, or on a statue of the deceased, known as the "Mouth-Opening Ritual." This was intended to give back to the dead person the use of the mouth and the body's other senses. A bull was then slaughtered and other offerings of food and drink were presented, before the body and its grave goods were finally buried.

Egyptian tombs had two parts. The body was interred along with its grave goods in a burial chamber below ground; this room was sealed after the funeral, and was supposed to be inaccessible from then on. Above ground was a chapel (or, in the case of royal tombs, an entire temple): here offerings could be made and prayers said for the deceased. The chapel was normally decorated with images of the deceased and scenes of people bringing offerings, and could consist of many rooms. Its focal point was usually a niched recess in the west wall, known as a "false door," with an offering slab placed in front of it. Through this niche, the spirit of the dead person could emerge from the burial chamber to partake of the nourishment (*k3w*) in the offerings (see Essay 7).

The ceremonies performed at the funeral were meant not only to restore the dead person's physical abilities but, more importantly, to release the ba from its attachment to the body, so that it could come and go at will. The ba was supposed to rejoin its life-force (the ka), so that the dead person could continue to live: the deceased are often called "those who have gone to their kas." Once this reunion had taken place, the deceased became an **akh** (𓅜𓏭 *3ḫj*) — literally, an "effective one," able to live on in a new, nonphysical form. Before this could happen, however, the deceased had to pass a final judgment.

In this trial, the heart of the dead person (𓄣) was weighed in a scale (𓍝) against a feather (𓆄), the hieroglyph for *m3ʿt* (Maat), an abstract noun meaning, among other things, "proper behavior." Ideally, the two sides of the scale should balance, showing that the person had lived a just and proper life. If they did, the deceased was declared 𓌷𓐙𓊤𓀁 *m3ʿ ḫrw* (abbreviated 𓐙 or 𓊤𓊤) "justified" (literally, "true of voice") and allowed to join the society of the dead. In funerary papyri such as the "Book of the Dead," this transition is represented in a scene where Horus, king of the living, formally presents the deceased to Osiris, king of the dead.

The Egyptians thought of the afterlife not as a kind of continual angelic state in some paradise but as a daily nonphysical existence on earth. The model for this new existence was the daily journey of the sun (see Essay 2). At night the sun descended into the Duat. In his journey through this nether region, he eventually came upon the mummified body of Osiris. The two gods joined and became one: from Osiris the sun received the power of new life, and through the sun Osiris was enabled to live again. Thus rejuvenated, the sun was able to continue his journey through the Duat and rise to new life again in the morning.

For each dead person, the burial chamber and its mummy were a kind of individual Duat and Osiris; this explains why preservation of the body was so important for the Egyptians, and why the deceased was often addressed as "Osiris." At night, the ba would rejoin the mummy in its tomb. Through this union, it would receive the power of new life and be able to wake up at sunrise and emerge from the tomb as an akh. During the day it could move about among the living, though on a different plane of existence, more like that of the gods, without the discomforts and hardships of physical existence. One text describes this ideal existence as follows:

> Becoming a living ba, which has control of bread, water, and air ... Your life happening again, without your ba being kept away from your divine corpse, and with your ba being together with the akhs ... You shall emerge each day and return each evening. A lamp will be lit for you in the night until the sunlight shines forth upon your breast. You shall be told: "Welcome, welcome, into this your house of the living!"

The ancient Egyptians felt themselves surrounded, and comforted, by the spirits of their ancestors living among them.

EXERCISE 8

Transliterate and translate the following phrases and sentences:

1. 
2.  — *šmꜥ* "chanter"
3. 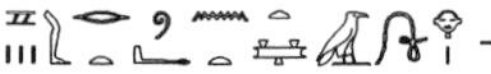 — *wꜥrt* "flight"
4.  — *pt* "sky"
5.  — *sḫmt* "Sekhmet," *rnpt* "year," *jdw* "pestilence"
6. 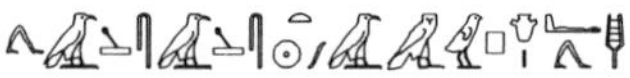 — *ꜥḥꜥ* "steadfast," *3t* "moment," *s3s3* "headlong attack"
7.  — *ḫt* "wake, aftermath" *j3w* "old age"
8.  — *wršy* "watchman," *jnb* "wall," *hrw* "duty"
9.  — *pḫrt* "remedy"
10.  — *zḥ* "advice"
11.  — *zḥ* "tent," *wḥyw* "tribe"
12.  — *hrw* "day," *sf* "yesterday"
13.  — *ḥtp* "peace"
14.  — *jrp* "wine," *mw* "water"
15.  — *m3ꜥt* "truth"
16. 
17. 
18. 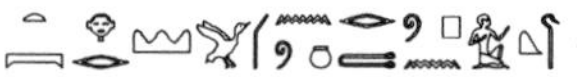 — *ḥq3* "ruler," *rṯnw* "Retjenu" (the region of Lebanon: see § 4.4)
19.  — *qdnw* "Qatna" (a town in Syria)
20. 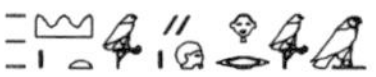 — *ḥrw* "Horus," *ḫ3st* "foreign land"
21.  — *st* "throne," *wmwt* "niche," *ḏꜥm* "electrum"
22.  — *ḫpš* "strong arm," *pḏt* "bow"
23.  — *sḫtj* "peasant," *mnḫ* "efficient"
24.  — *ḥm* "servant"
25.  — *nḥ* "prayer"
26. 
27. 
28. 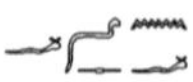

9. Numbers

9.1 Numerals

Ancient Egyptian used a decimal system of counting, as we do in English: that is, in ones, tens, hundreds, thousands, and so forth. Like English, too, Egyptian normally wrote numbers with **numerals** (numerical symbols) rather than by spelling out the words for each number. The two languages differ, however, in their approach to written numbers.

In English we use ten numerals (0–9) and a positional system of notation: the numeral 3, for example, means "three" if it is used by itself, but "thirty" if it is followed by another numeral (for instance, 36), "three hundred" if it is followed by two numerals (e.g., 328), and so forth. Egyptian uses six numerals and a repetitional system of notation. The six numerals are the following:

𓏺	1 — for units	𓆼	1,000 — for thousands
𓎆	10 — for tens	𓂭	10,000 — for ten-thousands
𓍢	100 — for hundreds	𓆐	100,000 — for hundred-thousands.

In hieroglyphic, each of these numerals is repeated the necessary number of times to indicate the number: for example, 𓏺𓏺 2, 𓆼𓆼𓆼 3,000, 𓂭𓂭𓂭𓂭𓂭𓂭𓂭 70,000.[1] The smaller signs (for 1, 10, and 100) are usually arranged in groups: for example, 𓏾 5, 𓍢𓍢𓍢𓍢𓍢𓍢 600. Numbers that combine more than one numeral are always arranged from the largest numeral to the smallest: for example,

𓆐𓂭𓂭𓂭𓂭𓂭𓆼𓆼𓍢𓎆𓎆𓏺𓏺𓏺 152,123 (= 100,000 + 5×10,000 + 2×1,000 + 100 + 2×20 + 3×1).

In texts written from left to right, like this example, the numerals follow the same order as English numerals; in those written from right to left, the order is the opposite: e.g., 𓏺𓏺𓏺𓍢𓍢𓍢𓍢𓍢𓍢𓆼𓆼 2,603.

In addition to the repetitional method of indicating numbers, Middle Egyptian sometimes employed a true multiplication system for numbers above 10,000:

𓆐𓏺𓏺𓏺𓏺 𓂭𓏺𓏺𓏺𓏺𓏺𓏺𓏺 470,000 — i.e., 4×100,000 + 7×10,000.

This system was also used to indicate numbers in the millions:

𓆐𓍢𓏺 10,100,000 — i.e., 101×100,000.

Originally there was a separate sign 𓁨 for 1,000,000, but this is more common in Middle Egyptian as a number of indefinite rather than precise value: "many," "a million."

As this system makes clear, the Egyptians had no regular symbol for zero. When subtractions resulted in zero in accounts and mathematical texts, scribes either left a blank space or wrote the sign 𓄤, an abbreviation for the word 𓄤𓆑𓂋𓅱𓏥 *nfrw* "depletion."

1 Hieratic developed separate signs for some of the multiples: i.e., one sign for 𓎆𓎆 "20" and another for 𓎆𓎆𓎆 "30." These are transcribed into hieroglyphic using the repetitional notation.

9.2 Cardinal numbers

Numbers used in counting are called **cardinal** numbers: in English, *one, two, three,* etc. In Egyptian, cardinal numbers are normally indicated in hieroglyphs by numerals rather than by words; only the number "one" is usually spelled out. It is rare to find the other numbers spelled out, but we are able to reconstruct the transliteration of the basic (one-word) numbers from Coptic:

	MASCULINE	FEMININE	COPTIC
one	𓌡𓂝𓏤 *wꜥ*	𓌡𓂝𓏏𓏤 *wꜥt*	ⲟⲩⲁ, ⲟⲩⲉⲓ
two	*snwj*	*sntj*	ⲥⲛⲁⲩ, ⲥⲛ̄ⲧⲉ
three	*ḫmtw*	*ḫmtt*	ϣⲟⲙ̄ⲛ̄ⲧ, ϣⲟⲙⲧⲉ
four	*jfdw*	*jfdt*	ϥⲧⲟⲟⲩ, ϥⲧⲟ
five	*djw*	*djt*	ϯⲟⲩ, ϯⲉ
six	*sjsw*	*sjst*	ⲥⲟⲟⲩ, ⲥⲉ
seven	*sfḫw*	*sfḫt*	ⲥⲁϣϥ, ⲥⲁϣϥⲉ
eight	*ḫmnw*	*ḫmnt*	ϣⲙⲟⲩⲛ, ϣⲙⲟⲩⲛⲉ
nine	*psḏw*	*psḏt*	ⲯⲓⲧ, ⲯⲓⲧⲉ
ten	*mḏw*	*mḏt*	ⲙⲏⲧ, ⲙⲏⲧⲉ
twenty	*mḏwtj*	*mḏwtt*	ϫⲟⲩⲱⲧ, ϫⲟⲩⲱⲧⲉ
thirty	*mꜥbꜣ*	*mꜥbꜣt*	ⲙⲁⲁⲃ, ⲙⲁⲁⲃⲉ
forty	*ḥmw*		ϩⲙⲉ
fifty	*djjw*		ⲧⲁⲓ̈ⲟⲩ
sixty	*sjsjw*		ⲥⲉ
seventy	*sfḫjw*		ϣϥⲉ
eighty	*ḫmnjw*		ϩⲙⲉⲛⲉ
ninety	*psḏjw*		ⲡ̄ⲥ̄ⲧⲁⲓⲟⲩ
one hundred		*št*	ϣⲉ
two hundred		*štj*	ϣⲏⲧ
one thousand	*ḫꜣ*		ϣⲟ
ten thousand	*ḏbꜥ*		ⲧⲃⲁ
one hundred thousand	*ḥfn*		—
one million	*ḥḥ*		—

The units (from *wꜥ* to *psḏw*) and the tens from *mḏw* to *mꜥbꜣ* have masculine and feminine forms; the rest of the cardinal numbers are masculine, except for *št* and *štj,* which are feminine. All the numbers behave like singular nouns, although *snwj/sntj, mḏwtj,* and *štj* were originally duals.

The cardinal numbers not on this list were formed by combining two or more one-word cardinals. For the most part, Egyptian seems to have been similar to English in this respect: for example, *ḫꜣ ḫmnw-št ḥmw-sjsw* "(one) thousand eight-hundred forty-six." In such compound numbers the one-word cardinals with two forms apparently used the masculine, except for the final cardinal, which could take either the masculine or the feminine form (if it had one): thus, *ḫmtw-št mꜥbꜣ* (m) and *ḫmtw-št mꜥbꜣt* (f) "three-hundred thirty."

In a few cases the formation of Egyptian compound numbers seems to have been different from that of their English equivalents. The cardinals from eleven to nineteen were compounds: for example, *mḏw-wꜥ* "eleven" (m), *mḏw-ḫmtt* "thirteen" (f). Although *štj* "two-hundred" was a single word (originally dual), the words for "two thousand" (*ḫꜣ snwj*) and "twenty thousand" (*ḏbꜥ snwj*: literally, "two ten-thousand") were compounds, with a word-order the reverse of that of other compounds. Since Egyptian uses different words for the thousands and ten-thousands, the compounds of the cardinals for ten thousand and higher are different than their English counterparts: for example, *djw ḏbꜥ* "fifty thousand" ("five ten-thousand"), *mḏw-snwj ḏbꜥ* "one-hundred-twenty thousand" ("twelve ten-thousand"). In keeping with the system noted at the end of § 9.1, above, the cardinal for "two million" was *štj ḏbꜥ* (literally, "two-hundred ten-thousand"); the original word is unknown, but was probably either *ḥḥwj* or *ḥḥ snwj*.

It is not necessary to learn all these number words in order to read hieroglyphic texts, since the cardinal numbers are usually represented in hieroglyphs by numerals. In transcription they are normally represented by English numerals rather than by the corresponding Egyptian number word: for example, *mḥ 30* (instead of *mḥ mꜥbꜣ*) "30 cubits."

9.3 Ordinal numbers

Words used to indicate numerical order in a series are called **ordinal** numbers: in English, *first, second, third*, etc. To form ordinal numbers in English, we add the ending *–th* to the cardinals except for the numbers 1 to 3, for which there are special words. In Egyptian, there is a special word only for "first," which is always spelled out: masculine *tpj* (, ,), feminine *tpt* (, ,). This is actually the same word as the prepositional nisbe *tpj* "standing atop" (§ 8.5.12).

The ordinals from "second" to "ninth" are formed by adding the endings *–nw* (, masculine singular) and *–nwt* (, feminine singular) to the **root** of the cardinal numbers:

snnw, snnwt	"second"	*sjsnw, sjsnwt*	"sixth"
ḫmtnw, ḫmtnwt	"third"	*sfḫnw, sfḫnwt*	"seventh"
jfdnw, jfdnwt	"fourth"	*ḫmnnw, ḫmnnwt*	"eighth"
djnw, djnwt	"fifth"	*psḏnw, psḏnwt*	"ninth."

These are usually written with numerals plus the ending (e.g., *2nw* "second," *6nwt* "sixth"), but they can also be spelled out: for example, *snw*[2] "second," *ḫmtnw* "third."

The rest of the ordinals, from "tenth" upwards, are formed by adding the words *mḥ* (, masculine singular) and *mḥt* (, feminine singular) before the cardinal number: for example, *mḥt-10* "tenth," *mḥ-200* "two-hundredth."

9.4 Use of the numbers

The cardinal numbers are grammatically nouns, and can be used by themselves and modified like other nouns: for example, *3 pn* "these 3," *kt 100* "another 100." The ordinal numbers are adjectives, but like other adjectives they can also be used by themselves as nouns: for example, *ḥr 2nwt.s* "upon its second one."

2 When the same two consonants came together in an Egyptian word without a vowel between them, they were written only once in hieroglyphs. Since *snnw* "second" is written *snw*, it was apparently pronounced **sVnnVw* (where *V* stands for a vowel). We will meet this rule again in Lesson 13.

When ordinal numbers modify a noun (or a noun phrase), they normally follow it, like other adjectives: *wḏyt 6nwt* "the 6th expedition," *zp tpj* "the first occasion." Occasionally, however, they come before the noun they modify: in that case, the noun either stands in apposition to the ordinal, or it is connected to it by an indirect genitive (§§ 4.11, 4.13.2): for example, *snwt.f j3t* "his second office" (literally, "his second one, the office"), *5nw n ḥ3b* "the 5th festival" (literally, "the 5th one of festival").

When cardinal numbers are used to modify a noun (or noun phrase), Egyptian writing normally uses what is called the "list form," with the noun first and the numeral second: for example, *rnpt 20* "20 years" (literally, "year, 20"). In measurements, the thing being measured is written first, followed by the unit of measurement and then the numeral: *ḥ(n)qt ds 100* "100 jugs of beer" (literally, "beer, jug, 100"). In measurements, both nouns are normally singular, as in this example. In other cases, however, the noun can also be plural (with numbers higher than 2): e.g., *zpw 4* "4 times."

The writing conventions for cardinal numbers seem to have come from accounts; English normally writes *$50* rather than *50 dollars* for similar reasons. As with *$50* in English, however, phrases like *rnpt 20* "20 years" and *zpw 4* "4 times" were probably pronounced with the number first: i.e., *mḏwtt rnpt* and *jfdw zpw*. For this reason, demonstratives that modify such phrases are always singular, since they agree with the numeral (which is singular) rather than the noun: for instance, *p3 t 1000* "the 1000 loaves of bread" (i.e., *p3 ḫ3 t*); *t3 t 100* "the 100 loaves of bread" (i.e., *t3 št t*); *p3(y).j ḫrdw 4* "my four children" (i.e., *p3y.j jfdw ḫrdw*).

Egyptian can use the words *wꜥ* and *wꜥt* "one," and the numerals (*ḫ3*) 1,000 and (*ḥḥ*) 1,000,000 before a noun, noun phrase, or pronoun. In that case, the number is connected to the following noun by the preposition *m* or the indirect genitive: for example, *1,000 m t* "1,000 loaves of bread" (literally, "1,000 in bread"), *ḥḥ n zp* "a million times" (literally, "a million of time"). With the words for "one," these two constructions have different meanings. The preposition *m* is used when *wꜥ* or *wꜥt* mean "one of many": *wꜥ m n3 n ꜥ3* "one of those donkeys," *wꜥ jm.ṯn* "one of you." The indirect genitive with *wꜥ* or *wꜥt* has the same sense as the normal construction in which the number modifies the noun directly: *dmj wꜥ* "one harbor," *wꜥ n mjṯn* "one path."

In the spoken language this last construction was also used to express the singular indefinite article ("a, an": see § 4.9); a few examples with this sense are found in the written language as well: *wꜥ n q3q3w* "a boat" (literally, "one of boat"). This is a development common to many languages: the indefinite articles in English, German, and French, for example, all come from the words for "one" in those languages.

9.5 *zp 2* "twice"

The phrase *zp 2* "two times, twice" is used in writing as a kind of "ditto" sign: for example, *ꜥš3 zp 2* "very often" (literally, "twice often"). In spoken Egyptian, was apparently replaced by the repeated word or phrase: i.e., *ꜥš3 ꜥš3* "often, often." The signs can also be used in the spelling of single words as a kind of abbreviation, indicating that the preceding signs are to be repeated: for example, (for) *sksk* "destroy."

9.6 Fractions

The ancient Egyptians expressed fractions in writing by the word *r* above a numeral: for example, 1/7 (*r-7*), 1/360 (*r-360*). There were special signs for a few fractions: 1/2 (*gs*), × 1/4 (*r-4*, also), 2/3 (*rwj*), and 3/4 (*ḫmt-rw*). Except for 2/3 and 3/4, all fractions had 1 as the numerator (the top part of the fraction). In order to express fractions with larger numerators, Egyptian combined several fractions: for example, 5 1/2 1/7 1/14 = 5 5/7 (i.e., 5 + 7/14 + 2/14 + 1/14 = 5 10/14 = 5 5/7). Except for 1/2, such fractions are relatively uncommon, and are mostly found in papyri of mathematics or accounts.

9.7 Weights and measures

Ancient Egypt used a number of different systems for measuring length, area, weight, and volume, much as we still do in English today. Measures of length, area, and weight (§§ 9.7.1–3) are fairly straightforward; those of length are the most common in Middle Egyptian texts. Measures of volume (§ 9.7.4) are more complicated, and are presented here only for reference.

1. Length

The standard Egyptian measurement of length was the cubit, equal to about 20 2/3 inches (52.5 centimeters). Its usual fractions and multiples were the following:

ḏbꜥ "finger"	=	1/28 cubit, 1/4 palm (0.74 in, 1.88 cm)
šzp "palm"	=	4 fingers, 1/7 cubit (2.95 in, 7.5 cm)
mḥ "cubit"	=	7 palms, 28 fingers
ḫt "stick, rod"	=	100 cubits (57.41 yards, 52.5 meters)
jtrw "river"[3]	=	20,000 cubits (6.52 miles, 10.5 kilometers).

2. Area

The standard measurement of area was the *sṯ3t* "aroura" (, also ,), equal to 100 square cubits (0.68 acre, 0.28 hectare).[4] Its most common fraction and multiple were the following:

mḥ-t3 "centaroura"	=	1/100 aroura (1×100 cubits)
sṯ3t "aroura"	=	100 centarouras
ḫ3-t3 "decaroura"	=	10 arouras (6.81 acres, 2.76 ha).

3. Weight

Weights were measured in terms of the deben (*dbn*), equal to approximately 3.21 ounces (91 grams). In the New Kingdom it had two fractions and no multiples:

šnꜥtj "ring"	=	1/12 deben (0.27 oz, 7.58 gm)
qdt "qite"[5]	=	1/10 deben (0.32 oz, 9.1 gm)

3 Also translated "schoenus" (pronounced "SKEE-nus"), from the Greek term for this measurement.

4 In Egyptian, however, the aroura was thought of as 100 strips of land each measuring 1×100 cubits, rather than as 100 squares of 1×1 cubit. This is the reason why the multiple of 10 arouras was known as the *ḫ3-t3* (literally, "thousand-land"): i.e., 1,000 strips of 1×100 cubits.

5 Pronounced "KEY-teh."

dbn "deben" = 12 rings, 10 qite.

The "ring" is apparently the earlier of the two, and is generally replaced by the qite after Dynasty 18. In the Middle Kingdom the deben had a lower value of only 0.48 oz (13.6 gm), and had no fractions. The change to the higher value seems to have occurred toward the end of Dynasty 12.

4. **Volume**

The Egyptians had different systems for liquid and dry measures of volume, as we do today. Liquids were measured in various kinds of jars, such as the *ds* for beer (see the example in § 9.4). The capacity of most of these is unknown, except for the *hnw* "hin," equal to about half a quart (0.48 liters).

The most common dry measure of volume was for grain. The standard unit of measurement was the *ḥq(3)t* "heqat" (also written , , ,), equal to 10 hin (4.36 dry quarts, 4.8 l). It had several different multiples:

, ,	*ḥq3tj* "double heqat"	=	2 heqat (8.72 dry quarts, 9.6 l)
, ,	*jpt* "oipe"	=	4 heqat (17.44 dry quarts, 19.2 l)
,	*ẖ3r* "sack"	=	10 heqat (43.59 dry quarts, 48 l).

In the Second Intermediate Period, the capacity of the "sack" was changed from 10 heqats to 4 oipe (= 16 heqat: 69.74 dry quarts, 76.8 l).

Egyptian employed several numerical systems in conjunction with these grain measures. The simplest, found mostly in hieroglyphic texts, was based on the heqat, and used regular numerals and fractions: for example, *ḥq3t 88½* "88½ heqat." Early Middle Kingdom hieratic texts (written from right to left) used mostly the sack and the heqat. Sacks were numbered with regular numerals, and heqats were counted with one to nine dots (10 heqat = 1 sack): for example, *jtj-mḥj ẖ3r 12.5* "northern barley, sack(s), 12.5" (i.e., 12 sacks, 5 heqat). Later hieratic texts (also written right to left) used mostly the heqat, double heqat, and oipe, and a special numbering system. Numerals placed **before** the measurement stood for multiples of 100: i.e., *3 ḥq3t* "300 heqat," *20 ḥq3tj* "2,000 double heqat" (= 4,000 heqat), *12 jpt* "1,200 oipe" (= 4,800 heqat). Numerals from 1 to 9 placed **after** the measurement stood for multiples of ten, while single heqats were indicated by dots: for example, *1 ḥq3t 64* "164 heqat." The fractions ½ and ¼ after the measurement stood for 50 and 25, respectively (i.e., ½ and ¼ of 100): for instance, *ḥq3t ½ 1 ¼ 8* "93 heqat" (i.e., 50 + 10 + 25 + 8).

Both hieratic systems also employed a special set of signs to indicate fractions. These were based on the (*wḏ3t*) "Sound Eye" of Horus (sometimes called the "Udjat Eye"). According to mythology, Horus's eye had been torn out by Seth, but was put back together by Thoth. The pieces of this Eye are used for the following fractions of grain measures:

=	½	=	⅛	=	1/32
=	¼	=	1/16	=	1/64

for example, *1 ḥq3t ½ 1 6 ½ ⅛ 1/32* "166 21/32 heqat" (i.e., 100 + 50 + 10 + 6 + 16/32 + 4/32 + 1/32).

9.8 Dates: months and days

The ancient Egyptians divided their year (*rnpt*) into three seasons (*tr*). The year began traditionally around mid-July, when the annual four-month inundation of the Nile started, and the names of the seasons reflect the Egyptian agricultural year: *3ẖt* "Inundation" (mid-July to mid-November), *prt* "Growing" (literally, "Emergence," mid-November to mid-March), and *šmw* "Harvest" (mid-March to mid-July). Each season was divided into four months (*3bd*) of thirty days each (, *sw*).[6]

The months also had names, but these are rarely used in hieroglyphic texts (see the Addendum at the end of this lesson). Instead, the Egyptians employed a three-part numerical system for indicating months and days:

1. the sign (for *3bd* "month") followed by a number from 1 to 4;
2. the name of the season; and
3. the sign ☉ (for *sw* "day") followed by a number from 1 to 30

for example, *3 3ẖt 7* "3 Inundation 7." The word *tpj* "first" was sometimes used instead of for "month 1," and the word *ᶜrqy* "last" was normally used instead of the numeral for the thirtieth day of the month: for instance, *tpj šmw 16* "first of Harvest 16," *2 prt ᶜrqy* "2 Growing last." The use of *tpj* "first (month)" and *ᶜrqy* "last (day)" indicates that the numbers in dates were probably pronounced as ordinals rather than cardinals: i.e., *ḫmtnw 3ẖt sfḫnw* "third (month) of Inundation seventh (day)."

The combination of Egyptian seasons, months, and days produced a year of 12 months (3×4) and 360 days (12×30). The ancient Egyptians recognized, however, that the year had 365 full days rather than 360. In order to accommodate this discrepancy, they added five extra days at the end of the year, after 4 *šmw* 30 and before 1 *3ẖt* 1. These were known as *ḥr(j)w-rnpt* "those over the year" (the number is a determinative; *ḥrjw* is a plural nisbe from the preposition *ḥr*); Egyptologists call them the "epagomenal" ("eppa-GOM-men-nal") days, meaning "added." Each epagomenal day was celebrated as the birthday of a particular god: (1) *mswt wsjr* "birth of Osiris," (2) *mswt ḥrw* "birth of Horus," (3) *mswt stẖ* "birth of Seth," (4) *mswt jst* "birth of Isis," and (5) *mswt nbt-ḥwt* "birth of Nephthys." In dates, these days could be recorded by their names, or by numbers: for example, *ḥr(j)w-rnpt 5* "epagomenal day 5." The first day of the year (*wpt-rnpt* "opening of the year" = 1 *3ẖt* 1) was celebrated as *mswt rᶜ* "the birth of Re."

The Egyptian day was divided into 24 hours (, *wnwt*), 12 for the day (, *hrw*) and 12 for the night (*grḥ*). The Egyptian day began at sunrise. Until the New Kingdom, the hours were not fixed in length but varied with the seasons: thus, in winter an "hour" of the day would be shorter than an "hour" of night, and vice-versa in summer. The hours had names, but these are used mostly in astronomical texts. In normal texts the hours were counted with the ordinal numbers: for example, *wnwt mḥt-10 nt hrw* "10th hour of the day" (about 4 PM); *wnwt 4nwt nt grḥ* "4th hour of the night" (about 10 PM).

6 This word means "day of the month." The word *hrw* means "day" or "daytime" as opposed to night. Each month had 3 weeks of 10 days each; the word for "week" is unknown.

9.9 Dates: years

The Egyptians numbered their years not from a single fixed point but by the reign of the current king. (If the British employed this system, they would refer to the year AD 1955 as "Year 2 of Queen Elizabeth II" rather than as 1955.) The system used in Middle Egyptian texts dates back to the end of the Old Kingdom. Before that time, years were numbered according to a census that was carried out every two years during a king's reign. This practice gave rise to the word for "year" that is used in dates: *ḥsbt* (or perhaps *rnpt-ḥsbt*; the older reading *ḥ3t-zp* is erroneous) literally, "(year of) counting." Full Middle Egyptian dates have the following form:

1. followed by the number of the king's regnal year;
2. the month, season, and day, as in § 9.8, above;
3. the phrase *ḫr ḥm n (n)swt bjt(j)* "during the incarnation of the King of Upper and Lower Egypt" (see § 8.2.13), followed by the king's throne name

for instance,

ḥsbt 2 3 3ḫt 1 ḫr ḥm n (n)swt bjt(j) N(J)-M3ᶜT-Rᶜ
"Year 2, 3 Inundation 1, during the incarnation of the King of Upper and Lower Egypt NI-MAAT-RE" (Amenemhat III).

More abbreviated dates leave out the specific reference to the king: *ḥsbt 24 2 prt ᶜrqy* "Year 24, 2 Growing last."

ESSAY 9. EGYPTIAN CHRONOLOGY

The modern view of time is linear, with the past at one end, the future at the other, and the present somewhere between. The ancient Egyptians viewed time as both linear and cyclical. Their linear view of time is expressed in the word *ḏt*, usually translated as "eternity." The concept underlying this term is one of eternal sameness. It refers to the pattern of existence that was established at the creation and will continue until the end of the world: the sky in place above the earth; the Nile flowing from south to north; the sun rising in the east and setting in the west; living things being born, growing, and dying. The Egyptian concept of cyclical time is embodied in the word *nḥḥ* (abbreviated), also translated as "eternity." In this view, time is eternally repeated and renewed: in the daily cycle of the sun, the yearly cycle of the seasons, and the cycle of birth and death among living things. In a sense, the Egyptian concept of time can be compared to a play: its script (*ḏt*) is fixed and unchanging, but each performance of the play (*nḥḥ*) is different, with new settings and new actors.

In their understanding of time, the Egyptians thought of each day, each year, and each accession of a new king as a new creation. This view underlies the Egyptian practice of dating their years by the reign of the current pharaoh (§ 9.9). Each time a new king came to the throne, a new cycle of year dates was begun: the start of each pharaoh's reign was the first year of a new creation and a new cycle of time.

While this method of counting years was satisfactory for the Egyptians, it is of limited use to modern historians. We fix historical events in relation to an absolute starting date of AD 1; this was calculated by Christians in late antiquity as the first year in the life of Jesus (AD stands for the Latin phrase *anno Domini* "in the year of the Lord"). Years after this date are numbered consecutively forward, so that AD 1945, for example, indicates the 1,944th year after AD 1. Years before AD 1 are numbered consecutively backward, beginning with 1 BC ("before Christ"; there is no Year 0).[7]

From ancient historical sources we know that the last Egyptian pharaoh, Cleopatra VII, died in 30 BC. From this point it might seem a simple matter to calculate when each preceding pharaoh ruled by adding the years of their reigns. Unfortunately, Egyptian sources do not always tell us how long each pharaoh ruled. Moreover, there were times in Egyptian history when more than one pharaoh ruled at a time, either as coregents or as rivals: in such cases, the ancient texts usually number each pharaoh's years independently, and we do not always know how many of these competing year dates overlapped. For these reasons, we cannot fix an Egyptian date such as Year 12 of Ramesses II in terms of years BC just by counting backwards from 30 BC.

Fortunately, Egyptian dating systems provide another clue to absolute dates. The Egyptian calendar consisted of 365 days (§ 9.8), but a true year (called a "solar year") is actually about 365¼ days long. We account for this difference by adding an extra day to our calendar every fourth year ("leap year"). Since the Egyptians had no leap years, their calendar moved backward in relation to the actual year by one day every four years: for example, if the Egyptian calendar day 1 Inundation 1 (1 *3ẖt* 1) corresponded to July 17 in a particular year, four years later the same calendar day would have fallen on July 16; eight years later, on July 15, and so forth.

No matter which calendar we use to record them, astronomical events always recur exactly one real (solar) year apart. The Egyptians were avid astronomers, and they kept careful records of their observations of the sun and the stars. One of the more important annual events they noted is called the rising of Sothis (*spdt*, the Egyptian name for the star we call Sirius). Sirius is visible in the Egyptian night sky for most of the year, but during a period of about seventy days in late spring it does not rise above the horizon; then, in mid-July, it reappears above the horizon just before sunrise. This reappearance of Sirius corresponded to the start of the annual inundation of the Nile, and marked the beginning of the year in ancient Egypt.

Ideally, the rising of Sothis should have occurred on 1 Inundation 1, which was the first day of the Egyptian calendar. Because the Egyptian calendar moved backward by one day every four years, however, the rising of Sothis also fell a calendar day earlier every four years. For four years the rising of Sothis might be observed on 1 Inundation 1, but during the next four years it would fall on Epagomenal Day 5 (the last day of the Egyptian calendar), then on Epagomenal Day 4 for four years, and so forth. It took about 1,453 years for the cycle to come full circle; Egyptologists call this span of time the "Sothic Cycle." From an observation made in late antiquity, we know that the rising of Sothis actually did occur on 1 Inundation 1 during the four-year period from AD 136–39. Calculating backward by the Sothic Cycle, we can determine that it also fell on 1 Inundation 1 during the four-year period from 1317–1320 BC and again in 2771–2774 BC.

7 Some modern historians prefer the term CE (for "common era") instead of AD, and BCE ("before the common era") instead of BC.

If a text records the rising of Sothis on a particular date of the Egyptian calendar in a king's regnal year, it is then a simple matter to calculate the actual date BC of this event (within four years) against these three fixed four-year periods. For pharaonic history there are only three such historical records. Two of these include the regnal year of a king as well as the month and day: on 2 Harvest 1 in Year 9 of Ptolemy III, and on 4 Growing 16 in Year 7 of Senwosret III. The first of these is 94 days before 1 Inundation 1: this dates Year 9 of Ptolemy III to the period between 240 and 237 BC (4×94 = 376 years earlier than AD 136–39; the actual date, which can be calculated from other sources, is 238 BC). The second is 140 days before 1 Inundation 1, and places Year 7 of Senwosret III about 1873–1876 BC (139×4 = 556 years earlier than 1317–1320).

Using these dates and other sources, Egyptologists are able to calculate the regnal years of most other ancient Egyptian kings in terms of actual years BC. The process is a complicated one, involving astronomy, king-lists, historical texts, biographical inscriptions, lunar dates of Egyptian festivals, and correspondences with Mesopotamian king-lists and the Hebrew Bible. Although Egyptian chronology is still the subject of much debate, most Egyptologists now agree that the dates of Egyptian pharaohs and dynasties from the Middle Kingdom onward are fairly certain, with a margin of error ranging from about 29 years in Dynasty 12 to near zero after 525 BC.

EXERCISE 9

1. Transliterate and translate the following list of booty from a military campaign of Thutmose III:

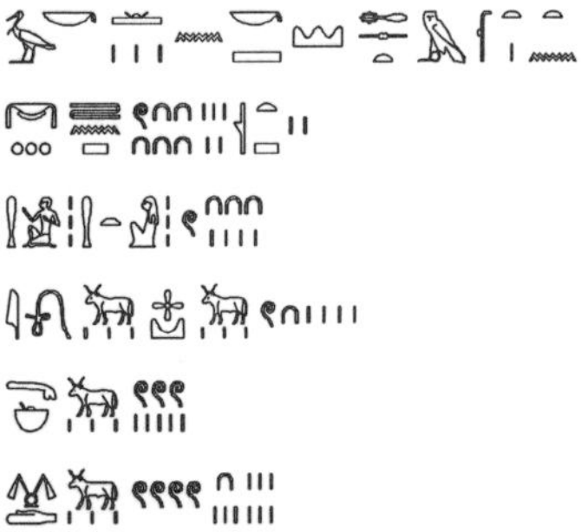

VOCABULARY:

jw3 "ox"
jḥ "cattle"
wnḏw "short-horned cattle"
b3kw "tribute"
nbw "gold"
ḥm / *ḥmt* "servant"
ẖzj "wretched"
k3 jdr "herd bull"
kš "Kuṣh" (northern Sudan)
dmd "total"

2. Transliterate and translate:
   a.  — *sḫm-k3-rᶜ*: throne name of a 13th-Dynasty king
   b.  — *zp* "time"
   c.  — *w3t* "path," *mw* "water," *jtj* "grain"
   d.  — *sḫtj* "peasant"
   e.  — *nḥsj* "Nubian"
   f. 
   g. 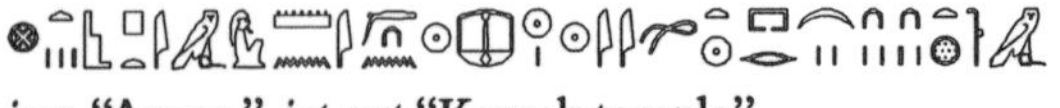 — *hrw-ḥ3b* "feast day, festival day" *jmn* "Amun," *jpt-swt* "Karnak temple"

h. 

i. 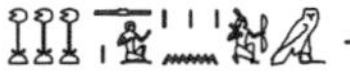 — *mšʿ* "expeditionary force," *zj* "man"

j.  — *jr* see § 8.2.7; *hrw* "day"

k.  — *wḏyt* "campaign," *nḫt* "victory"

l.  — *ḥtp* "peace"

m. 

n.  — *jb* "heart"

3. Write in hieroglyphs the ordinal counterparts of the following cardinal numbers:

a. 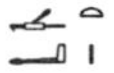 b.  c.  d.

e. f.  g.  h. 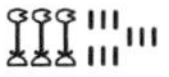

4. The following is an excerpt transcribed from a hieratic account in which amounts of something are tallied under the headings of certain kinds of cattle. Transliterate and translate it; in the translation, combine Egyptian fractions where necessary into a single fraction (i.e., $\frac{1}{3}\ \frac{1}{4} = \frac{7}{12}$).[8] See if you can figure out mathematically how the rows and columns are related.

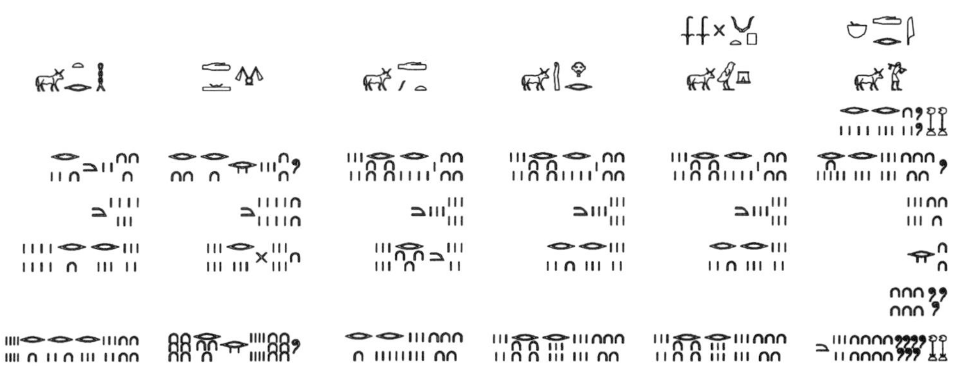

VOCABULARY:

jdr-mnjw "tended herd" (literally, "herder's herd")
wpt "splitting"
(n)g(3)w "steer"
ḥrj-ḏbʿ "hornless cattle"
ḥtr "team ox"
ḏrt "calf"
dmd "total"

8 To combine fractions with different denominators, find the lowest number into which all the denominators can be divided evenly, multiply the numerators by the number of times the denominator goes into this lowest number, then add all the numerators together. For example, to add $\frac{1}{3} + \frac{1}{5} + \frac{1}{6}$, change all the fractions to 30ths (30 is the lowest number into which 3, 5, and 6 can all be divided evenly): $\frac{1}{3} = \frac{10}{30}$, $\frac{1}{5} = \frac{6}{30}$, $\frac{1}{6} = \frac{5}{30}$. Then add the fractions: $\frac{10}{30} + \frac{6}{30} + \frac{5}{30} = \frac{21}{30}$.

Addendum: The Names of the Egyptian Months

Although the Egyptian calendar denoted months by numbers and seasons (§ 9.8), the months themselves had names. These are first attested in the Middle Kingdom, and seem to be the designations that were used in the Memphite region. The months are usually named after a festival that occurred in them or in the following month:

1 Inundation		*ṯḫj* "He of the Plumb-bob" (an epithet of Thoth)
2 Inundation		*mnḫt* "Clothing"
3 Inundation		*ḫnt ḥwt-ḥr(w)* "Voyage of Hathor"
4 Inundation		*nḥb-k3w* "Apportioner of Kas" (a god)
1 Growing		*šf-bdt* "Swelling of Emmer-Wheat"
2 Growing		*rkḥ-ᶜ3* "Big Burning"
3 Growing		*rkḥ-nḏs* "Little Burning"
4 Growing		*rnn-wtt* "Rennutet" (goddess of the harvest)
1 Harvest	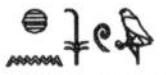	*ḫnsw* "Khonsu" (moon god)
2 Harvest		*ḫnt-ḫty-prtj* "Khentekhtai-perti" (a god)
3 Harvest		*jpt ḥmt* "She whose incarnation is select"
4 Harvest		*wpt-rnpt* "Opening of the Year."

In the New Kingdom most of the month-names were changed, in many cases to reflect festivals celebrated in Thebes. These names survived into Coptic, and are still used in the religious calendar of the Coptic church:

1 Inundation		*ḏḥwtj* "Thoth"	ⲑⲟⲟⲩⲧ
2 Inundation		*p(3)-n-jpt* "The one of Karnak"	ⲡⲁⲟⲡⲉ
3 Inundation		*ḥwt-ḥr(w)* "Hathor"	ϩⲁⲑⲱⲣ
4 Inundation		*k3-ḥr-k3* "Ka Upon Ka"	ⲕⲟⲓⲁϩⲕ
1 Growing		*t3-ᶜ(3)bt* "The Offering"	ⲧⲱⲃⲉ
2 Growing		*p(3)-n-p3-mḫrw* "The one of the censer"	ⲙϣⲓⲣ
3 Growing		*p(3)-n-JMN-ḤTP* "The one of Amen-hotep (I)"	ⲡⲁⲣⲙϩⲟⲧⲡ
4 Growing		*p(3)-n-rn(n)-wt(t)* "The one of Rennutet"	ⲡⲁⲣⲙⲟⲩⲧⲉ
1 Harvest		*p(3)-n-ḫnsw* "The one of Khonsu"	ⲡⲁϣⲟⲛⲥ
2 Harvest		*p(3)-n-jnt* "The one of the wadi"	ⲡⲁⲱⲛⲉ
3 Harvest	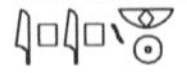	*jp(j)-jp(j)* (apparently from *jpt-ḥmt*)	ⲉⲡⲏⲡ
4 Harvest	(not attested)	*mswt-rᶜ* "Birth of Re"	ⲙⲉⲥⲟⲣⲏ.

The month names occur mostly in lists of festivals and in private letters. Although they are rare in normal texts, however, they were undoubtedly common in spoken Egyptian, just as we use names such as "April" instead of "Month 4."

10. Adverbial Sentences

10.1 Definitions

In §§ 7.1–7.2 and 7.6 we saw that the true predicate in English sentences such as *This plan is excellent* and *This plan is a disaster* is the adjective (*excellent*) or the noun or noun phrase (*a disaster*) that follows the verb *is*. English also has sentences in which the predicate is a prepositional phrase or an adverb: for example, *Jack is in the barn* and *Jill is here*. As in adjectival and nominal sentences, English requires the verb *is*, but the verb doesn't really add any information to the sentence: what is important is the part of the predicate after *is*. The word *here* is an adverb, and prepositional phrases such as *in the barn* can also function as adverbs (§ 8.11). Grammarians call a predicate such as *is in the barn* or *is here* an **adverbial predicate**.

Egyptian also has sentences in which the predicate is an adverb or a prepositional phrase. As in sentences with nominal or adjectival predicates, these are **nonverbal** sentences in Egyptian, without a verb that corresponds to the English verb *is*. Egyptologists call them **adverbial sentences**, short for the more accurate term "sentences with adverbial or prepositional predicates."

10.2 Basic patterns

In the Egyptian adverbial sentence the subject normally comes first and the predicate is second: for example,

 *ẖrwt.k m pr.k* "Your possessions are in your house,"

literally, "your possessions[1] in your house," where *ẖrwt.k* is the subject and the prepositional phrase *m pr.k* is the predicate. Occasionally the order of subject and predicate is reversed, mostly when the predicate is a prepositional phrase with *n* "to, for":

 *n k3.k jnw n sḫt* "For your ka is the produce of the field,"

where *jnw n sḫt* is the subject and *n k3.k* is the predicate (see the discussion of the ka in Essay 7).

Like nominal and adjectival sentences (§ 7.16), the adverbial sentence has no inherent tense. It can therefore refer to the past or future as well as to present situations: for example,

 *pꜥt m jmw* "The nobility were in mourning" (from a story)

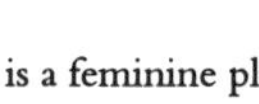 *wrrt.j n.s* "My crown shall be for her."

Unlike sentences with a nominal or adjectival predicate, those with an adverbial predicate can express wishes or commands as well as statements of fact:

 b3w.k r.f nṯr "May your impressiveness be against him, god!" (a wish)

 ḥr.k m ẖrw "Let your face be down!" (a command),

1 *ẖrwt* is a feminine plural reverse nisbe: literally, "those which you are under" (see §§ 8.8–8.9).

literally, "Your impressiveness against him, god!" and "Your face in down-ness!" (an abstract noun formed from the preposition *ẖr* "under"). Such adverbial sentences are actually closer to English usage than are those that state a fact, since English too can make wishes or commands without a verb: *A curse on both your houses!* (a wish), *Hands up!* (a command). As with nominal and adjectival sentences, there is nothing in the adverbial sentence itself to indicate whether it is a past, present, or future statement of fact or a wish or command. In most cases, however, the meaning is clear from the context in which the sentence is used.

10.3 The particle *jw*

Adverbial sentences that consist of just a subject and an adverbial predicate, such as those cited in the preceding section, are not very common in Middle Egyptian. Normally Middle Egyptian prefers to introduce adverbial sentences with one of a group of small words known as **particles**. Besides serving as an introductory word, each particle also adds a particular nuance to the sentence.

The most important Middle Egyptian particle is *jw* (spelled  or ). This word is used before a nominal subject or a demonstrative pronoun, or with the **suffix** form of a personal pronoun (§ 5.3): for example,

 *jw m(w)t m ḥr.j mjn* "Death is in my sight (literally, 'face') today"

 *jw n3 m sb(3)yt* "This is as an instruction"

 *jw.f m ꜥt* "It is in a room."

Although *jw* is very common in Middle Egyptian adverbial sentences, it usually cannot be translated into English. In fact, Egyptologists still debate about the exact meaning of *jw*, and no one has yet come up with a full explanation of why Egyptian uses it in some cases but not in others. One of the uses of *jw* that does seem clear, however, has to do with the difference between statements that are generally valid and those that are only temporarily true. English does not make this distinction: we use the same kind of sentence for both kinds of statements — for example, *The Eiffel Tower is in Paris* (always true) and *The President is in Paris* (temporarily true). Middle Egyptian, however, often does show the difference: in sentences with an adverbial predicate, *jw* generally marks a statement that is only temporarily true or one that is true in specific circumstances. The sentence *jw mwt m ḥr.j mjn* "Death is in my sight today," for example, might be true when it is spoken ("today") but is not always true. Similarly, *jw.f m ꜥt* "It is in a room" refers to the present location of something, not to its permanent location.

Besides its use in adverbial sentences, *jw* occasionally appears in sentences with an adjectival predicate. In such cases *jw* seems to have the same kind of meaning that it does in adverbial sentences: that is, to indicate that the adjectival statement is true only temporarily or in a specific circumstance; for example, 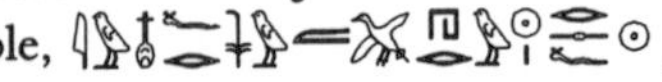 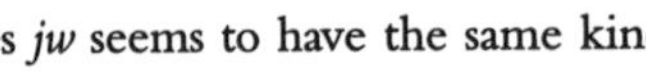 *jw nfr sw m p3 hrw r sf* "He is better today than yesterday" (literally, "He is good in this day with respect to yesterday"). In Middle Egyptian, *jw* is almost never used with nominal sentences. This is evidently because such sentences describe identifications that are not restricted to a particular time: *z3.j pw* "He is my son" (see § 7.16).

Since English does not make a distinction between statements that are generally or temporarily valid, the presence or absence of *jw* usually makes no difference to the translation. It was important to the Egyptians, however, and you should be aware of the difference.

10.4 **Other particles**

Besides *jw*, Middle Egyptian also uses a number of other particles to introduce adverbial sentences. As with *jw*, these particles also carry a nuance that the sentence does not have without them. They are used with the same kinds of subjects as *jw*, but when the subject is a personal pronoun they use the **dependent** form of the pronoun (§ 5.4) instead of the suffix form. The following are four of the most frequent particles:

1.  *m.k* (more properly, *mj.k*) "behold"

This particle, which always stands first, presumes that the sentence is being spoken to somebody. It has three forms, with a suffix pronoun indicating the gender and number of the person to whom the sentence is spoken:

2MS	*m.k*	, also  or 
2FS	*m.ṯ* or *m.t*	, , etc.
2PL	*m.ṯn* or *m.tn*	, , , etc.

The particle *m.k* is essentially used to present a statement, or to call it to the attention of the listener. Although it literally means "behold," this translation usually makes the statement sound too archaic or "biblical" to English ears. As a result, *m.k* is often best paraphrased in English, or left untranslated: for example,

 *m.k wj r gs.k*
"Here I am at your side" (literally, "Behold, I am at your side")

 *m.k sw ᶜ3 m ᶜ.j* "Look, he is here in my hand"

 *m.tn špswt ḥr šdw* "The noblewomen are on rafts."

2.  *nn* "not"

The particle *nn* is used to negate the adverbial sentence. It always stands before the subject, but it can be preceded by other particles itself (see no. 16 in the exercise, below):

 *nn mwt.k ḥnᶜ.k* "Your mother is not with you"

 *nn s(j) m jb.j* "It was not in my heart."

3. ,  *nḥmn* "surely"

The particle *nḥmn* is a stronger version of *m.k*, used to emphasize the truth of the adverbial sentence. It is always first in the sentence:

 *nḥmn wj mj k3* "I am really like a bull" ("Surely, I am like a bull").

4. ,  *ḥ3*; also  *ḥ3 3* and ,  *ḥwj 3* "if only, I wish, would that"

The particles *ḥ3*, *ḥ3 3*, and *ḥwj 3* are used to indicate that the adverbial sentence is a wish. Although the plain adverbial sentence can also be used as a wish (§ 10.2), the presence of these particles seems to imply some uncertainty about whether the wish will come true. They always stand first in the sentence:

 *ḥw(j) 3 wj jm* "I wish I was there" ("If only I was there").

10.5 Personal pronouns as subjects

With very few exceptions, **only the dependent or suffix form of the personal pronouns is used as subject in an adverbial sentence.** As a result, most Middle Egyptian adverbial sentences with a personal pronoun as subject are introduced by a particle of some sort: most often, by *jw* or *m.k*. The independent personal pronoun is used as the subject of an adverbial predicate only in a special kind of sentence, which we will meet toward the end of this book.

In Dynasty 17, written Egyptian began to use a new kind of independent personal pronoun as the subject of an adverbial sentence. This form seems to have come from the spoken language of Upper Egypt. Its paradigm consists of the element *tw* ( or ) plus the suffix pronouns for the first and second person, and dependent pronouns for the third person:

1S	*tw.j*	 (etc.)	"I"	1PL	*tw.n*		"we"
2MS	*tw.k*		"you"	2PL	*tw.tn*		"you"
2FS	*tw.(t)*		"you"				
3MS	*sw*	, 	"he, it"	3N	*st*	, 	"it, they"
3FS	*sj*		"she, it"				

This form is used only as subject and only in particular kinds of sentences, including those with an adverbial predicate. It always stands first in the sentence, and is not used after particles:

 *sw ḫr t3 n ͨ3mw, tw.n ḫr kmt*
"He has the land of the Asiatics. We have Egypt,"

literally, "He is under the land of the Asiatics" and "We are under Egypt" (see § 10.7, below). Since this pronoun is always used as the subject of a sentence, we can call it the **subject form** of the personal pronoun. You should note that it is not used before Dynasty 17 and does not appear in good, standard Middle Egyptian texts of the Middle Kingdom.

10.6 Adverbial sentences of identity

One of the most common kinds of adverbial sentence is used to identify the subject with something by means of the preposition *m*: for example,

 *m.k tw m mnjw* "You are a herdsman,"

literally, "behold, you (are) in a herdsman." For this kind of sentence we do not normally translate the preposition *m*. In Egyptian, however, it indicated that the subject was "in" the capacity or identity of something (see § 8.2.3): in this example, the subject *tw* "you" is "in" the function of "a herdsman."[2] Egyptologists sometimes call the preposition in this usage the "*m* of predication," meaning that the preposition makes it possible for the following noun to function as an adverbial predicate. In Egyptian, however, there was no difference between this meaning of *m* and the more understandable instances in which *m* means "in" a place or a state (see the examples in §§ 10.2, 10.3, and 10.4.2, above).

2 This may seem an odd way to express identity, but it is not peculiar to Egyptian. Scottish Gaelic uses a similar construction: *Tha thu nad bhuachaille* "You are a herdsman" — literally, "You are in your herdsman."

The existence of this kind of sentence means that Egyptian had two ways of expressing identity: with a nominal sentence (Lesson 7) or with an adverbial sentence using the preposition *m*. English forces us to translate both kinds of sentence in the same way: for example, *ntk r*^{c} "You are Re" (Exercise 7, no. 34) and *m.k tw m mnjw* "You are a herdsman." In Egyptian, however, the two constructions mean two different things. The nominal sentence is used when the identity is thought of as natural or unchangeable, and the adverbial sentence with *m* is used when the identification is seen as acquired or temporary. Thus, *ntk r*^{c} identifies who the subject is ("Re"), while *m.k tw m mnjw* identifies the subject's occupation (which is not necessarily permanent). In the same way, the sentence *ntk z3.j* "You are my son" implies that the speaker is talking to his real son, while *jw.k m z3.j* "You are my son" indicates that the person being addressed is acting as a son (whether he is the speaker's real son or not).

In § 10.3 we saw that Egyptian uses *jw* to distinguish statements that are only temporarily true from those that are always valid. The same kind of distinction underlies the contrast between adverbial sentences with the preposition *m* and nominal sentences of identity. In both cases, Egyptian makes a distinction that does not exist in English sentences, and which therefore cannot be translated directly into English. This is an instance in which the Egyptian language is richer — or at least, more precise — than English, and it is a good example of how the subtleties of a language can be lost in translation.

10.7 Adverbial sentences of possession

As we learned in § 6.9, the Egyptian language has no verb corresponding to the English verb of possession *have*. To say "I have cattle," Egyptian can use a nominal sentence with the noun *nb* "lord, master, owner": *jnk nb k3w* — literally, "I am an owner of cattle." More often, however, Egyptian prefers an adverbial sentence. The sentence quoted in § 10.5 is one example of how the language expresses possession by means of an adverbial predicate, with the preposition *ẖr*: to be "under" something is to possess it (see § 8.2.15). Alternatively, a predicate with the compound preposition "in the hand" can be used:

> *ẖrwt.j m* ^{c}*.j* "I have my possessions,"

literally, "My possessions are in my hand" (for *ẖrwt* "possessions," see n. 1 in this lesson).

The most common kind of adverbial predicate of possession involves the preposition *n* "to, for": for example,

> *nn jz n sbj* "The rebel has no tomb,"

literally, "A tomb is not for the rebel." In many instances this kind of sentence has a close parallel in English: thus, for the sentence just cited, we can also translate "There is no tomb for the rebel." Similarly,

> *ḫt.j nbt m š3 m nwt n sn.j*
> "My brother shall have all my things in the country and in the village,"

literally, "All my things in the country and in the village are for my brother" (a sentence taken from a man's will). Egyptologists often use the term **dative** (borrowed from Greek and Latin grammar) to refer to prepositional phrases such as *n sbj* and *n sn.j* in these examples.

These last two sentences are examples in which the preposition *n* governs a nominal object (*n sbj* "for the rebel," *n sn.j* "for my brother"). They show the normal word-order of adverbial sentences, with the subject (*jz*, *ḫt.j nbt m š3 m nwt*) first and the adverbial predicate second. When the object of *n* is a suffix pronoun, however, the order is usually reversed: for example,

 *jw n.k ꜥnḫ w3s* "Life and dominion are for you"

 *ḥ3 n.j šzp nb mnḫ* "I wish I had any effective image of a god,"

literally, "For you are life and dominion" and "Would that there were for me any effective image of a god." The normal word order is reversed because of a rule of Egyptian grammar: **a dative with a suffix pronoun tends to stand as close to the front of the sentence as possible.** In these examples, the datives *n.k* and *n.j* are second because the two particles, *jw* and *ḥ3*, must be first.

10.8 Adverbial sentences with the preposition *r*

Like other prepositions, the preposition *r* can be used in an adverbial predicate with the meanings it has in other uses (§ 8.2.7): for example,

 *jw.f r.j, jw.j r.f* "He is against me and I am against him."

When the adverbial predicate consists of *r* and a noun (or noun phrase) of place, the sentence often indicates the subject's destination:

 *jw.j r pt mḥtt* "I am bound for the northern sky"

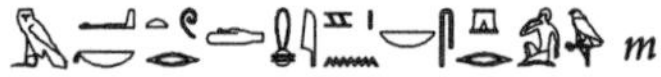 *m.k tw r dmj n nb-sgr*
"Look, you are headed for the harbor of the Lord of Silence,"

literally, "I am toward the northern sky" and "Behold, you are toward the harbor of the Lord of Silence" (i.e., you are courting death).

In the same way, when the object of *r* is a noun (or noun phrase) that denotes the occupation or function of a person, the sentence usually indicates a status "toward" which the subject is destined: for example,

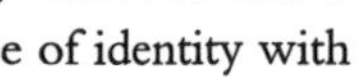 *jw.f r wꜥb nṯr pn* "He is to be a priest of this god,"

literally, "He is toward a priest of this god." This last kind of sentence is exactly analogous to the sentence of identity with the preposition *m*, which we considered in § 10.6. With *m*, the sentence indicates that the subject is "in" a particular role or function; with *r*, it indicates that the subject is "toward" (headed or destined for) the role or function.

10.9 Adverbial sentences without a subject

As in adjectival sentences (§ 8.5), Egyptian sometimes omits the subject in an adverbial sentence when it is clear from the context or when it doesn't refer to anything in particular:

 *jw mj sḫr nṯr* "It is like the plan of a god"

 *nn m jwms* "It is not an exaggeration."

The translation of such sentences usually has a "dummy" subject, *it*, because English grammar requires a subject. In Egyptian, however, the subject can just be left out. As these examples show, such sentences are always introduced by a particle of some sort.

10.10 Interrogatives as adverbial predicates

We have already seen how the interrogative adjective and pronouns are used as the predicate in adjectival and nominal sentences (§§ 7.5.4, 7.13). As you might suspect, the interrogative adverb *ṯnj* (§ 8.13) can be used as the predicate of an adverbial sentence:

 *jw jr.f tn(j)* "So, where is it?"[3]

In § 8.13 we also saw that the interrogative pronouns can be used as the object of a preposition. Such prepositional phrases can also serve as predicates in adverbial sentences:

 *sw mj jḫ* "What is it like?"

literally, "It is like what?" (for the subject, see § 10.5).

Essay 10. Maat

The concept of time that the ancient Egyptians called  *ḏt* represented their view that the pattern of existence was fixed, unchanging, and eternal (see Essay 9). The pattern itself they called 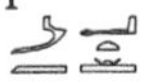 *m3ꜥt*, an abstract noun derived from the verb 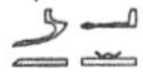 *m3ꜥ* "direct." The concept of *m3ꜥt* refers to the natural order of the universe, something like the notion of natural law in Western philosophy. It means essentially "the way things ought to be." This is a concept that is nearly impossible to translate accurately by one English word, so Egyptologists normally use the transcription of the Egyptian word ("Maat") rather than a translation.

The Egyptians saw Maat as a force of nature — in fact, the most fundamental of such forces. The hieroglyph , which appears in writings of the word, probably reflects this viewpoint. It seems to represent a socle or base on which an object such as a throne or a statue can stand, and perhaps for this reason it came to be used as an ideogram for something that is basic or fundamental. Like other natural forces, Maat was also divine (see Essay 4). As a goddess, Maat normally is represented in human form, identified (for unknown reasons) by the feather  she always wears tucked into her headband. From this association the feather also came to be used as an ideogram for *m3ꜥt*. The Egyptians seem to have used the feather, or the hieroglyph of the goddess wearing it (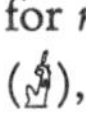), in art and writing only when they were thinking of Maat as a goddess. The socle was used as an ideogram or triliteral sign in writing the word *m3ꜥt* itself and related words, such as the verb *m3ꜥ* "direct" and the adjective *m3ꜥ*, which means "having the quality of Maat."

Like the other forces of nature, Maat was established at the creation, when the sun rose into the world for the first time; for this reason, the goddess is often called *z3t rꜥ* "the daughter of Re." To the Egyptians, it was the existence of Maat itself that ensured that the world would continue to exist as it had from the beginning of time:

> Maat is effective, lasting, and active; it is undisturbed since the time of him who made it.
> He who bypasses its laws is punished: it is the path even in the face of the ignorant. ...
> In the end it is Maat that lasts — something of which a man says: 'It is the legacy of my father.'

3 A subjectless sentence (see § 10.9). The prepositional phrase *jr.f* is used as a relational word, like English *so*.

Maat operated both in the world at large and in the world of human affairs. On the cosmic level it governed the proper functioning of the universe. Maat was what kept the world's elements fixed in their appropriate places, the seasons following in their natural order, night giving way to day, and each generation being succeeded by another. In the Egyptian view this ideal order did not mean that the more desirable parts of nature should eliminate the less desirable: instead, the concept of Maat was one in which all parts of nature lived in balance and harmony. The desert surrounding Egypt, for example, was a wild and dangerous place, yet it also served a purpose in isolating the country from its enemies for most of ancient Egyptian history. In the same way, life is clearly preferable to death, but death is also necessary if succeeding generations are to enjoy the same benefits and opportunities that their ancestors had.

Maat also governed the narrower world of human affairs. In that sphere Maat served as the yardstick against which the Egyptians measured most of their important experiences: their society's values, their relationships with one another, and even their own perception of reality. Depending on which of these areas of human activity it was used in, Maat corresponded to several different modern concepts, and can be translated by a number of English abstract nouns: "right"; "correct behavior," "order," "justice"; and "truth."

The opposite of Maat in each of these areas was  *jzft*: "wrong"; "incorrect or antisocial behavior," "disorder," "injustice"; and "falsehood." In our society the distinction between these opposites is determined by codes of religious commandments and civil laws. Ancient Egypt had no such codes. For the Egyptians the distinction was determined by practical experience: behavior that promoted balanced, harmonious relationships between people was *m3*^{c} ("right, correct, orderly, just, true"); that which did not, was a manifestation of *jzft*.

Although Maat was established by the creator, as part of the world's natural order, its opposite came from human beings themselves. In one Middle Kingdom text, the creator says:

> I made every man like his fellow (*mj snw.f*: see §§ 9.3–9.4).
> I did not command that they do *jzft*:
> it is their hearts that destroy what I have laid out.

In other words, the creator established a balanced universe ("I made every man like his fellow"); imbalance in the world comes about not through the existence of some evil force ("I did not command that they do *jzft*"), but through human behavior ("it is their hearts that destroy what I have laid out").

The sentence "I made every man like his fellow" has sometimes been taken as a sign that the Egyptians believed in a kind of natural equality, but this is not the case. The essence of Maat in the human sphere was not perfect social and economic equality but rather the harmonious coexistence of society's different levels (see Essay 3). Maat did not mean that the rich and powerful should become equal to the poor and weak, or vice-versa: in fact, texts that describe a society without Maat typically say things like "The beggars of the land have become rich men and the owners of things, those who have nothing." Instead, Maat meant that the rich and powerful should use their advantages not to exploit those less fortunate but rather to help them. Tomb biographies often echo this understanding in sentences such as "I have given bread to the hungry and clothing to the naked" and "I was a husband to the widow, and a father to the orphan."

It was the duty of all Egyptians to live in accordance with Maat. Only if they did so could they join the society of the dead when they died (see Essay 8). In the final judgment that every Egyptian (even the king) had to pass through, the heart of the deceased was weighed against a feather to determine if his or her actions in life (symbolized by the heart) were in balance with Maat (the feather). Unlike the final trial of Christian tradition, this was not a religious judgment but a social one: people who had been disruptive elements in the society of the living could hardly expect to be welcomed as members of the blessed society of the dead. Only when the comparison between the heart and Maat showed that the deceased was *m3ᶜ ḫrw* "true of voice" was the dead person formally transferred by Horus, king of the living, to the care of Osiris, king of the dead.

While normal Egyptians were responsible for conducting their lives in accordance with Maat, the king had a dual responsibility: not only to live his own life according to the same principle but also to maintain Maat in society as a whole. This larger responsibility had many different facets. It was the king's duty to keep Egypt's enemies at bay, so that the country could live in order and tranquility; to appoint just officials, who would keep society running smoothly and in harmony; to settle disputes between nomes, towns, and people; to manage the national grain supply, so that people would not go hungry between harvests; and to please the gods with temples and offerings, so that the forces of nature would continue to look kindly on the Egyptians. All of these actions, and others like them, were seen as part of the king's duty to his subjects and the gods — a duty summarized in texts by the phrase "putting *m3ᶜt* in place of *jzft*" and on temple walls by images of the king presenting the symbol of Maat () to the gods.

EXERCISE 10

Transliterate and translate the following sentences.

1.  — *jt(j)*: see § 7.8 n. 1; *ḫnw* "interior," *ᶜḥ* "palace"
2.  — future: *rn* "name," *ᶜnḫw* "the living"
3.  — *ms* "indeed," *jtrw* "river," *snf* "blood"
4.  — past; *ḥr(j) jb* "midst" (literally, "what is on the heart")
5.  — *wn(m)w* "food"
6.  — *ḥr* "face," *pt* "sky"
7.  — *nhw* "need"
8.  — *sḏmw* "obedient," *šms(w)* "follower," *ḥrw* "Horus"
9.  — *ḫ3t* "corpse," *qm3* "one that is thrown"
10.  — future: *ṯ3w* "air," *nḏm* "sweet," *mḥyt* "northwind"
11.  — past: *wᶜw* "soldier"
12.  — *ḥzwt* "blessing"; *ḥm.f* see Essay 3
13.  — *st* "place"

14. 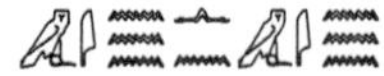 — a two-part question
15.  — *sḫ3* "memory"; *tp(j)w-t3* nisbe from *tp* "upon" and *t3* "earth"
16.  — *ᶜᶜft* "rate of payment," *qsn* "difficult"
17.  — past: *ḫnw* "the capital" (literally, "the interior"), *sgr* "stillness"
18.  — *j3w* "old man"
19. 
20.  — *wj* "mummiform coffin," *nbw* "gold," *ḫsbd* "lapis-lazuli"
21. 
22.  — *šmᶜ* "chanter," *ḫr ḥ3t* see § 8.3.1
23.  — *ḫt* see § 4.4
24. 
25.  — see §§ 8.10 and 10.2
26. 
27.  — *smsw* "eldest," *s3* "charge" (literally, "back"), *wḥyt* "tribe"
28. 
29.  — past: *wdpw* "waiter"; *jrt* see § 8.6.4
30.  — *b3ḥ* "presence"
31.  — past; *jr* "as for" (see § 8.2.7)
32.  — *nḏs* "commoner," *rnpt* "year"
33. 
34. 
35. 
36.  — *nhw* "loss," *mšᶜ* "expeditionary force"
37.  — *ᶜnḫ* "life"
38.  — past: *ẖt* "belly"
39.  — *tr* marks a question, not translated; *rm* "fish," *sbk* "Sobek"; see §§ 8.13 and 10.7
40.  — *3hw* "needy"
41. 
42.  — *ẖrd* "child"

11. Nonverbal Sentences

11.1 Definitions

Lessons 7 and 10 introduced us to three kinds of Egyptian sentence: those in which the predicate is adjectival, nominal, and adverbial. In each of these sentence-types the predicate is not a verb, although English forces us to translate them with one — usually, a form of the verb *be*. Because of this common feature Egyptologists group the three kinds of sentence together under the heading of "nonverbal sentences," which is short for the more accurate designation "sentences with a nonverbal predicate" (see § 7.1). In this lesson we will look at the three kinds of nonverbal sentences together, and at some further features of them.

11.2 Basic patterns and meanings

As we have seen, each of the three kinds of nonverbal sentence can have many different forms, depending on what is used as the subject and predicate. In general, however, each type has a basic pattern and meaning:

> **Adjectival sentences** have the normal pattern PREDICATE–SUBJECT, where the predicate is an adjective (always masculine singular or masculine dual). They express a **quality** of their subject: for example, *nfr sḏm* "Listening is good," where the predicate *nfr* describes a quality of the subject, *sḏm* "listening" — namely, that it is "good."
>
> **Nominal sentences** have two basic patterns: A B and A *pw* B, where either A or B can be the subject or predicate. They express the **identity** of their subject: *rꜥ pw* "He is Re" (where the predicate *rꜥ* tells who the subject, *pw* "he," is); *pḫrt pw ꜥnḫ* "Life is a cycle" (where the predicate *pḫrt* "a cycle" explains what the subject, *ꜥnḫ* "life," is).
>
> **Adverbial sentences** usually have the pattern SUBJECT–PREDICATE, where the predicate is an adverb or prepositional phrase; in some cases this pattern can be reversed, with the predicate preceding the subject. Despite their various forms, adverbial sentences all express essentially the **location** of their subject. This is self-evident in sentences such as *m.k tw ꜥꜣ* "You are here" (introduced by the particle *m.k*), but it is also true of a sentence such as *jw jtj.j m wꜥw* "My father was a soldier" (literally, "My father was in a soldier," introduced by the particle *jw*).

11.3 Marked and unmarked sentences

Each of the three kinds of nonverbal sentence basically expresses only a particular relationship — quality, identity, or location — between its subject and predicate. In their basic patterns, nonverbal sentences say nothing about when these relationships are supposed to be true, whether always or only at a particular time in the past, present, or future. Linguists call this kind of feature "unmarked." The English noun *pilot*, for example, is unmarked for gender: it can be used of a male pilot or a female one, because it says nothing about the sex of the person it refers to. (In contrast, the noun *actress* is marked for gender, because it can only refer to a woman). Egyptian nonverbal sentences are **unmarked for tense**.

When an element or construction of a language is unmarked for a particular feature, it can be used either without saying anything about that feature or with a more limited reference. In the English sentence *The pilot landed the plane safely* nothing is said about the pilot's sex, whereas the sentence *The pilot turned the controls over to her copilot* is clearly about a female pilot. Since Egyptian nonverbal sentences are unmarked for tense, they can be used either without reference to a particular time or with more limited reference to the past, present, or future.

In many cases nonverbal sentences express a generic relationship, one which is true regardless of time (see § 7.16): *nfr sḏm* "Hearing is good" (adjectival predicate); *pẖrt pw ꜥnḫ* "Life is a cycle" (nominal predicate); *z3 sḏmw m šmsw ḥrw* "An obedient son is a follower of Horus" (adverbial predicate). More limited relationships can be indicated by something in the sentence itself (as the pronoun *her* does for the noun *pilot* in the English sentence cited above): for example, *nfr n.f m hrw pn* "It is good for him *on this day*" (adjectival predicate: Exercise 8, no. 12), *jw mwt m ḥr.j mjn* "Death is in my sight *today*" (adverbial predicate: § 10.3). Often, however, it is only the context that determines whether the relationship expressed by a nonverbal sentence is meant as generic or as true in the past, present, or future.

The adverbial sentence *jw mwt m ḥr.j mjn* "Death is in my sight today" is clearly meant to be understood as true in the present, not generically or in the past or future. This temporal limitation is indicated not only by the adverb *mjn* "today" but also by the particle *jw*, which is typically used for statements that are true only temporarily or in particular circumstances. As we saw in § 10.3, *jw* can also be used in this way with an adjectival predicate: *jw nfr sw m p3 hrw* "He is good on this day." In both cases *jw* serves to **mark** the sentence as limited rather than generic in reference.

Here we come to an important difference between the various kinds of nonverbal sentences. Although all three are unmarked for tense, in Middle Egyptian normally only those with an **adverbial** or **adjectival** predicate can be marked to indicate that they have more limited reference to a particular time or circumstance. This has to do with the kind of relationship that each type of nonverbal sentence expresses. In Egyptian, quality and location are relationships that can be expressed either as unmarked for tense (in the basic adjectival and adverbial sentence) or as marked (for example, by *jw*) for reference to a more limited time or circumstance: *nfr sw* "He is good" vs. *jw nfr sw m p3 hrw* "He is good today"; *ẖrwt.k m pr.k* "Your possessions are in your house" vs. *jw.f m ꜥt* "It is in a room." For relationships of identity, however, Egyptian makes a distinction between marked and unmarked sentences. Nominal sentences can only express relationships of identity that are **unmarked** for tense: *ntk rꜥ* "You are Re." Naturally, since such sentences are unmarked they can be used not only for generic statements but also for statements that have a more limited applicability: *rꜥ pw* "He is Re," *ḥf3w pw* "It was a snake." Relationships of identity that are **marked** for reference to a more limited time or circumstance, however, can only be expressed by the adverbial sentence of identity with the preposition *m* (§ 10.6): *ntk ḥrw* "You are Horus" (unmarked) vs. *jw.k m ḥrw* "You are Horus" (literally, "You are in Horus": compare Exercise 10, no. 24).

As we have noted before, these distinctions that exist in Egyptian sentences normally make no difference to their English translations. It is important to be aware of them, however, not only because they do exist in Egyptian but also because they underlie some other differences in Egyptian grammar that we will meet in the next lesson.

11.4 The nonverbal negation of existence and adverbial sentences

In § 10.4.2 we saw that the particle *nn* "not" is used to negate the adverbial sentence. The same particle can also be used to negate existence in a sentence with the pattern *nn* A, where A is a noun, noun phrase, or pronoun, without any prepositional phrase or adverb after it: for example, *nn m3^{c}tjw* "There are no righteous men."[1]

When *nn* A contains a noun that has a suffix pronoun, the sentence amounts to the negation of possession: for example, *nn msw.f* "He has no children" (literally, "His children are not"). This construction is often found after an undefined noun (§ 4.9); in that case, *nn* can usually be translated by the English preposition "without": for example, *wsẖt nn ḥmw.s* "a barge without a rudder" (literally, "a barge, its rudder not").

In some cases what looks like a negated adverbial sentence is actually a *nn* A negation of existence with an adverb or prepositional phrase attached: for example, *nn tms ḥr.s* "There is no redness on it." Actually, there is no difference between this kind of sentence and a negated adverbial sentence such as *nn mwt.k ḥn^c.k* "Your mother is not with you." Just like the negation of existence, the negated adverbial sentence amounts to a denial that the subject exists in the situation specified by the adverbial phrase: i.e., as far as the situation *ḥn^c.k* "with you" is concerned, *mwt.k* "your mother" is nonexistent.

11.5 The negation of nominal sentences

In Middle Egyptian, nominal sentences are normally negated by **two** words together: the particle *nj* (without !) plus the particle *js*. These two elements stand on either side of the A part of the sentence — i.e., *nj* A *js* B, *nj* A *js pw*, and *nj* A *js pw* B: for example,

nj ntk js z(j) "You are not a man"

nj wsẖ js pw "It was not a broad one"

nj wr js pw wr jm "The great one there is not a great one."

These examples are negations of the sentences *ntk zj* "You are a man" (A B), *wsẖ pw* "It was a broad one" (A *pw*: see § 7.15), and *wr pw wr jm* "The great one there is a great one" (A *pw* B), respectively. Occasionally the *pw* part of a negated A *pw* sentence can be omitted: *nj z3.j js* "He is not my son" (negation of *z3.j pw* "He is my son").

The particles *nj* and *js* "bracket" the A part of the sentence, much like the negative particles *ne* (or *n'*) and *pas* do for French verbs (*Tu n'es pas un homme* "You are not a man"). Both *nj* and *js* are essential parts of the negation, even though they are separated from one another. The nominal sentence is not negated just by *nj* alone: apparent exceptions are really different constructions, as we will see below.

The particle *nn* is not normally found in sentences with a nominal predicate. In a few cases, however, it is used instead of *nj* or even by itself as a negation of the nominal sentence: for example, *nn z3.k js pw* "He is not your son" and *nn 3tpw pw ḥr rmnwj.tn* "It is not a load on your shoulders." This kind of negation, however, is normally found only in texts after Dynasty 12, and even there it is the exception rather than the rule.

1 *m3^{c}tjw* is a masculine plural nisbe from the noun *m3^{c}t* "Maat" (see Essay 10).

11.6 The negation of adjectival sentences

Besides its use in the negation of the adverbial sentence and in the *nn* A construction, the particle *nn* is also used to negate the adjectival sentence: for example,

 *m.ṯn nn šrr p3 t ḥ(n)qt*
"Look, that (amount of) bread and beer is not little,"

where *šrr* is the adjectival predicate and *p3 t ḥ(n)qt* is the subject. Such sentences are rare in Middle Egyptian. Normally the language prefers to use a nominal-sentence construction instead: for example, *nj wsḫ js pw* "It was not a broad one" (cited in the previous section), instead of *nn wsḫ st* "It was not broad."

The adjectival sentence of possession, *nj* A B (§ 7.5), is negated by *nj* ... *js*, like a nominal sentence:  *nj n(j)-wj js sp3t* "I do not belong to the nome." Other sentences that seem to contain an adjectival predicate negated by *nj* alone, without *js*, actually have a verbal predicate, not an adjectival one.

11.7 Other nonverbal negations

Besides negating nonverbal sentences, Egyptian can also negate individual words or phrases. English does this with the negatives *no* or *not*: for example, *No pets allowed* (negation of the noun *pets*), *not in living memory* (negation of the prepositional phrase *in living memory*). In Egyptian the particle *nj* is used to negate words: for instance,

 *nj ḫt pw* "It is nothing."

This is an A *pw* nominal sentence in which the A part is the phrase *nj ḫt* "nothing" ("no thing").[2] Although it looks like a negative nominal sentence, it does not conform to any of the patterns used for such a sentence (§ 11.5). Here only the word *ḫt* "thing" is negated, not the sentence itself: if Egyptian had wanted to negate the sentence, it would have written  *nj ḫt js pw* "It is not a thing."

When a word or phrase is negated in contrast to another word or phrase, Egyptian uses the negation , consisting of the negative *nj* and the particle *js* together. The negation *nj js* can normally be translated "not," "and not," "but not," or "except": for example,

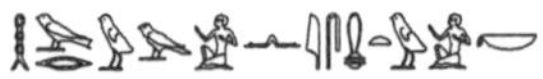 *ḥwrw nj js mjtw.k* "a poor man, not your equal"
(negation of the noun *mjtw.k*)

 *m m3ʿt nj js m grg* "in truth, and not in lying"
(negation of the prepositional phrase *m grg*)

 *rwd jnm.f nj js wrt* "his skin is firm, but not greatly"
(negation of the adverb *wrt*).

As these examples show, *nj js* negates both words and phrases, while *nj* alone negates words. The difference between *nj* and *nj js* as the negation of a word is that *nj js* is only used when the negation contrasts with or qualifies some other word or phrase, as can be seen in the examples given above.

2 The word *ḫt* is often written with plural strokes when it does not refer to any "thing" in particular.

11.8 Nonverbal negations: summary

For convenient reference, the nonverbal negations we have met in this lesson and the previous one can be summarized as follows:

NEGATIONS WITH *nj*

	negates words (§ 11.7)
	negates contrastive words or phrases (§ 11.7)
... 	negates nominal sentences (§ 11.5)
	negates adjectival sentences of possession (§ 11.6)

NEGATIONS WITH  *nn*

	negates existence (§ 11.4)
	negates adverbial sentences (§§ 10.4.2, 11.4)
	negates adjectival sentences (§ 11.6)
	negates nominal sentences (in later Middle Egyptian: § 11.5)
 ... 	negates nominal sentences (in later Middle Egyptian: § 11.5).

11.9 Nonverbal sentences of possession

Beginning in Lesson 6 we have seen different ways in which Middle Egyptian expresses the relationship between a possessor and a thing possessed without using a verb:

1. as nominal predicate
   - *nb* X "owner of X" (§ 6.9), where *nb* is the owner and X is the thing owned: for example,  *jnk nb k3w* "I own bulls" (literally, "I am an owner of bulls")
   - the *nfr ḥr* "beautiful of face" construction (§§ 6.5, 6.9), where *nfr* refers to the owner and *ḥr* is the thing possessed: for example, 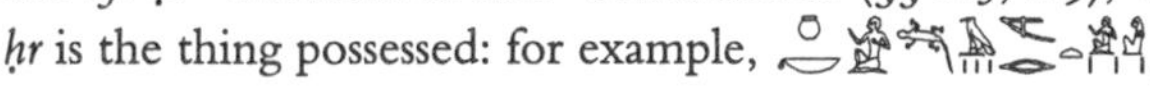 *jnk ꜥš3 mrwt* "I have many serfs" (literally, "I am many of serfs")
2. as adjectival predicate
   - *nj* A B "A belongs to B" or "B belongs to A" (§ 7.5), where either A or B can be the owner: for instance,  *n(j) wj rꜥ* "I belong to Re,"  *nnk pt* "The sky belongs to me"
3. as adverbial predicate
   - with the preposition *n* "to" and the prepositional phrases *n* X *jm(y)* "X's" and *m* ꜥ "in the hand of" (§§ 8.10, 10.7), where the object of the preposition or prepositional phrase is the owner: for example,  *nn jz n sbj* "The rebel has no tomb," 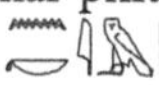 *n.k jm s(j)* "It is yours," 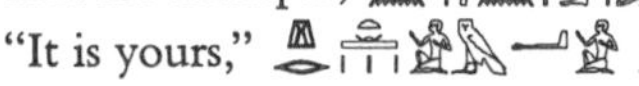 *ḫrwt.j m* ꜥ*.j* "I have my possessions"
   - with the preposition *ḫr* "under," where the object of the preposition is the thing possessed:  *tw.n ḫr kmt* "We have Egypt."

Note also the construction with *nn* followed by a noun with a suffix pronoun or possessive pronoun, discussed in § 11.4 above:  *nn msw.f* "He has no children."

Although most of these require a verb in the English translation ("own," "belong," "have," etc.), they are all nonverbal sentences in Egyptian, since Egyptian has no verb of possession.

11.10 Nonverbal sentences without a subject

In §§ 8.5 and 10.9, we saw that adjectival and adverbial predicates can both be used without a subject when the subject doesn't refer to anything in particular. Such sentences are normally translated into English using the "dummy subject" *it*: for example, *nfr n.tn* "It is good for you" and *jw mj sḫr nṯr* "It was like the plan of a god." Nominal sentences in Middle Egyptian must have an expressed subject, except in the negative, where the *pw* of an A *pw* sentence can be omitted: for instance, *nj z3.j js* "He is not my son" (§ 11.5). In this case the omitted subject actually refers to something ("he") but can still be omitted, perhaps for stylistic reasons.

11.11 Nonverbal interrogative sentences

In Lessons 7 and 10 we met examples of nonverbal sentences in which the predicate is an interrogative pronoun, adjective, or adverb, or a prepositional phrase containing an interrogative pronoun (§§ 7.13, 10.10). Egyptian can also make questions with nonverbal sentences that do not have these interrogative words. This can be done in two ways.

1. **Virtual questions**

Grammarians use the term "virtual" as the opposite of "real." A virtual question is one that has nothing to indicate it is a question other than its context: that is, a sentence that is really a statement but which functions as a question. This kind of question exists in English: for example, *Jack isn't here yet?*, which has exactly the same words and structure as the statement *Jack isn't here yet.* In English speech, of course, the two sentences are pronounced differently: in the question the voice rises at the end of the sentence, and in the statement it falls at the end (you can hear the difference by pronouncing the two sentences out loud). In writing, however, the only thing that distinguishes them is their final punctuation (question mark versus period).

Egyptian could also make virtual questions. Presumably they too were distinguished from statements by a difference in pronunciation, but we have no way of knowing if or how this was done. Since written Egyptian has no punctuation marks, virtual questions look exactly the same as statements. An example is the two-part sentence  from Exercise 10 (no. 14): *mw jm, nn mw jm* "Is water there, or is water not there?" This is really two statements that are used as questions: literally, "Water is there? Water is not there?"

Such virtual questions seem to be about as common in Egyptian as they are in English. Unfortunately, we have no way of knowing whether a nonverbal sentence is meant as a statement or as a question except from the context in which it is used. Even then the meaning is not always clear: In the example just cited, for instance, the sentence *nn mw jm* could also be understood as an answering statement "There is no water there."

2. **Questions with interrogative particles**

Although languages can make virtual questions, they also have overt ways of distinguishing questions from statements. In English, questions are normally indicated by reversing the subject and verb: for instance, *Is Jill here?* versus *Jill is here.* In Egyptian, real (nonvirtual) questions are usually marked by one or two particles:

 *jn* (also  and , *n*) — **at the beginning** of the sentence

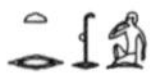 *tr* (also  and 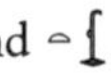,  *tj*) — **inside** the sentence, usually after the first word.

We have already met both of these particles: *jn* in questions with the interrogative pronoun *mj* (§ 7.13.1); and *tr* as part of the interrogative pronoun *ptr*, originally *pw-tr* (§ 5.11).

The particle *jn* can be used by itself or with *tr*, and seems to appear in questions with all kinds of predicates. It serves as a kind of Egyptian "question mark," and like a question mark is not normally translated. The particle *tr* also is usually not translated; occasionally however, it seems to mean something like "actually" or "really." Examples with a nominal predicate are:

> *jn mḫ3t pw* "Is it a scale?"[3] (an A *pw* sentence)
>
> *jn p3 pw ḫn n mdt*
> "Is this the phrase of speech?" (an A *pw* B sentence).

Sentences with an adverbial predicate regularly use the particle *jw* after *jn*: for example,

> *jn jw tr (j)t(j.j) ʿ3* "Is my father really here?"
>
> *jn jw n.k jtj.j r w3t* "Is my grain to be a path for you?"

Sentences with a nominal predicate can also have the particle *jw* after *jn*, unlike regular nominal sentences (§§ 10.3, 11.3): for instance,

> *jn jw qsnt pw* "Is it something difficult?" (an A *pw* sentence).

This is just about the only situation in which Middle Egyptian uses *jw* in a sentence with a nominal predicate.

When the particle *jn* is written, the sentence can look like a negative statement rather than a question: for example,

> *(j)n wr n.k ʿntjw* "Do you have a great deal of myrrh?"
>
> *(j)n jnk tr zm3.f* "Am I his confederate?"

Despite their appearance, we can be fairly certain that these are questions because they do not match the pattern for the negation of nonverbal sentences. The first example has an adjectival predicate (literally, "Is myrrh great to you?"), and should be a question because the few instances of negated adjectival sentences use the negations *nn* or *nj* ... *js*, not *nj* alone (§ 11.6). The second example is an A B nominal sentence, which is negated by *nj* ... *js* or less often by *nn* ... *js* or *nn*, but not by *nj* alone (§ 11.5).

These last two examples show how important it is to pay careful attention to the wording of an Egyptian sentence. Since hieroglyphic spelling is not standardized, we often have to rely on clues such as sentence patterns and word-order to understand what a particular sentence means. Sometimes we are fortunate enough to have several ancient copies of a particular text to guide us as well. The last example in the previous paragraph (from a Middle Egyptian story) is a case in point: in another copy of the story the same sentence has *jn jw* instead of , so we can be fairly certain that is in fact a spelling of *jn* and not the negation. But this kind of extra evidence is the exception rather than the rule. In most cases, we only have the structure of the sentence itself to guide us.

3 The spelling of *mḫ3t* is influenced by that of *m.k* (§ 10.4.1).

ESSAY 11. THE WORLD BEFORE CREATION

Egyptian texts frequently make reference to the gods and events involved in the creation of the world. There were many different creation accounts, and most of these were associated with the cult of a particular god in one of the major cities of ancient Egypt. Egyptologists used to think that these represented competing theologies, and to a certain extent this was true. In recent years, however, scholars have begun to recognize that the various accounts are less rival explanations of the creation than different aspects of a single, uniform understanding of how the world came to be. In the next few essays we will look at these different accounts, and the gods involved in them.

In Egyptian the creation was called *rk nṯr* "the time of the god," or more specifically *rk rᶜ* "the time of Re," but also *rk nṯrw* "the time of the gods." This reflects the Egyptian view that the creation involved both a single creator and the other gods as well: it was a cooperative effort among all the forces and elements of the universe.

Before the world was created the universe was a limitless ocean, whose waters stretched to infinity in all directions (see Essay 2). The Egyptians called this ocean *nw(j)* "the watery one." Like the other elements of the universe, it was a god (Nu, later Nun), who is often called *jt(j) nṯrw* "father of the gods" in recognition of his priority.

Although no one had ever seen this universal ocean, its features could be imagined by contrast with the created world. It was water (*nwj*), while the world contains dry land and air. Where the created world is active, it was inert (*n(j)n(j)*, source of the later name Nun). It was an infinite flood (*ḥḥw*), where the land of the world is finite. While the world is lit by the sun, it lay in perpetual darkness (*kkw*). And, in contrast to the tangible and knowable world, it was hidden (*jmn*) and lost (*tnm*).

Like the waters themselves, these qualities were seen as divine in their own right, and as male deities because their names are masculine. Some of them are mentioned in the earliest religious texts, dating to the end of the Old Kingdom. Because the waters themselves were an integral part of the creation — its background — the qualities of the waters could also be seen as creator gods. In texts of the First Intermediate Period and the Middle Kingdom we meet four of them in this role: Wateriness (*nwj*) and Infinity (*ḥḥw*), Darkness (*kkw*) and "Lostness" (*tnm*). Since the Egyptians equated creation with birth, the male qualities were given female counterparts. By the Late Period, the group consisted of four pairs: usually Nu (or Nun) and Naunet (see Essay 2), representing both wateriness and inertness (*njnj*); Huh and Hauhet, infinity; Kuk and Kauket, darkness; and Amun and Amaunet, hiddenness.

The eight gods together were worshipped as *ḫmnyw* "the Ogdoad" (a Greek word meaning "group of eight"). They are often shown with the heads of frogs (male) and snakes (female), two species of animal that the Egyptians associated with creative waters. The theology and worship of the Ogdoad was centered in the town of Hermopolis, which was called *ḫmnw* "Eight-town" in their honor. This name, which was pronounced ϢⲘⲞⲨⲚ in Coptic, has survived in the modern Arabic name of the site of ancient Hermopolis, el-Ashmunein.

The myths that concentrate on the Ogdoad's role in the creation are known as the Hermopolitan system. Most of what we know about this theology comes from texts of the Ptolemaic

Period. These call the group "the first originals ... the eldest gods, who started evolution ... who created the beginning in their time." In earlier texts the gods are simply mentioned by name. Although we lack early accounts of the Hermopolitan system, however, it is likely that the theology we meet in Ptolemaic texts existed already in the Old Kingdom, since the name *ḫmnw* "Eight-town" dates back to the Fifth Dynasty.

In one of the later texts the Ogdoad is described as "the fathers and mothers of the sundisk ... they floated in attendance on him and came to stand on the high hill from which the sun's lotus arose." This refers to one of the earliest known Egyptian images of the creation: a mound of earth that emerged as the first dry land when the primeval waters receded. It is tempting to see in this image the view of the early Egyptian farmers, watching the highest mounds of earth emerge as the annual floodwaters of the inundation receded from their fields. Just as the Nile's inundation left the land fertile and ready to grow new plants, so too the universal waters produced new life on the primeval mound, in the form of a lotus plant from whose blossom the sun emerged for the first time into the world, to give "light after the darkness."

The Egyptians worshipped this first lotus plant as the god Nefertum ( *nfr-tm*). The primeval hill itself they honored as the first "place" in the world, in the form of the god Tatjenen (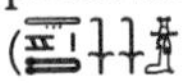 *t3-ṯnn(j)* literally, "land that becomes distinct"). Many Egyptian temples had a mound of earth in their sanctuary, which not only commemorated the primeval mound but which also was viewed as *the* primeval hill. Like the creation accounts themselves, these various mounds did not compete for recognition as the primeval hill but were viewed as alternative, and complementary, realizations of the "first place" (see the discussion of syncretism in Essay 4).

The image of the primeval mound is preserved not only in creation texts but also in hieroglyphs. The word "appear" is always written with the biliteral sign , representing the rays of the sun appearing over a mound of earth. In early hieroglyphs this sign has the form , where the image is even clearer.

EXERCISE 11

Transliterate and translate the following sentences.

1.  — past: *wḫ3* "fool"; *ḥrj-jb* see Exercise 10, no. 4
2.  — future: *sḫ3* "memory," *tpjw-t3* nisbe from *tp t3*
3.  — *q3 s3* "arrogant" (literally, "high of back")
4.  — *grt* "moreover," *2nw* "equal"
5.  — *b3gj* "being lazy"
6.  — *ṯ3z* "sentence," *jwms* "exaggeration"; for *mm* see § 8.2.5
7.  — *rmyt* "tears"
8. 
9.  — *3ḫ* "effective"

10.  — *jw* "complaint"

11.  — a negative question: "Is not …"; *jw* "error," *jwsw* "balance" (a scale with two pans ), *gs3w* "which tilts"

12.  — for *nf3* see §§ 5.8–5.9; *ꜥ3wt* "lump"

13. 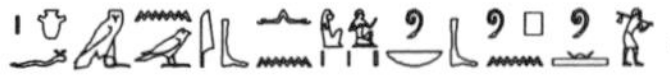 — *mnjw* "shepherd," *bw-nb* "everyone," *bjn* "bad"

14.  — *ḥmt* "servant," *špst* "noblewoman"

15.  — future: *mjtw* "equal, one who is like"

16.  — a metaphor for lawlessness: *nwt* "town," *ḥq3-ḥwt* "mayor" (literally, "ruler of the enclosure")

17.  — *ms* "offspring," *jwꜥw* "heir"

18.  — *šft* "respect"; *st* refers back to *rmṯ* and is not translated

19.  — *sf* "yesterday," *wzfw* "one who forgets things"

20.  — see no. 11

21.  — *ḏw* "evil"

22.  — *swt* "but" (comes inside the sentence in Egyptian, but first in English), *qn* "brave," *grḥ* "night" (see § 8.14)

23.  — *ḫnms* "friend," *zẖ* "one who cannot hear"

24.  — *sbḫt* "barrier"

25.  — *ḥ3tj-ꜥ* "high official"

26.  — *hrw nfr* "holiday" (literally, "good day"), *ꜥwn-jb* "greedy" (literally, "covetous of heart")

27. 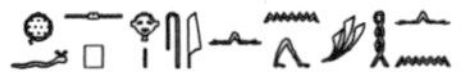 — *ḥn* "hurrying," *zp* "proper time"

28. 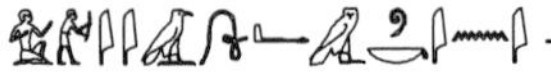 — *ꜥw3y* "robber"

29.  — *tjmḥj* "Libyan"

30. 

12. Nonverbal Clauses

12.1 Definitions

The preceding lessons have introduced us to many of the basic elements of an Egyptian sentence. Like all languages, Egyptian consists of **sounds**, which are combined into **words** of different kinds, such as nouns, pronouns, adjectives, prepositions, adverbs, and particles. Words, in turn, can be combined into **phrases**.

The sentences we have dealt with so far consist of words and phrases, some serving as the subject and others as the predicate of the sentence (at this point you may want to reread the discussion of subject and predicate in § 7.1). We have also seen some of the rules that Egyptian uses to make these combinations. The set of rules that a language uses to combine words into phrases and sentences is called **syntax**. It is a rule of Egyptian syntax, for example, that an adjectival predicate always comes before its subject, whereas English syntax normally dictates the reverse: *nfr st* "It is good."

Sentences in every language consist of one or more **clauses**. The term "clause" means "the combination of a subject and a predicate." Like phrases, clauses are combinations of words. The difference between them is that **a clause always contains a subject and predicate**, while a phrase does not. Some combinations can only be phrases or clauses: for example, *nfr r ḫt nb* "better than anything" (a phrase) and *nfr st* "It is good" (a clause). Others can be either a phrase or a clause, depending on how they are used (see § 7.17): for instance, *nfr ḥr* "good of face" (a phrase) or "The face is good" (a clause).

Almost all the sentences we have met so far have consisted of a single clause, with a single subject and predicate. This is the most basic kind of sentence in a language. All languages, however, have the ability to make sentences consisting of several clauses, not just one. The English sentence *Jack is happy when he is with Jill* has two clauses: *Jack is happy* (subject *Jack*, predicate *is happy*) and *when he is with Jill* (subject *he*, predicate *is with Jill*).

When a clause can stand by itself as a complete sentence, it is called a **main clause** or **independent clause**; a clause that cannot do this is known as a **subordinate clause** or **dependent clause**. In the sentence *Jack is happy when he is with Jill*, the first clause is independent because it can be a complete sentence (*Jack is happy*); the second clause, however, cannot stand by itself (*when he is with Jill*), so it is a dependent or subordinate clause. All sentences must have at least one main clause. A sentence with more than one clause can have a main clause and one or more subordinate clauses, or it can have several independent clauses. An English example of the latter kind of sentence is *Jack is happy, Jill is sad*. An Egyptian example is the sentence discussed in § 11.11.1: *mw jm nn mw jm* "Is water there, (or) is water not there?"

There are many different kinds of subordinate clauses, as we will see in the course of these lessons. This is true for Egyptian as well as English. In the next few sections we will discuss some of the subordinate clauses that have nonverbal predicates.

RELATIVE CLAUSES

12.2 Definitions

Lesson 6 introduced us to adjectives, which are words or phrases used to modify a noun (or noun phrase). Languages also use clauses in the same way. **A clause that is used like an adjective is called a relative clause.** In English such clauses usually contain a relative pronoun such as *who, which*, or *that*: for example, *a pilot who is experienced*. Here the relative clause *who is experienced* specifies what kind of pilot is meant, just as the adjective *experienced* does in the phrase *an experienced pilot*. This is an example of a relative clause with an adjectival predicate: *who* is the subject of the relative clause and *is experienced* is the predicate.

Like adjectives, relative clauses in English normally cannot be used by themselves. When they are used without a noun, English usually requires a word such as *one* or *ones* in place of the noun, just as it does for adjectives. Thus, English can say *They want a pilot who is experienced* or *They want one who is experienced* but not **They want who is experienced*, just as it can say *an experienced pilot* or *an experienced one* but not **an experienced*. Like adjectives, relative clauses always presume the existence of a noun or noun phrase that they modify, even if the noun or noun phrase is not actually expressed. This noun or noun phrase is called the **antecedent** of the relative clause: in the English expression *a pilot who is experienced*, the noun phrase *a pilot* is the antecedent.

Because they contain a subject and a predicate, relative clauses are more complicated than simple adjectives or adjective phrases, even though they are used like adjectives. One of the complicating factors is the relationship between the antecedent and the parts of the relative clause. In most cases a relative clause must contain something that refers to the same thing that the antecedent does: grammarians call this element the **resumptive** or the **coreferent**. Normally it is a pronoun, which has the same gender and number as the antecedent. Often the coreferent is the subject of the relative clause: in the English expression *a pilot who is experienced*, the coreferent is the relative pronoun *who* and it refers to the same person that the antecedent *a pilot* does. A relative clause in which the coreferent is the subject can be called a **direct relative clause**.

In many cases, however, the coreferent is not the subject of the relative clause. For example, in the English expression *a pilot whose crew is experienced*, the subject of the relative clause is the noun *crew* and the coreferent is the possessive relative pronoun *whose*; similarly, in the expression *a pilot on whom the crew can rely*, the noun *crew* is the subject of the relative clause and the coreferent, *whom*, is the object of the preposition *on*. A relative clause in which the coreferent is not the subject can be called an **indirect relative clause**.

The difference between direct and indirect relative clauses is often difficult to see in English because the syntax of English relative clauses is extremely complex. In Egyptian, however, relative clauses have a much simpler syntax.

12.3 The relative adjective *ntj*

The English words *who, which*, and *that* are relative pronouns. Like other pronouns, they "stand for" a noun or noun phrase (see § 5.1), but they also have the specific function of serving as the coreferent in a relative clause. Like other English pronouns, too, they have different forms, depending on how they are used in the relative clause. The pronoun *who* has three forms: *who*, used as the subject of a relative clause (like *he*, *she*, or *they*); *whose*, used as a possessive (like *his*, *her*, or *their*); and *whom*, used as the object of a verb or preposition (like *him*, *her*, or *them*). The pronouns *which* and *that* also have a possessive form *whose* but are otherwise invariable.

Middle Egyptian has no relative pronouns. Instead, it has two **relative adjectives**. Like other adjectives, these have three forms: masculine singular, masculine plural, and feminine (see § 6.2). The most common relative adjective has the following forms:

MASCULINE SINGULAR	*ntj*	, also 
MASCULINE PLURAL	*ntjw*	,  (also without plural strokes)
FEMININE	*ntt*	

The endings of these words are the same as those of the nisbe (§ 6.2). In fact, *ntj* is a nisbe: it is formed from the word  *nt*, which itself is nothing more than the feminine form of the genitival adjective (§ 4.13.2), used as a noun.

Like other adjectives, *ntj* agrees in gender and (if masculine) number with the word it modifies (in this case, its antecedent). In § 6.2, however, we noted that the feminine and plural forms of adjectives gradually disappeared from Egyptian, leaving only the masculine singular form. This is also true of *ntj*; occasionally, therefore, you will see the masculine singular form *ntj* used with plural or feminine antecedents as well.

The primary function of *ntj* can be stated very simply: it is a **relative marker**, which allows a sentence to serve as a relative clause. Such clauses normally have an adverbial predicate. Relative clauses with *ntj* rarely have a nominal or adjectival predicate in Middle Egyptian, for reasons that we will discuss later in this lesson.

12.4 Direct relative clauses with *ntj*

English uses the relative pronouns as subject in direct relative clauses. Middle Egyptian normally uses *ntj* in the same way in its direct relative clauses: for example,

 *ẖnt(j).f ntj m ḥwt-nṯr* "his statue, which is in the temple"

 *ḥnwt-t3 ntt m ꜥḥ.f* "the land's mistress, who is in his palace"

 *r(m)ṯ kmt ntjw jm* "people of Egypt who were there."

In these examples the relative adjective serves as the subject of the relative clause, just as the relative pronouns *which* and *who* do in their English translations. When a direct relative clause contains a negation, however, the subject has to be expressed by a pronoun, as we will see in § 12.8, below.

12.5 Indirect relative clauses with *ntj*

English and Egyptian handle indirect relative clauses in different ways. In English the coreferent is always combined with the relative marker, in the relative pronoun. Egyptian does something similar with *ntj* only in direct relative clauses. In indirect relative clauses the relative marker (*ntj*) and the coreferent (a pronoun) are separate: for instance,

 *wsḫ ntj z3-nswt ḥrw-dd.f jm.f*
"the barge in which King's Son Har-dedef was,"

where the suffix pronoun of *jm.f* is the coreferent of the antecedent *wsẖ*. The prepositional phrase *jm.f* is the predicate of the relative clause, and the subject is the noun phrase *z3-nswt ḥrw-dd.f*: literally, "the barge which King's Son Har-dedef was in it."

If we translate this sentence in more colloquial English — "the barge which King's Son Har-dedef was in" — you can see that the difference between Egyptian and (colloquial) English is fairly simple: Egyptian syntax normally requires the coreferent to be expressed by a pronoun, and English syntax does not. Occasionally, the syntax of the two languages is even closer, because Egyptian can also omit the coreferent in some cases: for example,

 *bw ntj nṯrw jm* "the place in which the gods are,"

or more colloquially "the place which the gods are in," using the prepositional adverb *jm* instead of the prepositional phrase *jm.f*.[1]

If you examine the relative clauses in these examples, you will see that they are nothing more than independent clauses — *z3-nswt ḥrw-dd.f jm.f* "King's Son Har-dedef was in it" and *nṯrw jm* "the gods are therein" — with the relative marker *ntj* in front of them. The same thing is true of all indirect relative clauses with *ntj*. The syntax of such clauses is very simple in Egyptian: *ntj* (or *ntt* or *ntjw*, depending on the gender and number of the antecedent) plus an independent clause. Unfortunately, the syntax of English is more complicated, because it requires the coreferent to be combined with the relative marker in a relative pronoun. To illustrate the difference, here are the steps involved in each language in producing the relative clause in the first example above:

EGYPTIAN: *wsẖ* modified by *z3-nswt ḥrw-dd.f jm.f*

- insert relative marker agreeing with the antecedent (masculine singular *ntj*): *wsẖ ntj z3-nswt ḥrw-dd.f jm.f*

ENGLISH: *the barge* modified by *King's Son Har-dedef was in it*

- insert relative marker (REL): *the barge* REL *King's Son Har-dedef was in it*
- combine relative marker and coreferent into relative pronoun (REL + *it* = *which*): *the barge which King's Son Har-dedef was in*
- move the preposition in front of the relative pronoun: *the barge in which King's Son Har-dedef was* (this step can be omitted in colloquial English).

In this example the coreferent is the object of the preposition *m* (which has the form *jm* with a pronominal suffix: § 8.2.3). This is not the only function the coreferent can have in the relative clause. It can also be the possessor of some element in the relative clause. In that case, English requires the possessive relative pronoun *whose*: for example,

 *z(j) ntj mrwt m ẖt.f* "the man in whose belly there are pains"

 *nṯr pn ntj ḥr.f m ṯzm* "this god whose face is a hound('s)."

Here again, Egyptian syntax simply puts the proper form of *ntj* in front of an independent clause: literally, "the man who pains are in his belly" and "this god who his face is a hound('s)."

1 English can also omit the relative pronoun in some cases: for example, *the place the gods are in*. Egyptian does this only when the antecedent is undefined, as we will see in § 12.11.

12.6 The relative adjective *ntj* with pronominal subjects

The examples in the preceding section all have a noun or noun phrase as subject of the relative clause (*z3-nswt ḥrw-dd.f*, *nṯrw*, *mrwt*, and *ḥr.f*). When the subject of an indirect relative clause is a personal pronoun, Egyptian normally uses the **suffix** forms: for instance,

 *bw ntj.f jm* "the place in which he is" (or "the place which he is in").

When the masculine singular form *ntj* has a pronominal suffix, the two strokes are often omitted. This produces a word that looks like the independent pronouns: for example,  *nt(j).k*,  *nt(j).f*,  *nt(j).sn*.

There are two exceptions to this rule: the **dependent** pronouns are used instead of the suffix forms for the first person singular (*wj* instead of *.j*) and for the neutral form *st* "it":

 *ꜥt tn ntt wj jm.s* "this room in which I am" (or "this room that I am in")

 *bw ntj st jm* "the place in which it was" (or "the place that it was in").

Very rarely, the dependent forms are used for other persons as well. Of course, for the plural pronouns there is really no way to know whether the suffix or dependent form is being used, since both forms look alike (see § 5.4): 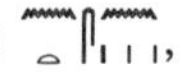, for example, could represent either *nt(j).sn* (suffix pronoun) or *nt(j) sn* (with the dependent pronoun). This is also true when the third-person feminine singular is spelled with just a uniliteral *s*: for example,  *ntj.s* or *ntj s(j)*.

12.7 The relative adjective *ntj* as a noun

Since it is an adjective, *ntj* can also be used as a noun, like other adjectives (see § 6.4). When it is used just by itself, without an antecedent or a following relative clause, *ntj* is a noun meaning "he who exists," "she who exists," "that which exists," or "those who exist, those which exist" (depending on its form). More often, *ntj* has a relative clause after it but no antecedent. In that case, the entire *ntj* clause functions as a noun, and *ntj* usually has to be translated as "one who," "he who," "that which," and so forth (see § 12.2): for example,

 *mj ntj m mr.f* "like one who is in his pyramid."

This is a direct relative clause with *ntj* as its subject; the entire clause serves as object of the preposition *mj* "like." An example of an indirect relative clause used in the same way is the following:

 *jn ntj mrwt m ẖt.f* "by the one in whose belly there are pains."

Here the subject of the relative clause is *mrwt* "pains" (compare the second-last example in § 12.5) and the entire *ntj* clause is the object of the preposition *jn* "by."

When it functions as a noun, *ntj* can be modified by the adjective *nb*, like other nouns. The phrase *ntj nb* (etc.) means "anyone who, everyone who, whoever," and so forth: for example,

 *ḥnꜥ ntt nbt jm.f* "together with everything that is in it"

 *n k3 n ntj nb rn.f ḥr wḏ pn*
"for the ka of everyone whose name is on this stela."

In the first of these examples *ntt* is the subject of the relative clause; in the second, the subject is *rn.f* (literally, "for the ka of every one-who his name is on this stela").

Theoretically, *ntj* can be used to make any adverbial sentence into a relative clause. Since the subject of an adverbial predicate can sometimes be omitted (§ 10.9), we can expect to find relative clauses where this is also true. An example is the expression  *ntj n.f* (using an older spelling of *ntj*). This means literally, "one who (there is something) for him." It is used as a noun meaning "one who has things" (see § 11.9.3), just as English makes a noun out of the verb *have* in the expression *the haves and the have-nots.*

12.8 Negative relative clauses with *ntj*

We saw in § 12.4 that Egyptian uses *ntj* as the subject of a direct relative clause. When such a clause is negated, however, a separate pronoun has to be used as its subject: for example,

 *ntt nn st m ḫnw.f* "that which was not inside it" —

This is an example of a relative clause used as a noun, without an antecedent (§ 12.7). It contains the independent sentence *nn st m ḫnw.f* "it was not inside it," with the pronoun *st* "it" as subject: literally, "that which it (*st*) was not in its interior (*ḫnw.f*)."

12.9 The relative adjective *jwtj*

The second relative adjective in Middle Egyptian has the following three forms:

MASCULINE SINGULAR	*jwtj*	, , , 
MASCULINE PLURAL	*jwtjw*	
FEMININE	*jwtt*	, , 

This is the only word in which  has the value *jw* or *jwt*; elsewhere is a biliteral with the value *nj* or an alternative writing of *n*. The endings are those of the nisbe, as with *ntj*, although the original word from which the nisbe is formed no longer exists in standard Middle Egyptian.

The relative adjective *jwtj* was originally the negative counterpart of *ntj*, meaning "who not, which not," etc. By the time of Middle Egyptian, however, negative relative clauses were usually made by using *ntj* and a negative sentence, as we saw in the preceding section. The older form *jwtj* still appears, however, in a few uses with nonverbal predicates:

- the expression 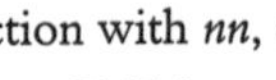 *jwtj-n.f.* This is the negative counterpart of *ntj n.f,* discussed at the end of the § 12.7, and means "a have-not": literally, "one who (there is) not (something) for him."
- the expression 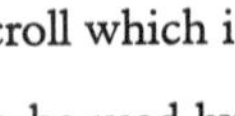 *jwtj-sw.* This is a variant of *jwtj-n.f* and means the same thing, although its syntax has not been satisfactorily explained.
- followed by a noun with a suffix pronoun. This is the relative counterpart of the independent construction with *nn,* discussed in § 11.4: for example,

   md3t jwtt zḫ3w.s "a scroll that has no writing,"

  literally, "a scroll which its writing is not."

Like *ntj, jwtj* can also be used by itself, without an antecedent or relative clause, as a noun meaning "he who does not exist," "that which does not exist," and so forth. The phrase *ntt jwtt* "that which is and that which is not" is an Egyptian idiom for "everything imaginable."

12.10 **Prepositional nisbes and relative clauses with *ntj***

Although we did not consider it as such, the prepositional nisbe (§§ 8.7–8.8) is also a kind of relative clause, since it offers another way for a clause with an adverbial predicate to be used like an adjective. Compare the following two examples:

 *nṯrw nt(j)w m pt* "the gods who are in the sky"

 *nṯrw jmjw pt* "the gods who are in the sky."

In the first example the relative clause consists of the relative adjective *ntjw* serving as subject of the adverbial predicate *m pt*. In the second, the prepositional part of the predicate has been converted to a nisbe. Indirect relative clauses and "reverse" nisbes (§ 8.9) can be compared in the same way: for instance,

 *ntt pr jm.s* "that in which the house is"

 *jmt-pr* "that in which the house is."

Even though prepositional nisbes and relative clauses with *ntj* can be translated the same way in English, however, they actually say different things. The difference between them is the same as that between independent adverbial clauses with and without *jw* (§ 10.3). The prepositional nisbe is an **unmarked** construction (§ 11.3). In the phrase  *nṯrw jmjw pt* the nisbe says nothing about the time or circumstances in which "the gods" are "in the sky" — much like the English construction in which a noun is modified by a prepositional phrase ("the gods in the sky"), which is also not specific about time or circumstances. The prepositional nisbe often has generic meaning, just like the unmarked sentence  *nṯrw m pt* "The gods are in the sky": both can imply that the sky is the normal location of the gods. On the other hand, the relative clause with *ntj* is **marked**. In  *nṯrw nt(j)w m pt* the relative clause corresponds to the marked independent clause  *jw nṯrw m pt* "The gods are in the sky." Both suggest a more limited relationship between the subject and predicate: implying, for example, that the gods are in the sky now but might be somewhere else at another time.

The relative adjective *ntj* can be considered as the relative-clause counterpart of the particle *jw*: Egyptian often uses *ntj* in relative clauses for the same reasons that it uses *jw* in main clauses, and a prepositional nisbe for the same reasons that it uses a main clause without *jw*. This is probably why relative clauses with *ntj* rarely have nominal or adjectival predicates in Middle Egyptian, just as such predicates are not normally used with *jw* in main clauses (§§ 10.3, 11.3).

12.11 **Relative clauses without *ntj***

When a relative clause with *ntj* is used without a preceding noun or noun phrase, it can be defined or undefined, like other nouns (§ 4.9): thus, the expression  *ntj m mr.f* can mean either "the one who is in his pyramid" (defined) or "someone who is in his pyramid" (undefined). When it is used as a modifier, however, its antecedent is usually **defined**: thus, the expression  *wsḫ ntj z3-nswt ḥrw-dd.f jm.f* normally means "**the** barge in which King's son Har-dedef was" and not "**a** barge in which King's son Har-dedef was." Egyptian often "reinforces" the definite nature of the antecedent by a demonstrative pronoun, as in  *nṯr pn ntj ḥr.f m ṯzm* "this god whose face is a hound('s)."

Undefined antecedents are normally modified by relative clauses without *ntj*. These are sometimes called "virtual" relative clauses (see § 11.11.1) because they look like main clauses. Unlike *ntj* clauses, they can have nominal and adjectival predicates as well as adverbial ones: for example,

 *qrft nbw jm.s* "a sack in which there is gold" —
literally, "a sack (which) gold is in it" (adverbial predicate)

 *srt jw.s m ḥᶜw* "a thorn that is in the flesh" —
literally, "a thorn (which) it is in the flesh" (adverbial predicate with *jw*)

 *nḏs ḏdj rn.f* "a commoner whose name is Djedi" —
literally, "a commoner (who) his name is Djedi" (nominal predicate)

 *špss pw ᶜ3 n.f ḫwt* "He was a noble who had much property" —
literally, "He was a noble (who) things were great to him" (adjectival predicate)[2]

 *wsḫt nn ḥmw.s* "a barge without a rudder" —
literally, "a barge (which) its rudder is nonexistent" (see § 11.4).

Although these clauses do not have *ntj* as a relative marker, they do have the other features of relative clauses: they follow the noun or noun phrase they modify, and they have a coreferential pronoun that agrees in gender and number with the antecedent. In form, however, they are identical to main clauses. The only thing that distinguishes them from main clauses is the fact that they follow undefined nouns. Although this may seem confusing, English actually does something similar with relative clauses that have a verb: we can say, for example, *a concert that I attended yesterday* (with the relative pronoun *that*) or *a concert I attended yesterday* (without a relative pronoun).

NOUN CLAUSES

12.12 Definitions

Just as a relative clause is a clause that functions like an adjective, a **noun clause** is one that functions like a noun. Nouns can have many different functions in a sentence: most often they serve as the subject, as a nominal predicate, or as the object of a verb or preposition. Although noun clauses can do the same things, usually they appear either as the object of a verb or a preposition.

English has a specific marker for noun clauses, just as it has for relative clauses: the mark of a noun clause is the word *that*, which is also used as a relative pronoun. Here are some examples of English noun clauses (in boldface) in various functions in a sentence:

AS SUBJECT: ***That Jill is a girl*** *shouldn't disqualify her* (compare the subject noun phrase in the similar sentence ***Jill's age*** *shouldn't disqualify her*).

AS PREDICATE: *It's not* ***that Jill is a girl****, just that she's too young* (compare the predicate noun phrase in the similar sentence *It's not* ***Jill's age****, just her inexperience*).

AS OBJECT OF A VERB: *Jack discovered* ***that Jill's age was a problem*** (compare the object noun phrase in the similar sentence *Jack discovered* ***Jill's age***).

2 Compare the sentence *(j)n wr n.k ᶜntjw* "Do you have a great deal of myrrh?" (§ 11.8.2).

12.13 Marked noun clauses

Just as English does with the word *that*, Egyptian normally has to mark the noun clause with something. Middle Egyptian does this in one of three ways.

1. **Noun clauses with *js***

Originally, the mark of a noun clause was the particle  *js*, which always stands **inside** the clause, after the first word or phrase. This particle apparently could be used to subordinate all three kinds of nonverbal sentence, but only those with nominal or adjectival predicate are normally attested, and the latter are rare. Examples of subordination by means of *js* still occur in Middle Egyptian, though mostly in religious texts: for instance,

 *ḏd.f z3.f js pw ḥr* "He says that his son is Horus"

 *rḫ.sn wr js nrw.f* "They will learn that his terror is great."

In the first example the noun clause contains the A *pw* B nominal sentence *z3.f pw ḥrw* "his son is Horus"; it serves as object of the verb *ḏd.f*, explaining what "he says." In the second, the noun clause contains the adjectival sentence *wr nrw.f* "the terror of him is great"; it serves as object of the verb *rḫ.sn*, and tells what "they will learn." In both cases the particle *js* allows the nonverbal sentence to function as a noun clause, just as the word *that* does in the English translations. Noun clauses marked by *js* generally serve as the object of a verb.

2. **Noun clauses with *ntt***

In Middle Egyptian the usual mark of a noun clause with a nonverbal predicate is the word  *ntt*. This is the same as the feminine form of the relative adjective *ntj*, just as English *that* is the mark of both a noun clause and a relative pronoun. Noun clauses with *ntt* are usually formed just by putting *ntt* in front of an independent clause. Unlike relative clauses with *ntt*, noun clauses introduced by *ntt* can have all three kinds of nonverbal predicate: nominal, adjectival, and adverbial. The following is an example with a nominal predicate:

 *m33.f ntt št3w pw ᶜ3*
"He saw that it was a great secret."

Here the noun clause serves as object of the verb *m33.f* "he saw" (telling what "he saw") and contains the nominal sentence *št3w pw ᶜ3* "It was a great secret" (see § 7.9).

A noun clause with *ntt* can occur as the object of prepositions as well as of verbs. The following combinations of *ntt* and a preposition or prepositional phrase are used:

m ᶜ ntt "seeing that" — literally, "with (the fact) that" (see § 10.7)
n ntt "for, because" — literally, "for (the fact) that" (§ 8.2.6)
r ntt "inasmuch as" — literally, "with respect to (the fact) that" (§ 8.2.7)
ḥr ntt "because" — literally, "upon (the fact) that" (§ 8.2.10)
ḫft ntt "in view of (the fact) that" (§ 8.2.11)
ḏr ntt "since" — literally, "since that" (§ 8.2.17).

Of these combinations, *n ntt*, *ḥr ntt*, and *ḏr ntt* are found most often in Middle Egyptian texts. Here are three examples of a noun clause as the object of a preposition, with all three kinds of nonverbal predicate:

 *ḥr ntt ntk jt(j) n nmḥ* "because you are a father to the orphan" (nominal predicate)

 *ḥr ntt nfr jb n b3k jm* "because the heart of yours truly[3] is happy" (adjectival predicate)

 *ḥr ntt mdw pw m ᶜ.j* "because this[4] staff is in my hand" (adverbial predicate).

When a noun clause introduced by *ntt* has a personal pronoun as the subject of an adverbial predicate, Egyptian normally uses the same forms of the pronoun that it does in indirect relative clauses with *ntj* (§ 12.6): that is, the suffix forms except for 1s *wj* and 3n *st*: for example,

 *ḏr ntt.f m wᶜ mm nw* "since he is one among these."

3. **Noun clauses with *ntt* and *js***

Noun clauses introduced by *ntt* occasionally have the particle *js* inside the noun clause as well. This kind of "double marking" seems to be a transition from the older construction marked by *js* to the newer form marked by *ntt*. The presence or absence of *js* in this case seems to make no difference to the meaning: for example,

 *n ntt jnk js b3 pw ᶜ3 n wsjr*

 *n ntt jnk b3 pw ᶜ3 n wsjr*

"for I am that great ba of Osiris" (for *pw* see n. 4).

These examples come from two different religious texts written close together on a single Middle Kingdom coffin.[5] In both of them the noun clause consists of an A B nominal sentence *jnk b3 pw ᶜ3 n wsjr* "I am that great ba of Osiris." They are virtually identical except for the presence of *js* in the first example but not in the second: apparently the scribe used an older construction in the first case but a more contemporary construction in the second.

12.14 Unmarked noun clauses

In some cases English can use independent clauses as noun clauses without the word *that* as a marker: for example, *Jack discovered Jill's age was a problem*, where the clause *Jill's age was a problem* is the object of the verb *discovered*. Egyptian can do the same thing: for instance,

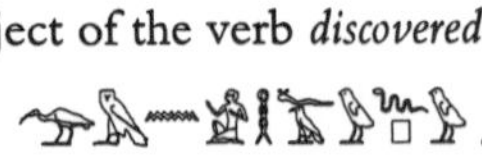 *gm.n.j ḥf3w pw* "I discovered it was a snake,"

where the A *pw* nominal sentence *ḥf3w pw* "It was a snake" is the object of the verb *gm.n.j* "I discovered." As with unmarked relative clauses, only the context — the fact that it follows a verb — indicates that this is a noun clause and not an independent statement: this is true both of the Egyptian sentence and of its English translation.

3 For *b3k jm* see § 8.10.

4 Demonstrative pronoun: § 5.8.

5 Spells 94 and 96 of the Coffin Texts. The gap in the second example does not occur in the original: it is inserted here only to show the difference between the two examples. Other copies of the first example also omit the *js*, while other copies of the second insert it.

ADVERB CLAUSES

12.15 Definitions

As its name indicates, an **adverb clause** is a subordinate clause that functions as an adverb. Just like adverbs, such clauses tell when, where, why, or how something happens or is true (§ 8.11). Adverb clauses are also known as **circumstantial** clauses, because they often describe the circumstances under which a main clause is true.

In the English sentence *Jack is happy today*, the adverb *today* tells when Jack is happy. Prepositional phrases also function as adverbs in many cases (§ 8.11): for example, in the English sentence *Jack gets depressed in the winter*, the prepositional phrase *in the winter* describes when Jack gets depressed. Adverb clauses have the same function as adverbs and prepositional phrases, as can be seen in the following English sentences: *Jack is happy when he is with Jill* (tells when Jack is happy), *Jack is happy because he is with Jill* (tells why Jack is happy).

English has two ways to make adverb clauses. Words such as *when* and *because* make it possible for an independent clause (such as *he is with Jill* in the examples just given) to serve as an adverb clause. In many cases, English can also make an adverb clause by turning its verb into an *–ing* form (and by omitting its subject, if it is the same as the subject of the main clause): for example, *Jack is happy being with Jill.*

Like English, Egyptian also has two ways of forming adverb clauses. As with relative clauses and noun clauses, such clauses can be **marked** by an initial word; or they can be **unmarked**, in which case their adverbial function comes from the context in which they are used.

12.16 Marked adverb clauses

We have already met one kind of marked adverb clause: that which consists of a preposition plus a noun clause with *ntt* (§ 12.10). Just as a preposition plus a noun can function as an adverb, so too can the combination of a preposition and a noun clause: for example,

3w jb n jmj-r pr nw m3ꜥ ḫrw ḏr ntt.f m wꜥ mm nw

"The heart of steward Nu, justified, is happy,[6] since he is one among these."

This sentence consists of two clauses: a main clause *3w jb n jmj-r pr nw m3ꜥ ḫrw* "The heart of steward Nu, justified, is happy," with an adjectival predicate; and an adverb clause *ḏr ntt.f m wꜥ mm nw* "since he is one among these," with an adverbial predicate. The adverb clause explains why the statement of the main clause is true.

Often, adverb clauses are marked by a particle at the beginning of the clause or by another particle inside the clause, or by a combination of both.

1. **Adverb clauses with *jsṯ***

This particle has several forms, as a result of sound changes in the history of the language. Originally the particle was 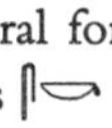 *sk*. Already in Old Egyptian, however, it also appears as 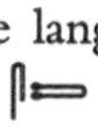 *sṯ* and  *jsṯ*, where the original *k* has changed to *ṯ*. Middle Egyptian uses all three forms, along with a

6 Literally, "The heart of the overseer of the house, Nu, justified, is long": the expression "long of heart" is an Egyptian idiom for "happy." For the title *jmj-r pr* "steward," see § 8.9; for *m3ꜥ ḫrw* "justified," see Essays 8 and 10.

fourth spelling,  *jst* (sometimes  *jstw* and  *stj*), where the final *ṯ* has changed to *t* (see § 2.8.3), and an archaizing form  *jsk*.

The particle *jsṯ* (etc.) stands at the head of the adverb clause and serves to mark it in the same way that *ntj* does for relative clauses and *ntt* does for noun clauses: for example,

 *ḥmt jty pw jsk ḥm.f m jnpw*
"She was the sovereign's wife when his incarnation was still (that of) a baby."

Here the main clause is the nominal sentence *ḥmt jty pw* "She was the sovereign's wife." The adverb clause has an adverbial predicate (*m jnpw*) and tells when the main clause was true.

Nonverbal clauses with *jsṯ* can have a nominal or adjectival predicate as well as an adverbial one: for instance,

 *jsṯ št3 wrt w3t* "although the road was very inaccessible,"

where the predicate of the adverb clause is adjectival (see § 7.4.1). Examples with adverbial predicate are the most common, however. When the subject of an adverbial predicate is a personal pronoun, the **dependent** forms are used: for example,

 *sk w(j) m šmsw.f* "while I was in his following."

You may have noticed that the preceding examples with *jsṯ* (etc.) were translated in English with different introductory words: "when," "although," and "while." The use of such words in translation is often a matter of personal preference on the part of the translator. In Egyptian the particle *jsṯ* merely serves to mark a clause as subordinate in some way. Sometimes the *jsṯ* clause is clearly adverbial in meaning — as it is, for example, in the sentence *ḥmt jty pw jsk ḥm.f m jnpw* "She was the sovereign's wife when his incarnation was still (that of) a baby." In other cases, however, the subordination is not so clear, and English has to resort to a less specific word to introduce the clause, such as "for" or "and." Occasionally the *jsṯ* clause is even best translated as an independent sentence without an introductory word, or with a vague word of relation such as "now" or "so": the clause *jsṯ št3 wrt w3t*, for example, can also be translated "Now, the road was very inaccessible."[7]

These are cases where English is more specific than Egyptian; we will meet them again when we discuss verbal clauses. For now, you should simply be aware that *jsṯ* serves to mark a clause as subordinate, and that such clauses often function specifically as adverbs, describing when, why, or how a main clause happens or is true.

2. Adverb clauses with *tj*

This particle, spelled  or , is apparently related to the word  "yes." Its meaning may be similar to that of the archaic English word *Yea* (as in "Yea, though I walk through the valley of the shadow of death": Psalm 23), but this rendering is not used in modern translations. Like *jsṯ*, *tj* stands at the head of an adverb clause and marks it as subordinate. Nonverbal clauses introduced by *tj* always seem to have an adverbial predicate, with a noun or a dependent pronoun as subject: for example,

7 Older translations often use the archaic word *Lo* to translate *jsṯ* in such cases, but this does not reflect the real meaning of *jsṯ*, and it is not very satisfactory in modern English.

 *jw.j m jr(j) rdwj.f tj sw ḥr prj*

"I was his attendant[8] while he was on the battlefield."

The particle *tj* is much less common than *jsṯ*. As in this example, most clauses introduced by *tj* are specifically adverbial, describing the circumstances under which a main clause is true. Like *jsṯ* clauses, however, those with *tj* are sometimes best translated as independent sentences.

3. **Adverb clauses with *js***

We have already met *js* as a subordinating particle in noun clauses (§ 12.13.1). The same particle is used to subordinate adverb clauses as well: for instance,

 *m3n.j njw ḥnᶜ jmn jnk js 3ḫj ᶜpr*

"I will see Niu and Amun, for I am an equipped akh."[9]

Here the adverb clause *jnk js 3ḫj ᶜpr* "for I am an equipped akh" explains why the speaker (who is deceased) is able to see the gods. Most examples of this construction are similar to this one: the adverb clause has a nominal predicate, and the clause supplies a reason why the main clause is true or an additional statement. Usually such clauses are best translated into English with the linking words "for" or "and" at the head of the adverb clause.

Since *js* is used to mark both noun clauses and adverb clauses, it cannot be described as a specific mark of either kind of clause. The particle does not make a clause into a noun clause or an adverb clause: instead, it is simply an indication that the clause is somehow subordinate.

4. **Adverb clauses with *jsṯ* and *js***

In a few cases adverb clauses are marked both by *jsṯ* at the head of the clause and by *js* inside it: for example,

 *jwᶜ.n.j 3ḫt nt rᶜ jsṯ jnk js nb-tm*

"I have inherited the Akhet of Re, for I am the Lord-of-All."[10]

The adverb clause here explains why the main clause is true. This kind of "double marking" is similar to that of noun clauses with both *ntt* and *js* (§ 12.13.3). As in the latter, the presence or absence of *js* apparently makes no difference to the meaning. Such clauses seem to occur primarily in religious texts.

12.17 Unmarked adverb clauses

Most adverb clauses in Egyptian have no special marking to indicate their function. They look just like independent sentences, and only the context in which they are used indicates that they are subordinate rather than main clauses. Such clauses can have a nominal, adjectival, or adverbial predicate. Examples with an adverbial predicate are by far the most common, however. They can consist of only a subject and a predicate, or they can be introduced by the particle *jw* (§ 10.3) or the negative *nn* (§§ 10.4.2, 11.4): for instance,

8 Literally, "one who was at his feet": *jr(j)* is a nisbe from the preposition *r*: see §§ 8.6.4 and 8.7.

9 In the main clause, *m3n.j* "I will see" is a verb with a 1s subject, and the noun phrase *njw ḥnᶜ jmn* is its object.

10 In the main clause, *jwᶜ.n.j* "I have inherited" is a verb with a 1s subject, and the noun phrase *3ḫt nt rᶜ* "the Akhet of Re" is its object. For *3ḫt* "the Akhet" see Essay 2.

 *m3 s3.k bjn mšʿ.j m s3.k*
"Your back will see evil, since my army is in back of you"[11]

 *ḏʿ pr jw.n m w3ḏ-wr*
"A storm came up, while we were at sea"[12]

 *w3ḥ.j st m wš3 nn r(m)t jm*
"I will leave it a ruin, with no people therein"[13]

In each of these examples the second clause describes an adverbial circumstance that applies to the first, main clause: *mšʿ.j m s3.k* "my army is in back of you" tells why *m3 s3.k bjn* "your back will see evil," *jw.n m w3ḏ-wr* "we were at sea" describes when *ḏʿ pr* "a storm came up," and *nn r(m)t jm* "people will not be therein" indicates how *w3ḥ.j st m wš3* "I will leave it a ruin."

Note that in each case the English translation provides a word to introduce the second clause ("since," "while," and "with"). Such words are supplied by the English translator: they do not exist in the Egyptian sentences. In fact, in each of these examples the second clause could theoretically be an independent sentence by itself; only the context indicates that it is actually subordinate to the preceding clause. Since this is so, the translation is partly a matter of preference, and other translations are often equally possible (though not always equally good): for example,

m3 s3.k bjn mšʿ.j m s3.k
"Your back will see evil, when my army is in back of you"
"Your back will see evil, for my army is in back of you"
"Your back will see evil, my army being in back of you"
"Your back will see evil: my army is in back of you"

ḏʿ pr jw.n m w3ḏ-wr
"A storm came up, when we were at sea"
"A storm came up, and we were at sea"
"A storm came up, we being at sea"
"A storm came up; we were at sea"

w3ḥ.j st m wš3 nn r(m)t jm
"I will leave it a ruin, without people therein"
"I will leave it a ruin, and no people will be therein"
"I will leave it a ruin, no people being therein"
"I will leave it a ruin; no people will be therein."

Obviously, unmarked adverb clauses in Middle Egyptian are less specific than English adverb clauses about the exact nature of the adverbial relationship with the main clause. In most cases the

11 In the main clause, *m3* "will see" is a verb, *s3.k* "your back" is its subject, and *bjn* "evil" is its object. The sentence, spoken by the pharaoh, means that the enemy to whom he is speaking will be defeated by the pursuing Egyptian army.

12 In the main clause, *ḏʿ* "a storm" is the subject of the verb *pr* "came up." "At sea" is literally "in the Great Blue-Green": *w3ḏ-wr* "Great Blue-Green" is the Egyptian name for both the Mediterranean Sea and the Red Sea.

13 In the main clause, *w3ḥ.j* "I will leave" is a verb with a 1s subject and *st* "it" is its object; *m wš3* is literally "in a ruin."

context only offers a range of possibilities. The adverb clause in the first example, for instance, could indicate either *why* the first clause is true ("since my army is in back of you") or *when* it is true ("when my army is in back of you"). In the second example, however, the adverb clause only describes *when* the first clause happened, not *why*.

To some extent, therefore, how you understand the context will determine how you translate an unmarked adverb clause — or whether you understand it as an adverb clause at all, rather than as an independent sentence. There are no hard and fast rules that can be offered to guide you, but you will discover that the context itself is generally a pretty good guide.

12.18 The position of adverb clauses

English can put an adverb clause either before or after the main clause: for example, "While we were at sea, a storm came up" and "A storm came up, while we were at sea." In Egyptian, only **marked** adverb clauses can precede the main clause. Such clauses can be marked by the particle *js* inside the adverb clause, or they can be introduced by the particles *jsṯ* (in its various forms) or *tj*, but they cannot be introduced by a preposition plus *ntt*.

ESSAY 12. THE CREATION OF THE WORLD

The Hermopolitan system discussed in Essay 11 seems to have been primarily concerned with the background of the creation, describing what the universe was like before creation began. The actual process of creation was the interest of theologians in another great Egyptian city, Heliopolis (near the site of modern Cairo).

Unlike the creation accounts of the Bible, those of ancient Egypt do not seem to have envisaged the possibility of something being created from nothing. Instead, the Egyptians believed that everything in the world — all its elements and forces — came from a single source, much like the primordial singularity in the "Big Bang" theory of modern physics. This original source of all things was known as the god Atum (*jtmw*, usually written). The god's name means "finisher," and refers to the fact that Atum "finished up" as the world. In recognition of his nature, Atum is called *nb tm* "Lord of Totality" (see the example in § 12.16.4) or more often, *nb-r-ḏr* "Lord to the Limit."

Before the creation, Atum existed from all time within the primeval waters in a state of inert potentiality — as the texts describe it, "alone with Nu, in inertness" and "in his egg." The creation happened when Atum evolved into the world, becoming the finite space of light and life within the infinite universal ocean (see Essay 2). This process is explained both as Atum's "self-evolution" — the god is often called *ḫpr ḏs.f* "he who evolved by himself" — and by the typical Egyptian metaphor of creation, birth.

The first act of creation involves the birth of two "children" from Atum: Shu (*šw*) and Tefnut (*tfnwt*, also *tfnt*). To explain how Atum could "give birth" to Shu and Tefnut by himself, the texts use the metaphors of masturbation or "sneezing" and "spitting," the latter based on a play on words (*jšš* "sneeze" = *šw* "Shu," *tf* "spit" = *tfnt* "Tefnut"). Shu is the atmosphere; his creation produced a dry (*šw*), empty (*šw*) space in the midst of the universal ocean, within which all life exists (Essay 2). Tefnut is the female counterpart of Shu; her role in the creation is essentially to serve as mother of the succeeding generations.

The creation of a void within the waters produced of necessity a bottom and a top where none had existed before. These are Geb (*gbb* or *gbw*), the earth, and Nut (*nwt*), the sky, the children of Shu and Tefnut. Together they define the physical structure and limits of the created world. In one text Shu says:

> I have lifted my daughter Nut atop me,
> that I might give her to my father Atum in his utmost extent.
> I have put Geb under my feet,
> and this god is knotting together the land for my father Atum.

The creation of the world's physical structure produced a place within which life could exist. The children of Geb and Nut are the primary forces of life: Osiris (*wsjr*, also and, after the Middle Kingdom,), the power of birth and regeneration; Isis (*jst*), the principle of motherhood; Seth (originally *stš*; by the Middle Kingdom *stẖ*; in the New Kingdom often *swtẖ*; in all periods usually written with the Seth-animal, or , as ideogram or determinative), the force of male sexuality; and Nephthys (, *nbt-ḥwt*), the female counterpart of Seth.

Together, Atum and his eight descendants are known as the Ennead, a Greek word meaning "group of nine." This is a direct translation of the Egyptian term *psḏt* "group of nine." The Egyptians understood this term figuratively as well as literally. When the gods of the Ennead are named, they occasionally amount to more than nine gods. This is apparently because the Ennead itself represents the sum of all the elements and forces of the created world. In early religious texts, the word *psḏt* "Ennead" is written , and it has been suggested that the term was seen not just as nine gods (× 9) but also as a "plural of plurals" (× 3), or an infinite number.

The Ennead was worshipped particularly in Heliopolis, often in the form of *jtmw ḥnꜥ psḏt.f* "Atum and his Ennead." The "tenth god" implicit in this phrase is Horus (*ḥrw*), the son of Isis and Osiris. Horus was the power of kingship. To the Egyptians this was as much a force of nature as those embodied in the other gods. It was manifest in two natural phenomena: the sun, the most powerful force in nature; and the pharaoh, the most powerful force in human society. Horus's role as the king of nature is probably the origin of his name: *ḥrw* seems to mean "the one above" or "the one far off" and is occasionally written , like the verb *ḥr(j)* "to be far off." This is apparently a reference to the sun, which is "above" and "far off" in the sky, like the falcon with which Horus is regularly associated (and with which his name is usually written).

The birth of the sun is actually the culmination of creation in the Heliopolitan system, as it is in the early myth of the primeval mound (see Essay 11). The sun's first rising into the newly created world-space marks the end of creation and the beginning of the eternal cycle of life, which the sun regulates (as king of nature) and makes possible through his heat and light. The Heliopolitan accounts therefore concentrate not only on Atum's "evolution" but also on the sun's role in the creation. As an element of nature, the sun is known simply as *rꜥ* "Sun" (usually transcribed "Re" or "Ra"). As the newly risen sun, he is often called *ḫpr(j)* "Khepri" (literally, "Evolver"); the beetle used to write this name is the source of the common depiction of the sun-god as a scarab. The sun at dawn is also known as  *ḥrw-3ḫtj* "Harakhti" (literally, "Horus of the Akhet")[14] or, combined with Re, as "Re-Harakhti" (sometimes written ). Since the sun is the culmination of Atum's "evolution" into the world, the two gods are occasionally combined in the form  *rᶜ-(j)tm(w)* "Re-Atum." Atum himself was often worshipped as the setting sun, apparently through association of his great age (as "oldest" of the gods) with the "old age" of the sun at this point in its daily cycle.

The Heliopolitan account of creation explained not only the origin of the world's structure, elements, and forces but also how its diversity evolved from a single source. Atum's generation of Shu and Tefnut is described as "when he was one and evolved into three." The Ennead itself is a metaphor of both physical relationship and dependency. Atum's "giving birth" to his "children" is a way of explaining how the elements of nature come from a single physical source, just as children derive their substance from that of their parents. The Ennead's generational scheme reflects the logical dependency of its parts: the creation of a void in the waters (Shu and Tefnut) produces a "bottom" and "top" (Geb and Nut, the children of Shu and Tefnut), and the void in turn makes possible the forces of life (Osiris and Isis, Seth and Nephthys, the children of Geb and Nut).

Although it is explained in generational terms, the Heliopolitan view of the creation is therefore less a "step-by-step" account than a kind of Egyptian "Big Bang" theory, in which all of creation happened at once, in the moment when Atum evolved into the world and time itself began. One Middle Kingdom text actually reflects this view of creation when it describes Shu as "the one whom Atum created on the day that he evolved."

EXERCISE 12

Transliterate and translate the following sentences.

1.  — *sšmw* "situation"
2.  — *n* "in," *qbw* "cool breeze," *rm* "fish," *šw* "sunlight"
3. 
4.  — *jt.n.j* "I took," *jm3m* "tent"
5.  — *jw* "island," *w3ḏ-wr*: see n. 12 above, *gs(wj).fj* "its two sides" (see § 5.7), *nwy* "waters"
6.  — *mdw.k* "you shall speak"
7.  — *wjn.sn* "they don't want to be"
8.  — *jr.n.(j)* "I did," *mj qd*: § 6.7; *jmj-jb* "confidant" (literally, "one who is in the heart")
9.  — *rḫ.n.(j)* "I learned of," *qd* "character," *zšj* "nestling"

14 *3ḫtj* is a nisbe from *3ḫt* "the Akhet" (see Essay 2). In the New Kingdom this name is written , where *3ḫtj* has been reinterpreted as a dual ("Horus of the Two Akhets").

10.  — *dpt* "boat," *sẖry* "pilot"

11.  — *srj* "official," *gs* "side"

12.  — *snf(3).n.j* "I have vented," *ẖt* "belly"

13. 

14.  — past

15.  — *sj3.n.j* "I recognized"

16.  — *wꜥb*: see Essay 5

17.  — *jw jr.n.(j)* "I spent," *ꜥḥꜥw* "lifetime," *ḥnwt* "mistress"

18. 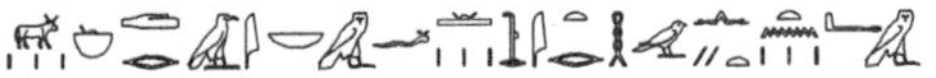 — *ḥtrj* "plow-team," *j3dr* "herd"

19.  — past

20.  — *stt* "boil," *nḥbt* "neck"

21.  — *ḏd.k* "you shall say," *h3b ṯw* "the one who sent you," *3ẖ* "effective," *ds* "knife"

22.  — *mr.ṯ sw* "you should love him"

23.  — *wdpw* "waiter," *rš* "delight," *rḥs* "butchering"

24. 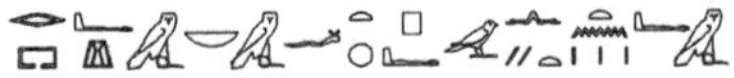 — *pꜥt* "loaf of bread," *mẖr* "food-storehouse"

25.  — *jw wp.n.f* "he opened," *b3ḥ* "presence"

26. 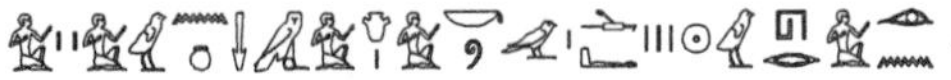 — *jr.n.j* "I spent," *wꜥ.kw* "alone," *snw* "companion" (literally, "second")

27.  — *3m.nj* "they burnt up"

28.  — past

29.  — *ẖnt(j)* "statue," *rd* "stairway," *jz* "tomb"

30.  — *rẖ* "know," *swḥt* "egg"

31.  — *wḏ* "stela"

32. 

33.  — *šndyt* "kilt"

34.  — past: *ꜥb* "flank" (of an army: literally, "horn"), *mḥtj* "northern," *mḥtj-jmntj* "northwest," *mjktj* "Megiddo" (a city in Israel)

35.  — past

13. Verbs

13.1 Introduction

Verbs are words that languages use to describe **actions.** In a clause or sentence, nouns and pronouns are normally the subject (what is being talked about), while verbs are usually the predicate (what is said about the subject: § 7.1). In English, every clause or sentence has a verbal predicate; Egyptian, however, can make clauses or sentences without verbs, as we have seen in the preceding lessons.

Verbs are the most complex part of any language. The other elements — nouns, pronouns, adjectives, prepositions, adverbs, and particles — have one or a few forms (such as singular and plural, masculine and feminine), but verbs typically have many different forms. The English verb *throw*, for example, has five simple forms (*throw*, *throws*, *threw*, *thrown*, and *throwing*), but also numerous compound forms such as *will throw*, *should throw*, *have thrown*, *had thrown*, *is thrown*, *is throwing*, *will be throwing*, *should have been thrown*, *were to have been throwing*, and so forth.

Because of this feature, verbs are typically the most difficult and time-consuming part of learning any language. This is as true for Middle Egyptian as it is for a modern language such as English. In some ways Egyptian verbs are simpler than those of English, but in other ways they are more complex. This lesson will give us an overview of the Middle Egyptian verb, but it will take the rest of this book for us to examine all the verb forms, their meanings, and their uses in Egyptian clauses and sentences.

13.2 Kinds of verbs

Egyptian, like English, has two different kinds of verbs, which grammarians call **transitive** and **intransitive**. The difference between these two categories has to do with the relationship between the action expressed by the verb and the verb's **agent**: that is, the person or thing that performs the action.

Transitive verbs are used to describe an action that is "transferred" from the agent. The English verb *throw*, for example, is transitive because it can be used in statements such as *the girl threw the ball*, where the action of the verb is "transferred" from the agent (*the girl*) to *the ball*. Transitive verbs typically involve two different parties: the agent who performs the action, and someone or something on whom the action is performed or to whom it is "transferred."

Intransitive verbs are used to describe an action that is not "transferred" but remains with the agent. Intransitive verbs typically involve only one party, the agent. Often they describe some kind of change in the agent's state or condition. An example is the English verb *fall*: a statement such as *the boy fell to the ground* describes a change in the state of the agent (*the boy*) — for instance, from sitting in a tree to lying on the ground. There are several different kinds of intransitive verbs. Some describe simply a change of state or condition, such as the English verbs *happen* and *rejoice*. **Verbs of motion** describe a change involving movement, such as *come*, *go*, and *fall*. **Adjective verbs** describe a change in quality: for example, *expand* and *diminish*.

The difference between transitive and intransitive verbs exists in the verb itself, no matter what form the verb appears in. Thus, the words *fall*, *falling*, and *fallen*, are all intransitive. Speakers of English are naturally aware of this difference, but it is not always easy to appreciate because very few verbs are strictly transitive or intransitive. Verbs are called transitive or intransitive based on their usual meaning: most are normally one kind or the other but some can occasionally be used in the opposite way. The English verb *sit*, for example, is basically intransitive, but it can also be used transitively (as in the expression *sit the child in his chair* or the idiom *sit a horse*, which means "sit on a horse").

Transitive verbs are usually more flexible than intransitive verbs in this respect. The English verb *sing*, for example, is transitive because it can be used in a statement such as *the soprano sang an aria*, where *an aria* is what is affected by the agent's action. But the same verb can also be used to describe an action involving only the agent, as in *the soprano sang*. In such cases, however, the verb is not intransitive but is merely used without specifying the thing affected by the action of the agent.

The person or thing affected by a transitive verb can also be identical with the agent of the verb. This is a special kind of construction known as **reflexive** use (because it "reflects back" on the agent). In English it is made by using a reflexive pronoun (with the suffix *–self*) to indicate the person or thing to whom the action is "transferred": for example, *the boy injured himself*. Even though the person or thing affected in this use is identical with the agent, the verb is still transitive because it describes an action performed on someone or something.

In general, a verb can be identified as transitive if it is normally used to describe an action performed on someone or something and not to describe a change in the state or condition of the agent (except reflexively). An intransitive verb can usually be recognized by the opposite criteria: if it is normally used to describe a change in the state or condition of the agent and not to describe an action performed on someone or something.

It is important to be aware of the differences between these various kinds of verbs, because they are often treated differently in grammar. In English, for example, only transitive verbs can be made passive: for example, *the boy was injured* but not **the boy was falled*. Similar grammatical differences exist in Egyptian, as we will see.

13.3 Features of verbs

Verbs describe not only action itself but also various features of an action. These features are grammatical: that is, they are indicated by the form the verb appears in rather than by the verb itself. Egyptian verbs can express four such features, which are also found in English verb forms.

1. Tense

The feature of tense indicates the **time** of a verb's action with respect to a particular point of reference. English has three basic tenses:

- **present** — indicates that the action is simultaneous with the point of reference **or** that it is not associated with any point of reference (generic: § 7.16.1): for example, *Jack wants to go* (Jack's desire exists at the time the sentence is spoken) and *Jill sings in the shower* (this is something Jill generally does, though it does not necessarily happen at the time the sentence is spoken).

- **past** — indicates that the action occurs before the point of reference: for example, *Jack threw the ball* (Jack's action happened before the sentence is spoken).
- **future** — indicates that the action occurs after the point of reference: for example, *Jill will sing an aria* (Jill's singing has not yet taken place when the sentence is spoken).

In each of these definitions, the point of reference was explained as the time at which the sentence is spoken: in other words, the moment of speaking. Past actions, for example, are those that occur before the moment of speaking, while future actions take place after it. This is sometimes known as "absolute tense." But the point of reference can also be another action. This can be called "relative tense." English has two relative tenses. The **pluperfect** or **past perfect** indicates that the action occurs before some point of reference in the past: for example, *Jack had left by the time Jill sang* (Jill's singing took place before the sentence is spoken, and Jack's leaving happened before Jill sang). The **future perfect** indicates that the action occurs before some point of reference in the future: for example, *Jack will have left by the time Jill sings* (neither action has taken place when the sentence is spoken, and Jack's leaving will happen before Jill's singing).

While English verbs express either absolute or relative tense, Egyptian verbs indicate only relative tense. Although their forms can be used to express absolute tense — for example, past or future — the same forms are also used to indicate the time of an action with respect to another action. Unlike English, Egyptian has no special pluperfect or future perfect forms. We will examine this feature in more detail when we discuss the individual forms.

2. **Aspect**

The term "aspect" refers to the **kind** of action indicated by a verb form. Egyptian verbs can express two kinds of aspect, which can also be expressed — in different ways — by English verbs:

- **completion** — used to indicate whether an action is completed or not. The English sentence *Jack has left*, for example, describes a completed action, while the sentence *Jack is leaving* describes an incomplete one.
- **repetition** (also called "extension") — used to indicate whether an action is done many times or not. The English sentence *Jill used to sing in the shower*, for instance, refers to many instances of singing, while the sentence *Jill sang in the shower* refers to only one.

In English, the verb form that denotes completion is called the **perfect** (*Jack has left*) and the form that expresses incomplete action is known as the **imperfect** (*Jack is leaving*). These forms also refer to the time of an action, but unlike the simple tenses they indicate whether the action is completed or not, rather than simply past, present, or future. English grammar has no special names for forms that express repetition.

In Egyptian, certain verb forms indicate whether an action is completed or incomplete, while others say nothing about these aspects. In grammatical terms, this means that forms indicating completed or incomplete action are **marked** forms (see the discussion in § 11.3). Studies of Egyptian grammar traditionally use the term **perfective** when speaking about completed action and **imperfective** for incomplete action. As we will see, however, the perfective forms do not necessarily imply that the action of the verb is completed; for that reason, we will use the English term **perfect** when speaking about completed action. The imperfective forms sometimes express an action that is incomplete, but other forms can do so as well; we will use the English term **imperfect** when speaking about incompleted action. The perfect, imperfect, and imperfective are all marked forms; the perfective is an unmarked form.

The feature of aspect is one of the major differences between the verbal systems of Egyptian and English. In Middle Egyptian, aspect is the primary feature of the verbal system and tense is secondary. The English verbal system is just the opposite: tense is the primary feature of English verb forms, while aspect is secondary. This means that Egyptian verb forms basically describe the kind of action, while those of English basically indicate tense.

3. **Mood**

The term "mood" refers to a value judgment that speakers place on verb forms. Both Egyptian and English have two moods:

- **indicative** — indicates that the action of the verb is a statement of fact: for example, *Jill sings in the shower* (Jill's singing actually happens).
- **subjunctive** — indicates that the action of the verb is possible, desirable, or contingent: for instance, *Jill might sing in the shower* (possible), *Jill should sing in the shower* (desirable), *Jill would sing in the shower if she wasn't so shy* (contingent).

Subjunctive forms are marked and indicative forms are unmarked. Verb forms are indicative unless they are specifically marked as subjunctive. The subjunctive can only indicate subjunctive mood, but indicative forms can sometimes be used to express possible, desirable, or contingent actions as well as statements of fact, because they are unmarked for mood.

4. **Voice**

The term "voice" refers to the relationship between the action of a verb and its subject. Both English and Egyptian have two voices:

- **active** — indicates that the subject performs the action: for example, *Jack threw the ball* (the subject, *Jack*, did the action of throwing).
- **passive** — indicates that the action is performed on the subject: for instance, *The ball was thrown by Jack* (the action of throwing was performed on the subject, *the ball*).

It is important to recognize that voice has to do with the relationship between a verb and its **subject**, not between a verb and its **agent**. In the active voice the subject and the agent are identical: in the sentence *Jack threw the ball*, *Jack* is both the subject of the verb and its agent. In the passive, however, the subject and agent are different: in the sentence *The ball was thrown by Jack*, the verb's subject is *the ball* and its agent (the one who did the throwing) is *Jack*. English indicates the agent of a passive verb with the preposition *by*, but it can also make passive statements in which the agent is not expressed: *The ball was thrown*. Egyptian uses the preposition *jn* to indicate the agent (§ 8.2.2), and it too can make passive statements in which the agent is not expressed.

13.4 Parts of verbs

English verb forms are made in two different ways: by changing the form of the verb or by adding different verb forms together. The first method, which grammarians call "synthetic," is used for the simple present and past tense and for participles: for example, *fall / fell / falling / fallen*, *call /*

called / calling / called. The second method, known as "analytic," is used for other tenses and forms of the verb: for instance, *is falling, did fall, would have fallen*, and so forth.

Middle Egyptian uses the same two methods for making its verb forms. Unlike English, however, most of its verb forms are synthetic. These are composed of five parts:

1. The **root** is the part of the verb that is found in dictionaries. In English, for example, *fall* is the root of the verb forms *falling, falls, fallen*, etc. (see the discussion of noun roots in § 4.2). An Egyptian example is the verb , meaning "like," "want," or "desire," which has the root *mrj*. There are several different kinds of roots, as we will see in the next section, and these determine some of the forms that the verb can have.

2. The **stem** is the most basic **form** of the verb. The English verb *fall*, for example, has two stems: *fall* and *fell*. There are two kinds of stems in Middle Egyptian verbs, used in different forms. The **base stem** is the simplest; for many verbs it is identical to the root. In the **geminated stem**, the last consonant of the base stem is doubled (or "geminated"). The base stem of *mrj* is *mr*, and its geminated stem is *mrr*.

3. **Endings** are one or more consonants that are added onto the end of the stem in various forms, in the same way that gender and number endings are added to nouns and adjectives. The form *mryt* "desired," for example, has the ending *–yt* added to the base stem.

4. **Suffixes** are one or two consonants that are added to the end of stems **after** any endings. In transliteration they are usually separated from the stem and endings by a dot, like the suffix pronouns. In the form *mrt.n.tw* "what was wanted," for example, the base stem *mr* has an ending *–t* and two suffixes indicating completed action (*n*) and the passive (*tw*).

5. The **prefix** is the consonant *j* (spelled or), added to the front of a verb form. Like the suffixes, it is usually separated by a dot in transliteration: for instance, *j.mz* "bring!," from the verb *mz* "bring in, introduce." The prefix is a common feature of verbs in Old and Late Egyptian but is rare in Middle Egyptian.

These elements are used in different combinations to make the various synthetic forms of the Middle Egyptian verb.

13.5 Root classes

Egyptologists divide Egyptian verbs into classes based on the form of their root. Each consonant of the root is called a "radical"; Middle Egyptian verbs can have from two to six radicals. In older studies of Egyptian grammar the root classes were given Latin names. These names, or their abbreviations, are still used in grammars; most English-speaking Egyptologists, however, normally use an English translation of the Latin name. The different root classes are the following:

1. **2-lit.** (biliteral) — verbs with two radicals (AB): example, *ḏd* "say." A few biliteral verbs have the "weak" consonant *j* as the final radical (A*j*); these are sometimes called second-weak verbs (abbreviated 2ae-inf., from the Latin *secundae infirmae* "of the second-weak (class)"): example, *zj* "go." In Middle Egyptian these are generally treated like other biliterals.

   Base stem: *ḏd, zj*
   Geminated stem: *ḏdd*; 2ae-inf. verbs have no geminated stem.

2. **2ae-gem.** (second-geminate; Latin *secundae geminatae*) — verbs with three radicals in which the second and third radicals are the same (ABB): example,  *m33* "see."[1]

   Base stem: *m3*
   Geminated stem: *m33*.

   Although they are different in writing, both stems probably had the two final radicals. In the base stem the two radicals would have been in contact, without a vowel between them (for example, *m3t* "seen" = **mV33Vt*; *V* stands for a vowel): hieroglyphic normally writes only one consonant in such cases (see n. 2 in Lesson 9). In the geminated stem the two identical radicals would have been separated by a vowel (for instance, *m33t* "seen" = **mV3V3Vt*).

3. **3-lit.** (triliteral) — verbs with three radicals (ABC): example,  *stp* "select." A few verbs of this class have the consonant *j* or *w* as the third radical: examples,  *dmj* "touch" and  *3bw* "brand." Most verbs with final *j* belong to the next class, however.

   Base stem: *stp, dmj, 3bw*
   Geminated stem: *stpp* (rare); verbs with final *j* or *w* have no geminated stem.

4. **3ae-inf.** (third-weak; Latin *tertiae infirmae*) — verbs with three radicals in which the third radical is the "weak" consonant *j* or *w* (AB*j*, AB*w*): examples,  *mrj* "like, want, desire" and  *z3w* "guard." Most verbs in this class have a final radical *j*; 3ae-*w* verbs are usually "strong" triliterals (3-lit.).

   Base stem: *mr, z3* or *z3w*
   Geminated stem: *mrr, z33*.

   Most 3ae-inf. verbs behave alike. A few verbs of this class, however, have no geminated stem, or geminate only rarely. The most common such verb is  *šmj* "go, walk."

5. **3ae-gem.** (third-geminate; Latin *tertiae geminatae*) — verbs with four radicals in which the third and fourth radicals are the same (ABCC): example,  *snbb* "converse."

   Base stem: none
   Geminated stem: *snbb*.

6. **4-lit.** (quadriteral) — verbs with four radicals (ABCD or ABAB): examples,  *wsṯn* "stride" and  *ptpt* "trample." Most 4-lit. verbs have the root pattern ABAB. These are known as **reduplicated** roots; many of them are related to biliteral roots with the same consonants: for example,  *snsn* "fraternize" and  *sn* "kiss, smell." Some reduplicated quadriliterals have the root pattern A*j*A*j*. These usually omit the "weak" consonant or write it only in final position: for example, 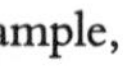 or  *ḥjḥj* "seek." These look like "geminated" biliterals (AA) or 3ae-inf. roots with identical first and second radicals (AA*j*), but they are 4-lit. roots because Egyptian has no verb roots with the patterns AA or AA*j*.

   Base stem: *wsṯn, ptpt, ḥjḥj*
   Geminated stem: none.

1 The "eye" sign is a determinative but it is normally written "inside" this verb to make a more compact grouping.

7. **4ae-inf.** (fourth-weak; Latin *quartae infirmae*) — verbs with four radicals in which the fourth radical is the "weak" consonant *j* (ABC*j*): example,  *msḏj* "hate." There are actually two kinds of 4ae-inf. verbs: some have only a base stem; others have a geminated stem as well. The verb *msḏj* is a geminating 4ae-inf. verb;  *ḥmsj* "sit down" is a non-geminating 4ae-inf. verb.

   Base stem: *msḏ*, *ḥms*
   Geminated stem: *msḏd* (geminating 4ae-inf. verbs only).

8. **5-lit.** (quinquiliteral) — verbs with five radicals. All verbs of this class are reduplicated from original 3-lit. or 3ae-inf. roots (ABCBC or AB*j*B*j*); often the non-reduplicated root is attested as well: examples, 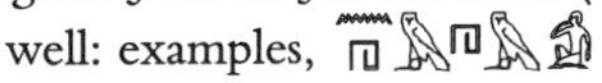 *nhmhm* and  *nhm* "yell," 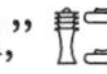 *ḏdjdj* and 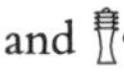 *ḏdj* "endure." Most 5-lit. verbs probably connote a more intense or extended action than their triliteral counterparts: thus, *nhmhm* "yell loudly, yell a lot" vs. *nhm* "yell." Verbs of this class seem to be uniformly intransitive.

   Base stem: *nhmhm*, *ḏdjdj*
   Geminated stem: none.

   Old Egyptian also possessed a few verbs with 6-lit. roots, which are fully reduplicated from triliteral roots — for example, *nḏdnḏd* "endure" — but Middle Egyptian uses only the partly-reduplicated root (*nḏdḏd*), with rare exceptions.

Causatives

Besides these eight root-classes Egyptian possessed a further seven classes known as **causatives.** These are formed from seven of the simple roots plus an initial radical *s*. Causatives generally denote causation of the action expressed by the root without *s*: for example, *sḫpr* "bring about, cause to happen," from *ḫpr* "evolve, happen, occur." Most causative roots have an attested simplex (root without *s*), but a few do not. Causatives are uniformly transitive. Their meaning can generally be translated by the verb "cause" plus the meaning of the simplex, but a few causatives have slightly different meanings: for example, *swḏ* "bequeath, hand over," from *wḏ* "command."

Although all causatives have an initial radical *s*, not all roots beginning with *s* are causative: *stp* "select," for example, is a 3-lit. root, not a causative. Egyptologists can generally determine if a verb is causative or not from its meaning, by the fact that it has an attested simplex (there is no verb **tp*, for example, that could be the simplex of *stp*), and by the fact that causative roots often behave differently than other roots with the same number and kinds of radicals. The seven causative classes are:

9. **caus. 2-lit.** (causative biliteral) — causatives of 2-lit. roots: example, 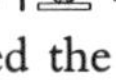 *smn* "fix, set," from  *mn* "become fixed, set." In Old Egyptian this class also included the causatives of 3-lit. roots with initial *w* or *j*, since these consonants were lost in the causative: for example,  *ssḫ* "broaden," from *wsḫ* "become broad." In Middle Egyptian, however, such roots are normally treated like other 3-lit. roots in the causative (*swsḫ*).

   Base stem: *smn*
   Geminated stem: none.

10 **caus. 2ae-gem.** (causative second-geminate) — mostly causatives of 2ae-gem. roots: example,  *sqbb* "cool, make cool" (transitive), from 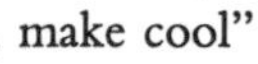 "cool, become cool" (intransitive). Some verbs of this class are from reduplicated 2-lit. roots: for example,  *sfkk* "devastate," related to  *fk* "become desolate" (the root **fkk* does not exist).

Base stem: *sqb* (rare)
Geminated stem: *sqbb*.

11. **caus. 3-lit.** (causative triliteral) — causatives of 3-lit. roots: example,  *sꜥnḫ* "give life, make live," from 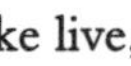 *ꜥnḫ* "live."

Base stem: *sꜥnḫ*
Geminated stem: none.

12. **caus. 3ae-inf.** (causative third-weak) — causatives of 3ae-inf. roots: example,  *sḫpj* "lead," from  *ḫpj* "walk."

Base stem: *sḫp*
Geminated stem: *sḫpp* (rare).

13. **caus. 4-lit.** (causative quadriliteral) — causatives of 4-lit. roots: example,  *s3ḫ3ḫ* "make verdant," from  *3ḫ3ḫ* "become verdant." This is one of the few verbs of this class that can be traced to a 4-lit. simplex. Other caus. 4-lit. verbs are reduplicated caus. 2-lit. roots: for example,  *sḫdḫd* "invert," from  *sḫd* "invert." No caus. 4-lit. verbs from nonreduplicated 4-lit. roots (*s*ABCD) are known.

Base stem: *s3ḫ3ḫ*
Geminated stem: none.

14 **caus. 4ae-inf.** (causative fourth-weak) — causatives of 4ae-inf. roots: example,  *sb3gj* "make weary," from  *b3gj* "become weary."

Base stem: *sb3g*
Geminated stem: none.

15. **caus. 5-lit.** (causative quinquiliteral) — causatives of 5-lit. roots: example,  *snḫbḫb* "cause to draw back," from  *nḫbḫb* "draw back." Some caus. 5-lit. roots are formed from reduplicated 3-lit. roots: for example,  *snšmšm* "file," from  *nšm* "cut."

Base stem: *snḫbḫb*
Geminated stem: none.

Each Middle Egyptian verb belongs to one of the fifteen root classes. Although the classes are numerous, they are not all equally well represented. The most common are those with 3-lit., 3ae-inf., and 2-lit. roots: about two-thirds of all verbs belong to one of these three classes. Verbs with more than three radicals are relatively infrequent, except for the 4ae-inf. class. The same is true for the causatives, with the exception of caus. 2-lit. verbs. It is theoretically possible that Egyptian possessed some caus. 3ae-gem. roots, but no verbs of this class have yet been found.

It is important to know the root class of a verb, because this determines the shape of many of its forms. Egyptian is similar to English in this respect. Speakers of English have to learn, for example, that *fall* is a "strong" verb and *call* is a "weak" verb: even though these two verbs look alike, they belong to different classes because they form their past tense and past participle differently (*fell* vs. *called*, *fallen* vs. *called*). Grammars of English do not teach the individual form of each verb in the language. Instead, they teach **paradigms** (see § 7.12 end). The paradigm of "weak" verbs, for example, indicates that their past tense and past participle is formed by adding *–ed* to the root. All "weak" verbs follow this paradigm: *call / called*, *dictate / dictated*, *synthesize / synthesized*, and so forth. It is up to the student of English to learn (from a dictionary) whether a particular verb is "weak" or not. Once this is known, the student can then produce all the proper forms of the verb by applying the paradigm.

Learning English is complicated by the fact that the class of a verb is not evident from its root: *fall* and *call*, for example, look quite similar. Moreover, not all "strong" verbs behave alike: *bring*, for instance, has the form *brought* in the past tense and past participle, while the similar-looking verb *sing* has the past tense *sang* and the past participle *sung*. Fortunately, Egyptian does not have these difficulties. The different root classes generally look different from each other, and all the verbs of a particular root class generally follow the same paradigm in producing their forms. This makes Egyptian verb forms easier to learn than those of English.

13.6 Anomalous verbs

Like most languages, Middle Egyptian has several irregular verbs, which do not behave like other verbs of their class. Most of these are irregular only in one particular form, and are therefore generally considered along with other verbs of the class. Two 3ae-inf. verbs, however, are markedly different from other verbs of this class in many respects. For this reason, they are considered separately, in a class of **anomalous** (anom.) verbs.

1. ***rdj* "give, put, cause"**

The verb *rdj* is spelled with the biliteral signs 𓏙 or 𓂞. The first of these signs originally had the value *ḏj*, but by Middle Egyptian it had become *dj* (see § 2.8.3). The second sign, which combines the first sign with a determinative 𓂝, has the value *dj*; it is often written 𓂝. The verb *rdj* has two base stems and an irregular geminated stem:

Base stem:	*dj*	(𓏙, 𓂞, 𓂝)
	rdj	(𓂋𓏙, 𓂋𓂞, 𓂋𓂝)
Geminated stem:	*dd*	(𓏙𓏙, 𓂞𓂞, 𓂝𓂝).

The two base stems are generally complementary — that is, *dj* is used in some verb forms and *rdj* in others — but some forms can use either base stem.

2. ***jwj* and *jj* "come, return"**

Egyptian originally had two verbs meaning "come, return": *jwj*, spelled with the biliteral sign 𓂻 *jw*, usually with a phonetic complement (𓂻𓅱, 𓂻𓏲, rarely just 𓂻); and *jj*, spelled with the sign 𓇋 *j*, often with a phonetic complement and determinative (𓇋𓇋𓂻, 𓇋𓂻 *jj*). Both verbs behave like 3ae-inf. roots in some respects, but the final radical of *jwj* is rarely written and that of *jj* (*jjj*) never is. They seem to be separate verbs in Old Egyptian, though the difference in meaning between them is not clear. By Middle Egyptian, however, they are mostly treated like different forms of a single verb:

Base stem: *j*, *jj* (, 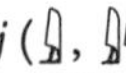, 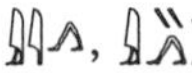)
jw (, , )
Geminated stem: *jw* (, , ), very rarely *jww* ().

The two base stems, *j*/*jj* and *jw*, are generally complementary, but some forms of this verb can use either base stem.

13.7 Defective verbs

Most verbs can be used in most forms of the Egyptian verbal system. A few verbs, however, can appear in only one or two forms. These are known as **defective** verbs. In English, the verb *can* (for example) is defective, because it only appears in the present and past tenses (*can*, *could*). Middle Egyptian has a number of defective verbs. The most important is the negative verb  *jmj* "not be, not do." Although this is a 3ae-inf. root, it is used in only two verb forms.

Essay 13. The Creative Word

The Heliopolitan creation accounts are concerned primarily with the physical evolution of Atum into the forces and elements of the world. Occasionally, however, the texts deal with the relationship between the physical aspect of creation and the intellectual component of the creator's will. In one text, for example, Atum says of himself:

I made my body evolve through my effectiveness.
I am the one who made me.
I built myself as I wanted, according to my heart.

To the ancient Egyptians, the heart was the seat of thought as well as emotion (see Essay 7). When Atum says "I built myself as I wanted, according to my heart," this implies that his physical evolution was the result of his initial concept of what the world would be like.

The link between the creator's idea of the world and its actual creation lies in the first sentence of this text: "I made my body evolve through my effectiveness." The term 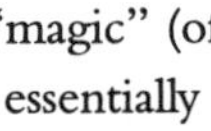 *3ḫw* "effectiveness" is an abstract noun related to the adjective 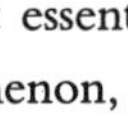 *3ḫ* "effective." This quality is often associated with intellectual activity or speech: an Egyptian official might say, for example, 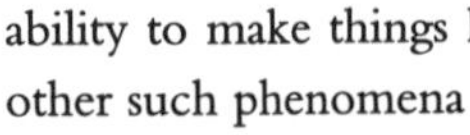 *jnk jqr sḫr 3ḫ n nwt.f* "I am one excellent of advice, effective for his town," or he might describe himself as 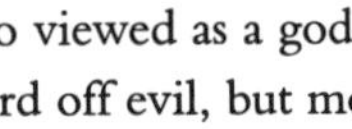 *3ḫ ḏd ḥr jb n nb.f* "effective of speech on the heart of his lord" (i.e., in his lord's opinion).

The quality of "effectiveness" is also closely related to the concept of  *ḥk3* "magic" (often plural 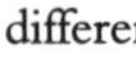 *ḥk3w* "magic spells, magic acts"). In ancient Egypt, "magic" meant essentially the ability to make things happen by indirect means. It was seen as a natural phenomenon, and like other such phenomena was also viewed as a god. Magic could involve physical means, such as the use of amulets or images to ward off evil, but most often it was associated with the power of creative speech: that is, speech that is "effective" enough to cause a desired result. The expressions "recite by magic" (*šdj m ḥk3w*) and "speak with effectiveness" (*ḏd m 3ḫw*) are often used together, as different ways of saying the same thing.

Ordinary people could make use of this force: in one text the creator describes how he made magic for people "as weapons to be a barrier against what might happen." But magic is most often associated with the king and the gods. In this respect it has two components, which the Egyptians called  *sj3* "perception" and 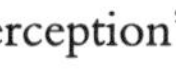 *ḥw* "annunciation." Perception is the ability to see what needs to be done, and annunciation is the power to make it happen through speech. The king's courtiers say to him, for example, "Annunciation is in your mouth, perception is in your heart: your speech is the shrine of Maat."

Just as the human king rules through the "effective" use of perception and annunciation, the sun rules the universe through the same forces. Images of the solar bark often show the sun accompanied by the gods Sia (Perception), Hu (Annunciation), and Heka (Magic). Such images reflect not only the sun's daily rule but also his daily re-creation of the world at sunrise (see Essay 9). And this in turn recalls the first act of creation, when the creator used the same forces to create the world at the very first sunrise: he "perceived" the world in his heart and brought it about by "announcing" his perception. The creation accounts often make reference to this process, when they have the creator say, for example, "I surveyed in my own heart," "I used my own mouth," and "I am the one who made what is, who caused what was not to evolve: when I spoke, Annunciation came into being."

This understanding of the creation as an act of perception and speech is quite similar to the one that underlies the story of creation in the Bible:

> God said, "Let there be light," and there was light [annunciation].
> God saw the light, that it was good [perception]. (Gen. 1:3–4)

In the Egyptian view, the creation of the world was an act of "magic." In fact, the creation of magic was sometimes seen as the first step in the creation itself. In one text the god Magic says: "I am the one whom the Sole Lord made before two things had evolved in this world ... when something came from his mouth ... when he took Annunciation in his mouth."

Although Perception, Annunciation, and Magic were seen as gods in their own right, the power of creative speech was most often associated with the god Ptah ( *ptḥ*), the patron deity of Memphis. This relationship was particularly common in the New Kingdom, but it appears already in an early Middle Kingdom text, where Ptah says of himself in relation to the creator:

>  *ḫr ntt jnk js ḥw tp(j) r.f sj3 jm(j) ẖt.f*
> "for I am Annunciation, who is in his mouth, and Perception, who is in his belly."

The reasons for this association will be discussed in the next Essay.

EXERCISE 13

For each of the following verbs, identify the root class and indicate (from the English translation) whether the verb is primarily transitive or intransitive.

1. *3ḫ* become effective
2. *jp* allot, assign
3. *jnj* fetch, use
4. *jrj* do, make
5. *jṯj* take possession of
6. *ꜥnḫ* live
7. *ꜥḥ3* fight
8. *ꜥḥꜥ* stand up
9. *w3ḥ* put, set
10. *wꜥb* become clean
11. *wnn* exist
12. *wḥm* repeat
13. *wdfj* be late, dawdle
14. *wḏ* command
15. *b3gj* become weary
16. *prj* go out, go up
17. *pḥrr* run
18. *psḏj* shine
19. *ptpt* trample
20. *f3j* carry
21. *m33* see
22. *mwt* die
23. *mrj* desire, want, like
24. *msḏj* hate
25. *mdwj* speak, talk
26. *njtjt* stammer
27. *nḥm* take away
28. *rwj* go away
29. *h3j* go down
30. *h3b* send
31. *ḥjḥj* seek
32. *ḥwj* hit
33. *ḥmsj* sit down
34. *ḥqr* hunger
35. *ḥtp* become calm, content
36. *ḫꜥj* appear
37. *ḫpr* evolve, happen
38. *ḫntj* go forward/upstream/south
39. *ḫr* fall
40. *ḫdj* go downstream/north
41. *s3ḫ* make effective
42. *sꜥnḫ* make live, nourish
43. *sꜥḥꜥ* erect
44. *sꜥq* introduce, bring in
45. *spdḏ* prepare
46. *sfḫḫ* loosen
47. *smn* set, fix
48. *smnḫ* make functional
49. *sn* smell, kiss
50. *snḏ* become afraid
51. *snḏm* sweeten
52. *srwj* remove
53. *sh3j* bring down
54. *sḫpr* bring about
55. *sḫm* gain control
56. *sḫr* fell, overthrow
57. *sšmj* lead
58. *stj* shoot
59. *sḏr* lie down, spend the night
60. *šmj* go, walk
61. *šmsj* follow
62. *šzp* receive
63. *šdj* take along
64. *qm3* throw
65. *qd* build
66. *qdd* sleep
67. *gmj* find
68. *gmgm* smash
69. *gr* become still
70. *tmm* close, shut
71. *ṯzj* pick up
72. *dr* remove, repulse
73. *ḏ3j* cross
74. *ḏd* say, speak

14. The Infinitival Forms

14.1 Definitions

When they are used in actual phrases, clauses, or sentences, verbs must appear in a particular form, just as nouns must be singular, plural, or dual, and adjectives must be singular or plural and masculine or feminine. In both Egyptian and English, verb forms are of two different kinds. Verb forms that describe action just as action, without reference to any tense, mood, aspect, or voice, are called **nonfinite** or **infinitival**. English has two such forms, the infinitive (for example, *to learn*) and the gerund (for example, *learning*). In many places these two forms can be used interchangeably: for instance, *To learn Egyptian requires patience* and *Learning Egyptian requires patience.* Middle Egyptian has three infinitival forms, each of which we will meet in this lesson: the infinitive, complementary infinitive, and negatival complement.

Most verb forms are **finite**: that is, they indicate an action that has a particular tense, aspect, mood, or voice (or combination of these features). In the English sentence *Jack was being summoned*, for example, the verb form *was being summoned* is past (tense), imperfect (aspect), indicative (mood), and passive (voice). The finite verb forms of Middle Egyptian will be covered in subsequent lessons.

THE INFINITIVE

14.2 Definition

The **infinitive** is a verb form used to refer to action just as action, without reference to any tense, mood, aspect, or voice. The infinitive actually belongs to a special class of words, known as **verbal nouns**, which are used to describe action as such.

English has not only the infinitive and gerund but also words such as *involvement* (the action of being involved), *condescension* (the action of being condescending), and *taxation* (the action of taxing), which are verbal nouns made from the verb root plus different suffixes, and words such as *fear, love,* and *hate* (the actions of fearing, loving, and hating), which are verbal nouns made just from the verb root itself. The infinitive in English has a special form that distinguishes it from other verbal nouns, consisting of the preposition *to* plus the verb root (as in *to learn, to involve, to fear,* and so forth).

Like English, Egyptian also has a number of different verbal nouns, one of which is the infinitive. The infinitive in Egyptian often corresponds to the English infinitive, but in other cases it is best translated by an English gerund or another verbal noun. Unlike the infinitive in English, the Egyptian infinitive cannot be recognized just by its form: in many cases it looks like other verbal nouns. What distinguishes the infinitive in Egyptian is its syntax: that is, the way it is used grammatically (see § 12.1). In the following sections we will look first at the form of the infinitive (which Egyptologists have determined by examining its different uses) and then at the various ways in which it is used.

14.3 The form of the infinitive

The Middle Egyptian infinitive has two forms: one with the base or geminated stem and no ending, and one with the base stem plus an ending *–t*. These two forms are complementary: some verbs use the form without an ending and others the form ending in *–t*. The choice of form depends on the verb class (§ 13.5) or, in some cases, the kind of verb. The paradigm of the infinitive is as follows:

1. **Regular forms**

2-LIT.	BASE	*ḏd* "to say, saying"
2AE-GEM.	GEMINATED	*m33* "to see, seeing"
3-LIT.	BASE	*nḥm* "to take away, taking away"
3AE-INF.	BASE + *t*	*jrt* "to do, doing"
3AE-GEM.	GEMINATED	*pḥrr* "to run, running"
4-LIT.	BASE	*wsṯn* "to stride, striding"
		ptpt "to trample, trampling"
4AE-INF.	BASE	*msḏ* "to hate, hating" (geminating verbs)
	BASE + *t*	*ḥmst* "to sit, sitting" (nongeminating verbs)
5-LIT.	BASE	*nhmhm* "to yell, yelling"
CAUS. 2-LIT.	BASE + *t*	*smnt* "to fix, fixing"
CAUS. 2AE-GEM.	GEMINATED	*sqbb* "to cool, cooling"
CAUS. 3-LIT.	BASE	*sḥtp* "to calm, calming"
CAUS. 3AE-INF.	BASE + *t*	*sẖpt* "to lead, leading"
CAUS. 4-LIT.	BASE	*sẖdẖd* "to invert, inverting"
CAUS. 4AE-INF.	BASE	*sm3w* "to renew, renewing"
CAUS. 5-LIT.	BASE	*snšmšm* "to file, filing"
ANOM.	BASE + *t*	, (rarely ,) *rdjt, djt* "to give, giving"
		, *jt, jjt* "to come, coming"
		, *jwt* "to come, coming."

Based on this chart, the general rule for forming the infinitive can be stated as follows: verbs with final-weak roots form their infinitive with the base stem plus *–t* (3ae-inf., 4ae-inf., caus. 3ae-inf., and anom. verbs), and the other classes have an infinitive that looks like the root. The exceptions to this rule are 4ae-inf. verbs that can have a geminated stem (§ 13.5.7) and caus. 4ae-inf. verbs, which behave like strong verbs (base stem with no ending); and caus. 2-lit. verbs, which behave like weak verbs (base stem plus *–t*). The anomalous verbs can use either of their base stems in the infinitive: the verb *jj/jwj* "come" has either *jjt* or *jwt*; the verb *rdj* "give" normally uses the base stem with *r* (*rdjt*). Note that the ending *–t* is usually written **before** the determinative.

2. **Special forms**

There are three special exceptions to the general paradigm of the infinitive, all of which have to do with phonology (how the words sounded) rather than morphology (how the infinitive was formed).

a. Like the feminine ending, the ending *–t* of the infinitive was eventually lost in pronunciation (see § 2.8.3). Sometimes, therefore, an infinitive that should end in *–t* is written without this ending. This is more common for caus. 3ae-inf. verbs than it is for other classes that use this form: for example,  *smsj* "to cause to give birth," from 3ae-inf. *msj* (the "dual strokes" in this form show that the word ended in a vowel). But it is occasionally found with the infinitives of other classes as well: for instance, 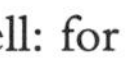 *ḥzj* "to sing" (3ae-inf.) and  *smn* "to fix" (caus. 2-lit.).

b. Verbs of the 2ae-gem. class usually have the geminated stem (i.e., the root) in the infinitive, but when the infinitive has a pronominal suffix the base stem is normally used instead: for example,  *wnn* "to exist, existing," but  *wn.f* "his existing." This variation between the two stems was probably due to the syllable structure of the two forms: the geminated stem was probably used in both forms, but in the suffixed form the geminated consonants were in contact and were therefore written only once (**wVnVn* vs. **wVnnVf*: see § 13.5.2).

c. The 2ae-gem. verb *m33* "see" also varies between geminated and base stems in the infinitive, like other verbs of the class:  *m33* (**mV3V3*) vs.  *m3.f* (**mV33Vf*). Unlike other 2ae-gem. verbs, however, *m33* sometimes uses the base form ( *m3*) in the infinitive even without a suffix. This is probably because the final *3* of the geminated stem was not actually pronounced as a consonant, and was therefore omitted in writing (see § 2.8.2): i.e.,  *m3(3)* = **mV3V*. The infinitive of *m33* sometimes also has a final *n*, usually before a pronominal suffix:  *m3n.f* "to see him." This *n* appears for the same reason that other Egyptian words sometimes vary between spellings with *3* and *n* (see § 2.8.3). It is nothing more than a variant spelling of whatever consonant is actually represented by *3* (see § 2.4): thus,  *m3.f* and  *m3n.f* both probably represent the spoken form **mV33Vf*. These various forms of the infinitive of *m33* can be summarized as follows:

WITH NO SUFFIX PRONOUN:	**mV3V3*	spelled , , rarely 
WITH A SUFFIX PRONOUN:	**mV33V*	spelled  or .

14.4 The subject of the infinitive

Like most other verb forms, the infinitive can have a subject, which is either a noun (or noun phrase) or a pronoun. In Middle Egyptian the subject of the infinitive can be expressed in two ways, each of which has a similar counterpart in English:

1. as an **agent**. When the subject is a noun or demonstrative pronoun, it is introduced by the preposition *jn* "by" (§ 8.2.2): for example,

 *nꜥt m ḫd jn ḥm.f* "traveling downstream by His Incarnation."[1]

1 The verb *nꜥj* "travel by boat" is 3ae-inf. The expression *m ḫd* "downstream" involves a verbal noun (not the infinitive) of 3ae-inf. *ḫdj* "go downstream": literally, "in going downstream."

When the agent is a personal pronoun, the **independent** form of the pronoun is used, without the preposition *jn* (which is not used with personal pronouns): for instance,

 *prt ntsn m s3 ḥm-k3.f* "emerging by them behind his ka-priest."

The pronoun here is actually the abbreviated form of the possessive construction with *n(j)* plus independent pronoun (§ 7.5.2), as can be seen from an example with the first-person singular form:

 *rwd nnk ḥr jb.f* "being firm by me in his opinion" —

literally, "being-firm belonging-to-me on his heart." Examples with a pronominal agent are relatively uncommon.

2. by the **direct genitive** (for nouns or demonstrative pronouns) or a **suffix** pronoun (for personal pronouns): for instance,

 *prt sm* "the emerging of the sem-priest" and

 *prt.s* "its emerging."

This construction is normal for intransitive verbs (such as *prj* "emerge"), but it can also be used for transitive verbs (see the next section). In rare cases the indirect genitive (§ 4.13.2) is used instead.

14.5 The object of the infinitive

The infinitive of transitive verbs can have an object as well as a subject: that is, a noun (or noun phrase) or pronoun indicating the person or thing on whom the action of the infinitive is performed. Like the infinitive's subject, its object can be expressed in two ways in Middle Egyptian:

1. by the **direct genitive** (for nouns or demonstrative pronouns) or a **suffix** pronoun (for personal pronouns). This construction is used when the subject of the infinitive either is not expressed or is expressed as an agent: for example,

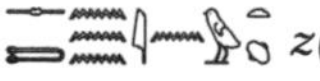 *z(3)t mw jn wt* "pouring water by the mortuary priest" and

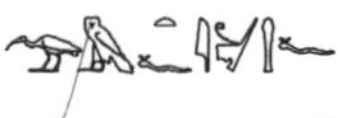 *gmt.f jn ḥm.f* "finding him by His Incarnation."

In each of these examples, the object is actually the possessor of the infinitive; English can use a similar possessive construction with its gerund: "the pouring of water by the mortuary priest" and "the finding of him by His Incarnation."

2. as a true object, by a noun, demonstrative pronoun, or **dependent** pronoun. This construction is used when the infinitive's subject is also expressed: for example,

 *jrt jst j3kb* "Isis's making mourning"

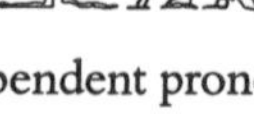 *ṯzt.j jb.j* "my lifting up my heart"

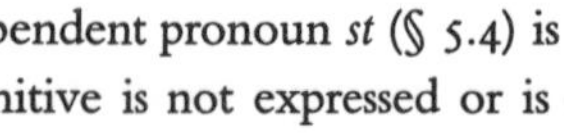 *rdjt.f wj m ḥ3t ẖrdw.f* "his placing me in front of his children."

The dependent pronoun *st* (§ 5.4) is also used as object of the infinitive, even when the subject of the infinitive is not expressed or is expressed as an agent, if the pronoun refers to things rather than people or to more than one person or thing: for instance,

 *rdjt st ḥr mrḥt* "adding it to oil" (literally, "putting it upon oil").

Here the pronoun refers to *msdmt* "galena" (a mineral), so *st* is used instead of the 3fs suffix-pronoun *.s* — i.e., instead of **rdjt.s ḥr mrḥt*, which we might otherwise expect according to the rule described in § 14.5.1.

14.6 Word-order

The first three examples in § 14.5.2 demonstrate the **basic rule of word-order** in Middle Egyptian verbal clauses: the verb comes first, followed by the subject and object. Grammarians call this a **VSO** word-order (Verb-Subject-Object); by contrast, English has an **SVO** word-order (as you can see from the translations of the three examples).

Although the subject normally comes before the object, pronouns also come before nouns. The basic pattern of Middle Egyptian verbal clauses is therefore actually **VsoSO**, where the small letters refer to pronouns and the capital letters to nouns. In this pattern the subject still comes before the object **except** when the subject is nominal and the object is pronominal: here the **VsoSO** rule requires the object to come before the subject (**VoS**): for instance,

rdjt sw rᶜ "Re showing himself" (literally, "Re giving himself"),

where *rᶜ* "Re" is the nominal subject and *sw* "him(self)" is the pronominal object.

Other elements, such as prepositional phrases and adverbs, normally follow the subject and object (as with *m ḥ3t ẖrdw.f* in the third example of § 14.5.2). The only exception to this order is the dative *n* with a suffix pronoun (**d**); this normally comes before everything except a pronominal subject (see § 10.7): for example,

rdjt n.f t-ḥḏ "giving him white-bread,"

jrt n.f st "to do it for him," and

rdjt.k n.j (n)swyt.k "your giving me your kingship."

When the preposition *n* is followed by a noun, however, it comes after the subject and object, like other adjuncts (**A**: prepositional phrases and adverbs): for instance,

rdjt mnṯw t3wj n jtj "Montu's giving the Two Lands to the sovereign."

The full word-order of a Middle Egyptian verbal clause is thus **VsdoSOA**. Although the order may seem complicated, it is actually quite logical. A pronominal subject (**s**) always comes first because suffix pronouns are actually part of the word they are attached to (§ 5.3). Pronominal datives (**d**) and objects (**o**) are separate words, but they were probably pronounced together with the verb, without a separate stress of their own. In this case, Egyptian was probably much like English. Thus, the clause *rdjt n.f t-ḥḏ* probably had only two stresses (one on *rdjt-n.f* and the second on *t-ḥḏ*), just as in the English translation ("GIVing-him WHITE-bread"); similarly, *rdjt.k n.j (n)swyt.k* probably had one stress on *rdjt.k-n.j* and a second on *(n)swyt.k* (as in the English translation "your-GIVing-me your-KINGship"), while *jrt n.f st* probably had only one (as in its English translation "to DO it for him"). Nominal subjects, objects, and datives, on the other hand, tend to be stressed separately: *rdjt mnṯw t3wj n jtj* "MONtu's GIVing the-Two-LANDS to-the-SOVereign."

It is important to memorize the normal **VsdoSOA** word-order. Although there are occasional exceptions to this order, they are rare. In Egyptian, as in English, the order of the words is sometimes the only thing that tells you what is the subject and the object in a verbal clause.

14.7 The infinitive with a direct genitive

The different constructions that Egyptian uses to express the subject and object of an infinitive seem quite complicated at first sight, but they are actually no more so than the various constructions that English uses for the same purpose. A noun introduced by *jn*, or an independent pronoun, is always the agent of the infinitive, while a dependent pronoun is always the object of the infinitive (§ 14.5.2).

Only a suffix pronoun or a noun used in a direct genitive with the infinitive of a transitive verb is ambiguous, since these can represent either the infinitive's subject or its object: thus, *gmt.f* (by itself) could be either "his finding" (subject) or "finding him" (object), and *rdjt mnṯw* (by itself) could mean either "Montu's giving" (subject) or "giving Montu" (object). The ambiguity actually exists in the genitival relationship itself, and it exists not only in Egyptian but in the English genitive as well. An English phrase such as *the assembling of an army*, for example, can refer both to an act of assembling performed by an army as the subject or an act of assembling in which an army is the object. In the same way, an Egyptian phrase such as *rdjt mnṯw* "the giving of Montu" could refer to the god Montu as subject or object. In both languages, only the context in which the phrase is used indicates which meaning is actually meant — although sometimes only one of the two meanings is likely: for example, *z3ṯ mw* "the pouring of water" probably refers to water as the thing that is poured (object), not the pourer (subject).

English can get around this ambiguity by using a passive gerund or infinitive, as in *the army's being assembled* or *for the army to be assembled*. In Egyptian, however, the infinitive is always active: there is no passive infinitive. This is true even though good English sometimes requires a passive translation of the Egyptian infinitive, as we will see in some of the following sections.

14.8 The infinitive as a noun

As we noted in § 14.2, the infinitive is actually a verbal noun: that is, a noun that describes the action of a verb. Because it is a noun, it can be used in most of the same ways that other nouns are used. We have already seen that the infinitive can be the first noun of a direct genitive and can have a suffix pronoun. Like other nouns, it can also be modified by an adjective or an indirect genitive: for example,

 *p3 ḫnt nfr n p3 ḥq(3)* "the good upstream sailing of the ruler."[2]

Unlike other nouns, however, the infinitive cannot be made plural and it is always **masculine**, even when it has the ending *–t*:

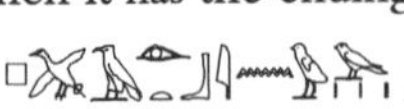 *p3 jrt bjnw* "this doing of bad things."

A form that does not conform to this rule is not the infinitive but another verbal noun, even though it may look like the infinitive: for instance, *prt.f tpt* "his first emergence." In many cases such apparent infinitives actually have a different form than the infinitive, with a weak consonant that is not written: thus, the verbal noun *ꜥḥꜥw* "stance" can be written like the 3-lit. infinitive *ꜥḥꜥ* "to stand up," and the verbal noun "love" can look like the 3ae-inf. infinitive *mrt* "to love."

2 The verb *ḫntj* "go upstream" is 4ae-inf. For *p3* "the," see § 5.10.3.

14.9 The infinitive in headings

Like English, Egyptian uses its infinitive in many different ways. We will examine all but one of these uses in the following sections; the remaining one is the subject of the next lesson.

The infinitive is often found in headings, such as the hieroglyphic labels to carved or painted scenes and the titles of texts: for example,

> *m33 k3t m jz* "Seeing the work on the tomb"
> (label of a scene showing the tomb-owner watching this activity)
>
> *prt m hrw* "Coming forth by day"
> (title of the collection of funerary spells known as the Book of the Dead)
>
> *srwḫ ᶜnwt nt s3ḫw ḏbᶜw* "Treating the nails of the toes and fingers"
> (title of a section in a medical papyrus).

The most common such heading, found in religious and magical texts, is (usually abbreviated) *ḏd-mdw* "recitation" — literally, "saying words." This normally introduces the text proper, after any other headings, or the speech of the various participants in a ceremony or scene. When such texts are written in vertical columns, sometimes stands at the head of each column as well as at the beginning of the text; in this case the heading serves as a kind of "quotation mark," and is not meant to be read.

14.10 The infinitive after the indirect genitive

Like other nouns, the infinitive can serve as the second noun of an indirect genitive, after the genitival adjective *n(j)*: for instance,

> *hrw pf n ᶜḥ3 rḥwj* "that day of the two companions' fighting"
>
> *r n wn sb(3) n b3* "Spell (literally, 'mouth') of opening a gate to the ba"
>
> *pẖrt nt sm3 ḫf(3)t* "Prescription for (literally, 'of') killing a snake."

When the first noun of the indirect genitive is undefined, the genitival phrase is often best translated as a relative clause with a passive verb: for example,

> *z(j) jqr n wb3 n.f jb* "an excellent man who can be confided in"
>
> *jty n ᶜbᶜb m rn.f* "a sovereign whose name can be boasted of" —

literally, "an excellent man of opening the heart to him" and "a sovereign of boasting about his name."

14.11 The infinitive as the object of a preposition

Since it is a noun, the infinitive can be used as the object of a preposition, like other nouns. Some examples of this use have special meanings.

1. after *ḥr* "upon"

The preposition *ḥr* followed by the infinitive sometimes has the meaning "because of" an action or "from" an action (see § 8.2.10), as in *ḥr st3s.j r m(w)t* "because of dragging me toward death" and *jt ḥm.j ḥr dr rṯnw* "the return of My Incarnation from repelling Retjenu." Most often, however, the combination of *ḥr* and an infinitive expresses

concomitant action: that is, action that goes on at the same time as that of a preceding clause. In this use, the prepositional phrase is usually best translated in English by an "...ing" form of the verb, with or without an introductory word such as "when" or "while": for example,

 *dbn.n.j ꜥf3y.j ḥr nhm*

"I went around my camp yelling" or "I went around my camp while yelling"

 *gm.n.f sw ḥr prt m sb3*

"He found him emerging from the gate."

Here the prepositional phrases *ḥr nhm* (literally, "upon yelling") and *ḥr prt m sb3* (literally, "upon emerging from the gate") describe an action that is concomitant with that of the past-tense actions *dbn.n.j ꜥf3y.j* "I went around my camp" and *gm.n.f sw* "he found him."

2. **after** *m* **"in"**

A prepositional phrase with the preposition *m* and the infinitive is also used to describe concomitant action: for instance,

 *gm.n.f sw m prt m sb3*

"He found him emerging from the gate" —

literally, "he found him in (the act of) emerging from the gate." The infinitive is less common after *m* than after *ḥr*. More often, *m* is used with a verbal noun (which can look like the infinitive): for example, *m ḫd* "going downstream, north" (the infinitive of 3ae-inf. *ḫdj* is *ḫdt*), *m ḫntyt* "going upstream, south" (the infinitive of 4ae-inf. *ḫntj* is *ḫnt*), and *m wḥm* "again" (literally, "in repeating").

3. **after** *r* **"to"**

The combination of the preposition *r* and the infinitive is normally used to describe **purpose**. It is regularly translated with the English infinitive, sometimes preceded by "in order": for example,

 *ḫnt.k(w) r jnt b(j3)w n nbw*

"I sailed upstream to get gold ore" or "I sailed upstream in order to get gold ore."[3]

This construction is very common in Middle Egyptian. It almost always indicates purpose, except in the expression *r ḏd*, which can mean "saying" (used to introduce a direct quotation) as well as "in order to say."

4. **after other prepositions**

The meaning of other combinations of a preposition and the infinitive is fairly straightforward: for instance,

 *ḏd mdw ḫft swrj pẖrt*

"Words to be said in accordance with drinking the prescription."[4]

This is also true of the infinitive plus a compound preposition, as in *m ḫt jt* "after returning" (literally, "in the wake of returning").

3 *ḫnt.k(w)* is a 1s form of the verb *ḫntj* "go upstream." This form, called the stative, will be discussed in Lesson 17.

4 The spelling of the 3-lit. infinitive *swr/swj* is etymological (originally *swr*, later *swj*): see § 2.8.3.

14.12 The infinitive as the object of a verb

Like other nouns, the infinitive can be used as the object of a transitive verb. This use is found most often after the following kinds of verbs:

- verbs of desire and emotion, such as *3bj* "desire," *mrj* "want," *snḏ* "fear"
- verbs of perception and cognition, such as *m33* "see," *rḫ* "know (how), learn (how)," *ḫmt* "think,"[5] *sḫ3* "remember," *k3j* "plan"
- verbs of speech and assignment, such as *wḏ* "command," *š3j* "determine," *rdj* "give," *ḏd* "intend, think" (literally, "say")
- verbs of starting and stopping, such as *3b* "stop," *wḥm* "repeat, do again," *š3ᶜ* "start, begin."

Most of these uses have similar counterparts in English: for example, *want to do, know how to do, remember to do, command* (someone) *to do* (something), *stop doing*. Examples in Egyptian are usually similar to English constructions: for example,

> *3b.n ḥm.j jrt mnw n (j)t(j).j jmn-rᶜ*
> "My Incarnation has desired to make a monument for my father Amun-Re"
>
> *k3.n.f ḥ3q mnmn.j* "He planned to plunder my herd"
>
> *wḏ.n.j n.k jrt st* "I have commanded you to do it"
>
> *wḥm.n.j m33 nḫtw.f*
> "I saw again (literally, 'I repeated seeing') his victories."

14.13 The infinitive in nonverbal sentences

Like other nouns, the infinitive can be used as the subject of a nonverbal predicate, or as the predicate in a nominal sentence: for example,

> *m.k nfr sḏm n r(m)ṯ* "Look, to listen is good for people"
>
> *nn n.s prt m jmnt* "Emerging from the West is not for her"
>
> *jr pšn ḏnnt.f jwd p3qt pw r p3qt nt ḏnnt.f*
> "As for splitting apart his skull, it is parting one plate of his skull from another."

In the first of these examples the infinitive *sḏm* "to hear" is the subject of the adjectival predicate *nfr* "good"; in the second, the infinitive phrase *prt m jmnt* "emerging from the West" is subject of the adverbial predicate *n.s* "for her" (see § 11.9.3).

The third example comes from a medical papyrus: it describes what is meant by the physician "splitting apart" the skull of a patient.[6] This is explained (literally) with the words "it is the parting of a plate with respect to a plate of his skull." Here the infinitive phrase *jwd p3qt* "the parting of a plate" is the predicate of an A *pw* nominal sentence, with the prepositional phrase *r p3qt nt ḏnnt.f* "from a plate of his skull" added. This kind of construction is common in explanations.

5 The "plural strokes" are a determinative, borrowed from the word *ḫmtw* "three" (§ 9.2).
6 *pšn* "splitting apart" is also an infinitive, object of the initial preposition *jr* "as for" (see § 8.2.7).

14.14 The infinitive in narration

Narration (the describing of past events) normally involves finite verb forms, but Middle Egyptian sometimes uses the infinitive for this purpose as well. Three such infinitival constructions are found in Middle Egyptian texts.

1. **In headings**

The beginning of a narration, or the beginning of major divisions within a narration, can use the infinitive to "set the scene" for the narration that follows. This use is especially common after dates: for example,

ḥsbt 2 ẖr ḥm n … (n)swt bjt(j) Ḫᶜ-SḪM-Rᶜ z3-r3 NFR-ḤTP … ḫᶜt ḥm.f ḥr st ḥrw m ᶜḥ

"Year 2 during the incarnation of … the King of Upper and Lower Egypt KHA-SEKHEM-RE, son of Re NEFER-HOTEP … Appearing of His Incarnation on the Horus-throne in the palace."[7]

This example comes from a stela of the 13th-Dynasty king Neferhotep I, which describes how the king appeared (*ḫᶜt*) in formal audience to issue a decree for the temple of Osiris at Abydos. This construction is similar to the use of the infinitive in other headings (§ 14.9).

2. **The "narrative" infinitive**

Some Middle Egyptian stories use the infinitive instead of a normal finite verb form within the body of a narration. Unlike the infinitive in headings, this use of the form normally has to be translated by a past tense in English, rather than by an infinitive or gerund: for example,

 *rdjt.f wj m ḥ3t ẖrdw.f* "He put me in front of his children" —

literally, "his placing me in front of his children." It is not always clear why such texts use the infinitive in place of a normal finite verb form,[8] but the construction seems to occur most often after major breaks in the narrative — at places where a modern novel might begin a new section or chapter. In that sense this use of the infinitive is comparable to the one described in the preceding paragraph.

3. **The *sḏm pw jr.n.f* and *sḏm pw jry* constructions**

The infinitive is also commonly used in narration in a special construction that Egyptologists call the *sḏm pw jr.n.f* construction. This is an A *pw* B nominal sentence in which A is an infinitive (such as *sḏm* "to hear") or infinitive phrase and B is the verb form 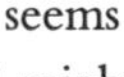 *jr.n* plus a noun or suffix pronoun as subject: for example, *jr.n.f*, meaning "what he did."[9] The construction *sḏm pw jr.n.f* means "what he did was to hear." It is often used in narration in much the same way that its translation is used in English narratives: for example,

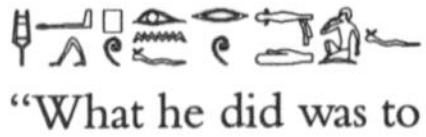 *ᶜḥᶜ pw jr.n.f r wšd.f*

"What he did was to stand up in order to address him."[10]

7 The omitted parts of this example contain the titulary and epithets of the king.

8 In other copies of this story the normal past-tense (finite) form *rdj.n.f* "he put" is used instead of the infinitive.

9 *jr.n.f* (etc.) is the verb form known as the perfect relative. It will be discussed in Lesson 24.

10 For *r wšd.f*, which also contains the infinitive, see § 14.11.3, above.

The *sḏm pw jr.n.f* construction also has a passive form, in which the verb form *jr.n.f* is replaced by the passive participle *jry*, meaning "what was done": for instance,

 *jwt pw jry r b3k jm* "What was done was to come for yours truly."

Like the narrative infinitive, the *sḏm pw jr.n.f* construction and its passive counterpart *sḏm pw jry* (which is much rarer) seem to occur after breaks in the narration — mostly at places where the translation might begin a new paragraph.

14.15 The infinitive after negations

The infinitive can be used like other nouns in the negation of existence, after the negative particle *nn* (§ 11.4) or the negative relative adjective *jwtj* (§ 12.9):

1. **after *nn***

The infinitive after the negative particle *nn* expresses an action whose existence is denied. This construction is most often found in unmarked adverb clauses (§ 12.17): for example,

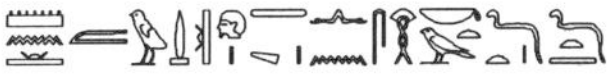 *mn m wḏ3 tp t3 nn skt ḏt ḏt*
"to remain in soundness on earth, without the body's expiring forever."

Here the first clause describes an action (using the infinitive *mn* "to remain") and the adverb clause indicates how that action is carried out.

2. **after *jwtj***

In § 12.9 we saw how the negative relative adjective *jwtj* followed by a genitival noun phrase expresses the non-possession of something as a relative clause. The same construction can be used, with a similar meaning, with an infinitive instead of a regular noun: for example,

 *jnk nṯr ꜥ3 ... jwtj ḫsf.f*
"I am the great god ... who is not barred,"

literally, "who his barring is not." In this case, and in most other examples of this construction, the suffix pronoun (or direct genitive, with a noun) is the object of the infinitive.

The Negative Infinitive and the Negatival Complement

14.16 Definition

In the negative constructions discussed in the preceding section, the infinitive itself is not negative: instead, it describes an affirmative action ("the body's expiring," "the barring of him") whose existence is negated (by *nn* or *jwtj*). English can negate the infinitive or the gerund itself: for instance, *the body's not expiring* and *to not bar him* (or *not to bar him*). In Egyptian the infinitive is made negative by using the infinitive of the 2-lit. verb *tm* (, ) "finish, fail, not be, not do" followed by a special verb form known as the **negatival complement**: for example,

 *tm m(w)t m wḥm* "Not dying again" or "To not die again."[11]

In this construction the negation is expressed by the infinitive *tm* "not, to not" and the verb itself by the negatival complement that follows it: here *m(w)t* "dying, die."

11 Title of a funerary spell. For *m wḥm*, literally "in repeating," see § 14.11.2.

14.17 The form of the negatival complement

The negatival complement of all verbs except those with geminated roots is formed with the base stem plus an ending *–w*, which is often not written; the negatival complement of verbs with geminated roots uses the geminated stem without an ending:

2-LIT.	*mḥ* "fill," *3dw* "be eager"
2AE-GEM.	*m33* "see"
3-LIT.	*wšb* "answer," *tw3w* "beseech"
3AE-INF.	*jt* and *jtw* "take" (originally *jṯ* and *jṯw*)
4AE-INF.	*mdw* and *mduw* "speak" (the root is *mdwj*); verbs of this class often show the final weak radical as *y*: for example, *b3gyw* "be weary"
5-LIT.	*nwtwtw* "totter"
CAUS. 2-LIT.	*sᶜrw* "cause to ascend"
CAUS. 3-LIT.	*sḫpr* "bring about"
ANOM.	*rdj* "give, put" (no examples with the *dj* stem or ending *–w*)
	jw "come" (no examples with the *jj* stem or ending *–w*).

14.18 Syntax of the negative infinitive

The negative infinitive can be used in most of the ways that the affirmative infinitive is used. It can also have the same kinds of subject and object as the affirmative form: for example,

tm m(w)t m ḫr(j)-nṯr jn z(j)
"Not dying in the necropolis by a man" (compare §§ 14.4.1, 14.9)[12]

r tm sᶜš3 mdwt
"in order not to multiply[13] words" (compare §§ 14.5, 14.11.3).

The subject and object follow the negatival complement, as these examples show. When the subject is a suffix pronoun, however, it is attached to the infinitive, not the negatival complement:

tm.f wn r.f pw "It means his not opening his mouth" (see § 14.13).

The negative infinitive is always active, like the affirmative; this is also true of the negatival complement. In some cases, however, English requires translation by a passive verb form, as in the following example (title of a funerary spell):

tm wn(m) z(j) jn ḥf3w m ḫr(j)-nṯr
"A man's not being eaten by a snake in the necropolis,"

or, more literally, "the not eating of a man by a snake in the necropolis" (see § 14.7).

12 Title of a funerary spell. The phrase *ḫr(j)-nṯr* "necropolis" means literally "the one that is under the god." It is masculine because it refers to an unexpressed antecedent *bw* "place": i.e., "(the place) that is under the god."

13 The caus. 3-lit. verb *sᶜš3* means literally "cause to be many"; the plural strokes are a determinative.

THE COMPLEMENTARY INFINITIVE

14.19 Definition

Egyptian has a special construction in which a verbal noun is used as an adverbial complement after another form of the same verb: for example,

 *wbn.k wbnt ḫpr.k ḫprt*
"You rise rising, you evolve evolving."[14]

Egyptologists call the verbal noun in this use the **complementary infinitive**. It is quite rare in Middle Egyptian and occurs almost exclusively in older religious texts.

14.20 The form of the complementary infinitive

The complementary infinitive always has the ending –*t*, as in the examples in the preceding section. This ending is attached to the base stem of most verbs, and to the geminated stem of geminating verbs. For final-weak verbs the ending seems to have been originally –*wt*, later –*yt*, attached to the base stem, but the weak consonants *w* and *y* are usually omitted in writing.

There are very few examples of the complementary infinitive in Middle Egyptian texts. The following are typical forms found in older religious texts:

2-LIT.	 *3ḫt* "becoming effective"
2AE-GEM.	 *wnnt* "existing"
3-LIT.	 *wbnt* "rising"
3AE-INF.	, ,  *mst, mswt, msyt* "being born"
4AE-INF.	 *psḏt* "shining"
ANOM.	 *jwt* "coming."

ESSAY 14. THE MEMPHITE THEOLOGY

The idea of creation by means of perception and the creative word is especially associated with the god Ptah, as noted in Essay 13. Why this should be so is not immediately clear.

Ptah was the chief deity of Memphis, Egypt's political capital from the beginning of pharaonic history. There he was known as 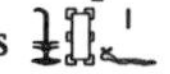 *rsw(j) jnb.f* "he who is south of his (city's) wall" (a *nfr ḥr* construction: § 6.5), from the location of his chief temple. Even in his earliest attestations, Ptah is associated with the mineral elements of the created world — metal ores and stone — and with the art of fashioning these elements into artifacts. He is shown with the same close-fitting skullcap that craftsmen wear in Old Kingdom tomb reliefs, and his high priest has the title  *wr ḫrp ḥmwt* "the chief one who manages craftsmanship." Ptah was especially revered as the patron of metal-workers, sculptors, and architects. His association with metal was often honored by uniting him with Sokar, the falcon-headed deity of meteoric ore, in the combined form Ptah-Sokar, and his

14 From a hymn to the rising sun: *wbn.k* and *ḫpr.k* are finite verb forms with the suffix pronoun as subject. For nouns used as adverbs, see § 8.14.

relationship to stone led to his union with the god Tatjenen (see Essay 11), in the form of Ptah-Tatjenen, particularly in the New Kingdom.

These characteristics explain why Ptah was often worshipped as a creator of the physical world, but not why this function should be associated with the nonphysical aspect of creation by thought and speech. Fortunately, chance has preserved for us a unique document that explains the association.

In the British Museum is a large piece of black granite known as the "Shabaka Stone," made for erection in Ptah's temple at Memphis. Although it was inscribed during the reign of the 25th-Dynasty pharaoh Shabaka (ca. 712–698 BC), its inscription purports to be much older, as the pharaoh's dedicatory text informs us:

> His Incarnation published this writing anew in the house of his father Ptah South of His Wall, since His Incarnation had found it as something that those before had made but as something that worms had eaten, and unknowable from beginning to end.

From this text it seems that the original found by Shabaka was written on papyrus or leather. This original was once thought to date to the Old Kingdom, but more recent analyses of its content indicate that it was probably composed during the reign of the 19th-Dynasty pharaoh Ramesses II, some 550 years earlier than Shabaka.

The text consists largely of a ritual commemorating the original unification of the Two Lands at Memphis (see Essay 1). At its end, however, is a shorter section devoted to the role of Ptah in the creation. This part of the text is often called the "Memphite Theology." It begins with a reference to the Heliopolitan creation account and the notion of the creative word: "Evolution into the image of Atum occurred through the heart and occurred through the tongue." The text then continues:

> But much older is Ptah, who enlivened all the gods as well as their life-forces ("kas") through this heart and through this tongue … His Ennead is in his presence in teeth and lips, which are the seed and hands of Atum: for Atum's Ennead evolved from his seed and his fingers, but the Ennead is teeth and lips in this mouth that pronounced the identity of everything and through which Shu and Tefnut emerged and gave birth to the Ennead.

Here the notion of creative thought and speech is given priority over the physical evolution of Atum into the forces and elements of the created world ("Atum's Ennead"). In effect, the text states that the creator's concept of the world and his creative utterance of that concept caused the "Big Bang" that resulted in Atum's evolution.

The text also clearly associates Ptah with the creator's thought and utterance. Like other accounts of Ptah's role in the creation, however, it does not actually identify Ptah as the creator himself. Rather, Ptah is an intermediary between the act of creative thought and speech and the result of that act, the evolution of Atum ("Ptah, who enlivened all the gods as well as their life-forces *through* this heart and *through* this tongue").

The key to Ptah's part in the creation lies in his role as patron of metalworkers, sculptors, and architects. These human acts of creation all involve an initial concept in the mind of the artisan — for example, of a statue or building — which is then given physical form through the use of the raw materials of metal or stone. In the end, the artisan's concept and craftsmanship or direction result in the "evolution" of the original raw material into a finished statue or building. To the Egyptians, Ptah was the divine force that made this evolution possible. In the same way, the force represented by Ptah made it possible for the creator's initial concept of the world ("heart," "perception") and his creative direction ("tongue," "announcement") to result in the evolution of Atum's raw material into the physical world. The text of the Memphite Theology puts it as follows:

> So has Ptah come to rest after his making everything as well as every divine speech ... So have the gods entered into their bodies.

It is significant that the text equates the creation of "everything" with the creation of "every divine speech." The term "divine speech" —  *mdw-nṯr*, literally, "speech of the god" — is the same term used to describe hieroglyphic writing (§ 1.4). As we have learned, hieroglyphs have a dual nature: they are images of things in the real world, but they are also representations of ideas. By using the term "divine speech" to describe the created world, the author of the Memphite Theology implies that everything in creation is itself a kind of hieroglyph of the creator's original concept. In the same way, the beginning of the text refers to "evolution into the image of Atum." The word "image" —  *tjt* — is also used of hieroglyphic signs (note the determinative: an adze, with which such signs could be carved). The physical world is thus an "image" of the original raw material of Atum in the same way that a hieroglyph is an "image" of a physical thing.

The Memphite Theology is one of the most sophisticated texts that has survived from ancient Egypt. It was written in a period of great intellectual creativity that flourished under Ramesses II, which produced another masterpiece of Egyptian thought that we will examine in Essay 15. In identifying Ptah as the intermediary between the creator's intellect and the physical evolution of the world, it anticipated the notion of the demiurge in Greek philosophy by more than 500 years — a notion that eventually found its way into Christian philosophy, as expounded in the opening words of the Gospel of John:

> In the beginning was the Word, and the Word was with God, and the Word was God. He was in the beginning with God. Through him all things came into being, and of all that has come into being not one thing came into being except through him. (John 1:1–3)

Just by itself, the Memphite Theology is enough to place Egyptian thought squarely in the line, and at the beginning, of the great traditions of Western philosophy.

EXERCISE 14

Transliterate and translate the following clauses and sentences, identifying the infinitives and their root class. To give you practice in using the dictionary, the meaning of individual words will no longer be given in the exercises: you can find them in the dictionary at the back of this book.

1.  — *jj.n.j* "I returned"
2.  — title of a funerary spell

3.  — *nfꜥ.n.j wj* "I took myself off"

4.  — *nj kꜣ.(j)* "I did not plan"

5.  — narrative

6.  — *mꜣꜣ.f wj* "he sees me"

7. 

8.  — *ḫmt.n.f* "he thought"

9.  — *sḫꜣ.n.k* "you have remembered"

10.  — see §§ 10.9 and 4.4

11.  — *wšb.k* "you should answer"

12. 

13.  — for  see Essay 6

14.  — *wrš.n.s* "she spent the day"

15.  — *wj jj.kw* "I have come"

16. 

17.  — *jw.f rḫ* "he knows," *ḥsq* "severed"

18.  — past

19.  — *jj.n.j* "I have come"

20. 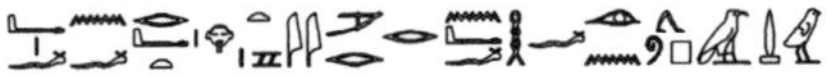

21.  — *ꜥḥꜥ.n sḏm.n.s ḫrw* "then she heard the sound"

22.  — *rꜥ-wsr* "Re-weser" (a name)

23. 

24.  — for see § 8.2.6; *r(w)d-ḏdt* "Rud-djedet" (a name)

25.  — title of a funerary spell

26.  — *wḏ.tw n.f* "let him be commanded"

27.  — title of a funerary spell

28.  — *mrr.k* "you wish"

29. 

30.  — 2 sentences

15. The Pseudoverbal Construction

15.1 Forms

In Lessons 10–12 we learned how Egyptian uses a prepositional phrase as an adverbial predicate in sentences and clauses, and in § 14.11 we saw that the infinitive can be used as the object of a preposition, like other nouns. As you might expect, therefore, the combination of a preposition and the infinitive can also be used as an adverbial predicate. Egyptologists call this kind of predicate the **pseudoverbal construction**: "verbal" because it involves a verb form (the infinitive), but "pseudo" because it is syntactically a nonverbal predicate (adverbial), even though part of the predicate is a real verb form (the infinitive).

Not every combination of a preposition plus the infinitive can be used in the pseudoverbal construction. In Middle Egyptian only three kinds of prepositional phrases occur in this use:

- ***ḥr* plus infinitive** — for example,  *ḥr jrt*: literally, "upon doing"
- ***m* plus infinitive** — for example, 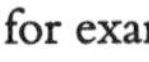 *m h3t*: literally, "in descending"
- ***r* plus infinitive** — for example,  *r prt*: literally, "toward emerging."

Of these, *ḥr* plus infinitive and *r* plus infinitive are very common in Middle Egyptian texts; *m* plus infinitive is used less often, and only with intransitive verbs. All three pseudoverbal constructions have Coptic descendants, known as the "First Present" (from original *ḥr* plus infinitive), "First Future" (from *m* plus infinitive), and "Third Future" (from *r* plus infinitive). Egyptologists sometimes use these names to refer to the Middle Egyptian constructions as well.

15.2 Basic meanings

Like all adverbial predicates, the pseudoverbal construction is essentially **nontemporal**: in itself it does not express a particular tense, but it can be used to describe past, present, or future actions (see § 11.3). It is also basically **indicative**, denoting a statement of fact (see § 13.3.3). These features are common to all three pseudoverbal predicates. Apart from these common features, however, the three pseudoverbal constructions have different basic meanings.

In Middle Egyptian the combination of *ḥr* plus infinitive as a pseudoverbal predicate most often expresses the **imperfect** (see § 13.3.2). It usually corresponds to the "progressive" forms of English verbs — that is, those which consist of a form of the verb *be* plus the gerund: for example, *ḥr jrt* "is doing, was doing." Like the English progressive, it normally indicates action **in process** ("progressing") either at the moment of speaking (for example, *Jill is doing the crossword puzzle*) or at the time of another action (for instance, *Jill was doing the crossword puzzle when Jack called*). Although this is the original, and most common, meaning, Egyptian eventually began to use *ḥr* plus infinitive to express simple action as well. Occasionally, therefore, *ḥr* plus infinitive corresponds to the simple present or past tense of English — particularly in **generic** statements, as in the English example *Jill does crossword puzzles*. This use begins to appear in texts at the end of Dynasty 12 and is most often found in Middle Egyptian texts from the New Kingdom.

The combination of *m* plus infinitive as a pseudoverbal predicate can also be translated with the English progressive: for example, *m h3t* "is descending." Rather than action in progress, however, it seems to denote **future** action, much like the English progressive does in a sentence such as *Jack is going to Alaska this summer.* Like *ḥr* plus infinitive, this construction also changed in meaning over the course of time. In texts from the New Kingdom, *m* plus infinitive often expresses the imperfect, like the pseudoverbal construction with *ḥr* plus infinitive.

The pseudoverbal construction with *r* plus infinitive denotes action that has yet to happen at the moment of speaking or with respect to another action: for example, *r prt* "will emerge, was to emerge." Usually this predicate implies an action that is **planned** or **inevitable**. In this respect it is similar to the English constructions with a form of the verbs *be* or *have* plus the infinitive, which also denote action that has yet to happen: for example, *Jill is to give the opening address* and *Jack has to leave*. The Egyptian pseudoverbal predicate with *r* plus infinitive can usually be translated with these English constructions as well as with the simple future: for example, *r prt* "is to emerge, has to emerge, was to emerge, had to emerge," and so forth, as well as "will emerge."

As is normal with adverbial predicates, the pseudoverbal construction comes **after** its subject (see § 10.2). It can be used in most of the ways that other adverbial predicates are used. These uses are described in the following sections.

15.3 The pseudoverbal construction in main clauses

Like other adverbial predicates, the pseudoverbal construction can be used in main clauses (or independent sentences: see § 12.1) without any introductory word: for example,

 *nb wr ḥr jtt* "A great lord is taking possession"

 *ˁwt ẖ3st r swrj ḥr jtrw nw kmt*

"A foreign land's flocks are to drink at the rivers of Egypt" (a prophecy).

This use is normally possible only with a nominal subject, as in these examples, or — in later Middle Egyptian texts — with special forms of the personal pronoun (see the next sections).

In most cases, main clauses with a pseudoverbal predicate have the same introductory words used with other adverbial predicates, such as *jw* and *m.k* (§§ 10.3–10.4): for example,

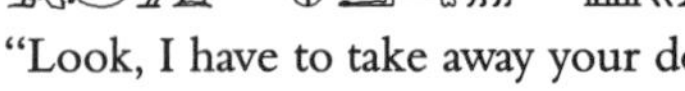 *jw sr(j)w ḥr rdjt n.k jw.k ḥr jtt*

"The officials are giving to you and you are taking"

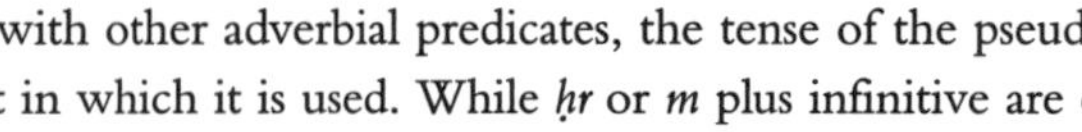

m.t wj m h3t r kmt r jnt ˁqw jm n ẖrdw.j

"Look, I am going down to Egypt to get supplies there for my children"

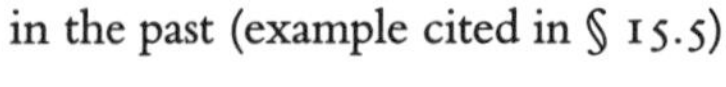 *m.k wj r nḥm ˁ3.k sẖtj*

"Look, I have to take away your donkey, peasant."

As with other adverbial predicates, the tense of the pseudoverbal construction depends on the context in which it is used. While *ḥr* or *m* plus infinitive are often best translated with the present tense, they sometimes express past actions (for examples, see §§ 15.6 and 15.8–15.9). Similarly, while *r* plus infinitive usually refers to future events, it can also denote an action that had yet to happen in the past (example cited in § 15.5).

15.4 **The pseudoverbal construction with subject pronouns**

A suffix or dependent pronoun after an introductory particle is normally used to express a pronominal subject in the pseudoverbal construction, as in the last three examples of the preceding section. In § 10.5 we met a special form of the personal pronoun that is used as the subject of an adverbial predicate in later Middle Egyptian texts. This pronoun can also function as the subject of a pseudoverbal predicate: for example,

 *tw.j r ṯḥn ḥnᶜ.f* "I am to engage with him (in battle)."

15.5 **The impersonal subject pronoun  *tw***

Besides the personal pronouns, Egyptian also has an impersonal pronoun  *tw* (also  and , rarely ). This pronoun is used **exclusively** as the subject of an adverbial predicate (including the pseudoverbal construction) or a verb form, either as a suffix or as a dependent pronoun. It can usually be translated by the English impersonal pronoun *one*, or its predicate can be translated by an English passive construction with the pronoun *it* as subject:[1] for example,

 *jw.tw r gmt mw*

"One had to find water" or "Water had to be found" (in a narrative)

 *m.k tw ḥr dd*

"Look, one is saying" or "Look, it is being said."

An example with *tw* as subject of an infinitive is  *jt.tw r ḏd n ḥm.f* "one's coming to say to His Incarnation": compare the use of the suffix pronouns as subject of the infinitive (§ 14.4.2).

With a pseudoverbal predicate, *tw* can be used by itself as subject without any introductory particle: for instance,

 *tw r šzp ḫᶜw nw ᶜḥ3*

"One is to take up tools of fighting" or "Tools of fighting are to be taken up."

This use of *tw* is restricted to pseudoverbal predicates with *r* plus infinitive, as in this example. In Middle Egyptian of the New Kingdom the subject pronoun has an impersonal form  *tw.tw* (or 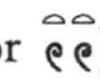). This is used, like the other subject pronouns, as the subject of any adverbial or pseudoverbal predicate: for example,

 *tw.tw ḥr 3s.n*

"One is hurrying us" or "We are being hurried."

Later Middle Egyptian sometimes uses *tw* not only as an impersonal pronoun but also as a substitute for nouns or noun phrases referring to the king. In this case, it is normally translated as "One" (capitalized): for example,

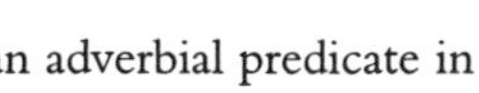 *hrw pn jw.tw m ᶜḥ* "this day, when One was in the palace,"

with an adverbial predicate in an adverb clause (see § 12.17). This use of the pronoun *tw* does not seem to occur earlier than the New Kingdom.

1 The French impersonal pronoun *on* has a similar twofold translation into English: *on dit* "one says" or "it is said."

15.6 The pseudoverbal construction after *ꜥḥꜥ.n* and *wn.jn*

The pseudoverbal predicate with *ḥr* plus infinitive is also used in main clauses with two introductory words that are not used in other kinds of adverbial-predicate clauses:  *ꜥḥꜥ.n* and  *wn.jn* (also spelled ). Both of these words mean "then," and they are found almost exclusively in narrative texts. Like *jw*, they are followed by a nominal or suffix-pronoun subject: for example,

 *ꜥḥꜥ.n.j ḥr j3š n mšꜥ ntj m dpt tn*
"Then I was calling to the expeditionary force that was in this boat"

 *wn.jn ḥm.f ḥr pg3 zẖ3w*
"Then His Incarnation was spreading open the writings"

 *wn.jn.tw ḥr ꜥḥ3 m t3 kmt*
"Then there was fighting in that (part of) Egypt."

These two introductory words are actually verb forms: *ꜥḥꜥ.n* means literally "stood up" and *wn.jn* "then existed." Thus, the examples just given mean literally "I stood up upon calling," "Then His Incarnation existed upon spreading open," and "Then one existed upon fighting." But when used to introduce a pseudoverbal predicate they have lost their literal meaning and denote simply subsequent action in a narrative (i.e., "then"). For that reason, the form *wn.jn* can also introduce an adjectival predicate:

 *wn.jn nfr st ḥr jb.sn* "Then it was good upon their heart(s)."

In texts of Dynasty 18, *wn.jn* is occasionally replaced by another verb form,  *wn.ẖr*, with the same syntax and apparently the same meaning: for example,

 *wn.ẖr.j ḥr šms jty* "Then I was following the sovereign."

All three introductory words are also used with verbal predicates, as we will see in Lessons 17–18.

15.7 The pseudoverbal construction without an infinitive

The preposition *ḥr* can be used as a pseudoverbal predicate without an infinitive when it introduces a direct quotation. In this case the infinitive *ḏd* "saying" is understood: for example,

 *ḥr-nb ḥr nb.n pw* "Everyone is (saying): 'He is our lord,'"

literally, "every-face is upon 'He is our lord.'"

15.8 The negated pseudoverbal construction

The pseudoverbal construction with *ḥr* plus infinitive can be negated by *nn*, like other adverbial predicates: for example,

 *nn wj ḥr sḏm st* "I was not hearing it."

With *r* plus infinitive, two constructions are attested:

 *nn sw r ḫpr* "He is not to come into existence"

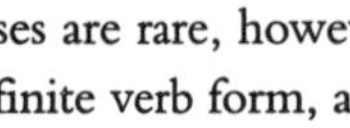 *nn jw.j r w3ḥ.t* "I'm not going to stop you (feminine)."

Such uses are rare, however. Normally the negation of the pseudoverbal construction is expressed with a finite verb form, as we will see in later lessons.

15.9 The pseudoverbal construction in adverb clauses

In Lesson 12 we saw how adverbial predicates can be used in both marked and unmarked adverb clauses. This is also true for pseudoverbal predicates. Examples are attested mostly with *ḥr* or *m* plus infinitive: for example,

1. **after** *jsṯ* (see § 12.16.1)

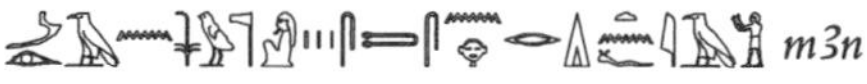 *m3n sw nṯrw sṯ sn ḥr rdjt n.f j3(w)*

"so that the gods may see him when they are giving him praise."[2]

2. **unmarked** (see § 12.17)

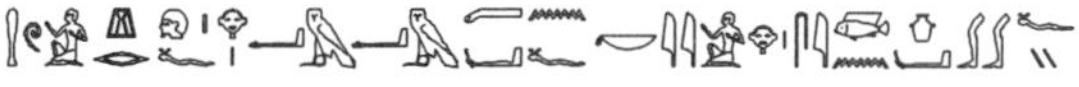

ḥmw ḥr tp.f ḥr ᶜmᶜm n.f ky ḥr sjn rdwj.fj

"A servant was at his head giving him a masssage, while another was rubbing his feet"[3]

 *sḏm.n.j ḫrw.f jw.f ḥr mdt*

"I heard his voice when he was talking"

 *hrw nfr jw.n m h3t r š3*

"A good day, as we are going down to the marsh!"

Note that the unmarked adverb clause with a pronominal subject is introduced by *jw*, while the the clause with a nominal subject has no introductory word. As a general rule, *jw*-clauses with a pronominal subject can be either main clauses or adverb clauses, while clauses with *jw* and a nominal subject are normally main clauses (or independent sentences). As with nonverbal adverb clauses, the translation of these adverb clauses is partly a matter of preference.

15.10 The pseudoverbal construction in relative clauses

Like other adverbial predicates, the pseudoverbal construction can be used in direct or indirect relative clauses, with or without the relative marker *ntj*. All three pseudoverbal predicates occur in this use: for example,

1. **with** *ntj* (see §§ 12.3–12.8)

 *m.tn zt pw ntt ḥr mn.s*

"Look, it is the woman who is suffering" (direct relative)[4]

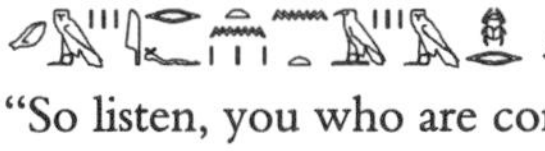 *sḏm jr.f tn ntjw m ḫpr*

"So listen, you who are coming into being (in the future)"[5] (direct relative)

 *pw-trj ntj tw r jrt*

"What is one to do?" or "What is to be done?" (indirect relative: literally, "What is that which one is to do?")[6]

2 *m3n* is a verb form to be discussed in Lesson 19; *sw* is its object and *nṯrw* its subject.

3 For the first clause see Exercise 14, no. 18. For the suffix of *rdwj.fj* "his two feet" see § 5.7.

4 Literally, "who is suffering her(self)": the verb *mn* "suffer" is transitive and is normally used with an object denoting the thing causing the suffering or, as in this case, with a reflexive pronominal object.

5 *sḏm jr.f* is an imperative construction, which will be discussed in Lesson 16; *tn* is the 2pl dependent pronoun.

6 For *pw-trj* "what?" see § 5.11; *ntj* is written for *ntt* "that which": see § 12.3.

2. **without** *ntj* (see § 12.11)

Relative clauses without *ntj* are used after undefined antecedents. When such clauses have a pseudoverbal predicate they are normally introduced by *jw* plus a suffix pronoun that refers back to the antecedent. This construction seems to be used only for direct relatives: for example,

jw.f m nḏs n rnpt 110 jw.f ḥr wnm t 50

"He is a commoner of 110 years (of age), who is eating 50 loaves of bread (a day)"

 *ḥf3w pw jw.f m jjt*

"It was a snake, who was coming"

ms pw n ḫn-nḫn jw.f r šzp ḥḏt jw.f r wṯz dšrt

"He is a child of southern Egypt, who is to take up the White Crown, who is to wear the Red Crown."[7]

When the relative clause comes immediately after its antecedent, *jw* and its suffix pronoun are omitted: for example,

 *z(j) ḥr mn r-jb.f* "a man suffering in his stomach."[8]

Although adverbial predicates can also be made into relative clauses by using a nisbe of the preposition (see § 12.10), this does not seem to be true for the pseudoverbal construction. The example just cited, therefore, has to be analyzed as a relative clause without a subject (like the English translation "a man suffering") rather than as a nisbe phrase **ḥr(j) mn* "who is upon suffering."

Since pseudoverbal predicates generally behave like other adverbial predicates, there would seem to be no syntactic reason why Egyptian should avoid expressions such as **ḥr(j) mn* "who is upon suffering" or **jrj šzp* "who is to take up." As we saw in § 12.10, however, the nisbe form of an adverbial predicate — such as *jmjw pt* "those who are in the sky" — is not specific about time or circumstances and often has generic meaning. Though they too are adverbial predicates, the pseudoverbal predicates are also finite verbal constructions, denoting actions that are in some way limited in their time or aspect. This is apparently why Egyptian did not use the nisbe form of such predicates.

15.11 The pseudoverbal construction in noun clauses

Although pseudoverbal predicates can be used like other adverbial predicates in noun clauses, few examples of such clauses are actually found in Middle Egyptian texts. There seem to be no examples of unmarked noun clauses with a pseudoverbal predicate (see § 12.14); those that do occur are introduced by *ntt* (see § 12.13.2) or by the word  *wnt* (also ), which has the same meaning as *ntt* and is used in the same way: for example,

 *ḏdw wnt.f ḥr ṯ3z.j* "of whom it is said that he is tying me together."[9]

7 *ḫn-nḫn* means literally "the interior of Hierakonpolis" and was a general term for the area of Egypt between Aswan and Thebes; *ḥḏt* "the white one" and *dšrt* "the red one" are feminine adjectives.

8 For *mn* "suffer" see n. 4 above; *r-jb* "stomach" means literally "mouth of the heart."

9 The *wnt* clause is the object of *ḏdw*, a verb form meaning "of whom it is said."

For noun clauses with *r* plus infinitive as predicate, two constructions are used. Texts of the Middle Kingdom use *ntt* or *wnt* plus the pseudoverbal construction: for example,

 *jw ḏd.n.sn wnt.sn r ḥḏt tpw*
"They have said that they are to smash heads,"

where *wnt* introduces the pseudoverbal construction as object of the verb form *jw ḏd.n.sn* "they have said." In texts of the New Kingdom the noun clause is introduced by *ntt jw*: for instance,

sspd ḫꜥw.tn r ntt jw.tw r ṯḥn r ꜥḥ3 ḥnꜥ ḫr pf ḫzj dw3
"Sharpen your tools, since one is to meet in order to fight with that wretched enemy in the morning,"

where the noun clause serves as object of the preposition *r* — literally, "with respect to (the fact) that."[10] Apart from the use of *wnt* or *ntt*, the difference between the later and earlier constructions is just the presence or absence of *jw* in the noun clause.

15.12 The pseudoverbal construction in questions

Like other adverbial predicates, the pseudoverbal construction can be used in questions as well as statements of fact. Most examples occur after the interrogative word *jn* (§ 11.11.2): for example,

 *jn jw.k ḥr m33* "Do you see?" (literally, "Are you seeing?").

The pseudoverbal construction is rare in other kinds of questions. The following is an exceptional instance, with an interrogative adverb at the beginning of the sentence:

 *mj mj jr.f z(j) nb ḥr sm3mw sn.f*
"So, why is every man killing his brother?"

The pseudoverbal sentence here is actually an adverb clause modifying the initial question, which has an unexpressed subject (compare Exercise 10, no. 39): literally, "So, (it is) like what, when every man is killing his brother?"[11]

ESSAY 15. THE CREATOR

Although they concentrate on different aspects of the creation, the accounts of Heliopolis and Memphis (Essays 12–14) are alike in one respect: the gods in both systems are actually part of the created world. Atum of Heliopolis is the material source of creation, which evolved into the world (as the Ennead), and Ptah of Memphis is the means through which that evolution happened. These gods are *immanent* in nature (see Essay 4). The gods of the Hermopolitan Ogdoad stand apart from the creation, but they too are immanent — not in the created world, but in the universal ocean that existed before creation and that still surrounds the world.

10 The initial verb form, *sspd* "sharpen," is an imperative, with the noun phrase *ḫꜥw.tn* "your weapons" as its object.

11 The prepositional phrase *jr.f* here acts like the English particle *so*; this use will be discussed in Lesson 16. The infinitive is from the 3-lit. root *sm3*. Its spelling reflects both the original root and the loss of the final consonant *3* in pronunciation; the final *w* shows that the infinitive ended in a vowel (i.e, **sVmV*, originally **sVmV3*).

The quality of immanence is a feature shared by all Egyptian gods, with one exception: the god Amun of Thebes. Amun appears already in texts from the late Old Kingdom, but we do not learn much about him until the Middle Kingdom, when he rose to prominence along with the pharaohs of Dynasties 11–12, which originated in Thebes. It was in Dynasty 18 (which also came from Thebes), however, that Amun first began to dominate Egyptian religion and, with it, Egyptian accounts of the creation.

The name "Amun" ( *jmn*, more fully  *jmnw*) means "hidden." Unlike all the other Egyptian gods, who were immanent in the phenomena of nature, Amun was *transcendent*: he existed above and apart from the universe, "hidden" from the created world. This quality of Amun is sometimes reflected in an epithet  *jmn(w)-rn.f* "He whose identity (literally, 'name') is hidden" (a *nfr ḥr* construction: § 6.5) and it is occasionally referred to in religious texts of the New Kingdom. The clearest statement of Amun's transcendence, however, comes from a hymn to the god that was written in Dynasty 19, probably during the reign of Ramesses II, on a papyrus that is now in the Netherlands National Museum of Antiquities in Leiden. This text explains Amun's "hidden" nature with the following words:

> He is hidden from the gods, and his nature is unknown.
> He is farther than the sky, he is deeper than the Duat.
> No god knows his true appearance,
> no image of his is revealed through inscriptions,
> no one testifies to him accurately.
> He is too secret to uncover his awesomeness,
> he is great to investigate, too powerful to know.

Unlike the other gods, Amun is not part of the created world ("He is farther than the sky, he is deeper than the Duat") and is therefore "hidden" — not just from human understanding but even from the knowledge of the gods themselves, who are also part of the created world.

Although Amun himself cannot be known, however, his existence can be deduced from the very fact that the world exists. As the only god who is independent of the universe, he is the true creator: the pre-existing god who thought of the world "through the heart" and commanded it to be "through the tongue." For this reason, all the other gods of creation — Atum and his Ennead, Ptah-Tatjenen, and even the Ogdoad of Hermopolis — are really just aspects of Amun himself. As the Leiden papyrus explains it:

> He began speaking in the midst of silence...
> that he might give birth to what is and cause them to live ...
> You began evolution with nothing ...
> The Ennead is combined in your body:
> your image is every god, joined in your person.
> You emerged first, you began from the start.
> Amun, whose identity is hidden from the gods;
> oldest elder, more distinguished than they ...
> *He* is the Great One in Heliopolis,

who is also called Tatjenen ...
Another of his evolutions is the Hermopolitans.
Original one who begot the original ones and caused the Sun to be born,
completing himself in Atum, one body with him.

The concept of Amun as a transcendent god whose existence can be seen in the phenomena of nature is summarized in the person of the god *jmn-rꜥ* "Amun-Re," who combines the notion of a transcendent god (Amun) with that of the greatest immanent force in nature, the sun (Re). Already in Dynasty 12, Amun-Re was recognized as the greatest of all the gods, the *nswt nṯrw* "king of the gods." In this role Amun-Re was also the source of the pharaoh's authority, the *nb nswt t3wj* "lord of the thrones of the Two Lands," and he was worshipped as such in the state temple at Karnak. Although there were many other temples to Amun throughout Egypt, Karnak was the most important. Perhaps as early as the Middle Kingdom, pharaohs were crowned there or had their coronation confirmed there, and during their reign most endeavored to add in some way to its splendor. Karnak became — and remained — the greatest of all Egyptian temples, because it embodied not only the shrine of Amun-Re but also the source of the Egyptian state itself.

Ultimately, the notion that every god could be seen as an aspect of Amun led to a kind of Egyptian monotheism: that is, the idea that all the gods are really one. This is different from the monotheism of Judaism and Islam, which accepts only one God, but it is similar to the notion of the Christian Trinity, which recognizes the existence of three different "persons" (Father, Son, and Holy Spirit) in a single God. The Leiden hymn to Amun, in fact, anticipated the Christian idea of a triune god by more than a thousand years, in the following words:

3 pw nṯrw nbw
jmn rꜥ ptḥ nn 2nw.sn
jmn rn.f m jmn
ntf rꜥ m ḥr ḏt.f ptḥ

"All the gods are three:
Amun, Re, and Ptah, without their second.
His identity is hidden in Amun,
his is Re as face, his body is Ptah."[12]

This passage, the most famous in the Leiden papyrus, recognizes the existence of a single god (in the singular pronoun "his") but accepts, at the same time, three separate aspects of the god: existing apart from nature (as Amun), yet visible in and governing nature (as Re), and the source of all things in nature (as Ptah). These lines have been regarded as the ultimate expression not only of Egyptian creation accounts but also of the entire 3,000-year history of Egyptian theology.

12 The four lines are separated by "verse points" in the hieratic original (see § 1.9). The first line is an A *pw* B nominal sentence, the second has an adverb clause with *nn* (§ 12.17), and the third has an adjectival predicate. The fourth line contains two sentences: the first has an adjectival predicate of possession (§ 7.5.2); the second is an A B nominal sentence (§ 7.8).

EXERCISE 15

Transliterate and translate the following clauses and sentences:

1.  — from a story
2. 
3. 
4.  — from a prophecy
5. 
6. 
7. 
8. 
9. 
10.  — from an autobiography
11. 
12.  — from a graffito in an alabaster quarry: *jn* "it is," *z3-nḫt* *ꜥḥ3-nḫt* a name (see § 4.15), *jrr* "who makes," *(j)m(j)-r š(j)* "overseer of the quarry," *sbk-m-ḥ3t* a name
13.  — heading from a temple archive
14. 
15. 

16. The Imperative and Particles

16.1 Definition and regular forms

The imperative is a verb form that is used to command action. It is always used by a speaker addressing someone (or something) in the second person, singular or plural. English has only one imperative form, which is used when addressing both one person (or thing) and more than one person (or thing): for example, *Behave yourself!* (singular) and *Behave yourselves!* (plural).

Written Middle Egyptian, for the most part, also has only one imperative form. For most verb classes, this is the **verb root**: for example,

2-LIT.	 *ḏd* "speak, say"
2AE-GEM.	 *m33* "see"; also with the base stem:  *m3* "see"
3-LIT.	 *sḏm* "hear"
3AE-INF.	 *jn* "get"
4-LIT.	 *nḏnḏ* "consult"
4AE-INF.	 *nḏr* "grab hold"
CAUS. 2-LIT.	 *srḫ* "make known, denounce"
CAUS. 3-LIT.	 *sḫpr* "bring about, make happen"
CAUS. 3AE-INF.	 *sꜥ3* "enlarge"
CAUS. 4AE-INF.	 *sḫnt* "promote (i.e., cause to be in front)"
ANOM.	 *jj* and  *jw* "come"
	,  *dj* "give, put"

This form is used when speaking to one person or more than one, male or female. Spoken Middle Egyptian, however, probably had four imperative forms: masculine and feminine, distinguished by vowels; and singular and plural, distinguished by the absence or presence of an ending. These features are preserved in the Coptic imperatives meaning "come!":

MS	**ⲁⲙⲟⲩ**	FS	**ⲁⲙⲏ**
MPL	**ⲁⲙⲱⲓ**	FPL	**ⲁⲙⲏⲓ.**

Of course, hieroglyphic shows no trace of the vowels that distinguished masculine and feminine imperatives, but the difference between singular and plural is sometimes reflected in writing. Imperatives addressed to more than one person can be written with plural strokes: for example,  *wḏ3* "proceed." An ending *–y* (ancestor of the Coptic plural ending **–ⲓ**) sometimes appears in the plural imperative of final-weak verbs: for instance,  *dgy* "look" (from 3ae-inf. *dgj*),  *dy* (from anom. *rdj*). Other roots rarely show the same ending:  *jtḥy* "pull" (from 3-lit. *jtḥ*).

16.2 Special forms

Besides the regular imperative forms discussed in the preceding section, Middle Egyptian also has a few special imperatives.

1. **Prefixed forms**

In Old Egyptian the imperative of some verb classes often had a prefix (see § 13.4.5). This feature is occasionally found in the imperative of some 2-lit. verbs in Middle Egyptian: for example, *j.z(j)* "go," *j.mz* "bring."

2. **The imperative *mj* "come"**

The regular imperatives of anom. *jj* and *jwj* "come," shown in § 16.1, are not often used. In place of these, Middle Egyptian normally uses the special imperative *mj* (the ancestor of Coptic ⲁⲙⲟⲩ, etc.; also spelled). In most texts this imperative is spelled , where the "arm" sign is a biliteral *mj* (more properly : see the next paragraph). Like other final-weak imperatives, the plural of *mj* can be written with an ending: for example, *my* "come!"

3. **The imperative *jmj* "give"**

The regular imperative of *rdj* "give, put" is also rare. Instead, most Middle Egyptian texts use the imperative *jmj*. In this word, the sign was originally a biliteral *jm*, with the first two signs as its phonetic complements and the final sign as determinative.[1] Eventually, however, it came to be used as a uniliteral *m* (like : § 2.3). As a result, texts of the New Kingdom and later sometimes spell the imperative *jmj* as if it had two *ms*: , .

4. **The imperative *m* "take"**

The verbs *šzp* "take" (3-lit.) and *jtj* "take possession" (3ae-inf.) have regular imperatives. In addition to these, however, Middle Egyptian has an imperative *m* (originally *jm*), also meaning "take!" This imperative is found exclusively in religious texts, and almost always with a following dative: for example, *m n.k jrtj.k* "Take to you your two eyes." The imperative and the following dative were apparently pronounced as one word; as a result, the imperative *m* and the preposition *n* are usually written together, with the biliteral sign *mn*:[2] for instance, *m-n.k jrt.k* "Take to you your eye."

16.3 Object and subject of the imperative

The object of the imperative is expressed by a noun (or noun phrase) or pronoun; for personal pronouns the **dependent** form is used: for example,

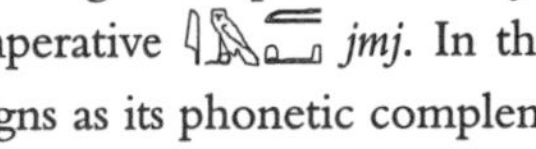 *jᶜ tw, jmj mw ḥr ḏbᶜw.k*

"Wash yourself; put water on your fingers,"

where the 2ms pronoun *tw* "you, yourself" is object of the imperative *jᶜ* "wash" and the noun *mw* "water" is object of the imperative *jmj* "put." Clauses with the imperative follow the rules of word order described in § 14.6: for instance,

1 Although was originally a determinative in this word, because of its use here it came to be viewed as a biliteral with the value *mj*. This is why (as well as) is often found in spellings of words that begin with *m*, such as *m.k* (§ 10.4.1) and *mḫ3t* "scale" (Lesson 11, n. 3).

2 Compare the use of biliteral *ns* in writings of *n(j)-sw*, *n(j)-sj*, and biliteral *nw* in writings of *n(j)-wj*: § 7.5.1.

 *j.z(j) jn n.j jfd m pr.j*
"Go, get me a sheet from my house"

 *j.z(j) jn n.j sw* "Go, get him for me,"

where the pronominal dative *n.j* "for me" precedes both the nominal object *jfd* "a sheet" (**VdO**) and the pronominal object *sw* "him" (**Vdo**); and

 *jmj mrwt.k n t3-tmw* "Give your love to everyone"[3]

 *jmj n.n ḫnt.n nfrt* "Give us our good outcome,"[4]

where the nominal dative *n t3-tmw* "to everyone" follows the nominal object *mrwt.k* "your love" (**VOD**) but the pronominal dative *n.n* "to us" precedes the nominal object *ḫnt.n nfrt* "our good outcome" (**VdO**).

In Egyptian as in English, the subject of the imperative ("you") is normally understood but not expressed. When it is expressed, however, Egyptian uses the **dependent** pronouns **after** the imperative: for instance,

 *wḏ*ᶜ *tw ḏs.k z3-mrw* "You decide by yourself, son of Meru"[5]

 *wḏ3 tn r* ᶜ*ḫnwtj* "You (all) proceed to the audience-hall."

As the translations of these examples show, English can also express the subject of the imperative with a pronoun ("you").

The second-last example also illustrates how Egyptian can use a noun or noun phrase referring to the imperative's subject (in this case, *z3-mrw* "son of Meru," referring to the person being addressed). The noun or noun phrase in this use is known as the **vocative**. A vocative can be used with the imperative even when the subject is not expressed, and unlike the subject it can come before or after the imperative: for instance,

 *mww my* "Dancers, come!"

 *my rḫw* "Come, companions!"

16.4 Negation of the imperative

Middle Egyptian has two ways to express a negative imperative. Both use the negation  *m* (usually spelled just ), which is actually the imperative form of the negative verb *jmj* (one of the two forms in which this defective verb can appear: § 13.7). In the simpler negation, *m* is followed by the negatival complement (§ 14.17): for example,

 *h3 r ḫrw, m h3w ḥr tp.f*
"Descend to below: don't descend on his head!,"

where *m h3w* "don't descend" is the negative counterpart of the imperative *h3* "descend." Besides the simple negatival complement, *m* can also be followed by the negatival complement of the verb *jrj* "do" plus a verbal noun: for instance,

3 *t3-tmw* "everyone" is a noun phrase meaning literally, "the land complete."
4 There is an extra *t* in *ḫnt.n*: the feminine ending is written twice, once in the noun *ḫnt* and once before its suffix.
5 For *ḏs.k* "yourself," a noun phrase used adverbially, see § 8.14.

 *ḫ3y m jr nwdw* "Measuring-line, don't deviate!"

literally, "don't do deviation." The two-part construction (*m* plus negatival complement) is common in earlier Middle Egyptian texts. The three-part form (*m jr* plus verbal noun) begins to replace this construction already in the Middle Kingdom, and by the New Kingdom it has become the standard way of negating the imperative, particularly in less formal texts. In this respect the history of Middle Egyptian is similar to that of English, where an original two-part construction (*go not!*) has also been replaced by one that uses the verb *do* (*do not go!*, *don't go!*).

The negated imperative follows the same rules as the affirmative form (§ 16.3), with one addition: when the imperative being negated is from an adjective verb (§ 13.2), the negatival complement can have a third-person subject. In this case, *m* has to be translated as "don't let" rather than just "don't": for example,

 *m ꜥ3 jb.k ḥr rḫ.k*
"Don't let your heart get big because of your knowledge,"

where *jb.k* is the subject of the negatival complement *ꜥ3* "get big." The relationship between the adjective verb and its subject in this construction is similar to that between the adjective and a following noun in the *nfr ḥr* construction (§ 6.5): literally, perhaps, "don't get big of your heart." Note that the adjective verb describes a **process** ("get big"), not a simple quality ("be big").

PARTICLES

16.5 Definitions

The category of particles is used as a kind of catchall for words that do not fit readily into the other categories of Egyptian words (nouns, pronouns, adjectives, prepositions, adverbs, and verbs). We have met some of these words over the course of the previous lessons.

Egyptian particles are usually categorized by where they occur in the clause or sentence. Some particles are always the first element in a clause or sentence: these are known as **proclitic** particles (from a term of Greek grammar, meaning "leaning forward"). Other particles can only occur inside a clause or sentence, usually as the second element: these are called **enclitic** particles ("leaning in"). **Interjections** are particles that can stand alone, or that can be omitted from a clause without substantially changing its meaning.

Egyptian particles other than interjections can also be divided into categories on the basis of meaning. Those that have a syntactic function, such as marking a kind of clause, are known as "converters." The remaining particles have no specific syntactic function, but they do add a nuance of meaning to a clause or sentence: these can be called "statement auxiliaries."

16.6 Proclitic particles

1.  *jw*

This is the most common of all Egyptian particles. We have already met it in connection with adverbial and adjectival sentences (§ 10.3); it is also used in verbal sentences, as we will see in later lessons. The particle *jw* basically serves to assert that a statement is true from the speaker's point of view or with respect to another statement. It is almost always the first element in its clause, although it can occasionally follow another proclitic particle.

2.  *jn* (also , , )

So far we have seen how *jn* is used to introduce a nonverbal question (§§ 7.13.1, 11.11, 15.12); it also introduces verbal questions, as we will see in later lessons. Besides this function, *jn* serves to mark the subject in particular kinds of sentences, a use we will also examine in Lessons 19 and 23. This particle is probably the same word as the preposition *jn*, which indicates the agent of a passive verb or the infinitive (§§ 8.2.2, 14.4.1).

3.  *jḫ* "then"

This particle is used to mark sequential action. It is used almost exclusively before one particular verb form, which we will discuss in Lesson 19.

4.  *jsw* "behold"

The particle *jsw* has the same meaning as *m.k* (§ 16.6.7), and is used in much the same way: for example,

 *jsw ḏw pw mḏr ḏꜥ*
"Behold, he is a mountain that turns the stormwind."[6]

It is much less common than *m.k*, but it survived into Coptic (as **ⲉⲓⲥ** "behold") long after *m.k* disappeared from the spoken language.

5.  *jsṯ* (also , 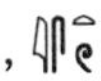, , , )

As we have already seen, the particle *jsṯ* (etc.) can be used to mark a clause as dependent on a preceding clause or sentence (§§ 12.16.1, 12.16.4, 15.9), usually as an adverb clause. In this respect, *jsṯ* can be considered a converter. In many cases, however, the connection with a preceding clause or sentence is less obviously adverbial, and for this reason *jsṯ* is probably best viewed as a statement auxiliary. Its use in verbal clauses is the same as that for clauses with nonverbal predicates.

6.  *wnt* "that"

The particle *wnt* is used to mark a clause with a nonverbal or verbal predicate as a noun clause (§ 15.11). Although it is classed as a particle, *wnt* is probably a form of the verb *wnn* "exist." It is less common than *ntt*, which has the same use (§ 16.6.11).

7.  *m.k* (etc.) "behold"

We have already met this particle in our discussion of nonverbal sentences (§ 10.4.1), and it is used in verbal sentences in the same way. It always serves to introduce a main clause (or independent sentence) and seems to call its clause to the attention of the person or persons being spoken to. For this reason it normally has the form *m.k* (2ms), *m.ṯ* or *m.t* (2fs), *m.ṯn* or *m.tn* (2pl), with the second-person suffix pronouns. Rarely, the form  *mj* is used by itself, without a suffix pronoun. In that case, it has the meaning "although" or "whether": for example,

 *mj wj m ẖnw m wj m st tn*
"whether I am at home (literally, 'in the interior') or whether I am in this place."

The particle *mj* may have started out as an imperative meaning "see!" or the like; it was originally followed by dependent pronouns, like an imperative (§ 16.3), rather than the suffix forms.

6 This sentence is from a hymn in praise of the king; *mḏr* is a participle, a verb form we will meet in Lesson 23.

8. *nj* and *nn* "not"

These are the two major negative words of Middle Egyptian. We have already seen how both of them are used in the negation of words and of nonverbal clauses and sentences (§§ 11.8, 12.17). They are also used to negate verb forms, as we will learn in future lessons. The particle *nn* can also be used by itself to contrast with a preceding phrase or clause, with the meaning "or not":

ḏ3t jtrw m s3 tbwtj ḏ3t nfr nn
"Crossing the river on sandals is a good crossing or not?"[7]

Most Middle Egyptian texts clearly distinguish the negative particles *nj* and *nn* by their spelling: is used only in the spelling of *nn*, and *nj* is spelled with alone. The particle *nn* is a creation of Middle Egyptian: Old Egyptian had only the particle *nj*, which was used like both of the later negations *nj* and *nn*. Some early Middle Egyptian texts still have remnants of this older system, and use *nj* where standard Middle Egyptian texts would use *nn*. There is also reason to believe that older texts sometimes use as a spelling of *nj* — i.e., *n(j)*, with as a phonetic complement. Although you can usually rely on the spelling to indicate whether *nj* or *nn* is meant, therefore, you also need to be aware of the different constructions in which both negations are used (for nonverbal sentences, see § 11.8; their use in verbal sentences will be summarized in Lesson 26). If one of the negations appears in a construction for which it is not normally used, there is a chance that is being used for *nn*, as it was in Old Egyptian, or that is being used as a spelling of *nj*, particularly in early texts (before Dynasty 12).

9. *nfr* "not"

The particle *nfr* is an infrequent negation in Middle Egyptian texts. It is found in only three constructions:

- *nfr pw*, used in the construction *nfr pw* X "there is no X at all": for example, *nfr pw m3ʿ tk3 jm* "There was no offering of a taper at all there," or "There was not even the offering of a taper there." This is a stronger negation than the more common *nn* X "there is no X" (§ 11.4).
- , *nfr n* "not, that not," used with a following verb form. This is an Old Egyptian construction, normally replaced by the negative verb *tm* (§ 14.16) in Middle Egyptian.
- *nfr 3* "not at all, not even," used mostly with a following verb form. This construction is found in a few early Middle Egyptian texts.

The particle *nfr* is related to the noun *nfrw* "depletion" (see § 9.1 end).

10. *nḥmn* "surely"

We have met this particle in connection with adverbial sentences (§ 10.4.3). It is always used in main clauses or independent sentences, with nonverbal or verbal predicates, and emphasizes the truth of the statement made in the clause or sentence.

7 An A B nominal sentence (see § 7.8.2) used as a virtual question (§ 11.11.1); *ḏ3t* is the infinitive of 3ae-inf. *ḏ3j* (masculine: see § 14.8). The sentence is ironic: "crossing the river on sandals" (literally, "on the back of two sandals") rather than by boat is clearly impossible, and therefore not "a good crossing." A freer translation might be "Are sandals a good means for crossing the river, or not?"

11. *ntt* "that"

The particle *ntt* is used to mark a clause with a nonverbal or verbal predicate as a noun clause (§§ 12.13.2–12.13.3); it corresponds to the English word *that,* which has the same function. Although it can be considered a particle, *ntt* is actually the feminine form of the relative adjective *ntj.*

12. *ḥ3, ḥ3 3, ḥwj 3* "if only, I wish, would that" (also ,)

As we saw in § 10.4.4, these particles are used to mark a main clause or independent sentence as a wish when there is some uncertainty about whether the wish will come true. They are used with verbal as well as nonverbal predicates.

13. *ẖr* "then" (also ; originally)

The particle *ẖr* has several functions in Middle Egyptian. It serves mostly as a statement auxiliary, with nonverbal or verbal predicates, to indicate the inevitable result of an action described in some preceding clause: for example,

 *wbn.f ẖr t3 m ḥꜥꜥwt*

"He rises, and then the land is in excitement."[8]

As a statement auxiliary, *ẖr* normally marks a subordinate clause — as in this example, where it introduces a clause with an adverbial predicate. Syntactically, *ẖr* can be used as a converter to allow a prepositional phrase to stand at the beginning of a sentence: for example,

ẖr m ḫt mšrw ḫpr, jwt pw jr.n p3 nḏs

"Then later, when evening had fallen, along came the commoner."

Here *ẖr* introduces the prepositional phrase *m ḫt* "after" (literally, "in the wake"), used adverbially, at the beginning of the sentence: literally, "Then after(wards), evening having happened, what the commoner did was to come."[9] In this use *ẖr* always marks the beginning of a sentence. The distinction between the two uses of *ẖr* is easy to recognize: when it is followed directly by a prepositional phrase, *ẖr* is a converter and marks the beginning of a sentence; otherwise, it is a statement auxiliary and introduces a subordinate clause denoting inevitable result.

14. *smwn* "perhaps, maybe, probably"

The particle *smwn* introduces a main clause (or independent sentence) with nonverbal or verbal predicate. It indicates that the statement of the clause or sentence is uncertain: for example,

 *nb.j smwn sḫtj.f pw*

"My lord, it is probably his peasant,"

where *smwn* introduces an A *pw* nominal sentence after the vocative *nb.j* "my lord." It has been suggested that the particle *smwn* derives from an adverbial sentence *s(j) m wn* "it is something that may be"; in this respect it would be similar to the English word *maybe,* which comes from the expression "it may be."

8 *wbn.f* is a verb form we will discuss in Lesson 25.

9 The clause *mšrw ḫpr* "evening happened," is used as an adverb clause; *ḫpr* is the stative, a verb form we will meet in the next lesson.

15.  *k3* "then" (also )

This particle, like *jḫ* (§ 16.6.3), marks a clause with a verbal or nonverbal predicate as the future result of the action of some preceding clause. Like *jḫ*, too, it is mostly used with one particular verb form, to be discussed in Lesson 19.

16) ,  *tj*

As we saw in § 12.16.2, *tj* serves to mark a clause with adverbial predicate as an adverb clause; it is also used for the same purpose with a verbal predicate.

16.7 Enclitic particles

1.  *3*

This particle can be used to emphasize a preceding word or phrase: for example,

 *4nw zp 3 m spr n.k* "the *fourth time* of petitioning to you!"

This is also the meaning it has in the combined particles *nfr 3* "not at all" and *ḥ3 3 / ḥwj 3* "if only" (§§ 16.6.9, 16.6.12). Most instances of *3* occur in sentences with a verbal predicate; in these it serves not only as an emphasizer but also to indicate that the action of the verb is contrary to fact, as we will see in Lesson 18.

2.  *jr.f*, 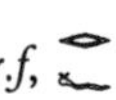 *r.f* (etc.) "so"

Besides the uses we have already met (§§ 8.2.7, 10.8, 14.11.3, 15.1.2), the preposition *r* can also act like an enclitic particle when it governs a suffix pronoun: e.g., *jr.f*, more often *r.f* (§ 8.2.7). In this case the prepositional phrase usually appears as the second element in the clause (or sentence), like other enclitic particles, rather than in the normal position of prepositional phrases at the end of the clause. This use is very common in Egyptian texts, though mostly for clauses with a verbal predicate.

The enclitic use of *jr.f* (etc.) derives from the basic meaning of the preposition *r* "with respect to" (§ 8.2.7). The suffix pronoun *.f* refers to some previous clause or sentence, and the prepositional phrase serves to relate its clause to the preceding one: for example,

nn jꜥš n ḥ3t m wnwt.sn "There is no pilot in their hour."
jn jw r.f tnj mjn "So, where is he today?"[10]

The enclitic here relates the question in the second sentence to the statement of the first: *r.f* means literally, "with respect to it," where the suffix pronoun refers to the preceding sentence. As the translation indicates, this relational value of *r.f* can often be conveyed by the English particle *so*. The third-person pronoun is usually masculine singular *.f*; feminine singular (*r.s*) is rarely used instead.

With a first or second-person suffix, the enclitic serves to relate the action of the verb to the speaker (first person) or the person(s) being addressed (second person) rather than to a preceding statement. This use is very common with imperatives: for example,

 *sḏm r.k n.j* "Listen to me!"

literally, "listen, with respect to yourself, to me!"

10 The expression *jꜥš n ḥ3t* "pilot" literally means "caller of the front": i.e., the man who stands at the bow of a boat and watches for obstructions in the river. The phrase "in their hour" means "when they are on duty." The subject of the second sentence is omitted (see §§ 10.9–10).

Enclitic *jr.f* is used not only by itself, as in the preceding examples, but also in conjunction with other particles. The combination  *jst r.f* is especially common. It is normally used to introduce a new topic or additional information in the course of a narrative, and often corresponds to the English particle *now*, which has a similar function (see § 12.16.1): for example,

 *jst r.f jr p3 mw, jw.f m mḥ 12*
"Now, as for the water, it was 12 cubits (deep)."

Clauses with *jst r.f* are syntactically subordinate, but often have to be translated as main clauses.

3. *js*

The particle *js* is a syntactic element. We have already met it as part of the nonverbal negations *nj ... js* (§ 11.5) and *nj js* (§ 11.7), and as a marker of nonverbal noun clauses (§§ 12.13.1, 12.13.3) and adverb clauses (§§ 12.16.3–12.16.4). These same functions are also found in clauses with a verbal predicate. Essentially, *js* indicates that the clause in which it occurs is subordinate. This is easiest to see in noun clauses and adverb clauses, but it is also true of the negations *nj ... js* and *nj js*. As we have seen (§ 11.7), the negative particle *nj* can be used to negate a word: for example,

 *nj ḫt pw* "It is nothing."

The addition of *js* to such a clause indicates that the negation applies to the entire clause, not just to the word that follows *js*, as in

 *nj ḫt js pw* "It is not a thing."

The sentence *nj ḫt pw* is an **affirmative** sentence: literally, "It is a non-thing." The sentence *nj ḫt js pw* is a **negative** sentence: it means that the statement *ḫt pw* "it is a thing" is not true. The presence of *js* in the negation *nj ... js* indicates that the **entire clause** (*ḫt pw*) is subordinate to the negation, not just the **word** (*ḫt*) that follows *nj*.

We have also seen how the negation *nj js* is used to negate a word or phrase in contrast to something (§ 11.7), as in

 *ḥwrw nj js mjtw.k* "a poor man, not your equal."

Here too *js* is a marker of subordination: it indicates that the phrase in which it is used (*nj js mjtw.k* "not your equal") is dependent — by contrast — on that which precedes it (*ḥwrw* "a poor man"). The use of *js* to subordinate a single word or phrase is occasionally found in affirmative sentences as well: for example,

 *n.k jm s(j) mjtt ṯzmw.k js*
"It is yours as well, being your hounds."[11]

Here *js* subordinates the noun phrase *ṯzmw.k* "your hounds" to the preceding clause *n.k jm s(j) mjtt* "It is yours as well." This use, which is not too common in Middle Egyptian, is difficult to translate literally; in most cases, it can be paraphrased using the word "as" before the subordinated phrase: "It is yours as well, as your hounds."

11 For *n.k jm s(j)* see §§ 8.10 and 10.7. The word *mjtt* "as well" is an adverb formed from the adjective *mjtj* "similar," which in turn is a nisbe of the preposition *mj* "like": see § 8.14. The sentence refers to a foreign country as subject to the pharaoh.

4.  *w* "not"

This particle is a rare negation that has survived as a holdover from Old Egyptian. It is found almost exclusively in religious texts, and only with particular verb forms (see § 26.29.4)

5.  *wnnt* "really, indeed" (also  *wnt*)

This particle is used mostly in nominal sentences and only rarely with a verbal predicate. Its meaning corresponds fairly closely to that of English emphasizing adverbs such as *really*, *actually*, *indeed*, *truly*, *in fact*: for example,

 *jnk wnnt sr(j) ꜥ3 n jb.f* "I am truly an official great of heart."

6. , ,  *mj* "please, now"

The enclitic particle *mj* is probably just the proclitic particle *mj* (§ 16.6.7) used enclitically. It is used after the imperative or (rarely) the subjunctive (Lesson 19): for instance,

 *mj mj jb.j* "Come now, my heart!"

7.  *ms* "surely, indeed" (also  *msw*, )

This particle is used mostly in main clauses, with both verbal and nonverbal predicates. It implies astonishment, reproach, objection, or particular persuasiveness, and corresponds fairly closely in meaning to the English adverb *surely*, which has much the same connotation: for example,

jw ms r(m)ṯ mj gmw, zbw ẖt t3
nn ms ḥḏ ḥbsw m p3(y).n rk

"The people are surely like black ibises, and dirt is throughout the land:
there is surely no one with white clothes in our time!"[12]

The phrase 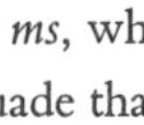 *jw ms*, which begins the first sentence of this example, was so associated with sentences used to persuade that it eventually became an idiom for "exaggeration" (i.e., the kind of claim made by snake-oil salesmen for their products): see Exercise 11, no. 6.

8. *ḥm* "and, also, moreover" (also , 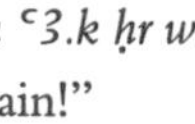)

This particle is found in clauses with nonverbal or verbal predicates. It indicates that the clause in which it occurs is an additional statement to one that has been made earlier: for example,

 *m.k ḥm ꜥ3.k ḥr wn(m) jtj.j*

"And look, your donkey is eating my grain!"

9. 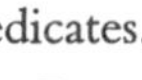 *swt* "but"

The particle *swt* normally occurs in the second of two phrases, clauses, or sentences and indicates a contrast with the preceding one, like English "but." It is used with nonverbal or verbal predicates. For examples, see Exercise 11, no. 22, and Exercise 15, no. 8.

10.  *grt* "now, moreover, but"

The particle *grt* is used in clauses with nonverbal or verbal predicates. It has much the same English translation as the particle *ḥm* (§ 16.7.8), but unlike the latter it normally marks a new topic or a new line of thought. For an example, see Exercise 11, no. 4.

12 *ḥḏ ḥbsw* is a *nfr ḥr* construction (§ 6.5): literally, "there is not one white of clothes." For *p3(y).n* "our" see § 5.10.5.

11.  *tr* (also  and ,  *tj*)

This particle occurs exclusively in questions, as we have seen in previous lessons (§§ 7.13.1–7.13.2, 7.13.4, 11.11.2). It is usually not translated, although it occasionally seems to mean something like "actually" or "really" (see § 11.11.2). It is used in clauses with verbal and nonverbal predicates.

16.8 Interjections

1.  *j* "oh!" (also , , , , and  *j3*)

This interjection is used before a vocative: for example,

 *j ꜥnḫw tp(j)w t3* "Oh, (you) living who are on earth!"

2. 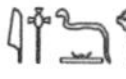 *j.nḏ ḥr* "hail to!" (also , etc.)

This interjection always occurs first in the sentence, and is always used with a second-person suffix pronoun attached to *ḥr* — i.e., *j.nḏ ḥr.k*, *j.nḏ ḥr.ṯ*, and *j.nḏ ḥr.ṯn* — as well as with a following vocative: for example,

 *j.nḏ ḥr.k ḏḥwtj* "Hail to you, Thoth!"

Although it is used (in this form) only as an interjection, it may derive from an original verbal expression *j.nḏ.j ḥr.k* (etc.), meaning something like "May I inquire about you," with the first-person suffix unwritten. It is used almost exclusively in religious texts.

3.  *m-bj3* "no!" (also  and )

This interjection occurs only as a separate word, like the English interjection "no!": for an example, see Exercise 15, no. 11.

4.  *h3* "oh!" (also , influenced by the verb *h3j* "descend")

The interjection *h3* is used like *j* before a vocative. It is less common than *j*, and occurs mostly in religious texts, usually before the name of the deceased and often followed by the demonstrative *pn* (feminine *tn*) or *pw* (feminine *tw*): for example,

 *h3 wsjr (r)ḫ-(n)sw(t) z3-sbk pn ꜥḥꜥ*

"Oh, Osiris Royal Acquaintance Si-sobek, stand up!"

literally, "Oh this Osiris (see Essay 8) Royal Acquaintance Si-sobek."

5.  *tjw* "yes!"

Like its negative counterpart *m-bj3* (§ 16.8.3), this interjection is used only as an independent word, like the English "yes!": for an example, see Exercise 15, no. 11.

Essay 16. Heresy

The Egyptian view of the world and its creation, as discussed in Essays 4–5 and 11–15, was fundamental to Egyptian civilization and remained basically unchanged throughout the more than 3,000 years of that civilization's history — with one exception. For two decades at the end of the Eighteenth Dynasty, one Egyptian king tried to introduce a different understanding of reality into his country's culture.

When the pharaoh Amenhotep III died, around 1350 BC, he was succeeded by his son of the same name, whom Egyptologists call Amenhotep IV. Three years into his rule, the new pharaoh made a stunning break with tradition by erecting a new temple within the precinct of the state temple of Amun at Karnak (see Essay 15), decorated in a radically new style of art and dedicated not to Amun but to a new form of the solar deity Re-Harakhti (Essay 12). This new god was depicted not as the falcon or falcon-headed human by which Re-Harakhti was traditionally represented, but in the image of the solar disk (*jtn*) with its life-giving rays extending to earth:

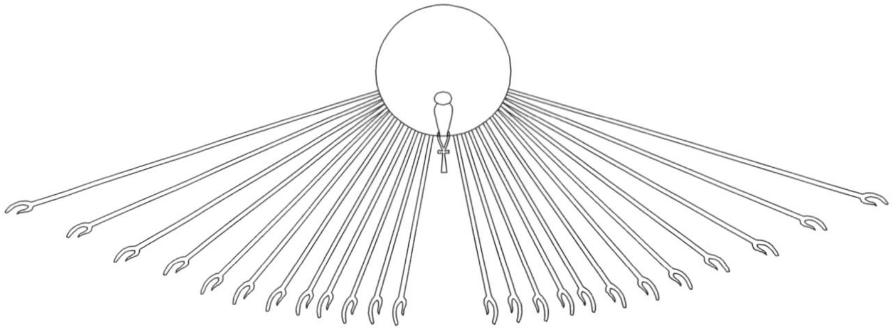

The god's name was also given a new form. It was now presented not simply as *rʿ-ḥrw-3ḫtj* "Re-Harakhti" but as a longer formula, enclosed in two cartouches like the names of a king:

"The living one (*ʿnḫ*), Re-Harakhti (*rʿ-ḥrw-3ḫtj*), who becomes active (*ḫʿj*) in the Akhet (*m 3ḫt*), in his identity as the light (*m rn.f m šw*) that is in the sun-disk (*ntj m jtn*)."

New as he was, this deity was rooted in the theology of Dynasty 18, which had placed increasing emphasis on the life-giving role of the sun. In the traditional theology this emphasis was incorporated in the combined form of the deity Amun-Re (see Essay 15). The new theology of Amenhotep IV, however, ignored Amun. The sun was now seen not as the physical manifestation of the god Amun but as the vehicle for a new supreme deity, who was not the invisible, unknowable, and transcendent Amun but the visible power of Light. Although the new deity is often called simply *jtn* or *p3 jtn* "the sun-disk," the disk itself was merely its vehicle, the means through which light comes into the world — much as the sun (*rʿ* "Re") had been for the life-giving power of Amun in traditional theology. The image of the solar disk that dominates scenes of the new theology is not meant as a depiction of the sun but as a *hieroglyph*, a more complex form of the normal hieroglyph for "light" ( ).

In his fifth year on the throne Amenhotep IV made yet another break with tradition, designed to emphasize even further the supreme status of his new god. He began construction of a new capital city designed to replace both the political capital of Memphis (associated with Ptah) and the religious capital of Thebes (city of Amun). This new city, called Akhetaten (*3ḫt-jtn* "Place where the sundisk becomes effective"), was built in Middle Egypt, on virgin land that had no previous divine associations. At the same time, the king changed his personal name from Amenhotep (*jmn-ḥtp* "Amun is Content") to Akhenaten (*3ḫ-n-jtn*), meaning "He who is effective (*3ḫ*) for the sundisk." Modern excavators have named Akhenaten's capital Tell el-Amarna, after the name of a nearby settlement. The name "Amarna" is used in Egyptological literature to refer not only to the site itself but also to the two-decade period of Akhenaten's religious experiment.

Although Akhetaten was intended to establish the supremacy of the new god, the worship of the traditional gods, including Amun, was still tolerated. Sometime between the ninth and eleventh year of Akhenaten's rule, however, a new policy came into effect. The god's name was changed to a new form:

meaning "The living one (*ꜥnḫ*), the Sun (*rꜥ*), ruler of the Akhet (*ḥq3 3ḫtj*), who becomes active (*ḥꜥj*) in the Akhet (*m 3ḫt*), in his identity as the light (*m rn.f m ḥ3jt*) that comes in the sun-disk (*jj m jtn*)."[13] This change served two purposes: it removed the reference to Re-Harakhti and substituted the neutral word *ḥ3jt* "light" for *šw* (which was also the name of the god Shu), and it made even clearer the sun-disk's role as the *vehicle*, not the *origin*, of Light. Both these changes were meant to establish Light as not just the supreme god but the only god. This new emphasis was also reflected in a campaign of active persecution against the traditional theology: on monuments throughout Egypt, Akhenaten's minions began to erase the names of Amun and his consort, Mut, and to change the plural *nṯrw* "gods" to the singular *nṯr* "god." To judge from later inscriptions, the temples of the older gods may have been closed as well, and their priesthoods disbanded.

Along with his religious reforms Akhenaten also introduced a host of cultural changes. The art of his reign not only has a new style but new subject matter as well: in place of the formal, timeless poses of the king before the gods, it shows Akhenaten and his family in the intimate scenes of everyday life. Under Akhenaten, the contemporary spoken language began to appear increasingly in writing, an innovation that led eventually to Late Egyptian (§ 1.2). The temples of Akhenaten's new god were not dark, mysterious buildings housing an inaccessible image of the god, but broad courts open to the sunlight. These structures were built not of the massive multi-ton blocks of traditional Egyptian architecture, but of small blocks that could be handled by a single workman; Egyptologists call these blocks *talatat* (an Arabic word). All of these changes reflect Akhenaten's

13 The word *3ḫtj* is a nisbe, written as a "false dual": see n. 14 in Lesson 12. The writing of the word *ḥ3jt* "light" uses the sun hieroglyph as an ideogram; the grouping of the signs in this word is dictated by the need to conserve space in the cartouche.

emphasis on the visible, tangible, here-and-now rather than the more spiritual and timeless forms of traditional Egyptian art.

Despite its emphasis on reality, however, the new artistic style in which Akhenaten's monuments were decorated also exaggerated the forms of the king and his family. This last feature was long thought to reflect a physical deformity of the king, but it is now known to have been merely an artistic convention meant to emphasize the difference between the royal family and mere mortals: as the new art matured it became less exaggerated, and images from the end of the king's reign show him with a normal human physique.

Akhenaten's immediate family consisted of his mother, Queen Tiya; his Chief Queen, Nefretiti; their six daughters, the most important of whom were the eldest, Meret-aten, and the third oldest, Ankhes-en-pa-aten; a minor queen, named Kiya; and probably another daughter by her, whose name is not known. Akhenaten's successors Smenkh-ka-re and Tut-ankh-amun were also from the royal family. Although their exact relationship to Akhenaten is uncertain, they were most likely his sons, perhaps by Kiya: they were probably brothers, and Tut-ankh-amun is attested late in Akhenaten's reign as "king's son of his body, his beloved, Tut-ankhu-aten."

Toward the end of his reign there is some evidence that Akhenaten elevated Nefretiti from Chief Queen to co-pharaoh. Her rule, as the pharaoh Nefer-neferu-aten, lasted at least three years, including perhaps a brief period of sole rule after the death of Akhenaten. She was followed by Smenkh-ka-re, who was married to Meret-aten. After a short reign of a year or less, he was succeeded by Tut-ankh-aten, who had married Ankhes-en-pa-aten. By his third year of rule, Tut-ankh-aten had abandoned Akhet-aten, changed his name to Tut-ankh-amun and that of his wife to Ankhes-en-amun, and reestablished the worship of Amun and the other traditional gods of Egypt.

Akhenaten's attempt to establish the worship of a single god did not survive his own reign. Already toward the end of his life there is evidence of an attempt to reconcile the new religion with the worship of Amun at Thebes, under the patronage of Nefer-neferu-aten. His successor Tutankhamun reopened the temples and established new priesthoods, and an active campaign to dismantle Akhenaten's monuments began under Haremhab, the last king of Dynasty 18. Eventually even the name of Akhenaten and those of his immediate successors were deleted from official records; later kinglists jump from Amenhotep III directly to Haremhab. When it was necessary to refer to Akhenaten at all, he was mentioned only as "the heretic of Akhetaten."

Akhenaten's reforms have been the subject of much speculation, not all of it well considered or well informed. Although the precise meaning and motive of his revolutionary changes are still debated, it now seems clear that Akhenaten did not attempt to establish a kind of monotheism like that of the early Hebrews. Instead of promoting a single transcendental god, Akhenaten emphasized the predominance of a single immanent force of nature — Light — as the only true god. In theological terms this was a step backward from the intellectual progress that had been achieved in the theology of Amun (see Essay 15). More importantly, the impersonal nature of Akhenaten's deity left the Egyptians without a god to whom they could relate as they had to Amun and the other gods. This, more than anything, seems to have been the reason why Akhenaten's reforms did not survive him and why later generations of Egyptians considered them not a revelation but a heresy.

EXERCISE 16

Transliterate and translate the following sentences:

1. 
2. 
3. 
4. 
5. 
6. 
7. 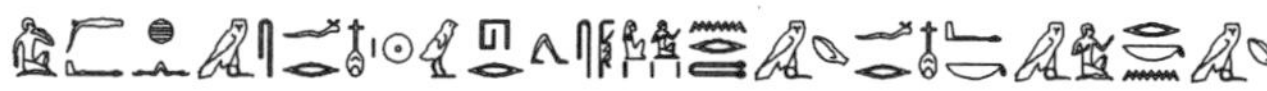
8. 
9. 
10. 
11. 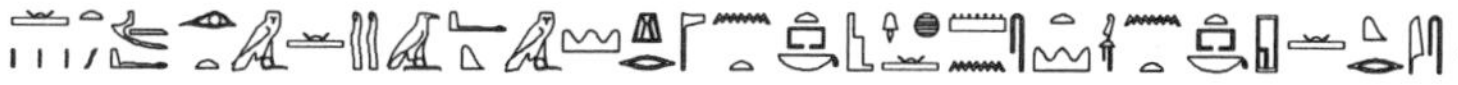 — one sentence
12. 
13.  — *nfrtj* personal name
14.  — *jnpw* personal name "Anubis"
15. 
16. 
17. 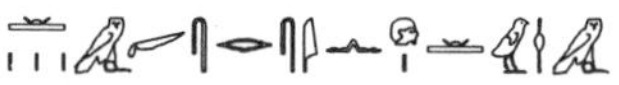
18.  — *kt* ... *kt* "one ... the other"
19.  ( § 9.5)
20.  — said by a servant giving a woman a drink from a jar
21. 
22.  — from a hymn in praise of the king
23.  — from a story: *nmtj-nḫt* personal name
24. 
25.  — two sentences, from a description of adverse times
26. 
27.  — *tpj* § 8.6.12
28. 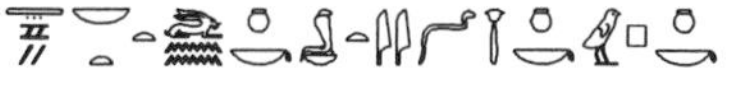

29. 

 — from a description of a journey in the sun's boat

30. 

31. 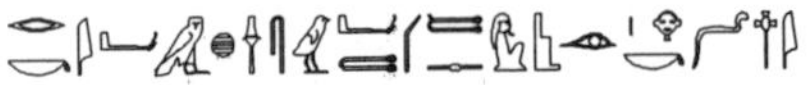

32.  — *jmnt* "the West," here personified as a goddess

33. 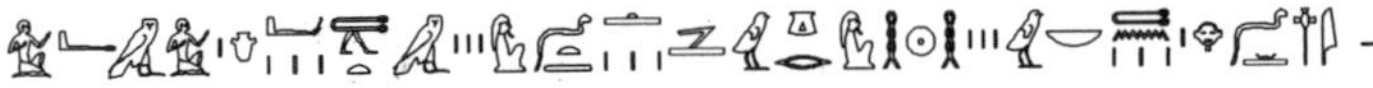 — *nḥḥ* and *ḏt* see Essay 9; *grg* "founder"

34. 

 — *šmsw* "who follow," *r nmtwt.f* "in his footsteps," for the preposition *n* (§ 8.2.6), *kt-ḫj* § 6.7,  *rꜥ* "Re, the Sun"

17. The Stative

17.1 Definition and basic meaning

The stative is a verb form used to express a **state of being** in which its subject is, was, or will be. Originally, the stative expressed the perfect tense: that is, completed action (§ 13.3.2). By Middle Egyptian, however, other verb forms were used for that function, and the stative had come to express instead the **result** of a completed action. In this respect, the stative is similar to the English past participle. In the sentence *The table is set*, for example, the past participle *set* describes both a state in which its subject (*the table*) is and the result of a prior action (in this case, of someone setting the table). Because of this similarity, the stative is sometimes called the **pseudoparticiple**. The stative still retains its older meaning of completed action in one use in Middle Egyptian, and for this reason it is also known as the **old perfective**.

Like the English past participle, the stative expresses two different relationships between the verb and its subject. When the verb is **transitive**, the stative normally expresses the result of a prior action performed **on** its subject. In the example given above, for instance, the past participle *set* describes the state resulting from a prior action that was performed on the subject, *the table*. When the verb is **intransitive**, the stative expresses the result of a prior action performed **by** its subject. In modern English the verb *go* is practically the only intransitive verb with a past participle that is used in this way: for example, *Jack is gone*, where the past participle *gone* describes the state resulting from a prior action performed by the subject, *Jack*. Even though most English intransitive verbs have a past participle, this form can only be used to express **action**, not a state of being: for example, *The sun has appeared* (completed action) but not **The sun is appeared* (state). Languages such as French and German, however, normally use the past participle of intransitive verbs to express a state of being, as in *Le soleil est paru* (French) and *Die Sonne ist erschienen* (German), both of which mean, literally, "the sun is appeared." In this respect Egyptian is like French and German rather than English: the stative of intransitive verbs basically expresses state, not action.

The stative is one of the most common Egyptian verb forms, and it existed in all stages of the language, from Old Egyptian through Coptic (where it is often called the **qualitative**). It is also one of the most flexible of all verb forms, appearing in many different uses and constructions. As we will learn in the course of this lesson, English often requires different translations for the stative, depending on how it is used, because of grammatical differences between the two languages. Despite these differences, however, you should try to remember that the basic meaning of the form in Middle Egyptian is always an expression of state, even when there is no practical way to translate this basic meaning into good, grammatical English.

The stative is a form that Egyptian shares in common with most of the Afro-Asiatic languages to which it is related (§ 1.1), from ancient Akkadian to modern Arabic and Berber. This relationship helps us to understand some of the features of the stative, even though there are often major differences in syntax and meaning between the Egyptian verb form and its Afro-Asiatic relatives.

17.2 The stative suffixes

The stative differs from all other Egyptian verb forms in one important respect: it is **always** combined with a pronominal suffix (some Egyptologists refer to this as the "ending" of the stative). The suffix pronouns used with the stative have a special form, which is found only in combination with the stative and nowhere else:

1S *.kw* — , , also , , , , or simply
The seated man is a determinative, as in *jnk* (§ 5.5). The spelling represents *.kw*, not *.kwj*: the reed-leaf in this case is used in place of the seated man. The Old Egyptian form was *.kj* (or); this spelling is occasionally found in older Middle Egyptian texts as well.

2S *.tj* — , , often simply ; often in New Kingdom texts
Used for both masculine and feminine. When the suffix is spelled it is usually written **before** the determinative: for example, *pr.t(j)* "you have come." When the verb itself ends in *t*, the suffix can be omitted, probably because it came next to the *t* of the verb, without a vowel between (see the discussion at the end of this section), and the combination *tt* was written with only one *t*: for example, *nḫt.(tj)* "successful" (2ms).

3MS *.w* — or ; **usually not written**
This suffix is normally written **before** the determinative: for example, *h3.w* "descended." The Old Egyptian form was *.j*; this spelling is occasionally found in older Middle Egyptian texts as well.

3FS *.tj* — , , often simply ; often in New Kingdom texts
When the suffix is spelled it is usually written **before** the determinative: for example, *mḥ.t(j)* "full." When the verb itself ends in *t*, the suffix is often omitted, as in the 2s (see above): for example, *m(w)t.(tj)* "dead."

1PL *.wjn* — , , rarely
The original form was *.nw*, which appears once in Old Egyptian as and a few times in early Middle Egyptian texts as . The Middle Egyptian suffix *.wjn* may derive from an adjectival predicate: e.g., *ḥtp.wjn* "we are content," originally probably *ḥtpwj n* "how content we are" (see §§ 7.2–7.3).

2PL *.tjwnj* — ,
Used for both masculine and feminine. The bird is the *tjw*-vulture (G2, sometimes in the form), not the *3*-bird (G1).

3PL *.wj* — or , sometimes with plural strokes; also *.y*; **usually not written**
The ending is normally written before the determinative: for example, *šn.w* "encircled." Old Egyptian also had a separate form *.tj* for the 3fpl, written like the singular, and two dual forms: 3mdu *.wjj* (,) and 3fdu *.tjj* (,). These older forms rarely appear in Middle Egyptian; most Middle Egyptian texts use the form *.wj* (or *.y*) for the third-person plural or dual, masculine or feminine.

Transcriptions of Egyptian words in other ancient languages, survivals of the stative in Coptic, and parallels from related languages (see the end of § 17.1), all give us an idea how the different forms of the stative were actually pronounced. Using the verb *ḥtp* "become content," these can be reconstructed as follows (the "accented" vowel *á* shows which syllable was stressed):

1S	**ḥatpáku*	1PL	? (originally **ḥatpánu*)
2MS	**ḥatpáta* or **ḥatápta*	2MPL	**ḥatpátunu* or **ḥatáptunu*
2FS	**ḥatpáti* or **ḥatápti*	2FPL	**ḥatpátina* or **ḥatáptina*
3MS	**ḥátpa* (Coptic ϩⲟⲧⲡ̄)	3PL	**ḥátpu*
3FS	**ḥatápta* or **ḥatpáta*		

As you can see, the stative suffixes probably distinguished between masculine and feminine in the second person by vowels, which of course are not visible in hieroglyphs. All the suffixes probably ended in a vowel, which is why their final "weak" consonants (*w* and *j*) — which reflect these vocalic endings — are often omitted in writing. These reconstructions are given here to help you appreciate the relationship between the various written forms and the actual spoken forms they were meant to represent.

17.3 **The stative stem**

Most verb classes use the base stem in forming the stative, with a few peculiarities in some classes. The following examples are representative of the forms found in Middle Egyptian texts:

2-LIT. *mḥ.(w)* "full" (3ms)

2AE-GEM. *qb.tj* "cool" (3fs). Occasionally the geminated stem is used: for example, *gnn.tj* "soft" (3fs). The two forms may reflect a difference in pronunciation: i.e., *qabbáti* = *qb.tj* but *ganánti* = *gnn.tj*. There seems to be no difference in meaning or use between them.

3-LIT. *snb.t(j)* "healthy" (2s)

3AE-INF. *h3.w* "descended" (3ms). The third-person masculine forms (singular and plural) often have a final *y* instead of the suffix *w*: for example, *h3y* (3ms). In rare cases the geminated stem is used instead of the base: for instance, *h33.(w)* (3ms). The reasons for this are not clear, but there seems to be no difference in meaning or use from the regular forms.

3AE-GEM. *špss.kw* "ennobled" (1s) — geminated stem

4-LIT. *p3ḫd.tj* "inverted" (3fs)

4AE-INF. *ḥms.(w)* "seated" (3ms). The third-person masculine forms (singular and plural) sometimes have a final *y* instead of the suffix *w*: for example, *w3sy* "ruined" (3ms).

5-LIT. *nḏ3ḏ3.tj* "runny" (3fs)

CAUS. 2-LIT. *sʿq.t(j)* "brought in" (3fs)

CAUS. 2AE-GEM.	*sšmm.(w)* "heated" (3ms) — geminated stem
CAUS. 3-LIT.	*sʿnḫ.t(j)* "vivified" (3fs)
CAUS. 3AE-INF.	*sṯn.k(w)* "distinguished" (1s)
ANOM.	Both *rdj* "give, put" and *jwj/jj* "come" can use either base stem:
	rdj.t(j) "put" (3fs) and *dj.t(j)* "put" (2ms)
	jw.t(j) "come" (2ms) and *jj.t(j)* "come" (3fs)
	Like other final-weak verbs, these occasionally have a final *y* instead of the suffix *w* in the 3ms and 3pl: for example, *dy* "put" (3pl).

17.4 The subject of the stative

Although the stative always has a pronominal suffix, it is often used with a separate subject, which is a noun (or noun phrase) or pronoun placed **before** the stative itself. This combination is known as the **SUBJECT-stative construction**: for example,

t3 3q.w r 3w "The entire land is ruined."

As this example demonstrates, the stative (here, 3ms *3q.w* "ruined," from the verb *3q* "go to ruin") agrees as far as possible in gender and number with its subject (here, the singular noun *t3* "land"). Note also that the stative tends to be as close to its subject as possible: in this case, *3q.w* stands next to *t3* and before the modifier *r 3w* "entire" (§ 6.7). Similarly,

jtrw šw.(w) nw kmt "The river of Egypt is dried up,"

where the 3ms stative *šw.(w)* "dried up" (from the verb *šwj* "dry up") stands next to its subject, *jtrw* "river," and before the indirect genitive *nw kmt* "of Egypt."[1]

When the subject of the stative is a personal pronoun it is normally introduced by a particle of some sort. In this respect the SUBJECT-stative construction behaves like an adverbial sentence (§ 10.5), and it is used with the same particles (§§ 10.3–10.5, 16.6): for example,

jw.f mḥ.(w) ẖr nfrwt nbt "It is filled with all good things"

m.k wj 3tp.kw m jʿnw "Look, I am loaded with woe,"

with statives from the verbs *mḥ* "fill" and *3tp* (originally *3ṯp*) "load" as predicates. Like adverbial sentences, too, the stative is used in later Middle Egyptian texts with the subject pronoun as subject (§ 10.5): for instance,

tw.n qb.wjn ẖr t3(y).n kmt
"We are calm in our (part of) Egypt,"[2]

with the 1pl stative *qb.wjn* "calm" (literally, "cooled," from the 2ae-gem. verb *qbb* "cool, cool off, cool down, calm") as the predicate.

1 The spelling of *jtrw* is irregular. The indirect genitive *nw* is plural because nouns denoting liquids are often treated as plurals, even when the nouns themselves are singular.

2 Literally, "we are calmed under our (§ 5.10.5) Egypt." The spelling of the stative suffix *.wjn* with the determinatives of the verb between *wj* and *n* is unusual, but it reflects the probable origin of this suffix in the adjectival-predicate construction *qbwj n* "how cooled we are" (§ 17.2).

As these examples show, the syntax of the SUBJECT-stative construction is essentially the same as that of adverbial sentences, except that the predicate is a stative form instead of an adverb or prepositional phrase. For that reason, grammars of Middle Egyptian sometimes describe the SUBJECT-stative construction as a form of the pseudoverbal construction (Lesson 15); this is not quite accurate, however, since the stative is a real verbal predicate, unlike the pseudoverbal predicates with preposition plus infinitive.

17.5 The stative as an expression of state

As we saw in the first section of this lesson, the stative in Middle Egyptian essentially expresses a state of being, usually one that results from some previous action. This is true of all the examples given in the previous section: "the land is ruined" (i.e., in a state of ruin), "the river is dried up" (i.e., in a state of dryness), "it is filled" (in a state of fullness), "I am loaded" (in a state of encumbrance), "we are calm" (in a state of calmness). In these examples the state of being expressed by the stative is more important than the action that produced the state, even though the state has actually resulted in each case from a previous action — i.e., "going to ruin" (*3q*), "drying up" (*šwj*), "filling" (*mḥ*), "loading" (*3tp*), and "becoming calm" (*qbb*).

Although it often presupposes a previous action, therefore, the stative itself does not actually express this action. Instead, it simply denotes a state. As such, **the stative has no tense**. In the same way that adverbial predicates can express a past, present, or future location (§§ 11.2–11.3), the stative can be used to express not just a present state (as in the examples of § 17.4) but also a state in the past (as we will see in the next section) or, as the following example shows, in the future:

 *ḥ3 t3 mḥ.(w) m mjt(w)w.f*
"If only the land would be filled with those like him!"

Here the stative of the verb *mḥ* "fill" describes a state that does not exist at the time of speaking.[3]

17.6 The SUBJECT-stative construction as a past tense

Although the stative itself is basically the tenseless expression of a state, the SUBJECT-stative construction is regularly used in Middle Egyptian to express the past or perfect tense of **intransitive** verbs, particularly verbs of motion: for example,

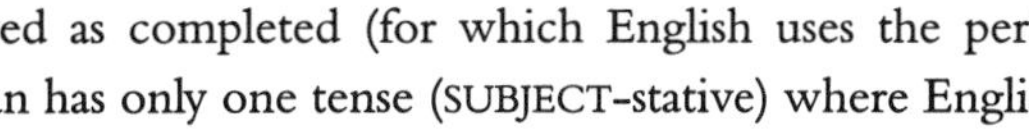 *ḏ*ᶜ *pr.(w) jw.n m w3ḏ-wr*
"A storm came up, while we were at sea"[4]

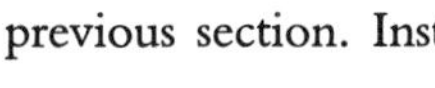 *m.k wj jj.kw* "Look, I have come."

As these examples show, the SUBJECT-stative construction can be used to describe an action that happened in the past (for which English uses the past tense: "a storm came up") or an action that is viewed as completed (for which English uses the perfect tense: "I have come"). Note that Egyptian has only one tense (SUBJECT-stative) where English has two (past and perfect).

This use of the stative does not contradict what was said about the basic meaning of the form in the previous section. Instead, it illustrates a fundamental difference between the grammar of

3 Compare the sentence *jw.f mḥ.(w) ẖr nfrwt nbt* "It is filled with all good things," cited in § 17.4.
4 The second clause in this sentence, *jw.n m w3ḏ-wr*, is an adverb clause (literally, "we were in the Great Blue-Green"): see § 12.17.

Egyptian and that of English. Middle Egyptian regularly expresses both the past and the perfect tense of an intransitive verb not by describing past or completed **action** but by describing the **state** that results from that action. Thus, the examples just given mean literally "a storm was emerged" (stative of the verb *prj* "come forth") and "I am come" (stative of the verb *jj* "come"). In contrast to Egyptian, modern English describes the past or perfect of such verbs as an **action**, not the resulting state: "a storm came up," "I have come." In older English, however, the past or perfect tense of an intransitive verb could also be expressed as a state: for instance, *sumer is icumen in* (old English song: "summer has come in"). This is also the case in modern colloquial French and German, as we saw in § 17.1.[5]

When it is used as a past tense (but not as the perfect), the SUBJECT-stative construction is often introduced by the words *ʿḥʿ.n*, (or) *wn.jn*, or *wn.ḫr* "then," which we have already met in pseudoverbal sentences (§ 15.6): for example,

 *ʿḥʿ.n.(j) h3.kw r mryt* "Then I went down to the shore"

 *wn.jn p3 smn ʿḥʿ.(w)* "Then that goose stood"

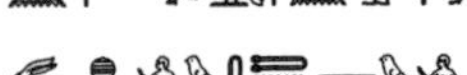 *wn.ḫr.j wsṯn.kw* "Then I strode forth."

These examples have exactly the same syntax as those with an adverbial predicate: that is, the introductory word is followed by a noun or suffix pronoun as subject, and then by the predicate — in this case, the stative rather than an adverb or prepositional phrase.

The use of the stative to express a past or perfect tense is primarily a feature of **intransitive** verbs (§ 13.2): transitive verbs use a different form, which we will meet in the next lesson. The stative can be used for the past or perfect tense of a transitive verb in the **passive**, however — that is, to describe a past action performed on the subject rather than by the subject (§ 13.3.4): for example,

 *ʿḥʿ.n.j rdj.kw r jw jn w3w n w3ḏ-wr*
"Then I was put on (literally, "given to") an island by a wave of the sea."

This use of the stative is also common, but usually with a personal pronoun as the subject (here, the suffix pronoun of *ʿḥʿ.n.j*); nominal subjects are normally used with a different passive verb form, which we will discuss in Lesson 21. In this case too the stative actually expresses a state, not an action: here, something like "then I was situated at an island."

To summarize, the SUBJECT-stative construction is normally used to express the past or perfect tense for the following kinds of verbs and subjects:

- **intransitive** verbs, with any kind of subject. The relationship between the stative and its subject is **active**: for example, *ḏʿ pr.(w)* "a storm came up," *m.k wj jj.kw* "I have come."
- **transitive** verbs, with a **personal pronoun** as subject. The relationship between the stative and its subject is **passive**: for example, *ʿḥʿ.n.j rdj.kw* "then I was put."

5 In literary French and German, constructions such as *Le soleil est paru* and *Die Sonne ist erschienen* express only the perfect tense, and a different form is used for the past: *Le soleil parut*, *Die Sonne schien* "the sun appeared." This form is rarely used in everyday speech and writing.

17.7 The stative of adjective verbs

Like an adjectival predicate, the stative of an adjective verb (§ 13.2) describes a quality of its subject: for example,

 *wn.jn jb.f nfr.(w) r ḫt nbt*
"Then his heart was better (i.e., happier) than anything,"

where the stative of the verb *nfr* "become good" describes a quality (goodness, happiness) of the subject *jb.f* "his heart."

In English such predicates have much the same translation as a true adjectival predicate: compare, for example, the following sentence:

 *wn.jn nfr st ḥr jb.f r ḫt nbt*
"Then it was better on his heart than anything."

In Egyptian, however, the two constructions are different, and they involve slightly different connotations as well. While both the adjectival stative and the true adjectival predicate express a quality of their subject, the stative of an adjective verb has the additional nuance of a prior action that produced the quality. Thus, in the two examples given here, the adjectival-predicate construction *nfr st* means simply "it was good," while the stative construction *jb.f nfr.(w)* "his heart was good" implies that the quality "good" has resulted from the prior action of "becoming good." This is not a distinction that can easily be expressed in English, except by paraphrasing the stative: i.e., *jb.f nfr.(w)* "his heart had become, and was now, good" vs. *nfr st* "it was good."

Even though English usually requires similar translations for an adjectival predicate and the stative of an adjective verb, therefore, you should be aware that there is a subtle difference in meaning between the two constructions in Egyptian.

17.8 The stative of *rḫ* "know"

In § 17.6 we saw that the stative of a transitive verb normally has passive meaning, expressing the result of an action performed *on* its subject. There is one major exception to this rule in Middle Egyptian. The stative of the transitive verb *rḫ* always has **active** meaning, expressing an action performed **by** its subject: thus, *jw.j rḫ.kw* means "I know" (or "I knew"), not "I am known." Like other active verbs the stative of *rḫ* can have a direct object denoting the thing that is "known" by the subject. This object can be a noun (or noun phrase or noun clause) or a pronoun; when it is a personal pronoun, the **dependent** forms are used: for example,

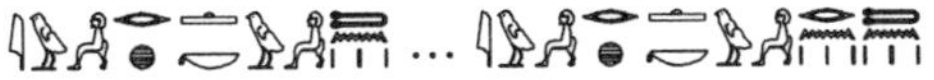 *jw.j rḫ.kw ṯn … jw.j rḫ.kw rnw.ṯn*
"I know you … I know your names."

The reason for this exception has to do with the basic meaning of *rḫ*. Although this verb is translated by the English verb "know" in many of its forms, it really means to "experience" or "learn about" something. The stative is translated as "know" because it expresses the state that results from experiencing or learning about something — which, of course, is a state of knowledge. Thus, a sentence such as *jw.j rḫ.kw rnw.ṯn* really means something like "I am experienced about your names." Ancient Egyptian does not actually have a verb that corresponds exactly to the English verb *know*.

17.9 The SUBJECT-stative construction in main clauses

As we have seen in the preceding sections, the SUBJECT-stative construction has essentially the same syntax as that of sentences with an adverbial or pseudoverbal predicate. Examples given in §§ 17.4 and 17.6 demonstrate the use of this construction in main clauses without an introductory word. This use is particularly common in proper names: for example, 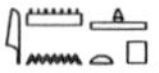 *jmn-ḥtp.(w)* "Amun is contented" (Amenhotep), 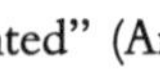 *ḏḥwtj-ms.(w)* "Thoth is born" (Thutmose), 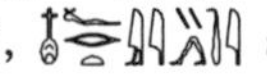 *nfrt-jj.tj* "The beautiful one has come" (Nefretiti).

Other examples given above show how the SUBJECT-stative construction is used after the particles *jw*, *m.k*, *ḥ3*, and the words *ᶜḥᶜ.n*, *wn.jn*, and *wn.ḫr*. It is found in main clauses after other particles as well, which are the same ones used to introduce main clauses with an adverbial or pseudoverbal predicate: for example,

 *nḥmn z3.f ᶜq.(w) r ᶜḥ*
"His son has surely entered the palace" — cf. § 10.4.3

 *smwn msḥ pn ḥ3.(w)*
"This crocodile is probably dangerous" — cf. § 16.6.14

 *jw ms m(w)tw ᶜš3w qrs.w m jtrw*
"Truly, many dead are buried in the river" — cf. § 16.7.7.

Adverbial or pseudoverbal sentences are usually introduced by a particle of some sort in Middle Egyptian (§§ 10.3, 15.3), and the same is true for the SUBJECT-stative construction. Examples without such an introductory word are normally possible only when the subject is a noun (or noun phrase), a demonstrative pronoun, or the subject pronoun. When two main clauses are combined in a single sentence, however, both the introductory word **and the subject** of the stative can be omitted in the second clause: for example,

 *jw.j rḫ.kw ṯn, rḫ.kw rnw.ṯn*
"I know you, and know your names."

This is known as a **compound sentence.** As the translation shows, it exists in English as well as Egyptian. The second clause in such a sentence is not a dependent clause (§ 12.1) but a second main clause with its subject omitted. In English the two main clauses are joined by *and*; Egyptian, which has no regular word for "and," simply puts the second clause after the first. The subject can be omitted in the second clause because it is easily understood from the first one.

Like an adverbial predicate (§ 10.9), the stative can also have its subject omitted after a particle when the subject does not refer to anything in particular: for instance,

 *m(j), h3 jm, jw nfr.w* "Come, go down there: it is good."

This use occurs mostly with the stative of adjective verbs, as in this example.

17.10 The SUBJECT-stative construction in relative clauses

In relative clauses the SUBJECT-stative construction is normally introduced by the relative adjective *ntj*, like adverbial and pseudoverbal predicates (§§ 12.4–12.7, 15.10). In direct relative clauses (§ 12.4), *ntj* itself serves as the subject of the stative: for example,

 *ꜥt nbt nt z(j) ntt mr.tj* "every limb of a man that is sick,"

where the relative clause *ntt mr.tj* "that is sick" (literally, "that has become sick") modifies the feminine antecedent *ꜥt nbt* "every limb." In indirect relative clauses (§ 12.5), *ntj* serves as the relative marker, and the subject of the stative is expressed separately: for instance,

 *ḏw pf b3ḫw ntj pt tn rhn.tj ḥr.f*
"that mountain, (named) Bakhu, on which this sky is propped up,"

literally, "which this sky is propped up on it," where the suffix pronoun of the prepositional phrase *ḥr.f* "on it" is the coreferent of the antecedent *ḏw pf* "that mountain" (the proper noun *b3ḫw* is in apposition to *ḏw pf*: § 4.11); in the relative clause, *pt tn* "this sky" is the subject and the stative *rhn.tj* "propped up" (from the verb *rhnj* "lean, depend") is the predicate.

The SUBJECT-stative construction can also appear without *ntj* in relative clauses after an undefined antecedent (cf. § 12.11): for example,

 *m sm3 z(j) jw.k rḫ.tj 3ḫw.f*
"Don't kill a man whose effectiveness you know."

This is an example of the SUBJECT-stative construction in an indirect relative clause: literally, "a man you know his effectiveness," where the suffix pronoun of *jw.k* is the subject of the relative clause and the suffix pronoun of *3ḫw.f* "his effectiveness" is the coreferent of the undefined antecedent *zj* "a man." An example of the construction in a direct relative clause is the following:

jw.f m nḏs n rnpt 110 jw.f ḥr wnm t 50 … jw.f rḫ.(w) ṯ3z tp ḥsq
"He is a commoner of 110 years (of age), who is eating 50 loaves of bread (a day) … who knows (how) to tie on a severed head."

literally, "he knows tying on a severed head," similar to *jw.f ḥr wnm t 50* "he is eating 50 loaves of bread" (we have already met the first part of this sentence in § 15.10.2).

17.11 The SUBJECT-stative construction in noun clauses

When it is used in a noun clause, the SUBJECT-stative construction is normally introduced by *ntt* or *wnt* "that," as are noun clauses with an adverbial or pseudoverbal predicate (§§ 12.13.2, 15.11): for instance,

 *ḥr ntt wj ṯb.kw m ṯbtj ntj zkr*
"because I am shod with the sandals of Sokar"[6]

 *j.ḏd.k n ḥrw wnt wj ḥꜥ.kw m m3ꜥ ḫrw.f*
"You should say to Horus that I am excited about his justification."[7]

In the first of these examples, the noun clause is the object of the preposition *ḥr*; in the second, it is the object of the verb form *j.ḏd.k* "you should say."

6 Literally, "because of (the fact) that I am sandaled with the two sandals of Sokar." For *ḥr ntt* see § 12.13.2; *ntj* is the old feminine dual form of the indirect genitive (not the relative adjective *ntj*).

7 *j.ḏd.k* is a verb form we will meet in Lesson 19. The expression *m3ꜥ ḫrw*, literally, "true of voice," refers to the justification of Horus over his enemies (see Essay 8).

In § 12.14 we saw how an independent sentence with adverbial predicate can function as a noun clause without any introductory word. This is also true for the SUBJECT-stative construction. Examples in Middle Egyptian occur mostly in the following uses:

1. as object of the compound preposition *m ḫt* "after" (literally, "in the wake of"): for instance,

jw ḫrp.n.(j) jtj-šmʿj n jnj n ḥf3t m ḫt jw-m-jtrw sʿnḫ.t(j)

"I directed Upper Egyptian barley to Ini and to Hefat, after Iu-em-itru was fed."[8]

Here the sentence *jw-m-jtrw sʿnḫ.t(j)* is used as the object of the compound preposition *m ḫt*, just as the English translation uses the sentence "Iu-em-itru was fed" as the object of the preposition "after" without an introductory word.

2. as the A element in an A *pw* nominal sentence: for example,

 *ḫ3 pw ḫr.(w) ḥr ḫrw ṯ3w.s*

"It means a thousand have fallen at the sound of its wind."[9]

In this case the entire sentence *ḫ3 ḫr.(w) ḥr ḫrw ṯ3w.s* "a thousand have fallen at the sound of its wind" is used as a nominal predicate (A). As usual in an A *pw* sentence, *pw* is placed as close to the front of the sentence as possible (§ 7.9): here, immediately after *ḫ3* "a thousand," which is the subject of the stative *ḫr.(w)* "have fallen." Compare the use of the infinitive as predicate in an A *pw* sentence, which we met in § 14.13.

3. as the object of a verb, for example:

jn jw m3ʿt pw p3 ḏd jw.k rḫ.tj ṯ3z tp ḥsq

"Is the saying (that) you know how to tie on a severed head the truth?"

This is an A *pw* B nominal sentence, used in a question (§ 11.11.2), where A is the noun *m3ʿt* "the truth" and B is the noun phrase *p3 ḏd jw.k rḫ.tj ṯ3z tp ḥsq* "the saying you know tying on a severed head." In the noun phrase, the sentence *jw.k rḫ.tj ṯ3z tp ḥsq* "you know tying on a severed head" is the object of the infinitive *p3 ḏd* "the saying" (see § 14.8).

In each of these cases, the SUBJECT-stative construction is used like a noun — as the object of a preposition, as the predicate in a A *pw* sentence, and as the object of a verb — even though it is a complete sentence in itself, with its own subject and predicate.

8 *jw ḫrp.n.(j)* "I directed" is a verbal construction we will meet in the next lesson. The stative *sʿnḫ.t(j)* means literally "caused to live": the verb *sʿnḫ* is often used as an idiom meaning "to feed" someone; the stative is feminine because its subject, the proper name of a town, is treated as feminine (§ 4.4). The words *jnj* and *ḥf3t* are names of towns in Upper Egypt, south of Thebes. The name *jw-m-jtrw* means "Island in the River"; since it was pronounced as one word, the preposition *m* and the first consonant of *jtrw* were often combined in the biliteral sign *mj* (as in this example). This text comes from the stela of an official who lived in *jw-m-jtrw*, and describes how he took care of neighboring towns after first caring for his own.

9 Literally, "it is (that) a thousand have fallen at the sound of its wind." The possessive pronoun of "its wind" refers to a throwstick, used to hunt birds. The full context of the sentence is: "Waterfowl shall come to you in the thousands, and settle on your path. Once you have thrown your throwstick at them, it means a thousand have fallen at the sound of its wind." This passage occurs in an idealized description of hunting in the marshes in the afterlife.

17.12 The SUBJECT-stative construction in adverb clauses

In previous lessons we have seen how adverbial sentences and those with a pseudoverbal predicate can function as adverb clauses, either with an introductory particle or without one (§§ 12.16–12.17, 15.9). The SUBJECT-stative construction can be used in exactly the same way. The following is an example with the introductory particle *jsṯ*:

wḏ3 pw jr.n ḥm.f m dpt-nṯr, jst ꜥḥꜥw pn grg.(w) m skwt

"What His Incarnation did was to proceed in the god's boat, while this flotilla was furnished with troop-ships."[10]

In most cases an adverb clause with the stative is unmarked: that is, it looks just like a main clause, or independent sentence, but is identified as an adverb clause by the context in which it is used (compare the same use of adverbial and pseudoverbal predicates in unmarked adverb clauses: §§ 12.17 and 15.9.2). The following are two examples with nominal and pronominal subject:

 *nꜥt m ḫd jn ḥm.f, jb.f 3w.(w)*

"Sailing downstream by His Incarnation, his heart happy"[11]

 *jnk šꜥd ḏrt.f, jw.f ꜥnḫ.(w), m b3ḥ ḥm.f*

"I was the one who cut off his hand, while he was (still) alive, (right) in front of His Incarnation."[12]

Each of these examples could be an independent sentence — *jb.f 3w.(w)* "his heart was happy," *jw.f ꜥnḫ.(w)* "he was alive" — but the context in which they are used shows that they are adverbial. Both are circumstantial clauses (§ 12.15), describing a state pertaining when the action of the main clause took place.

17.13 The SUBJECT-stative construction in clauses of result

Most adverb clauses describe circumstances in which a preceding clause happens or is true. In some cases, however, an adverb clause describes a circumstance that results from the action of a preceding clause. We use the past participle of some verbs this way in English: for example, in the sentence *The hunters shot the lion dead*, the past participle *dead* describes a state that results from the action of the main clause *The hunters shot the lion* (the lion was dead only after the hunters shot him, not before). Note that this meaning is determined by context, not by the verb form itself: the same form can be used to describe a circumstance in which the action of the main clause happens, as in *The hunters found the lion dead* (the lion was dead when the hunters found him).

Egyptian uses its stative form in much the same way. In some cases, an adverb clause with the SUBJECT-stative construction describes the result of another action rather than an existing circumstance: for example,

10 From a description of a river-procession of the image of Osiris. The sentence indicates that the king sailed in the boat with the god's image, accompanied by a flotilla of troop-ships. For *wḏ3 pw jr.n ḥm.f*, see § 14.14.3.

11 Literally, "his heart lengthened": *3wj jb* "lengthening the heart" is an Egyptian idiom for "happiness." The form *nꜥt* is an infinitive: see § 14.4.1.

12 From a passage describing how the author saved the king from a rampaging elephant. The word "hand" refers to the elephant's trunk. The word *šꜥd* "the one who cut off" is a participle, a verb form we will meet later.

 *st.n.j sw, ʿḥ3w.j mn.(w) m nḥbt.f*
"I shot him, with my arrow stuck in his neck."[13]

The adverb clause here expresses a state that results from the action of the main clause, not one that exists when the action of the main clause is performed.

As this example shows, adverb clauses of result look the same as, and obey the same rules as, other adverb clauses: only the context indicates that they express result rather than a circumstance in which the main clause happens. It is not always easy to translate such clauses literally into English. In most cases they make better sense if they are paraphrased as the second clause of a compound sentence or if they are preceded by the words *so that*: "I shot him, and my arrow was stuck in his neck"; "I shot him, so that my arrow was stuck in his neck."

17.14 The SUBJECT-stative construction in questions

In questions the SUBJECT-stative construction is normally preceded by the particles *jn jw*: for example,

 *jn jw.f trj sḏr.(w)* "Is he really asleep?"

In this use the SUBJECT-stative construction behaves like sentences with an adverbial or pseudoverbal predicate (§§ 11.11, 15.12).

17.15 The SUBJECT-stative construction negated

Like the pseudoverbal construction (§ 15.8), the SUBJECT-stative construction is rarely negated: instead, it is normally replaced by another verb form in negated sentences. Nonetheless, there are a few examples of the construction after the negative particle *nn* in Middle Egyptian: for instance,

 *nn sw wn.(w)* "He does not exist,"

literally, "he is nonexistent," using the stative of the 2ae-gem. verb *wnn* "exist."

17.16 The stative without a preceding subject

In the uses of the stative we have examined so far, the verb form has a separate subject preceding it (SUBJECT-stative). We have seen that this subject can be omitted in the second clause of a compound sentence or when it does not refer to anything in particular (§ 17.9). In such cases the stative still has a separate subject, even if this is understood rather than expressed in actual words: for example, in the compound sentence *jw.j rḫ.kw ṯn, rḫ.kw rnw.ṯn* "I know you, and know your names," the second *rḫ.kw* has the same subject as the first (*jw.j*), even though the subject is only expressed in the first clause — just as the second verb "know" in the English translation has the same subject as the first ("I"), even though the subject is only expressed in the first clause.

These therefore are actually uses of the SUBJECT-stative construction, in which the subject has been omitted, and not uses of the stative without a preceding subject. There are, however, several uses in which a stative that appears without a preceding subject actually has no separate subject. These are not instances in which the subject has been omitted: instead, they represent uses of the stative by itself. In such cases the subject of the stative is its own suffix pronoun rather than a separate word. These uses of the stative are examined in the following sections.

13 *st.n.j* is a verb form we will meet in the next lesson; *mn.(w)* is the stative of *mn* "become fixed, set, stick."

17.17 The stative in main clauses

In Middle Egyptian the stative can be used by itself, without a separate subject, as the predicate of a main clause (or independent sentence). In this use the stative has two basic meanings:

1. **as a past tense**

As noted in § 17.1, the stative was originally a form used to express completed action. In Old Egyptian the stative could be used without a separate subject in main clauses to express completed or past action rather than a state. Echoes of this original use are still found in some older or archaizing Middle Egyptian texts. Examples are attested only for the first-person singular or, in a few cases, for the third-person masculine singular: for example,

 *jj.kw m ḥtp, mšꜥ.j ꜥḏ.(w)*
"I came (back) in peace, with my expeditionary force intact"

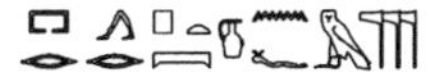
pr.(w) r pt, ẖnm.n.f m nṯrw
"He went up to the sky and joined with the gods."[14]

As these examples show, the stative in this use usually describes an action that happened in the past, corresponding to the simple past tense of English ("I came back," "he went up"). At the beginning of a narrative, however, it can be translated with the English pluperfect (§ 13.3.1), describing the background of the story that follows: for instance,

 *šm.kw r bj3 n jtj*
"I had gone to the mining country for the Sovereign."[15]

In most cases the stative used in this way has essentially the same meaning as in the normal SUBJECT-stative construction used as a past tense (§ 17.6). Thus, when the stative is from a transitive verb, it is normally passive, as in the following example:

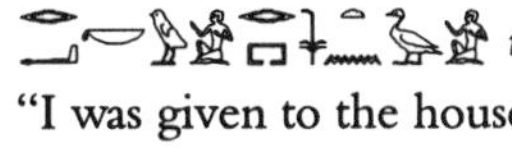 *rdj.kw r pr z3-nswt*
"I was given to the house of a king's-son" (compare the last example in § 17.6).

The only regular exception to this rule is the stative of the transitive verb *rḫ*, which has active meaning as it does in the SUBJECT-stative construction: for example,

 *rḫ.k(w) ṯn, rḫ.k(w) rnw.ṯn*
"I know you, and know your names" (compare the example in § 17.8).

Sometimes, however, the stative of transitive verbs other than *rḫ* also has active rather than passive meaning: for instance,

 *wd.k(w) rn.j r bw ẖr(j) nṯr*
"I have set my name at the place where the god is,"[16]

14 *ẖnm.n.f* is a past-tense verb form we will meet in the next lesson.

15 From the beginning of a story. In the preceding sentence the narrator says "Let me tell you something similar that happened with me," and the rest of the story follows the sentence cited as an example here. For the spelling of *jtj* "sovereign," see Essay 6.

16 The noun phrase *bw ẖr(j) nṯr* means literally, "the place that is under the god" (§ 8.8).

where the stative *wd.k(w)* (from the verb *wdj* "set") is active ("I have set") rather than passive ("I have been set"). This kind of active use is another holdover from Old Egyptian. In Middle Egyptian it occurs mostly in early Middle Kingdom autobiographies that follow the Old Kingdom model. In form and syntax it is no different from the stative that has passive meaning, such as *rdj.kw* "I was given," in the fourth example above. Unfortunately, the only way to know whether such a stative has passive or active meaning is by its context or by the fact that it has an object, such as *rn.j* "my name" in this example. Fortunately, however, this ambiguity is present only in the first-person stative without a preceding subject: in the more usual SUBJECT-stative construction the stative of transitive verbs (except *rḫ*) is always passive.

2. **as a wish or command**

The stative with a second-person suffix (singular or plural) can be used in main clauses without a separate subject as a wish or command: for instance,

 *ḥrj.tj r.sn, ᶜr wj, m33 wj*
"Be far from them: approach me, see me!"

As this example shows, the stative in this use is often best translated as an imperative. Where the imperative is used to command action, however ("approach," "see"), the stative is used to command or request a state: thus, *ḥrj.tj* (from the verb *ḥrj* "become distant") means "be far!" or "you should be far" (state) rather than "go away!" (action).

This use of the stative is also represented in some common Middle Egyptian idioms, including *jj.tj* "welcome" (literally, "be come"), *snb.tj* "farewell" (literally, "be healthy"), and *z3.tj ḥr* or *z3.tj r* "beware of!" (literally, "be guarded about," "be guarded against"): for example,

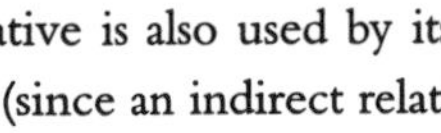 *j.tj m ḥtp 3ḫj ᶜpr* "Welcome in peace, equipped akh!"

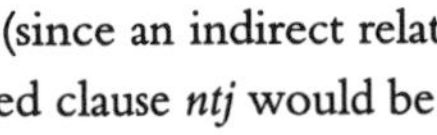 *snb.t(j) snb.t(j) nḏs* "Farewell, farewell (§ 9.5), commoner!"

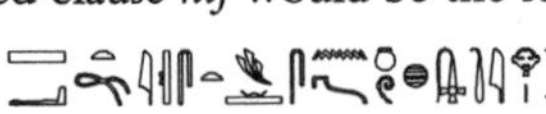 *z3.tj ḥr ḫsf m nf* "Beware of punishing wrongly."

17.18 The stative in relative clauses

We have already seen how the SUBJECT-stative construction is used in relative clauses (§ 17.10). The stative is also used by itself as the predicate of relative clauses, but only of those which are **direct** (since an indirect relative clause would require a separate subject) and **unmarked** (since in a marked clause *ntj* would be the subject): for example,

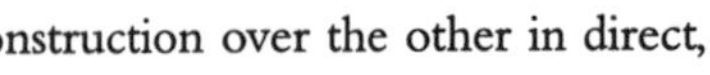 *šᶜt jst snwḫ.tj ḥr mrḥt*
"an old papyrus-scroll, which has been boiled with oil."

As you can see from this example, the meaning of the stative in this use is no different from that of the SUBJECT-stative construction in the same use. It is not always clear why Egyptian prefers one construction over the other in direct, unmarked relative clauses. In most cases, however, the stative used by itself, without a preceding subject, comes immediately after its antecedent noun or noun phrase (as in this example). We have already seen the same phenomenon in relative clauses with a pseudoverbal predicate after an undefined antecedent: for example, *zj ḥr mn r-jb.f* "a man suffering in his stomach" (§ 15.10.2).

17.19 The stative in adverb clauses

In § 17.12 we examined the use of the SUBJECT-stative construction in adverb clauses. In marked adverb clauses, such as those introduced by *jsṯ*, the stative always has a preceding subject. In **unmarked** adverb clauses, however, the stative can also be used by itself, without a preceding subject: for example,

jr.n.j hrw 3, wʿ.kw, jb.j m snw.j, sḏr.kw m ẖnw n k3p n ḫt

"I spent 3 days alone, with my heart my (only) companion, lying inside a thicket"[17]

This example has three circumstantial clauses, describing how the action of the main clause ("I spent 3 days") took place. The second adverb clause has an adverbial predicate; the first and third, a stative predicate: *wʿ.kw* "(I was) alone" (stative of the verb *wʿj* "be alone," related to the number *wʿ* "one"), and *sḏr.kw* "(I was) lying" (stative of the verb *sḏr* "lie down").

The stative is very often used in an adverb clause without a preceding subject after the verbs  *wrš* "spend the day,"  *sḏr* "lie down, go to bed, go to sleep, spend the night," and  *gmj* "find." With *wrš* and *sḏr*, the stative's subject is normally identical with the **subject** of the preceding verb, and the stative describes the state in which the subject "spends the day" or "lies, spends the night": for example,

 *wrš.s ḥqr.t(j)* "She should spend the day hungry"[18]

 *m.tn nb ḫwt sḏr.(w) jb.(w)*

"Look, the property-owner has gone to bed thirsty."

In the first of these examples the adverb clause explains how the subject (*.s* "she") is to "spend the day": namely, *ḥqr.t(j)* "hungry" (from *ḥqr* "hunger, become hungry"). In the second, the stative *jb.(w)* "thirsty" (from *jbj* "thirst, become thirsty") describes how the subject (*nb ḫwt*, literally "the owner of things") has "gone to bed": the main clause is a SUBJECT-stative construction expressing the past tense with an intransitive verb (§ 17.6). When the stative is used in an adverb clause after *gmj* "find," its subject is normally the same as the **object** of the verb: for instance,

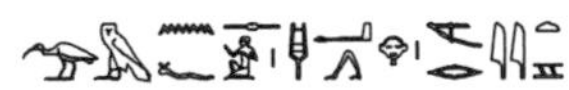 *gm.n.f z(j) ʿḥʿ.(w) ḥr mryt*

"He found a man standing on the riverbank."

Here the stative *ʿḥʿ.(w)* "standing" describes the state that the man was in when he was found: *z(j)* "a man" is the object of *gm.n.f* "he found."

The stative without a preceding subject can also express result in an adverb clause, like the SUBJECT-stative construction (§ 17.13): for example,

 *ʿḥʿ.n jn.n.f sw, rdj.(w) n ḥnwt.f*

"Then he fetched it, and it was given to its mistress"[19]

17 Literally, "I did 3 days, alone, my heart as my second, lying in the interior of a shelter of tree(s)." The first part of this example was presented in Exercise 12, no. 26; *jr.n.j* "I spent" (literally, 'I did') is a verb form we will meet in the next lesson.

18 *wrš.s* "she should spend the day" is a verb form we will meet in Lesson 19.

19 *jn.n.f* is a verb form we will meet in the next lesson. For the spelling of *n* "to," see § 8.2.6.

Here the stative *rdj.(w)* describes the state ("given") that resulted from the action of the main clause ("he fetched it"), not a circumstance that existed when the action of the main clause happened. As with the SUBJECT-stative construction in this use, the stative here makes better sense if it is translated as the second clause of a compound sentence (as in the example above) rather than as an adverb clause ("Then he fetched it, given to its mistress").

As in relative clauses, it is not always clear why Egyptian prefers the SUBJECT-stative construction in some unmarked adverb clauses and the stative without a preceding subject in others. In most cases, however, when the stative is used without a preceding subject its subject has already appeared in some form in an earlier clause. This relationship can be seen in each of the examples cited above. In fact, it is much more common for an adverb clause with the stative as predicate to have a subject that has already been mentioned in a preceding clause than to have an entirely new subject. As a result, **in most adverb clauses the stative has no preceding subject**: examples of the SUBJECT-stative construction in unmarked adverb clauses are actually much less frequent than those of the stative by itself.

The following can therefore be offered as a good rule of thumb for adverb clauses with the stative as predicate:

- when the subject of the stative has not already appeared in a preceding clause, naturally it has to be expressed, and the SUBJECT-stative construction is used (§ 17.12, second example, and § 17.13);
- when the stative's subject is identical with something that has been previously mentioned in the sentence, the stative is normally used by itself, without a preceding subject (as in the examples in this section).

There are no exceptions to the first part of this rule. The second part of the rule is generally true, but there are some cases where it is not — for instance, the last example in § 17.12. You should also note that this rule applies only in **unmarked** adverb clauses. When the adverb clause is marked by a particle such as *jsṯ*, the SUBJECT-stative construction is used, whether the stative's subject has already been mentioned in a preceding clause or not.

17.20 The stative in epithets

A special kind of unmarked dependent clause using the stative without a preceding subject occurs as an epithet after nouns or proper names. Unlike an unmarked relative clause, this can be used after defined nouns or noun phrases (proper names are always defined: § 4.9). There are two major uses of such clauses in Middle Egyptian:

1. **expressions for "whole, complete, entire"**

   The stative of the verbs *tm* "complete," *dmdj* (originally *dmḏj*) "coalesce," and *t(w)t* "reconcile" can be used as an equivalent of the English adjectives "whole, complete, full, entire": for example, *psḏt tm.tj* "the complete Ennead," *nwt dmd.t(j)* "the whole village," *sp3t.s t(w)t.(tj)*[20] "her entire nome." The stative in this use is actually a kind of adverb clause: literally, "the Ennead, completed," "the village, coalesced," and "his nome, reconciled."

20 For the spelling of the stative, see § 17.2 (3fs).

2. **wishes for life and health**

In § 17.17.2 we saw how the second-person stative can be used as a wish or command. The third-person stative can also be used as a kind of wish after proper names or certain nouns or noun phrases. The most common examples of this use involve the expressions *ꜥnḫ.tj* "alive," *ꜥnḫ.(w) ḏt* "alive forever," and (an abbreviation for) *ꜥnḫ.(w)-wḏꜣ.(w)-snb.(w)* "alive, sound, and healthy." The first of these is often placed after the names of queens and princesses; the second and third, after the name of the king: for example,

nṯr nfr ḪPR-KꜢ-Rꜥ ꜥnḫ.(w) ḏt
"The good god, KHEPER-KA-RE (Senwosret I), alive forever."

The third expression, commonly abbreviated "lph" in translations,[21] is also placed after words referring to the king, such as *ḥm.f* "His Incarnation" and *jty* "sovereign" (see Essay 6); after words or phrases referring to the palace, such as *pr-ꜥꜢ* "big house" (see Essay 3), *pr-nswt* "king's house," and *stp-zꜢ* "palace"; and after the phrase *nb* or *nb.j* "the lord, my lord," referring either to the king or to a high official: for instance,

tjw, jw.j rḫ.kw jty ꜥnḫ.(w)-wḏꜣ.(w)-snb.(w) nb.j
"Yes, I know, sovereign lph, my lord."

Related to this use is the expression *snb.t(j) ꜥnḫ.t(j)* "you being healthy and alive" or "may you be healthy and alive," which is used as a polite wish to soften a request, somewhat like the English expression "if you please": for example,

ntk hꜢb.k ḥr mdwt m ḥr.k, snb.t(j) ꜥnḫ.t(j)
"You are the one who should send (word) about your responsibilities, if you please."[22]

This expression is mostly found in Middle Kingdom letters written to a superior.

17.21 Meaning and syntax of the stative: summary

Because the stative is used so widely and in so many different ways in Middle Egyptian, the preceding discussion has been of necessity fairly complicated. To help you remember the main points more easily, they can be summarized as follows:

1. **meaning**
   - the stative normally expresses a **tenseless state** in which its subject is, was, or will be
   - the stative can be used to express **past or completed action**: for intransitive verbs the stative is the normal form used for this meaning; for transitive verbs this meaning is normally possible only with a pronominal subject or with no preceding subject (§§ 17.6, 17.17.1)
   - the second-person stative with no preceding subject can be used to express a **wish or command** (§ 17.17.2)
   - the stative with no preceding subject can be used as an **epithet** (§ 17.20)

21 From the older translation "may he live, be prosperous, and be healthy."

22 *hꜢb.k* is a verb form we will meet in Lesson 19. *mdwt m ḥr.k* "your responsibilities" means literally "the matters in your face": *rdj mdt m ḥr* "put a matter in the face" of someone is an idiom for making someone responsible for something.

2. **voice**
   - the stative of **intransitive** verbs is **active**, describing the result of a prior action performed by its subject
   - the stative of **transitive** verbs is normally **passive**, describing the result of a prior action performed on its subject
   - the stative of **adjective** verbs describes a **quality** that results from a prior action (§ 17.7)
   - the stative of the transitive verb *rḫ* is **active**, and corresponds in meaning to the English verb "know" (§ 17.8)
   - the first-person singular stative of other transitive verbs can be **active** when used as a past tense without a preceding subject (§ 17.17.1)

3. **syntax**

The stative is used either with a preceding subject or without one. In the first case the stative's suffix agrees in gender and number with the subject, insofar as possible (§ 17.4); in the second, the stative's suffix itself is the subject (§ 17.16). The following table shows the various kinds of clauses and sentences in which these two constructions are used:

	SUBJECT-stative	**stative**
main clause	✓	✓ (archaic; 1s, rarely 3ms)
wish or command	—	✓ (2s/2pl)
question	✓	—
negated	✓ (rare)	—
relative clause	✓	✓ (unmarked only)
noun clause	✓	—
adverb clause	✓	✓ (unmarked only)
epithet	—	✓

As this summary makes clear, the stative is normally used with a preceding subject in Middle Egyptian, except in wishes or commands and epithets. The stative without a preceding subject has a much more limited range of use; only in unmarked relative and adverb clauses is it more common than the SUBJECT-stative construction.

ESSAY 17. PHONOLOGY AND WRITING

Lessons 1–3 introduced us to the fundamental principles of Egyptian phonology and writing. Throughout succeeding lessons, however, we have also encountered numerous unusual spellings of Egyptian words, where the relationship between the hieroglyphs and the words they represent is not immediately evident from the basic principles alone. These exceptional writings illustrate two tendencies that were constantly at odds with one another in the minds of the ancient scribe: on the one hand, the tendency to preserve older, "etymological" spellings of words; and on the other, the tendency to reflect the contemporary pronunciation of words. In this respect Middle Egyptian writing is comparable to that of modern American English, which exhibits the same conflict in words such as *lite* vs. *light* and *thru* vs. *through*. While such English spellings are mostly relegated to the world of advertising, others have become a standardized part of the written language: examples are the words *honor* and *archeology*, which have been simplified from the older, etymological spellings *honour* and *archaeology* (still used in British publications).

We have now reached the point in our studies where we can examine Middle Egyptian spelling in more detail. As we have already seen in § 2.8, most exceptional spellings involve sounds that were lost or altered between the time of the Old Kingdom, when hieroglyphic writing was first standardized, and the Middle Kingdom, when Middle Egyptian became the standard written language. Originally, most Egyptian words began and ended with a consonant — with the probable exception of some shorter words such as  *j* "oh" (perhaps just **a*), and some pronominal suffixes, as we have seen in this lesson (§ 17.2). Within words, each syllable also began with a single consonant and ended either with a vowel or a single consonant — i.e., either CV or CVC. Clusters of more than one consonant were possible only when two CVC syllables came together: for example, the feminine adjective  *nfrt* "good," probably pronounced **nafrat* (CVC–CVC); the masculine form  *nfr* had the structure CV–CVC (probably **nafir*).

With the loss of some consonants in pronunciation, however, many Middle Egyptian words began or ended with a vowel rather than a consonant. Thus, for example, the loss of the feminine ending *t* and syllable-final *r* (§ 2.8.3) meant that  was pronounced **nafra* (CVC–CV) and  something like **nafi* (CV–CV). The hieroglyphic system had no regular way of indicating such vocalic endings. In writing these words, scribes could ignore the sound changes and use the traditional spelling — in the same way that standard English still writes *light* even though the *gh* sound is no longer pronounced. Often, however, a scribe would attempt to "modernize" the spelling. A final vowel could be indicated in various ways:

- by omitting the lost consonant: for example,  for older ; or  for older 
- by spelling the word as if it had originally had a final *j* (§ 2.4): for example,  *tj* for the particle  *tr* (§ 16.7.11). For a lost final *r* (as in this word), older and newer spellings were often combined, as in  *trj* (i.e., *tr* > *tj*).
- by adding the "curl *w*" to the end of the word: for example,  for older . This method probably originated in the masculine plural ending of nouns, which seems to have been simply a vowel (probably **u*).

The use of an extra "curl *w*" was especially common in hieratic texts; it was used increasingly over time and is very often found in New Kingdom texts, even those in hieroglyphic.

The loss of the feminine ending *t* was not universal: when a feminine word had a suffix, or was combined in pronunciation with a following word beginning with a vowel, the feminine ending was preserved. This gave rise to spellings such as 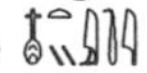 for the name *nfrt-j.tj* "Nefretiti" (§ 17.9), which contemporary transcriptions in cuneiform (the wedge-shaped writing of Mesopotamia) show was pronounced something like **naftíta* (originally **nafratíta*). To indicate that it was preserved in pronunciation, the ending *t* was sometimes written with a second *t* (or *ṯ*) or with an extra "curl *w*" before a suffix pronoun: for example, *jzwt.ṯn* for *jzwt.n* "our crew," *jntw.f* for *jnt.f* "that it should fetch" (a verb form).

Egyptologists are divided about how to represent such phonetic spellings. Some ignore them and transliterate the words as if they were written normally; the feminine ending with an extra "curl *w*" is sometimes transliterated with a special sign (*ṯ*). In this book, words are usually represented as they are written: omitted consonants are added in parentheses, and the "curl *w*" is transliterated: thus,  *nf(r)* and  *nfrw*.

Phonetic spellings are particularly common in the writings of foreign names or loanwords borrowed from other languages. To write such words Egyptian scribes often employed a system known as **group writing**. In this system, foreign words could be spelled out by using similar-sounding Egyptian words. We do much the same thing when we indicate the pronunciation of unfamiliar words by using common English words: for example, "JOE-sir" for *Djoser* (a king of Dynasty 3).

Two systems of group writing are known from Egyptian texts, one used in the Middle Kingdom and the other in the New Kingdom. The Middle Kingdom system was primarily "alphabetic," with the occasional addition of biliteral signs or short Egyptian words for CVC and CV syllables. The uniliteral signs generally had the same values as in Egyptian words, with the following special conventions: doubled consonants (CC) could be written twice; , , or  was used for a syllable beginning or ending with a vowel;  or  was used for *y* at the beginning of words as well as  for *y* in the middle or end ( almost never occurs at the beginning of Egyptian words);  normally represented the consonant *l* or *r*; was used for *d* as well as *r* (the latter also as , from the Egyptian word **ra* "mouth"); was used for *l* as well as *n*; and the "curl *w*" was used to indicate that a syllable or word ended in a vowel. Some examples of foreign names written in this system are:

-  *y3-mt* for *Yarmut*, the name of a city southwest of Jerusalem; the Egyptian word  *m(w)t* "death" is used for the second syllable
- 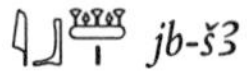 *jb-š3* for *Abi-šar*, a Canaanite personal name meaning "My Father is King"; the Egyptian word  *š3* "marsh" is used for the second part of the name
-  *jk-zp-j* for *Aksapi*, the name of a city west of Galilee (Biblical Achsaph); the Egyptian word  *zp* "time, occasion" is used for the second syllable
-  *ḫn-ḏr* for *Ḫanzir*, the personal name of a pharaoh of Dynasty 13 (conventionally transcribed as Khendjer; the Semitic name means "wild boar"); the Egyptian preposition *ḏr* "since" is used for the second syllable
-  *y-tn-hddw* for *Yattin-Haddu*, an Amorite personal name meaning "Haddu (a god) Gives"; the Egyptian word  *tn(j)* "distinct" is used for the second syllable
-  *ꜥprw-js-jpj* for *ꜥAbdu-Asꜣapi*, a Canaanite personal name meaning "Servant of As'aph"; the Egyptian word *ꜥprw* "equipped" is used for the first part of the name.

By the New Kingdom the practice of using short Egyptian words in group writing had been largely abandoned in favor of a new system based on CV syllables. Where possible, these syllables were written with biliteral signs; the final vowel was represented by , 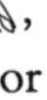 (less often ), and  or . The consonant *l* was no longer written with  but as , 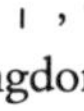, or 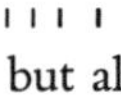. This system was used not only for spelling out foreign names, as in the Middle Kingdom, but also for writing the many loanwords that had come into Egyptian from Semitic languages to the East. The following are some typical examples of the New Kingdom system of group writing:

-  *j3-ywj-r* for *ayyala* "stag" (Hebrew *ayyal*)
-  *yw-mj* for *yamma* "sea, lake" (Arabic and Hebrew *yam*)
-  *bw-nr* for *balla* "outside" (Arabic *barra*)
-  *mj-r-k3-bw-tj* for *markabata* "chariot" (Arabic *markaba*)
-  *s3-r-qw* for *thalgu* "snow" (Arabic *thalg*)
-  *š3-r-mj* for *šalama* "peace" (Arabic *salam*, Hebrew *šalom*)
-  *t-r* for *tilla* "mound" (Arabic *tell*, Hebrew *tel*); the Egyptian word 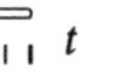 *t* "bread" is used to write the CV group *ti*.

Such loanwords, like the system used to write them, first appear in texts of the late Second Intermediate Period, and are mostly found in the New Kingdom and later. They are also much more frequent in Late Egyptian texts than in those written in Middle Egyptian.

The attempt to reflect the actual pronunciation of words, both native Egyptian and foreign, is one of the more interesting features of ancient Egyptian writing, because it gives us a few clues to how the language actually sounded. While it can sometimes make the reading of hieroglyphic texts more difficult, particularly for beginners, it is also a nice reminder that Egyptian is not just a curious artifact of ancient history but a language that was once spoken and written by real people.

EXERCISE 17

Transliterate and translate the following sentences:

1. 
2. 
3. 
4. 
5. 
6.  — from a story: *zb.n ḥm.f mšꜥ* "His Incarnation had sent an expedition,"  *smsw* "eldest"
7. 
8.  — for *r.j* see § 16.7.2
9.  — *rd.f* "he flourishes"
10.  — *ꜥḥꜥ* "wait"
11. 
12. 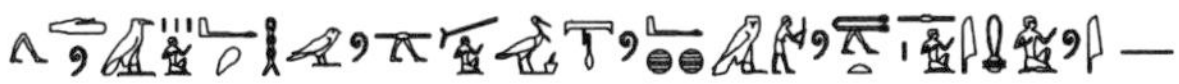 — from a story: *jtw* "overtaken"

13.  — *z3-nht* "Sinuhe," a personal name, meaning "Son of the Sycamore";  *ʿ3m(w)* "Asiatic"

14. 

15. 

16. 

17. 

18. 

19. 

20.  — *mf3kt* for *mfk3t* "turquoise," *ḥr* "in"

21.  — *gm.n.f* "he found"

22. 

23.  — *s3ḫbw* a city near Heliopolis

24. 

25. 

26. 

27. 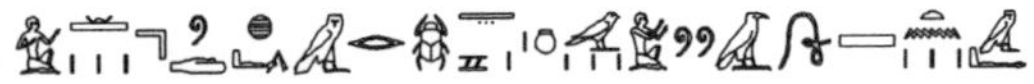

28. 

29.  — *ʿḥʿ n* "wait for, expect," *ḥr* "in," *t3* "this (part of)"

30. 

31.  — *r.j* "for me"

32. 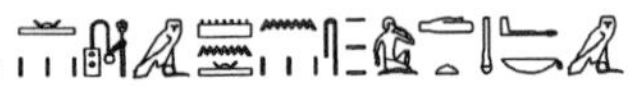

33. 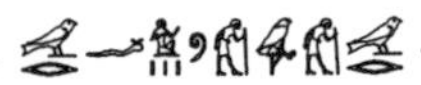 —  in both instances is an ideogram, read *wr*

34.  — spoken by a god to the king: *n m3* "at seeing," infinitive; *MN-ḪPR-Rʿ* throne name of Thutmose III

35.  — *dj.n.j* "I have given," *jwtj sw* § 12.9

18. The Perfect

18.1 **Definition**

The English perfect is a verb form used to express completed action. Most such actions are past from the point of view of the speaker: an example is the sentence *Jill has done her homework*, where the verb form *has done* indicates that the action of Jill doing her homework is completed. But an action can be described as completed even if it did not happen in the past: for example, in the English sentence *Jack can watch television after he has done his homework*, the verb form *has done* describes the action of Jack doing his homework as completed with respect to the action of the main clause even though it has yet to happen from the speaker's point of view.

The perfect does not necessarily have to refer to a past event because it primarily expresses an aspect rather than a tense (§ 13.3). As such, it is different from the past tense, which always describes past action: for example, the sentence *Jack did his homework* can only refer to a past event, not one that has yet to happen.

The Middle Egyptian perfect is similar to that of English. It basically describes **completed action** and is an aspect, not a tense. In English the perfect has to be marked for tense, like most English verb forms: either as the present perfect (*has done*), the past perfect (*had done*), or the future perfect (*will have done*). The Egyptian perfect, however, expresses **only** aspect, not tense. For that reason, it is translated not only by the English present perfect but sometimes by the other perfect forms, or even by nonperfect verb forms, depending on how it is used.

The perfect is one of twelve Middle Egyptian verb forms that Egyptologists group into a category called the **suffix conjugation**. Although the twelve forms all have different meanings and uses, they behave alike with regard to their subject and the word order of the clauses they are used in. Verb forms of the suffix conjugation can have a noun (or noun phrase) or pronoun as subject, and this always **follows** the verb itself. When the subject is a personal pronoun, it is expressed as a **suffix pronoun** attached directly to the verb form, after any endings or other suffixes: hence the name "suffix conjugation."

18.2 **Form**

The perfect is one of the easiest verb forms to recognize. It is always marked by the consonant *n* (spelled or ) added directly as a suffix to the verb: for example,  *sḏm.n* "has heard." This suffix is attached directly to the stem of the verb itself, before any other suffixes.

The subject of the perfect follows the verb form itself: for example,  *sḏm.n nṯr* "the god has heard,"  *sḏm.n.f* "he has heard." Using the verb *sḏm* "hear" as a model, Egyptologists refer to the perfect as the *sḏm.n.f* ("sedgem-EN-ef") form.

The perfect often looks exactly like a second verb form, called the perfect relative (or *sḏm.n.f* relative). The two forms can usually (but not always) be distinguished by how they are used. For the present we need not be concerned about the difference, but we will learn in Lesson 25 how to tell the two forms apart.

Most verb classes use the base stem in the perfect, with a few exceptions. The following are typical forms found in Middle Egyptian texts:

2-LIT.	*ḏd.n.f* "he has said"
2AE-GEM.	*3mm.n.f* "he has grasped" — geminated stem; occasionally base stem: for instance, *wr.n.s* "it has become large." The verb *m33* "see" normally uses the base stem: for example, *m3.n.j* "I have seen"; but also geminated *m33.n.k* "you have seen."
3-LIT.	*nḥm.n.j* "I have taken"
3AE-INF.	*jr.n.j* "I have done"
3AE-GEM.	*špss.n.(j)* "I have become distinguished"
4-LIT.	*sksk.n.k* "you destroy"
4AE-INF.	*ḫnt.n.(j)* "I have advanced"
CAUS. 2-LIT.	*sḫr.n.f* "he has felled"
CAUS. 2AE-GEM.	*sqbb.n* "has cooled" — geminated stem
CAUS. 3-LIT.	*sʿnḫ.n.j* "I have nourished"[1]
CAUS. 3AE-INF.	*sms.n.sn* "they had caused to give birth"
CAUS. 4AE-INF.	*sḫnt.n.f* "he has promoted"
ANOM.	The verb *rdj* "give, put" uses either base stem: for instance, *rdj.n.j*, *dj.n.j*, *rdj.n.(j)*, *dj.n.(j)* "I have given." The verb *jwj/jj* "come" normally uses the stem *jj*, rarely the *jw* stem: for example, *jj.n.sn* "they come," *jw.n.n* "we have come." The latter is mostly found in religious texts.

As these examples illustrate, the suffix is regularly written **after** the determinative. Sometimes, however, it is placed before the determinative, particularly with verbs whose stem ends in *n*: for instance, as well as *qn.n.f* "it embraced."

The 3ae-inf. verb *jnj* "get, fetch" which has no determinative, normally has two signs in the perfect, the first of which is a phonetic complement of the biliteral sign used to write the verb's stem (§ 3.1): i.e., *jn.n.j* "I have fetched." Occasionally, however, only the perfect suffix is written: *jn.n.j* "I have fetched." When the perfect of *jnj* has an unwritten 1S suffix pronoun and is followed immediately by the dative (§ 14.6), only two signs are written, one for the perfect suffix and the other for the preposition *n* of the dative: for example, *jn.n.(j) n.k* "I have fetched for you." When the suffix pronoun is written out, however, the normal spelling is used: *jn.n.j n.k* "I have fetched for you." A spelling such as *jn.n.(j) n.k* is avoided because Egyptian normally reserves three signs in a row for the word or determinative *mw* "water."

1 Literally, "I have caused to live": see Lesson 17, n. 8.

18.3 The meaning of the perfect

As noted at the beginning of this lesson, the perfect expresses basically the aspect of **completed action**. Even though most instances of the perfect have to be translated by an English verb form denoting past action (the English perfect and past tenses), **the perfect itself is tenseless**: it can express completed action not only in the past, but also in the present or even the future, as we will see in the course of this lesson. In each case, the perfect denotes only completion; the tense with which the form has to be translated in English comes from the context in which it is used, not from the form itself.

Egyptian has two forms that express completion: the stative and the perfect. As we saw in the last lesson, the stative describes the state of being that results from a completed action. This is so even in cases where English grammar forces us to translate the stative by a verb form expressing action (§ 17.6). The perfect, on the other hand, expresses completed **action.** This distinction can be difficult for English speakers to appreciate, because modern English allows only the expression of completed action for most verbs, transitive or intransitive: for example, *The train has reached the station* (transitive) and *The train has arrived* (intransitive). Only the common English verb *go* still allows for the distinction between completed action and state: for example, *The train has gone* (completed action) and *The train is gone* (state) — but not **The train is arrived.*

Unlike English, Egyptian can make the distinction between state (the stative) and completed action (the perfect) for most if not all of its verbs. Nevertheless, Egyptian prefers the stative when the verb is intransitive and the perfect when it is transitive.[2] This preference means that **the stative and the perfect often act as counterparts of each other**: transitive verbs use the perfect where intransitive verbs normally use the stative, and vice versa: for example,

ḫnt.kw pḥ.n.j 3bw, ḫd.kw pḥ.n.j mḥt

"I have gone upstream and reached Elephantine;

I have gone downstream and reached the Delta,"

with the intransitive verbs *ḫntj* "go upstream" and *ḫdj* "go downstream" in the stative and the transitive verb *pḥ* "reach" in the perfect.

Despite this general preference, however, Egyptian could on occasion use the stative of a transitive verb, as we saw in the last lesson (§ 17.17.1), or the perfect of an intransitive one. Like the perfect of transitive verbs, that of intransitive verbs expresses completed action: for example,

 *jw ḫnt.n.(j) r ḥ3t* "I have advanced to the fore,"

with the perfect of the intransitive verb *ḫntj* used after the particle *jw*.[3] The difference between *ḫnt.n.j* and *ḫnt.kw* cannot be expressed in English, but it exists in Egyptian nonetheless: the former expresses completed action; the latter, the state resulting from that completed action.

2 In this respect the Middle Egyptian perfect is quite similar to the perfect of modern colloquial French and German, which is also used for transitive verbs (*j'ai atteint, ich habe erreicht* "I have reached") where intransitive verbs use an expression of state (*je suis allé, ich bin gegangen* "I have gone," literally "I am gone").

3 Despite the difference in translation, the verb *ḫntj* in this passage is the same as that in the preceding example. The verb *ḫntj* means basically "go forward": when it is used of travel it means "go upstream" (on the Nile) or "go south" because the Egyptians oriented themselves facing south (see Essay 2).

It is important to keep in mind that the perfect always expresses completed **action**, particularly when you encounter the perfect of an intransitive verb. When an adjective verb (which is always intransitive) is used in the perfect, it expresses the **acquisition** of a quality rather than the quality itself (which is expressed by the adjective or by the stative: § 17.7). Thus, a form such as  *špss.n.(j)*, for example, means "I have become distinguished," not "I have been distinguished."

The perfect of intransitive verbs has a much more restricted range of usage than that of transitive verbs, as we will see in the course of this lesson. Most examples of an intransitive perfect involve the perfect relative form, not the perfect itself.

18.4 Subject, object, and word order in clauses with the perfect

As noted in § 18.2, the perfect normally precedes its subject. This word order, with the verb first, is the opposite of that with which we have become familiar in clauses that have a pseudoverbal or stative predicate, but it is the normal order for clauses with a verbal predicate in Middle Egyptian. The **VsdoSOA** rule we met in our discussion of the infinitive (§ 14.6) applies to all clauses with a verbal predicate. Examples with the perfect are:

 *rdj.n.j ḥknw n mntw* "I gave praise to Montu" **(VsOA)**

 *sj3.n wj mjtn(w)* "The scout recognized me" **(VoS)**

 *mz.n.j n.f jnw pn* "I presented this cargo to him" **(VsdO)**

 *ꜥḥꜥ.n rdj.n.f n.sn st* "Then he gave it to them" **(Vsdo)**

 *ꜥḥꜥ.n 3w.n n.f z3-nswt ḥrw-dd.f ꜥwj.fj*
"Then King's Son Har-dedef extended his arms to him" **(VdSO)**.

Note that when the object is a personal pronoun the **dependent** form is used (*wj* "me," *st* "it").

Exceptions to this word order are rare. When the subject is a long noun phrase, however, Egyptian tends to put it before the verb; in such cases the preposed ("put in front") subject is also repeated after the verb by a personal pronoun: for example,

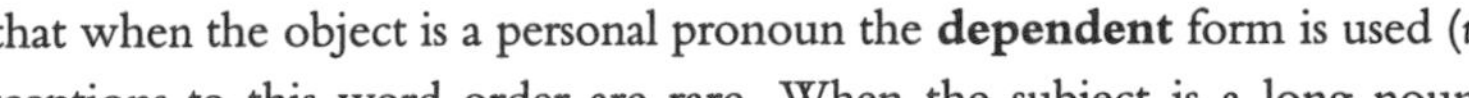
w3yw r ḏwt k3y(w) sbjw sḫr.n.sn rw.sn n snḏw.f
"Those who fell into evil and plotted rebellion have lowered their voices for fear of him"[4]

Here the subject is the noun phrase *w3yw r ḏwt k3y(w) sbjw* "those who fell into evil and plotted rebellion"; it is repeated by the suffix pronoun of the verb form *sḫr.n.sn* "they have lowered."

In most cases the preposed subject is a fairly long noun phrase, as in this example. A shorter subject, however, can be preposed for stylistic reasons, or to focus attention on it: for instance,

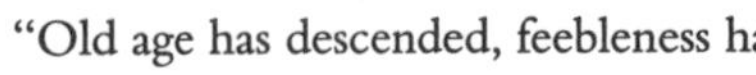 *j3w h3.w, wgg 3s.n.f wj*
"Old age has descended, feebleness has overtaken me."

Here the subject of the second clause, *wgg* "feebleness," has been placed in front of the perfect in order to form a stylistic balance with the SUBJECT-stative construction in the first clause.

4 *w3yw* "those who fell" and *k3y(w)* "those who plotted" are participles, a verb form we will meet in Lesson 23. *sḫr.n.sn rw.sn* "they have lowered their voices" means literally, "they have caused their mouths to fall."

Preposing an element of the clause in order to focus attention on it is known as **topicalization**. This can be done simply by putting the topicalized element first in the clause: for example,

 *jnw nb nfr n rṯnw jf.n.j st r ꜣw*
"All the good produce of Retjenu, I have plundered it completely."

Here the initial noun phrase *jnw nb nfr n rṯnw* "all the good produce of Retjenu" is the object, repeated by the dependent pronoun *st* after the verb *jf.n.j* "I have plundered." Topicalized elements can also be marked by the initial preposition *jr* "as for": for instance,

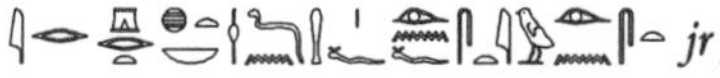 *jr grt ḫt nb wḏ.n ḥm.f jr.(j) n.f st jw jr.n.(j) st*
"Moreover, as for everything His Incarnation commanded I do for him, I did it."[5]

In this example the topicalized noun phrase *ḫt nb wḏ.n ḥm.f jr.(j) n.f st* "everything His Incarnation commanded I do for him" is the object, and is repeated by the dependent pronoun *st* as object of the verb *jr.n.(j)* "I did." Note that English grammar also allows for topicalization in the same way that Egyptian does, as can be seen in the translations of these examples.

18.5 The perfect with omitted subject

As we have seen in earlier lessons, the 1s suffix pronoun can be omitted in writing, and this is also true when it is the subject of the perfect. The 1s suffix is often unwritten when it is followed immediately by the 1s dependent pronoun *wj* as the verb's object: for example,

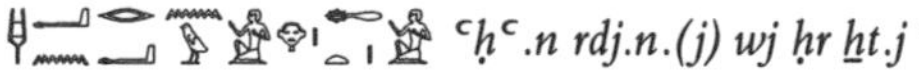 *ꜥḥꜥ.n rdj.n.(j) wj ḥr ẖt.j* "Then I put myself on my belly."

The reason for this is probably the fact that the 1s suffix was simply the vowel *i* (§ 5.3). It is often omitted when followed by the dependent pronoun *wj* probably because the latter was pronounced together with the verb form as a single word, and the suffix pronoun was heard simply as a vowel between the two consonants *n* and *w* (i.e., **rVdiniwi*).

Even when it is not the first-person singular, the perfect's subject can be omitted if it is clear from the context. Normally this feature is an option only when the subject has been mentioned previously: for example, in a compound sentence (§ 17.9):

jw.jn r.f sḫtj pn r spr n.f 4nw zp, gm.n sw ḥr prt m sbꜣ n ḥwt-nṯr
"So then this peasant came to petition to him a 4th time, and found him emerging from the gate of the temple."[6]

Here the subject of the perfect *gm.n* in the second clause is omitted because it has already been mentioned in the first clause (*sḫtj pn* "this peasant"), just as the English translation omits it for the same reason ("and found"). The subject can also be omitted if it does not refer to anything in particular, corresponding to the English "dummy" subject *it*: for instance,

5 *wḏ.n ḥm.f jr.(j) n.f st*, literally, "which His Incarnation commanded I do it for him," is a relative clause with the perfect relative form (*wḏ.n*); we will consider this form in Lesson 24. The relative clause itself contains another clause, *jr.(j) n.f st* "that I do it for him," serving as object of *wḏ.n*; *jr.(j)* is a verb form we will meet in the next lesson.

6 *jw.jn* is a verb form we will meet in Lesson 22.

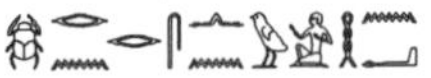 *ḫpr.n r.s nn wj ḥnᶜ(w)* "It happened when I was not with them."[7]

Sometimes the perfect with an omitted subject has a special form in which the perfect suffix is written *nj*. Like other examples with omitted subject, this form is normally used only when the subject has been mentioned in a previous clause: for example,

pr.n n3 m ḫt … 3m.nj nn wj m ḥr(j) jb.sn

"Those went up in fire … They burnt up when I was not in their midst."[8]

This special form of the perfect suffix is related to the regular perfect suffix *n* in the same way that the prepositional adverb *nj* is related to the preposition *n* (§ 8.2.6). Since the prepositional adverb can also be spelled simply, it is possible that all examples of the perfect without a subject also had the same special form of the suffix: thus, perhaps, *gm.n(j)* and *ḫpr.n(j)* in the second and third examples of this section. For the first-person singular, however, the subject is **unwritten**, not omitted: thus, the first example in this section is *rdj.n.(j)*, not *rdj.n(j)*.

18.6 The perfect with the suffix *tw*

The impersonal pronoun *tw* (§ 15.5) can also be used as the subject of the perfect. In such cases it behaves like a suffix pronoun: for example,

 *jr.n.t(w) n.j ḥtpwt*

"One has made offerings for me" or "Offerings have been made for me."

In this example the perfect with the suffix *tw* can be translated either as an active form with the impersonal subject "one" or as a passive. In many cases, however, the suffix *tw* is used to make a real passive form of the perfect: for example,

 *rdj.n.tw n.j nn n ṯ3ww jn nn n ḥwnwt*

"Those winds have been given to me by those girls."

Here the prepositional phrase *jn nn n ḥwnwt* "by those girls" shows that the noun phrase *nn n ṯ3ww* "those winds" is the subject of *rdj.n.tw* and not its object (the translation "one has given me those winds by those girls" makes no sense). When the verb form used in this way has a personal pronoun as its subject, the pronoun is attached as a suffix pronoun **after** the suffix *tw*: for instance,

 *qd.n.tw.k n ḥ3b* "You have been built for a festival."

In this case the suffix pronoun *.k* can only be the subject of the verb, since the dependent form of the personal pronoun is used as direct object (§ 18.4).

The *tw* form of the perfect has a rather limited use in Middle Egyptian. The normal passive counterpart of the perfect is a different verb form, which will be introduced in Lesson 21. In most cases, in fact, the form with the suffix *tw* is not the regular perfect at all, but the perfect relative form.

7 *r.s* is a less common form of the enclitic particle *jr.f/r.f* (§ 16.7.2); *nn wj ḥnᶜ(w)* is a negated sentence with adverbial predicate (§§ 8.2.9, 8.15), serving as an unmarked adverb clause (§ 12.17).

8 Here too the adverbial sentence *nn wj m ḥr(j) jb.sn*, literally, "I was not one upon their heart," serves as an unmarked adverb clause; *ḥr(j)* is a prepositional nisbe (§§ 8.6–8.7).

18.7 The perfect expressing completed action

The perfect is often used to denote an action that is viewed as completed from the standpoint of the speaker: that is, a past action viewed as completed in the present. In this it is similar to the English present perfect tense, with which it is often translated. One very common example of this meaning occurs in royal hieroglyphic inscriptions, in the formula  *dj.n.(j) n.k* "I have given to you." This formula occurs in scenes of the king before a god or goddess, recording the deity's recitation (*ḏd-mdw*: § 14.9) to the king (see no. 28 in this lesson's exercises). The following is an example of the formula addressed to the female pharaoh Hatshepsut:

ḏd-mdw jn ḥwt-ḥrw mwt-nṯr nbt pt ḥnwt nṯrw dj.n.(j) n.ṯ ꜥnḫ ḏd w3s nb ḫrj.(j)

"Recitation by Hathor, the god's mother, lady of the sky, mistress of the gods:
I have given you all life, stability, and dominion that I have."[9]

In such cases the action of "giving" is expressed as completed from the point of view of the deity who speaks the words.

The perfect also expresses completed action in another formula common in royal hieroglyphic inscriptions, which is placed on buildings, statues, and other monuments as a dedicatory text. This is known as the *jr.n.f m mnw.f* formula, from its opening words. It typically has three parts: (1) *jr.n.f m mnw.f n jt.f* "He has made, as his monument to his father," followed by the name of a god or royal ancestor; (2) *jrt n.f* "the creation for him," with the infinitive *jrt* "making" (or the infinitive of another verb), followed by a description of the monument; and (3) *jr.f dj ꜥnḫ* "that he might achieve given-life."[10] The dedicatory inscription of Thutmose III from one of his temples is a good example:

jr.n.f m mnw.f n (j)t.f rꜥ-ḥrw 3ḫtj nṯr ꜥ3 nb pt
jrt n.f ḥwt-nṯr m jnr n rwḏt
jr.f dj ꜥnḫ ḏt

"He has made, as his monument to his father Re-Harakhti, the great god, lord of the sky, the creation for him of a temple in sandstone, that he might achieve given-life forever."[11]

Note that this formula's three parts normally all begin with a form of the verb *jrj* "make, and that these forms are past *(jr.n.f)*, atemporal *(jrt)*, and future *(jr.f)* in reference.

For transitive verbs the perfect is the normal form used to express a past action as completed from the speaker's point of view. Although it can appear without an introductory particle (as in the *dj.n.j n.k* formula just discussed), in normal usage the perfect is introduced by the particles *jw* or *m.k*: for example,

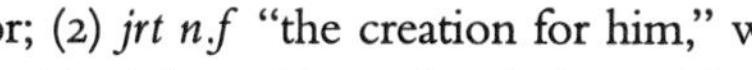 *jty ꜥnḫ.(w)-(w)ḏ3.(w)-s(nb.w) nb.j jw jn.n.j ḏdj*
"Sovereign lph, my lord, I have fetched Djedi"

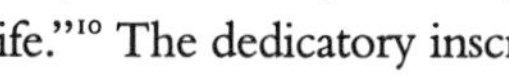 *m.k pḥ.n.n ḫnw* "Look, we have reached home."

9 *ḫrj.(j)* is a prepositional nisbe (§ 8.6): literally, "which is by me."

10 *jr.f* "that he might achieve (literally, 'make') is a verb form discussed in the next lesson; for the expression *dj ꜥnḫ* "given life," see § 23.15).

11 For Re-Harakhti see Essay 4. *jnr n rwḏt* "sandstone" means literally, "stone of sturdiness."

In each of these examples the speaker reports the action as completed from his point of view. Each action — "fetching," "reaching" — took place before the sentence was spoken, and is therefore past from the standpoint of the speaker. The speaker, however, is not reporting it as an historical past event but as an action that has been completed from the viewpoint of the present, at the time the sentence is spoken. The aspect of completion is more important than the fact that the actual action took place in the past: the perfect denotes completion, not tense.

Since the perfect does not express tense, it can also be used to describe an action as completed from the viewpoint of another action or situation. When that point of reference is in the past, the perfect corresponds to the English past perfect tense ("had done"): for example,

r s3 msyt pw, ḫ3w ḫpr.(w), šzp.n.j wnwt nt nfr jb

"It was after supper, when evening had come, and I had started the hour of relaxation."[12]

Here the perfect *šzp.n.j* expresses the action of "starting (literally, "receiving") the hour of relaxation" as completed in the past, "after supper, when evening had come."

18.8 Actions contrary to fact

In English the past perfect can be used not only to describe an action as completed in the past but also to express an action that never happened at all. Egyptian uses its perfect in the same way; for example, after the particle *ḥ3* (§ 16.6.12):

 *ḥ3 r.f jr.n.j ḫrw.j m t3j 3t*

"If only I had used (literally, 'made') my voice at that moment!"

Such uses are known as "contrary to fact." They express the action of the verb as completed from the standpoint of a hypothetical past action or situation (the speaker never actually used his voice).

The same hypothetical relationship underlies the use of the perfect in sentences where it corresponds to a form of the English future perfect tense ("would have done"). Such sentences are often marked as contrary to fact by the particle *3* (§ 16.7.1): for example,

jr šzp.j 3 st, ḫˁw m ḏrt.j, jw dj.n.j ḫt ḥmw

"If I had received it with weapons in my hand, I would have made the cowards retreat."[13]

This sentence refers to an attack in which the speaker was taken by surprise, without weapons to defend himself. The perfect form *jw dj.n.j* expresses the action of "making the cowards retreat" as completed with respect to the action of the first clause, *šzp.j* "my receiving." Since that action is marked as hypothetical by the particle *3*, however, the completed action expressed by the perfect is contrary to fact (the speaker never actually "made the cowards retreat").

12 From a narrative. The first clause is an A *pw* sentence with the prepositional phrase *r s3 msyt* "after supper" (literally, "at the back of supper") as A. The second is a SUBJECT-stative construction used as an unmarked adverb clause: literally, "evening having evolved." The term *nfr jb* "relaxation" means literally "goodness of heart."

13 Literally, "As for my hypothetically (*3*) receiving it, weapons in my hand, I have given that the cowards retreat." In the first clause, *šzp.j* "my receiving" is the infinitive, used as object of the preposition *jr* "as for"; the pronoun *st* "it" is the object of the infinitive, and refers to an attack (mentioned in a previous sentence). The second clause, with an adverbial predicate, is an unmarked adverb clause. In the third clause, *ḫt ḥmw* "that the cowards retreat" is a verb form used as object of *dj.n.j*; we will meet this construction in the next lesson.

There are not many examples of the perfect used to express an action contrary to fact, and most of them are marked in some way — such as by the particles *ḥꜣ* or *ꜣ* — to distinguish them from normal statements of completed action.

18.9 **The perfect as a past tense**

As we saw in § 18.7, the perfect often denotes a past action, although it expresses that action as completed rather than as a past event. To express an action as a past event, English uses the past tense rather than one of its perfect tenses: for example, *Jack did his homework*. Middle Egyptian, however, has no separate past tense form: instead, it uses the perfect for this function.[14] Like the stative of intransitive verbs (§ 17.6), the perfect of transitive verbs is used not only to denote completed action but also to express an action as a past event: for example,

ꜥḥꜥ.n.(j) šm.kw r smjt st, gm.n.j sw rḫ.(w) st

"Then I went to report it, and I found him (already) aware of it."

Here the perfect *gm.n.j* "I found" in the second clause, like the stative in the first clause, expresses the action of the verb as a past event. Even though the basic meaning of the form is still that of completed action, a translation with the English present perfect is impossible in this case (*"Then I went to report it, and I have found him aware of it").

When the perfect is used as a past tense it can be the first word in the sentence or clause, as in the last example, but more often it is preceded by a particle or an introductory word, as it is when it expresses completed action. Examples introduced by *m.k* usually express completed action, but *jw* often introduces the perfect as a past tense, as in the following example from a story:

jw wp.n.f r.f r.j, jw.j ḥr ẖt.j m bꜣḥ.f

"He opened his mouth toward me, while I was on my belly in his presence."

Most often, however, the perfect used as a past tense is introduced by  *ꜥḥꜥ.n*. We have already met this word introducing sentences with a pseudoverbal or stative predicate (§§ 15.6, 17.6). In those constructions *ꜥḥꜥ.n* is followed by a suffix pronoun or a noun (or noun phrase or demonstrative pronoun), which is the subject of the pseudoverbal or stative predicate. When it introduces the perfect, however, *ꜥḥꜥ.n* precedes the verb form itself, since the subject normally follows the verb. The difference can be seen in the following example:

ꜥḥꜥ.n.s šm.tj r jkn n.s nhj n mw, ꜥḥꜥ.n jt.n sj msḥ

"Then she went to scoop up for herself a little water. Then a crocodile took her."

Sentences with a pseudoverbal or stative predicate can also be introduced by *wn.jn*, but this word is hardly ever used with the perfect. Like *ꜥḥꜥ.n*, however, it is followed by the verb form itself, not by its subject: for example,

14 In this respect, Middle Egyptian is similar to modern French and German. In these languages, too, the perfect is used both for completed action and to report a past event: for example, *j'ai trouvé* (French) and *ich habe gefunden* (German) mean both "I have found" and "I found." French and German still have a separate past tense form (*je trouvai, ich fand*), but it is used mainly in formal writing (such as novels) and not in everyday speech.

 *wn.jn ḫn.n sdb.f ḥr mw*

"Then its fringe landed on the water."[15]

Both *ꜥḥꜥ.n* and *wn.jn* are used with the perfect only when it denotes a past event, not when it expresses completed action. After the particles *jw* and *m.k*, or without an introductory word, the perfect can have either meaning; in this case the context usually indicates which meaning is intended. Some passages, however, lend themselves to a translation with either the English present perfect or the past tense. This is often the case in biographies, where an official describes his deeds: for example,

 *jw dj.n.(j) t n ḥqr ḥbsw n ḥ3t(j)w*

"I have given bread to the hungry and clothes to the naked," or

"I gave bread to the hungry and clothes to the naked."

In such cases, however, the ambiguity exists only in the English translation: in Egyptian the perfect is a single verb form, regardless of its use.

18.10 The perfect of *rḫ* "know"

In the last lesson we saw how the stative of the verb *rḫ* "experience, learn" corresponds to the English verb "know" because it denotes the state (knowledge) that results from experiencing or learning about something (§ 17.8). The perfect of this verb also corresponds to the English verb "know," because it expresses the action of experiencing or learning about something as completed: for example,

 *m3.n.j ꜥfdt nt sj3, rḫ.n.j jmt.s*

"I have seen the box of Sia, and I know what is in it"[16]

literally (and perhaps better in this case), "I have learned what is in it." Although both the stative and the perfect of *rḫ* mean "know," the latter seems to be used when the action of learning or experiencing something is more important than the resulting state of knowledge — as it is here.

18.11 The perfect in adverb clauses

Besides expressing completed action or past events in main clauses, the perfect is also commonly used in unmarked adverb clauses to denote **prior circumstance**. In this function the perfect basically indicates an action that has been completed with respect to the action or the circumstance described in the main (or governing) clause. Such clauses can have various translations in English: for example,

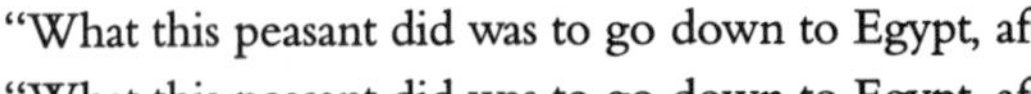

h3t pw jr.n sḫtj pn r kmt, 3tp.n.f ꜥ3w.f

"What this peasant did was to go down to Egypt, after he had loaded his donkeys" or

"What this peasant did was to go down to Egypt, after loading his donkeys" or

"What this peasant did was to go down to Egypt, having loaded his donkeys."

15 For the spelling of *ḫn.n* see § 18.2. This is an example with the perfect of an intransitive verb, expressing past action rather than the state resulting from that action: see § 18.3.

16 For the god Sia, see Essay 13. *jmt.s* "what is in it" is a feminine prepositional nisbe used as a noun (§§ 8.6–8.7).

Whichever translation is used, the perfect in the adverb clause describes an action that was completed before the action of the main clause took place (the peasant loaded his donkeys before setting off). When the perfect of the verb *jnj* "get, fetch" is used in an adverb clause it can often be translated by the English gerund "bringing": for example,

 *m.ṯn wj j.kw, jn.n.j n.f ꜥrtj*
"Look, I have come, bringing him two jawbones."

Although the translation "bringing" suggests an action that happens at the same time as that of the main clause, however, this is only a feature of English. In Egyptian the adverb clause denotes prior circumstance, as can be seen in the more literal translation "having gotten two jawbones for him."

Sometimes the action described by the perfect not only precedes that of another clause but also provides the reason for it. In such cases the adverb clause can be translated with the introductory words "because," "since," or "for": for instance,

 *ꜥḥꜥ.n rdj.n.f n.(j) nn, rḫ.n.f jqr st ꜥ.(j)*
"Then he gave me this, because he knew the excellence of my action."[17]

Such clauses can be translated in English not only with an introductory word denoting causality (such as "because") but also in the same way as other clauses of prior circumstance: in this case, "having learned of the excellence of my action," similar to "having loaded his donkeys" and "having gotten two jawbones for him" in the previous examples. This is because the notion of causality comes from the context, not from the verb form itself.

Middle Egyptian also uses the perfect in marked adverb clauses, usually after the particles *jsṯ* or *tj*: for example,

 *tj ḥm.f jt.n.f jwꜥt.f, ḥtp.n.f ṯntt-ḥrw*
"Once His Incarnation had taken his inheritance, he occupied the dais of Horus,"[18]

where the adverb clause is introduced by *tj*, which allows it to stand in front of the main clause (see § 12.18). Such marked clauses, however, are relatively unusual. In most cases, adverb clauses with the perfect are unmarked, with the verb form itself as the first word in the clause.

The fact that most adverb clauses with the perfect are unmarked can make it difficult to interpret the sequence of events in some passages. Compare, for example, the following two sentences:

ꜥḥꜥ.n.j mt.kw n.sn, gm.n.j st m ẖ3yt wꜥt
"Then I died because of them, after finding them as one pile of corpses"[19]

ꜥḥꜥ.n.(j) šm.kw r smjt st, gm.n.j sw rḫ.(w) st
"Then I went to report it, and I found him (already) aware of it."

17 The noun phrase *st ꜥ*, literally, "place of the arm," is an idiom for "action."
18 The subject in the first clause is topicalized (§ 18.4).
19 This sentence describes the grief of the speaker at finding his family destroyed in a conflagration. "Then I died" is meant metaphorically: "then I died of grief."

In the first example the *gm.n.j* clause describes an event that happened before that of the main clause (the speaker first found the "pile of corpses," then "died" of grief); in the second example it describes an event that happened after that of the main clause (the speaker first "went to report it" and then "found him aware of it"). There is nothing in the verb forms or the syntax of either example to indicate this sequence of events: only the logic of the sentences themselves reveals it.

The reason for this apparent ambiguity lies in a basic difference between the grammar of Egyptian and that of English. Our language forces us to treat the *gm.n.j* clause in the first example as a marked subordinate (or dependent) clause: "after finding them" (or "when I found them"). In Egyptian, however, it is only **contextually** subordinate: it is dependent because it follows another clause to which it is logically related. In another context it could be an independent clause in its own right ("I found them as one pile of corpses"). This kind of relationship can be difficult for speakers of English to appreciate. Our language allows grammatically independent clauses to be contextually subordinate in noun clauses or relative clauses (for example, *he said he didn't do it* and *the year she went to Paris*) but not in adverb clauses. Egyptian, however, does allow contextual dependence in adverb clauses, as the first example above illustrates. Even though we analyze the *gm.n.j* clause in the first example as an adverb clause of prior circumstance, therefore, it is actually no different grammatically from the *gm.n.j* clause in the second example, which describes action that happened after that of the main clause. Only the context indicates which sequence of events is intended, just as it indicates that the first *gm.n.j* clause is subordinate to the preceding clause rather than an independent statement in its own right.

18.12 The perfect in relative clauses

Middle Egyptian uses the perfect only in two kinds of relative clauses: indirect relative clauses after *ntj* (§ 12.5) or unmarked relative clauses after an undefined antecedent (§ 12.11), either direct or indirect: for example,

m.ṯn nn šrr p3 t ḥ(n)qt ntj rdj.n.j n.ṯn sw

"Look, the (amount of) bread and beer that I have given you is not little"[20]

 *bnr š3ᶜ.n.f r(w)d*

"a date that has started to harden" (direct)[21]

 *mj z(j) smt.n sw ḫnws*

"like a man whom a stinging insect has tormented" (indirect).[22]

Examples of the construction with *ntj* are not common. Instead of a clause with *ntj* plus the perfect, Egyptian normally uses the perfect relative form; we will examine the use of this form in relative clauses in Lesson 24.

The perfect is not used in direct relative clauses with a defined antecedent: for that function Middle Egyptian uses a different verb form, which we will meet in Lesson 23.

20 A negated adjectival sentence (§ 11.6). The relative clause means literally "which I have given it to you."
21 Literally, "a date it has started to harden"; *r(w)d* is an infinitive serving as object of *š3ᶜ.n.f*.
22 Literally, "like a man a stinging insect has tormented him."

18.13 The perfect in noun clauses

When it is used in a noun clause the perfect is sometimes preceded by the noun-clause markers *ntt* or *wnt* — for example, as the object of a verb or a preposition:

 *j(w).k rḫ.t(j) ntt ḏd.n jdw* "You know that Idu said ..."

 *n ntt sḏm.n.f jhm* "because of (the fact) that he heard shouting."

The perfect can also be used in unmarked noun clauses as the object of a verb or preposition: for instance,

 *jr gm.k ṯ3z.n.f ḥr gs.f wnmj*

"If you find it has knotted up on its right side"[23]

 *nmj.k w3ḏ-wr ṯb.t(j) mj jr.n.k tp t3*

"You shall traverse the sea sandaled, like you did on land."[24]

In other uses only the unmarked form of the noun clause with the perfect is attested — for example, as the A element of an A *pw* nominal sentence:

jr z3wt sbjw ḥtm.n.tw zm3yt swtj pw

"As for the guarding of the rebels, it means that the gang of Seth has been annihilated,"[25]

Here the entire sentence *ḥtm.n.tw zm3yt swtj* "the gang of Seth has been annihilated," with the *tw* form of the perfect, serves as the nominal predicate of the A *pw* sentence: literally, "it is (that) the gang of Seth has been annihilated."

18.14 The negated perfect

In Middle Egyptian the perfect is often used after the negation  *nj*. Like the perfect itself, the negated perfect is tenseless. Although it expresses the negation of completed action, however, it is **not** equivalent to the English perfect or past tenses. Instead, it normally corresponds to the **present tense** in English, denoting the negation of **action**, **ability**, or **necessity**, either as something that is generally true or as something that is true only at the moment of speaking: for example,

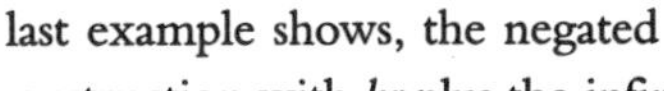 *nj nmꜥ.n ẖwd m pr.f*

"He who is rich in his house does not show partiality" or

"He who is rich in his house does not have to show partiality."[26]

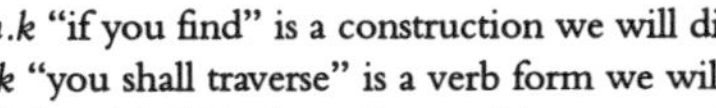 *m.k wj ḥr spr n.k, nj sḏm.n.k st*

"Look, I am petitioning to you, (but) you can't hear it" or

"Look, I am petitioning to you, (but) you don't hear it."

As the last example shows, the negated perfect serves as the negative counterpart of the pseudo-verbal construction with *ḥr* plus the infinitive, which is normally not negated itself (§ 15.8).

23 *jr gm.k* "if you find" is a construction we will discuss in the next lesson.

24 *nmj.k* "you shall traverse" is a verb form we will meet in the next lesson; *nmj* is a 3-lit. verb with final *j* (§ 13.5.3). *ṯb.t(j)* "sandaled" is the stative used in an unmarked adverb clause.

25 *swtj* is a New Kingdom form of the name of the god Seth (Essay 12).

26 This sentence refers to the tendency of judges to show favoritism to rich defendants, who could pay bribes to secure a favorable verdict.. A wealthy judge, according to the speaker, is likely to be free of such partiality.

The perfect can also be negated by *nn*. This construction is much less common than the normal negation with *nj*, and seems to have the same meaning: for instance,

 *wnf jb n hrw r 3w.f nn grg.n.f pr*

"He who is frivolous for the whole day cannot establish a household."[27]

This negative construction seems to be a feature of particular texts rather than of Middle Egyptian in general.

As we saw above (§ 18.3), Egyptian normally uses the stative of intransitive verbs as the counterpart of the perfect of transitive verbs. After the negative particles *nj* or *nn*, however, the perfect of intransitive verbs is used, not the stative: for example,

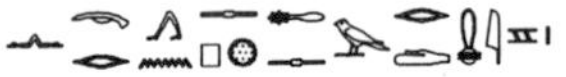 *nj spr.n zp ẖz r dmj*

"An unworthy cause cannot arrive at the harbor" (i.e., cannot succeed).

This is because the negated perfect expresses action, not state: "cannot arrive, does not arrive," not "is not in a state of arrival." The stative itself is negated only in the SUBJECT-stative construction, and even there only rarely (§ 17.15).

Examples of the perfect with the suffix *tw* are also common after the negative: for instance,

 *jw ms ḥmwt wšr.(w), nj jwr.n.tw*

"Surely, the women are barren: no one can conceive,"

literally, "one cannot conceive" or "one is not conceiving" (from a description of adverse times). Most examples of the perfect without an expressed subject also occur in negations: for instance,

 *ḫnmsw nw mjn nj mr.nj*

"The friends of today do not love."

In this case the subject *ḫnmsw nw mjn* "the friends of today" has been topicalized; in place of the usual suffix pronoun repeating the subject after the verb, the subject of the verb is omitted and the verb has the special form of the perfect suffix that is used when the subject is omitted (§ 18.5).

Although it is normally translated with the present tense, as these examples show, the negated perfect can be used in contexts that require a past tense in the English translation: for example,

wn.jn.s ḥr dbn t3 ˁt, nj gm.n.s bw jrrw st jm

"Then she was going around the room,
(but) she couldn't find the place in which it was being done."[28]

Despite the past reference of such examples, however, the construction still denotes the negation of action or ability ("she couldn't find"), not the negation of a past event ("she didn't find"). Egyptian uses a different negation for the latter, which we will meet in Lesson 20.

27 The subject, *wnf jb n hrw r 3w.f*, is preposed because of its length. The expression *wnf jb* "frivolous" means literally "loose of heart"; *wnf* means "loose-fitting" (of clothes: hence the determinative).

28 *bw jrrw st jm*, literally, "the place that it was done in," is a relative construction containing a verb form we will meet in Lesson 23.

If it seems odd that the negated perfect has a different translation than the perfect elsewhere, you should remember that the perfect expresses the aspect of completion and not a tense. Its negation therefore denotes the negation of completion, not the negation of completed or past action. An expression such as *nj sḏm.n.k* actually means something like "you do not complete hearing": therefore, "you do not hear" or "you cannot hear." Similarly, *nj gm.n.s* in a past context means something like "she did not complete finding": therefore, "she could not find" or "she was not finding."

18.15 The negated perfect in adverb clauses

Like the affirmative (nonnegated) perfect, the negated perfect can be used not only in main clauses (or independent sentences) but also in subordinate clauses. Examples in adverb clauses are almost always unmarked. They look just like main clauses, and are only subordinate by virtue of their context (that is, because they are logically related to a preceding clause): for example,

 *jw.f ḥr ꜥḥ3 ḏr rk ḥrw, nj qn.n.f*
"He has been fighting since the time of Horus, without being able to prevail."

Here the clause *nj qn.n.f* "he cannot prevail" describes how the action of the main clause happens.

The use of the negated perfect in adverb clauses is similar to that of the negative particle *nn* plus the infinitive (§ 14.15.1). Compare the following two examples:

 *r gr.(w), nj mdw.n.f*
"The mouth is silent, without being able to speak"

 *ꜥḥꜥ.n.s gr.tj, nn ẖnt*
"Then she was still, without rowing."[29]

The adverb clause in each of these sentences describes how the action of the preceding clause happens or is true. Although the two negative constructions express the negation of action, the negated perfect normally has the connotation of inability ("without being able to speak"), while *nn* plus the infinitive expresses the negation of action itself ("without rowing"). Thus, the adverb clause *nj qn.n.f* in the first example in this section means "without being able to prevail" rather than simply "without prevailing," since the latter could have been expressed by *nn* plus the infinitive (*nn qnt*).

In many cases, the negated perfect can be translated either as an adverb clause or as an independent statement: for example, "The mouth is silent, without being able to speak" or "The mouth is silent: it cannot speak" (second example in this section); similarly "Then she was going around the room, without being able to find the place in which it was being done" or "Then she was going around the room, (but) she couldn't find the place in which it was being done" (last example in the previous section). This is because the negated perfect in itself is simply a statement. Its function as an independent statement or an adverb clause depends solely on the context in which it is used — and on how the translator understands that context.

29 The verb *gr* means basically "become still." When it is used with reference to action, it means "become still"; with reference to speaking, it means "become silent."

18.16 The negated perfect in noun clauses

Noun clauses with the negated perfect are rare, but Middle Egyptian has a few examples introduced by the noun clause marker *ntt* "that": for instance,

m.ṯn rḫ.n.ṯn ntt jr ḫt nbt ddt sr(j) nb nḏs nb r ḥwt-nṯr m tp(j) n šmw.f nj nḏm.n n.f ḫtḫt jm

"Look, you know that, as for anything that any official or any commoner gives for the temple from the first of his harvest, the reversal of it cannot become pleasant for him."[30]

This is a good example of a fairly complex Middle Egyptian sentence. Everything after *rḫ.n.ṯn* "you know" (or "you have learned": § 18.10) is a noun clause serving as its object. The predicate of the noun clause is the negated perfect *nj nḏm.n* "cannot become pleasant"; its subject is *ḫtḫt* "the reversal" (infinitive). In the noun clause, the expression *ḫt nbt ddt sr(j) nb nḏs nb r ḥwt-nṯr m tp(j) n šmw.f* "anything that any official or any commoner gives for the temple from the first of his harvest" is topicalized and marked as such by the preposition *jr* "as for" (§ 18.4). The topicalized expression is repeated after the verb (*nḏm.n*) by *n.f* "for him," referring to *sr(j) nb nḏs nb* "any official or any commoner" and by the prepositional adverb *jm* "of it," referring to the topicalized expression as a whole.

18.17 The negated perfect in relative clauses

Like the perfect itself, the negated perfect can be used in unmarked relative clauses, direct or indirect, after an undefined antecedent: for example,

 *dpy nb snḏw mm mw nj tkn.n.tw.f*

"a crocodile, a lord of fear among the waters, who cannot be approached" (direct)

 *zt jt.n.s rnpwt ꜥšꜣ nj jj.n n.s ḥzmn.s*

"a woman who has matured,[31] for whom her menstruation does not come" (indirect).

In the first example, the coreferent of the antecedent is the suffix pronoun *.f*, which is the subject of the perfect: literally, "a crocodile … he cannot be approached." The second example has two relative clauses after the antecedent *zt* "a woman": the first direct, the second indirect. The coreferent in both is the suffix pronoun *.s*: in the first clause, it serves as the subject (literally, "she has taken many years"); in the second, it is both the object of the preposition *n* and the possessor of the noun *ḥzmn* (literally, "her menstruation does not come for her").

The negated perfect is only rarely used in marked relative clauses (after *ntj*): an example in a direct relative clause is

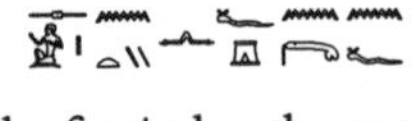 *z(j) ntj nj fgn.n.f* "the man who cannot urinate."

Instead of *ntj* plus the negated perfect, Middle Egyptian more often uses the perfect after the negative relative adjective *jwtj* "who not, which not" (§ 12.9). This construction is used mostly after defined antecedents, in both direct and indirect relative clauses: for example,

30 *ddt sr(j) nb nḏs nb r ḥwt-nṯr m tp(j) n šmw.f* is a relative clause modifying *ḫt nbt* "anything." It uses a verb form (*ddt*) we will meet in Lesson 24; *sr(j) nb nḏs nb* is the subject of the relative clause. For *tp(j)* "first" see § 9.3. The sentence means that no official or commoner who gives a donation to the temple likes to see it appropriated for some other purpose.

31 Literally, "has taken many years."

 *nṯr pw jwt(j) mjn.n.f* "that god who cannot die" (direct)

 *j3t twy nt 3ḫ(j)w jwtt sw3.n.ṯw ḥr.s*

"that mound of the akhs, by which one cannot pass"[32] (indirect) —

literally, "who he cannot moor"[33] and "which one cannot pass by it." Note that *jwtj*, like *ntj*, agrees in gender and number with its antecedent.

In Middle Egyptian, *jwtj* plus the perfect is the normal construction for negative relative clauses with the perfect when such clauses modify a defined antecedent. The rarer construction with *ntj nj* plus the perfect is a variant form of *jwtj* plus the perfect: for all practical purposes, *jwtj* is functionally equivalent to *ntj nj* in this use.

18.18 The perfect in questions

There are two kinds of questions with a verbal predicate: those in which the action of the verb itself is questioned, and those in which some other element is questioned. An English example of the first kind of question is *Has Jack done his homework?*; examples of the second kind are *When did Jack do his homework?* and *What did Jack do?*. The first kind of question can be called a **predicate question**; the second, an **adjunct question**.

For the most part, English treats both kinds of questions alike. In Egyptian, however, they are treated differently. When the perfect is used in a predicate question, it is usually preceded by the particles *jn jw*, less often by *jn* alone: for example,

 *jn jw srwḫ.n.k ꜥtj* "Have you treated the two limbs?"

 *jn d3.n.k n.j z(j)* "Have you ferried a man for me?"

The negated perfect can also be used in a predicate question, in which case it is introduced by the interrogative particle *jn*: for example,

 *jn nj ḫn.n.tn* "Can't you row?"

In an adjunct question the perfect is normally the first word in the sentence: for instance,

 *j.n.ṯn tn(j)* "Where have you come (from)?"

 *jr.n.k r.s mj jšst* "So how did you do (it)?"[34] —

literally, "you have come where?" and "so you did (it) like what?" (see §§ 5.11, 8.13, 10.10).

The difference between predicate and adjunct questions actually involves more than just the presence or absence of *jn jw* or *jn*. Although it looks just like the perfect, the verb form used in adjunct questions is actually the perfect relative. Why this is so need not concern us here, but will be discussed in Lesson 25.

32 The suffix *tw* of the perfect is written *ṯw* in this example: see § 2.8.3. For *twy* "that" see § 5.10.1.

33 The verb *mjnj* "moor" (a boat: the first determinative is a mooring stake) is a euphemism for "die." It is normally spelled *mnj*, as here, but the reed-leaf is the second radical, not the last: the verb belongs to the 4ae-inf. class, which does not show the final radical *j* in the perfect. For *pw* "that" see § 5.8.

34 The object "it" is omitted. For *r.s* "so" see n. 7.

ESSAY 18. EGYPTIAN LITERATURE

One of the advantages of studying Middle Egyptian is that a knowledge of the language gives you firsthand access to a whole world of ancient thought and literature. We are fortunate that the Egyptian climate has preserved so much of that literature for us — not only in the hieroglyphs carved on stone monuments or painted on tomb walls, but especially in the much more fragile texts inscribed on wood or written in ink on papyrus.

The hieroglyphic examples presented in these lessons are all taken from real ancient Egyptian texts, ranging from mundane documents of everyday life to sophisticated treatises on philosophy and theology. Because our knowledge of Middle Egyptian is completely dependent on the written word, it is important to understand the cultural background of these texts: why they were composed in the first place, how they were transmitted, and what they meant to the people who wrote them. In this essay we will look at Egyptian literature as a whole; subsequent essays will discuss the various kinds of Egyptian texts in more detail.

Middle Egyptian literature reflects a number of different layers of the Egyptian language, from the spontaneous conversation of fieldworkers to the most carefully crafted literary compositions. Such layers (also known as registers) exist in all languages. In English, for example, contractions such as *can't* or *won't* are more common in everyday speech and writing than in formal literary compositions. In modern French and German, the past tense belongs to the layer of formal language and is largely absent from everyday speech (see n. 14 above). The difference is even more pronounced in modern Arabic, which uses one set of words and grammar for writing and formal speech and a different set for everyday conversation; the first set, called Standard Literary Arabic, is uniform across the Arabic-speaking world, but the second, known as Colloquial Arabic, differs from country to country. Politicians giving a speech in Arabic sometimes switch between these two layers deliberately: for example, by using the formal language to appear statesmanlike and the colloquial to identify themselves with the common people.

Middle Egyptian seems to have been similar to modern Arabic, and probably often had significant differences between the spoken and written language. For a number of reasons, however, it is not always easy, or even possible, to distinguish the various layers from one another in an Egyptian text. Some layers are less well represented than others in preserved texts; and as the language changed with time, words or grammatical constructions from one layer were adopted into others. Because of these difficulties, Egyptologists have not devoted much effort to identifying the different layers of speech that might be present in a text. Along with other factors such as dialect (§ 1.3) and the change in language over time, however, such differences probably account for some of the more unusual constructions we have met in this and past lessons.

The base of all communication, of course, was the speech used in everyday conversation. Of all the layers, this is the least well represented in Middle Egyptian texts. We know it primarily through occasional labels in tomb scenes, which record the conversation of workers depicted in the scenes. Unlike written Middle Egyptian, it seems to have had a definite article (*p3*, *t3*, *n3* "the": § 5.10.3), and perhaps an indefinite article as well (*wᶜ*, *wᶜt* "a": § 9.4 end). Over time these two features were gradually adopted in the written language. When we come across them in a

Middle Egyptian text, however, it is not always clear whether their presence reflects this historical process or whether it was meant as a deliberate use of the "colloquial" layer.

The Egyptians themselves were conscious of the different layers in their speech. The language of official documents was viewed as a standard not only for written texts but also for the speech of the upper classes (see the text cited in § 5.10.3). The Egyptians were also aware of the difference between ordinary conversation or writing and the kind of carefully crafted language that we call literature. The latter was known as  *mdwt nfrt* "beautiful speech" (much like the French term *belles lettres*), and those who could compose it were called  *nfr mdw* "beautiful of speech." It is a nice reflection on Egyptian society that the possession of this talent was not felt to be limited to the upper classes or the educated. One of the most famous pieces of Egyptian literature is a series of discourses on the nature of Maat, expounded by a peasant from one of the oases (the "boondocks" of ancient Egypt); and another text tells us that "Beautiful speech is more hidden than gemstones, yet it is found with servant-women at the millstones."

Like the English-speakers of Shakespeare's time, the Egyptians delighted in the clever use of language, not only in content but also in style. We have already met a good example of the latter in Exercise 17:

 *wr wr wrw.f wr.(w)* "Great is a great one whose great ones are great."

As with the different layers that are probably present in many texts, we are not always able to recognize the kind of deliberate craftsmanship involved in literary style. We can see, however, many of the devices found in the literature of more familiar cultures, including allegory, metaphor, puns, and phonetic features such as alliteration. One common feature of Egyptian literature is the use of what has been called "thought couplets," in which the thought of one sentence or clause is repeated in different words or expanded in the following sentence or clause: for example,

 *ꜥḥꜥ jb pw m 3t s3s3*
 *ꜥnw pw nj rdj.n.f s3.f*
"He is one steadfast of heart in the moment of attack;
he is a repeller who does not show his back."[35]

This feature is also found in the literature of other ancient Near Eastern cultures; it is most familiar to us from the poems of the Bible, especially the Psalms.

Some of what we — and probably the Egyptians themselves — would consider "beautiful words" includes recognizable literary genres such as stories and poems, but it also encompasses less obvious kinds of texts such as tomb biographies and even some letters. When one such text had a particularly well crafted sentence, it was often copied in other texts of the same kind. Many of the more important works of Egyptian literature exist in several copies. In some cases this is because parts of them were used to train schoolboys in the art of writing; but works of literature were also copied by more well-educated scribes simply for their own enjoyment, and we owe our knowledge of some of the best creations of Egyptian literature, which exist in only one copy, to this latter motive.

35 From a poem in praise of the king. Note the alliteration between the final words of both sentences (*s3s3* ~ *s3.f*).

Egyptian literary texts are often inscribed at the end with a colophon giving the name of the copyist, but the names of the authors are usually not recorded. Nevertheless, the Egyptians were usually aware of their identity, and they revered their literary giants as much as we do the authors of our own great literature. The most poignant illustration of this reverence is preserved for us in a literary composition of the Ramesside Period, naming some of the famous writers from the golden age of Middle Egyptian literature:

> As for those learned writers since the time that came after the gods,
> those prophets of what was to come, their names have become fixed forever …
>
> They did not make pyramids of copper with stelae of metal;
> they were not able to leave a heritage of children.
> Yet their names are pronounced:
> they made for themselves a heritage of writings, of the teachings they made …
>
> Is there one now like Hardedef? Is another like Imhotep?
> No one has come in our time like Neferti or Khety, their best.
> I will let you know the name of Ptahemdjehuti and Khakheperseneb.
> Is another like Ptahhotep, or Kaires? …
>
> They are gone, their names forgotten,
> but writings make them remembered.

EXERCISE 18

Transliterate and translate the following sentences:

1. 
2.  — *ḥtw* personal name
3. 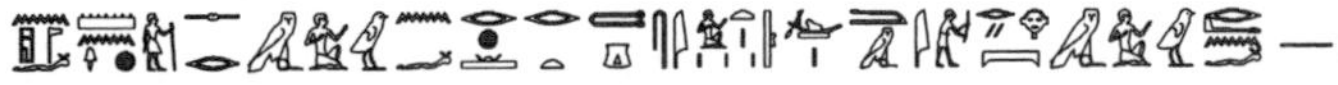 — from an autobiography
4.  — from a letter: *rn.f-snb* and *z3-nb* are personal names (see § 4.15); for the measurements, see § 9.7.4
5. 
6. 
7.  — *nn* "this," meaning "this situation you are in"
8. 
9. 
10.  — *jb* "mind" (see Essay 7)
11.  — *ẖnn* "rower"

12. [hieroglyphs] — from a description of the king as an athlete

13. [hieroglyphs] ... [hieroglyphs]

14. [hieroglyphs]

15. [hieroglyphs] — *jnbw-ḥq3* name of a frontier fort (§ 4.15)

16. [hieroglyphs]

17. [hieroglyphs]

18. [hieroglyphs]

19. [hieroglyphs]

20. [hieroglyphs]

21. [hieroglyphs]

22. [hieroglyphs]

23. [hieroglyphs]

24. [hieroglyphs] — *p3* "do in the past," uses the infinitive as its object

25. [hieroglyphs] ... [hieroglyphs]

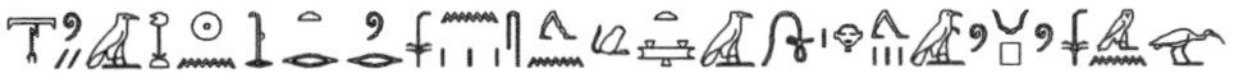

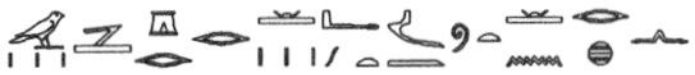

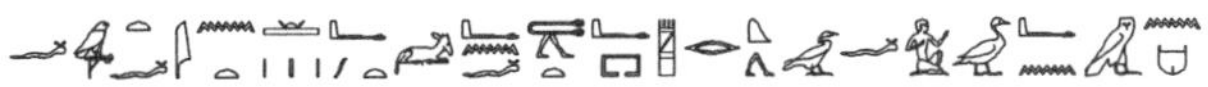

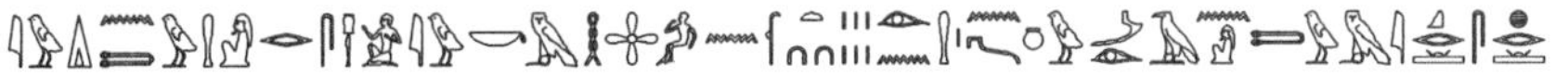

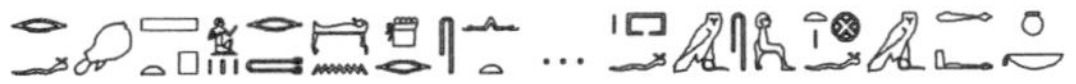

26. The following is a damaged dedicatory inscription from a temple of Thutmose III in Nubia. Using § 18.7, see if you can restore the lost hieroglyphs (indicated by hatching), transliterate, and translate:

[hieroglyphs] ... [hieroglyphs] — *bhn* "Buhen" (a Nubian site), *ḥ(3)bt* nisbe from *ḥ3b* "festival"

27. [hieroglyphs]
[hieroglyphs]
[hieroglyphs]

[hieroglyphs] — from a temple of Thutmose III at Thebes: *nb nswt t3wj* see Essay 15, *ḫnt(j)* nisbe, *sj* for *st*, the dependent pronoun *sw* (referring to *mnw*) has been omitted after *gm.n*.

28. Transliterate and translate the texts in the scene on the following page. Vocabulary:
Right: *NB-M3ᶜT-Rᶜ* "Neb-maat-re" ("Lord of Re's Maat," throne name of Amenhotep III); *n ẖt.f* "bodily" (literally, "belonging to his body"); *mr.f* "his beloved"
Left: *(n)swyt* "kingship"

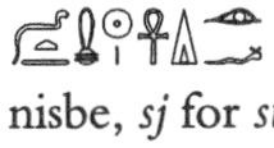

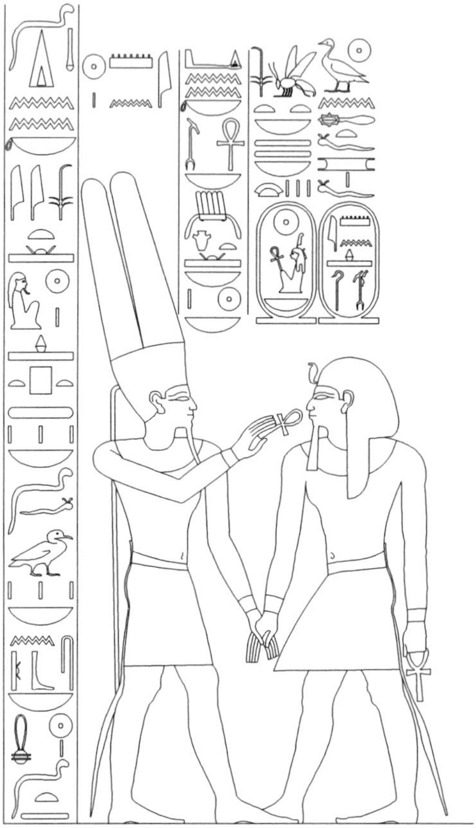

Amenhotep III Receiving Life from Amun-Re

19. The Subjunctive

19.1 Definition

One of the features of the Egyptian verbal system, as we saw in Lesson 13, is that of mood: indicative forms are used in statements of fact; subjunctive forms mark the statement as contingent, possible, or desirable (§ 13.3.3). Most English verb forms are indicative, but English also has several different subjunctive forms. In Middle Egyptian there is only one subjunctive form. The indicative forms of Middle Egyptian can sometimes be used for statements that do not express a fact (see §§ 17.17.2, 18.8), because they are unmarked for mood. The subjunctive, however, is a marked form: it always indicates that a statement is in some way possible, desirable, or contingent on some other action or situation.

Like most Middle Egyptian verb forms, the subjunctive expresses action rather than state and is essentially tenseless: it denotes a mood rather than a specific tense. Nonetheless, actions that are contingent, possible, or desirable are most often seen as lying in the future, either with respect to the speaker's viewpoint or with respect to some other action. As a result, the subjunctive is often translated by an English future form, and for that reason it is also known as the **prospective** ("looking forward"). This book uses the name "subjunctive" not only because it describes the basic meaning of the form but also because the term "prospective" is better applied to a different verb form, which we will meet later.

19.2 Form

Unlike the perfect, the subjunctive is not marked by a special suffix. Instead, it usually has to be recognized by how it is used rather than by how it looks. We know from Coptic however, that the subjunctive was distinguished in actual speech by a stressed final vowel *a* after the verb stem: for example, **ᶜanḫáf* "he shall live." Of course, this feature is not visible in hieroglyphs. In most verb classes, the subjunctive looks just like the **base** stem of the verb (§ 13.4). The following table shows the typical forms found in Middle Egyptian texts.

2-LIT.	*ḏd.j* "I shall say." Rarely prefixed: *j.ḏd.k* "you shall say." The prefixed form is found mostly in early Middle Egyptian texts (with the prefix spelled), as a holdover from Old Egyptian, and in texts after the Middle Kingdom (with the prefix usually spelled), where it anticipates some Late Egyptian forms.
2AE-GEM.	*gn.j* "I shall become soft."[1] The verb *m33* "see" has both the normal form and a special form with the stem *m3n*: *m3.k* and *m3n.k* "you shall see." The stem *m3n* is the same one used occasionally in the infinitive (§ 14.3.2).

1 Probably representing **gannái* — i.e., *AVBBái* (see § 13.5.2).

3-LIT.	 *wḥm.j* "I shall repeat"
3AE-INF.	 *ms.s* "she shall give birth." Coptic shows that the 3ae-inf. base stem had a final *i* in the subjunctive: i.e., **misiás*. This vowel is occasionally reflected in hieroglyphs by a final double reed-leaf, probably because it was heard as a consonant (i.e., **misyás*):  *sky.f* "he would have wiped out." Unlike other 3ae-inf. verbs, the verb *jnj* "get, fetch" has a special form in the subjunctive, with the ending *t*:  *jnt.f* "he should fetch." The ending *t* is sometimes spelled *tw*, probably to show that the *t* was actually pronounced (see Essay 17):  *jntw.f* "it should fetch."
3AE-GEM.	 *snbb.sn* "they may converse" — geminated stem
4-LIT.	 *wstn.k* "you shall stride";  *ẖtẖt* "should revert"
4AE-INF.	 *ḥms.s* "she should sit"; occasionally with final double reed-leaf:  *rnpy* "shall become young"
CAUS. 2-LIT.	 *swḏ.ṯn* "you might bequeath"
CAUS. 2AE-GEM.	 *sqbb.k* "you might cool off" — geminated stem
CAUS. 3-LIT.	 *swꜥb.k* "you should clean"
CAUS. 3AE-INF.	 *sq3.k* "may you heighten"; also with final double reed-leaf:  *sq3y.k* "may you heighten"
CAUS. 4-LIT.	 *smnmn.ṯn* "you shall cause quaking"
CAUS. 4AE-INF.	 *sḫnt.f* "may he promote"
ANOM.	The verb *rdj* "give, put, allow" uses only the base stem *dj*:  *dj.k* "you should give,"  *dj.j* "I will allow." The verb *jwj/jj* "come" uses only the base stem *jw* and always has the ending *t*, like the 3ae-inf. verb *jnj* "get, fetch": 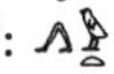 *jwt* "shall come."

19.3 Subject, object, and word order in clauses with the subjunctive

The subjunctive, like the perfect, belongs to the category of the suffix conjugation (§ 18.1). It is one of six verb forms in this category that are not marked by a special suffix such as the *n* of the perfect (§ 18.2). Egyptologists commonly refer to these six verb forms collectively as the *sḏm.f* ("sedgem-EFF"). The subjunctive is therefore also known as the subjunctive *sḏm.f* (or the prospective *sḏm.f*). Clauses with the subjunctive follow the normal rules with regard to the subject of the verb and the word order of other elements in the clause, which we reviewed in our discussion of the perfect (§ 18.4).

Like the perfect, the subjunctive can be used without an expressed subject when its subject is obvious from the context or when it does not refer to anything in particular; we will meet an example of this use later in the lesson. Unlike the perfect, however, the subjunctive is rarely used with a preposed or topicalized subject.

19.4 The subjunctive with the suffix *tw*

Like the perfect, the subjunctive can be used with the impersonal suffix pronoun *tw* as its subject: for example,

 *njs.tw n.k m ḫrt-hrw ḥr wḏḥw n wnn-nfr.(w)*
"One shall call to you daily from the offering-table of Wenen-nefer."[2]

The suffix *tw* is also used to make the **passive form of the subjunctive**. In this case the verb form is followed by a noun (or noun phrase) or pronoun as its subject: for example,

 *st3.tw n.k tk3 m grḥ* "A taper shall be lit for you at night."

When the subject is a personal pronoun it takes the form of the suffix pronoun and is attached to the verb **after** the suffix *tw*: for example,

 *ḥw.tw.f m šsm 50* "He will be beaten with 50 lashes."

When the suffix *tw* is attached to the subjunctive *jnt* "get, fetch," only one *t* is written: i.e., 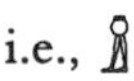 *jn.tw* "should be brought" (not  *jnt.tw*). The subjunctive *jwt* "come," however, shows the ending *t* before the suffix *tw*:  *jwt.tw* "one shall come."

19.5 The subjunctive in main clauses

Like the perfect, the subjunctive can be used as the verb form in a main clause or independent sentence. In this use it has two basic meanings:

1. **as a wish or command**

Because the subjunctive marks the action of the verb as contingent, possible, or desirable, it is the form that Middle Egyptian normally uses in main clauses to express a **wish**: for example,

j (j)tm(w) jmj ḥwt-ꜥ3t jty nṯrw nḥm.k wj m ꜥ nṯr pw ꜥnḫ m ḫryt
"Oh, Atum, who is in the Great Enclosure, sovereign of the gods,
may you save me from that god who lives on slaughter."[3]

The subjunctive is also used to express a **polite command**, corresponding to English constructions with the verb *should*: for instance,

 *m.k wj m ꜥ.k, jp.k wj*
"Look, I am in your hand(s): you should take account of me."

It can also be used to express an **exhortation**, corresponding to English constructions with the verb *let*: for example,

 *jrjw-ꜥ3 ḥr šm.n ḥ3q n.n*
"The doorkeepers are saying: 'Let's go and plunder for ourselves.'"[4]

2 *ḫrt-hrw* is a nisbe phrase used as a noun (object of the preposition *m*): literally, "in what is under the day." *wnn-nfr.(w)* "Wenen-nefer" (or "Onnophris," the Greek pronunciation) is an epithet of Osiris, meaning literally "he who is continually young."

3 *ḥwt-ꜥ3t* is the name of a temple in Heliopolis. *ꜥnḫ* "who lives" is a verb form we will meet in Lesson 23.

4 *jrjw-ꜥ3* "doorkeepers" is literally "those who pertain to the door" (§ 8.7). For *ḥr* "are saying," see § 15.7.

The final clause in this example (*ḥ3q n.n* "and plunder for ourselves") is an instance of the subjunctive with omitted subject: the 1pl suffix *.n* is omitted because it is clear from the preceding clause (*šm.n* "let's go").

Of these three uses, the last (exhortation) is only expressed by the subjunctive; but other verb forms can be used to express wishes and commands. As a command, the subjunctive is softer or more polite than the imperative: Egyptian tends to use it instead of the imperative when the command is addressed to a superior, such as a high official, the king, or a god: for example,

 *wḏ3 ḥm.k r prw nw zẖ3w*
"Your Incarnation should proceed to the houses of writings" or
"May Your Incarnation proceed to the houses of writings" or
"Let Your Incarnation proceed to the houses of writings."

The subjunctive differs from the stative in expressing a wish or command because it denotes action, whereas the stative denotes a state: thus, subjunctive *šm.k* "you should go" but stative *šm.tj* "you should be gone" (i.e., "begone!") — both of which also contrast with the simple imperative *šm* "go!"; similarly, subjunctive *ᶜnḫ.f* "may he live" versus stative *ᶜnḫ.(w)* "may he be alive" and imperative *ᶜnḫ* "live!"

2. **expressing the future**

The subjunctive is frequently used to express an action that is to take place in the **future**, as in the following example from a prophecy:

jw dpt r jjt m ẖnw, sqdw jm.s rḫ.n.k
šm.k ḥnᶜ.sn r ẖnw
"A ship is to come from home, with sailors in it whom you know,
and you will go home with them."[5]

This example illustrates two means of expressing the future in Middle Egyptian: with the pseudoverbal construction of *r* plus the infinitive (§ 15.2), in the first clause; and with the subjunctive *šm.k*, in the last clause. Although both constructions refer to future actions, they have different connotations. The pseudoverbal construction is an **involuntary** future: it describes a future action over which the actor has no control, one that is in some way compulsory or inevitable. The subjunctive is a **voluntary** future: it denotes actions that are intended or willed by the actor. In the example given above, the future action in the first clause is expressed with the pseudoverbal construction both because it is prophesied (and therefore inevitable) and because it is involuntary: the actor (*dpt* "a ship") normally has no control over its actions. In the last clause the future action is expressed with the subjunctive both because the actor (*.k* "you") is a human being, who can control his actions, and because the future action is viewed as voluntary: the actor will in fact want to "go home with them."

5 The second clause is a sentence with adverbial predicate, used as an adverb clause; *rḫ.n.k* is the perfect relative form, to be discussed in Lesson 24.

When the actor is the first person the pseudoverbal construction often expresses **compulsion** or **necessity**: for instance, when a peasant's donkey eats someone's grain, the owner of the grain says

m.k wj r nḥm ʿ3.k sḫtj ḥr wnm.f šmʿ(j).j

"Look, I have to take away your donkey, peasant, because of its eating my barley."[6]

When the subjunctive is used as a future with first-person subject, it often denotes the actor's **intention**: for example, the pharaoh Kamose, speaking of an enemy who has invaded Egypt, says

tw.j r ṯhn ḥnʿ.f, sd.j ẖt.f
jb.j r nḥm kmt ḥ(w)t ʿ3mw

"I have to engage with him (in battle): I intend to cut open his belly.
My intention is to take (back) Egypt and smite the Asiatics."[7]

By using the pseudoverbal construction in the first clause, the pharaoh indicates that he has no choice but to fight with the enemy. The subjunctive *sd.j* in the second clause, however, expresses a future action that the king himself intends to happen.

English also expresses voluntary and involuntary future actions with different verbal constructions, which are actually quite similar to those of Egyptian. The pseudoverbal construction usually corresponds to the English constructions *is to* and *have to* with the infinitive, which denote inevitable and compulsory actions. When it is used to express the future, the subjunctive normally corresponds to the English future tense: *you will go*, for example, is actually derived from the construction *you will to go*, in which the action is described as willed by its actor.

19.6 The subjunctive after particles

Since the subjunctive indicates that the action of the verb is contingent, possible, or desirable, it is not used with the particle *jw*, which basically marks its clause as a statement of fact (§ 16.6.1). The subjunctive can be used with the introductory particle *m.k*, however; in such cases the verb form is usually future, though it sometimes expresses a wish, command, or exhortation: for example,

 *m.k swrj.j m jrp n k3mw.k*

"Look, I intend to drink of the wine of your vineyard"

 *m.t n jr.n 3t jm.s* "Look, let's us spend some time in it."[8]

The subjunctive is also used after the particle *ḥ3* (and its variants *ḥw*, *ḥwj*, *ḥwj 3*, etc.) — as might be expected, since *ḥ3* marks its clause as a wish (§ 16.6.12): for instance,

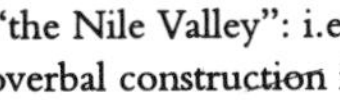 *ḥwj 3 mry wj k3.k* "Would that your ka might desire me!"

The subjunctive is often associated with three particles in Middle Egyptian that deserve special consideration:

6 *wnm.f* "its eating" is the infinitive, used as object of the preposition *ḥr* "because of." The noun *šmʿj* is a nisbe related to *šmʿw* "the Nile Valley": i.e., "Upper Egyptian barley."

7 For the pseudoverbal construction in the first clause, see § 15.4. In the third clause, *jb.j* "my intention" means literally "my heart"; *nḥm* and *ḥ(w)t* are both infinitives, objects of the preposition *r*.

8 Literally, "Look (2fs), we, we should make a period of time in it," with the 1pl subject topicalized (§ 18.4).

1. **the subjunctive after** *jḫ*

The particle *jḫ* introduces a clause of future consequence, corresponding to English clauses in which the future tense is introduced by the words *thus, so,* or *then.* It is used almost exclusively with the subjunctive as an expression of the future: for example,

sb3 r.k sw r mdt ẖr ḥ3t, jḫ jr.f bj(3)w n msw srjw
"So, teach him to speak (well) in the beginning:
then he will be a model for the children of officials."[9]

Normally, the clause introduced by *jḫ* describes an action that the speaker desires or expects to happen as the consequence of some preceding action or situation, as in this example.

2. **the subjunctive after** *ẖr*

The particle *ẖr* can introduce clauses with several kinds of predicates (§ 16.6.13). When the subjunctive is used in such clauses, it denotes future consequence: for instance,

wbn.f m nwt ḥqr, ẖr s3.sn m jnw n š3w
"When he rises in the town of hunger,
then they will become sated with the products of the fields."[10]

Unlike *jḫ*, the particle *ẖr* signals an inevitable consequence of some preceding action or situation: thus, the sentence just cited means that the rising of the inundation will inevitably bring an end to hunger. The subjunctive is not very common after *ẖr*; most Middle Egyptian texts use a different verb form or construction, which we will meet in the next lesson.

3. **the subjunctive after** *k3*

The particle *k3* is used mostly with the subjunctive, in clauses or sentences expressing future consequence: for example,

ḥw jry.k ḫft ḏd.j, k3 ḥtp m3ꜥt r st.s
"If only you will do as I say! Then Maat will come to rest at its (proper) place."[11]

Clauses with *k3* denote simple future consequence, without the notions of desire or expectation (indicated by *jḫ*) or inevitability (signaled by *ẖr*).

19.7 The subjunctive in conditional sentences

Conditional sentences pose a condition under which the action or situation of the main clause is true: for example, *If you do that, you'll be sorry*, where the main clause *you'll be sorry* is true under the conditions stated by the first clause (*if you do that*). Such sentences always consist of two clauses: the conditional clause is known as the protasis, and the main clause is called the apodosis. In Middle Egyptian the protasis is normally introduced by *jr*; this can be translated as "if,"

9 The prepositional phrase *ẖr ḥ3t* "in the beginning," means literally "under the front."
10 From a description of the inundation; *wbn.f* is a verb form we will meet in Lesson 25.
11 *ḏd.j* is the infinitive, used as object of the preposition *ḫft*: literally, "according to my saying."

"when," or "as," although it is actually the full form of the preposition *r* "as for, with respect to" (§ 8.2.7). When the protasis is introduced by *jr*, it always comes first in the sentence, before the apodosis.

The contingent meaning of the subjunctive makes it a natural form for conditional sentences. It can appear in both the protasis (after *jr*) and the apodosis: for example,

jr jwt pt tn m rsw(j), ḥms ḏḥwt(j)-nḫt.(w) pn ḥr rsw.s

"If this sky comes with a southwind, this Djehutinakht will sit on its south,"[12]

with the subjunctives *jwt* "comes" and *ḥms* "will sit." Because the subjunctive itself expresses contingent action, it is sometimes used as the protasis on its own, without *jr*: for instance,

j ᶜnḫw ... sw3t(j).sn ḥr jz pn, mr.ṯn ᶜnḫ msḏ.ṯn ḫpt, jw.ṯn r drp n.j m ntt m ᶜ.ṯn

"Oh (you) living ... who shall pass by this tomb! As you love to live and hate to pass on, you are to offer to me from what you have."[13]

Here the protasis contains two subjunctive forms, *mr.ṯn* "you love" and *msḏ.ṯn* "you hate," and the apodosis is expressed with the pseudoverbal construction of *r* plus the infinitive. In such sentences the conditional sense of the protasis is conveyed by the context instead of a specific introductory word. English has similar conditional sentences: for example, *You do that and you'll be sorry.*

19.8 The subjunctive in adverb clauses

In Middle Egyptian, adverb clauses with the subjunctive are almost exclusively **unmarked**. Such clauses have three basic uses:

1. **to express purpose**

Clauses of purpose state the reason for the action of another clause. In English they are normally introduced by the phrases *in order that, so that,* or *that.* In Egyptian such clauses are often expressed by the subjunctive alone, without an introductory word: for example,

 *jr.n.f ṯ3w n jb, ᶜnḫ fnḏw.sn*

"He has made air for the heart, so that their noses might live,"

where the subjunctive *ᶜnḫ fnḏw.sn* "so that their noses might live" describes the purpose of the action in the main clause. We have already met another way of expressing purpose, by means of the preposition *r* plus the infinitive (§ 14.11.3). Egyptian uses the subjunctive instead of the infinitive construction when it needs or wants to express the actor of the verb in the purpose clause, as in this example. The use of the subjunctive to express purpose is extremely common, and it is the most frequent use of the subjunctive in an adverb clause.

12 From a funerary text: *ḏḥwtj-nḫt.w* is the name of the deceased. *rswj* "southwind" is a nisbe from *rsw* "south": literally, "southerner" (compare the New England term *nor'easter*).

13 *ᶜnḫw* "living ones" and *sw3t(j).sn* "who shall pass" are different kinds of participles, a verb form we will discuss in Lesson 23. *ᶜnḫ* "to live" and *ḫpt* "to pass on" are infinitives (see § 14.12). For *m ᶜ.ṯn*, literally "in your hand(s)," see § 10.7; the form of the arm-sign reflects the idea of a hand presenting an offering (a pot of water).

2. **to express result**

Clauses of result express the outcome of an action or situation. In English such clauses are normally introduced by the words *so that*. Egyptian uses the subjunctive alone for this purpose, without an introductory word: for example,

jtrw šw.(w) nw kmt, ḏ3y.tw mw ḥr rdwj

"The river of Egypt is dried up, so that the water is crossed on foot,"[14]

where the subjunctive *ḏ3y.tw mw* "the water is crossed" expresses the result of the situation described in the first clause. We have already seen how the stative can also be used to express result, either by itself or with a preceding subject (§§ 17.13, 17.19). The subjunctive is used when the result is an action; the stative, when it is a state. Note that the tense of the verb in such clauses is not necessarily future, as this example demonstrates.

3. **to continue an imperative**

When Egyptian wants to express more than one command, it often uses the imperative followed by the subjunctive, rather than two imperatives: for example,

m.k mdwt.sn mn.(w) m zẖ3w, pg3 šd.k

"Look, their words are set in writing. Open (the scrolls) and recite."

In many cases the subjunctive in an adverb clause is capable of more than one translation. Thus, in the last example it is also possible to translate "open, that you may read," with a clause of purpose. Similarly, two translations are possible for the following example:

 *jr n nṯr, jr.f n.k mjtt*

"Act for the god, so that he may do the same for you" (purpose) or

"Act for the god, and he will do the same for you" (result).

The subjunctive in an adverb clause simply expresses action that is contingent on that of another clause. All three of the meanings described above are actually the same in Egyptian, since Egyptian uses the simple subjunctive for each of them. The different connotations — purpose, result, or continuation of an imperative — depend on the context. In some cases the context is precise enough to rule out all but one meaning: for example, the subjunctive in § 19.8.2 can only express result, not purpose. Others, however, are not so clear, and in those cases the translation is simply a matter of how the translator understands the sentence.

19.9 The subjunctive in noun clauses

Middle Egyptian frequently uses the subjunctive in noun clauses, as the subject of another predicate or as the object of a verb. Such clauses can be marked (by *ntt* "that"), but most are unmarked. The following is an example of the subjunctive used as the subject of another predicate:

 *twt wrt jr.k mnw.k m jnw*

"It is very fitting that you should make your monument in Heliopolis,"

14 For the first clause, see § 17.4; *rdwj* is literally "two feet" (dual): the plural strokes are superfluous.

where the subjunctive clause *jr.k mnw.k m jnw* "you should make your monument in Heliopolis" is the subject and the adjective *twt wrt* "very fitting" is the predicate.

The subjunctive is used most often in noun clauses as the object of a verb. Such clauses typically occur after verbs such as *wḏ* "command," *mrj* "desire, wish, like," and *z3w* "beware," where the action of the noun clause is always **subsequent** to that of the governing verb: for example,

wḏ.n nṯr jr.f pr n.f ẖr.s
"The god has commanded that he act as revealer of it for him"[15]

jw ms wr šrj ḥr mr.j m(w)t.j
"Truly, the great and the small are saying (§ 15.7): 'I wish I would die' "[16]

z3w sj3t.k jtj-mḥ(j) ḫ3r jm
"Beware of shorting a sack of northern barley from it."[17]

The verb *z3w* "beware" often has the sense of English "lest" before the subjunctive: for instance,

rdj.n.t(w).k r dnjt n m3jr z3w mḥ.f
"You have been put to (be) a dam for the poor man, lest he become flooded."[18]

The subjunctive can also be used as the object of verbs of perception or speech, such as *rḫ* "learn, know" and *ḏd* "say": for example,

sw3ḏ.n.f n.f jw(ʿ)t.f m ẖt, rḫ.n.f nḏ.f r ḥr.f
"He has bequeathed his inheritance to him in the womb,
knowing he would consult about him"[19]

ḏd.n.f ʿḥ3.f ḥnʿ.j "He said he would fight with me."

In such cases too, the subjunctive always describes an action that is subsequent to the action of the governing verb.

The use of the subjunctive in an unmarked noun clause as the object of a verb is one of the prime examples of contextual subordination in Middle Egyptian. In each case, the clause with the subjunctive could be a main clause or independent sentence in its own right, but it is subordinate because of the context in which it is used. Such clauses can sometimes be translated with a construction that is contextually subordinated in English: thus, *mr.j m(w)t.j* "I wish I would die," *rḫ.n.f nḏ.f r* "knowing he would consult," *ḏd.n.f ʿḥ3.f* "he said he would fight." In other cases, however, English requires a real dependent noun clause (introduced by *that*), or some other construction

15 Literally, "that he make one who emerges for him under it": *prj ẖr* "emerge under" is an idiom for "reveal"; *pr* "one who emerges" is a verb form we will meet in Lesson 23.

16 *mr.j* "I wish" is also the subjunctive: literally, "I would like that I die."

17 Literally, "beware (that) you short"; *sj3t* "cut short" is a caus. 3-lit. verb; for *jtj-mḥj ḫ3r* see § 9.4.

18 This sentence is addressed to an official, and is meant to remind him of his duties. The image is metaphorical: i.e., "your responsibility is to prevent the poor from being overwhelmed by the powerful."

19 This sentence refers to the king receiving the inheritance of a god. *sw3ḏ* is a frequent New Kingdom "misspelling" of *swḏ* "bequeath." For *rḫ.n.f* "knowing," see §§ 18.10–18.11. *nḏ r*, literally, "inquire the mouth," is an idiom for "consult."

where the correspondence between the Egyptian subjunctive and its translation is even less clear: thus, *wḏ.n nṯr jr.f* "the god has commanded that he act," *z3w sj3t.k* "beware of shorting." These different translations are only necessary, however, because of differences between Egyptian and English. Egyptian is actually more consistent than English, since it allows contextual subordination of the subjunctive after most verbs.

19.10 The subjunctive after *rdj*

By far the most common use of the subjunctive in an unmarked noun clause involves the use of this form as object of the verb *rdj* "give, put." The combination of *rdj* plus the subjunctive has **causative** meaning: for example, *rdj sḏm.f* "cause that he hear," "have him hear," "make him hear," "allow him to hear" — literally, "give (that) he hear," where *sḏm.f* is the subjunctive. In this construction, the verb *rdj* itself can appear in any verb form: for example,

m.tn rdj.n.j j3ᶜš.tw n.tn r rdjt ḏᶜr.tn n.j z3.tn

"Look, I have had you called in order to have you seek out for me a son of yours."

This sentence contains two examples of *rdj* plus the subjunctive: *rdj.n.j j3ᶜš.tw n.tn* "I have had you called" (literally, "I have given that one call to you"), with the perfect of *rdj*, and *r rdjt ḏᶜr.tn* "in order to have you seek out" (literally, "to give that you seek out"), with the infinitive of *rdj*. In the following example, *rdj* itself is in the subjunctive:

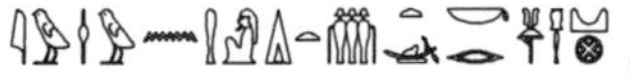 *jw wḏ.n ḥm.j dj.t(w) ḫnt.k r t3-wr 3bḏw*

"My Incarnation has commanded that you be made to sail south to Tawer and Abydos."

Here *dj.t(w)* is the subjunctive as object of the verb *wḏ* "command," and *ḫnt.k* is the subjunctive as object of *dj.t(w)*: literally, "My Incarnation has commanded (that) one give (that) you sail south." The subjunctive of *rdj* is used in a main clause in the following example:

 *ḏd.j wrt, dj.j sḏm.tn st*

"I will say something important, and I will let you hear it,"

literally, "I will give (that) you hear it"; both *dj.j* and *sḏm.tn* are subjunctive forms (as well as *ḏd.j* in the first clause). The imperative of *rdj* (§ 16.2.3) is frequently used with the subjunctive as well: for example,

 *jm(j) rḫ.f rn.k* "Let him know your name,"

literally, "give (that) he know your name"; so also with *rdj* itself as the object of the imperative: for instance,

 *jm(j) dj.tw m3ᶜ t 1000*

"Have 1000 loaves of bread presented,"

literally, "give (that) one give the presenting of 1000 loaves of bread," where *dj.tw* is the subjunctive as object of *jmj* (*m3ᶜ* is the infinitive as object of *dj.tw*).

In our initial discussion of the verb we saw that many Egyptian verb roots have a causative counterpart (§ 13.5.9–13.5.15): for example, *h3j* "descend" and *sh3j* "cause to descend." The construction of *rdj* plus the subjunctive has the same basic meaning as the causative:

e.g., *rdj h3j* "cause to descend." All Egyptian verbs can be used in the subjunctive as the object of *rdj*, but not all of them have a causative root. This is true for some of the most common Egyptian verbs, including *jwj* and *jj* "come," *jnj* "fetch," and *rdj* itself. For such verbs the causative has to be expressed with *rdj* plus the subjunctive: *rdj jwt* "cause to come" (not **sjwj* or **sjj*), *rdj jnt* "cause to fetch" (not **sjnj*), and *rdj dj* "cause to give" (not **srdj*). Because *rdj* plus the subjunctive was such a common construction, it eventually became the normal means of expressing the causative. In Coptic most of the older causative roots have disappeared, and the language has developed a new causative root formed with **т** (a descendant of *rdj*) and the descendant of the subjunctive: for example, **тϩιο** "cause to fall," from *rdj h3j* "cause to descend."

The verb *rdj* plus the subjunctive is one of the most frequent constructions of Middle Egyptian, so it is important that you be able to recognize it in order to translate texts correctly.

19.11 The subjunctive in negations

Middle Egyptian has several different negations of the subjunctive, corresponding to the different uses and meanings of this verb form in affirmative clauses. The three most important are:

1. **the subjunctive with nn**

In most cases the subjunctive is negated simply by putting the negative particle *nn* in front of it. This negation has **future** meaning: for example,

 *nn dj.j jt.t sw m ˁ.j* "I will not let you take him from me,"

literally, "I will not give (that) you (2fs) take him from me" (both *dj.j* and *jt.t* are subjunctive). The negation *nn* plus the subjunctive is the negative counterpart of the subjunctive used to express the future (§ 19.5.2): i.e., *dj.j* "I will give" versus *nn dj.j* "I will not give."

The negation *nn* plus the subjunctive is also the negative counterpart of the pseudoverbal construction with *r* plus the infinitive: for example,

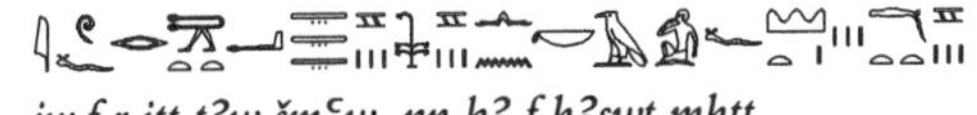

jw.f r jtt t3w šmˁw, nn k3.f ḫ3swt mḥtt

"He is to take possession of the lands of the Nile Valley:

he will not consider the northern countries."

This counterpart relationship exists because the pseudoverbal construction with *r* plus the infinitive is normally not negated itself (§ 15.8).

The negation *nn zp* "never" is also used with the subjunctive, as a stronger version of *nn* plus the subjunctive. Like the latter, it has future meaning:

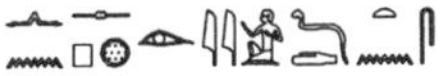 *nn zp jry.j ḏdt.n.s* "I will never do what she said."[20]

This negation actually involves two verbs in the subjunctive: the word *zp* itself is a verb meaning "happen," which is used in the subjunctive after *nn*, and the subjunctive that follows *zp* is actually the first word of a noun clause serving as the subject of *zp*. Thus, the example given here means literally "(that) I will do what she said will not happen." The negation *nn zp* is much rarer than the normal negation with *nn*.

20 *ḏdt.n.s* "what she said" is a form of the perfect relative, which we will discuss in Lesson 24.

2. **the negative construction**  *jm.f sḏm*

The negative verb *jmj* is a defective verb (§ 13.7), used in only two forms. We have already met one of these, the negative imperative *m* "don't" (§ 16.4). The other form in which this verb is used is the subjunctive  (or ) *jm* "should not, may not". Like the negative imperative, it is followed by the negatival complement (§ 14.17): thus,  *jm.f sḏm* "he should not hear, may he not hear, let him not hear." This construction is used as the negative counterpart of the subjunctive expressing a **wish or command**: for example,

 *z3.k pw ... jm.k jwd jb.k r.f*
"He is your son ... you should not separate your heart from him."

In this construction *jm* itself is the subjunctive, so it can take a suffix pronoun as its subject (*jm.f sḏm*), like the subjunctive of other verbs. When the subject is a noun, however, it normally comes after the negatival complement (*jm sḏm* NOUN), not after *jm*: for instance,

 *jm sḫpr jb.j pn ḏbꜥw pn ḏw r.j*
"May this heart of mine not create this bad reproach against me,"

where *jb.j pn* "this heart of mine" is the subject and *sḫpr* "create" (literally, "cause to evolve") is the negatival complement.

In Old Egyptian *jm.f sḏm* was also used as the negative counterpart of the subjunctive in purpose clauses. This use can still be found in some Middle Egyptian texts as well: for example,

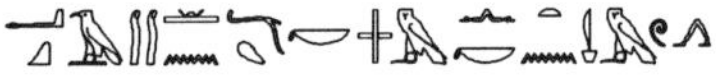 *ꜥq3 ns.k, jm.k tnmw*
"Let your tongue be straight, so that you do not go astray."

The normal negation of purpose clauses in Middle Egyptian, however, is the construction discussed in the next section.

3. **the subjunctive negation**  *tm.f sḏm*

Unlike *jmj*, which has only two forms (imperative and subjunctive), the negative verb *tm* can appear in the same forms as other Middle Egyptian verbs. We have already met the infinitive of this verb, which is used with the negatival complement as the negation of the infinitive (§ 14.16). The subjunctive of *tm* serves as a negative counterpart of the subjunctive in **dependent clauses**: this includes all the functions of the subjunctive itself **except** main clauses (or independent sentences) expressing the future or a wish or command. Like *jmj*, the subjunctive of *tm* is followed by the negatival complement and can take a suffix pronoun or a noun as its subject; nominal subjects usually follow the negatival complement (*tm.f sḏm*, *tm sḏm* NOUN).

The following examples illustrate some of the uses of the subjunctive negation *tm.f sḏm* in Middle Egyptian texts:

 *jw.j r jrt nj3j, jḫ tm.f ḫzw*
"I am to make a shelter: then he won't get cold" — after *jḫ* (§ 19.6.1)

 jr tm.sn rdw, nn msy.s
"If they do not grow, she will not give birth" — conditional (§ 19.7)[21]

21 The determinative of the negatival complement *rdw* (2-lit.) is borrowed from *rwd* "become firm" (3-lit.).

 *m k3hsw ḫft wsr.k, tm spr bw ḏw r.k*

"Don't be harsh when you are powerful, so that evil doesn't reach you" or
"Don't be harsh ... and evil won't reach you" — purpose or result (§§ 19.8.1–19.8.2)[22]

 *jw wḏ.n gbb (j)t(j) wsjr tm.j wn(m) ḥs*

"Geb, father of Osiris, has commanded that I not eat excrement" — object of *wḏ* (§ 19.9).

Because *tm* is a verb in its own right, its subjunctive form can even be negated by *nn*, like the subjunctive of other verbs:

 *nn tm.f jr bw nfr*

"He will not not do goodness" — i.e., "He will not fail to do goodness."

4. **summary of negations with the subjunctive**

The various negative constructions with the subjunctive, and their affirmative counterparts, are summarized in the following table:

AFFIRMATIVE	NEGATIVE
main clause, future	*nn sḏm.f*
main clause, wish or command	*jm.f sḏm*
purpose and result clauses	*tm.f sḏm*; rarely *jm.f sḏm*
all other uses of the subjunctive	*tm.f sḏm*.

The subjunctive is used in one other normal Middle Egyptian negation besides these, which we will meet in the next lesson.

19.12 The subjunctive in questions

Like the perfect, the subjunctive can be used in both predicate and adjunct questions (§ 18.18). In predicate questions (when the action of the verb itself is questioned), the sentence is normally introduced by *jn*: for example,

 *jn ꜥw3.tw.j r.f m ḏ3tt.f*

"So, shall I be robbed in his estate?"

The negative construction *nn sḏm.f* can also be questioned in the same way: for instance,

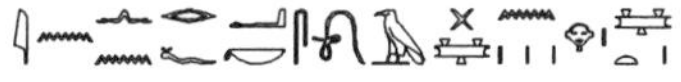 *jn nn r.f dj.k sw3.n ḥr w3t*

"So, won't you let us pass on the path?"

In adjunct questions (when some other element of the sentence is questioned), the subjunctive is normally the first word in the sentence: for example,

 *ḥrwj, jry.j mj* "How terrible! What shall I do?"[23]

The subjunctive is not very common in adjunct questions: normally a different verb form is used for such questions, which we will meet in Lesson 25.

22 *ḫft wsr.k* is literally "in accordance with your being strong" (*wsr* is the infinitive). The second clause means literally "so that evil doesn't arrive at you" or "and evil won't arrive at you"; *bw ḏw* is an abstract formed from the adjective *ḏw* "bad": literally, "a bad thing."

23 *ḥrwj* is an adjectival predicate (§ 7.2) without an expressed subject: "How terrible (it is)!" For *mj* "what?" see § 5.11.

19.13 The subjunctive of *wnn*

The 2ae-gem. verb *wnn* (, ) "exist" is a verb in its own right, and like other verbs it can be used in the subjunctive (ungeminated *wn*): for example,

 *wn.j ḥnᶜ nb-ᶜnḫ* "I shall exist with the Lord of Life."

Usually the important part of the clause is not the verb itself but the adverb or prepositional phrase that accompanies it. In such cases, **the subjunctive of *wnn* allows an adverbial predicate to function like a subjunctive.** When the verb *wnn* is used in this way it normally corresponds to a form of the English verb *be* rather than *exist*: for example,

 *wn k3wt(j)w.k m ḥᶜᶜw*
"Your workers will be in jubilation" (future: § 19.5.2)

 *jj.n.(j) wn.j m z3.k*
"I have come that I might be your protection" (purpose: § 19.8.1)

 *dj.k wn.j m šmswt ḥm.k*
"May you let me be in the following of Your Incarnation" (object of *rdj*: § 19.10).

The subjunctive of *wnn* can also be accompanied by the stative. This combination makes it possible for the stative to function like a subjunctive: for instance,

 *dj.j wn.sn ḫw.(w) mk.w*
"I will make them be exempted and protected."

Here the subjunctive *wn* allows the statives *ḫw.(w) mk.w* "they are exempted and protected" to serve as the object of *rdj* — something that the stative cannot do by itself.

Although it looks like a subjunctive construction, the negation  *nn wn* is normally not future. It may contain a different verb form, which we will discuss in the next lesson.

Essay 19. Middle Egyptian Wisdom Literature

Insofar as their works are known, the famous writers mentioned at the end of the last essay were all authors of the kind of texts that we call wisdom literature. The Egyptians called this genre  *sb3yt* "instruction," and it seems to have been the most popular form of literature among the Egyptians themselves. More compositions of this type have come down to us than any other form of ancient Egyptian secular literature.

Although we have only one copy of some wisdom texts, most survive in more than one copy, from several to more than a hundred. Some of the copies we have were written on papyrus by accomplished scribes, for preservation or perhaps for their own pleasure. The best of these date to the Middle Kingdom. Most, however, were written on flakes of limestone, called "ostraka" (singular "ostrakon"), by New Kingdom schoolboys copying a master text or taking dictation from their teacher. Being school texts, they are often full of errors, and this makes the understanding of many passages conjectural or even impossible; but they also provide a witness to the affection and reverence the Egyptians had for this particular form of their literature.

Middle Egyptian wisdom texts can be divided into three categories. The oldest are instructions for living, in which the author records his advice for a proper and successful life. Most were written by — or more likely, in the name of — famous officials, for the edification of their sons. The earliest are attributed to three officials of the Old Kingdom: an unnamed vizier instructing his sons, one of whom, named **Kagemni**, is said to have become vizier under Snefru in Dynasty 4; **Hardjedef** (or Djedefhor), a son of Snefru's successor, Khufu; and **Ptahhotep**, a vizier of the pharaoh Isesi, from the end of Dynasty 5. These are often said to have been composed during the Old Kingdom, perhaps during Dynasty 6, but the earliest manuscripts are written in Middle Egyptian and date from the beginning of the Middle Kingdom or just before it, so there is some doubt as to the actual age of the original compositions.[24]

Whatever may have been the historical origin of their instructions, Hardjedef and Ptahhotep were venerated by later generations of Egyptians as the authors of the wisdom texts ascribed to them. The name of the author — real or fictional — of the instruction for Kagemni is lost, but it may have been Kaires, a revered author whose work is unknown (see the end of Essay 18). Another early instruction that has not survived was ascribed to Imhotep, architect of the Step Pyramid of Djoser (Dynasty 3), who was later deified as the patron of scribes and physicians.

These instructions include a range of advice, from correct behavior in social situations to proper conduct toward superiors and subordinates. Their purpose is the transmission of Maat — right and proper behavior — both for its own sake and as the key to a happy and successful life. The individual who lives according to Maat is often described as *gr* "the still man" or "the silent man" — that is, the calm and self-effacing person — or *rḫ* "the knowledgeable man," as opposed to *wḫꜣ* "the fool."

Several later Middle Kingdom instructions also belong in this category. These include the anonymous and fragmentary **Instruction of a Man for his Son**; another anonymous instruction on loyalty to and reverence for the kingship (known as the **Loyalist Instruction**); and the **Instruction of Khety**, another of the revered ancient sages. The last is the most well-attested of all wisdom texts, surviving in more than a hundred copies, most of which were written as exercises by schoolboys. Its popularity as a school text no doubt derives from the fact that it is a commentary on ancient Egyptian trades, contrasting the miserable life of manual workers, from fishermen to artisans, with the comfortable and respected occupation of a scribe.

A second type of wisdom literature deals with the proper conduct of the kingship. This category includes two texts supposedly written by kings for their successors. The **Instruction for Merikare** is addressed to a pharaoh of Dynasty 10 by his father, and may date to the First Intermediate Period. Besides advice on the management of the country and subordinates, this text includes a long discourse on the relationship between human beings and the god (cited in part at the end of Essay 5). The **Instruction of Amenemhat** contains advice of Amenemhat I, first king of Dynasty 12, for his son and successor, Senwosret I. It is famous for its description of an attempted assassination of Amenemhat by elements of the royal guard, which may or may not have been successful. Based on this experience, the king warns his son not to be too trusting of subordinates.

24 Hardjedef and Ptahhotep are historical figures. No vizier named Kagemni is known for Dynasty 4, but a vizier of this name served under the pharaoh Teti in early Dynasty 6.

The third category of Middle Egyptian wisdom literature is often called "admonitions." These texts are descriptions or prophecies of adverse times in Egypt, when the country is overrun by outsiders and the normal social order is turned upside down. The earliest such text is probably the **Prophecies of Neferti**. This is set in the time of the pharaoh Snefru and details the predictions of a sage named Neferti about a future time when Egypt will be thrown into chaos by the incursion of Asiatics into the Delta. In the end, Neferti foretells the coming of a king from southern Egypt who will reunite the country and bring order and prosperity. Since the king is named Ameny — a nickname of Amenemhat I — this text is generally viewed as a composition of early Dynasty 12, intended to contrast the reign of the new dynasty with the chaos of the First Intermediate Period; the earliest copies, however, date to the beginning of Dynasty 18.

The text called the **Admonitions of Ipuwer** is similar to the Prophecies of Neferti in content. It survives only in a single lengthy manuscript, dating to Dynasty 19; its beginning and end are lost. Although it too bemoans a time when the country is in chaos, it contains no specific historical references; certain features of its grammar and vocabulary, however, point to a Middle Kingdom origin. The **Lamentations of Khakheperre-seneb** are also preserved in a single copy, of 18th-Dynasty date, which reproduces only the beginning of the text. The original was probably composed in the early Middle Kingdom; the name of its author honors the pharaoh Senwosret II, whose throne name was Kha-kheper-re. Like Ipuwer's admonitions, its complaints are general in character; the author several times calls upon his heart to relieve his anxiety by explaining how to bear up under his misery.

Another unique Middle Egyptian text, known as the **Dialogue of a Man with his Ba**, is closely related to the genre of admonitions, particularly the Lamentations of Khakheperre-seneb. This is of undisputed Middle Kingdom origin, since its sole surviving copy was written early in Dynasty 12; its beginning is lost. The text takes the form of a debate between a man and his ba (see Essay 7) — essentially, therefore, a dialogue of a man with himself. The man is torn between life in this world, which is certain but full of misery, and the attraction of life after death, which promises to be happy but which is also unknown and uncertain. In the end, the ba advises the man to accept his life while looking forward to a better existence in the next world.

Despite their differences in content, the three categories of Middle Egyptian wisdom texts have several features in common. The single theme underlying them all is that of Maat (see Essay 10). The instructions for living explain how to behave in accordance with Maat in order to achieve happiness and success; the royal instructions contain advice for the proper and successful conduct of kingship; and the admonitions promote Maat by describing the disastrous state of a world in which this principle of order is ignored.

Common to all the wisdom texts as well is a general rather than specific view of the divine. Instead of invoking specific deities, the texts usually just refer to *nṯr* "the god." It is a matter of some debate whether this is meant as a general term — i.e., "any god" — or as a more specific reference to the underlying unity of all gods (see Essays 4 and 15). Conceivably, however, the use of this term simply reflects the secular origin of wisdom literature, composed by officials and learned men who meant their compositions for a wide audience and who had themselves a broader or more general view of the divine than that of any one theological system.

Exercise 19

Transliterate and translate the following sentences. A number of the examples are taken from texts of Middle Egyptian wisdom literature.

1. 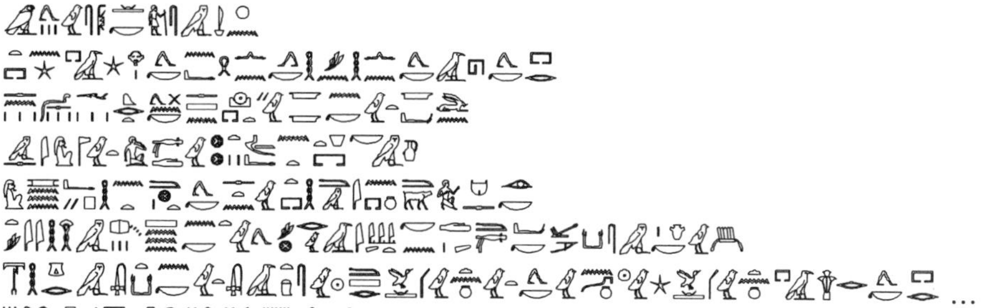
 … — from a series of wishes for the afterlife: *wsḫt nt m3ʿtj* refers to the hall of judgment (see Essay 8) *jjwj* "welcome!"

2. 

3. 

4. 

 … — a metaphor for proper behavior

5. 

6. 

7.  — threat of the pharaoh Kamose against *jppj* "Apophis," ruler of the Hyksos

8.  — from the Dialogue of a Man with his Ba

9.  — from the Instruction for Merikare: *ḫmt* "think"

10.  — from the Instruction for Merikare

11. 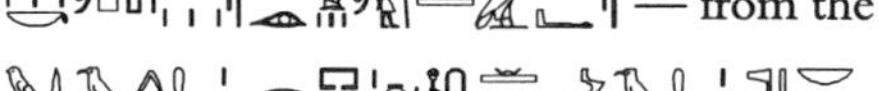

12. 

13. 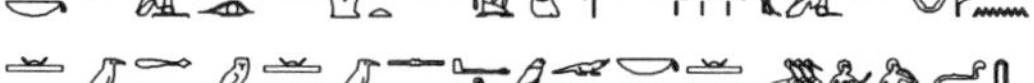

14. 

15.  — *wnt ḫr.f* "what he had," literally "what was by him"

16. 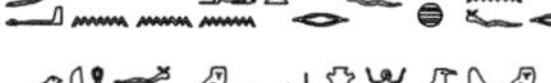 — from the Instruction of Ptahhotep

17. 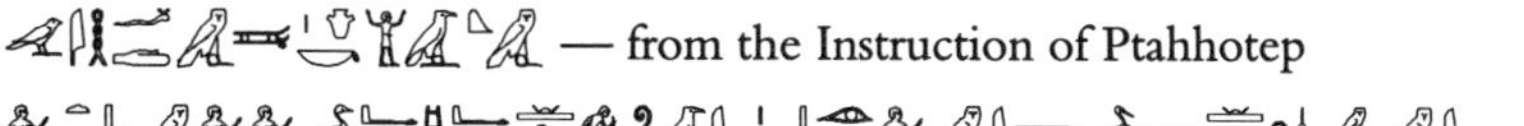 — from the Instruction of Ptahhotep

18.  — from the Instruction of Ptahhotep

19.  — from the Instruction of Ptahhotep: *n sjm3* "at the pleasure"; *jrt* infinitive used instead of the negatival complement

20.  — from the Lamentations of Khakheperre-seneb

21.  — from the Lamentations of Khakheperre-seneb: *rḫ wḫdw* "one that knew how to bear up"; *jrj sḫnj* "make landing" (in the sense of coming to rest)

22. 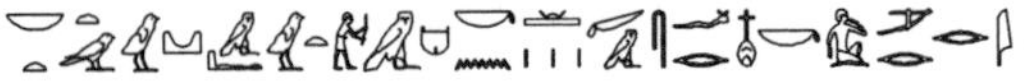 — from the Instruction of Ptahhotep

23.  — from the Instruction of Ptahhotep

24.  — from the Instruction of Ptahhotep: for *tr* "time" see § 8.14

25.  — *wp-w3wt* "Wepwawet," a god who guided the other gods; his name means "He who parts the ways"

26. 

27. 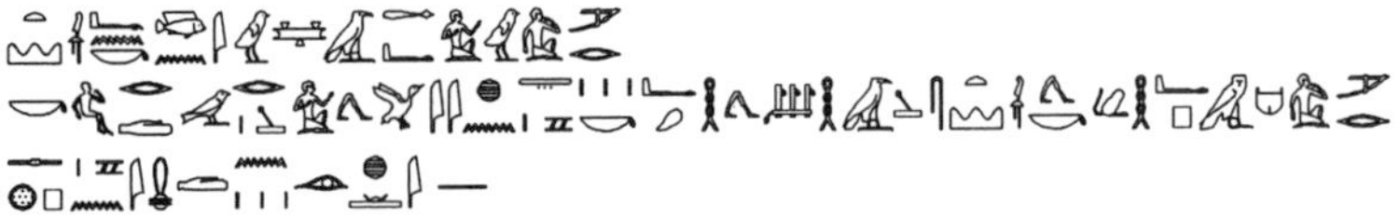 —
speech of the ba at the end of the Dialogue of a Man with his Ba: *jmnt* "the West" is the land of the dead; *s3ḥ t3* "touch land" is an idiom for "be buried"; *wrd* "weariness" is a metaphor for death

28.  — from the Instruction of a Man for his Son: *pḥw* "results"

29.  — from the coffin of a woman

30.  — from the Instruction of Khety

20. The Perfective and Imperfective

20.1 Definitions

The perfective and imperfective are two verb forms of the *sḏm.f* belonging to the suffix conjugation (§§ 18.1, 19.3). They look like the subjunctive in many verb classes, but they have different uses and different meanings than the subjunctive.

The perfective is a verb form that simply expresses **action**, without any indication of tense or mood. Although it is used almost exclusively with reference to past actions, and therefore usually corresponds to the English past tense, its past tense comes from the constructions and contexts in which it is used and is not a feature of the verb form itself. Note that the perfective is *not* the same as the perfect, which expresses completed action, as we saw in Lesson 18.

The imperfective expresses **imperfective or repetitive action**: action that is in some way ongoing, incomplete, or repeated. This is an aspect rather than a tense (§ 13.3.2). Like the perfective and many other Middle Egyptian verb forms, the imperfective is essentially tenseless. It often has to be translated by an English present tense, but it can be used with reference to past or future actions as well.

Many Egyptologists use the terms **indicative** (or indicative *sḏm.f*) instead of perfective and **circumstantial** (or circumstantial *sḏm.f*) instead of imperfective when referring to these forms. Although the perfective is an indicative form, most other Egyptian verb forms are also indicative. The imperfective is frequently used to express circumstance, as we will see below, but it has other uses as well. The names "indicative" and "circumstantial" are therefore too broad in one case and too narrow in the other. For that reason, this book uses the older terms perfective and imperfective, which are much more descriptive of the basic meaning of the two forms.[1]

20.2 Forms

The perfective, imperfective, and subjunctive of most verbs and verb classes look exactly alike, although the three forms can be distinguished from each other by how they are used. The following tables are therefore limited to verbs and classes for which formal differences can actually be seen. The forms of other classes are the same as those of the subjunctive (§ 19.2).

1. **Perfective**

2-LIT.  *ḏd.j* "I said" — no prefixed forms

2AE-GEM.  *wn* "existed" — ungeminated, like the subjunctive. The verb *m33* "see" uses both *m3* and, less often, *m3n*: for example,  *m3.t(w).f* and 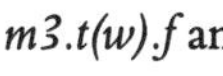 *m3n.tw.f* "it has been seen."

1 Those of you familiar with Gardiner's *Egyptian Grammar*, which has long been the standard reference for Middle Egyptian grammar, should be aware that his use of the terms "perfective" and "imperfective" are **not** the same as in this book. More recent studies have shown that Gardiner's "perfective *sḏm.f*" is actually two forms, which we have called the subjunctive and the perfective, while his "imperfective *sḏm.f*" includes not only the form we have called the imperfective but also two others, which we will meet in Lessons 21 and 25.

3AE-INF. *šd.j* "I took" — base stem. No forms with final *y*, either in this class or in the other final-weak classes. The verb *jnj* "get, fetch" has the normal form: *jn* "got."

ANOM. The verb *rdj* "give, put, let" always uses the base stem *rdj*: *rdj* "gave," *rdj* "let." The verb *jwj/jj* "come" uses both base stems: *jw* "came," *j* "has come."

2. **Imperfective**

2-LIT. *ḏd.f* "he says." Rarely prefixed, like the subjunctive: and *j.ḏd.f* "he says."

2AE-GEM. *m33.f* "he sees" — geminated. The verb *wnn* "exist" is also geminated: *wnn.s* "it exists."

3AE-INF. *šd.f* "he takes" — base stem. Occasionally, examples in this and other final-weak classes have a final *y*: for example, *mḥy.j* "I worry." The verb *jnj* "get, fetch" has the normal form: *jn.tw* "one gets."

ANOM. The verb *rdj* "give, put, let" always uses the base stem *dj*: *dj.sn* "they give," *dj.f* "it makes." The verb *jwj/jj* "come" uses both base stems, the stem *jj* normally with a final single or double reed-leaf: *jw.f* "it comes," *jj* "comes," *jy.f* "he was returning."

20.3 Subject and word order

Since the perfective and imperfective are forms of the suffix conjugation, they behave like the perfect and the subjunctive with respect to their subject and the word-order of their clauses. Both forms can be used with the suffix *tw* as an impersonal subject: for example, *jn.tw* "one gets." The suffix *tw* is also used to make **the passive form of the perfective and imperfective**, in the same way that it is used to form the passive of the subjunctive (§ 19.4). In this case, the subject is a noun (or noun phrase) or pronoun: for instance, *m3.t(w).f* "it has been seen."

20.4 The perfective in main clauses

In Old Egyptian the perfective of **transitive** verbs was often used in main clauses to denote actions that happened in the past, like the past tense of English. In Middle Egyptian this function was taken over by the perfect of transitive verbs, as we have seen (§ 18.9). Nevertheless, the older construction with the perfective is still found in some Middle Egyptian texts: for example,

rdj (w)j ḥm.f r zẖ3 n ṯm3, ḥz wj ḥm.f ḥr.f r ʿ3t wrt

"His Incarnation gave me to (be) scribe of the cadaster;

His Incarnation blessed me because of it very greatly,"[2]

2 The dependent pronoun *wj* in the first clause is written irregularly, without its normal initial consonant. The "scribe of the cadaster" (*zẖ3 n ṯm3*) was an official in charge of records showing the ownership and yield of agricultural land. For *r ʿ3t wrt* "very greatly" see § 8.14.

where the perfectives *rdj* "gave" and *ḥz* "blessed" describe past events in the life of the speaker. In the same way, the perfective is sometimes used instead of the perfect after *ꜥḥꜥ.n* or *wn.jn* (§ 18.9): for instance,

 *ꜥḥꜥ.n rdj.f wj m r.f*

"Then he put me in his mouth" (from a story about a giant serpent)

 *wn.jn ꜥḥꜥ.sn ḥms.sn ḫft*

"Then they stood and sat accordingly."

Old Egyptian could also use the perfective of **intransitive** verbs with a noun subject in main clauses to express completed action. In Middle Egyptian the SUBJECT-stative construction is normally used for this purpose (§§ 17.6, 18.3), but the older construction is occasionally used in some texts: for example,

ḫꜥ sbkw, ḥq(3).n.f pt, mḥ.n.f t3wj m wsrw.f

"Sobek has appeared, he has begun to rule the sky,
and has filled the Two Lands with his might."

Here the intransitive perfective *ḫꜥ sbkw* "Sobek has appeared" is used in parallel with the transitive perfect forms *ḥq(3).n.f* "he has ruled" (i.e., "he has begun to rule") and *mḥ.n.f* "he has filled."

Neither of these uses of the perfective is very common in Middle Egyptian. The intransitive use is found primarily in religious texts, and is probably a conscious archaism (like the English use of *thou* and *thee* in prayers). The transitive use occurs mostly in early Middle Egyptian tomb biographies and in some early literary texts. Rather than an archaism, however, it may be a dialectical feature. In Late Egyptian the perfective is once again used as the regular past tense of transitive verbs, while the older perfect has disappeared. This later use of the perfective is sometimes reflected in Middle Egyptian texts from the Second Intermediate Period onward, where it occasionally appears as a past tense instead of the transitive perfect.

20.5 The negated perfective

By far the most frequent use of the perfective in Middle Egyptian — and just about the only use of this form in most texts — is in the negation  *nj sḏm.f*. This construction is the negative counterpart of the perfect. It is used for the negation of **past or completed action**: for example,

jrt.j šmt m ḫntyt, nj k3.j spr r ḫnw pn

"I made my way upstream; I did not plan to arrive at that capital"[3]

jw.j ḥr mꜥq ḏr p3wt, nj m3.j mjtj zrw pn

"I have been roasting (birds) since the creation,
and I have never seen the like of this goose."[4]

3 From a story: *jrt.j* is the "narrative" infinitive (§ 14.14.2) and *šmt* is an infinitive used as its object: literally, "my making a going."

4 Speech of a man roasting a goose over a fire. *p3wt* "the creation" means literally "the original time."

As with the perfect (§ 18.9), the translation of the negated perfective by an English past tense (*nj k3.j* "I did not plan") or perfect (*nj m3.j* "I have not seen") depends on the context. The Egyptian form itself simply describes the negation of action.

The negated perfective of three verbs merits special attention. The negation  *nj rḫ.f*, with the perfective of *rḫ*, means "he did not learn, he has not learned" and therefore "he does not know" (see §§ 17.8, 18.10): for example,

 *nj rḫ.j sw* "I do not know him."

The verb  *p3* means "do in the past," and is used with the infinitive as its complement: for instance, 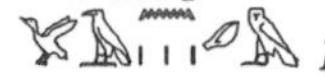 *p3.n sdm* "we once heard" — literally "we did hearing in the past." The negated perfective of this verb has the meaning "not once, never": for example,

 *nj p3 d3yt mjn zp.s*
"Wrongdoing has not once moored its cause" —

literally, "wrongdoing has not done in the past the mooring of its occasion" (i.e., has never made its cause arrive successfully).

The perfective negation  *nj zp* is a more common way of expressing "never." In the last lesson we met the similar construction  *nn zp* (§ 19.11.1) as a future negation, where *zp* is the subjunctive of a verb meaning "happen." In the negation *nj zp* it is the perfective, and therefore has past meaning: for example,

 *nj zp jry.j ḫt nbt ḏwj r r(m)ṯ nb*
"I have never done anything badly against any people."[5]

As in the future negation *nn zp*, the perfective negation *nj zp* is used with the subjunctive of another verb as its subject: here, *jry.j* — literally, "(that) I would do anything badly against any people did not happen." Note that this is a construction in which the subjunctive has to be translated by a past tense ("I have done" or "I did") rather than the future. This use of the subjunctive to refer to past events is possible because the subjunctive itself does not express a specific tense.

20.6 The perfective in subordinate clauses

When we first examined subordinate clauses in Lesson 12, we saw that they are essentially main clauses (or independent sentences) that have been converted to function as nouns (noun clauses), adjectives (relative clauses), or adverbs (adverb clauses), either by means of some introductory word (marked dependent clauses) or by context alone (unmarked dependent clauses). Just as the perfective is not very common in main clauses in Middle Egyptian (§ 20.4), so too it is rarely found in dependent clauses. The negated perfective, however, is occasionally used in such clauses: for example,

- a marked noun clause, after *ntt*

   *ḥr ntt nj ḥr.j st, nj ḫmt.j st*
  "because I didn't anticipate it and didn't consider it"

5 Since it does not have a feminine ending, *ḏwj* is not an adjective (*ḫt nbt ḏwt* "anything bad," "any bad thing") but an adverb "badly" (see § 8.14).

- a marked relative clause, after *ntj*

   *ntj nj m3.t(w).f* "one who has not been seen"[6]

- an unmarked relative clause, after an undefined antecedent

   *t3 w3 nj rḫ sw r(m)ṯ* "a far land that people don't know."[7]

Middle Egyptian normally uses other verb forms instead of the perfective in subordinate clauses: the (intransitive) stative or (transitive) perfect in unmarked relative clauses (§§ 17.18, 18.12); the same forms in adverb clauses (§§ 17.19, 18.11); and the perfect relative or perfective relative (forms we will meet Lesson 24) in noun clauses and relative clauses after a defined antecedent.

20.7 The imperfective in main clauses

Unlike the perfective, the imperfective has a fairly broad range of uses in Middle Egyptian. In main clauses or independent sentences it is used to express actions that are generally or always true, and usually corresponds to the simple present tense in English: for example,

 *mr sw nwt.f r ḫʿw.⟨sn⟩*
"His town loves him more than (they do) themselves."[8]

Such examples, where the imperfective is the first word in the clause, are relatively rare. Usually the imperfective is introduced by a particle of some sort, most often *jw*: for example,

 *jw jn.tw ʿqw, wn 3q*
"Close friends are brought when there is a disaster."[9]

The imperfective is well suited to such generalizations both because it is tenseless and because it expresses extended action.

Because the imperfective is tenseless, however, it can also be used with reference to past events. In that case it usually has to be translated with the English construction *used to*, describing habitual past action, or the English past imperfect (*was* or *were* plus the ...*ing* form of the verb), denoting ongoing or incomplete past action: for example,

 *jw jr.j m mtt nt jb n nb rʿ nb*
"I used to act with correctness of heart for the lord every day" (habitual action)

 *jw ḥms.tw ḥr dmj n ḥwt-wʿrt*
"The harbor of Avaris was being besieged"[10] (ongoing past action).

By themselves, of course, these examples contain nothing to indicate that they refer to past actions: the tense comes from the contexts in which they are used (in this case, a tomb biography and a historical text, respectively). The imperfective itself simply denotes extended action, and says nothing about when the action takes place.

6 Literally, "one who he has not been seen" (direct relative).
7 Literally, "a far land people don't know it" (indirect relative).
8 Literally, "His town loves him with respect to ⟨their⟩ body"; the suffix pronoun *sn* is omitted.
9 I.e., one turns to friends in times of trouble. *ʿqw* "close friends" means literally "those who enter": i.e., those who have access to a person. The clause *wn 3q* "when there is a disaster" is discussed in § 20.16.3.
10 Literally, "one was sitting on the harbor of Avaris."

20.8 The SUBJECT-imperfective construction

Like the perfect, the imperfective can have its subject or object preposed (§ 18.4), either because of its length or to topicalize it: for example,

 *wp(w)tj ḫdd(j) ḫnt(j) r ẖnw 3b.f ḥr.j*

"The messenger going north or going south to home used to stop by me."[11]

Here the subject *wp(w)tj ḫdd(j) ḫnt(j) r ẖnw* "the messenger going north or going south to home" is preposed before the verb because of its length, and is repeated by the suffix pronoun on the verb *3b.f* "he used to stop" itself.

Most cases of the imperfective with a preposed subject, however, are examples of a special verbal construction, known as the SUBJECT-imperfective or SUBJECT-*sḏm.f* construction. This construction, which is quite common in Middle Egyptian, is used either in **generalizations** or to express the **imperfect**. Like the imperfective itself, it is normally introduced in main clauses by a particle of some sort, most often *jw*: for example,

 *jr šm grg, jw.f tnm.f*

"When lying walks, it goes astray"[12] (generalization)

 *jw.f 3tp.f šmw.f r ẖnw dpt*

"He was loading his harvest into a boat" (imperfect).

In the first of these examples the SUBJECT-imperfective construction describes a generalization, something that is generally or always true. The second example (from a story) is not a generalization but a description of ongoing or incomplete action.

We have now seen three ways in which Middle Egyptian could express generalizations and the imperfect: with the SUBJECT-imperfective construction, with the imperfective itself (§ 20.7), and with the pseudoverbal construction of *ḥr* plus the infinitive (§ 15.2). Theoretically, the generalization *jw.f tnm.f* "it goes astray" could also have been expressed as *jw tnm.f* (imperfective) or as *jw.f ḥr tnm* (pseudoverbal construction), and the imperfect action *jw.f 3tp.f* "he was loading" could also have been expressed as *jw 3tp.f* (imperfective) or as *jw.f ḥr 3tp* (pseudoverbal construction). It is not always clear why the language uses one of these constructions rather than another. There is, however, some historical background to their use.

The imperfective itself was probably originally used both for generalizations and for imperfect actions, and it retains both of these meanings throughout Middle Egyptian (e.g., *jw tnm.f* "it goes astray" and "it is/was going astray"). Sometime in or before the Old Kingdom, Egyptian started to use the SUBJECT-imperfective construction instead of the plain imperfective to express the imperfect (*jw.f tnm.f* "it is/was going astray"), and the construction still has this meaning in some early Middle Egyptian texts. During Dynasty 5 the pseudoverbal construction came into the language and began to replace the SUBJECT-imperfective construction as the normal way of expressing the imperfect (*jw.f ḥr tnm* "it is/was going astray"). As this happened, the older SUBJECT-imperfective construction started to be used for generalizations. This is the situation we find in most Middle

11 *ḫdd(j)* "going north" and *ḫnt(j)* "going south" are imperfective participles, a form we will meet in Lesson 23.

12 The verb *šm.f* in the first clause is subjunctive: see § 19.7.

Egyptian texts: generalizations expressed by the SUBJECT-imperfective construction and the imperfect by the pseudoverbal construction (*jw.f tnm.f* "it goes astray," *jw.f ḥr tnm* "it is/was going astray"). Toward the end of its lifetime as a spoken language, however, Middle Egyptian began to use the pseudoverbal construction for generalizations as well (*jw.f ḥr tnm* "it goes astray"): most examples of this use come from later Middle Egyptian texts. Eventually the language lost both the imperfective and the SUBJECT-imperfective construction, and the pseudoverbal construction was used to express both the imperfect and generalizations, as the older imperfective had once been used (*jw.f ḥr tnm* "it is/was going astray" and "it goes astray").

Middle Egyptian not only changed during the five hundred or so years it was spoken, but some of its dialects probably retained older constructions longer than others did, and the authors of Middle Egyptian texts sometimes deliberately used older forms. In reading Middle Egyptian texts, therefore, you have to be aware not only of the basic meaning of verb forms and constructions, but also of the fact that those meanings sometimes changed in the course of time. As with tense, however, the context of a sentence is usually a good clue as to its meaning. The two passages cited above are good examples: just from their wording alone, it would be difficult to mistake the first sentence as an example of the imperfect or the second as a generalization.

20.9 The SUBJECT-imperfective construction after particles

As noted in the preceding section, the SUBJECT-imperfective construction is normally introduced by the particle *jw* in main clauses or independent sentences. It can also be used after other introductory words or particles: for instance,

 *m.k m3ꜥt wtḫ.s ẖr.k, nš.t(j) m st.s*

"Look, Maat is fleeing (from) under you, expelled from its place"

 *wn.jn ḥm.f wšd.f wj ꜥḏ.f bjt nt rꜥ nb*

"Then His Incarnation used to address me, so that he might learn about the character of every day."[13]

Two particles that are sometimes used with the SUBJECT-imperfective construction deserve special attention:

1. the SUBJECT-imperfective construction after  *ḫr*

In the previous lesson we saw that the particle *ḫr* used before the subjunctive signals an inevitable consequence of some action or situation (§ 19.6.2). With the SUBJECT-imperfective construction, *ḫr* denotes **necessity**. The construction *ḫr.f sḏm.f* can usually be translated as "he must hear" or "he has to hear": for example,

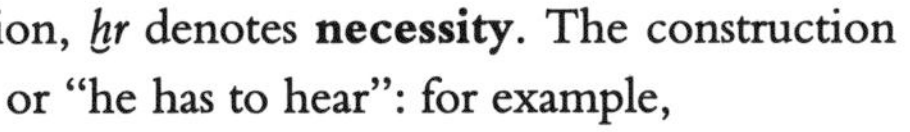 *jr m ḫt jꜥ.s ḥr.s rꜥ nb, ḫr.s gs.s ḥr.s jm*

"After she washes her face every day, she has to oil her face with it."[14]

The subjunctive is rarely used after *ḫr*, but the *ḫr.f sḏm.f* construction, with the imperfective, is quite common in Middle Egyptian texts.

13 I.e., the king used to ask me about the day's events every day. *ꜥḏ* "learn about" literally means "reel in."

14 From a prescription for an ointment to erase wrinkles. The first clause means literally "as for after she washes her face every day": *jꜥ.s* is a verb form we will meet in Lesson 25.

2. **the SUBJECT-imperfective construction after** *k3*

The particle *k3* can also introduce the SUBJECT-imperfective construction. This combination normally denotes **subsequent action**. The construction *k3.f sḏm.f* can usually be translated "then he hears" or "then he will hear": for example,

jr m ḫt ḥtp ḥm n nṯr pn šps m ḫt.f, k3.tw dj.tw pr ᶜḥᶜ n wdn ᶜpr.(w) m ḫt nb n wnwt-ḥwt-nṯr

"After this august god becomes satisfied with his thing(s), then one has the heap of offering(s), equipped with everything, go forth to the hourly staff of the temple."[15]

It is often hard to see how the meaning of the *k3.f sḏm.f* construction differs from that of *k3* plus the subjunctive (§ 19.6.3). The latter, however, denotes future **consequence**, while *k3* followed by the SUBJECT-imperfective construction expresses **subsequent** action rather than consequence. This is often best expressed by a future tense but it need not be, as the example cited here shows.

Although the subjunctive and imperfective of most verbs look the same, it is easy to distinguish the two forms after the particles *ḫr* and *k3*: the subjunctive always follows the particles directly (*ḫr sḏm.f, k3 sḏm.f*), while the imperfective is always preceded by its subject (*ḫr.f sḏm.f, k3.f sḏm.f*). As the examples above demonstrate, when the subject is a personal pronoun it is expressed by a suffix pronoun added directly to the particle.

20.10 The imperfective in adverb clauses

Although the imperfective is often used in main clauses or independent sentences, it is even more common in adverb clauses. In this use the imperfective always expresses **concomitant action**: that is, action going on at the same time as that of the preceding or governing clause. Both the imperfective itself and the SUBJECT-imperfective construction are used in adverb clauses, and in this use both have the same meaning. The adverb clause can be marked, usually by the particles *jsṯ* (or *jst, sk*, etc.) or *tj*: for example,

jw.sn [ḥr ḥ3q] mjktj m t3 3t,

jst jtḥ.tw p3 ḫrw ḫzj n qdš ḥnᶜ ḫrw ḫz(j) n dmj pn m ḫ3z r sᶜqt st r dmj.sn

"They were plundering Megiddo at that moment,

while that wretched enemy of Qadesh and the wretched enemy of that town were being pulled up in haste to bring them into their town"[16]

15 I.e., the temple priesthood (*wnwt-ḥwt-nṯr* "the hourly staff of the temple") are to receive the offerings after they have been presented to the god. For *jr m ḫt* "after" see n. 14. The second clause means literally "then one gives that the heap of offering(s) go forth": *pr ᶜḥᶜ n wdn* is the subjunctive serving as object of *dj.tw* (§ 19.10). The clause *ᶜpr.(w) m ḫt nb* is an adverb clause with the stative (§ 17.19); the stative is 3ms because it refers to *ᶜḥᶜ n wdn* "the heap of offering(s)."

16 From a description of Thutmose III's battle at Megiddo, in northern Israel; the words *ḥr ḥ3q* "were plundering" are restored. The sentence relates how the Egyptian army sacked Megiddo after a battle outside its walls. The enemy leaders, rulers of Megiddo and Qadesh, had fled back to the town's walls and were being hauled up onto its battlements by the town's defenders. In a previous sentence, Thutmose III expresses his displeasure that the Egyptian army started to plunder the town instead of going after the enemy leaders.

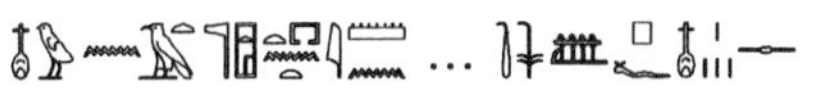

nfrw(j) n t3 ḥwt-nṯr nt jmn … tj sw šzp.f nfrw.s

"How good it is for the temple of Amun … when he is receiving its beauty."

The first of these examples shows the imperfective used after *jst*; in the second, the SUBJECT-imperfective construction is used after *tj*.

Most adverb clauses with the imperfective or SUBJECT-imperfective construction are unmarked. They look just like main clauses but are adverbial by virtue of the context in which they are used: for example,

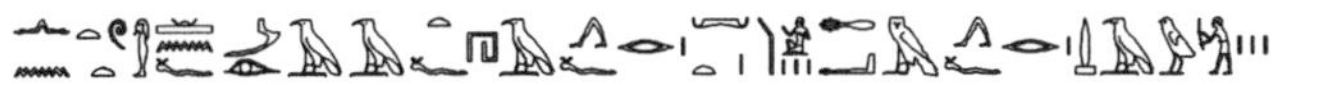

nn twt n.f, m33.t(w).f h3.f r-pḏt(j)w, ẖꜥm.f r-ḏ3w

"There is none equal to him when he is seen charging archers and engaging opposition"

 *sḏm.n.j ḫrw.f, jw.f mdw.f*

"I heard his voice as he was speaking."[17]

The first example contains three adverb clauses with the imperfective: *m33.t(w).f* modifies the main clause *nn twt n.f,* describing **when** "there is none equal to him" (namely, "when he is seen"); *h3.f* and *ẖꜥm.f* modify the first adverb clause, describing **how** "he is seen" (namely, "charging" and "engaging"). In the second example the adverb clause *jw.f mdw.f,* with the SUBJECT-imperfective construction, tells **when** "I heard his voice."

In each of the four examples cited in this section, the action of the adverb clause is concomitant with that of the governing clause. The marked clauses in the first two examples can only be adverbial, but the unmarked clauses in the two examples just above could be main clauses in a different context: e.g., *h3.f r-pḏtjw* "he charges archers," *jw.f mdw.f* "he was speaking." Just as with the other unmarked adverb clauses we have examined in previous lessons, they are subordinate only by virtue of their context, and not because of anything in the clause or the form of the verb or verbal construction itself.

Such adverb clauses of comcomitant action are among the most frequent uses of the imperfective in Middle Egyptian. They are particularly appropriate after verbs such as *m33* "see" and *gmj* "find," where they describe the action going on when something is "seen" or "found." An example with *m33* has been cited above; the following is an example after *gmj*:

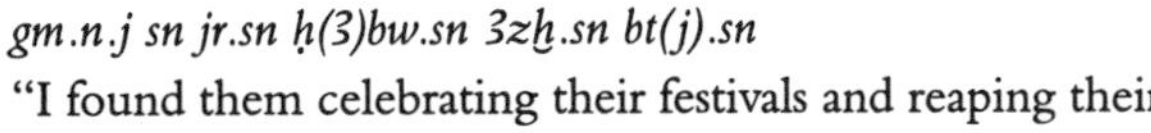

gm.n.j sn jr.sn ḥ(3)bw.sn 3zẖ.sn bt(j).sn

"I found them celebrating their festivals and reaping their emmer wheat."

Note that the imperfective always describes an **action**: as such, it contrasts in adverb clauses with the stative, which expresses a state (§§ 17.12, 17.19). Also, the imperfective always describes a **concomitant** action in adverb clauses and therefore contrasts with the perfect, which denotes a prior action in such clauses (§ 18.11).

17 This passage, from a Middle Egyptian story, is a good example of how the SUBJECT-imperfective construction and the pseudoverbal construction can both express the same thing in Middle Egyptian: another copy of the same passage has *sḏm.n.j ḫrw.f, jw.f ḥr mdt* "I heard his voice as he was speaking."

20.11 The imperfective in captions

A special use of the imperfective occurs in the captions to scenes such as those found on the walls of temples and tombs. Such scenes are usually labelled with an infinitive phrase explaining the action depicted (§ 14.9) and with captions identifying the action's participants. Often, the latter include not just a name and epithets but also a clause describing what the person named is doing. For example, a scene showing the goddess Amaunet embracing the pharaoh Hatshepsut has the following caption:

jmnt nbt pt ḥrt jb jpt-swt sḥtp.s jb dj.s ꜥnḫ w3s nb

"Amaunet, mistress of the sky and resident in Karnak,
contenting the heart and giving all life and dominion."[18]

Such captions always consist of a name (with or without epithets) followed by the imperfective — in this case, two imperfectives: *sḥtp.s* "she contents" and *dj.s* "she gives." They can be understood either as the SUBJECT-imperfective construction or as adverbial uses of the imperfective: i.e., in the example above either "Amaunet … is contenting the heart and giving all life and dominion" or "(This is) Amaunet … contenting the heart and giving all life and dominion." A third possible analysis is discussed in § 20.14, below.

20.12 The imperfective in noun clauses

Middle Egyptian rarely uses the imperfective in noun clauses. Examples occur mostly in older texts, in marked noun clauses with the SUBJECT-imperfective construction: for instance,

ḫw 3 ḏd n mwt.(j) tw ntt wj snḏ.k(w) wrt jw.k(w) m pf gs, ntt wḏꜥ 3d.f wj

"If only that mother of mine had been told that I am very afraid and marooned on yonder side, and that the Condemned One is raging at me."[19]

Here the SUBJECT-imperfective construction *wḏꜥ 3d.f wj* "the Condemned One is raging at me" is used in the second of two noun clauses; both are introduced by *ntt*, and both are subjects of the passive verb form *ḏd*. Note that the SUBJECT-imperfective construction expresses an action ("is raging") while the SUBJECT-stative construction in the first clause expresses a state ("am afraid"). A possible example of the SUBJECT-imperfective construction used as an unmarked noun clause is discussed in § 20.14, below.

20.13 The imperfective in relative clauses

In relative clauses with defined antecedents the imperfective is normally replaced by other forms, which we will meet later. The following is a rare example of the SUBJECT-imperfective construction in an indirect relative clause marked by *ntj*:

18 The nisbe *ḥrj jb* "who is in the heart" followed by a temple name is regularly used for gods and goddesses who are honored in a temple but whose primary shrine or temple is elsewhere. The name of the temple of Karnak, *jpt-swt*, means "the (most) select of places."

19 Speech of Horus as a child, from a religious text. *ḏd* "had been told" is the passive, a form we will meet in the next lesson. *wḏꜥ* "the Condemned One" refers to the god Seth, and is often used instead of the god's name. The verb *3d* "rage" can be transitive in Egyptian, as it is here.

 *jw sptj.j ḏd.sn wrt m ntt ḏḥwtj zẖ3.f jm*

"My lips say a Great Thing from that which Thoth writes about."

This sentence contains two instances of the SUBJECT-imperfective construction: one in the main clause (*jw sptj.j ḏd.sn* "my lips say") and one in the relative clause (*ḏḥwtj zẖ3.f* "Thoth writes"). The relative clause itself is the object of the preposition *m* "from."

The imperfective is much more common in relative clauses with **undefined** antecedents. Such clauses normally use the verb form itself as their first word: for example,

smw snwtt rn.s rd.s ḥr ẖt.s mj q3dwt, jw jr.s ḥrt mj zšn(j)

"A plant called *snwtt*, which grows on its belly like creepers:
it makes a flower like the lotus."

This sentence has two unmarked relative clauses after the undefined antecedent *smw* "a plant": *snwtt rn.s*, with a nominal predicate (see § 12.11); and *rd.s ḥr ẖt.s mj q3dwt*, with the imperfective. Both clauses could be separate sentences by themselves — *snwtt rn.s* "its name is *snwtt*" and *rd.s ḥr ẖt.s mj q3dwt* "it grows on its belly like creepers" — but here they are relative clauses by virtue of the context they are used in. Note the difference between the second relative clause, which has the imperfective by itself (*rd.s*), and the main clause, in which the imperfective *jr.s* "it makes" is introduced by *jw*.[20]

Like all relative clauses in Egyptian, those with the imperfective do not have to have an expressed antecedent. Examples of this use are mostly limited to nominal sentences of the pattern *jnk sḏm.f* "I am (or was) one who hears": for example,

 *jnk mr.f nfrt msḏ.f ḏwt*

"I am one who loves what is good and hates what is evil."

Such sentences are common in Middle Kingdom biographies of officials. The suffix subject of *mr.f* and *msḏ.f* is masculine because the speaker is a man: it refers to an unexpressed antecedent such as *zj* "man" — i.e., *jnk (zj) mr.f nfrt* "I am (a man) who loves what is good."

20.14 Special uses of the imperfective in relative clauses

The imperfective can be used as an unmarked relative clause not only after undefined antecedents but also after vocatives (§ 16.3): for example,

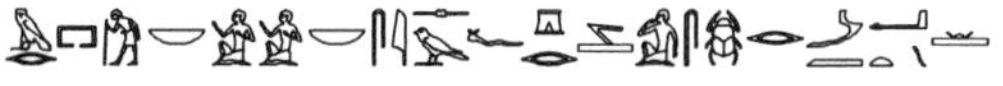

(j)m(j)-r pr wr nb.j, nb sjz.f grg, sẖpr m3ʿt

"Chief steward, my lord! (You) lord who makes lying easy! Bring about Maat!"[21]

Here the noun phrase *nb sjz.f grg* — literally, "a lord who makes lying easy" — is used as a third vocative after *(j)m(j)-r pr wr* "chief steward" and *nb.j* "my lord."

20 The first part of this sentence, *smw snwtt rn.s rd.s ḥr ẖt.s mj q3dwt* "a plant called *snwtt*, which grows on its belly like creepers," is actually the subject of *jr.s* "it makes": it has been preposed because of its length, and is repeated by the suffix pronoun of *jr.s* (feminine because it refers to *snwtt* rather than *smw*).

21 The title *jmj-r pr wr* "chief steward" is literally "great overseer (§ 8.9) of the house." The verbs *sjzj* and *sẖpr* are causatives: literally, "cause to be easy" and "cause to happen."

The imperfective is also used as an unmarked relative clause after proper names. The most common example of this use occurs on stelae, where the clause  *ḏd.f* "who says" (rarely also  or  *j.ḏd.f*) follows the name of the person honored on the stela and precedes that person's speech: for instance,

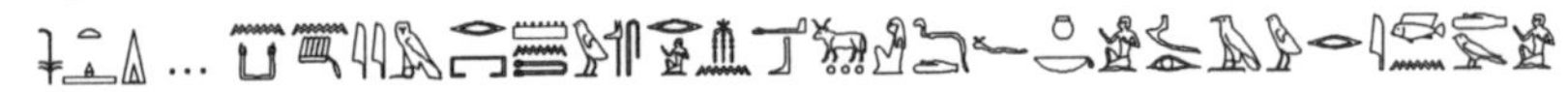

ḥtp-dj-(n)swt … n kꜣ n jmꜣḫy (j)m(j)-r pr mnṯw-wsr.(w) ms.n ꜥb-jḥw ḏd.f, jnk mꜣw r jnd
"A royal offering … for the ka of the honored steward Mentu-woser, born of Ab-ihu, who says: I am one who looks after the afflicted."[22]

It is possible to interpret the imperfective in captions (§ 20.11) as the same kind of relative clause: thus, *jmnt … sḥtp.s jb dj.s ꜥnḫ wꜣs nb* "Amaunet … who contents the heart and gives all life and dominion."

Several different translations are also possible for the following example from a ritual text, in which the imperfective is used in an A *pw* nominal sentence:

 *ḥrw pw šd.f jrt.f m ꜥ stḫ*
"This is Horus, who takes his eye from Seth" or
"This is Horus taking his eye from Seth" or
"This means that Horus is taking his eye from Seth."

In the first translation, the *šd.f* clause is taken as an unmarked relative clause modifying *ḥrw*; in the second, it is interpreted as an unmarked adverb clause, as in captions. In both of these translations, the A part of the sentence is the noun *ḥrw* "Horus," and the *šd.f* clause is added. A third possibility is to understand the A part of the sentence as the SUBJECT-imperfective construction *ḥrw šd.f jrt.f m ꜥ stḫ* "Horus is taking his eye from Seth," serving as an unmarked noun clause, which is the nominal predicate of *pw* (compare the use of the SUBJECT-stative construction as an unmarked noun clause in the same kind of sentence: § 17.11).

In the end, of course, these differences of interpretation only concern the English translation. No matter how the sentence is understood, the words in Egyptian are the same: *ḥrw pw* followed by a clause with the imperfective. This points up the need to remember the **basic** meaning of Egyptian verb forms. The imperfective is a single verb form, expressing basically imperfective action. This is true whether it is used in generalizations or for the imperfect; by itself or in the SUBJECT-imperfective construction; and in main clauses, noun clauses, adverb clauses, or relative clauses. Different English translations are necessary for these various uses only because of differences between the Egyptian and English languages, not because of differences in Egyptian itself.

20.15 The imperfective in negations

The normal negative counterpart of the imperfective is the negated perfect, which expresses the same kinds of generalizations or imperfect actions that the imperfective does (§ 18.14). Compare, for example, the use of the affirmative SUBJECT-imperfective construction and the negated perfect in the following sentence:

22 *ḥtp-dj-nswt* is a formula we will examine in Lesson 24. *ms.n ꜥb-jḥw* means literally "whom Ab-ihu birthed": *ms.n* is the perfect relative, which we will also discuss in Lesson 24. *mꜣw* "one who looks" is a noun.

jr z(j) nb nt(j) jm, j(w).f mꜣꜣ.f wsjr rꜥ nb, ṯꜣw m fnḏ.f, nj mjn.n.f ḏt

"As for any man who is there, he sees Osiris every day, with air in his nose, and he does not die forever."[23]

In dependent clauses the imperfective is negated by using the imperfective of the negative verb *tm* plus the negatival complement: for example,

 *kt smꜣꜥ mwyt tm.s mꜣꜥw*

"Another (method) of making urine regular when it is not regular."[24]

We have already met a similar construction as the negative counterpart of the subjunctive in dependent clauses (§ 19.11.3). The two constructions have the same syntax, except for the form of *tm* (imperfective vs. subjunctive). Although the imperfective and subjunctive of *tm* look the same, they can be distinguished by their meaning. In the example cited here, the *tm* clause clearly expresses concomitant action (imperfective) rather than purpose or result (subjunctive).

It is uncertain whether the imperfective itself was ever negated. Occasional examples of the negation *nj sḏm.f* seem to express a generalization or imperfect action, like the imperfective, rather than past or completed action, like the negated perfective (§ 20.5): for instance,

nj jn.tw ḥtpt r dmj, jw jn.tw ꜥqw wn ꜣq

"Contentment is not brought to harbor,
and close friends are brought when there is a disaster."[25]

The verb forms in the first two clauses here have the same meaning (generalization) and look the same (*jn.tw*): since the form after *jw* is the imperfective, the negated form in the first clause may be the imperfective as well. Although the negated perfect normally refers to a past or completed action, however, the perfective itself simply denotes action, without any reference to time or completion. It is possible, therefore, that the occasional examples of *nj sḏm.f* with nonpast meaning, such as the one cited here, also contain the negated perfective. The question could be settled by examples with distinctive imperfective forms, such as 2ae-gem. *mꜣꜣ* (vs. perfective *mꜣ* or *mꜣn*) or anom. *dj* (vs. perfective *rdj*), but none have yet been identified with certainty in Middle Egyptian texts.[26] This is one of the areas in which our understanding of Middle Egyptian grammar is still not complete.

23 The word *jw.f* is spelled like the noun *jf* "flesh": this is a common spelling of the particle *jw* with the 3ms suffix pronoun in early religious texts. The clause *ṯꜣw m fnḏ.f* "air in his nose" is an adverbial sentence serving as an adverb clause. The 4ae-inf. verb *mjnj* "moor" is a common euphemism for "die"; the verb is often spelled *mnj* (as it is here), but the reed-leaf represents the second radical, not the last.

24 From a medical text. *smꜣꜥ* is an infinitive, serving as the second noun of a direct genitive. The word *pḫrt* "prescription, method" is understood after *kt*.

25 From a wisdom text describing the value of friends. The first clause means "contentment never lasts"; for the second clause, see § 20.7.

26 There are examples of *nj mꜣꜣ*, but these involve another verb form, which we will meet in the next lesson. A good example would have to have fairly clear general or imperfect meaning and would have to come from a text that makes the normal Middle Egyptian distinction between the negations *nj* and *nn* (see § 16.6.8).

20.16 The perfective of *wnn*

Like other verbs, the 2ae-gem. verb *wnn* "exist" has a perfective,  *wn*. This form is sometimes used like that of other verbs, with reference to the past in main clauses and after the negation *nj*. Often, however, *wn* is used in ways that the perfective of other verbs is not.

1. **as a regular perfective**

The perfective *wn* can have two meanings, like the subjunctive of *wnn* (§ 19.13). It is sometimes used to express the past existence of something: for example,

 *nj wn kj ḥr.j*
"Clamor over me did not exist" or "There was no clamor over me."[27]

More often, however, an accompanying prepositional phrase or adverb, or a following verb form such as the stative or imperfective, is the important part of the clause rather than the verb *wn* itself. In this case, *wn* normally corresponds to the English verb forms *was* or *were*: for instance,

 *wn.j m smr* "I was a courtier."

 *wn.j wšd.j ḥmwt ḥr.s* "I kept addressing the craftsmen about it."

As we have seen, adverbial predicates can refer to past situations as well as to those that are true in the present or are generally true (§ 10.2), and the imperfective can be used for past as well as present actions (§ 20.7–20.8). Theoretically, therefore, these sentences could have been expressed simply as *jw.j m smr* "I was a courtier" and *jw.j wšd.j* "I kept addressing." The perfective *wn*, however, provides a way to indicate that the adverbial predicate and the imperfective refer **specifically** to a past situation and action, rather than allowing the context alone to supply the past reference.

2. **as a perfect**

The verb *wnn* is unusual in that it apparently has no regular perfect form (i.e., **wn.n*).[28] In its place Egyptian uses the perfective *wn*. The perfective of *wnn* thus appears in some uses that are typical of the perfect rather than the perfective — for example, as a past perfect, with reference to a situation that existed before that of another past action (cf. § 18.7):

ms.n.f jt(j).f jmn ḥr jnjwb3 13 ... jw grt wn ḥm n nṯr pn šps ẖr ḥ3t ḥr jnjwb3 11
"He produced his father Amun on 13 carrying-poles ... Now, the incarnation of this noble god had been previously on 11 carrying-poles."[29]

Since *wnn* is an intransitive verb, its perfective can express completed action, like the perfective of other intransitive verbs (§ 20.4). It is probably for this reason that Egyptian uses the perfective *wn* rather than a regular perfect form.

27 Meaning "I was not the cause of any commotion"; *kj* is the infinitive of a 2ae-inf. verb (§ 13.5.1).

28 Although it does have a perfect relative form, which we will meet in Lesson 24.

29 This passage describes how the king had 13 carrying-poles made for the processional bark of the god Amun (see Essay 5); the verb *msj* "give birth" is often used of the production of statues and other paraphernalia. The word *jnjwb3* "carrying-pole" is in group writing (see Essay 17). The prepositional phrase *ẖr ḥ3t* "previously" means literally "under the front." The spelling of *jtj.f* "his father," with two determinatives (a god and a king) and the suffix pronoun before them, is unusual.

3. **in generalizations**

The perfective *wn* is often used to express the existence of something in general, not just in the past. When *wn* has this function in main clauses it is usually preceded by the particle *jw*, like other generalizations (§ 20.7); the construction *jw wn* normally means "there is" or "there exists": for instance,

 *jw wn ḫf3w ḥr wpt ḏw pf*
"There is a snake on the brow of that mountain."

The negative counterpart of *jw wn* as a general statement of existence is  *nn wn*. Although this looks like the subjunctive negation *nn sḏm.f* (§ 19.11.1), it normally means "there is not" or "there does not exist" rather than "will not exist": for example,

 *nn wn šw m ḫrwy* "There is no one who is free of an enemy"

 *nn wn jz n ꜥwn-jb* "There is no tomb for the greedy of heart."

We have already met a nonverbal construction with similar meaning: namely, *nn* plus a noun (or noun phrase) or adverbial sentence (§ 11.4). Theoretically, Egyptian could also say *nn šw m ḫrwy* "There is no one who is free of an enemy" and *nn jz n ꜥwn-jb* "There is no tomb for the greedy of heart" (compare the second example in § 10.7). There seems to be little difference in meaning between the negative constructions with and without *wn*, and it is not clear why Egyptian sometimes prefers one negation and sometimes the other. The verbal construction *nn wn* is used almost exclusively in main clauses (or independent sentences), however, while the construction with *nn* alone has a broader use (§§ 12.11, 12.17).

The perfective *wn* is also common as a general expression of existence in dependent clauses. The following are two examples in marked relative and adverb clauses:

jr m3ꜥt n nb m3ꜥt, ntj wn m3ꜥt nt m3ꜥt.f
"Do Maat for the lord of Maat, the Maat of whose Maat exists"[30]

kš ḫzt w3.tj r bšt … sṯ wn wr ḥr mḥtt kš ḫzt w3.f r ṯr ḫnrtt
"Miserable Kush has gone off to rebellion … there being a chief on the north of miserable Kush who is going off to a time of criminality."[31]

Middle Egyptian often uses *wn* as a general expression of existence in unmarked adverb clauses, as in the following example, cited in § 20.7 above:

 *jw jn.tw ꜥqw, wn 3q*
"Close friends are brought when there is a disaster,"

30 An indirect relative clause: literally, "who the Maat of his Maat exists." This is a somewhat convoluted way of saying "the lord of Maat, from whom all Maat comes."

31 The adjective *ḫzt* is feminine because names of places are normally feminine: § 4.4. The verb *w3.f* is an imperfective used in an unmarked relative clause after the undefined antecedent *wr* "a chief" (§ 20.13). The noun *ḫnrtt* "criminality" is a nisbe formed from the noun *ḫnrt* "prison": the literal meaning is something like "that which pertains to prison."

literally, "when disaster exists." In this use *wn* expresses **concomitant** circumstance: that is, the existence of something at the same time as the action or situation of the governing clause. When the action or situation of the governing clause is present, as in this example, *wn* is also present. When the governing clause refers to a past event or situation, *wn* is past: for instance,

 *ḥḏ.n.j, wn hrw* "I set off when it was day,"

literally, "when day existed." This use is possible because, like other perfectives, *wn* itself simply denotes action and not a specific tense.

20.17 The imperfective of *wnn*

The verb *wnn* also has a regular imperfective,  *wnn*. This form has a much more restricted use than the perfective *wn*. Unlike *wn*, it does not seem to be used to express the existence of someone or something. Instead, it is normally accompanied by a prepositional phrase or adverb, which is the important part of the clause. In this use it expresses the **imperfect** — action that is in some way habitual, incomplete, or ongoing: for instance,

 *wnn t3 m znj mnt* "The land was continually in distress."[32]

Here the imperfective *wnn* denotes an ongoing state of distress (hence the translation "was continually"). This is a connotation that could not be expressed either by a nonverbal sentence such as *jw t3 m znj mnt* "the land (was) in distress" or by the more specific perfective construction *wn t3 m znj mnt* "the land was in distress."

The imperfective of *wnn* can also be used to add an imperfect connotation to the stative, in much the same way that the subjunctive of *wnn* allows the stative to function like a subjunctive (§ 19.13): for example,

m.t gm.n.j ḥm-(n)sw(t) sbkw-m-ḥ(3)b, m.t wnn.f w^{c}r.(w), m.t rdj.n.j sw n ḫnt n sḏm
"Look, I have found the royal servant Sebek-em-hab. He used to be a fugitive.
I have given him to the prison for trial."[33]

Here *wnn.f* indicates that the stative *w^{c}r.(w)*, from the verb *w^{c}r* "flee," refers to an ongoing state that existed before the fugitive was apprehended: literally, "he was continually in flight." The normal SUBJECT-stative construction *m.t sw w^{c}r.w* would mean simply "he had fled" (§ 17.6).

Like the imperfective of other verbs, *wnn* can also be used in dependent clauses. The following is an example in an unmarked adverb clause:

 *nnk tm, wnn.j w^{c}.k(w)*
"Everything belonged to me while I was alone."[34]

Here again the imperfective indicates that the stative *w^{c}.k(w)* "I was alone" refers to an ongoing state: the creator's eternal existence alone before the creation. The imperfective adds a note of continuity that would not be expressed by an adverb clause such as *jw.j w^{c}.kw* "when I was alone."

32 The expression *znj mnt* "distress" is a compound noun meaning literally "the surpassing of suffering."
33 From a letter addressed to a woman (see § 10.4.1). The word *sḏm* "trial" is an infinitive: literally, "for hearing."
34 Speech of the creator. For *nnk* "belonged to me," see § 7.5.2.

20.18 The perfective and imperfective of *wnn*: summary

As the discussion in the preceding two sections indicates, the perfective and imperfective of *wnn* are like those of other verbs in some respects: the perfective can be used as a past tense in main clauses and after the negation *nj*, and the imperfective expresses the imperfect. The major difference between *wnn* and other verbs is that Middle Egyptian uses the perfective of *wnn* in generalizations, while other verbs use the imperfective or the SUBJECT-imperfective construction for this function (§§ 20.7–20.8).

Both forms of *wnn* are also different in that they are often used not as verbs in their own right but as a way to give adverbial predicates or the stative the meanings expressed by the perfective and imperfective. Thus, the perfective can be used to indicate that an adverbial predicate or stative has specific past reference, and the imperfective can be used to give them the connotation of ongoing, incomplete, or habitual action.

By itself, an adverbial predicate simply describes the situation of its subject, and the stative just denotes a state. Thus, a statement such as *jw.s m pr* or *m.k sj m pr* simply relates the subject, *.s* or *sj* "she," to the situation *m pr* "in the house"; and a statement such as *jw.f šm.w* or *m.k sw šm.w* just relates its subject, *.f* or *sw* "he," to the state *šm.w* "gone." Such statements say nothing about the time, mood, or aspect of the relationship: this is why they can be used for different tenses as well as for statements of general validity. When the perfective is added to such statements, it indicates that the relationship pertains to a past or completed situation or state, and when the imperfective is added, it indicates that the relationship is somehow ongoing, incomplete, or habitual.

Sometimes it seems as if there is little difference in translation between an adverbial predicate or stative by itself and the same predicates introduced by the perfective or imperfective of *wnn*. The adverb clause "while I was alone," for example, can be expressed in at least three ways in Middle Egyptian:

-  w^{c}*.kw* — stative (cf. § 17.19)
-  *wn.j* w^{c}*.kw* — stative with the perfective of *wnn*
-  *wnn.j* w^{c}*.kw* — stative with the imperfective of *wnn*.

Although each of these can be translated the same way, however, they are different constructions in Egyptian, with different meanings. The first is a simple adverb clause, meaning something like the English "I being alone." The perfective in the second indicates that the state w^{c}*.kw* refers to the past, somewhat like English "when I was alone." The imperfective in the third marks the state as ongoing or habitual, and can be paraphrased by the English "during the time I was alone" or "when I used to be alone."

A single English translation — "while I was alone" — would make sense for all of these; but this does not mean that Egyptian had several different ways of saying the same thing. The English constructions "I being alone," "when I was alone," and "during the time I was alone" also mean essentially the same thing as "while I was alone," but each has a slightly different meaning. In the same way, each of the Egyptian constructions has a slightly different meaning as well, although all of them can be translated in much the same way. You should try to be aware of these differences and to reflect them, insofar as possible, in your translations.

20.19 The imperfective in questions

In predicate questions (when the verb itself is questioned), the perfective, and sometimes the imperfective, are introduced by the particle *jn*: for example,

 *jn ḫm.k m h3w.j*

"Are you unaware of my situation?" — perfective[35]

 *jn gs3 jwsw*

"Does a balance tilt?" — imperfective.

More often the imperfective, and the SUBJECT-imperfective construction, are introduced by the particles *jn jw* in predicate questions: for instance,

 *jn jw šd.tw ẖnnw m ẖnw pr*

"Are troublemakers received inside a house?"

 *jn jw k3 mr.f ᶜḥ3*

"Is the bull wanting to fight?"

The particles *jn jw* also introduce the perfective of *wnn* in predicate questions about the existence of something: for example,

 *jn jw wn ky nḫt ᶜḥ3 r.f*

"Is there another champion who could fight against him?"[36]

Middle Egyptian does not use the perfective and imperfective in adjunct questions (when something other than the verb is questioned); instead, it uses different forms, which we will meet later.

Essay 20. Middle Egyptian Stories

Like all human cultures, the Egyptians told stories for entertainment and to convey a moral message — usually both. Storytelling in Egypt is undoubtedly as old as the civilization itself, but the earliest written stories we have date from the Middle Kingdom and were composed in Middle Egyptian, the classical language of Egyptian literature. Several of these have survived only in fragments, but four works have been preserved more or less complete.

The oldest Egyptian story known is that of the **Shipwrecked Sailor**. It exists in a single copy, on a papyrus now in St. Petersbug, Russia, which was written in the late 11th or early 12th dynasty. The story begins abruptly (the beginning of the papyrus may have been cut away) with an unnamed member of an expedition speaking to his leader, who is also unnamed. Their expedition has returned to Egypt safely, but apparently without achieving its mission, and the leader is despondent. To cheer him up, the narrator tells him how he himself once triumphed over adversity.

He had gone on another expedition by sea and the boat in which he was traveling was destroyed by a storm, leaving him the only survivor, washed up on a deserted island. After spending "three days

35 *ḫm* is the opposite of *rḫ* "know," and denotes the nonacquisition of knowledge. The perfective *ḫm.k* "you are unaware" thus means literally "you did not learn."

36 *ᶜḥ3* "who could fight" is a verb form we will meet in Lesson 23.

alone, with my heart my (only) companion," the sailor encounters a giant serpent. Although the sailor is at first terrified, the serpent reassures him by telling him his own story of how he had persevered when his entire family was destroyed by a meteor. The serpent then predicts the arrival of a ship that will bring the sailor back to Egypt. When this prophecy is fulfilled, the sailor returns to Egypt together with a cargo of marvelous goods from the island; he presents these to the king, and is rewarded with a promotion and servants.

The story ends with the narrator encouraging his leader to take heart from these examples of triumph over adversity. But the leader refuses to be consoled, saying "What's the point of giving water to a goose at dawn when it's going to be slaughtered that morning?" The tale of the Shipwrecked Sailor is unusual not only for this adverse ending, but also for the anonymity of its characters and for the literary device of a story within a story within a story.

By far the most famous ancient Egyptian tale — in the ancient Egyptians' eyes as well as our own — is the story of **Sinuhe** (*z3-nht* "Son of the Sycamore"). It was composed in the early Middle Kingdom but survives in many copies, dating from Dynasty 12 to the Ramesside Period. The story is set in the reign of Senwosret I and is presented in the form of a tomb biography of Sinuhe, who was a servant of the queen.

At the beginning of the tale Sinuhe is on a military campaign in the Libyan desert, led by Senwosret, who at this point is still the heir apparent. During the campaign Senwosret's father, Amenemhat I, dies, and Senwosret is informed of the fact secretly by messengers from the palace. Sinuhe overhears the message. Fearing that rival factions will kill Senwosret and his followers, he flees to the coast of Syria. There he is adopted by a local sheikh and eventually becomes a tribal ruler in his own right. After many years, he is challenged to battle by the head of a rival clan. The account of their fight — which Sinuhe wins by killing his challenger — foreshadows in some respects the Biblical tale of David's victory over Goliath, just as the story of Sinuhe's long exile abroad resembles that of Moses in the story of the Exodus.

After this success, Sinuhe begins to long for home. His situation is reported to Senwosret, and the king sends him a letter (which the story reproduces in full) urging him to come back. Sinuhe rejoices over the pharaoh's invitation and returns to Egypt, though he is still afraid of punishment for doubting Senwosret's ability to gain control after his father's death. In an audience before the king, Sinuhe is championed by the queen and the royal children. Senwosret pardons him, gives him the property and station of a high official, and orders a pyramid built for him in the royal cemetery. The story ends with the words "I was under the blessing of the king until the day of mooring (i.e., dying) came."

Although it is couched in the form of a tomb biography, the story of Sinuhe is clearly a careful literary composition. It is primarily written in the form of "thought couplets" (see Essay 18), and can be considered as much a poem as a prose tale. The elegance of its language was probably one of the reasons for its popularity: a number of the copies we possess were written by schoolboys as scribal exercises.

The other two great works of Middle Kingdom fiction are written in the third person. The tale of the **Eloquent Peasant** is preserved on four papyri dating from the end of the Middle Kingdom, although it is set in the time of the pharaoh Nebkaure Khety (Dynasty 10). It tells the story of a peasant from the oasis of Wadi Natrun (northwest of modern Cairo), who loads his donkeys with produce and sets out for Herakleopolis, the capital of Dynasty 10 in Middle Egypt. On the way he passes the land of a tenant farmer, who covets the peasant's goods. The farmer has some linen spread out on the road at a point where it passes between his grainfield and the bank of a canal. To avoid the linen, the peasant leads his donkeys through the field, and one of them eats a wisp of the grain. The farmer uses this as an excuse to seize the peasant's donkey as "payment" for its transgression.

The peasant then goes to petition to the farmer's landlord, who is the chief steward in charge of the king's state property. The steward is so impressed with the peasant's eloquence that he reports it to the pharaoh. The king then orders the steward not to reply to the peasant's complaint, so that he will be forced to continue his eloquent petitions. The bulk of the story is taken up by eight more lengthy petitions, each of which is a literary discourse on the nature of Maat. After the ninth petition, the steward finally grants the peasant's request. His petitions are recorded on papyrus and given to the king, "and they were better on his heart than anything that is in this entire land." The story ends with the steward ordering the property of the covetous farmer to be given to the eloquent peasant.

The last great work of fiction written in Middle Egyptian, like the first, exists only in a single copy, on a papyrus dating from the Hyksos Period (Dynasty 15), now in the Egyptian Museum in Berlin. It is is commonly known as **Papyrus Westcar**, after the name of its first modern owner. The beginning and end of the papyrus are lost. The surviving portion contains five related stories set in the Old Kingdom, during the reign of Khufu (Dynasty 4), builder of the Great Pyramid. Three of these are tales of magicians, told to Khufu by his sons, and the fourth relates wonders performed for Khufu himself. At the end of the fourth tale, the magician predicts to Khufu the birth of three kings of the next dynasty, to nonroyal parents. The fifth tale is about the miraculous birth of these kings and subsequent events in the life of their mother.

Middle Egyptian literature undoubtedly possessed many more stories than just these. Some have survived merely in fragments, including the beginning of a story about a herdsman who meets a strange goddess in the marshes, and pieces of a tale about a pharaoh's adventures in the Fayum oasis. The tradition of stories also continued well after the Middle Kingdom, and we possess a number of other tales written in Late Egyptian and Demotic.

There are significant similarities and differences among the four great works of Middle Egyptian storytelling. Each of them was written not merely for entertainment but also, if not primarily, to convey a "moral." The story of the Shipwrecked Sailor is about perseverance in the face of adversity; the tale of Sinuhe reflects a genre of early Middle Kingdom texts extolling the virtue of loyalty to the king; the travails of the Eloquent Peasant are a vehicle for sermons on the nature of Maat, particularly in relations between officials and their dependents; and the stories of Papyrus Westcar contrast the power of kingship with the greater powers that mere commoners can possess through learning, magic, or the intervention of the gods.

All of the stories are written in Middle Egyptian, but they differ in the kind of language used and its literary refinement. Sinuhe and the Eloquent Peasant are careful compositions, each crafted by an author in full command of the highest form of classical Middle Egyptian and the literary arts. The Shipwrecked Sailor and the stories of Papyrus Westcar, on the other hand, are closer to the spoken language of their time, and read more like oral narratives committed to writing than deliberate literary compositions. Between them, the four works span the full range of classical Middle Egyptian. The tale of the Shipwrecked Sailor shows us literary Middle Egyptian in its earliest form, those of Sinuhe and the Eloquent Peasant reflect the language at its literary apex, and the stories of Papyrus Westcar give us a look at the speech of the Middle Kingdom on its way to becoming Late Egyptian.

EXERCISE 20

Transliterate and translate the following sentences. A number of the examples are taken from Middle Egyptian stories.

1. 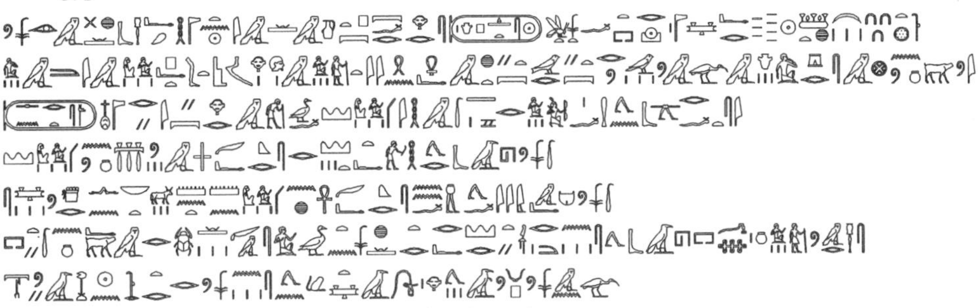
 ... — beginning of the story of Sinuhe: *SḤTP-JB-Rᶜ* throne name of Amenemhat I; *jr* "the one who made"; *Z(J)-N-WSRT* Senwosret (I); *ḫpr* "that had happened."
2.  — description of the king, from the story of Sinuhe: *wmt* "thick" (a "thick" heart is a courageous one); *ᶜš3t* "multitude" (of enemies)
3.  — from the story of Sinuhe: *jb* "the thirsty"
4.  — from the story of Sinuhe: *jwt* "there came" (§ 14.14.2); *(r)tnw* "Retjenu" (see Exercise 8, no. 18)
5.  — from the story of Sinuhe: *ḫr-nswt* "king's possessions"
6.  — from the story of Sinuhe: *jrt.n.k* "that which you have done"; the second verb in each line is subjunctive (§ 19.8.2).
7.  — from the story of Sinuhe: *zḫz m s3* "run after" (a fugitive); *ṯ3z ḥwrw* "hue and cry" (literally, "a poor sentence")

8.  — from the story of Sinuhe (speaking to the king)

9. 
 — from Papyrus Westcar: for *jr m ḫt* see n. 14 in this lesson; *h3w* "goes down"

10. 

11. 

12.  — *nḫt-sbkw* "Nakht-Sobek" (personal name)

13. 

14.  — from the story of Sinuhe: *ḫprt* "something that has happened"

15.  — *r pw* "either" (see § 4.12)

16. 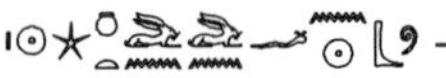 — a prophecy about the sun

17.  — beginning of the Eloquent Peasant: *zj pw wn.(w)* "there was a man" (literally, "it is that a man existed"); *ḫw.n-jnpw* a name meaning "He whom Anubis has protected"

18.  — from Papyrus Westcar: *ḏd-SNFRW* "Snefru Endures," a town near Memphis

19.  — from the serpent's story in the Shipwrecked Sailor

20.  — from the Shipwrecked Sailor

21. 

22.  — from the story of the Herdsman

23. 

24.  — from the story of the Herdsman

25. 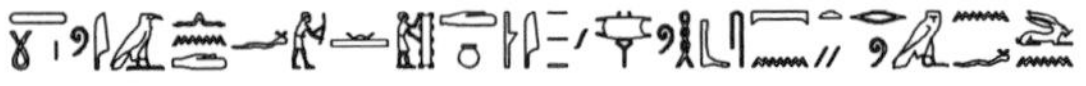 — description of a builder, from the Instruction of Khety: *m rwtj n* "out in" (literally, "in the outside of")

26.  — from a medical text

27.  — title of a prescription for encouraging a baby to nurse

28. 

21. The Prospective and Passive

21.1 Definitions

In this lesson we will consider three further forms of the *sḏm.f* (§ 19.3): the prospective, the prospective passive, and the passive. These can look like the other *sḏm.f* forms we have met in the last two lessons, but they have different meanings and uses.

The prospective denotes **action that has not yet happened**, either at the time of speaking or with respect to another action or situation. This is an aspect, not a tense. The prospective usually corresponds to the future tense in English, but it can also refer to an action in the past, which had not yet happened from the viewpoint of another past action or situation. This form is a holdover from Old Egyptian. In Middle Egyptian it has largely been replaced by the subjunctive or the pseudoverbal construction with *r* plus the infinitive (*jw.f r sḏm*). It is mostly found in older religious texts, but still survives in a few common Middle Egyptian constructions. The prospective also has a passive counterpart, the prospective passive, which is even rarer than the prospective itself in Middle Egyptian.

The passive denotes **completed action.** It is the normal passive counterpart of the perfect, and has largely the same meanings and uses as the perfect. In the past few lessons we have seen that verb forms of the suffix conjugation can be made passive by adding the suffix *tw* to the active form: i.e., active *sḏm.f* "he hears," passive *sḏm.tw.f* "he is heard." In such cases the suffix *tw* adds the feature of passive voice (§ 13.3.4) to what are otherwise active forms. The passive, however, is **always** passive: it is passive in itself, and does not need the suffix *tw* to make it passive.

The Prospective

21.2 Forms

As noted above, the prospective is actually two forms: an active and a passive. In most verb classes both forms have the ending *w* (𓅱 or 𓏲), which is added directly to the verb stem. Because of this ending the prospective is sometimes called the "*sḏmw.f*" ("sedgem-OO-eff") although that is a misnomer, since the 3-lit. class (to which *sḏm* belongs) is one of the few classes that actually do not have the ending *w*. The verbs of the 2-lit., 2ae-gem., and 3-lit. classes do not have an ending in the prospective; the anomalous verbs *rdj* "give" and *jwj/jj* "come" rarely do.

Because it is a "weak" consonant (§ 2.8.2), the *w* ending of the prospective can be omitted in writing. The prospective can therefore appear with no ending at all, even if the verb belongs to a class that can have the *w* ending. The ending can also be written as *y* (𓇌) rather than *w*. This is particularly common in verbs of the 3ae-inf. and 4ae-inf. classes and their causatives.

The prospective passive looks like the active in classes that have an ending and in the 2ae-gem. class. Verbs of the 2-lit., 3-lit., and 4ae-inf. classes are easily recognized in this form by their unusual geminated stem; because of this feature, the prospective passive is sometimes known as the *sḏmm.f* ("sedgem-EM-eff").

The following table shows examples of typical prospective forms for the various verb classes in Middle Egyptian:

1. **Prospective Active**

2-LIT.	*pḥ* "will reach" — no prefixed forms
2AE-GEM.	*m33.k* "you will see," *wnn.j* "I will be" — always geminated
3-LIT.	*ḥw3.sn* "they will rot"
3AE-INF.	*h3w* "will go down," *h3y.k* "you will go down"
4-LIT.	*gmgmw* "will break"
4AE-INF.	*ḥmsw* "will sit"
5-LIT.	*nznznw.j* "I will burn up"
CAUS. 2-LIT.	*smḫw* "will forget," *snqy.s* "she will suckle"
ANOM.	The verb *rdj* "give, put, make, allow" always uses the base stem *rdj*: *rdj.j* "I will make"; the ending *w* is rare: and *rdjw.t(w)* "will be allowed." The verb *jwj/jj* "come" uses only the base stem *jw*: *jw.f* "it will come"; rarely with the ending *y*: *jwy.f* "let him come."

2. **Prospective Passive**

2-LIT.	*pḥḥ* "will be reached" — geminated stem
2AE-GEM.	*3mm* "will be seized" — geminated stem
3-LIT.	*nḥmm.f* "he will be taken away" — geminated stem
3AE-INF.	*jṯw.f* and *jṯy.f* "he will be taken"
4AE-INF.	*nḏrr.j* "I will be grabbed"
CAUS. 2-LIT.	*sḫdw.j* "I will be inverted"
CAUS. 4-LIT.	*sḫdḫdw* "will be inverted," *sḫdḫdy.f* "he will be inverted"
ANOM.	The verb *rdj* "give, put, make, allow" normally has the same form as the active: *rdj.k* "you will be put"; rarely with the ending *w*: *rdjw.j* "I will be given."

As these tables show, the ending of the prospective, when there is one, is normally written **before** the determinative.

21.3 Subject and word order

The prospective forms behave like other forms of the suffix conjugation with respect to their subjects and the word-order of their clauses (§ 18.4). Middle Egyptian can use the suffix *tw* to form the passive of the prospective, as it does with the subjunctive (§ 19.4) and the perfective and imperfective (§ 20.3): for example,  *nḏrw.t(w).j* "I will be grabbed." This form has exactly the same meaning and uses as the prospective passive itself: thus,  *nḏrw.t(w).j* and  *nḏrr.j* both mean "I will be grabbed." In the first case, the passive is made by adding the suffix *tw* to the active (*nḏrw* + *tw*); in the second, it is expressed by means of the prospective passive (*nḏrr*), which is passive in itself. Originally the prospective formed its passive only by means of the prospective passive. By Middle Egyptian, however, the prospective passive was largely an obsolete form and the newer construction, with the suffix *tw*, was used in its place.

21.4 The meaning of the prospective

As noted in § 21.1, the prospective denotes action that has not yet happened. In this respect it is essentially the original indicative counterpart of the subjunctive. When the subjunctive is used with reference to an action that has not yet occurred, it marks that action as somehow contingent, desirable, or uncertain (§§ 19.1, 19.5.2). The prospective is an indicative form: it simply indicates that the action has yet to happen, without any notion of uncertainty or desirability.

The prospective is largely obsolete in Middle Egyptian. Its original uses, which can be observed in Old Egyptian texts, have been mostly taken over in Middle Egyptian either by the subjunctive or by the pseudoverbal construction with *r* plus the infinitive. With few exceptions, when we do find the prospective in Middle Egyptian it is in a use or construction for which the language normally uses the subjunctive or the pseudoverbal construction. Most examples of the prospective occur in early Middle Egyptian texts or in those that reflect an older stage of the language, such as religious texts, but there are a few cases in which standard Middle Egyptian still uses the prospective form.

21.5 The prospective negated

In our discussion of the subjunctive we saw that the negative construction of *nn* plus the subjunctive is the normal negation of the future in Middle Egyptian: for example, 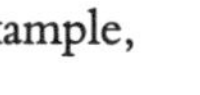 *nn dj.j* "I will not give" (§ 19.11.1). This construction is the standard negative counterpart of both the subjunctive, expressing voluntary action, and the pseudoverbal construction with *r* plus the infinitive, which denotes action that is somehow compulsory or inevitable (§ 19.5.2).

The subjunctive negation was originally used only for voluntary actions, and a different negation, with the prospective, was used for the regular future. This construction involves the negative particle *nj* () and the prospective forms, both active and passive: for example,

 *nj ḫfꜥ.ṯn-wj, nj 3mm.ṯn-wj*
"You will not grasp me, you will not seize me."[1]

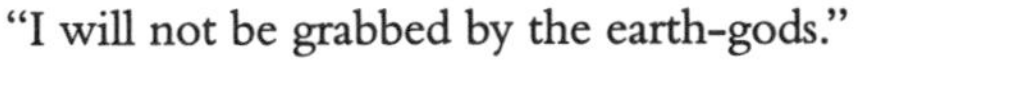 *nj ḫfꜥꜥ.j jn šw, nj 3mm.j jn 3krw*
"I will not be grasped by Shu, I will not be seized by the earth-gods."[2]

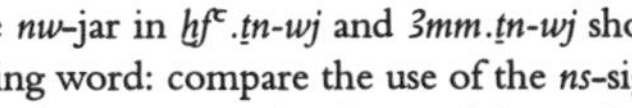 *nj nḏrw.t(w).j jn 3krw*
"I will not be grabbed by the earth-gods."

1 The *nw*-jar in *ḫfꜥ.ṯn-wj* and *3mm.ṯn-wj* shows that the dependent pronoun *wj* was pronounced as part of the preceding word: compare the use of the *ns*-sign in the adjectival predicate *n(j)-sw* (§ 7.5.1).

2 The *3krw* represent the forces of the earth, often imagined as serpents.

Each of these negations expresses a statement of fact about action that has not yet happened, rather than the desire or intention of the verb's subject. The difference is somewhat difficult to see in English, which does not normally make such a distinction, but it exists in the Egyptian constructions nonetheless.

The future negation with the prospective is found mostly in older texts that do not make the regular Middle Egyptian distinction between the negatives *nj* and *nn* (see § 16.6.8). As a result, it is not always possible to know whether a future negation in such texts is using the prospective *nj sḏm.f* or the subjunctive *nj sḏm.f* (the ancestor of Middle Egyptian *nn sḏm.f*). In the first example cited above, for instance, *nj ẖfꜥ.ṯn* could involve either form: only the parallel negation *nj 3mm.ṯn* in the second clause indicates that the verb is prospective, since the subjunctive would have the form *nj* (later *nn*) *3m.ṯn* (2ae-gem.: see § 19.2).

21.6 Other uses of the prospective

The future negation with the prospective is one of the few uses in which the prospective passive can still be found in Middle Egyptian. The active form (and the passive with *tw*), however, is somewhat more frequent in regular Middle Egyptian texts. In most cases it occurs in the same kinds of constructions as those for which the subjunctive is normally used: for example,

 *jr m33.k, m.k pẖrt pw nt wn m3ꜥ*

"Do (it) and you will see: it is a true remedy"[3] — result clause (§ 19.8.2)

 *ḥ3 rdj.t(w) swḏ3.j jb.k*

"If only I will be allowed to inform you"[4] — after *ḥ3* (§ 19.6)

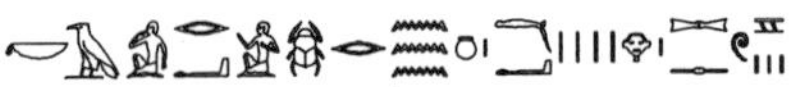 *k3 rdj.j ḫpr mw nw mḥ 4 ḥr ṯ3zw*

"Then I will make water of 4 cubits happen upon the sandbanks" — after *k3* (§ 19.6.3).

Each of these examples involves a context in which Middle Egyptian normally employs the subjunctive. Only the form of the verb shows that the prospective rather than the subjunctive is being used: *m33.k* "you will see" instead of subjunctive *m3.k* "you will see," *rdj.t(w)* "will be allowed" instead of subjunctive *dj.tw* "might be allowed," and *rdj.j* "I will make" instead of subjunctive *dj.j* "I will make."

The most common use of the prospective as an alternative to the subjunctive is in the protasis of conditional sentences, after *jr* "if" (see § 19.7): for instance,

jr jw ... z(j) nb n h3w.j r mdt m t3 jmt-pr ... m rdj sḏm.tw n.sn

"If any man of my family will come to contest this will ... don't let them be listened to."[5]

Here the form of the verb after *jr* shows that it is the prospective (*jw*) rather than the subjunctive (*jwt*: cf. the first example in § 19.7). The distinction in meaning between the two forms is probably not much different than that of English "if any man will come" (prospective *jw*) versus "if any man should come" (subjunctive *jwt*).

3 Literally, "look, it is a remedy of true existence."

4 Literally, "if only it will be given that I make sound your heart" (cf. § 19.10).

5 Literally, "don't give that one listen to them"; *mdwj m* "contest" means literally "speak in" (the matter).

One place in which Middle Egyptian still seems to use the prospective and not the subjunctive is an adverb clause of **future circumstance**: for example,

jw.f r smr mm sr(j)w, rdj.t(w).f m q3b šnyt

"He is to be a courtier among the officials, for he will be put in the midst of the court."

Here the second clause, with the prospective, describes how "he is to be a courtier among the officials," but with reference to something that has not yet happened. This use is impossible to translate literally as an adverb clause in English; instead, we have to use a second main clause such as "for he will be put" or "and he will be put." The prospective is used instead of the subjunctive because the subjunctive in an adverb clause expresses purpose or result rather than future circumstance (§ 19.8). Such clauses with the prospective are fairly rare: normally Middle Egyptian uses a form describing concomitant circumstance, such as the imperfective (§ 20.10).

21.7 The prospective of *wnn*

Although the prospective of most verbs is used only occasionally in Middle Egyptian, the prospective of *wnn* "exist" is still a regular part of the Middle Egyptian verbal system. This form can be used as a verb in its own right, to express the future existence of its subject: for example,

 *ꜥnḫ.j ꜥnḫt, wnn.j wnnt*

"I shall truly live, I shall truly exist."[6]

Most often, however, it is used like the subjunctive, perfective, and imperfective of *wnn*: with a following adverb, prepositional phrase, or stative as the important part of the clause rather than the verb itself. In such cases **the prospective of *wnn* allows an adverbial predicate or stative to function like a prospective.**

Usually the prospective of *wnn* corresponds to the simple English future "will be," and indicates specifically that the situation expressed by the adverbial predicate or the state expressed by the stative has not yet happened: for instance,

 *jnk z3b jq(r) tp t3, wnn.j m 3ḫ(j) jq(r) m ẖrt-nṯr*

"I am an excellent official on earth; I will be an excellent akh in the necropolis"

 *wnn ḏd r pn ꜥnḫ.(w) m ẖrt-nṯr*

"He who says this spell will be alive in the necropolis."[7]

In the first of these examples, the prospective allows the adverbial predicate of the second clause to function as a specific future statement in contrast to the atemporal statement of the nominal predicate in the first clause; in the second, it allows the atemporal stative *ꜥnḫ.(w)* "alive" to refer specifically to the future.

The prospective of *wnn* can also make it possible for an adverbial predicate or the stative to function in ways that the normal adverbial sentence or SUBJECT-stative construction cannot — for instance, as the protasis of a conditional sentence:

6 *ꜥnḫt* and *wnnt* are complementary infinitives (§§ 14.19–14.20).

7 *ḏd* "he who says" is a verb form we will meet in Lesson 23.

 *jr wnn jb.f r ᶜḥ3, jmj ḏd.f ḫrt jb.f*

"If his mind will be toward fighting, let him say what he has in mind."[8]

Here the prospective *wnn* allows the adverbial sentence *jb.f r ᶜḥ3* "his mind is toward fighting" to serve as the protasis after *jr* — something that the adverbial sentence cannot do by itself. The prospective of *wnn* also allows a pseudoverbal predicate to function in the same way:

jr grt wnn mr-snfrw ḥr mrt wnn m s3 n3 n jḥw, ḫr.k dj.k sw m s3 jr(j)

"Now, if Mer-Snefru will be wanting to be in charge of those cattle,
you'll have to put him in charge of them."[9]

The prospective (*wnn*) is the normal form of the verb *wnn* after *jr* "if, when" in Middle Egyptian, rather than the subjunctive (*wn*).

The prospective of *wnn* is also used in the negation *nj wnn* "will not exist" or "will not be": for example,

jr grt ḥm-k3 r(m)ṯ nbt ḫnnt(j).sn st, nj wnn.f, nj wnn z3.f ḥr nst.f

"Now, as for the ka-priest of any people who shall disturb it,
he will not exist; his son will not be in his place."[10]

The verb *wnn* is unusual in Middle Egyptian because it still regularly uses the older prospective negation *nj wnn* as the negation of the future instead of the standard Middle Egyptian negation with the subjunctive after *nn* that is used by other verbs. As we saw in the last lesson (§ 20.16.3), *nn wn* normally expresses generalizations ("there is not") rather than the future, even though it looks like the normal subjunctive negation *nn sḏm.f* (§ 19.11.1).

THE PASSIVE

21.8 Form

Unlike the prospective, which has two forms (active and passive), the passive is a single form. It often looks like the active forms of the *sḏm.f* and has to be distinguished by the context in which it is used rather than by its appearance. In many verb classes the Middle Egyptian passive apparently had an ending *w* ( or ), added directly to the verb stem as in the prospective. The passive can have this ending even in classes that do not have an ending in the prospective, such as the class of 2-lit. verbs. Like the prospective, the passive can have the ending *y* () rather than *w*, but in normal Middle Egyptian texts this ending appears only on verbs with a final radical *j*, such as those of the 3ae-inf. class and the anom. verb *rdj*.

The following table shows typical examples of the passive for the different verb classes in Middle Egyptian:

8 Literally, "If his heart will be toward fighting, give that he say (§ 19.10) what his heart has"; *ḫrt* is a nisbe of the preposition *ḫr* "near, by, with."

9 The second *wnn* is an infinitive, object of *mrt* (§ 14.12). *m s3* "in charge" means literally "in back of"; *jr(j)* is a prepositional adverb: literally "thereunto" (§ 8.15). For *ḫr.k dj.k* "you'll have to put" see § 20.9.1.

10 *ḫnnt(j).sn* "who shall disturb" is a verb form discussed in Lesson 23. *ḥr nst.f* "in his place" means "as his successor."

2-LIT.	*wn* "has been opened," *šꜥw* "was cut off" — no prefixed forms
2AE-GEM.	*m3* "has been seen" — base stem
3-LIT.	*šzp* "has been taken," *wḥmw* "has been repeated"
3AE-INF.	*jr* "was made," *jrw* "have been made," *jry* "was made"
4-LIT.	*gmgm* "have been broken"
4AE-INF.	*ꜥw3* "has been robbed," *ḫwsw* "was built"[11]
CAUS. 2-LIT.	*sẖr* "was felled"
CAUS. 3-LIT.	*sꜥḥꜥ* "was installed"
CAUS. 3AE-INF.	*sḥr* "has been driven off," *sḫꜥw* "was made to appear"
CAUS. 4AE-INF.	*sm3w* "were renewed" (root *sm3wj*), *sḫntw* "was sent upstream"
ANOM.	The verb *rdj* "give, put, cause" uses both base stems: *rdj* "was caused," *rdjw* "was caused," *rdjw* "has been given," *rdy* "were put," *dj* "were put," *djw* "was caused."

As with the prospective forms, the ending of the passive, when there is one, is normally written **before** the determinative.

21.9 Subject and word order of the passive

The passive follows the normal rules for forms of the suffix conjugation with respect to its subject and the word order of its clause (§ 18.4). Since it is a form that already has passive meaning, it is not used with the passive suffix *tw*. The passive is quite often used without an expressed subject, especially when the subject does not refer to anything in particular (corresponding to the English "dummy" subject *it*): for example,

jw jr mj ḏd.f "It was done as he said,"

literally, "(it) was done like his saying" (*ḏd* is the infinitive). The agent of the passive, when it is expressed, is introduced by the preposition *jn* (see § 8.2.2; for an example see § 21.14 below).

One important peculiarity of the passive is that it is rarely used with a personal pronoun as subject. Normally the subject of the passive is a noun (or noun phrase) or demonstrative pronoun, but not a suffix pronoun. **Middle Egyptian regularly uses the stative instead of the passive when the subject is a personal pronoun**: for example,

ṯ3.kw, ꜥꜥb šnw.j "I was shaved, my hair was combed."

Here the verb in the second clause, with a nominal subject (*šnw.j* "my hair"), is the passive, while that in the first clause is the stative because it has a personal pronoun as its subject: thus, *ṯ3.kw* rather than **ṯ3w.j* "I was shaved."[12]

11 The first "arm" sign is for the biliteral sign *ḫw*.

12 The verb *ṯ3j* is 3ae-inf.; it actually refers to hairs being plucked out rather than to shaving.

21.10 The meaning of the passive

In Lesson 18, we saw that the suffix *tw* could be used to make a passive form of the perfect. This is actually a specialized form of the passive: in most cases the *sḏm.n.tw.f* is not the perfect itself but the perfect relative, which we will discuss in detail later. The normal passive counterpart of the perfect is the passive with a nominal subject, or — as we have just seen — the stative when the subject is a personal pronoun: e.g.,

SUBJECT	ACTIVE	PASSIVE
nominal[13]	*m3.n r*^{c} "Re saw"	*m3 r*^{c} "Re was seen" (passive)
personal pronoun	*m3.n.f* "he saw"	*m3.w* "he was seen" (stative).

As the normal passive counterpart of the perfect, the passive has essentially the same meaning as the perfect (§ 18.3). It denotes completed action, and as such it often corresponds to an English perfect or past tense. Thus, a passive such as *m3 r*^{c} can mean "Re was seen" (past), "Re has been seen" (present perfect), or "Re had been seen" (past perfect), depending on context. Like the perfect, however, the passive expresses an aspect, not a tense; it can therefore refer to the present or future as well as to past actions.

Since the passive voice indicates that an action is performed **on** its subject (§ 13.3.4), only transitive verbs can appear in the passive: intransitive verbs can only denote an action performed **by** the subject (§ 13.2). Egyptian, like English, however, has some verbs that can be either transitive or intransitive. An English example is the verb *join*: it is transitive in the sentence *Jack joined the two parts together* and intransitive in the sentence *The two parts joined together nicely*. The Egyptian verb  *zm3* "join" is used in the same way. This peculiarity can make it difficult to know whether a particular example of the *sḏm.f* of such a verb is the passive (transitive) or an active (intransitive) form. In the sentence  *zm3 3ḫt.j m 3ḫt.f*, for instance, the verb could be passive or active: "My Sacred Eye has been joined with his Sacred Eye" or "My Sacred Eye has joined with his Sacred Eye" (perfective). In an example like this, without any context, it is impossible to decide between the two. Fortunately, however, the context usually provides some clues as to which form is meant. It is also important to remember how the various forms are used: in the sentence just cited, for example, the passive is more likely because it is a common Middle Egyptian form, while the perfective is unusual in main clauses (§ 20.4).

21.11 The passive in main clauses

As the passive counterpart of the perfect, the passive is used in the same constructions as the perfect, and with the same meanings. The following examples illustrate the use of the passive in main clauses expressing completed action and as a past tense (cf. §§ 18.7, 18.9):

 *šzp ḫrpw, ḥ(w) mjnt*

"The mallet has been taken (in hand), the mooring-post has been hit"

 *dj sr(j)w r* ^{c}*ḥ*^{c}*w.sn*

"The officials were put at their stations."

13 That is, a noun or noun phrase, anything that is equivalent to a noun or noun phrase (such as an infinitive or a noun clause), or any pronoun except a personal pronoun.

Like the perfect, the passive in main clauses is usually preceded by an introductory word of some sort, most often *jw*, *m.k*, or *ʿḥʿ.n* (cf. §§ 18.7, 18.9): for example,

jw ḫwsw n.j mr m jnr "A pyramid of stone was built for me"

m.k ms n.k ẖrdw 3 "Look, 3 boys have been born to you"

ʿḥʿ.n šʿw nḥbt.s "Then its neck was cut."

The passive can also express an action contrary to fact, like the perfect (§ 18.8):

ḥw zn zẖ3w "If only the writings had been opened."

21.12 The passive in dependent clauses

The uses and meaning of the passive are also comparable to those of the perfect in dependent clauses. The following are two examples in marked dependent clauses:

bjk ʿẖ.f ḥnʿ šmsww.f, nn rdjt rḫ st mšʿ.f, jst h3b r msw-nswt
"The falcon was flying off with his followers, without letting his army know it, although the king's children had been sent for"[14] — adverb clause after *jsṯ* (cf. § 18.11)

ḥr ntt r.f wḥmw ḏddwt
"because in that respect what has been said has been repeated"[15] — noun clause marked by *ntt* (cf. § 18.13).

Most dependent clauses with the passive are unmarked adverb clauses. Like the perfect (§ 18.11), the passive in this use expresses **prior circumstance**: for example,

jʿ.jn.sn sw, šʿd ḫp3.f
"Then they washed him, after his umbilical cord had been cut."[16]

The passive can also be used like the perfect in an unmarked relative clause after an undefined antecedent (cf. § 18.12): for instance,

sbj gm zḫw.f "a rebel whose plots have been discovered."

This use is possible only for indirect relative clauses, as in this example. For direct relative clauses, and those after a defined antecedent, Egyptian uses different forms, which we will meet later.

Unlike the perfect (§ 18.13), the passive is rarely used in unmarked noun clauses as the object of a verb or preposition. Examples that appear to be the passive in such uses are usually other forms, such as the infinitive: for instance,

m rdj sṯ3.f [ḫr] p3 srj "Don't let him be brought before the official."

Here the object of *rdj*, *sṯ3.f*, is probably the infinitive (literally, "don't allow the bringing of him") rather than the passive because it has a suffix pronoun (cf. § 21.9).

14 For the first two clauses see Exercise 20, no. 1. The passive in the final clause has no subject: literally, "(it) was sent for the king's children."

15 For *r.f* "in that respect" see § 16.7.2. The subject of the passive, *ḏddwt* "what has been said," is a verb form we will meet in Lesson 23.

16 From the description of a birth; *jʿ.jn.sn* "then they washed" is a verb form we will meet in the next lesson.

21.13 The negated passive

Like the perfect, the passive can be negated by the negative particle *nj*. This construction expresses the negation of **action**, **ability**, or **necessity** and is normally translated by the **present** tense in English, as in the corresponding construction with the perfect (§ 18.14): for example,

 *nj nḥm tp.j m ꜥ.j* "My head cannot be taken away from me."

Although it usually corresponds to the English present tense, however, the negated passive can occur in contexts that require a past tense in translation: for instance,

nj srḫ.tw.j mm šnyt, nj gm wn.j m rw-prw

"I was not denounced in the court, no fault of mine could be found in the temples."

Note the difference here between the past negation *nj srḫ.tw.j* "I was not denounced," with the passive form of the perfective (§§ 20.3, 20.5), and the negated passive *nj gm* "could not be found": the former expresses the negation of a past event; the latter, the negation of ability.

Like the negated perfect, the negated passive can also be used in dependent clauses: for instance,

[swḏ3 jb pw] n nb.j ꜥnḫ.(w) (w)ḏ3.(w) s(nb.w) ḥr ntt nj gm n3 n ẖrdw

"It is (a communication) to inform my lord, lph, about the fact that those boys could not be found"[17]

 *jry ḫ3yt jm.sn, nj rḫ ṯnw*

"A heap of bodies was made of them, the number being unknown."

In the first example the negated passive is used in a marked noun clause introduced by *ntt*. In the second, it is used in an unmarked adverb clause. Note that the passive of *rḫ*, like the perfect, expresses the idea of "knowing" as the completed action of "learning" (§ 18.10): *nj rḫ ṯnw* means literally "the number could not be learned" — thus, "could not be known."

The negated passive is one construction in which the passive is sometimes used with a suffix pronoun as its subject: for example,

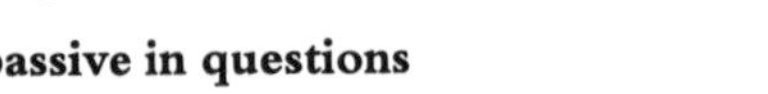 *jw.f rdj.w n.j, nj nḥm.f m ꜥ.(j)*

"It has been given to me; it cannot be taken away from me."

Normally, however, Middle Egyptian prefers the passive form of the perfect (e.g., *nj nḥm.n.tw.f*) in such cases. In fact, the negated passive itself is relatively uncommon in Middle Egyptian, except in religious texts: the normal passive counterpart of the perfect after the negative particle *nj* is the *sḏm.n.tw.f* form, not the passive.

21.14 The passive in questions

Like the perfect, the passive can be used in predicate questions, where the action of the verb itself is questioned (§ 18.18). In this use it is usually introduced by the particles *jn jw*: for example,

17 Literally, "It is making sound the heart of my lord" (see n. 4 above): *swḏ3 jb* is a noun clause with the infinitive, used as the A part of an A *pw* nominal sentence.

(j)n jw wḏ sḏm jṯꜣ jn r(m)ṯ nbt wpw ḥr (j)m(j)-r-šnt

"Has it been ordered that a thief be tried by any people except the sheriff?"[18]

The passive is not normally used in adjunct questions: for these Middle Egyptian prefers the *sḏm.n.tw.f* form, which is actually the perfect relative. This use will be discussed in Lesson 25.

THE *SḎM.F* FORMS

21.15 Forms

We have now met all six forms of the *sḏm.f*: perfective, imperfective, subjunctive, prospective, prospective passive, and passive. As you have seen, these forms often look alike in many classes. In fact, there is no verb class in which each of the six forms has a distinctive appearance. But each class does have at least two written forms, as you can see by comparing the tables in this and the past two lessons. To help you remember what the six *sḏm.f* forms look like in each of the major classes, the following table compares all six, using a sample verb from each class:[19]

	PERFECTIVE	IMPERFECTIVE	SUBJUNCTIVE	PROSPECTIVE	PROSPECTIVE PASSIVE	PASSIVE
2-LIT. *ḏd* "say"	*ḏd*	*ḏd* (*j.ḏd*)	*ḏd* (*j.ḏd*)	*ḏd*	*ḏdd*	*ḏd(w)*
2AE-GEM. *tmm* "close"	*tm* *mꜣn**	*tmm*	*tm* *mꜣn**	*tmm*	*tmm*	*tm*
3-LIT. *nḥm* "remove"	*nḥm*	*nḥm*	*nḥm*	*nḥm*	*nḥmm*	*nḥm(w)*
3AE-INF. *jṯj* "take"	*jṯ*	*jṯ* (*jṯy*)	*jṯ*, *jṯy* *jnt**	*jṯ(w)*, *jṯy*	*jṯ(w)*, *jṯy*	*jṯ(w)*, *jṯy*
4/5-LIT. *gmgm* "break"	*gmgm*	*gmgm*	*gmgm*	*gmgm(w)*	*gmgm(w)*	*gmgm(w)*
4AE-INF. *nḏrj* "grab"	*nḏr*	*nḏr* (*nḏry*)	*nḏr*, *nḏry*	*nḏr(w)*, *nḏry*	*nḏrr*	*nḏr(w)*
CAUS. 2/3/4-LIT. *sẖr* "fell"	*sẖr*	*sẖr*	*sẖr*	*sẖr(w)*, *sẖry*	*sẖr(w)*, *sẖry*	*sẖr(w)*
CAUS. 2AE-GEM. *sqbb* "cool"	*sqbb*	*sqbb*	*sqbb*	*sqbb(w)*, *sqbby*	*sqbb(w)*, *sqbby*	*sqbb(w)*
CAUS. 3/4AE-INF. *shꜣj* "bring down"	*shꜣ*	*shꜣ* (*shꜣy*)	*shꜣ*, *shꜣy*	*shꜣ(w)*, *shꜣy*	*shꜣ(w)*, *shꜣy*	*shꜣ(w)*
ANOM. *rdj* "give, put, cause"	*rdj*	*dj*	*dj*	*rdj* (*rdjw*, *rdy*)	*rdj* (*rdjw*, *rdy*)	*rdj(w)*, *dj(w)* (*rdy*, *dy*)
ANOM. *jwj/jj* "come"	*jj*, *jw*	*jw*, *jy*, *jj*	*jwt*	*jw* (*jwy*)	—	—

18 Literally, "has the hearing of a thief been ordered": *sḏm* is the infinitive, serving as the subject of the passive *wḏ*. The noun *rmṯ* "people" is sometimes treated as a collective (§ 4.6), and therefore feminine. The title *jmj-r šnt* "sheriff" means literally "overseer of disputes."

19 When there is more than one written form, the most common is listed first. Parentheses indicate an optional feature: thus, *ḏd(w)* means that the form can either be *ḏdw* or *ḏd*. Parentheses around an entire form means that it is rare. An asterisk marks forms that are special to particular verbs.

As you can see from this table, there are very few written forms that are used for only one of the six *sḏm.f* forms: these include the geminated 2-lit, 3-lit., and 4ae-inf. forms, which are used only for the prospective passive; the *–w* forms of 2-lit. and 3-lit. verbs, which are used only for the passive; the *–t* forms of the verbs *jnj* "fetch" and *jwj* "come" (*jnt, jwt*), which are used only for the subjunctive; the forms *djw* and *dy* of the verb *rdj* "give," which are used only for the passive; and the rare form *jwy* of the verb *jwj* "come," which is used only for the prospective. All the other written forms are used for at least two forms of the *sḏm.f*, and some can be used for all six.

Despite this drawback of the Egyptian writing system, however, Egyptologists have been able to identify the six forms of the *sḏm.f* by means of their paradigms (see § 7.12 end). The perfective and subjunctive, for example, look exactly alike in most classes, but the differences that exist in the 3ae-inf. verb *jnj* "fetch" (perfective *jn* vs. subjunctive *jnt*) and the anomalous verbs *rdj* "give" and *jwj/jj* "come" (perfective *rdj* vs. subjunctive *dj*, perfective *jj* or *jw* vs. subjunctive *jwt*) point to the existence of two distinct *sḏm.f* forms beneath the single written form of the other classes. The spoken language, of course, probably distinguished between all six forms of the *sḏm.f* in ways that are not reflected in writing: for example, by the use of different vowels or by differences in which syllable of the form was stressed, or both.

21.16 Meanings

Of course, the identification of the six *sḏm.f* forms also depends on their meaning. We have been able to identify the subjunctive as a distinct form, for example, not only by its distinctive written form in the 3ae-inf. verb *jnj* and the anomalous verbs but also by the fact that this distinctive form has a different meaning and use than the corresponding forms of the perfective. If it did not, we would have to conclude (as earlier Egyptologists did) that the perfective and subjunctive were only a single form, and that the three verbs *jnj*, *rdj*, and *jwj/jj* had two written representations of this form for reasons unknown, such as optional or dialectical differences in pronunciation.

Through careful study of Middle Egyptian texts, however, Egyptologists have been able to discover not only the six different paradigms but also the fact that these six paradigms do in fact correspond to consistent differences in meaning. This has been — and still is — an ongoing process of refinement in our understanding of Middle Egyptian. The prospective, for example, was first identified as a distinct form in the 1950s, and its full paradigm has been known only since 1979.

To help you remember the different meanings of the six *sḏm.f* forms, their basic values can be summarized as follows:

- PERFECTIVE — action; normally used with reference to past actions
- IMPERFECTIVE — imperfective action (incomplete, habitual, or ongoing); often present
- SUBJUNCTIVE — action viewed as contingent, possible, or desirable; often future
- PROSPECTIVE — action that has not yet happened; usually future
- PROSPECTIVE PASSIVE — passive counterpart of the prospective
- PASSIVE — completed action performed on its subject; normally perfect or past

Each of these meanings represents a mood (subjunctive) or an aspect, not a specific tense. As a result, all of the forms can be used with reference to past, present, or future actions even though they are normally associated with one or another of these tenses.

Except for the subjunctive, each of the six *sḏm.f* forms is indicative, expressing the action of the verb as a statement of fact. The other form of the suffix conjugation we have met, the perfect, is also indicative: it denotes completed action performed by its subject; the passive *sḏm.f* is the passive counterpart of this form. The six forms of the *sḏm.f*, as well as the perfect, all describe action. As such, they contrast with the stative, which basically denotes a state.

ESSAY 21. HISTORICAL TEXTS

The ancient Egyptians did not write history in the modern sense of the word: that is, as an objective recounting of past events. Many Egyptian texts do in fact record historical events, from those of national importance, such as military campaigns of the pharaohs, to the more personal texts in tombs and on stelae that recount significant events in the lives of their authors. But such texts normally were not written as an attempt to record or understand what happened in the past. When historical events are mentioned in texts, from the deeds of the pharaohs to official autobiographies, they are intended to demonstrate the exemplary behavior of their subjects.

In their biographical inscriptions officials usually record their material achievements, the successful completion of assignments, and their recognition by superiors or the king himself. These often sound vain or exaggerated to modern ears: for example,

> I am wealthy and well supplied with fine things: there is nothing I am missing in all my things. I am an owner of cattle, with many goats, an owner of donkeys, with many sheep. I am rich in barley and emmer, fine in clothing: there is nothing missing from all my wealth.
>
> I returned from the sea having done what His Incarnation had commanded, bringing for him every product I found on the shores of the god's land ... Never was the like of this done by any king's acquaintance sent on a mission since the time of the god.

The Egyptians themselves were somewhat aware of this tendency: occasionally biographies include statements such as "This is what I really did: there is no boasting and no lie in it."

Such autobiographies, however, were not written as egotistical memoirs. Their purpose is associated with a concept expressed by the Egyptian word *jm3ẖ*: they were meant to demonstrate that their author was *jm3ẖy*, an adjective meaning the same thing as the noun phrase *nb jm3ẖ* "possessor of *jm3ẖ*." The concept of *jm3ẖ* cannot be rendered easily by a single English word. It denotes a dependency relationship between two individuals in which the one who is *jm3ẖy* is worthy of the attention, respect, and care of the other. The relationship itself is expressed by means of the preposition *ẖr* "by, near." An official can be *jm3ẖy ẖr* "worthy of attention by" the king or a god; a wife can be *jm3ẖyt ẖr* "worthy of respect by" her husband. The possession of this quality entitled a person to be remembered by future generations and to receive the concrete expression of that remembrance in the form of funerary offerings at the tomb. Its acquisition was based on a person's behavior and accomplishments during life: this is what the autobiographies are meant to establish.

During the Old Kingdom most such autobiographies were inscribed on the walls of the tomb chapel, where they could be read by visitors; for this reason they are often called "tomb biographies." This practice continued after the Old Kingdom, but during the First Intermediate Period biographies were often inscribed on stelae instead, and most Middle Kingdom biographical texts are preserved on such stelae. These were erected not just at the tomb itself but in many cases at a private memorial chapel (called a "cenotaph") near the temple of Osiris in Abydos. Most of the Middle Kingdom stelae now in museums around the world come from these Abydos cenotaphs.

Closely related to the biographies in form and content, though not in intent, is the genre of graffiti. These were inscribed on cliff walls and rocks at various significant locations throughout Egypt. The most important groups of such graffiti are to be found in the ancient alabaster quarries at Hatnub, in Middle Egypt; in the Wadi Hammamat, a valley route through the desert from the Nile to the Red Sea, just north of Thebes; on granite boulders at Aswan, the southern border of ancient Egypt; and in several ancient mines and quarries in Nubia, south of Aswan. They record the visits of expeditions to and through these sites, and range from the simple names and titles of expedition members to longer texts describing the purpose of the expedition and extolling the accomplishments of its leaders.

Because they describe notable events in the lives of their authors, the biographical texts and graffiti are a primary source for our knowledge of Egyptian history. Often they provide the only record of historical events that are not mentioned, or have not survived, in official accounts. Even when they do reflect events known from other sources, they offer a valuable perspective on such events from the viewpoint of people who lived through or participated in them. The graffiti are particularly important in this respect. Those dating to the beginning of the Middle Kingdom tell us about the political and economic situation in Egypt during the period when the Theban Dynasties 11 and 12 were trying to regain control of the entire country after the divisions of the First Intermediate Period — struggles that are barely reflected in the official records of the kings themselves.

Like the biographies and graffiti of officials, the royal inscriptions that mention historical events were written not to record those events but to demonstrate the pharaoh's role in creating and preserving Maat (see Essay 10). One example of this purpose is the genre of texts describing the restoration of order. Often composed during a king's first year on the throne, these inscriptions contrast the chaotic situation that existed in the country before the king's accession with the peace and order established by the new regime. They reflect the Egyptian view of the accession as the equivalent of the creation, when the order of the world was first established after the chaos of the precreation universe (see Essays 9 and 11). The most famous example of this genre is the Restoration Stela of Tutankhamun, which describes that king's efforts to restore the traditional religious institutions of Egypt after the disruption of Akhenaten's reforms (see Essay 16).

Many royal historical texts deal with the king's military campaigns. These usually describe wars and battles in the countries surrounding Egypt — Asia Minor to the east, Libya to the west, and Nubia in the south — but in some cases they record struggles within Egypt itself, such as those of Dynasty 17 and early Dynasty 18 against the Hyksos domination of the north (see Essay 1). Such campaigns often occupied the king's first few years on the throne, when foreign powers were tempted to test the ability and resolve of the new pharaoh. Although they are often described as the king's efforts to  *swsḫ t3šw* "broaden the borders" of Egypt, these campaigns seem usually to have been motivated not by the desire for conquest but by the need to establish and maintain control over access to Egypt by foreign peoples. Many texts of this type come from Dynasty 18, when the pharaohs attempted to create a "buffer zone" of Egyptian influence in Asia Minor, as a hedge against the kind of immigration or invasion that had led to the Hyksos control of northern Egypt during the Second Intermediate Period. For similar reasons, the pharaohs of Dynasty 12 established a series of frontier forts along the river in northern Nubia, an accomplishment that is recorded in several royal stelae from these forts.

By far the most extensive military records come from the reign of the pharaoh Thutmose III of Dynasty 18. During the course of his 54-year reign (ca. 1479–1425 BC), Thutmose III conducted sixteen separate military campaigns, mostly in Asia Minor, at one point reaching the banks of the Euphrates River in Mesopotamia, where he set up a stela commemorating the achievement. Officials accompanying the pharaoh on these campaigns kept a kind of daily diary of events. Such records were probably kept in one form or another by all pharaohs, but almost none have survived. We know of Thutmose III's day book only because he eventually had it transcribed on the walls of the temple of Amun at Karnak. The text records each campaign in order, describing the pharaoh's progress and battles at various sites and ending with a list of tribute received as a result of each victory. One of its more abbreviated entries reads as follows:

> Year 30, when His Incarnation was in the mountain country of Retjenu on the sixth campaign of victory of His Incarnation. Arrival at the town of Qadesh, destroying it, cutting down its trees, plundering its grain. Proceeding past Rayat, arrival at the town of Tsumura, arrival at the town of Arad, doing the same to it. List of tribute brought to His Incarnation by the chiefs of Retjenu ...: children of the chiefs brought in this year: 36 men; male and female servants, 181; horses, 188; chariots wrought with gold and silver and painted, 40.

More often, the battle at each site is described in detail. Here again, however, the purpose of the inscription is not to record history but to demonstrate the pharaoh's fulfillment of his duty to defend Egypt. In fact, the important part of the text is not what we would regard as its historical accounts but the list of tribute, most of which was given to the temple of Amun.

Because such texts were not written as purely historical accounts, scholars need to be careful in using them to reconstruct ancient history. They give us only one side of the story, and even that in a way we would not always regard as accurate. The best example is Ramesses II's account of the battle at the Syrian town of Qadesh, which took place in his Year 5 (ca. 1274 BC). Camped outside the city in preparation for a siege, the king and his army were surprised and nearly annihilated by an attack of Hittite chariotry. Ramesses managed to survive and eventually fight the Hittites to a stalemate, but the battle is presented in Egyptian records as a great victory. In a sense it was, since it eventually led to a peace treaty between the Egypt and the Hittites — one of the first such treaties in recorded history. What was important to the Egyptians was not the historical reality of the battle itself, but the fact that it demonstrated once again the pharaoh's success in maintaining the order and harmony of Maat.

EXERCISE 21

Transliterate and translate the following sentences.

1. 
 — from Papyrus Westcar

2. 

3.  — *wḏt nbt ḥm.f* "all that His Incarnation commanded"

4. 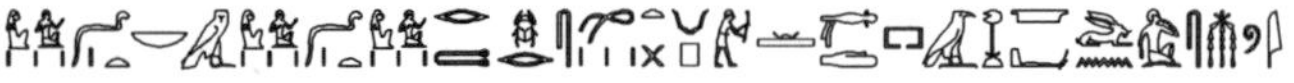

5. 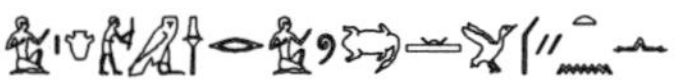

6. 

7.  — *j3dw* "Iadu" a region in the netherworld

8. 

9. 

10.  — *pḥ* "he who reaches," *st* and *jm* refer to the next life

11.  — *zpp zj* "when a man survives"

12. 

13. 

14. 

15.  — *wḥmw n wᶜrt mḥtt* "herald of the northern sector" (a representative of the king, stationed in northern Thebes)

16. 

17. 

18. 

19. 

20. 
 ... — description of a temple procession: *ḥwt-nbw* "enclosure of gold" (the shrine)

22. Other Forms of the Suffix Conjugation

22.1 Definitions

We have now met seven forms of the suffix conjugation: the perfect and the six forms of the *sḏm.f*. Besides these, the Middle Egyptian verbal system has another four forms that Egyptologists classify as belonging to the suffix conjugation. These generally occur less often than most of the seven forms we have already considered, but like the perfect they are relatively easy to identify. Unlike the perfect and the six *sḏm.f* forms, none of them has a common or self-evident name. Egyptologists refer to them by means of a hypothetical example based on the verb *sḏm* "hear," in the same way that the perfect is often called the *sḏm.n.f*.

Three of the forms are marked by a suffix, like the perfect: the *sḏm.jn.f*, with the suffix *jn*; the *sḏm.ḫr.f*, with the suffix *ḫr*; and the *sḏm.k3.f*, with the suffix *k3*. These biliteral suffixes behave exactly like the suffix *n* of the perfect (§ 18.2): they follow the verb stem itself, and precede any other suffixes. Because of their common feature of a biliteral suffix, we can refer to the *sḏm.jn.f*, *sḏm.ḫr.f*, and *sḏm.k3.f* collectively as the **biliteral suffixed forms**. The fourth form is marked by the ending *–t* attached directly to the verb stem; it is known as the *sḏmt.f* ("sedgem-TEFF"). This form can be used with passive as well as active meaning. The *sḏmt.f* with passive meaning has the same ending and often looks the same as the active; it is called — for obvious reasons — the passive *sḏmt.f*.

For the most part, the *sḏm.jn.f* and *sḏm.k3.f* express **subsequent or consequent action**: that is, action that happens after or as the result of another action. The *sḏm.jn.f* is normally past ("then he heard") but can be used for other tenses; the *sḏm.k3.f* is regularly used with reference to future events ("then he will hear"). The *sḏm.ḫr.f* expresses **necessary or normative action**; it can usually be translated with an English present tense using the auxiliaries *must* or *have to* ("he must hear, he has to hear"). Despite their usual associations with particular tenses, however, these three forms are not tenses in themselves: like the other forms of the suffix conjugation — and unlike English verb forms — they do not necessarily associate the verbal action with a particular point in time.

The *sḏmt.f* expresses **completed action**, like the perfect and the passive. Unlike the latter two forms, however, its use is very restricted in Middle Egyptian. In general, the *sḏmt.f* is complementary to the perfect and passive: it is used in constructions and with meanings that the perfect and passive are not.

THE *SḎM.JN.F*

22.2 Forms

Like the perfect, the *sḏm.jn.f* is easily recognized by its suffix, *jn* (𓇋𓈖 or 𓇋[hieroglyph]), which is added directly to the verb stem, before any other suffixes. The verb stem itself appears in the base stem in most classes. The following are typical examples of the *sḏm.jn.f* for the various verb classes in Middle Egyptian:

2-LIT.	 *ḏd.jn.f* "he said"
2AE-GEM.	 *m3.jn.f* "he saw," 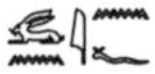 *wn.jn.f* "he was" — base stem
3-LIT.	 *ḥpt.jn* "embraced"
3AE-INF.	 *jᶜ.jn.sn* "they washed"
4-LIT.	 *hbhb.jn.k* "you knead"
CAUS. 2-LIT.	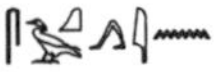 *sᶜq.jn* "introduced"
ANOM.	The verb *rdj* "give, put, allow" regularly uses the base stem *rdj*:  *rdj.jn.sn* "they put"; the base stem *dj* is much less common:  *dj.jn.f* "he put." The verb *jwj/jj* "come" normally uses the base stem *jw*:  *jw.jn* "came"; the base stem *jj* is rare:  *j.jn* "came."

As these examples illustrate, the suffix *jn* is always written **after** any determinative that the verb stem may have.

22.3 Subject and word order

The *sḏm.jn.f* follows the normal rules regarding its subject and the word order in its clause. It can be used with the suffix *tw* as the impersonal subject "one": for example,

 *jw.jn.ṯw r smj n ḥm.f*
"Then one came to report to His Incarnation."[1]

The same suffix is used to make **the passive form of the** *sḏm.jn.f*: for instance,

 *jn.jn.tw.f n.f ḥr ᶜ*
"Then it was fetched for him immediately."[2]

22.4 Meaning and use of the *sḏm.jn.f*

The *sḏm.jn.f* normally denotes past action that is **subsequent or consequent** to a preceding action or state, a notion that English expresses by means of the adverb *then* plus the past tense ("then he heard"): for example,

ḏd.jn ḥm.f ᶜnḫ.(w)-(w)ḏ3.(w)-s(nb.w) j.z(j) jn n.j sw
st3.jn.tw.f n.f ḥr ᶜwj
wn.jn.f ḥr ẖt.f m b3ḥ ᶜ ḥm.f ᶜnḫ.(w)-(w)ḏ3.(w)-s(nb.w)
"Then His Incarnation, lph, said: 'Go, get him for me.'
Then he was brought to him immediately.
Then he was on his belly before His Incarnation, lph."

1 The suffix *tw* is written *ṯw*: see § 2.8.3.
2 *ḥr ᶜ* (or dual *ḥr ᶜwj*) "upon the hand/hands" is a common idiom for "immediately": compare the English expression *at first hand*.

As these examples illustrate, the *sḏm.jn.f* is used exclusively in independent sentences (or main clauses) and is normally the first word in the sentence. It occurs most often in narration (as here), where its function seems to be to move the story from one event to the next. In this respect the *sḏm.jn.f* has much the same meaning as the introductory word  *ꜥḥꜥ.n* "then" plus a verbal or pseudoverbal predicate (§§ 15.6, 17.6, 18.9, 20.4, 21.11).

In most cases there seems to be little or no difference in meaning between the *sḏm.jn.f* and an *ꜥḥꜥ.n* construction. While both can denote subsequent action, however, the *sḏm.jn.f* sometimes has the extra connotation of consequence — action that results from a previous action or situation rather than one that simply follows. A good example of the difference is the first passage cited in Exercise 21, where *wn.jn* plus the SUBJECT-stative construction follows three sentences introduced by *ꜥḥꜥ.n*:

> *ꜥḥꜥ.n jn n.f smn wḏꜥ ḏꜣḏꜣ.f*
> *ꜥḥꜥ.n rdj pꜣ smn r gbꜣ jmntj n wꜣẖj ...*
> *ꜥḥꜥ.n ḏd.n ḏdj ḏdwt.f m ḥkꜣw*
> *wn.jn pꜣ smn ꜥḥꜥ.(w) ḥr ḥbꜣbꜣ*
> "Then a goose whose head had been severed was fetched for him.
> Then the goose was put on the west side of the columned hall ...
> Then Djedi said his sayings of magic.
> Then (as a result) the goose stood up waddling."

Each of these sentences describes an action that happened in sequence, one after the other. In the first three sentences, with *ꜥḥꜥ.n*, the action is simply sequential; in the fourth sentence, with *wn.jn*, however, the action is not only sequential but also the result of the preceding one.

The *sḏm.jn.f* of *wnn* "exist" is normally used not as a verb in its own right ("then he existed") but as a means of allowing another verb form or construction to function like the *sḏm.jn.f*. Examples can be seen in the two passages cited in this section, where *wn.jn* is used with an adverbial predicate and the SUBJECT-stative construction.

Constructions with *wn.jn* are actually one of the most common uses of the *sḏm.jn.f* form in Middle Egyptian. Most examples of the *sḏm.jn.f* in Middle Egyptian texts involve either a *wn.jn* construction or the *sḏm.jn.f* of the verb *ḏd* "say" followed by a direct quote (as in the first sentence cited in this section). For other verbs — and for *ḏd* when it is not followed by a direct quote — Middle Egyptian usually prefers a verb form introduced by *ꜥḥꜥ.n* (or *wn.jn*) rather than the *sḏm.jn.f* of the same verb: thus, in the passage cited just above, *ꜥḥꜥ.n jn*, *ꜥḥꜥ.n rdj*, *ꜥḥꜥ.n ḏd.n*, and *wn.jn pꜣ smn ꜥḥꜥ.(w)* rather than *jn.jn.tw*, *rdj.jn.tw*, *ḏd.jn*, and *ꜥḥꜥ.jn*.

Although it is most often used in contexts that require a past tense in the English translation, the *sḏm.jn.f* itself is tenseless. As a result, it can also express subsequent or consequent action in nonpast contexts: for example,

>  *jr ẖꜣ.k z(j) ḥr mn r jb.f, rdj.jn.k ḏrt.k ḥr.f*
> "If you examine a man suffering in his stomach, and you put your hand on it."[3]

Most examples of this use occur in particular medical texts, such as the one cited here.

3 The verb *ẖꜣj* "examine" is abbreviated 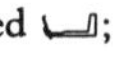; for the first clause, see § 15.10.2.

THE *SḎM.ḪR.F*

22.5 Forms

The *sḏm.ḫr.f* is distinguished by the suffix  *ḫr*, which is added directly to the verb stem, before any other suffixes. The verb stem is generally the same as that of the *sḏm.jn.f*. The following are typical examples of this form in Middle Egyptian:

2-LIT.	 *ḏd.ḫr.k* "you have to say"
2AE-GEM.	 *m33.ḫr.k* "you have to see" — geminated stem. The verb *wnn* "exist" normally uses the base stem:  *wn.ḫr* "has to be"; the geminated stem is common in New Kingdom texts:  *wnn.ḫr* "has to be."
3-LIT.	 *tnm.ḫr.f* "he must be going astray"
3AE-INF.	 *jr.ḫr.k* "you have to make"
4-LIT.	 *h3h3.ḫr.tw* "one has to winnow"
4AE-INF.	 *nḏr.ḫr.k* "you have to fasten"
CAUS. 2-LIT.	 *smn.ḫr.tw* "one has to set"
CAUS. 2AE-GEM.	 *sšmm.ḫr.k* "you have to heat" — geminated stem
CAUS. 3-LIT.	 *srwḫ.ḫr.k* "you have to treat"
ANOM.	The verb *rdj* "give, put, allow" uses the base stem *rdj*:  *rdj.ḫr.k* "you have to put." The verb *jwj/jj* "come" uses the base stem *jw*: 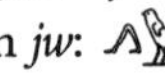 *jw.ḫr* "had to come."

As with the suffixes of the perfect and the *sḏm.jn.f*, the suffix of the *sḏm.ḫr.f* is written after any determinatives that the verb may have.

22.6 Subject and word order

As a form of the suffix conjugation, the *sḏm.ḫr.f* follows the normal rules regarding its subject and the word order in its clause. The *sḏm.ḫr.f* can be used with the suffix *tw* as the impersonal subject "one": for example,

 *ḏd.ḫr.t(w) n.f j.nḏ ḥr.k* "One has to say to him: Hail!"[4]

The same suffix is used to make **the passive form of the** *sḏm.ḫr.f*: for instance,

 *rdj.ḫr.t(w).f ḥr gs.f wꜥ* "He has to be put on his one side."

22.7 Meaning and use of the *sḏm.ḫr.f*

The *sḏm.ḫr.f* is the ancestor of two constructions we have already met: *ḫr sḏm.f*, with the subjunctive (§ 19.6.2), and *ḫr.f sḏm.f*, with the imperfective (§ 20.9.1). The two younger constructions have replaced the *sḏm.ḫr.f* in standard Middle Egyptian, but religious and scientific texts seem to prefer the older verb form, and it shows up occasionally in other Middle Kingdom texts as well.

4 For *j.nḏ ḥr.k* "hail!" see § 16.8.2.

Like the *sḏm.jn.f*, the *sḏm.ḫr.f* is usually the first word in its clause, and is used in main clauses or independent sentences. The *sḏm.ḫr.f* basically expresses **necessary action**, like the *ḫr.f sḏm.f* construction, and can generally be translated in English with the expressions "must" or "have to" before the verb itself: for example,

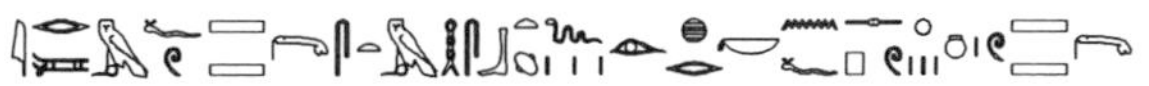

jr tm.f wšš st m ḥsbwt, jr.ḫr.k n.f zpw nw wšš
"If he doesn't excrete them as worms, you have to make for him concoctions for excretion."[5]

Like the *ḫr sḏm.f* construction, the *sḏm.ḫr.f* can also denote the inevitable (i.e., necessary) result of some action or situation: for instance,

 *jr swrj.f mw, stp.ḫr.f* "If he drinks water, he inevitably gags."

In such cases the *sḏm.ḫr.f* is often better translated by the English present tense (as in this example) than by the English "must" or "have to" constructions. The same translation is usually appropriate in cases where the *sḏm.ḫr.f* denotes **normative action** — that is, action that is normally (and thus necessarily) true: for example,

jr r.f m tr n mšrw pnꜥ.ḫr.f jrt.f r rꜥ, ḫpr.ḫr ꜥḥꜥw m jzwt
"So, at the time of evening, he inevitably overturns his eye against Re, and a stoppage inevitably happens in the crew (of the sun-boat)."[6]

Although it can usually be translated by an English present-tense construction, the *sḏm.ḫr.f* itself is actually tenseless. For that reason it can also be used with reference to past or future actions: for instance,

wn.j wšd.j ḥmwt ḥr.s, sbqw(j) ntj m bj(ꜣ) pn, ḏd.ḫr.sn jw mfkꜣt m ḏw r nḥḥ
"I kept addressing the craftsmen about it (with the words) 'How precious is what is in this mine!' and they inevitably said: 'Turquoise is in the mountain forever.' "[7]

nḥm.k wj m ꜥ nṯrwj jpwj ꜥꜣwj ... ḏd.ḫr.sn ꜥꜣwj sw
"May you save me from those two great gods ... and they will have to say: 'How great is he!.' "[8]

In these examples the tense is set by the verb form or construction in the first clause, and this in turn influences the tense of the *sḏm.ḫr.f* form: *wn.j wšd.j ... ḏd.ḫr.sn* "I was addressing ... and they inevitably said," *nḥm.k wj ... ḏd.ḫr.sn* "May you save me ... and they will have to say."

5 For the construction in the first clause, see § 19.11.3.
6 From a description of the sun's nightly journey. The one who "overturns his eye against Re" is the serpent who seeks to stop the progress of the sun-boat. The first clause means literally, "so, as for in the time of evening."
7 The first clause contains the perfective of *wnn* followed by the imperfective *wšd.j*: see § 20.16.1. *ḥmwt* "craftsmen" is a collective (§ 4.6).
8 *jpwj* is an archaic dual form of the demonstrative pronoun *pw* (cf. § 5.10.2).

The *sḏm.ḫr.f* of the verb *wnn* "exist" is normally used not as a verb in its own right (e.g., "he has to exist," "he inevitably exists") but as a means of allowing other verb forms and constructions to function like the *sḏm.ḫr.f*. In the following sentence, for example, it imparts the meaning of the *sḏm.ḫr.f* to a pseudoverbal predicate (in the first clause) and the SUBJECT-stative construction (in the second clause):

wn.ḫr.f ḥr sjn ḥʿ(w).f jm, wn.ḫr ḥʿw.f w3d.(w) mj wʿ jm.sn nb

"He has to be rubbing his body with it, and his body is inevitably freshened like every one of them."[9]

Such uses occur mostly in Middle Kingdom texts; by the time of the New Kingdom, *wn.ḫr* often seems to be little more than a stylistic variant of *wn.jn* (see §§ 15.6, 17.6).

THE *SḎM.K3.F*

22.8 Forms

The *sḏm.k3.f* is distinguished by the suffix *k3*, which is added directly to the verb stem, before any other suffixes. The suffix is regularly written , with two uniliteral signs, and not with the biliteral sign *k3*. The verb stem itself is generally the same as that of the *sḏm.jn.f* and *sḏm.ḫr.f*. The following are typical examples of this form in Middle Egyptian:

2-LIT.	*ḏd.k3* "will say"
2AE-GEM.	*wn.k3* "will be" — base stem (no other 2ae-gem. verbs are attested in the *sḏm.k3.f* form)
3-LIT.	*ʿḥʿ.k3.k* "you will stand up"
3AE-INF.	*gm.k3.k* "you will find"
4-LIT.	*wnwn.k3* "will move about"
4AE-INF.	*ḥms.k3* "will sit down"
CAUS. 2-LIT.	*sḥḏ.k3.k* "you will brighten"
CAUS. 3-LIT.	*swḏ3.k3.t(w)* "will be made sound"
ANOM.	The verb *rdj* "give, put, cause" uses the base stem *rdj*: *rdj.k3.t(w)* "will be put," *rdj.k3.j* "I will cause." The verb *jwj/jj* "come" uses the base stem *jw*: *jw.k3.f* "he will come."

As with the suffixes of the perfect and the *sḏm.jn.f* and *sḏm.ḫr.f*, the suffix of the *sḏm.k3.f* is written after any determinatives that the verb may have.

9 This text has several unusual spellings, including the writing of the suffix of the *sḏm.ḫr.f* with a bookroll determinative and the *d*-sign spelling out the final radical of *w3d* "become fresh" (a variant form of the verb *w3ḏ*: see § 2.8.3). For *wʿ jm.sn* "one of them," see § 9.4; *nb* "every" modifies *wʿ*, even though it is placed after the prepositional phrase *jm.sn*.

22.9 Subject and word order

As a form of the suffix conjugation, the *sḏm.k3.f* follows the normal rules regarding its subject and the word order in its clause. The suffix *tw* is used to make **the passive form of the *sḏm.k3.f***: for example,

 *nḥm.k3.t(w) stpwt ḥr ḫ3wt nṯrw*
"The choice cuts of beef will be taken off the gods' altars."

22.10 Meaning and use of the *sḏm.k3.f*

The *sḏm.k3.f* is the ancestor of two constructions we have already met: *k3 sḏm.f*, with the subjunctive (§ 19.6.3), and *k3.f sḏm.f*, with the imperfective (§ 20.9.2). These two younger constructions have replaced the *sḏm.k3.f* in standard Middle Egyptian. The older form is mostly limited to religious texts and a few royal inscriptions that use archaic language, but it sometimes appears in other Middle Egyptian texts as well.

Like the *sḏm.jn.f* and *sḏm.ḫr.f*, the *sḏm.k3.f* is almost always the first word in its clause. It basically expresses **future consequence**, like the *k3 sḏm.f* construction. In most cases it is used in the apodosis of a conditional sentence (see § 19.7): for example,

 *jr gm.k nṯrw ḥms.y, ḥms.k3.k r.k ḥnʿ.sn*
"If you find the gods seated, you shall sit down with them."[10]

Less often the *sḏm.k3.f* expresses **subsequent action**, like the *k3.f sḏm.f* construction: for instance,

jṯ.k š(j)wj dmdwj, ʿḥʿ.k3.k r.k ḥr wʿrt tw wrt ḫntt jzkn
"You shall take possession of the two united lakes, and then you shall come to stand on that great desert flank that is in front of *jzkn*."[11]

The *sḏm.k3.f* always seems to refer to future action. Nevertheless, it is probably tenseless, like the other forms of the suffix conjugation, denoting merely consequence or subsequent action rather than the future tense specifically.

The negative counterpart of the *sḏm.k3.f* can be expressed by means of the *sḏm.k3.f* of the negative verb *tm* plus the negatival complement: for example,

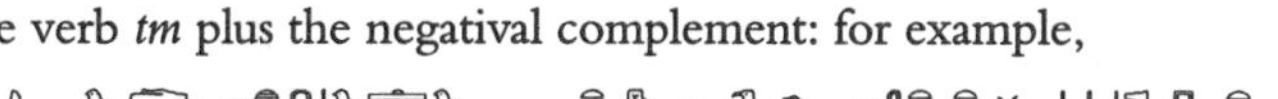
jr wdf ḫt(m) wḏ pw … tm.k3 ʿq stpwt r nmt-nṯr
"If the sealing of this decree is delayed …
choice cuts of beef will not enter the god's slaughterhouse."

Usually, however, it is expressed by the future negation *nn sḏm.f*, with the subjunctive, or the older future negation *nj sḏm.f*, with the subjunctive or prospective (see § 21.5). Thus, a different version of the text just cited has 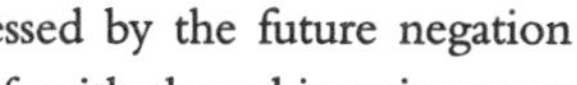 *nj ʿq stpwt r nmt-nṯr* "choice cuts of beef and fowl will not enter the god's slaughterhouse," with the prospective negation *nj ʿq*.

10 For *r.k* see § 16.7.2.

11 *jṯ.k* "you shall take possession" is a subjunctive; *dmdwj* "united" is a verb form we will meet in the next lesson. The "two united lakes" refers to the day and night sky (see Essay 2). *jzkn* is a region of the eastern sky near the horizon. The passage as a whole refers to the deceased's identification with the sun in its daily cycle.

22.11 The suffixed forms of the suffix conjugation

As we saw in § 21.15, the six forms of the *sḏm.f* are distinguished by differences in the verb stem itself or by means of an ending, or both. In contrast to these, the *sḏm.jn.f*, *sḏm.ḫr.f*, *sḏm.k3.f*, and the perfect (*sḏm.n.f*) are distinguished primarily by means of a suffix. The shape of the verb stem itself is therefore of less importance in these four forms. As it turns out, the four suffixed forms generally use the same verb stem. In most classes this is the base stem (§§ 18.2, 22.2, 22.5, 22.8), although the classes with geminated roots (2ae-gem., 3ae-gem., and caus. 2ae-gem.) generally use the geminated stem, as far as they are attested at all.

The major differences between the four suffixed forms in terms of their verb stem occur in the 2ae-gem. verbs *m33* "see" and *wnn* "exist, be" and the anom. verbs *rdj* "give, put cause" and *jwj/jj* "come." These can be summarized as follows:

m33 "see"	base stem in the perfect and *sḏm.jn.f*: *m3.n.j*, *m3.jn.f* geminated stem in the perfect (rare) and *sḏm.ḫr.f*: *m33.n.k*, *m33.ḫr.k*
wnn "exist, be"	base stem in most forms: *wn.jn.f*, *wn.ḫr*, *wn.k3* (no perfect: § 20.16.2) geminated stem in the *sḏm.ḫr.f*: *wnn.ḫr* (New Kingdom texts)
rdj "give, put, cause"	base stem *rdj* in all forms: *rdj.n.j*, *rdj.jn.sn*, *rdj.ḫr.k*, *rdj.k3.j* base stem *dj* also in the perfect and *sḏm.jn.f*: *dj.n.j*, *dj.jn.f*
jwj/jj "come"	base stem *jw* in most forms: *jw.n.n* (rare), *jw.jn*, *jw.ḫr*, *jw.k3.f* base stem *jj* in the perfect: *jj.n.sn* — rare in the *sḏm.jn.f*: *jj.jn*.

As you can see from this list, Middle Egyptian is generally consistent in the verb stem it uses for the four suffixed forms. There are only a few cases in which a suffixed form appears with more than one verb stem: these include the perfect of 2ae-gem. verbs (base and geminated stems), the *sḏm.ḫr.f* of *wnn*, and the perfect and *sḏm.jn.f* of *rdj* and *jwj/jj*.

No one has yet discovered why this duplication occurs. In some cases it is apparently chronological. Thus, the *sḏm.ḫr.f* of *wnn* usually appears with the base stem in Middle Kingdom texts and the geminated stem in New Kingdom sources; similarly, some New Kingdom copies of Middle Kingdom texts also use a geminated form of the perfect of *m33* (*m33.n.f*) rather than the normal Middle Egyptian form with the base stem (*m3.n.f*). This and the other instances of duplicate stems could also reflect different dialects, in the same way that English dialects sometimes vary between verb forms (for example, *dove* and *dived* as the past tense of the verb *dive*). In any case, for those suffixed forms that do have more than one verb stem there is no perceptible difference in meaning between the two stems.

THE *SḎMT.F*

22.12 Forms

The *sḏmt.f* is distinguished by the ending *t*, which is added directly to the verb stem. This feature is identified as an ending rather than a suffix because it is normally written as part of the verb stem itself, before any determinatives, unlike the suffixes *n*, *jn*, *ḫr*, and *k3*. The *sḏmt.f* has the following forms in Middle Egyptian:

2-LIT. — *rḫt.f* "he knew"

2AE-GEM. — *ꜥnnt* "were tied up" — geminated stem. The verb *wnn* uses the base stem: *wnt* "was"; *mꜣꜣ* has the form *mꜣnt* "saw."

3-LIT. — *sḏmt* "heard"

3AE-INF. — *jrt.j* "I made." The final radical *j* can be written as a double reed-leaf — usually in the passive *sḏmt.f* but rarely also in the active: *jryt* "was made" *hꜣyt.ṯn* "you have gone down."

4AE-INF. — *ḥmst.j* "I sat down"

CAUS. 2-LIT. — *srdt.k* "you have caused to grow"

CAUS. 3-LIT. — *snḫnt.j* "I reared"

CAUS. 5-LIT. — *snḫḫt.j* "I caused to mature" (root *snḫjḫj*)

ANOM. — The verb *jwj/jj* "come" normally uses the stem *jj*, but examples with the stem *jw* also occur: *jt*, *jyt* "came," *jjt.f* "it came," *jwt.n* "we have returned." The verb *rdj* "give, put, allow" does not seem to be attested in the *sḏmt.f* form.

The active and passive *sḏmt.f* usually look alike except in the 3ae-inf. class, where the passive normally has a double reed-leaf before the ending *–t*. The ending *–t* is sometimes written as *–tw*, to show that it was pronounced (see Essay 17): for example, *sḏmtw.j* "I have heard" (for *sḏmt.j*). Only rarely is it omitted, but this can happen when the verb stem ends in *t* or *d*: *wtt* "were begotten" (probably for **wVttVt* or **wVtVttV*),[12] *rd* "grew" (perhaps for **rVdtV*).

22.13 The *sḏmt.f* negated

The most common use of the *sḏmt.f* in Middle Egyptian is after the negative particle *nj*. The construction *nj sḏmt.f* is normally used in adverb clauses, where it has the meaning "before he heard," "before he has heard," or "before he had heard": for example,

ḫpr rn.k, nj msyt r(m)ṯ, nj ḫprt nṯrw
"Your identity evolved before people were born, before the gods evolved"

or "before people had been born, before the gods had evolved." Such adverb clauses are usually unmarked, as in this example. Rarely, however, they can be marked by *jsṯ*: for instance,

jnk wꜥ m nw n fnṯw qmꜣw.n jrt nb-wꜥ, jsṯ nj ḫprt jst
"I am one of those worms that the Sole Lord's Eye created even before Isis evolved."[13]

Besides its adverbial function, *nj sḏmt.f* can also be used in relative clauses. In this case the construction usually has to be translated as "not yet" with an English perfect tense ("he has/had not yet heard"). The following is an example in a marked relative clause:

12 The root is 3-lit. *wtt*, originally *wtṯ*.
13 *qmꜣw.n* is a verb form we will meet in Lesson 24.

 *m w3 ntt nj jjt* "Don't brood over what has not yet come."[14]

The *nj sḏmt.f* construction has the same meaning in unmarked relative clauses: for instance,

 *jw.f mj z(j) nj kmt.f bsw*
"He is like a man who has not yet completed emerging."

Like other unmarked relative clauses, this use of *nj sḏmt.f* occurs after an undefined antecedent, as in this example.

22.14 The *sḏmt.f* after prepositions

Besides the negation *nj sḏmt.f*, the *sḏmt.f* is also used as the object of a few prepositions in Middle Egyptian. The most common of these is the preposition *r* "with respect to." The construction *r sḏmt.f* means "until he has/had heard" or "until he heard": for example,

m.k tw r jrt 3bd ḥr 3bd r kmt.k 3bd 4 m ẖnw n jw pn
"Look, you are to spend month upon month until you have completed 4 months in the interior of this island."

Less often the *sḏmt.f* is used after the preposition *ḏr* "since." The construction *ḏr sḏmt.f* means "since he has/had heard" or "since he heard": for instance,

 *ḏd rn.j, jn z3ṯw, ḏr ẖndt.k ḥr.j*
"'Say my name,' says the ground, 'since you have stepped on me.' "[15]

The preposition *ḏr* with the *sḏmt.f* normally means "since" in the sense of "because," as in this example, rather than "since the time of."

The *sḏmt.f* does not seem to be used after other prepositions. With rare exceptions, possible examples of such a use have been found only for verbs of classes that have an infinitive with the ending –*t* (see § 14.3), and are therefore probably the infinitive rather than the *sḏmt.f*: for instance,

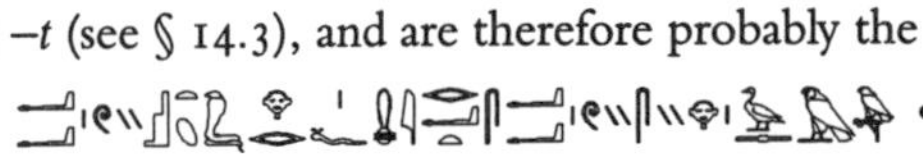 *ʿwj jst ḥr.f mj rdjt.s ʿwj.sj ḥr z3.s ḥrw*
"Isis's hands are on him, like she puts her hands on her son Horus,"

literally, "like her putting her hands on her son Horus" (see § 14.5.2).

22.15 The *sḏmt.f* of *wnn*

Like that of other verbs, the *sḏmt.f* of the 2ae-gem. verb *wnn* "exist" is used most often in the negation *nj wnt*. Unlike the normal *nj sḏmt.f* construction, however, *nj wnt* does not seem to be used with the meaning "before" or "not yet." Instead, it regularly expresses the nonexistence of its subject, like *nn* and *nn wn* (§§ 11.4, 20.16.3): for example,

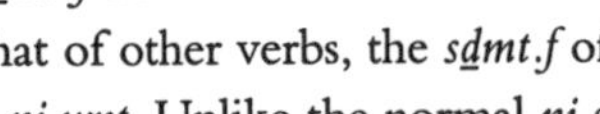 *nj wnt js[w n] ʿwn jb* "There is no tomb for the greedy."

There seems to be little difference in meaning between *nj wnt* and the other two negations: compare *nn jz n sbj* "There is no tomb for the rebel" (§ 10.7) and *nn wn jz n ʿwn jb* "There is no tomb for the greedy" (§ 20.16.3). While the negation with *nn* alone can be used in main and dependent

14 The subject of *jjt* is not expressed because it is clear from the context: literally, "that which (it) has not yet come."
15 *jn* "says" is discussed later in this lesson.

clauses and the negation *nn wn* occurs mostly in main clauses, however, *nj wnt* usually appears in dependent clauses in Middle Egyptian. These are most often unmarked adverbial clauses or unmarked relative clauses (after an undefined antecedent): for example,

jr gm.k qs.f wḏ3.(w), nj wnt pšn thm jm.f

"If you find his bone sound, with no split or perforation in it"

 *smr wᶜ, nj wnt snw.f* "a unique courtier without equal."

literally, "there existing no split or perforation in it" and "there existing no second of his." As the three examples cited here demonstrate, *nj wnt* is regularly used with a nominal subject.

The negation *nj wnt* also has a noun-clause counterpart, with the negative word  *jwt* "that not" in place of *nj*: for example,

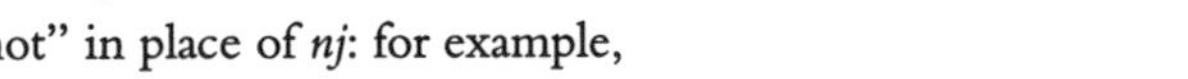

jw.k rḫ.t(j) jwt wnt.(j) mm j3tjw

"You know that I am not among the mound-dwellers,"

In this case the important part of the noun clause is not the verb *wnt* itself but the prepositional phrase that accompanies it. The noun clause does not deny the existence of the subject itself, but the subject's existence in the situation specified by the prepositional phrase (see § 11.4).

The *sḏmt.f* of *wnn* can also serve as the object of a preposition, like the *sḏmt.f* of other verbs. Here too *wnt* has a slightly different meaning than the normal *sḏmt.f*. The construction *r wnt.f* means "until he is" rather than "until he has existed": for example,

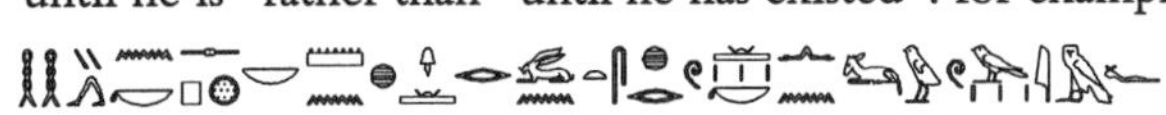

ḥ(j)ḥj n.k zp nb mnḫ r wnt sḫrw.k nn jww jm.f

"Seek out for yourself every worthwhile deed, until your conduct is without wrong."[16]

In most such cases, *wnt* is not used as a verb in its own right but as a means for some other predicate to function as a *sḏmt.f*. In the following sentence, for instance, it allows the SUBJECT-stative construction to function like a *sḏmt.f* after the preposition *ḏr* "since":

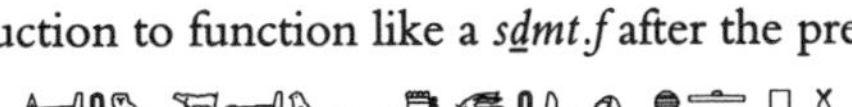

dj n.ṯ s(j) m ḫnw ᶜwj.ṯ, ḏr wnt.s j.t(j) 3ḫ.t(j) ᶜpr.t(j)

"Put her inside your arms, since she has come, effective and equipped."

This "colorless" use of *wnt* is the origin of the word *wnt* "that," which we have already met as a marker of noun clauses (§§ 15.11, 17.11).

22.16 The meaning of the *sḏmt.f*

The *sḏmt.f* seems basically to express the action of the verb as completed. This is easiest to see in the construction *ḏr sḏmt.f* "since he has heard" but it is true of the other two main uses of the *sḏmt.f* as well. Thus, the construction *r sḏmt.f* means something like "up to (the point of) his completing hearing," and *nj sḏmt.f* can be understood as "he has not yet completed hearing." Even

16 Literally, "until your conduct exists, no wrong being in it." For the first clause, see Exercise 21, no. 12.

though it is translated differently, the *sḏmt.f* of *wnn* may also have the same basic meaning: for example, a statement such as *nj wnt jsw n ꜥwn jb* "A tomb for the greedy has not yet existed" is the same as saying "There is no tomb for the greedy."

As we have already seen, Middle Egyptian also uses the perfect to express completed action. Both forms are used in the same kinds of constructions, but mostly with different meanings: the negated perfect does not have the "before" or "not yet" meaning of the negated *sḏmt.f*, and the *sḏmt.f* rather than the perfect is the normal form after the prepositions *r* "until" and *ḏr* "since."

It has been suggested that the *sḏmt.f* is an older form than the perfect, and may once have been the regular means by which Egyptian expressed completed action. If so, that stage of the language predates the first written texts, since already in Old Egyptian the *sḏmt.f* has much the same role it has in Middle Egyptian. Historically, however, the perfect could have replaced many of the original functions of the *sḏmt.f*, in much the same way that the newer pseudoverbal construction has taken over some of the functions of the older prospective. In fact, we can occasionally see traces of such a process of replacement still happening in Middle Egyptian — for example, when a text uses the perfect rather than the *sḏmt.f* after the preposition *r* "until":

 *r ẖpr.n z3.s m nẖt-ꜥ* "until her son had come of age."[17]

Such uses are rare, however. For the most part, the *sḏmt.f* has only a few very specific functions in Middle Egyptian, and those functions are almost exclusively limited to the *sḏmt.f*.

The Parenthetics

22.17 Definition

The speech of someone that is quoted within a text is known as a "direct quotation." In English such direct quotations are common features of stories and novels, where they are usually set off from the rest of the text by quotation marks. The speaker of the direct quotation is introduced by a word such as *said*: for example,

> "I can't make head or tail of this," said Dr. Livesey,

where the words "I can't make head or tail of this" are the direct quotation and "Dr. Livesey" is the speaker.[18]

Since hieroglyphic writing has no quotation marks, it relies on other means to mark a direct quotation. In Middle Egyptian narratives, direct quotations are most often introduced by the words *ḏd.jn* or *ꜥḥꜥ.n ḏd.n* "then said" followed by the name of the speaker or by a noun or pronoun referring to the speaker (see the first example in § 22.4, above). Occasionally, however, Middle Egyptian puts the reference to the speaker **after** the direct quotation (or after its first few words). In that case the speaker is introduced not by a form of the verb *ḏd* "say" but by one of three special words that are used only for this particular function. These introductory words are known as "**parenthetics**."[19]

17 Literally, "had become as one forceful of arm" — i.e., able to take care of himself.

18 This example is taken from the novel *Treasure Island*, by Robert Louis Stevenson.

19 Referring to the term *parenthesis*, which Webster's Dictionary defines as "A word, phrase, or sentence, by way of comment or explanation, inserted in, or attached to, a sentence grammatically complete without it."

22.18 Forms

The three Middle Egyptian parenthetics, in their most common form, are 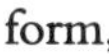 *jn*,  *ḫr*, and  or  *k3*. The last of these appears only in one form (*k3*) and may be identical with the particle *k3*, which we have already met (§§ 16.6.15, 19.6.3, 20.9.2, 21.6). The other two look like the prepositions *jn* and *ḫr* (§§ 8.2.2, 8.2.13) but they sometimes have slightly different forms, which point to a different origin.

The parenthetic *jn* is occasionally spelled , , , or . This is actually the 3ms stative of an old verb *j* "say," which is used only as a parenthetic, followed by the preposition *jn*: i.e., *j.(w) jn*. When the speaker is feminine, the 3fs form  *j.t(j) jn* can be used. In addition, the normal form  can be followed by the 3pl pronoun  *sn*. In this case,  is probably the perfect *j.n.sn* rather than the prepositional phrase *jn.sn*, since the preposition *jn* is not used with personal pronouns (§ 8.2.2). The parenthetic *jn* thus has the following forms in Middle Egyptian:

	*jn* NOUN: for example,  *jn r*ᶜ "says Re"
 (etc.)	*j.(w) jn* NOUN: for example,  *j.(w) jn wsjr* "says Osiris"
	*j.t(j) jn* NOUN: for example,  *j.t(j) jn jmnt* "says the West"
	*j.n.sn*: for example,  *j.n.sn* "they say"
	j.n.sn NOUN: for example,  *j.n.sn nṯrw* "say they, the gods."

The first and last of these are the most common. The form  NOUN may represent the perfect *j.n* with a nominal subject, but it could also derive from the stative constructions *j.(w) jn* NOUN and *j.t(j) jn* NOUN with the stative omitted.

The parenthetic *ḫr* occasionally has the fuller spellings , , or , like the noun *ḫrw* "voice," to which it may be related. It is always used with a suffix pronoun, sometimes followed by a noun, or with the impersonal pronoun *tw*: for example,

 *ḫr.f* "he says"

 *ḫr.sn nṯrw* "say they, the gods"

 *ḫr.tw* "they say" (literally, "says one").

Sometimes *ḫr* appears in the form  or  *ḫr.fj*. This is always followed by a dependent pronoun, a dependent pronoun with a following noun, or a noun: for instance,

 *ḫr.fj sw* "said he,"  *ḫr.fj st* "said they"

 *ḫr.fj sn nṯrw* "say they, the gods"

 *ḫr.fj ḏḥwtj* "says Thoth."

The parenthetic *k3* always seems to be used with a suffix pronoun, without a following noun, or with the impersonal pronoun *tw*: for example,

 *k3.k* "you shall say"

 k3.tw "one will say."

22.19 Meaning and use of the parenthetics

All three parenthetics correspond to the English verb *say* in its parenthetic use, and are usually translated by a form of this verb. The parenthetics *jn* and *ẖr* can be either present or past ("says," "said"); *k3* seems to be exclusively future ("will say").

The parenthetics are only used with a direct quotation. They either follow the entire quotation or are inserted near its beginning, but they never precede it. An example of *jn* inside a direct quotation has already been cited in § 22.14, above. Examples with *ẖr* and *k3* are:

m.k ḏd.n n.j (j)m(j) r ḥwt-nṯr ttj, m.k rdj.n.j wḏ3 jb.f r.s gr, ẖr.fj sw

"Look, the temple-overseer Teti said to me: 'Look, I have also informed him about it,' he said"[20]

k3 h3b.k n.j ḥr.s, nj jn.tw m db(3)w jrj, k3.k n.j ḥr.s gr

"Then you shall send (word) to me about it. 'Nothing has been brought as replacement for them,' you shall say to me about it also."[21]

In Middle Egyptian the parenthetic *jn* seems to be limited to religious texts, but it becomes quite common again in Late Egyptian in the form  *j.n.f* "he said." The parenthetics *ẖr* and *k3* occur throughout Middle Egyptian.

You may have noticed the similarity between the three parenthetics and the suffixes of the *sḏm.jn.f*, *sḏm.ẖr.f*, and *sḏm.k3.f*. On the basis of form and meaning there can be little doubt that the parenthetic *k3* and the *sḏm.k3.f* are related, and that both are related in turn to the particle *k3*. In fact, the parenthetic can be regarded as a use of the *sḏm.k3.f* or the *k3.f sḏm.f* construction with the verb *ḏd* "say" left unexpressed: i.e., *k3.k* "you shall say" = *(ḏd).k3.k* or *k3.k (ḏd.k)*. In this respect the parenthetic *k3* is comparable to the preposition *ḥr* used for *ḥr (ḏd)* "saying" (§ 15.7).

The relationship between the suffixed forms and the other two parenthetics is less certain. Although the parenthetics *jn* and *ẖr* are often spelled like the suffixes of the *sḏm.jn.f* and *sḏm.ẖr.f*, they are probably not related to those suffixes. Parenthetic *jn* comes either from the perfect of the old verb *j* "say" (*j.n*) or from the related construction *j.(w)/j.t(j) jn* with the stative omitted, and parenthetic *ẖr* seems to be derived from the noun *ẖrw* "voice," but there is no evidence that the verbal suffixes *jn* and *ẖr* have the same origins. Moreover, the parenthetic *ẖr* does not have the necessary or normative connotation of the *sḏm.ẖr.f*.

20 Literally, "I have caused his heart to become sound with respect to it also." For *gr* "also," see § 8.12.

21 For *k3 h3b.k* see § 19.6.3. *nj jn.tw m db(3)w jrj* means literally "one has not brought as replacement thereunto," with the negated perfective (§ 20.5); *jrj* is a prepositional adverb (§ 8.15).

ESSAY 22. RELIGIOUS TEXTS

Throughout these lessons we have seen many forms and constructions of Middle Egyptian grammar qualified with the remarks "found mostly in religious texts" or "limited to religious texts." Such forms and constructions usually represent holdovers from an earlier stage of the language, which have been replaced by different forms and constructions in other kinds of Middle Egyptian texts. We should not be surprised at this kind of linguistic conservatism. The same phenomenon exists in our own culture, which still uses archaic forms such as *thou art* in hymns and prayers.

Religious texts are a major part of Egyptian literarature for a number of reasons, not least because religion itself was an important factor of everyday life (see Essay 4). Secular texts were usually written on papyrus, and most have perished along with the libraries, homes, and offices in which they were stored. Religious texts, however, were often inscribed in more permanent media, such as tomb walls or stone stelae; even those written on papyrus or wood were often deliberately buried, and so have survived in greater numbers than their secular counterparts.

Ancient Egyptian religious texts generally fall into one of two categories: funerary and devotional. The latter includes primarily hymns and prayers, which will be discussed in Essay 23; the former is the subject of the present essay.

Funerary texts are the oldest and most extensively preserved of all ancient Egyptian literary genres. They begin with the **Pyramid Texts** of the Old Kingdom, a collection of rituals and magical texts first inscribed on the walls of the burial chamber and other rooms and corridors inside royal pyramids of the 5th and 6th Dynasties. Egyptologists refer to the individual texts as spells or "utterances" (from the term *ḏd-mdw*, with which most of them begin: see § 14.9). Altogether nearly a thousand spells of the Pyramid Texts are known, ranging in length from a few words to several pages in a modern translation. Despite their great number, they all belong to one of three general categories.

Offering spells are texts that were recited during the presentation of individual offerings. In these the deceased is generally addressed as "Osiris" and the offering itself, which is mentioned at the end of the spell, is referred to as the "Eye of Horus." Such spells are usually quite short, and they often contain a "pun" on the name of the offering itself: for example,

 *wsjr WNJS m-n.k jrt ḥr(w), nj šꜥ.s jr.k | šꜥt 2*

"Osiris UNIS, take to you the Eye of Horus: it cannot be cut from you. Cut-bread, 2."

The Offering Ritual began with a series of spells designed to 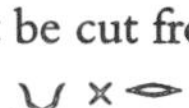 *wpt r* "open the mouth" of the deceased, so that the mummy could magically recover the senses and physical powers it had during life, before the offerings themselves were presented.

The Resurrection Ritual is a series of longer texts, also recited to the deceased. Beginning with the words "You have not gone away dead, you have gone away alive," they were intended to release the ba from its attachment to the mummy so that it could begin its daily cycle of rebirth in the world of the living (see Essay 8). These texts, along with the Offering Ritual, were usually inscribed in the burial chamber itself, on the walls surrounding the sarcophagus containing the mummy.

The remaining spells of the Pyramid Texts line the walls of the other rooms and corridors of the royal tomb. These were meant to be spoken by the deceased's ba as it made its way through the night toward its rebirth at dawn, and they gave it the magical words and instructions it needed to pass safely through the dangers along its way. Originally composed in the first person, these "personal" spells were often edited into the third person for each tomb, substituting the name of the deceased for the original first-person pronouns.

Although the Pyramid Texts were inscribed only in royal tombs during the Old Kingdom, the texts themselves were probably used for nonroyal burials as well. Scenes from the tombs of officials often show the same kinds of rituals being performed that are reflected in the Pyramid Texts. In place of the Offering Ritual such tombs regularly have an "offering list," in which the names of the individual offerings and their amounts are laid out in a series of rectangles. Although the offering spells are not included, these charts show the same offerings mentioned in the Offering Ritual of the Pyramid Texts, and usually in the same order.

During the First Intermediate Period, officials began to have the Resurrection Ritual and some of the personal spells from the Pyramid Texts inscribed on the walls of their own burial chambers and coffins. These older spells are often accompanied by new personal spells of the same type. Because they are most often inscribed on coffins, these newer funerary texts are known as **Coffin Texts**. There are nearly twelve hundred individual spells of the Coffin Texts. Most of them are personal spells, in the first person. Like those of the Pyramid Texts, they were meant to give the deceased's ba the means to pass safely from the tomb to its new life as an akh. Most of the Coffin Texts are written in an early form of Middle Egyptian, and they give us a good understanding of the beginnings of this stage of the Egyptian language.

The Coffin Texts also contain a new type of funerary text, known as the "Netherworld Guides." These provide a description of various places in the Duat (see Essay 2), along with the words that the ba needs to pass safely through them. The most elaborate of these guides is known as the **Book of Two Ways**, and is usually illustrated by a map of the regions described.

During the Second Intermediate Period, the funerary texts began to be separated into several distinct compositions. The most important of these is known as the **Book of the Dead**. This is a modern name: the ancient Egyptians themselves called it 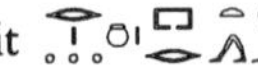 *rw nw prt m hrw* "Spells of coming forth by day." Most copies of the Book of the Dead contain a hundred or so spells of the personal type (also called "chapters"), including some descended from spells of the Pyramid Texts and Coffin Texts. The Book of the Dead was generally written in cursive hieroglyphs (§ 1.9) on papyrus, accompanied by illustrations (called "vignettes").

The two most important texts of the Book of the Dead were the spells now given the numbers 17 and 125. Spell 17 was entitled  *prt m hrw* "Coming forth by day," a name it gave to the Book of the Dead as a whole. A descendant of Spell 335 of the Coffin Texts, it deals with the sun-god, Re, and his nightly reunion with Osiris, the principle of new life. This spell was so important that in most copies its clauses and sentences are interspersed with explanatory texts (known as "glosses") describing what the text means: for example,

> I am the great god who evolved by himself.
>
> *Who is he? He is Nun, the father of the gods. Another explanation: he is Re.*

Spell 125 deals with the final judgment, in which the heart of the deceased is weighed against a feather, symbol of Maat (see Essay 8). Judging the weighing are 42 gods seated on either side of a hall. The central text of the spell is the "Negative Confession," in which the deceased addresses each of the judges in turn with a specific denial of wrongdoing during life: for example,

> Oh, Shadow-Swallower who comes from Qernet: I have not killed people.

The end of the judgment (which is always successful) is a vignette showing the deceased being formally transferred by Horus, king of the living, to the jurisdiction of Osiris, king of the dead.

The Book of Two Ways of the Coffin Texts gave rise to several similar Netherworld Guides, most of which are inscribed in the royal tombs of the New Kingdom and Ramesside Period. These include the composition Egyptologists call the **Amduat** (from the Egyptian *jmj dw3t* "he who is in the Duat") and several texts dividing the netherworld into twelve separate sections (for the hours of the night), such as the **Book of Gates** and the **Book of Caverns**. Although these first appear in the New Kingdom, they are written in Middle Egyptian.

From the earlier ritual texts is descended the New Kingdom composition known as the **Mouth-Opening Ritual**. Inscribed mostly in private and royal tombs of the New Kingdom, it contains 75 separate "scenes" or "acts," in which priests "open the mouth" of a statue of the deceased and provide it with various offerings. A number of its texts are direct descendants of original spells in the Pyramid Texts.

Besides their tendency to use older grammatical forms, the funerary texts have a number of other features in common. The original Pyramid Texts, and most of the New Kingdom texts other than the Book of the Dead, are written in hieroglyphs, either carved or (in the New Kingdom) painted on tomb walls. The Coffin Texts and Book of the Dead were mostly written in cursive hieroglyphs, or sometimes hieratic, on papyrus or wood coffins. All of the funerary texts tend to be written in vertical columns of text rather than in horizontal lines. In some cases these texts are arranged retrograde, meaning that the signs face the end of the text rather than its beginning (see § 1.6).

In some copies of the Pyramid Texts and Coffin Texts, signs of dangerous beings such as snakes were occasionally mutilated to prevent them from harming the occupant of the tomb: for example, the  snake is sometimes cut in two (). During a short time from the end of the Dynasty 12 and into Dynasty 13, this practice was extended to all signs of living beings in copies of the Coffin Texts. Such signs, known as "mutilated hieroglyphs," show only a part of the whole, usually just the upper portion of the body. The following is an example of such an inscription:

j dbn jmj swḥt.f, sḏ3.k wj mj sḏ3t.k tw ḏs.k

"Oh, encircled one who is in his egg! May you transport me like you transport yourself."[22]

Although this practice was short-lived, New Kingdom funerary texts still occasionally "kill" dangerous signs by means of a stroke or a knife (e.g., ,).

22 *dbn* is a verb form we will meet in the next lesson. *sḏ3t.k* is an infinitive: literally, "like your transporting yourself."

EXERCISE 22

Transliterate and translate the following sentences.

1. 
2. 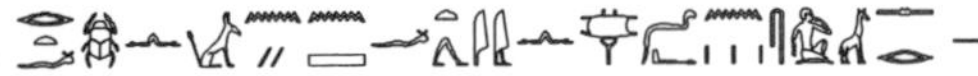 — *sr.sn* "they could predict" (imperfective)
3. 
4. 
5.  — *ḏdtj.tn* "what you might say"
6. 
7. 
8. 
9.   — *ḫ3j* () "examine," *wt* "bandage"
10. 
11. 
12. 
13. 
14.  — *wšd* impersonal passive (subject not expressed)
15. 
16. 
17. 
18. 
    Chapter 6 of the Book of the Dead: *jpn* for *pn*; the English letter *N* stands for the name of the deceased; *jrrwt jm* "that is done"
19. 
20. 

23. The Participles

23.1 Definitions

When we were first introduced to relative clauses in Lesson 12, we learned that they are clauses that are used like adjectives (§ 12.2). In subsequent lessons we have seen that many verb forms can be used in such clauses — not only when the clauses are marked by means of an introductory word such as *ntj* in Egyptian or *who* in English but also when they are unmarked and their relative function is indicated only by virtue of the context in which they occur. These clauses represent just one use of a particular verb form. In most cases the verb form used in a relative clause can serve as the predicate in a main clause, noun clause, or adverb clause as well.

Participles are verb forms that are specifically designed to serve as adjectives. English has two such forms, usually known as the present participle (e.g., *burning*) and the past participle (e.g., *burnt, melted, frozen*). Like other adjectives, both of these can be used to modify nouns, as in *a burning log* and *burnt toast*. Because participles are verb forms that serve as adjectives, they are equivalent to relative clauses: thus, the phrases *a burning log* and *burnt toast* can also be expressed as *a log that is burning* and *toast that has been burnt*. In fact, **participles are simply concise ways of expressing a relative clause in a single word**.

Despite their names, the English present and past participles actually express aspects rather than specific tenses: the present participle denotes ongoing action and the past participle refers to completed action. Because they do not express a specific tense, they can be used with reference to any tense: for example, in the sentence *Jack extinguished the burning log*, the present participle *burning* refers to a past action; similarly, the past participle *burnt* denotes an action that lies in the future in the sentence *Tomorrow the cook will serve burnt toast.*

The two English participles also express different voices. The present participle is active, describing an action performed **by** the noun it modifies: thus, in the phrase *a burning log*, the log is doing the burning. The past participle of intransitive verbs is also active: in a phrase such as *a grown boy*, the boy has done the growing. The past participle of transitive verbs is passive. It describes an action done **to** the noun it modifies: for example, in the phrase *burnt toast*, the participle *burnt* denotes something that has been done to the toast.

Middle Egyptian has five participles. One of them refers exclusively to action that is yet to happen, and can be called the **prospective participle**. The other four are distinguished by features of aspect (perfective or imperfective) and voice (active or passive), and are called the **perfective active**, the **imperfective active**, the **perfective passive**, and the **imperfective passive** participles. The active participles describe action done by someone or something; the passive participles, action done to someone or something. The aspectual feature is the same as in the perfective and imperfective *sḏm.f* (§ 20.1): the perfective participles simply describe action, without any indication of tense or aspect, while the imperfective participles denote action that is in some way repeated, ongoing, or incomplete.

23.2 Gender and number

All five Middle Egyptian participles can be used to modify a preceding noun. Since they are adjectives, they normally agree with the noun they modify. Like other Egyptian adjectives, the participles have three basic forms — masculine singular, masculine plural, and feminine (§ 6.2) — which are marked by means of gender and number endings: for example,

MASCULINE SINGULAR	*z3 mr* "the loving son"
MASCULINE PLURAL	*z3w mrw* "loving sons"
FEMININE	*z3t mrt* "the loving daughter"
	z3wt mrt "loving daughters."[1]

Like other adjectives, the participles used with a plural noun can be written with plural strokes, but they are just as often found without them: thus, in addition to the plural forms shown above, we also find writings such as  *z3w mrw* "loving sons" and  *z3wt mrt* "loving daughters." Like other adjectives, too, the participles eventually lost all but the masculine singular form, so we can also find writings such as  *z3w mr* "loving sons" and  *z3wt mr* "loving daughters" in Middle Egyptian texts.

This way of marking agreement applies to the perfective and imperfective participles. The prospective participle also agrees with the noun it modifies, but it uses a different way of marking that agreement, by means of suffix pronouns rather than the normal gender and number endings:

MASCULINE SINGULAR	*.f* or *.fj* — written  or 
FEMININE SINGULAR	*.s* or *.sj* — written , , or , ; rarely 
PLURAL	*.sn* — written , , , or .

These are nothing more than the regular third-person suffix pronouns (§ 5.3). The extra ending *–j* in the singular forms is the same as that which is occasionally added to these pronouns when they are used with dual nouns (§ 5.7). It appears in the prospective participle because this participle always has the ending *–tj* added to the verb stem (which makes it look like a feminine dual); we will see examples in § 23.8, below.

23.3 Basic translations

When the participles modify nouns, they can sometimes be translated by an English participle, as in the example *z3 mr* "the loving son" from the preceding section, where the Egyptian participle *mr* is translated by the English participle "loving." Because of the differences between Egyptian and English grammar, however, such direct, one-to-one translations are often impossible. In the similar phrase  *wp(w)tj ḫdd(j)* "the messenger who used to go north," for example, the participle *ḫdd(j)* has to be translated with a relative clause because English does not allow a construction such as *"the used to go north messenger." Translations with a relative clause are possible because participles are simply concise ways of expressing such clauses in a single word. In fact, most Egyptian participles are usually best translated as relative clauses.

1 The last was originally *z3wt mrwt*, but the feminine plural form seems to be obsolete in Middle Egyptian: see the discussion in § 6.2.

Like most other Egyptian adjectives, the participles can also be used by themselves as nouns, without modifying a preceding noun (see § 6.4). In this function they usually have to be translated by a relative clause, since English does not normally allow its participles to serve as nouns: for example, *mr* "the one who loves," *ḫddj* "the one who used to go north." Sometimes an Egyptian participle used as a noun can be translated with a kind of word that grammarians call the "noun of agent."[2] This is a noun that refers to someone or something that performs an action: for instance, *mr* "lover." Egyptian also has nouns of agent: for example, *sḏmw* "hearer." Such nouns sometimes look like participles that are used as nouns: thus, the word used by itself could either be the participle *sḏm* "one who hears" or the noun of agent *sḏm(w)* "hearer." In the course of this lesson we will learn ways to distinguish the various participles from other words that are not participles, as well as from one another.

Depending on how they are used, therefore, the Egyptian participles can be translated in three different ways:

- by an English **participle**: for example, *z3 mr* "the loving son"
- by a **relative clause**: for example, *z3 mr* "the son who loves," *mr* "the one who loves"
- by a **noun of agent**: for example, *mr* "lover."

In some cases, more than one of these translations is possible: for example, *z3 mr* "the loving son" or "the son who loves." Often, however, the way in which a participle is used allows for only one of the three translations in English, as we will see in the course of this lesson.

23.4 Forms: the verb stem

The prospective participle is usually easy to recognize because it has a distinctive ending (*–tj*) and uses the third-person suffix pronouns to mark gender and number. We will examine the form of this participle in detail in § 23.8, below.

The perfective and imperfective participles were undoubtedly distinguished from each other in the spoken language, but the Egyptian writing system usually does not reflect such distinctions. Nevertheless, hieroglyphs do show some differences in the verb stem or endings of these participles, which sometimes allow us to distinguish between the two forms.

In some verb classes the perfective and imperfective participles can be distinguished by the verb stem they use. As a general rule, the classes with geminated or final-weak roots (2ae-gem. and 3ae-gem., 3ae-inf. and 4ae-inf., and their causatives), as well as the anom. verb *rdj* "give, put, cause," use the **base stem for the perfective participles** and the **geminated stem for the imperfective participles**: for example, perfective *mr* "loving" (active) and *mr* "loved" (passive) vs. imperfective *mrr(j)* "loving" (active) and *mrr(w)* "loved" (passive), from the 3ae-inf. verb *mrj* "love." In addition, the class of 2-lit. verbs sometimes uses the geminated stem for the **perfective passive** participle, though it regularly uses the base stem for all four forms: for instance, *ḏd* "speaking" (perfective active), *ḏd(j)* "speaking" (imperfective active), *ḏd(w)* "spoken" (perfective and imperfective passive), but also *ḏdj* "spoken" (perfective passive).

2 Some grammars use the Latin term *nomen agentis*, meaning "noun of agent" (plural *nomina agentis* "nouns of agent").

23.5 Forms: stem endings

In all verb classes the perfective and imperfective participles are distinguished by their endings as well. Besides the regular endings that mark gender and number, Middle Egyptian also uses five different sets of stem endings for the participles. Four of these are used for the perfective and imperfective forms, and the fifth is used for the geminated perfective passive participles of 2-lit. verbs. They can be summarized as follows, using the "strong" verb 𓆓𓂧 *ḏd* "speak" (2-lit.) and the "weak" verb 𓌸𓂋𓀁 *mrj* "love" (3ae-inf.) as examples.

1. **perfective active** — no special ending other than those of gender and number: for example,

MASCULINE SINGULAR	*ḏd* "who speaks"
	mr "who loves"
MASCULINE PLURAL	*ḏdw* "who speak"
	mrw "who love"
FEMININE	*ḏdt* "who speaks, who speak"
	mrt "who loves, who love."

2. **imperfective active** — all verbs have the ending *–j* (𓏭) or *–y* (𓇌) in the masculine forms, no special ending in the feminine: for example,

MASCULINE SINGULAR	*ḏdj, ḏdy* "who speaks"
	mrrj, mrry "who loves"
MASCULINE PLURAL	*ḏdjw, ḏdyw* "who speak"
	mrrjw, mrryw "who love"
FEMININE	*ḏdt* "who speaks, who speak"
	mrrt "who loves, who love."

3. **perfective passive** — strong verbs have the ending *–w* (𓅱, 𓏲), rarely *–y* (𓇌), in the masculine singular and no special ending in the masculine plural or feminine; weak verbs have the ending *–y* (𓇌) in all forms: for example,

MASCULINE SINGULAR	*ḏdw* "which is spoken," rarely *ḏdy*
	mry "who is loved"
MASCULINE PLURAL	*ḏdw* "which are spoken"
	mryw "who are loved"
FEMININE	*ḏdt* "which is/are spoken"
	mryt "who is/are loved."

4. **imperfective passive** — all verbs have the ending *–w* (𓅱, 𓏲) in the masculine singular and no special ending in the masculine plural or feminine: for example,

MASCULINE SINGULAR	*ḏdw* "which is spoken"
	mrrw "who is loved"
MASCULINE PLURAL	*ḏdw* "which are spoken"
	mrrw "who are loved"
FEMININE	*ḏdt* "which is/are spoken"
	mrrt "who is/are loved."

5. **geminated perfective passive**, 2–lit. verbs — the masculine forms have the ending *–j* (𓏭); the feminine has no special ending: for example,

MASCULINE SINGULAR	*ḏdḏj* "which is spoken"
MASCULINE PLURAL	*ḏdḏjw* "which are spoken"
FEMININE	*ḏdḏt* "which is/are spoken."

As you can see from these tables, the stem ending, when there is one, is either *–j*, *–y*, or *–w*. The following chart can be used as another guide to help you remember which participial forms these endings are used with:

	ACTIVE PERFECTIVE	ACTIVE IMPERFECTIVE	PASSIVE PERFECTIVE	PASSIVE IMPERFECTIVE
–j (𓏭)	—	ms/mpl	ms/mpl (2-lit. gem.)	—
–y (𓇌)	—	ms/mpl	ms/mpl/f (weak verbs) ms (strong verbs, rare)	—
–w (𓅱, 𓏲)	—	—	ms (strong verbs)	ms.

All of these stem endings are "weak" consonants (§ 2.8.2). As a result, they are unfortunately often omitted in writing: *–j* appears almost exclusively in masçuline singular forms; *–y* is most often found in the perfective passive participles, less commonly in the imperfective active forms; and *–w* usually occurs in the imperfective passive forms, less often in the perfective forms.

When a participle is written without a stem ending it is often impossible to know for certain which form it is. The masculine singular form 𓆓𓂧, for example, could represent any of four different participles: perfective active *ḏd*, imperfective active *ḏd(j)*, perfective passive *ḏd(w)*, or imperfective passive *ḏd(w)*. For this reason, Egyptologists normally do not supply the missing endings, and transcribe a form such as 𓆓𓂧 simply as *ḏd*.

Even when they are written, it is important to remember which stem endings are used with which participles. Egyptian nouns of agent can also have the endings *–w* or *–y*. In the expression *z3 sḏmw* "a son who listens," for example, the word *sḏmw* must be such a noun and not an active participle, because the masculine singular active participles do not end in *–w*: even though we translate *sḏmw* in this expression as a participle ("who listens"), the literal translation is actually "a son, a listener." Similarly, in the expression *sdyt qs* "bone-breaker," the word *sdyt* (from 2-lit. *sd* "break") must be a noun of agent rather than an active participle, since the feminine active participles do not have the stem ending *–y*.

Sound changes can also affect the way a participle is written, particularly in texts written after the Middle Kingdom. New Kingdom scribes sometimes added the ending 𓏲 (rarely 𓅱) to masculine singular participles, probably to indicate that they ended in a vowel (see Essay 17): for example, *sm3mw* "that kills" (for imperfective *sm3j*), *rdjw* "who put" (for perfective *rdj*). In some 3ae-inf. verbs the middle radical *3* became *y* in pronunciation, and later spellings of such verbs can reflect this sound change: for instance, *h3yt* "what has descended" (for perfective *h3t*). Taken by themselves, these three words could also be verbal nouns, but the constructions they are used in indicate that they are participles, despite their unusual endings.

23.6 Forms: the active participles

The following table shows typical examples of the active participles for the various verb classes as they appear in Middle Egyptian texts:

2-LIT.	PERFECTIVE	*ḏd* "who speaks"
	IMPERFECTIVE	*ꜥqt* "that enters," *rḫyw* "who know." Rarely prefixed, mostly in the expression *j.ḫm(j)-sk(jw)* "imperishable (star)" — literally, "who does not know destruction."
2AE-GEM.	PERFECTIVE	*m3w* "who saw," *wnt* "that which was"
	IMPERFECTIVE	*m33(j)* "who sees," *wnnyw* "who exist"
3-LIT.	PERFECTIVE	*šꜥd* "who cut off"
	IMPERFECTIVE	*ḏꜥr(j)* "that seeks," *ꜥḥ3y* "that fights"
3AE-INF.	PERFECTIVE	*prt* "that emerged"
	IMPERFECTIVE	*prrt* "that emerges," *ḫddj* "that goes north"
4AE-INF.	PERFECTIVE	*msḏ* "who hates"
	IMPERFECTIVE	*msḏḏ(j)w*, *msddyw* "who hate," *ḫnt(j)* "who used to go south," *ḥmsyw* "who sit"
CAUS. 2-LIT.	PERFECTIVE	*smn* "who fixed"
	IMPERFECTIVE	*sꜥqyw* "those who introduce"
CAUS. 2AE-GEM.	IMPERFECTIVE	*sgnn(j)* "who softens." This class does not seem to have an ungeminated form.
CAUS. 3-LIT.	PERFECTIVE	*sḫpr* "who brings about"
	IMPERFECTIVE	*stwt(j)* "he who reconciles"
CAUS. 3AE-INF.	PERFECTIVE	*sqd* "who sailed"
	IMPERFECTIVE	*sqdd(j)* "who sails," *sjddy* "who quells"
CAUS. 4AE-INF.	PERFECTIVE	*sb3q* "who brightened"
	IMPERFECTIVE	*sḫnt(j)w* "who promote"
ANOM.	PERFECTIVE	*rdj*, rarely , *dj* "who gave, who put"; , , *jj*, *jy* "who comes"[3]
	IMPERFECTIVE	, , *dd(j)* "who gives, who used to give"; *jwy* "who comes"

3 The final *-j* or *-y* of *jj/jy* is part of the stem of this verb, not an ending.

23.7 Forms: the passive participles

The following table shows typical examples of the passive participles for the various verb classes as they appear in Middle Egyptian texts:

2-LIT.	PERFECTIVE	*ḏdt* "said," *ḏdw* "said"; *ḏddt* "what has been said," *ḏddj* "said"
	IMPERFECTIVE	*ḏdt* "what is said"
2AE-GEM.	PERFECTIVE	*m3* "seen"
	IMPERFECTIVE	*m33*, *m33w* "seen"
3-LIT.	PERFECTIVE	*h3b* "sent," *njsw* "the one who has been summoned," *h3by* "sent"
	IMPERFECTIVE	*zftw* "slaughtered"
3AE-INF.	PERFECTIVE	*ms* "born," *jry* "made," *jryt* "what has been made"
	IMPERFECTIVE	*jrr* "that are done," *jrrw* "done"
4AE-INF.	PERFECTIVE	*ꜥw3* "he who was robbed"
	IMPERFECTIVE	*msddt* "the one who is hated"
CAUS. 2-LIT.	PERFECTIVE	*swḏt* "what has been bequeathed"
CAUS. 3AE-INF.	PERFECTIVE	*sḫ3yt* "what has been recalled"
	IMPERFECTIVE	*sqddt* "sailed"
CAUS. 4AE-INF.	PERFECTIVE	*sḫnty* "promoted"
ANOM.	PERFECTIVE	*rdy*, *rdj*, *dy*, *dj* "given," *dy* "put"
	IMPERFECTIVE	*ddw* "put," *ddt* "what is put"

The stem of the active and passive participles of the 3ae-inf. verb *jrj* "make, do" is normally spelled *jr* in the perfective and *jrr* in the imperfective, but a few texts use the spelling for the perfective *jr* and for the imperfective *jrr*. Only a few 4ae-inf. verbs use the geminated stem in the imperfective participles, active and passive.

Except for the geminated 2-lit. forms, the active and passive participles use the same pattern of base and geminated stems. The stem endings are therefore an important clue as to whether a particular participle is active or passive. Since the endings themselves are frequently omitted in writing, however, we often have to depend on the context to distinguish active from passive forms.

23.8 Forms: the prospective participle

The prospective participle is a single verb form, almost always active in meaning. It has three parts: the verb stem, the stem ending *–tj*, and the suffix pronouns that are used to mark gender and number agreement. We have already met the suffix pronouns earlier in this lesson (§ 23.2). The stem ending *–tj* is normally spelled or , less often ; in plural forms it sometimes appears as or , where the plural strokes are simply a determinative. In Old Egyptian the stem ending was *–wtj* rather than *–tj* for final-weak verbs, verbs with more than three radicals, and causatives; this older ending is still occasionally found in Middle Egyptian.

The following table shows typical examples of the prospective participle for the various verb classes in Middle Egyptian:

2-LIT.	*ꜥqt(j).sn* "who shall enter."
2AE-GEM.	*m33t(j).sn* "who shall see," *wnntj.sj* "which will be."
3-LIT.	*sḏmtj.sn* "those who will hear."
3AE-INF.	*mkt(j).sn* "who shall protect." Occasionally with the stem ending *–wtj*: *h3wt(j).f* "who shall go down."
4AE-INF.	*sw3t(j).sn* "who shall pass."
CAUS. 2-LIT.	*sḫ3t(j).fj* "one who shall remember."
ANOM.	, *rdjt(j).f* "who will give." *jwt(j).sn* "who will come."

The verb stem is the same as that which is used for the prospective active *sḏm.f* (§ 21.2.1), and it is probable that these two verb forms are related.

Even though they are suffixes rather than endings, the pronouns that are used to mark the gender and number of the prospective participle are a normal part of this form.[4] Sometimes, however, the participle appears without a suffix pronoun, just as the verb forms of the suffix conjugation can occasionally be used without an expressed subject. In such cases the stem ending is normally spelled out, as 𓏏𓏭 or 𓇌. Such forms usually occur when the participle is used by itself, as a noun referring to a general state of affairs rather than to a specific person or thing: for example, *ḫprtj* "what would happen," *ḏdtj* "what should be spoken."

23.9 Syntax of the participles

Participles can be used like other adjectives, as single words that either modify a noun or stand by themselves as nouns: i.e.,

z3 nfr "the good son"	*nfr* "the good one"
z3 mr "the loving son"	*mr* "the loving one"
z3 mry "the beloved son"	*mry* "the beloved one"
z3 mrtj.fj "the son who will love"	*mrtj.fj* "the one who will love."

Egyptian adjectives themselves, in fact, are nothing more than active participles of adjective-verbs: thus, the adjective *nfr* "good, the one who is good" is an active participle of the verb *nfr* "become good, be good," just as the participle *mr* "loving, the one who loves" is an active participle of the verb *mrj* "love." Because you are already well acquainted with adjectives, you already know a good deal about how participles work.

Participles, however, are more than simple one-word adjectives. They are also verb forms, and like other verb forms they can be used as the predicate in a clause of their own, with the same kinds of objects, datives, adverbs, and dependent clauses that accompany other verb forms. Unlike

4 Because of its distinctive form, the prospective participle is also known as the *sḏmtj.fj* (sedgem-TEE-fee).

other kinds of clauses with a verbal predicate, however, participial clauses do not have a separate subject. This is because the participle contains in itself both the verb and its subject. To see how this is so, look at the following two pairs of clauses:

MAIN CLAUSE, ACTIVE	*wbn rʿ m pt*	"The sun rises in the sky"
PARTICIPIAL CLAUSE, ACTIVE	*wbn m pt*	"he who rises in the sky"
MAIN CLAUSE, PASSIVE	*m33.tw rʿ m pt*	"The sun is seen in the sky"
PARTICIPIAL CLAUSE, PASSIVE	*m33 m pt*	"he who is seen in the sky."

As these examples demonstrate, the only differences between the main clause and the participial clause are the form of the verb and the presence or absence of a separate subject.

The rules of word order that govern other verbal clauses (§§ 14.6, 18.4) also govern participial clauses: for example,

dd(j) n.f st "the one who gives it to him" (**Vdo**)

dd(j) n.f j3w "the one who gives him praise" (**VdO**)

dd(j) ṯn ḥr 3ḫt "the one who puts you on land" (**VoA**)

dd(j) sn.f m t3 "the one who puts his brother in the ground" (**VOA**).

Like other verb forms, participles can also govern dependent clauses of their own, such as noun clauses and adverb clauses: for instance,

dd(j) jr.s bw bjn "the one who makes her do evil"

jt(j)w mwwt wnnyw ḥnʿ.j jst wj m nw
"the fathers and mothers who existed with me when I was in the Primeval Waters."[5]

In the first example, the participle *dd(j)* governs a noun clause with the subjunctive *jr.s* (§ 19.10): literally, "the one who gives that she do badness." In the second example, the participial phrase *wnnyw ḥnʿ.j* "who existed with me" is followed by a marked adverb clause describing when the action of the participle took place.

Besides the fact that they do not have a separate subject, participial clauses can also differ from other kinds of verbal clauses in one other respect: when a participle is used by itself, as a noun, it can be modified by the adjective *nb* "all, each, every, any," like other nouns: for example, *jrrt nbt* "all that is done," with the passive participle — literally, "every(thing) done." When the participial clause has other elements, such as a dative, object, or prepositional phrase, *nb* tends to come as close to the participle as possible, although a pronominal dative or object can come before *nb*: for example,

wjnt(j).f nb p3 ʿqw "anyone who will reject these rations"[6]

jrt(j).f n.s nb "anyone who will act for her,"

literally, "any one-who-will-reject these rations" and "any one-who-will-do (something) for her."

5 For *nw* "Primeval Waters," see Essay 11.

6 The stem ending of *wjnt(j).f* is written twice, once before the determinative and once after it.

23.10 Meaning of the participles

The **prospective participle** is normally associated with action that is yet to happen, like the prospective *sḏm.f* (§ 21.4). In most cases, this means that the prospective participle is translated by the future tense in English, as the examples cited in §§ 23.8–23.9 demonstrate. Like the prospective, however, the prospective participle is not specifically future. It can also be used to refer to action that has already occurred but had yet to happen at some point in the past: for example,

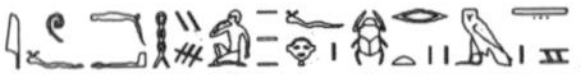 *jw.f mḥj.f ḥr ḫprtj m tꜣ*
"He was thinking about what would happen in the land."[7]

Because this sentence comes from a narrative of past events ("he was thinking"), English requires us to translate the participle *ḫprtj* (§ 23.8 end) as "what would happen" rather than "what will happen." In another context this same sentence could be translated "He is thinking about what will happen in the land" (see § 20.8).

The **perfective participles** simply describe action without any indication of tense or aspect, like the perfective *sḏm.f*. They are the most common of the participles, and can be used with reference to any tense: for example,

 *msw.s … mꜣw ḥr n ḫntj nj ʿnḫt.sn*
"her children … who saw the face of the Butcher before they lived" (past)

 *mꜣt mꜣt šdt ḫwt m kkw*
"the lioness who sees and takes things in the dark" (generic present)

 *nn ꜣyt ḥr n mꜣ ḥr.k*
"The face of him who might see your face will not blanch" (future).

Because the participles in these examples are translated with a relative clause, English requires us to choose a specific tense. The participles themselves, however, are tenseless, like the English present participle. You can see this by using a different translation, with the English participle instead of a relative clause: "her children … seeing the face of the Butcher before they lived," "the lioness seeing and taking things in the dark," "the face of the one seeing your face."

The **imperfective participles** are also tenseless, but unlike the perfective participles they carry the extra connotation of incomplete, ongoing, or repeated action. In most cases, they are used to describe habitual or customary actions: for example,

 *nfrt nbt jnnt n ḥm n nb.j*
"every good thing that was brought to the incarnation of my lord" (past)

 *mj jrrt n nṯr* "like that which is done for a god" (present)

 *rḫ jrrt n ḥbsyt nt z(j)*
"What should be done for the wife of a man is known" (future).

Here again, translation with an English participle shows the tenseless nature of these forms: "every good thing brought to the incarnation of my lord," "like that done for a god," "that done for the wife of a man is known."

7 The spelling of *mḥj* "think" is influenced by the nouns *mḥ* "cubit" (§ 9.7.1) and *mḥj* "flax."

The imperfective participles are less common than their perfective counterparts. It is not always clear why Egyptian prefers one over the other. Often the perfective and imperfective forms have the same English translation: for example,

nḫt pw grt jr m ḫpš.f … wꜥf ꜥb pw sgnn ḏrwt

"Moreover, he is a champion who acts with his strong arm …

he is a horn-deflecter who weakens the hands (of his enemies)."

In this passage, from a hymn in praise of the king, both the perfective active participle *jr* "who acts" and the imperfective active participle *sgnn* "who weakens" refer to customary action. The only difference between them seems to be the fact that the perfective form is used with a singular adjunct (*m ḫpš.f* "with his strong arm") while the imperfective participle has a plural object (*ḏrwt* "hands"). In this case Egyptian apparently thinks of the action of "weakening" as being performed on each of the plural objects "hands," and therefore as repeated — i.e., imperfective. This kind of relationship between the imperfective forms and the plural is quite common.

Although they are all essentially tenseless, the different participles do tend to be associated with some tenses more than others. The prospective participle is naturally used for future actions. The perfective forms are normally used either for generic actions (those that are normally or always true) or for single, one-time past actions: for example,

 *jr jtj sḫpr btj*

"the one who makes barley, who brings about emmer" (active, generic)

 *jr pt smn [st]*

"the one who made the sky, who set it (in place)" (active, past)

 *nswtyw sꜣ.t(j) m jrt n.sn*

"Royal tenants are sated with what is done for them" (passive, generic)[8]

 *dj.n.f ḥꜣw ḥr jryt ḏr bꜣḥ*

"He has given more than what was done previously" (passive, past).

The imperfective forms are most often used with reference to generic actions: for instance,

 *šsꜣ nṯr m jrr-n.f*

"The god is aware of the one who acts for him" (active)[9]

 *mj jrrt n nṯr* "like that which is done for a god" (passive).

When they refer to past events, the imperfective forms denote repeated or habitual actions rather than single past acts: for example,

 *wp(w)tj ḫdd(j) ḫnt(j) r ḫnw ꜣb.f ḥr.j*

"The messenger who used to go north or south to home used to stop by me" (active).[10]

8 *nswtyw* is a plural nisbe from the noun *nswt* "king," and refers to the tenant farmers of royal lands. The 3fs stative *sꜣ.t(j)* shows that it is treated here as a collective.

9 The seated man indicates that the participial phrase *jrr n.f* was thought of as a single word.

10 A SUBJECT-imperfective construction: § 20.8.

Similarly, in the example *nfrt nbt jnnt n ḥm n nb.j* "every good thing that was brought to the incarnation of my lord" cited earlier in this section, the imperfective passive participle *jnnt* shows that the writer is thinking of several past acts of "bringing" rather than just one — i.e., "every good thing that was (normally) brought" rather than "every good thing that was (once) brought."

As you can see from these examples, there is a good deal of overlap in meaning between the perfective and imperfective forms, except in reference to past actions. Unless the participle comes from a class that distinguishes the two forms in writing, it is therefore often impossible to know whether a particular form is perfective or imperfective on the basis of its meaning alone. In some cases, however, the form can be identified on the basis of a parallel form. Thus, we can be fairly certain that the active participle *ḫnt(j)* in the last example is imperfective because it is parallel to the distinctive imperfective form *ḫdd(j)*, while the active participles *sḫpr* and *smn* in two earlier examples are probably perfective since they are parallel to the perfective form *jr*.

As demonstrated by the example at the top of the preceding page, however, parallel constructions are not always a reliable guide to identifying the form of a particular participle. Fortunately, whether a participle is perfective or imperfective usually does not make a great deal of difference in translation, since English does not distinguish between these two aspects in the same way that Egyptian does. It is far more important for you to be able to recognize a form as an active or passive participle than to know whether it is perfective or imperfective.

23.11 Participles as adjectival predicates

We have already seen how participles can be used as adjectives to modify a preceding noun (examples in §§ 23.9–23.10). Besides this use, participles can also serve as adjectival predicates, like other adjectives (§§ 7.2–7.3). Only the perfective participles appear in this function and, like other adjectives, they are used in the masculine singular form: for instance,

 *ḥꜥ st jm.f r nṯr.sn*
"They are more excited about him than (about) their god" (active)

 *ꜥrq sw r ḫnt*
"He was bent forward" (passive),

with the active participle of *ḥꜥj* "become excited" and the passive participle of *ꜥrq* "bend."

The perfective participles can also be used, like other adjectives, in the masculine dual form as an exclamatory adjectival predicate: for example,

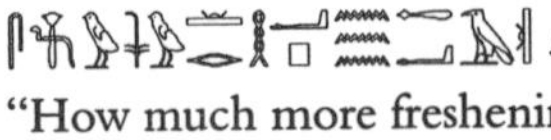 *sw3ḏw(j) sw r ḥꜥp(j) ꜥ3*
"How much more freshening he is than a high inundation!"[11]

literally, "he is doubly freshening with respect to a big inundation," with the active participle of the caus. 3-lit. verb *sw3ḏ* "cause to become fresh." The most common example of this use is the expression  (etc.) *jjwj* "welcome!" — literally, "doubly come" (for an example, see the last sentence in Exercise 19, no. 1).

11 The first bookroll is a determinative of *sw3ḏw(j)*. It is placed after *sw* either because of a scribal error or because the phrase *sw3ḏwj sw* was considered as a single word.

23.12 Participles as nouns

As we have already noted, participles, like other Egyptian adjectives, can be used by themselves, as nouns. In this use they are usually translated by an English relative clause: for example,

m3t "the one who saw, she who saw"

m33w "the one who is seen, he who is seen"

m33tj.sn "the ones who will see, they/those who will see."

As a noun the participle occasionally has a determinative, as in *m3t* "she who saw." The feminine participle used as a noun is often equivalent to an English neuter. This use is particularly common for the passive participle, which is often written with plural strokes: for instance, *jrrt* "that which is done, what is done," *jryt* "that which was done, what has been done."

The participial noun has the same functions as other nouns. It can serve, for example, as the second noun of an indirect genitive (§ 23.10, fourth example), as the object of a preposition (several examples in § 23.10), and as the subject of a verb (§ 23.10, seventh example). It can also be used as the object of a verb: for instance,

nj rḫ.n ẖprt ẖt t3
"We don't know what is happening throughout the land."

Since participles themselves can have objects (§ 23.9), participial nouns can even be used as the object of another participle: for example,

qd qd sw, ms ms sw
"who built the one who built him, who birthed the one who birthed him,"

where the participial phrases *qd sw* "the one who built him" and *ms sw* "the one who birthed him" are used as objects of the participles *qd* "who built" and *ms* "who birthed."[12]

Like other nouns, participles can also be used as the predicate in a nominal sentence: for example,

swsẖ t3šw pw
"He is one who widens the borders (of Egypt)"

ẖsrw ḏwt pw sr(j)w
"Officials are those who dispel evil"

jnk ḏd nfrt wḥm mrrt
"I am one who says what is good and repeats what is loved."

In the first of these examples, the participial phrase *swsẖ t3šw* is the predicate of an A *pw* nominal sentence; in the second, the participial phrase *ẖsrw ḏwt* is the first part of an A *pw* B sentence. In the third example, the participial phrases *ḏd nfrt* and *wḥm mrrt* are the predicate of an A B sentence; note also the parallel use of the adjective *nfrt* "what is good" and the imperfective passive participle *mrrt* "what is loved."

12 These phrases refer to a king who made statues of a god. The verbs *qd* "build" and *msj* "give birth" are used here with reference to both the king's birth and the creation of the statues. The god is the king's father, who "built him" and "birthed him" (*qd sw, ms sw*), while the king is the one who "built" and "birthed" (*qd, ms*) the statues.

23.13 The participial statement

Participles are also used as nouns in a special kind of nominal sentence that is known as the "participial statement." This has the pattern A B, with the following elements:

A an independent pronoun (§ 5.5), or
the particle  (§ 16.6.2) plus a noun (or noun phrase), or
the particle  plus the interrogative pronoun *mj* (§ 5.11)

B the masculine singular perfective active participle, or
the masculine singular imperfective active participle.

In the participial statement the A part of the sentence is always emphasized. When A is an independent pronoun or *jn* plus a noun (or noun phrase), this emphasis is usually reflected in English by translations such as "A is the one" or "It is A." The participle in the B part of the sentence is always active; always masculine singular, regardless of the gender or number of the element in A; and is normally translated by a relative clause. The following examples illustrate how this works:

 *jnk jr ṯn*
"I am the one who made you" or "It is I who made you"

 *jn nṯr jrr jqr*
"It is the god who makes success" or "The god is the one who makes success"

 *jn mj jr.f rdj pr.k*
"So, who made you go out?" — literally, "who is it who gave that you go out?"

As these examples show, in the participial statement the perfective participle normally refers to single past acts, and the imperfective participle to generic actions. In past contexts, however, the imperfective participle can also be used for habitual past acts: for instance,

 *ntf dd n.f st*
"He is the one who used to give it to him" or "It was he who used to give it to him."

The future form of the participial statement uses the prospective participle, as you might expect: for example,

 *jr grg sn, ntf wnnt(j).fj m t3 pn*
"As for the one who establishes them, he is the one who will exist in this land."

This construction is extremely rare, however. In its place Middle Egyptian normally uses a similar construction in which the A part of the participial statement is followed by the subjunctive or prospective *sḏm.f*: for example,

 *jnk nḏ.j sw m ᶜ ḫftjw.f*
"I am the one who will save him from his enemies"

 *jn n3 n wḥᶜw 3bw šd.sn mr pn ṯnw rnpt*
"Those fishermen of Elephantine are the ones who shall dredge this canal every year"

 *jn mj r.f jn.f n.j sj*
"So, who will get it for me?"

As these examples demonstrate, the verb form always has a suffix-pronoun subject that agrees in gender and number with the A part of the sentence.

Like other nominal sentences, the participial statement can also be negated by means of the negation *nj ... js* or *nn ... js* (see § 11.5). The two particles bracket the first word in the sentence, which is either an independent pronoun or the particle *jn*: for example,

 *nj jnk js prr r 3ḫt*
"I am not the one who goes forth to the Akhet"

 *nj jn js rᶜ pr m ḥtrw*
"Re is not the one who emerged from the yoke."

Note that the negation applies to the sentence as a whole (see § 11.7), not to the participial clause. The examples just cited do **not** mean "I am the one who does not go forth to the Akhet" or "Re is the one who did not emerge from the yoke." Later in this lesson we will see how Egyptian negates the participial clause itself.

23.14 The participial statement vs. other kinds of nominal sentences

It is easy to recognize the participial statement when the A part consists of *jn* plus a noun or *jn mj*, since no other kind of nominal sentence has this pattern. When A is an independent pronoun, however, the participial statement looks like the regular A B nominal sentence (compare the last example in § 23.12). A sentence such as the following can therefore be understood with two different meanings, as indicated by boldface in the translation:

 *jnk jr pt*
"**I** am the one who made the sky" (participial statement) or
"I am **the one who made the sky**" (regular nominal sentence).

We have already met this kind of ambivalence in A B sentences where B is a noun rather than a participle (see § 7.12). In both cases the difference in meaning corresponds to a difference in the predicate of the sentence. In the participial statement, the independent pronoun in A is always the predicate: "**I** am the one who made the sky" (answers the question "Who is the one who made the sky?"). In the other kind of nominal sentence, B is the predicate: "I am **the one who made the sky**" (answers the question "Who are you?").[13] Just as in the English sentence *I am the one who made the sky*, there is nothing in the Egyptian sentence *jnk jr pt* itself to indicate which of the two possible meanings is intended.[14] In most cases we have to depend on the sentence's context for this information. There are, however, two features that distinguish the the two kinds of A B sentence.

In the third person the participial statement always uses the independent pronoun, as it does in the first and second person: for instance,

 *ntf d3jr ḫ3swt*
"He is the one who repels the foreign lands."

13 The alternative translation "It is I who made the sky" is only possible for the participial statement. It can be used to answer the question "Who is the one who made the sky?" but not the question "Who are you?" This is because English uses this construction to mark the predicate, which is always the word or phrase that follows *it is*.

14 The two were probably distinguished when spoken, however, as they are in the English sentence: see § 7.12.

The nominal sentence that is not a participial statement uses the A *pw* construction, as in the following example, cited in § 23.12 above:

 *swsḫ t3šw pw*
"He is one who widens the borders (of Egypt)."

In the first of these examples, *ntf* is the predicate (the sentence answers the hypothetical question "Who is the one who repels the foreign lands?"); in the second, the participial phrase is the predicate (answering the hypothetical question "Who is he?"). This same distinction between *ntf* B and A *pw* is made in nominal sentences where B and A are nouns (§ 7.12).

In the participial statement there is agreement in gender and number between the pronoun in A and any pronouns in B that refer back to it: for instance,

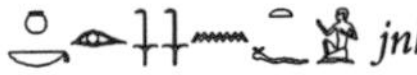 *jnk jr nn n (j)t(j).j*
"I am the one who made this for my father,"

where the suffix pronoun of *(j)t(j).j* "my father" refers back to *jnk*. In the other kind of nominal sentence, however, such pronouns in B are always in the third person: for example,

 *jnk ḫsf ꜥw3 m 3t.f*
"I am one who bars robbery by his wrath,"

where the suffix pronoun of *3t.f* "his wrath" is in the third person. English has a similar rule of agreement, as can be seen in the two translations. Egyptian sentences like the first of these two examples are fairly rare, but the second kind, with third-person pronouns, is very common. This feature is a good way of telling when a nominal sentence is **not** a participial statement.

Egyptian also has another kind of nominal sentence that is similar to the participial statement in meaning. This construction has the pattern A *pw* B, where A is an independent pronoun and B is an active participle (or participial clause): for example,

 *jnk pw mdwy n.k*
"The one who is speaking to you is I."

Since it uses *pw* between A and B, this is not strictly an example of the participial statement; but it has the same effect as the participial statement, by making the independent pronoun the predicate (see § 7.12.3). The difference between this kind of sentence and the participial statement is the same as that between the two English translations:

jnk mdwy n.k	"I am the one who is speaking to you" (participial statement)
jnk pw mdwy n.k	"The one who is speaking to you is I."

The English sentence *The one who is speaking to you is I* is perfectly grammatical and understandable, but that kind of sentence is not very common in English. The same is true of the sentence *jnk pw mdwy n.k* in Egyptian.

23.15 Special features of the passive participles

As noted at the beginning of this lesson, the passive participles describe action done to someone or something. This is true both when the participles are used to modify a preceding noun and when they are used as nouns by themselves: for example,

 *ḏwt jryt r.f jn sn.f stẖ*

"the evil done against him by his brother Seth"

 *ḥ3w ḥr jryt ḏr b3ḥ*

"more than that done previously."

In both of these examples the perfective passive participle *jryt* refers to an act of "doing" that has been performed on something: on *ḏwt* "the evil," in the first example, and on an unexpressed antecedent, in the second. The English past participle works the same way: in the translations of these examples, the past participle *done* describes an action that has been performed on each of the antecedents it modifies: "the evil" and "that."

English also uses the past participle of some verbs in a slightly different way, where the action of the participle is **not** performed on the antecedent. Compare, for example, the use of the participle *spoken* in the following two sentences:

Words spoken in haste are soon regretted.

Friends spoken to rudely are quickly lost.

In the first sentence the participle is used in the normal way, to describe an action performed on its antecedent (*words*). In the second sentence, however, the action of the participle is not performed on the noun it modifies (*friends*) but on something else that is not expressed. Although it has the same structure as the first example, this sentence is actually a concise way of saying "Friends to whom words are spoken rudely are quickly lost," where the true antecedent of the participle (*words*) is expressed.

Middle Egyptian can use its passive participles in the same way, and it can do so for all verbs, not just a few as in English. Egyptian also differs from English in requiring a pronoun in the participial clause that refers back to the noun being modified: for example,

 *sn jrr(w) ḥn^{c}.f ḫpr.(w) m ḫft(j)*

"The brother acted with has become an enemy,"

or more loosely, "The brother with whom one used to do things has become an enemy": literally, "the brother done with him has evolved (3ms stative) into an enemy." The suffix pronoun of *ḥn^{c}.f* refers back to the noun *sn* "brother," which the imperfective passive participle *jrr(w)* modifies.

In this example the thing on which the action of the participle is performed is not actually mentioned, either in Egyptian or in English. A few English verbs, however, do allow the object of the participle's action to be expressed: for example, *The student given encouragement learns quickly* and *The student found fault with soon loses interest*, where the nouns *encouragement* and *fault* express the thing on which the action of the past participles *given* and *found* is performed. These are actually more concise ways of saying "The student to whom encouragement is given" and "The student with whom fault is found," with relative clauses in which the nouns *encouragement* and *fault* are the subjects of passive verbs.

Middle Egyptian also uses its passive participles in this way. In Egyptian, however, this construction can be used for all transitive verbs, not just a few. Here again, Egyptian requires a pronoun in the participial clause that refers back to the noun being modified: for example,

mj šmsw nb n nb.j ꜥnḫ.(w)-(w)ḏꜣ.(w)-s(nb.w) ddw n.f swḏꜣ jb
"like any follower of my lord, lph, to whom a communication is given"[15]

 *r(m)ṯ jry nn r gs.sn*
"the people beside whom this was done,"

literally, "any follower ... given to him a communication" and "the people done this beside them." The first of these examples could be translated with the past participle in English ("any follower ... given a communication"), but the second cannot, even though both are the same construction in Egyptian.

A frequent example of this kind of construction is the expression  *ḏdw n.f*, feminine 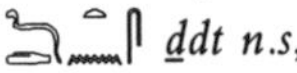 *ḏdt n.s*, which is used between two proper names, to introduce a person's nickname: for instance,

 *jn-(j)t(j).f ḏdw n.f jw-snb.(w)* "Intef, called Iu-seneb"
 *šftw ḏdt n.s ttj* "Sheftu, called Teti."

The literal meaning of the expression A *ḏdw n.f* B is "A, said to him B": thus here, "Intef, said to him Iu-seneb" and "Sheftu, said to her Teti."[16]

Note that each of the four preceding examples has a pronoun in the participial clause that refers back to the noun being modified. Such a pronoun is required even when the participle does not have an expressed antecedent. In this case, the gender and number of the pronoun agree with that of the participle (which, of course, reflects the gender and number of the unexpressed antecedent): for example,

 *ḏdw n.f mdt ḥꜣpt*
"one to whom a concealed matter is said"

 *rdyt ꜥntjw r šnj.sn*
"those (women) on whose hair myrrh has been put,"

literally, "one said to him a concealed matter" (*n.f* referring to masculine singular *ḏdw*) and "those given myrrh to their hair" (*r šnj.sn* referring to feminine plural *rdyt*).

There are only a few exceptions to the rule requiring the participial clause to have a pronoun that refers back to the antecedent. When the pronoun would be the object of the preposition *m*, it is usually omitted: for instance,

 *gmḥwt 3 stt tkꜣ jm* "3 wicks with which a lamp is lit,"

literally, "3 wicks lit a lamp therewith," with the preposition adverb *jm* instead of the prepositional phrase *jm.s*.[17] Another common exception occurs in phrases such as  *dj ꜥnḫ* "given life" and

15 For *ꜥnḫ.(w)-(w)ḏꜣ.(w)-s(nb.w)* "lph," see § 17.20.2. The expression *swḏꜣ jb* "communication" means literally "making sound the heart": see Essay 25.

16 The two male names mean "He whom his father got" (with a verb form we will meet in the next lesson) and "He who comes healthy" (with the imperfective active participle *jw*). The meaning of the feminine names is uncertain.

17 *jm.s* rather than *jm.sn* because the pronoun would refer to the number *3* (*ḫmtt*): see § 9.4.

 *dj ʿnḫ ḏd w3s* "given life, stability, and dominion," which are frequently used after the name of the king: for example,

 *(n)swt bjt(j)* *ḎSR-K3-Rʿ dj ʿnḫ ḏt*

"the King of Upper and Lower Egypt DJESER-KA-RE, given life forever."[18]

These were such common expressions that they came to be used as a noun, in the phrase  *jr.f dj ʿnḫ* "so that he (the pharaoh) might achieve 'given life'" (see § 18.7), and so forth. An example is the following caption accompanying a scene of the pharaoh presenting myrrh to a god:

ḥnk m tpj ʿntjw w3ḏ n jmn rʿ nb nswt t3wj nb pt, jr.f dj ʿnḫ ḏd w3s snb, 3w jb.f, mj rʿ ḏt

"Dedication with the best of fresh myrrh for Amun-Re, lord of the thrones of the Two Lands, lord of the sky, so that he might achieve given life, stability, dominion, and health, with his heart happy, like Re forever."[19]

The expression *dj ʿnḫ* is probably a short form of *dj n.f ʿnḫ* "to whom life has been given," with the dative *n.f* omitted. Note that English "given life" has exactly the same structure.

Passive participial clauses with a following noun look just like clauses with the passive *sḏm.f*, except that the verb form is a passive participle. In fact, it is sometimes difficult to tell the difference between the two kinds of clauses: for example,

 *zt-ḥmt ḏd grg r.s*

"a woman about whom a lie has been told."

Here the verb form *ḏd* is actually the passive *sḏm.f*, used in an unmarked relative clause after an undefined antecedent (§ 21.12). The only thing that distinguishes it from a passive participle is the fact that it does not have the feminine ending *–t* to agree with the noun it modifies.

You can even think of passive participial clauses such as those in the above examples as main clauses that have been converted to serve as adjectives by changing a passive verb form to the passive participle. Like clauses with the passive *sḏm.f*, they obey the normal rules of word order. The only exception is when the participle is used with a following personal pronoun instead of a noun. In this case the **dependent** form of the pronoun is normally used: for example,

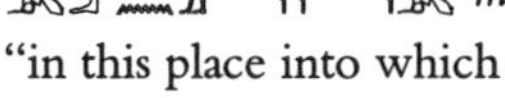 *nj gm.n.s bw jrrw st jm*

"She could not find the place in which it was done,"

literally, "the place done it therein," with the dependent pronoun *st*. The similarity between the two kinds of clauses is so strong, however, that there are sometimes exceptions to the exception, where the passive participle has a suffix pronoun, like a verb form in a main clause: for instance,

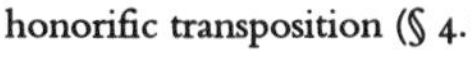 *m bw pn jny.k jm*

"in this place into which you have been brought,"

literally, "this place brought you therein," where *jny.k* is used instead of *jny ṯw*.

18 Djeser-ka-re is the throne name of the pharaoh Amenhotep I of Dynasty 18 (ca. 1525–1504 BC).

19 The adverb clause *3w jb.f* means literally "his heart being long." In the phrase *mj rʿ* "like Re," the name of the god is in honorific transposition (§ 4.15). For *jr.f* "so that he might achieve" (literally, "make"), see § 19.8.1.

23.16 The passive participle of intransitive verbs

The English construction discussed in the preceding section can also occur with the past participle of an intransitive verb, which is not otherwise passive: for example, *Decisions arrived at in haste are often regretted*. Middle Egyptian has a similar construction, in which intransitive verbs appear in a passive participle, even though such verbs cannot otherwise be made passive: for example,

 *nṯr wʿ ʿnḫw ḫr sšm.f*
"sole god, under whose guidance one lives"

 *ʿnḫ.f m m(w)tt ḫr.s*
"He lives on that from which one dies,"

literally, "sole god, lived under his guidance" and "He lives on that died under it." As in the construction with the passive participle of transitive verbs, such participial clauses require a pronoun that refers back to the antecedent, whether the antecedent is expressed, as in the first example, or unexpressed, as in the second. Unlike the transitive construction, such clauses never have a noun (or dependent or suffix pronoun) following the passive participle.[20] As the two examples cited here illustrate, they usually have to be translated by a relative clause with the impersonal pronoun "one" as the subject of the intransitive verb.

Transitive verbs are sometimes used in the same way as intransitive verbs in this construction: for instance,

 *rʿ pw, m33w m stwt.f*
"He is the sun, by whose rays one sees."

This sentence could also be translated as "He is the sun, seen in his rays." The context in which it occurs, however (a hymn of praise to the king), shows that the verb *m33* "see" is used here intransitively rather than with the antecedent *rʿ* "sun" as its object.

23.17 The participles of *wnn* and *p3*

The verb *wnn* "exist, be" has perfective, imperfective, and prospective active participles, and these can be used like other active participles (for examples, see §§ 23.9 and 23.13). Unlike those of most other verbs, however, the participles of *wnn* can also be used to allow other verbal constructions to function like participles: for example,

 *t3w fnḫw wnw w3.(w) r tkk t3šw.j*
"the lands of the Phoenicians, who had started to violate my borders"

 *ršy gmḥtj.f wnntj.f ḥr šms nswt*
"He who will observe and who will be following the king will rejoice."

In the first of these examples the perfective active participle *wnw* is used as the subject of the stative *w3.(w)*, allowing the SUBJECT-stative construction to function as a participle. This expresses a past perfect action "had started," in contrast to the normal past meaning of the simple perfective active participle *w3w* "who started." In the second example the prospective participle *wnntj.f* is

20 What looks like the same construction with a following noun or suffix pronoun actually involves a different verb form, as we will see in the next lesson.

used as the subject of the pseudoverbal predicate *ḥr šms*, allowing it to serve as a participle. This construction has the normal imperfect meaning of the pseudoverbal construction ("will be following"), where the prospective participle *šmstj.f* would mean simply "who will follow."

The verb *p3* "do in the past," which we met in Lesson 20, can also be used as a perfective active participle with a following infinitive (see § 20.5): for instance,

sj3.n wj mjtn jm p3 wnn ḥr kmt

"The scout there, who had once been in Egypt, recognized me."[21]

In this case the past perfect could have been expressed by the participial phrase *wn ḥr kmt* "who had been in Egypt," with the perfective active participle of *wnn*, but the use of *p3* adds the extra connotation expressed by the English adverb *once* in the translation.

23.18 The negation of the participles

All Middle Egyptian participles are negated by means of the participles of the 2-lit. negative verb *tm* followed by the negatival complement (§§ 14.16–14.17), or less often, the infinitive: i.e.,

m3 "who saw"	*tm m33* "who did not see" (perfective active)
m33 "who sees"	*tm m33* "who does not see" (imperfective active)
m3w "who was seen"	*tmmj m33* or *tmw m33* "who was not seen" (perfective passive)
m33w "who is seen"	*tmw m33* "who is not seen" (imperfective passive)
m33tj.f "who will see"	*tmtj.f m33* "who will not see" (prospective).

The following sentences show how these constructions work in actual Middle Egyptian texts:

 *tm gm sk3w m nb mnmn*

"He who could not find a plow-team is (now) the owner of a herd"

jw.j rḫ.kj psḏt jnw tmmt bs wr-m3w ḥr.s

"I know the Ennead of Heliopolis, to which (even) the Greatest of Seers has not been introduced"[22]

jr grt fẖt(j).fj sw tmt(j).f ꜥḥ3 ḥr.f, nj z3.j js

"But as for him who shall lose it, who shall not fight for it, he is not my son."[23]

In the first of these examples, *tm* is the perfective active participle (negative counterpart of *gm sk3* "he who could find a plow-team"). In the second, *tmmt* is the perfective passive participle used in the passive construction discussed in § 23.15. The third sentence shows both affirmative and negative examples of the prospective participle.

21 The word *kmt* "Egypt," literally means "black," referring to the soil of the Nile Valley (see Essay 2). This is why Egyptian uses the preposition *ḥr* "on" rather than *m* "in": *ḥr kmt* means literally "on the blackland."

22 *rḫ.kj* is the older form of the 1s stative *rḫ.kw* (§ 17.2). For the term *psḏt* "Ennead," see Essay 12. *wr-m3w* "Greatest of Seers" was the title of the high priest of Heliopolis. The verb *bs* "introduce" uses the preposition *ḥr* "upon" rather than "to" as in English.

23 *nj z3.j js* "he is not my son" is a negated A *pw* sentence without *pw*: see § 11.5.

23.19 A final word about the participles

This lesson has been the longest you have encountered so far in this book. There are two reasons why this is so. First, the forms of the Middle Egyptian participles are more numerous than those of the other verb forms. They are also more complicated, because they can have different verb stems **and** different sets of endings, whereas the other verb forms generally have only a single form. There are therefore a lot of participial forms to learn.

Second, participles are the most versatile and widely used of all Egyptian verb forms. Being able to recognize a participial form is only half the battle: it is also necessary to understand the various ways Egyptian uses them. These are often quite different from the ways English uses its participles. Only occasionally can an Egyptian participle be translated directly by one of the two English participles. As you have seen from the examples above, Egyptian often uses a participle where English requires a more complicated relative clause.

At the beginning of this lesson, you learned that participles are concise ways of expressing relative clauses in a single word. In fact, **participles are the normal way that Middle Egyptian uses to express a relative clause that has a verbal predicate**. This is one of the major differences between Egyptian and English. Marked relative clauses with *ntj* plus a verb form — which correspond more closely to the relative clauses of English — are actually fairly uncommon. Such clauses are mostly used for nonverbal predicates. Unmarked relative clauses with a verb form are more common, but they are used mostly after undefined nouns, while participles can be used to modify any kind of antecedent.

Even though an Egyptian participle can sometimes be translated by an English one, you need to be aware that the reverse is often not true. Just as an Egyptian participle often cannot be translated by English participle, so too English uses its participles in some ways that Egyptian cannot.

Both languages are similar in using their participles as adjectives modifying nouns: for example, 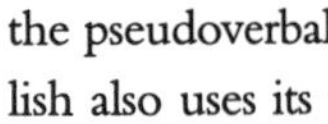 *wp(w)tj ḫdd(j)* "the messenger going north" and 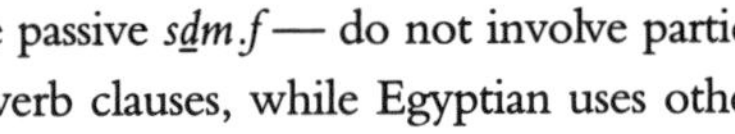 *ḏwt jryt r.f* "the evil done against him," where the Egyptian participles *ḫdd(j)* (imperfective active) and *jryt* (perfective passive) are translated by the English participles *going* and *done*. In other cases, however, the English participles correspond to a different kind of verb form in Egyptian. The English present participle is part of the imperfect tenses (*He is reading*, *She was talking*), while the past participle is used to make passive verb forms (*The ball was thrown*). The Egyptian counterparts to these constructions — such as the pseudoverbal construction (§ 15.2) and the passive *sḏm.f* — do not involve participles at all. English also uses its participles as predicates in adverb clauses, while Egyptian uses other verb forms for this purpose: for instance,

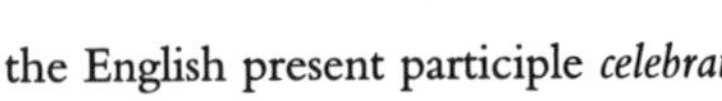 *gm.n.j sn jr.sn ḥ(3)bw.sn*
"I found them celebrating their festivals" (§ 20.10)

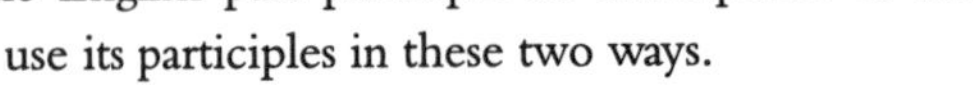 *gm.n.f p3 nḫ3w w3ḥ.(w) ḥr p3qyt*
"He found that fish-pendant set on a sherd" (Exercise 17, no. 21)

where the English present participle *celebrating* is used to translate the imperfective *sḏm.f* form *jr.sn* and the English past participle *set* corresponds to the Egyptian stative *w3ḥ.(w)*. Egyptian could never use its participles in these two ways.

It is important to be aware of these differences between the two languages when you are using existing translations to help you understand the grammar of an Egyptian text (as Egyptologists themselves often do). One way to tell if an English form in a translation corresponds to an Egyptian participle is to replace it by a relative clause: if the replacement makes sense without changing the meaning of the sentence, the Egyptian form is probably a participle; if it does not, it is probably some other form.

ESSAY 23. HYMNS AND POETRY

Besides funerary texts, which were discussed in Essay 22, Middle Egyptian religious literature also consists of devotional texts. Very few of these are prayers. Although the Egyptians certainly prayed to their gods, most of the prayers that have been preserved to us date from the Ramesside Period and later, and were composed in Late Egyptian. For Middle Egyptian the great majority of devotional texts fall into the category that Egyptologists call "hymns."

The key concepts in this literary genre are the words *dw3* "worship" and *j3jw* "praise," which often appear in the titles of hymns: for example, *dw3 wsjr* "Worshipping Osiris" and *djt j3jw n wsjr* "Giving Praise to Osiris." Although hymns, like prayers, can be addressed directly to a god, unlike prayers they are almost exclusively devoted to praising him (or her); only occasionally do they also beseech the deity for intercession, favors, or blessings.

Hymns are among the most carefully composed of all Egyptian literary forms. They normally consist of short lines arranged conceptually into "thought couplets" (see Essay 18), or sometimes triplets (the technical terms for such groups are "distich" and "tristich"). The lines themselves are often participial phrases describing the god being "worshipped" or "praised." A typical example is the following, from the beginning of the "Hymn to the Inundation," ascribed to the Middle Kingdom author Khety (the second line of each distich is indented):

> Worshipping the Inundation.
> Hail to you, Inundation,
>   who emerges from the ground and comes to make Blackland live;
> hidden of conduct, dark in the daytime,[24]
>   to whom his followers sing;
> who waters the fields that Re creates,
>   in order to make all the flocks live;
> who sates the hills that are far from water,
>   whose dew is what comes from the sky;[25]
> whom Geb desires, who manages Nepri,
>   who makes green the craft of Ptah.[26]

24 The inundation is "hidden" because it is unpredictable; the silt that the inundation carries makes it "dark."

25 A reflection of the increased humidity that the inundation brings.

26 Geb is the earth, Nepri is the god of grain, and Ptah is the god of minerals and stone. The image behind this couplet is that of the inundation producing green crops from sandy soil.

This passage also illustrates another feature of the hymns. Most such compositions are not just random collections of eulogies, but carefully arranged expositions of Egyptian thought about the nature and significance of the god being "praised." The authors of such texts usually tried to incorporate into them as many of the different aspects of the god as possible. These aspects are sometimes expounded by means of a play on words that associates a particular characteristic of the god with one of the forms under which he was worshipped. An example is the following, from a hymn to the god Amun:

> who made the whole (*tmw*) land, the creator (*sḫpr*) who made all that exists,
> in this your identity of Atum-Khepri (*jtmw-ḫprj*).

Hymns, in fact, are the prime vehicle through which the theologians of ancient Egypt preserved and transmitted their thinking about the nature of the gods and their activity in the world. As such, they are the ancient Egyptian equivalent of the philosophical writings of the Greeks and the theological treatises of medieval scholars. Much of what we know about ancient Egyptian religion and philosophy comes from such texts.

Hymns were written not only in praise of the gods but also to honor the king. There is even a papyrus of the Hyksos Period that preserves a set of hymns to the royal crowns and headgear. One of the more important works of Middle Kingdom literature is a series of six short hymns in honor of the pharaoh Senwosret III. This collection begins with the pharaoh's titulary followed by the words "as he takes possession of the Two Lands in justification" (see no. 1 in the Exercise, below), suggesting that the hymns were composed either in honor of the king's accession or to be recited during the festival celebrating his thirtieth year on the throne.

There is not a great deal of information about how the hymns were actually used. Those composed in honor of a god were presumably recited, or perhaps sung, during temple rituals. The word  *dw3* "worship" is possibly related to the noun  *dw3w* "morning." If so, hymns with this word in their title may have been recited at dawn, the beginning of the Egyptian day; some sun-hymns, in fact, have specific titles such as 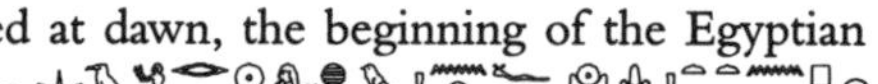 *dw3 rᶜ ḫft wbn.f m 3ḫt j3btt nt pt* "Worshipping Re at his rising from the eastern Akhet of the sky." The titles of other hymns tell us they were meant to be recited at midday or sundown, and there are also some collections with hymns for each hour of the day and night.

The verse structure of Egyptian hymns, with its short lines and couplets, is similar to that of modern poetry. Some hymns even have specific refrains and "choruses," suggesting that they were recited or sung by alternating performers. Although they certainly qualify as poetry, however, the Egyptian hymns are not poetry of the type found in most English hymns and songs. As far as we can tell, they did not use end-rhymes, and they were usually written in continuous lines like other texts. A few of the six hymns in honor of Senwosret III, mentioned above, are a rare exception: their individual lines each occupy a single horizontal line of text, much like the arrangement of modern poems.

Hymns represent just about all that has survived of Middle Egyptian poetry. The famous Egyptian love poems were composed in the Ramesside Period, and are written in Late Egyptian. A few nonreligious Middle Egyptian songs have survived, however, including snatches of workmen's songs recorded in tomb reliefs. The most famous Middle Egyptian composition of this genre is known as the Harper's Song. It is preserved in two New Kingdom copies, where it is entitled "The song that is in the mortuary temple of (King) Intef, justified, in front of the singer on the harp" — indicating that the original (now lost) was inscribed on a wall in a royal tomb-complex of Dynasty 11 or 17 (both of which had kings named Intef), before the picture of a harpist. The song itself consists of two verses and a refrain: the first verse describes the ravages of time on monuments and memory, and the second advises listeners to enjoy life while they can; the refrain, with which the song ends, repeats both themes:

> Make holiday — don't weary of it!
> Look, there is no one allowed to take his things with him,
> and there is no one who goes away who comes back again.

Similar, much shorter, songs are found on a few Middle Kingdom stelae, accompanied by the picture of a blind harpist. These, and the description of the original in the tomb of King Intef, show that the composition was certainly sung to the accompaniment of a harp, but we have no information about the context or occasion in which it was performed.

EXERCISE 23

Transliterate and translate the following passages, and identify the participles in each.

1. From a hymn to Senwosret III; the arrangement reflects that of the original hieratic papyrus (cols. 1–5 and 7–10):

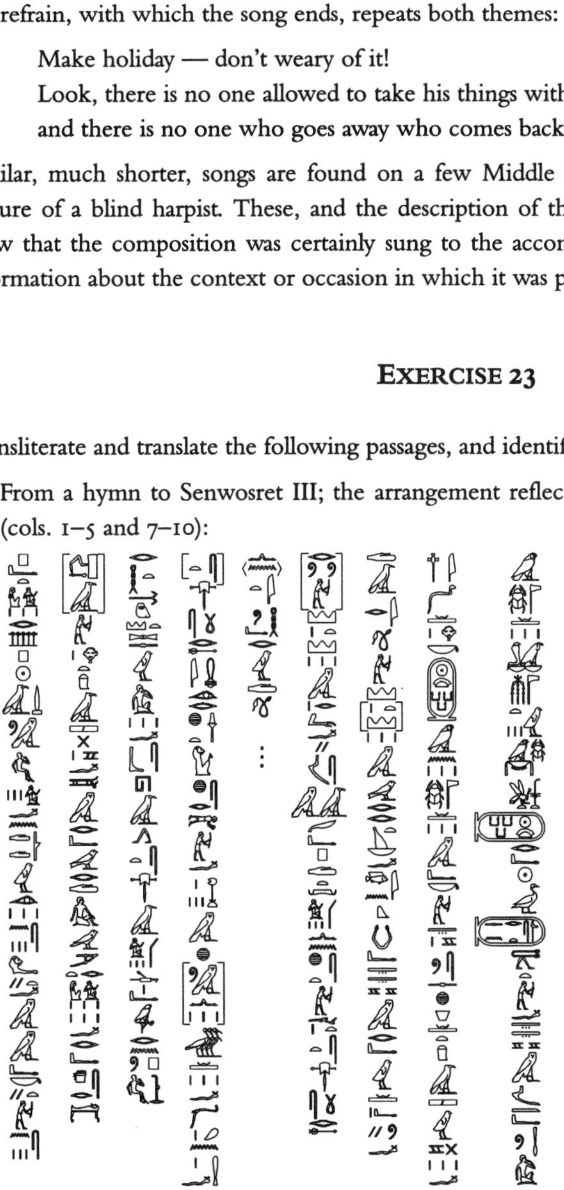

for the king's titulary, see Essay 6:
- *nṯrj ḫprw* "Divine of Evolution"
- *bjk-nbw ḫpr* "Gold Falcon Who Has Evolved"

mj jrr sḫmt "as Sekhmet does"

ḥ3w m see § 9.4

ns … ḫnt and *ṯ3zw.f … sttjw* are A B nominal sentences used adverbially

ḫnt "Upstream" (Nubia)

wʿ rnpw "unique youngster" (literally, "young unique one")

mrwt.f has an extra pair of plural strokes

rdj sḏr the verb form *rdj* also governs the next clause: read *(rdj) ḏ3mw.f n qddw.sn*

2. 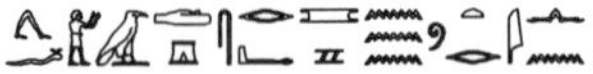

3. 

4.  — two clauses, contrasting past and present; ignore the plural strokes after *jwtj*

5. 

6.  — from a hymn in praise of the king

7.  — from a hymn in praise of the king

8.  — *nj* for *nn*; *p3* "such"

9.  — not a complete sentence

10. 

11. 

12.  — *ḥr ḫw.k* "except you"

13. 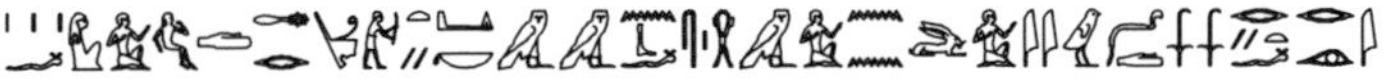 — *ḏdwy.j* "which I say"

14. 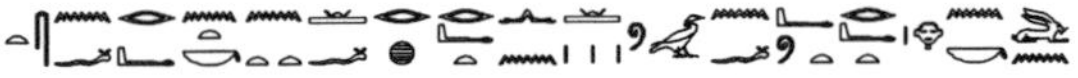

15. 

16. 

17. 

18. 

19.  — for the first *n* see § 4.13.2

20.  — two sentences

21.  — *ḏdj* and *r(w)d-ḏdt* are personal names

22.  — read *(j)n mj*: § 7.13.1

23. 

24. 

25. 

26. 

27.  — *f3j* ᶜ is an act of homage

28. 

24. The Relative Forms

24.1 Definitions

In the preceding lesson we saw that participles are a concise way of expressing a relative clause in a single word. This is why participles can be paraphrased by relative clauses. In English as well as Egyptian, participles denote both a verb and its subject. For example, the active participle *ꜥnḫw* and its English counterpart "the living" both mean "those who (subject) are alive (verb)," and the passive participle *mryt* and its English counterpart "beloved" both mean "she who (subject) is loved (verb)." The relative clause says the same thing as the participle, but with the verb and its subject divided into separate words.

Egyptian and English participles correspond to **direct** relative clauses — those in which the subject of the verb is the same as the antecedent (§ 12.2). For example, in the phrase *z3 sḏm* "the son who listens," the antecedent *z3* "the son" is the same as the subject of the verb expressed in the active participle *sḏm* "who listens"; and in the phrase *z3t mrrt* "the daughter who is loved," the antecedent *z3t* "daughter" is identical with the subject of the verb expressed in the passive participle *mrrt* "who is loved."[1]

As we saw in Lesson 12, however, both English and Egyptian also have **indirect** relative clauses, in which the subject of the verb is not the same as the antecedent. An English example is *the father to whom his son listens*: here the subject of the relative clause (*his son*) and the antecedent (*the father*) refer to two different people. English has no verb forms that combine an indirect relative clause into a single word in the way that participles do for direct relative clauses. When the subject of the relative clause is not the same as the antecedent, English can only use a relative clause, and not some form like a participle: thus, we can only say *the father to whom his son listens*, not something like **the father listening his son to*. In Egyptian, however, such forms do exist. They are known as **relative forms**.

We therefore need to refine the statement made in § 23.19: participles are the normal way that Middle Egyptian uses to express a **direct** relative clause that has a verbal predicate, and **relative forms are the normal way that Middle Egyptian uses to express an *indirect* relative clause that has a verbal predicate**. The difference can be illustrated by the following examples:

 *z3 sḏm n jt(j).f*

"the son who listens to his father" or "the son listening to his father"

 *jt(j) sḏm n.f z3.f*

"the father to whom his son listens" — literally, "the father who his son listens to him."

In the first example, *sḏm* is an active participle. In the second, *sḏm* is a relative form, with *z3.f* "his son" as its subject.

1 You may want to review the difference between the subject and the agent of a passive verb (§ 13.3.4). In the phrase *z3t mrrt* "the daughter who is loved," the **agent** of the verb (the person doing the loving) is not expressed.

Like participles, the relative forms consist of a verb stem and an ending. Unlike the participles, the relative forms also have a separate subject, which can be either a distinct word (such as *z3.f* "his son" in the example above) or a suffix pronoun attached directly to the relative form. While Middle Egyptian has five participles, it has only three relative forms: the **perfective relative**, the **imperfective relative**, and the **perfect relative**. The perfective and imperfective relative generally look like the perfective and imperfective passive participles, and the perfect relative looks like the perfect of the suffix conjugation. Egyptologists often call the first two the perfective and imperfective relative *sḏm.f*, and the third the relative *sḏm.n.f*.

24.2 Endings

Like participles, the relative forms are essentially adjectives. As such, they normally agree in gender and number with the noun they modify. The endings that express this agreement are the same as those of other adjectives and the perfective and imperfective participles: for example,

MASCULINE SINGULAR	 *z3 mrr.f* "the son whom he loves"
MASCULINE PLURAL	 *z3w mrrw.f* "the sons whom he loves"
FEMININE	 *z3t mrrt.f* "the daughter whom he loves"
	 *z3wt mrrt.f* "the daughters whom he loves."

As in the adjectives and participles, the relative forms modifying plural nouns can also have plural strokes, and the feminine ending can sometimes be omitted.

Besides these endings some relative forms can also have a stem ending, like those of the participles (§ 23.5). There are two sets of stem endings, for the perfective and imperfective relative forms. They can be summarized as follows, using the "strong" verb  *ḏd* "say" (2-lit.) and the "weak" verb  *mrj* "love" (3ae-inf.) as examples.

1. **perfective relative** — strong verbs have no ending other than those of gender and number; weak verbs have the ending *–y* (): for example,

MASCULINE SINGULAR	*ḏd.f* "(that) which he says"
	mry.f "(the one) whom he loves"
MASCULINE PLURAL	*ḏdw.f* "(those) which he says"
	mryw.f "(those) whom he loves"
FEMININE	*ḏdt.f* "(that/those) which he says"
	mryt.f "(the one/ones) whom he loves."

2. **imperfective relative** — all verbs have the ending *–w* () in the masculine singular and no special ending otherwise, rarely the ending *–y* (): for example,

MASCULINE SINGULAR	*ḏdw.f*, rarely *ḏdy.f* "(that) which he says"
	mrrw.f, rarely *mrry.f* "(the one) whom he loves"
MASCULINE PLURAL	*ḏdw.f*, rarely *ḏdyw.f* "(those) which he says"
	mrrw.f, rarely *mrryw.f* "(the ones) whom he loves"
FEMININE	*ḏdt.f* "(that/those) which he says"
	mrrt.f, rarely *mrryt.f* "(the one/ones) whom he loves."

3. The **perfect relative** has no special ending, other than those of gender and number:

MASCULINE SINGULAR	*ḏd.n.f* "(that) which he said"
	mr.n.f "(the one) whom he loved"
MASCULINE PLURAL	*ḏdw.n.f* "(those) which he said"
	mrw.n.f "(those) whom he loved"
FEMININE	*ḏdt.n.f* "(that/those) which he said"
	mrt.n.f "(the one/ones) whom he loved."

As you can see from these charts, the stem ending, when there is one, is either –*y* or –*w*. With some exceptions, –*y* is a mark of the perfective form and -*w* a mark of the imperfective. Originally both the perfective and imperfective ended in –*w*, like the passive participles (§ 23.5), but this ending is rarely found with the perfective forms in Middle Egyptian. The ending –*y* is the result of a sound change from –*w*: thus, perfective *mry.f* was originally *mrw.f* and imperfective *mrry.f* is simply a variant of *mrrw.f*.[2] A good example of this change is the form *ḏdwy.j* "which I say," which shows both the original ending –*w* and the later ending –*y* (i.e., *ḏdw.j* > *ḏdy.j*), much like the writing *swrj* "drink" reflects both the original radical *r* and its Middle Kingdom pronunciation *j* (i.e., *swr* > *swj*: see § 2.8.3).

Because the stem endings are "weak" consonants, they are often omitted in writing. Since it is impossible to know whether the omitted ending was –*w* or –*y*, Egyptologists normally do not supply it in transliteration: thus, a form such as perfective is simply transliterated as *mr.f*, and imperfective is transliterated as *mrr.f*. In New Kingdom texts the ending (or) is sometimes added to the masculine singular, even where no such ending is normally present: for example, *mnw pn nfr jrw.n.k* "this beautiful monument you have made." In such writings the –*w* probably indicates a vowel rather than a formal ending (see Essay 17).

In the perfective relative the feminine ending –*t* is sometimes written or instead of : for example, *ḏdtj.f* "that which he might say." Since forms with this ending normally have prospective meaning (as in this example), some Egyptologists have identified them as examples of a fourth relative form, called the prospective relative. Whether such a form existed is still a matter of debate. A difference in writing can only be seen in the feminine, and the normal written form of the perfective relative often has prospective meaning (as we will see). For these reasons, we will err on the side of caution and view such forms only as unusual writings of the feminine perfective rather than as examples of a separate prospective relative.

24.3 Forms

As noted at the beginning of this lesson, the perfective and imperfective relative forms generally look like the perfective and imperfective passive participles, and the perfect relative looks like the perfect of the suffix conjugation. The following tables show typical examples of these forms for the various verb classes as they appear in Middle Egyptian texts.[3]

2 This variation may be due to dialect as well as chronology. A similar variation can be seen in the modern Egyptian Arabic participle meaning "wanting": some speakers say *ꜥawiz*; others, *ꜥayiz*.

3 Because of the wide variety of English translations that the relative forms demand, only the verbal part of each form in the tables has been translated, and not the relative words "that, which, who, whom," etc.

1. **Perfective and imperfective**

2-LIT. PERFECTIVE ⟨hieroglyphs⟩ *wḏt* "commanded."

IMPERFECTIVE ⟨hieroglyphs⟩ *ḏdw* "say," ⟨hieroglyphs⟩ *ḏdy.k* "you say." Rarely prefixed: ⟨hieroglyphs⟩ *j.ḏdw* "say."

2AE-GEM. PERFECTIVE ⟨hieroglyphs⟩ *wn.k* "you will exist."

IMPERFECTIVE ⟨hieroglyphs⟩ *m33t.k* "you see," ⟨hieroglyphs⟩ *wnn.k* "you will exist," ⟨hieroglyphs⟩ *wnnw* "exists."

3-LIT. PERFECTIVE ⟨hieroglyphs⟩ *t3z.n* "we assembled."

IMPERFECTIVE ⟨hieroglyphs⟩ *wršw* "spends the day," ⟨hieroglyphs⟩ *ḫndy.k* "you tread."

3AE-INF. PERFECTIVE ⟨hieroglyphs⟩ *mr.k* "you want," ⟨hieroglyphs⟩ *mry.s* "she wants."

IMPERFECTIVE ⟨hieroglyphs⟩ *mrrw* "wants," ⟨hieroglyphs⟩ *jrr* "does," ⟨hieroglyphs⟩ *jrry.k* "you do."

4AE-INF. PERFECTIVE ⟨hieroglyphs⟩ *rhnt* "can depend."

IMPERFECTIVE ⟨hieroglyphs⟩ *w3ḫḫw* "is inundated."

CAUS. 2-LIT. PERFECTIVE ⟨hieroglyphs⟩ *swḏ* "has bequeathed."

IMPERFECTIVE ⟨hieroglyphs⟩ *smjw* "reports."

CAUS. 3-LIT. IMPERFECTIVE ⟨hieroglyphs⟩ *sdmj* "adheres."

CAUS. 3AE-INF. PERFECTIVE ⟨hieroglyphs⟩ *sḫ3y.k* "you mention."

CAUS. 4AE-INF. PERFECTIVE ⟨hieroglyphs⟩ *sḫnt* "promoted."

IMPERFECTIVE ⟨hieroglyphs⟩ *sb3q.f* "he brightens."

ANOM. PERFECTIVE ⟨hieroglyphs⟩ *rdj.k* "you put"; ⟨hieroglyphs⟩ *djt.f* "he gives," ⟨hieroglyphs⟩ *djt.j* "I might put."

⟨hieroglyphs⟩ *j* "come."

IMPERFECTIVE ⟨hieroglyphs⟩ *ddw.sn* "they give," ⟨hieroglyphs⟩ *dd.f* "he puts," ⟨hieroglyphs⟩ *ddyt.f* "he gives."

⟨hieroglyphs⟩ *jww*, ⟨hieroglyphs⟩ *jw* "come"; rarely ⟨hieroglyphs⟩ *jyw* "come."[4]

2. **Perfect**

2-LIT. ⟨hieroglyphs⟩ *ḏdt.n.f* "he said."

2AE-GEM. ⟨hieroglyphs⟩ *m3t.n.j* "I have seen," ⟨hieroglyphs⟩ *wnt.n.f* "he was."

3-LIT. ⟨hieroglyphs⟩ *sb(3).n.k* "you have taught."

3AE-INF. ⟨hieroglyphs⟩ *gmt.n.f* "he found."

4-LIT. ⟨hieroglyphs⟩ *sꜥsꜥt.n.f* "he has wrecked."

4AE-INF. ⟨hieroglyphs⟩ *mdwt.n.j* "I have spoken."

---

4   Probably from an original *jww* > *jyw* (see § 24.2).

CAUS. 2-LIT. 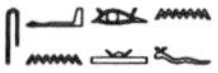 *sꜥn.n.f* "he has beautified."

CAUS. 3-LIT.  *sspd.n.k* "you have sharpened."

CAUS. 3AE-INF.  *sḥ3.n* "has bared."

CAUS. 4AE-INF.  *sẖnt.n* "promoted."

ANOM. ,  *rdj.n.j* "I have given"; rarely 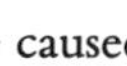 *dj.n.f* "he caused."
 *jt.n.f* "he came,"  *jj.n.sn* "they came."

As you can see by comparing these tables with those in §§ 23.7 and 18.2, the stems of the perfective and imperfective relative forms are generally the same as those used in the perfective and imperfective passive participles, and the stem of the perfect relative form is comparable to that of the perfect. As in the participles, the 3ae-inf. verb *jrj* "make, do" is normally spelled *jr* in the perfective and 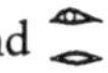 *jrr* in the imperfective relative.

24.4 Word order in clauses with relative forms

Like participles, the relative forms can be used both as adjectives, modifying a preceding noun, or as nouns by themselves, without an expressed antecedent: i.e.,

z3 mr.f "the son he wants"	*mr.f* "the one he wants"
z3t mrrt.f "the daughter he loves"	*mrrt.f* "the one he loves"
z3w mrw.n.f "the sons he wanted"	*mrw.n.f* "the ones he wanted."

As verb forms, the relatives obey the normal rules of word order for clauses with a verbal predicate (§§ 14.6, 18.4): for example,

 *mduw ḏdw nṯrw dw3tjw n nṯr pn*
"the words that the Duat-gods say to this god" (**VSD**)

 *mduw ḏdw n.sn nṯr pn*
"the words that this god says to them" (**VdS**)

 *nn n zẖ3w rdj.n wj wp(w)tj n ḥm.k ḥr.s*
"this writing which the messenger of Your Incarnation assigned me to" (**VoS**).[5]

When they are used by themselves, as nouns, the relative forms can be modified by the adjective *nb* "all, each, every, any": for instance,

 *ḫnt.(j) nbt jm*
"wherever I might land" — literally, "any(where) that I might land in"

 *mrrt nbt k3.j* "all that my ka loves"

 *h3bt.n.j n.k nb ḥr.s*
"everything I have written to you about" — literally, "all that I have sent to you about it."

As these examples show, *nb* tends to come as close to the relative form as possible, though a pronominal dative can come between them. This is the same as the word order in clauses where *nb* modifies a participle used as a noun (§ 23.9).

5 Literally, "which the messenger of Your Incarnation put me on it," meaning "assigned me to do."

24.5 Syntax of the relative forms

Like participles, the relative forms are ways that Egyptian uses to express a relative clause that has a verbal predicate. As we saw in Lesson 12, relative clauses always contain some element (known as the coreferent) that refers to the same thing as the antecedent, whether or not the antecedent itself is expressed (§ 12.2). Participles are always the equivalent of **direct** relative clauses, in which the coreferent is the **subject** of the verb. In normal participial clauses this coreferent is not expressed by a separate word, because the participle itself denotes both the verb and its subject (§ 24.1), but it is reflected by the gender and number ending of the participle: i.e.,

> *nṯrt mrrt rmṯ* "the goddess who loves people" and
> *mrrt rmṯ* "she who loves people" (active)
>
> *ḏwt jryt jn stẖ* "the evil which was done by Seth" and
> *jryt jn stẖ* "that which was done by Seth" (passive).

In each of these examples, the subject of the relative clause is the same as the antecedent: in the first set, the one doing the loving (*nṯrt* "the goddess" and unexpressed "she"); in the second, the thing which was done (*ḏwt* "the evil" and unexpressed "that").[6]

Relative forms are the equivalent of **indirect** relative clauses, where the coreferent is not the subject but some other element of the relative clause. In such clauses the antecedent is normally identical with one of four elements in the relative clause:[7]

1. **direct object of the relative form**

This is the most common construction in relative clauses with a relative form. In this case **the coreferent is not expressed**: for example,

>  *z3t ktt*^{A} *jnt.n.j m zš3*
> "the little daughter^{A} I got through prayer"
>
>  *mj m3t.n ḥm.j m zẖ3w.f*
> "like that which My Incarnation has seen in his writings."

This construction is only possible when the relative form is a transitive verb, since only transitive verbs can have a direct object. Note that English also does not express the coreferent in this case: we do not say *"the little daughter^{A} I got her^{C}" or *"(a thing^{A}) which My Incarnation has seen it^{C}," just as Egyptian does not say **z3t ktt*^{A} *jnt.n.j sj*^{C} or **m3t.n st*^{C} *ḥm.j*.

2. **object of a preposition**

The antecedent can also be identical with the object of a preposition in the relative clause. In this case the coreferent is normally expressed: for example,

>  *ẖnw*^{A} *ḫpr.n.k jm.f*^{C}
> "the home^{A} in which you grew up" or "the home^{A} you grew up in"

6 The special uses of the passive participle discussed in §§ 23.15–23.16 have a different relationship between the antecedent and the coreferent. This relationship will be discussed in § 24.7.

7 In the following discussion the antecedent is marked by a superscript A and the coreferent by a superscript C (when they are expressed), so that you can identify both elements more easily.

 *ḏdw n.f*[C] *ḏḥwtj j3wt*
"one to whom Thoth gives praise,"

literally, "the home[A] which you grew up in it[C]" and "(a person[A]) who Thoth gives him[C] praise." As the translations of these examples show, the coreferent is not expressed in English, though Egyptian normally requires it. When the coreferent is the object of the preposition *m*, however, it can also be omitted in Egyptian: for instance,

 *bw*[A] *jn.n.f sw jm*
"the place[A] he brought him from"[8]

 *ḫt*[A] *nb nfrt wꜥbt ꜥnḫt nṯr jm*
"every good and pure thing[A] that a god lives on"

Compare the first of the two preceding examples, where the coreferent is expressed: *ẖnw*[A] *ḫpr.n.k jm.f*[C] "the home[A] you grew up in."

3. **a possessive**

The antecedent occasionally is identical with a suffix pronoun attached as possessive to a noun in the relative clause. English normally requires the translation of such clauses with the relative word *whose* or *of whom*, without an expressed coreferent: for example,

 *nṯr*[A] *pf mnḫ wnnw snḏ.f*[C] *ḫt ḫ3swt mj sḫmt*
"that efficient god[A], fear of whom is throughout the foreign lands like Sekhmet"

 *dmd b3w jnw r mswt.f*[C] *r jrt (n)swt n (n)ḥḥ*
"one at whose birth the bas of Heliopolis united in order to make a king of eternity,"

literally, "that efficient god[A] who his[C] fear is throughout the foreign lands" and "(a king[A]) who the bas of Heliopolis united at his[C] birth." In this case **the coreferent is always expressed** in Egyptian. In English it is usually subsumed into the relative pronoun *whose*, which comes from the phrase *who his*[C].

4. **part of a dependent clause governed by the relative form**

Like the participles (§ 23.9), the relative forms can govern a dependent clause of their own, such as a noun clause or an adverb clause. The antecedent of the relative clause can be identical with some element in such dependent clauses: for example,

 *sḏr*[A] *rdj.n.k rs.f*[C]
"a sleeper[A] whom you have caused to awake"

 *k3t.n.f jrt st*[C] *r.j*
"what he intended to do to me."

In the first of these examples the coreferent is the subject of a subjunctive used as object of the relative form *rdj.n.k*: literally, "a sleeper[A] whom you have caused that he[C] awake." In the second example the coreferent is the object of the infinitive *jrt*, which itself is the object of the relative form *k3t.n.f*: literally, "(the thing[A]) that he intended to do it[C] to me." These examples show how

8 Note that the object of the relative form, *sw* "him," is expressed in this case because it is not the coreferent.

Egyptian expresses the coreferent where English usually omits it. Like English, however, Egyptian can also omit the coreferent in such constructions: for instance,

 *ḏꜥm*[A] *dj.n.f jnt ḥm.j*

"the electrum[A] he caused My Incarnation to get"

 *ḥꜥ sw m šꜣt.n.j jrt*

"He is excited about what I have decided to do."

In the first of these examples the relative form *dj.n.f* governs a subjunctive, and the unexpressed coreferent is the object of the subjunctive; this could also have been expressed as *ḏꜥm*[A] *dj.n.f jnt sw*[C] *ḥm.j* — literally, "the electrum[A] which he caused that My Incarnation get it[C]." In the second example the relative form *šꜣt.n.f* governs an infinitive and the unexpressed coreferent is the object of the infinitive; Egyptian could also have said *šꜣt.n.j jrt st*[C] — literally, "(the thing[A]) that I have decided to do it[C]." Unlike the other three constructions with relative forms, there are no hard and fast rules that determine when Egyptian expresses the coreferent in a dependent clause and when it omits it.

24.6 Translating relative forms

As the examples in the previous section illustrate, relative clauses with a relative form often require an English translation whose syntax is quite different from that of Egyptian. This is because the syntax of English relative clauses is much more complicated than that of Egyptian — as we have already observed in our discussion of relative clauses with a nonverbal predicate (§ 12.5). Like nonverbal relative clauses, those with a verbal predicate (i.e., a relative form) can be understood as statements that have been converted to function as relative clauses. The rules for doing this are actually fairly simple in Egyptian. They can be illustrated by the following example:

 *ḥḏt*[A] *ꜥꜣt ḥꜥꜥt psḏt m nfrw.s*[C]

"the great white (crown[A]), at whose beauty the Ennead is excited."

In Egyptian and in English this construction is formed from two parts: the antecedent *ḥḏt ꜥꜣt* "the great white one," and the statement *ḥꜥ psḏt m nfrw.s* "the Ennead is excited at her beauty." In Egyptian the statement has been converted to modify the antecedent by two simple rules:

- change the verb form to a relative form: *ḥꜥ psḏt m nfrw.s* ⇒ *ḥꜥꜥ psḏt m nfrw.s*
- add a gender and number ending to agree with the antecedent: *ḥꜥꜥt psḏt m nfrw.s* (this step is eventually omitted in spoken Middle Egyptian).

In contrast, the same procedure requires four rules in English:

- insert a relative marker (REL): *the great white one* REL *the Ennead is excited at her beauty*
- move the coreferent phrase after the relative marker: *the great white one* REL *her beauty the Ennead is excited at*
- combine the relative marker and coreferent into a relative pronoun (REL + *her* = *whose*): *the great white one whose beauty the Ennead is excited at*
- move the preposition in front of the relative pronoun: *the great white one at whose beauty the Ennead is excited* (this step can be omitted in colloquial English).

As you can see, the syntax of clauses with an Egyptian relative form is much simpler than corresponding relative clauses in English. The difference between the two languages is especially pronounced when the coreferent is part of a dependent clause governed by the relative form: for example,

 *nbt*^{A} *ḥtpwt ḥ*^{cc}*t wsjr m33.f s(j)*^{C}

"the mistress^{A} of offerings, at whom Osiris is excited when he sees her^{C}"[9]

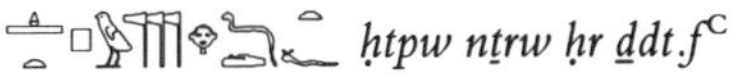 *ḥtpw nṯrw ḥr ḏdt.f*^{C}

"he^{A} who because of what he^{C} says the gods are content."

In the first of these examples the coreferent *s(j)* is the object of *m33.f*, which is an imperfective *sḏm.f* in an unmarked adverb clause dependent on the relative form *ḥ*^{cc}*t wsjr* — literally, "the mistress^{A} of offerings, who Osiris is excited when he sees her^{C}." In the second, both *ḥtpw* and *ḏdt.f* are relative forms, and the coreferent is the subject of *ḏdt.f* — literally, "he^{A} who the gods are content because of what he^{C} says." Although both examples are relatively straightforward constructions in Egyptian (as can be seen from their literal translations), they are quite difficult to translate into the convoluted relative constructions that proper English requires. In the first case this is possible only by inserting a preposition (*at*) that does not exist in the Egyptian; the translation given for the second example is even more contorted, and only marginally grammatical.

Because the two languages handle relative clauses so differently, students of Egyptian — and even experienced Egyptologists — usually have more trouble with relative forms than with any other part of Middle Egyptian grammar. The best way to understand clauses with relative forms is by keeping in mind the simple and straightforward nature of the Egyptian constructions. When you are confronted with relative forms, don't try to put them immediately into proper English. Instead, you should first translate them literally, word for word, and only then convert your translation into grammatical English.

24.7 Passive relative forms

In English the verb form in a relative clause can be passive as well as active: for example, we can say not only *the student whose essay the teacher praised* but also *the student whose essay was praised by the teacher*. Egyptian relative forms, however, are normally **active**. To make a passive relative, Egyptian sometimes adds the suffix *tw* to a relative form: for example,

^{c}*šw n s*^{c}*ḥw.n qrs.tw w*^{c}*b[w] m jnw.sn*

"cedars for our privileged, with the produce of which the pure are buried."[10]

This is simply the normal active relative form with the impersonal pronoun *tw* "one" (§ 15.5) as its subject: literally, "cedars^{A} ... which one buries the pure in their^{C} produce."

This kind of passive relative is not very common, and is mostly found in texts written after the Middle Kingdom. To express a passive relative Middle Egyptian normally uses the passive participles in the special construction we met in the preceding lesson (§ 23.15): for example,

9  is a spelling of *wsjr* "Osiris" peculiar to the Coffin Texts, from which this example is taken.

10 Better wood coffins were made of cedar planks (the "produce" of cedars) imported from Lebanon.

ḏdw n.f mdt ḥ3pt
"one to whom a concealed matter is said"

rdyt ᶜntjw r šnj.sn
"those on whose hair myrrh has been put."

On the surface these look like passive relatives — that is, like indirect relative clauses in which the verb form is passive: "(one^{A}) who a concealed matter is said to him^{C}," where the coreferent is the object of a preposition (compare § 24.5.2); and "(women^{A}) who myrrh has been put on their^{C} hair," where the coreferent is the possessor of a noun in the relative clause (compare § 24.5.3). In fact, however, they are direct relative clauses, like all participial clauses. The verb forms are not relative forms but passive participles describing an action that is done to their antecedents. The coreferent is actually an unexpressed subject of the participle, as it is in other participial clauses (see § 24.5, beginning): i.e., "(one) told a concealed matter" and "(women) given myrrh for their hair." For all practical purposes, of course, the difference is academic, and you can think of such uses as passive relatives if you like — as long as you remember that the verb forms are passive participles and not passive relative forms.

24.8 Meaning of the relative forms

The perfect relative has the same meaning as the perfect of the suffix conjugation. It describes completed action, and normally corresponds to the past or perfect tenses of English: for example,

j3dw m3.n.f ḫnt
"the boy he saw previously" (past)

m.k m3 n3 n k3wt jr.n.k
"Look, those works you have done have been seen" (perfect)

wn.jn.s ḥr wḥm sḏmt.n.s nbt
"Then she was repeating all she had heard" (past perfect).

The perfect relative of *rḫ* "learn" describes the completion of the act of "learning," and therefore usually means "know" (present), like the perfect of this verb: for instance,

šm b3 r bw rḫ.n.f
"The ba goes to the place it knows."

The same is true for the verb *ḫm* "not know," the opposite of *rḫ*.

The basic meaning of the perfective and imperfective relative forms is the same as that of the perfective and imperfective participles (§ 23.10). The perfective relative describes action without any indication of tense or aspect, and can therefore be used with reference to any tense: for instance,

jr mj qd m mrt.f
"It has been done completely as that which he wanted" (past)

mry ᶜš3t mnmnt nbt
"whom the multitude of every herd desires" (present)

wnn nn n ḫwt n z3.k wᶜ mr.k
"These things shall be for the one son of yours you will want" (future).

The imperfective relative is also tenseless, but it carries the extra connotation of incomplete, repeated, or ongoing action. In most cases it is used to describe customary or habitual action: for example,

jr ḥms.k ḥnᶜ ᶜš3t, msd t mrr.k

"When you sit down (to eat) with a crowd, hate the bread you love,"

in other words, make a good impression by not eating too much of the things *mrr.k* "you (normally) love" to eat.

Although they are both essentially tenseless, however, the perfective and imperfective relatives tend to be associated with some tenses more than others, like their participial counterparts. The **perfective** is often used to describe **prospective** action and the **imperfective** normally corresponds to the English **present** tense: for example,

 *ḏd n.j jrt.ṯn r.s*

"Tell (§ 16.1) me what you will do about it"

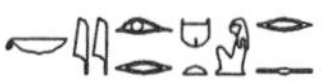 *ky jrr ḥmt r.s*

"Another (remedy) that a woman does for it."

When the two forms are used with reference to the **same** tense, however, the perfective denotes a single action and the imperfective describes repeated or ongoing actions. A good example of this contrast can be seen in a common set of relative clauses used to describe someone as an individual whom people "love" (*mrj*) or "bless" (*ḥzj*): for example,

 *mry nswt, mrrw nwt.f, ḥzzw nṯrw.s nbw*

"one whom the king loves, whom his town loves, and whom all its gods bless."

The perfective relative is used in the first clause and the imperfective in the next two clauses not because they express a difference in tense but because of the subjects they have. The perfective *mry* is used with the singular subject *nswt* "the king" because it is thought of as a single instance of "loving." With the collective subject *nwt.f* "his town" and the plural subject *nṯrw.s nbw* "all its (the town's) gods," however, the imperfectives *mrrw* and *ḥzzw* are used because these subjects refer to more than one actor and therefore more than one instance of "loving" and "blessing."

The verb *mrj* "want, love" is a good illustration of the basic aspectual difference that exists between the two relative forms (and between perfective and imperfective forms in general). Both forms of this verb can be used with the same antecedent and the same subject: for example,

 *ḥmt.f mrt.f mrrt.f*

"his wife, whom he loves and whom he continues to love."

In this case the perfective form is simply the normal way of saying "whom he loves," while the imperfective expresses the same action as ongoing: we can paraphrase this as "his wife, whom he loves now (*mrt.f*) and always (*mrrt.f*)." In the same way, a son can be called both  *z3.f mr.f* and  *z3.f mrr.f*. Both of these mean "his son, whom he loves," but the first is a general statement while the second emphasizes the continued nature of the "loving."

24.9 Some common uses of the relative forms

We have already met the perfect relative *jr.n.f* as part of the construction *sḏm pw jr.n.f* "what he did was to hear" (§ 14.14.3). Relative forms with a god's name as subject are common in proper names, often with the god's name in honorific transposition: for example, *mry-rʿ* "He whom Re loves," *ddt-jmn* "She whom Amun gives," *ẖw.n-jnpw* "He whom Anubis has protected." The perfect relative *stp.n-rʿ* "whom Re has chosen" is part of many New Kingdom royal names. An example is *wsr-m3ʿt-rʿ stp.n-rʿ*, the throne name of Ramesses II (Dynasty 19, ca. 1279–1213 BC), meaning "Powerful one of the Maat of Re, whom Re has chosen." The personal name of this king also contains a perfective relative form: *rʿ-ms-sw mr-jmn(w)*, meaning "Re is the one who gave him birth (perfective active participle), whom Amun loves." We have the actual pronunciation of both these names thanks to a transcription in cuneiform, where the vowels are written: *was-muʿa-riʿa satipna-riʿa* and *riʿa-masi-sa may-amana.*[11]

Individuals often added the names of their parents after their own by means of the relative forms *jr.n* and *ms.n*: for instance,

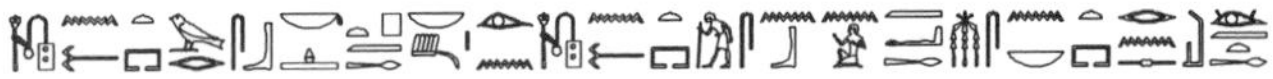

zẖ3 n ẖnrt wr sbk-ḥtp.(w) m3ʿ ẖrw nb jm3ẖ, jr.n zẖ3 n ẖnrt wr snb-n.j m3ʿ ẖrw,
ms.n nbt pr rn.s-rs.(w) m3ʿt ẖrw

"Chief prison-scribe Sebek-hotep, justified, possessor of honor,
begotten of the chief prison-scribe Seneb-ni, justified,
born of the house-mistress Renes-res, justified."[12]

The clauses *jr.n* X and *ms.n* Y mean "whom X made" and "to whom Y gave birth," but they are normally translated "begotten of" and "born of" because the length of the phrases that serve as their subject usually makes a literal translation somewhat clumsy in English.

Kings are often described as "beloved" of a particular god by means of the perfective relative form *mry* with the god's name as subject (often in honorary transposition): for example,

(n)swt bjt(j) NBW-K3W-Rʿ mry wsjr-ẖnt(j)-jmntjw dj ʿnẖ

"King of Upper and Lower Egypt NUB-KAU-RE, beloved of Osiris
the foremost of Westerners, given life."[13]

Here too the expression *mry* X is translated "beloved of X" rather than "whom X loves" because the length of the god's name and epithets would often require too much of a separation between "whom" and "loves." Sometimes the perfect relative *mr.n* is used in this context: for example,

11 The pronounced form of the throne name shows the loss of the final *r* of *wsr* and the feminine *t* of *m3ʿt*; in the personal name the *r* of *mr* has changed to a *y* (see § 2.8.3). The stress was probably on the second-last syllable in all four parts: i.e., "wass-moo-ah-REE-ʿah sah-tip-nah-REE-ʿah, ree-ʿah-mah-SEE-sah migh-ah-MAH-nah."

12 The adjective *wr* "chief" is written two different ways; it modifies *zẖ3* "scribe" (masculine), not *ẖnrt* "prison" (feminine). The names mean "Sobek is content" (stative), "Become healthy for me!" (imperative), and "Her name is awake" (stative). For *m3ʿ ẖrw* "justified" see Essay 8; for *nb jm3ẖ* "possessor of honor" see Essay 21.

13 For *dj ʿnẖ* "given life," see § 23.15. Nub-kau-re ("The golden one of the sun's life force") is the throne name of Amenemhat II (Dynasty 12, ca. 1929–1892 BC). Egyptologists often transcribe *nbw* "gold" as "Nub" in proper names to distinguish it from *nb* "lord."

 *(n)swt bjt(j)* DSR-ḪPRW-Rᶜ STP.N-Rᶜ *mr.n jmn*
"King of Upper and Lower Egypt DJESER-KHEPERU-RE SETEPEN-RE,
whom Amun has loved."[14]

This does not mean that the god has finished "loving" the king. Instead, *mr.n* means something like "wanted" — i.e., "whom Amun wanted (for his son and successor as king)." It is also possible to read  as *mr(y) n jmn* "the beloved (one) of Amun," where *mr(y)* is a perfective passive participle. This is clearly the reading in other instances: for example,

mry n (j)t(j).f, ḥzy n mwt.f, mrrw snw.f snwt.f
"beloved of his father, blessed of his mother, whom his brothers and sisters love."

In this case the verb forms in the first two clauses must be passive participles with a following indirect genitive, because the perfect relative form does not have a masculine singular ending *y*. In the third clause, however, *mrrw* is the imperfective relative.

24.10 The *ḥtp-dj-nswt* formula

One of the most common uses of the relative forms is in a dedicatory formula found on coffins, stelae, and other funerary objects. This is known as the *ḥtp-dj-nswt* formula, from its opening words. The following is a typical example, from a stela of the late Middle Kingdom:

ḥtp-dj-(n)swt wsjr ḫnt(j) jmntjw nṯr ᶜ3 nb 3bḏw wp-w3wt nb t3 ḏsr
dj.sn prt-ḫrw t ḥnqt k3w 3pdw šsr mnḫt, ḫt nbt nfrt wᶜbt ddt pt qm3(t) t3 jnnt ḥᶜp(j)
ᶜnḫt nṯr jm, ḥtpwt ḏf3w ṯ3w nḏm n ᶜnḫ
n k3 n rḫ-(n)swt snbj šrj m3ᶜ ḫrw ms.n nbt pr juwj m3ᶜt ḫrw
"A royal offering of Osiris, foremost of Westerners, the great god, lord of Abydos,
and of Wepwawet, lord of the Sacred Land,
giving an invocation offering of bread and beer, cattle and fowl, linen and clothing —
every good and pure thing that the sky gives, the earth creates, the inundation
brings, on which a god lives — offerings, food, and the sweet air of life,
for the ka of the king's acquaintance Senebi Jr., justified, born of the house-mistress
Iuui, justified."

This formula underwent many changes in the course of Egyptian history and it has many different versions, but most examples have four elements in common:

1. **the dedication**

The formula always begins with the expression  (sometimes ). This is a relative clause, *ḥtp-dj-(n)swt*: literally, "an offering that the king gives," with *(n)swt* "king" in honorary

14 This is the throne name of Haremhab (Dynasty 18, ca. 1323–1295 BC). It means "Sacred one of Re's evolutions, whom Re has chosen."

transposition. It identifies the object on which it is inscribed as a funerary item theoretically authorized by the king himself: in effect, a royal funerary gift. Some inscriptions specifically say as much: for example,

jr qrst tn jn (n)swt [dj] n.j st m [...] m ḥtp-dj-nswt
"As for this burial, the king is the one who gave it to me as [...],
as an 'offering that the king gives.'"[15]

Because of its practical meaning and the way it is normally associated with the rest of the formula, *ḥtp-dj-(n)swt* is often better translated as "a royal offering" rather than literally, as a relative clause.

2. **the agent**

The king's "gift" is normally made not by the king personally but by a local funerary establishment. The god of such establishments, usually Osiris or Anubis, is understood as the agent of the gift. His participation is usually recognized in the formula by the appearance of his name and epithets as a direct genitive after *ḥtp-dj-(n)swt*. The example given here, which was erected at Abydos, cites two gods in this way: Osiris, king of the dead ("foremost of Westerners") and chief god of Abydos; and Wepwawet, guardian of the cemetery at Abydos (the "Sacred Land").

Sometimes the god's name is introduced by the indirect genitive or the preposition *jn* "by": for example, *ḥtp-dj-(n)swt n jnpw* "a royal offering of Anubis," *ḥtp-dj-(n)swt jn wsjr* "a royal offering by Osiris." Occasionally the name of the god is incorporated directly into the dedication in place of the word *(n)swt*, as in  *ḥtp-dj-jnpw* "an offering that Anubis gives." This alternative can also be combined with the normal dedication: for instance,  *ḥtp-dj-(n)swt ḥtp-dj-jnpw* "an offering that the king gives and an offering that Anubis gives."

3. **the offerings**

The list of gifts included in the *ḥtp-dj-nswt* can be the most extensive part of the formula. It either follows directly after the agent or is introduced by *dj.f* (plural *dj.sn*) "giving," an imperfective *sḏm.f* referring to the agent or agents (see § 20.14).

There are two basic gifts: burial and offerings. The first is commonly associated with "a royal offering of Anubis" and is usually described as  *qrst nfrt m z(mj)t jmntt* "a good burial in the western cemetery." The second, normally "a royal offering of Osiris," is an "invocation offering," which the presenter calls the deceased's spirit to come and partake of: this is described in Egyptian as *prt ḫrw* "sending forth the voice." At its most basic, the offering consists of  *prt-ḫrw t ḥnqt k3w 3pdw* "an invocation offering of bread and beer, cattle and fowl." Other elements can be added to this, such as the *šsr mnḫt* "linen and clothing" mentioned in the example cited here. The offerings are often summarized by the phrase *ḫt nbt nfrt wꜥbt* "every good and pure thing"; this can be further qualified by clauses with relative forms, such as *ddt pt qm3(t) t3 jnnt ḥꜥp(j) ꜥnḫt nṯr jm* "that the sky gives, the earth creates, the inundation brings, on which a god lives" in the example above.

15 The shading  is a convention used to show portions of an inscription that are lost and for which no restoration has been supplied. Its size corresponds to that of the missing text: here, a single group.

4. **the beneficiary**

The *ḥtp-dj-(n)swt* formula ends with the name of the deceased person to whom the "royal offering" is made. This is preceded by the dative *n* "for" or the fuller expressions *n jm3ḫy* "for the honored," *n k3 n jm3ḫy* "for the ka of the honored," or (as here) *n k3 n* "for the ka of." The deceased's name is usually followed by the phrase *m3ꜥ/m3ꜥt ḫrw* "justified," sometimes also by the expression *nb/nbt jm3ḫ* "possessor of honor."

The *htp-dj-nswt* formula is one of the most commonly occurring of all Middle Egyptian texts, so you should take special care to familiarize yourself with its construction.

24.11 The relative forms of *wnn* and *p3*

The verb *wnn* "exist, be" can be used in one of the three relative forms as a verb in its own right: for example,

 *swt pw wnn t-ḥḏ.f*

"He is the one whose white-bread exists."[16]

Such uses are quite rare, however. Normally the relative forms of *wnn* are used to allow adverbial predicates to function as relatives: an example has been cited in § 24.5.3 above.

The verb *p3* "do in the past," which we met in § 20.5 and again in § 23.17, can be used as a relative form with a following infinitive: for example,

nj ḫpr mjtt n b3kw p3.n nb.sn ḥzt st

"The like did not happen to servants whose master had ever blessed them,"

literally, "who their master once did blessing them." This could also have been expressed with the perfect relative of *ḥzj* — *b3kw ḥzw.n st nb.sn* "servants whose master had blessed them" — but the use of *p3* here adds the extra connotation of "ever" (see § 20.5).

24.12 The negation of the relative forms

Like the participles (§ 23.18), the relative forms are negated by means of the negative verb *tm*. The negative verb occurs in the relative form, followed by the negatival complement (or, less often, the infinitive) of the verb being negated: i.e.,

m3t.f "what he will see"	*tmt.f m33* "what he will not see" (perfective)
m33t.f "what he sees"	*tmt.f m33* "what he does not see" (imperfective)
m3t.n.f "what he has seen"	*tmt.n.f m33* "what he has not seen" (perfect).

The following is an example in which the perfect relative is negated:

 *nn mdt tmt.n.f ꜥrq sj*

"There is no matter that he did not understand."

Note that the coreferent, *sj* "it," is expressed here because it is the object of the negatival complement *ꜥrq* and not the object of the relative form *tmt.n.f* itself.

16 I.e., who has white-bread. For *swt* see § 5.5; for the sentence construction see § 7.12.3.

ESSAY 24. NONLITERARY TEXTS

Besides the various genres of Egyptian literature that we have discussed in the past five essays, there is also a large body of Middle Egyptian texts that fall outside the realm of pure literature. Where literary texts were composed with an eye to style as well as content, these nonliterary documents are generally concerned with content alone. As such, they are often closer to the contemporary spoken language than most literary compositions. Almost all were written on papyri. Some were meant to be preserved as archival or reference documents, but many were undoubtedly written to be temporary records and have survived only through chance.

The largest group of such texts are those that we might call "scientific" documents. These are mostly of two kinds: mathematical treatises and medical texts. Middle Egyptian mathematical treatises are represented by four papyri and two wood tablets. Of these, the most important is the **Rhind Mathematical Papyrus**, which contains a table of the division of 2 by odd numbers from 3 to 101 and a series of 84 problems in arithmetic and plane and solid geometry. The title tells us that the papyrus was copied during the reign of the Hyksos pharaoh Apophis (ca. 1560 BC) "in conformance with a writing of old made in the time of the King of Upper and Lower Egypt NI-MAAT-RE" (Amenemhat III of Dynasty 12, ca. 1844–1797 BC). Its contents are typical of those found in the other mathematical texts.

There are 12 major Middle Egyptian papyri that deal with medicine. Five of these were written during the Middle Kingdom but are only partially preserved, and the remainder were copied during the New Kingdom and Ramesside Period. The two most important are the **Edwin Smith Papyrus** and the **Ebers Papyrus**, both 18th-Dynasty copies. The Ebers Papyrus is one of the longest papryi we have from ancient Egypt, with 110 pages of text. Its scribe claims that it was copied "as what was found in writing under the feet of Anubis in a shrine and brought to" a king of the First Dynasty. Despite this attribution, the earliest preserved medical texts are all written in Middle Egyptian and were undoubtedly composed after the end of the Old Kingdom.

The medical papyri are mostly concerned with the practical treatment of ailments. Ebers and two others deal with general medicine, and the rest cover specific areas, including trauma, ophthalmology, gynecology, obstetrics, and veterinary medicine. They give instructions for the treatment of specific conditions, including pharmacological prescriptions. Despite their practical nature the medical papyri also include magic spells that the physician was to recite as part of the treatment. The Egyptians thought that nontraumatic diseases were caused by malevolent spirits and needed to be cured not only by practical means but also by driving off the inimical agents. Balancing this approach, however, several of the papyri also contain extended treatises on anatomy and physiology, including a rudimentary description of the circulatory system.

Middle Egyptian "scientific" documents also include astronomical texts. The Egyptians placed great importance on the calculation of astronomical events related to monthly festivals and the beginning of the annual inundation, but only a few of their writings in this area have survived. These are preserved for the most part not on papyri but on the lids of Middle Kingdom coffins and the ceilings of later tombs and mortuary monuments. They record the position, names, and movement of stars and planets, and include many of the constellations that we recognize today.

Other nonliterary texts are represented primarily by administrative documents, legal texts, and letters. The last will be discussed in the next essay. The category of administrative documents covers a wide variety of texts, including accounts. Some of the more interesting are a series of 12th-Dynasty records from the fortresses in northern Nubia, unfortunately preserved only in fragments, which detail the daily movement of traffic and trade; and the **Reisner Papyri**, a group of four early Middle Kingdom papyri from the site of Nagᶜ ed-Deir, north of Thebes, containing records of personnel and labor connected with a building project and dockyard.

Legal documents are the least well represented of all genres of Middle Egyptian texts. From the Middle Kingdom we have a few private wills, written on papyrus. There is also a unique legal text, known as the **Karnak Juridical Stela**, that was inscribed during the reign of the pharaoh Nebirierau of Dynasty 17 (ca. 1600 BC). This describes a lawsuit over the right of succession to the mayoralty of the town of el-Kab, south of Thebes, and was erected in the temple of Karnak to publicize and preserve the decision in the case. There are many such legal texts from later periods of Egyptian history, including a series of papyri recording the investigation and trial of tomb robberies, but these are written in Late Egyptian and Demotic. The Karnak Juridical Stela is one of the few such records to survive from earlier phases of Egyptian history.

EXERCISE 24

Transliterate and translate the following passages, and identify the relative forms and coreferent (where present) in each.

1. 
2.  — first person
3. 
4. 
5. 
6. 
7.  — not a complete sentence
8. 
9. 
10. 
11. 
12. 
13. 
14.  — imperative and vocative
15. 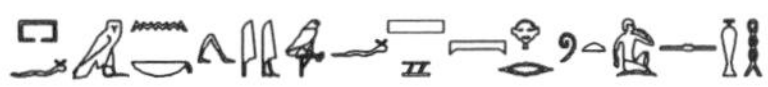

16. 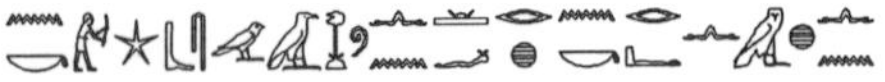

17. 

18.  (past)

19. 

20.  — *ḫft ḫsf.f* "when he punishes"

21. 

22.  — *jr.tw* "put";  *nḫt* "victory"

23. 

24. 

25. 

26. 

27. 

28. 

29. 

30.  — *zn* passive *sḏm.f*

31. 

32. 

33.  — spoken to a god

34. 

35.  — *n.j* dative

36. 

37. 

38. 

39.  — *m33* "regard"

40.  — *wnn-nfr.(w)* "Wenennefer," an epithet of Osiris meaning "He who exists perfect (imperfective active participle plus stative)"; the proper names are *sbkw-nḫt.(w)* Sebek-nakht ("Sobek is victorious"), *m3t* Mat ("New," feminine), *jnj* Ini (meaning uncertain, feminine), and *z3t-sty(t)* Sit-Satis ("Daughter of Satis," feminine); the determinative of the primary beneficiary's name is written after the phrase identifying his mother.

25. Special Uses of the Relative Forms

25.1 Nonattributive uses of the relative forms

In the last lesson we saw how Egyptian uses its relative forms to express relative clauses that have a verbal predicate. In this use the relative forms always have an antecedent, whether it is expressed or not. They also can have an ending that reflects the gender and number of the antecedent. Even when the antecedent is not expressed, the ending of the relative form still refers to it: for example, the feminine relative *m33t.f* "the one whom he sees" or "that which he sees" reflects an unexpressed feminine noun such as *ḥmt* "woman" or *ḫt* "thing."

The relative forms have such endings because they are being used as adjectives, which normally agree in gender and number with the thing they modify. When the relative forms are used in this way, they are said to have **attributive** function: that is, they attribute the action expressed by the relative form to a particular antecedent, just as adjectives attribute a particular quality to the noun or noun phrase they modify.

Egyptian also uses its relative forms **nonattributively**. In this function the relative forms are not adjectives: they do not express relative clauses, and they do not have antecedents (expressed or unexpressed). There are two kinds of nonattributive uses of the relative forms in Middle Egyptian, which Egyptologists call **nominal** and **emphatic**.

25.2 Forms and meanings

In both nonattributive functions the relative forms have one thing in common: **they have no gender and number endings**. This is because they have no antecedent to modify, expressed or unexpressed. When the relative forms have nominal or emphatic function, **only the masculine singular form is used, without an ending**: thus,

	NONATTRIBUTIVE	MS ATTRIBUTIVE (§ 24.2)
PERFECTIVE	*ḏd.f*; *mr.f*	*ḏd.f*; *mry.f* or *mr.f*
IMPERFECTIVE	*ḏd.f*; *mrr.f*	*ḏdw.f*, *ḏdy.f*, or *ḏd.f*; *mrrw.f*, *mrry.f* or *mrr.f*
PERFECT	*ḏd.n.f*, *mr.n.f*	*ḏd.n.f*, *mr.n.f*.

Because of these differences in appearance, some Egyptologists prefer to think of the nonattributive forms not as special uses of the relatives but as separate forms of the suffix conjugation, which they call the "nominal" or "emphatic" *sḏm.f* and *sḏm.n.f*. There are, however, good historical reasons for analyzing them as the relative forms, which we will discuss in the next lesson. In any case, what they are called makes no difference to the nominal and emphatic *uses* of these forms, which are universally recognized.

Despite their slight difference in appearance, the nonattributive relative forms have the same basic meanings that they do in their attributive function (§ 24.8). The perfective form describes action without any specific indication of tense or aspect; the imperfective expresses incomplete, repeated, or ongoing action; and the perfect denotes completed action.

Nominal Uses

25.3 The relative forms in noun clauses

As we saw when we first met them in § 12.12, noun clauses are clauses that have the function of a noun. Like regular nouns or noun phrases, they can serve as the object of a preposition or verb, as the second part of a direct or indirect genitive, as the subject of another predicate, as the predicate of a nominal sentence, and even by themselves as headings or captions, like the infinitive. Middle Egyptian frequently uses its relative forms nonattributively in **unmarked** noun clauses. The nonattributive relative forms appear in all of the functions that such clauses can have:

1. **object of a preposition**

The nonattributive relative forms can be used as the object of both simple and compound prepositions (§ 8.3): for example,

jr.sn n.k ẖt nbt nfrt rʿ nb mj mrr b3k jm

"May they do for you everything good every day, as your humble servant wishes"

 *wḏ n jrryw r jrt ẖft š3.n.k*

"Command to the doers to do according as you have decided"

m ẖt rdj n.j wnwt-ḥwt-nṯr p3 t-ḥḏ

"after the hourly temple staff give me that white-bread."

These examples show the imperfective relative *mrr* used as the object of *mj* "as," the perfect relative *š3.n.k* used as the object of *ẖft* "according as," and the perfective relative *rdj* used after the compound preposition *m ẖt* "after."

Like other prepositional phrases, such uses of the relative forms normally appear within or at the end of sentences, as in the first two examples. The perfective and imperfective relative forms of *mrj* "want, love," however, can be used after the preposition *m* at the beginning of a sentence, with the sense of a conditional ("if") or comparative ("as") clause: for example,

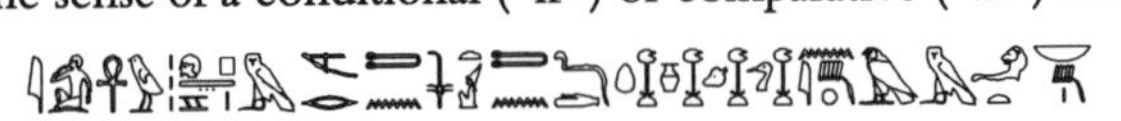

j ʿnẖw tp(jw) t3 m mr.ṯn (n)swt.ṯn, ḏd t 1000 ḥnqt 1000
k3 1000 3pd 1000 n jm3ẖ ḥrw-m-ḥ3t nb jm3ẖ

"Oh living who are on earth, as you love your king, say: 1000 bread, 1000 beer, 1000 cattle, 1000 fowl for the honored Hor-em-hat, possessor of honor"

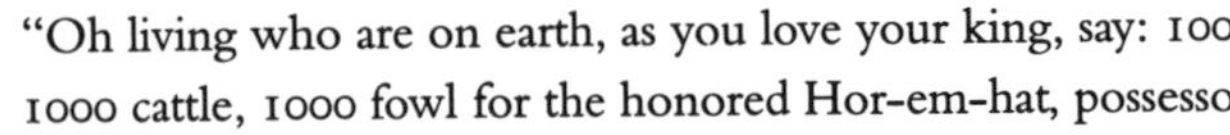

ḏd.jn ḥm.f m mrr.k m3.j snb.kw, swdf.k sw ʿ3

"Then His Incarnation said: 'As you wish to see me healthy, you should delay him here.'"[1]

The literal meaning of this construction is similar to that of English noun clauses beginning with *in that*: i.e., "in that you love your king" and "in that you wish to see me healthy."

1 *m3.j* is an infinitive with the suffix pronoun as object: § 14.5.1.

2. **second part of a genitival phrase**

The nonattributive relative forms can also be used as the second part of a direct or indirect genitive. Examples with the direct genitive mostly involve compound prepositional phrases, such as *m ḫt rdj n.j wnwt-ḥwt-nṯr p3 t-ḥḏ* "after the hourly temple staff give me that white-bread," cited in § 25.3.1 — literally, "in the wake of the hourly temple staff give me that white-bread." The following are examples with the indirect genitive:

 *jw.f mj rᶜ hr(w) n ms.tw.f*

"He is like Re on the day he was born"

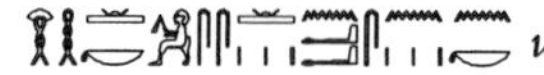 *w3ḥ.k špssw n ḏd.sn n.k*

"You shall keep the finery they give to you,"

literally, "on the day of he was born" and "the finery of they give to you." As these examples show, the genitival constructions are not directly translatable as such into English.

3. **object of a verb**

The relative forms are also used nonattributively as the object of a verb. This function is mostly limited to the imperfective form: for instance,

 *jw ḥmt.j rḫ.tj ntrr.f*

"My Incarnation knows that he is divine"[2]

 *jb n ḥm.k r qbb nj m33 ḫnn.sn*

"The heart of Your Incarnation is to become calm at seeing them row."[3]

In Lessons 18 and 19 we saw how the perfect and the subjunctive can be used in an unmarked noun clause as the object of a verb. The *sḏm.n.f* in such clauses (§ 18.13) is probably the perfect relative rather than the perfect of the suffix conjugation. The subjunctive in noun clauses is not a relative form, however. Even though the subjunctive and the imperfective relative of some verbs look the same, we can generally tell the two forms apart by their meaning. The subjunctive is used when the action of the noun clause is **subsequent** to that of the governing verb (§ 19.9), while the imperfective relative is used when the action of the noun clause is **simultaneous** with that of the governing verb. The form that is used as the object of *rdj* "cause" is also the subjunctive (§ 19.10) rather than the imperfective relative.

4. **subject of another predicate**

Unmarked noun clauses with the relative forms can be used as the subject of another predicate: for example,

 *ḥnwt.j m.tn zt pw ntt ḥr mn.s, qsn ms.s*

"My mistresses, look: it is a woman, who is suffering. It is hard for her to give birth"[4]

2 *ḥmt.j* and the stative *rḫ.tj* are feminine because they refer to the female pharaoh Hatshepsut. *ntrr.f* is the imperfective relative of the 4ae-inf. adjective-verb *nṯrj* "be/become divine."

3 *nj* is a spelling of the preposition *n* (§ 8.2.6); *m33* is an infinitive.

4 *mn* "suffer" is used with the direct object of the thing being suffered from. In this case the suffix pronoun *s* refers back to *zt* "woman": literally, "who is suffering her(self)."

ḫpr.n swt wnn ḥm n (n)sw(t) bjt(j) SNFRW *m3ᶜ ḫrw m nswt*

"Now, it happened that the incarnation of the King of Upper and Lower Egypt SNEFRU, justified, used to be king."

In the first of these examples the perfective relative *ms.s* is used as subject of the adjectival predicate *qsn*: literally, "that she gives birth is hard." In the second, a noun clause with the imperfective relative *wnn* is the subject of the perfect *ḫpr.n*: literally, "that … SNEFRU, justified, used to be king happened."

The subjunctive can also be used as the subject of another predicate (§§ 19.9, 19.11.1, 20.6). Here again, the subjunctive seems to be used when the action of the noun clause is subsequent to that of the main predicate, while the nonattributive relative forms are used when it is simultaneous (as in the two examples above) or prior.

5. **predicate of a nominal sentence**

The nonattributive relative forms are sometimes used as predicate in an A *pw* nominal sentence: for example,

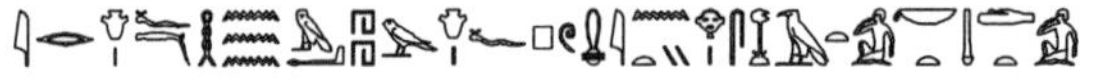

jr jb.f mḥ.(w), mhh jb.f pw mj ntj ḥr sḫ3t kt mdt

"As for 'his heart is flooded,' it means that his heart forgets,
like one who is thinking of another subject,"

literally, "it is that his heart forgets," where the noun clause *mhh jb.f*, with the imperfective relative, is the predicate of *pw*.[5] A similar example has been cited in § 18.13, with what is probably the perfect relative form.

This construction is commonly used in religious texts, with the perfective relative *ḫpr*, to explain how certain customs or natural phenomena came to be: for example,

jw.j gr r rdjt jnḥ.k ptj m nfrw.k m ḥḏwt.k, ḫpr jᶜḥ pw n ḏḥwtj

"'I am also going to make you embrace the two skies with your beauty
and with your light': that is how the moon of Thoth evolved,"[6]

literally, "it is that the moon of Thoth evolved." The construction is also common in the phrase  *jw.f pw* or  *jw.s pw* "that is how it goes" (literally, "it is that it comes," with the imperfective relative *jw*), in colophons at the end of literary texts (see Essay 18): for instance,

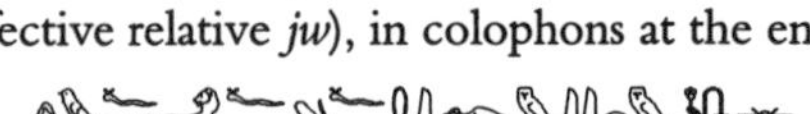

jw.f pw ḥ3t.f r pḥ(wj).fj mj gmyt m zḫ3

"That is how it goes, (from) its beginning to its end, like that found in writing."

5 This sentence is an explanation of what is meant by the idiom *jb.f mḥ.w* "his heart is flooded": i.e., he is preoccupied.

6 From a speech of the creator to Thoth. The last clause explains how the moon came to be associated with Thoth. The *ptj* "two skies" are those of the world and the Duat (see Essay 2). The explanation involves a pun between the words *jnḥ* "embrace" and *jᶜḥ* "moon."

6. **headings**

In Lesson 14 we saw how the infinitive is used in headings, such as the captions of scenes and the titles of texts (§ 14.9). The imperfective relative form can also be used instead of the infinitive in this function: for instance,

 *jrr z(j) mrrt.f m ẖrj-nṯr*

"How a man does what he wants in the necropolis" (title of Spell 221 of the Coffin Texts).

The infinitive is the normal form in this function, and can even be used with a subject: thus, this heading could also have been worded *jrt z(j) mrrt.f m ẖrj-nṯr* "A man's doing what he wants in the necropolis," with the infinitive *jrt* (see § 14.14.2). The infinitive, however, is a nonfinite verb form: it expresses just the action of the verb, without reference to any tense, mood, aspect, or voice (§ 14.1). The use of the imperfective relative *jrr* instead of the infinitive *jrt* makes it possible to add the aspectual connotation of the imperfective — here, the notion of normal or habitual "doing" rather than simply "doing" per se.

25.4 The meaning and use of relative forms in noun clauses

As you can see from the examples in the previous section, the relative forms used nonattributively are normally translated as clauses beginning with *that* or *how*, or without any introductory word, depending on the construction, and not as relative clauses. It may seem odd that Egyptian uses its relative forms in this way, but English has a similar practice. We can use an unmarked clause both as a relative clause and as a noun clause: for example, the clause *Jill loves to sing* is a relative clause in the sentence *Jack hates the kinds of songs Jill loves to sing* and a noun clause in the sentence *Jack knows Jill loves to sing*. We can also use the word *that* to mark both relative clauses and noun clauses, as in *Jack hates the kinds of songs that Jill loves to sing* and *Jack knows that Jill loves to sing.*[7]

Several Middle Egyptian verb forms with a nominal or pronominal subject can be used in noun clauses, but only three such forms normally occur as the **first** word in an **unmarked** noun clause: the infinitive, the subjunctive, and the relative forms. Although there is thus some overlap in usage, there are a number of ways to tell which form is being used in a particular example.

The infinitive is used in the same kinds of noun clauses as the relative forms (see §§ 14.9–14.13). As a general rule, **the relative forms are preferred if the verb has an expressed subject; otherwise, the infinitive is used.** Because the infinitive of some verb classes can look like the perfective or imperfective relative and can also have a subject, however, it is not always possible to know for certain which form is being used in a particular example. For instance, the 3-lit. verb form *sḫm* in the title  *sḫm z(j) m ḥk3w.f* could be either the infinitive with a genitival subject ("A man's gaining control of his magic") or the imperfective relative ("How a man gains control of his magic"). In such ambiguous cases the presence of an expressed subject usually shows that the verb is a relative form rather than the infinitive, unless the form of the verb itself indicates otherwise. In the example cited in § 25.3.6, the verb form *jrr* can only be the imperfective relative, since the infinitive of this verb has a different form (*jrt*).

7 In standard English the word *how* can also introduce noun clauses (*Jack knows how Jill loves to sing*) but not relative clauses. In some nonstandard dialects, however, *how* can also introduce a relative clause: *He showed her the way how to do it.*

The subjunctive can also be used as the first word in an unmarked noun clause. Here again it is not always possible to know whether a particular example is the subjunctive or a relative form, since the subjunctive can look like the perfective relative in most verb classes. This use of the subjunctive, however, is much more restricted than that of the relative forms: it is basically limited to noun clauses that serve as the object of a verb or as the subject of another predicate. For the most part Middle Egyptian seems to prefer the relative forms in both of these functions, with a few exceptions: the subjunctive is the normal form as subject in the negation *nj/nn zp* (§§ 19.11.1, 20.5) and as object after *rdj* "cause" or when the action of the noun clause is subsequent to that of the governing verb (§ 25.3.3).

In the last of these functions, however, a relative form can also be used instead of the subjunctive: for example,

 *jw grt wḏ.n ḥm.f prr.(j) r ḫ3st*

"Moreover, His Incarnation has commanded that I go out to the desert."

This example illustrates how prevalent the relative forms actually are in noun clauses. As the preceding discussion indicates, **the nonattributive relatives are the normal forms that Middle Egyptian uses in unmarked noun clauses that have a verbal predicate.** In practical terms this means that unless there is good evidence to the contrary, a *sḏm.f* or *sḏm.n.f* that stands at the beginning of an unmarked noun clause is most likely to be one of the three relative forms rather than an infinitive or a form of the suffix conjugation.

25.5 The negation of the nonattributive relative forms

The relative forms are negated in nominal uses just as they are in relative clauses, by means of the relative form of the verb *tm* plus the negatival complement: for example,

jnk dr bẖbẖ m q3 s3, sgr q3 ḫrw r tm.f mdw

"I am one who removes arrogance from the haughty (literally, 'high of back'), who silences the boisterous (literally, "high of voice") so that he does not speak"

jr nj šzp.n jwf.f wt, tm šzp jwf.f pẖrt pw m ꜥ šmmt ntt ḥr jwf.f

"As for 'his flesh does not accept a bandage,' it means that his flesh does not accept the prescription because of the heat that is on his flesh."

In the first of these examples the relative *tm.f mdw* is used as object of the preposition *r* (literally, "with respect to that he does not speak"); in the second, the relative *tm šzp jwf.f pẖrt* is used as predicate in an A *pw* sentence (literally, "it is that his flesh does not accept the prescription").

The relative forms are also used after the negative relative adjective *jwtj* "who not, which not" (§ 12.9): for instance,

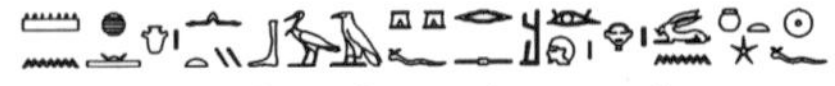

mnḫ jb, jwtj b3gg.f, rs tp ḥr wnwt.f

"one who is efficient of heart, who does not become lazy, who is vigilant at his hour (of duty)"

ᶜḏ pw 3w 3w, jwt(j) m3 rᶜ-(j)tm(w) ḥ3t.f

"Oh long, long ichneumon, whose front Re-Atum does not see!"[8]

In the first of these examples the imperfective relative *b3gg.f* (from 4ae-inf. *b3gj*) is used in a direct relative clause; in the second, the perfective relative *m3* is the predicate in an indirect relative clause. The *sḏm.n.f* can also be used after the negative relative adjective *jwtj* (§ 18.17), but in this case it is not clear whether the verb form is the perfect or the perfect relative.

EMPHATIC USES

25.6 Subject and predicate vs. theme and rheme

As we have learned in the course of these lessons, every clause or sentence contains both a subject and a predicate (see §§ 7.1 and 12.1). Normally, the subject of a clause or sentence is what is being talked about, and the predicate is what is said about the subject. Everything else in the clause or sentence is secondary to these two main pieces of information; grammarians sometimes group such "extra" elements under the general heading of "adjuncts." In the English sentence *Jill likes to sing in the shower*, for example, the noun *Jill* is the subject (the thing being talked about), the verb phrase *likes to sing* is the predicate (that which is said about *Jill*), and the prepositional phrase *in the shower* is an adverbial adjunct (telling where *Jill likes to sing*).

These definitions of subject and predicate are normally true, but they are not necessarily true for every sentence. Normally, for example, English uses a sentence such as *Jill likes to sing in the shower* to tell what Jill does. But the same sentence can also be used in a different way, to tell where Jill likes to sing. Even though the written sentence remains the same, we recognize these two different meanings by two different patterns of intonation in the spoken language. When the sentence is used in the normal way, to tell what Jill does, the three main elements — subject, predicate, and adverbial adjunct — each receive approximately equal emphasis: *JILL likes to SING in the SHOWER*. When the sentence is used to tell where Jill likes to sing, however, the adverbial adjunct receives much greater emphasis than the other parts: *Jill likes to sing IN THE SHOWER*.

This difference in spoken emphasis corresponds to a difference in the information conveyed by the sentence. In the normal pattern, the sentence tells us something about Jill. In the other pattern, however, the sentence tells us something about the statement *Jill likes to sing*. The two patterns also correspond to different kinds of questions. The normal speech pattern answers a question such as "What does Jill like to do?"; the other pattern answers the question "Where does Jill like to sing?"

In terms of the information it conveys, a clause or sentence has two main parts, which can be called the **theme** and the **rheme**. The theme is what is being talked about, and the rheme is what is said about the theme. These terms also correspond to the notions of given and new information: the theme is always **given** information, something that has already been mentioned or that is taken as given; the rheme is always **new** information, something additional that is said about the theme. In the normal meaning of our English example, *Jill* is the theme and the rest of the sentence is the

8 The ichneumon is an animal similar to the mongoose. For *pw* "oh" see § 5.10.1.

rheme. In the second meaning, however, *Jill likes to sing* is the theme and the adverbial adjunct *in the shower* is the rheme: that Jill likes to sing is a given; the new information the sentence tells us is where she likes to sing.

The theme and rheme of a sentence are not necessarily the same as its subject and predicate. In a normal sentence the two sets of terms do refer to much the same thing: thus, in the normal meaning of our example, *Jill* is both the theme and the subject, and the rheme *likes to sing in the shower* contains both the predicate and an adverbial adjunct. But this relationship is not true for every sentence. In the second meaning of our example, the theme is the statement *Jill likes to sing*, which contains both the subject and the predicate of the sentence, and the rheme is the adverbial adjunct *in the shower.*

It is essential to keep this difference in mind. The terms "subject," "predicate," and "adjunct" refer to **syntactic** functions — to the way in which a clause or sentence is put together. These remain the same no matter what kind of information the clause or sentence is meant to convey. The terms "theme" and "rheme" refer to the sentence **information**. They can be different parts of a clause or sentence, depending on its meaning.

25.7 Emphatic sentences

In studies of Egyptian grammar, clauses or sentences in which the predicate is **not** part of the rheme are known as "**emphatic**."

English has two ways of making an emphatic sentence: by intonation alone, or by special syntactic constructions. In the first method the sentence looks like a normal, nonemphatic statement, but the rheme is given special emphasis in speech: for example, *Jill likes to sing* IN THE SHOWER. In writing, of course, such sentences have no distinguishing features. We normally depend on the context to identify them, or on devices such as making the rheme boldface: for instance, *Jill likes to sing* ***in the shower***. The second method involves what is known as a "cleft sentence," in which the rheme is separated ("cleft") from the rest of the sentence by various means, such as *Where Jill likes to sing is in the shower* or *It is in the shower that Jill likes to sing.*

Middle Egyptian uses two similar methods to make emphatic sentences. One method probably involved a normal sentence in which the rheme was spoken with special emphasis. Although we have no access to the spoken language, we can see occasional examples of normal sentences in which something other than the predicate is clearly the rheme: for example,

jmj sspd.tw t3 šzpt ntt m p3 š(j), m.k wj jj.kw r ḥmst jm.s

"Have the pavilion that is in the garden made ready: look, I have come to sit in it."

The sentence *m.k wj jj.kw r ḥmst jm.s* has a subject (*wj*), predicate (*jj.kw*), and an adverbial adjunct (*r ḥmst jm.s*). Normally, the stative construction *m.k wj jj.kw* would be used to report a past action ("look, I have come": § 17.9). Here, however, the speaker is not just telling the listener that "I have come": this is obvious, since the speaker has just issued a command to the person being addressed. Instead, the important part of the sentence is the adverbial adjunct *r ḥmst jm.s* "to sit in it," which tells **why** "I have come." The subject and predicate *m.k wj jj.kw* together are the theme, the given or old information in the sentence. The new information, the rheme, is the adverbial adjunct. Although this is syntactically a normal sentence, the context identifies it as emphatic. As in English, however, the rheme may also have been given special emphasis when the sentence was spoken.[9]

Such emphatic uses of normal sentences are not distinguished by anything special in the sentence itself. We can only identify them by paying close attention to the meaning of the sentence in its context. Like English, however, Egyptian also has special constructions that can be used for emphatic sentences. When such sentences have a verbal predicate, these constructions involve the use of **the nonattributive relative forms in place of the normal verb forms**. This use of the nonattributive relative forms is very common in Middle Egyptian, even more so than the nominal use of these forms, so we need to examine it in some detail.

There are five major kinds of emphatic sentences (or clauses) with a verbal predicate in Middle Egyptian, which we will discuss in the five following sections. In each of these the predicate is one of the three nonattributive relative forms, and the important part of the sentence — the emphasized element, or rheme — is something other than this predicate.

25.8 Sentences with emphasized interrogatives

Interrogative words are always the rheme in any sentence. This is because interrogatives always ask for new information; everything else in the sentence is a given, part of the theme. In the English sentence *Where did Jack go?*, for example, the fact that Jack went somewhere is taken as given: what the speaker or writer wants to know is **where** he went. The theme in this sentence is *did Jack go*, which contains both the subject (*Jack*) and the predicate (*did go*); the rheme is the adverbial interrogative *where*.

Sentences with an adverbial interrogative are the easiest of all emphatic sentences to recognize. When such sentences have a verbal predicate, they use one of the three nonattributive relative forms for the verb: for example,

 *ms.s jr.f z(j) nw*
"So, (at) which time will she give birth?"

 *dd.tn n.f ḥr mj*
"Why do you give to him?"

ꜥḥꜥ.n wšd.n.j nꜣ n mḏꜣyw r ḏd, j.n.ṯn tn(j)
"Then I questioned those Medjay, saying: 'Where have you come (from)?' "[10]

The first of these examples shows the perfective relative *ms.s*, with the interrogative *z(j) nw* "(at) which time?" used adverbially (see §§ 5.11, 8.14). In the second, the imperfective relative *dd.tn* is used with the interrogative prepositional phrase *ḥr mj* "why?" (literally, "on account of what?"). The third example has the perfective relative *j.n.ṯn* with the interrogative adverb *tn(j)* "where (from)?" (§ 8.13). In each case, the interrogative is the rheme and the subject and predicate together are the theme of the sentence.

9 We will see some evidence for the spoken emphasis of the rheme at the end of this lesson.
10 The *mḏꜣyw* "Medjay" were a nomadic people of Nubia. For *r ḏd* "saying" see § 14.11.3.

25.9 Sentences with emphasized adverbs or prepositional phrases

Just like the interrogative words in questions, other kinds of adverbs and prepositional phrases can be the rheme in a declarative sentence. When such sentences have a verbal predicate, Middle Egyptian uses the nonattributive relative forms for the verb: for example,

 *ntk ḥmw n t3 r ḏr.f, sqdd t3 ḫft wḏ.k*
"You are the rudder of the entire land: the land sails according as you command" or
"You are the rudder of the entire land: it is according as you command that the land sails."

In the second clause (or sentence) of this example, the rheme is the prepositional phrase *ḫft wḏ.k* "according as you command" (with the imperfective relative: § 25.3.1). That "the land sails"[11] is a given: what is important is that it does so "according as you command." Egyptian shows this by using the imperfective relative *sqdd t3* instead of a normal verbal predicate such *sqd t3, jw sqd t3,* or *jw t3 sqd.f* (see §§ 20.7–20.8).

Such "emphatic" sentences can often be recognized by the form of the verb: in this example, for instance, *sqdd* can only be a relative form, since the active *sḏm.f* of 4ae-inf. verbs such as *sqdj* "sail" does not use the geminated stem (§ 21.15). Context can also be a good indication of an emphatic sentence: for example, the answer to a question. Two of the questions cited in § 25.8 are followed by such emphatic sentences as answers:

 *ms.s m 1 prt 15*
"She will give birth on 1 Growing 15 (§ 9.8)" or
"It is on 1 Growing 15 that she will give birth"

 *ʿḥʿ.n ḏd.n.sn j.n.n ḥr ḫnmt jbhyt*
"Then they said: 'We have come from the well of Ibhyt' " or
"Then they said: 'It is from the well of Ibhyt that we have come,' "

with the perfective relative *ms.s* "she will give birth" and the perfect relative *j.n.n* "we have come," reflecting the same forms used in the preceding questions. As in the corresponding questions, the fact that "she will give birth" and the fact that "we have come" are both given: what is important in the sentences is **when** "she will give birth" and **where** "we have come" from.

When the form of the verb itself is ambiguous, context is often the only clue that an adverbial adjunct is the real rheme of the sentence: for example,

 *ḥtp n.j nswt n kmt,*[12] *ʿnḫ.j m ḥtpwt.f*
"May the king of Egypt be gracious to me, (for) I live by his grace" or
"May the king of Egypt be gracious to me, (for) it is by his grace that I live."

The important part of the second clause is the prepositional phrase *m ḥtpwt.f* "by his grace," which reflects the subjunctive *ḥtp* "be gracious" of the first clause. Although *ʿnḫ.j* "I live" could be an imperfective or subjunctive *sḏm.f,* the context indicates that it is the imperfective relative form, serving as the predicate of an emphatic sentence.

11 Metaphorically, of course: compare the English metaphor of the "ship of state."
12 *kmt* has a superfluous *t*.

25.10 Sentences with emphasized adverb clauses

Since entire clauses can have adverbial function in a sentence, such clauses can also be the rheme of an emphatic sentence. In this case, the main clause uses a nonattributive relative form to express a verbal predicate, since the verb itself is not the rheme: for example,

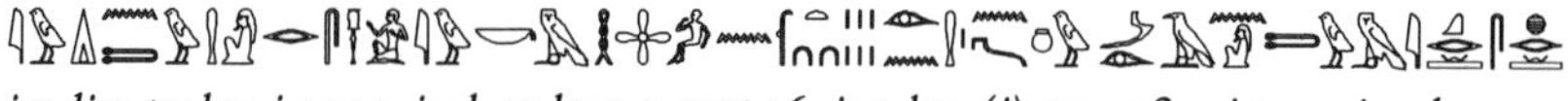

jw dj.n ṯw ḥm.j r smr, jw.k m ḥwn n rnpt 26, jr.n ḥm.(j) nw, mꜣ.n.j ṯw m jqr sḫr
"My Incarnation has given you to (be) a courtier, though you are a youth of 26 years.
My Incarnation has done this because I have seen you as one who is excellent of advice."

This passage is a good illustration of the difference in meaning between nonemphatic and emphatic sentences. The syntax of its two sentences is similar, consisting of a main clause followed by an adverb clause (for the adverb clauses, see §§ 12.17 and 18.11). The first sentence, which is nonemphatic, tells what the king did: the new information is given by the predicate of the main clause (*dj.n*), which is therefore the rheme. In the second sentence, however, the main clause does not report new information: the fact that the king "has done this" is a given, since it has already been reported by the preceding sentence. Here the sentence rheme, the new information, is the adverb clause, which tells **why** the king acted. Even though their syntax is similar, therefore, the two sentences have quite different meanings. Their verb forms are also different, though they too look the same: in the first sentence the predicate of the main clause is the perfect, because it is the rheme; in the second sentence the predicate of the main clause (*jr.n*) is not the rheme, and is therefore the perfect relative form rather than the perfect.

The second sentence in this example can also be translated with an English cleft sentence: "It is because I have seen you as one who is excellent of advice that My Incarnation has done this." You can often use this English construction to test whether an Egyptian sentence is emphatic or not, because it only makes sense when the adverb clause (or adverbial adjunct) is emphasized — as you can see by trying it with the first sentence of the example (*"It is though/while/as you are a youth of 26 years that My Incarnation has given you to (be) a courtier").

In the emphatic sentence of this example, the main clause *jr.n ḥm.(j) nw* "My Incarnation has done this" does not add any new information. Sometimes, however, both the main clause and the adverb clause of an emphatic sentence convey new information: for example,

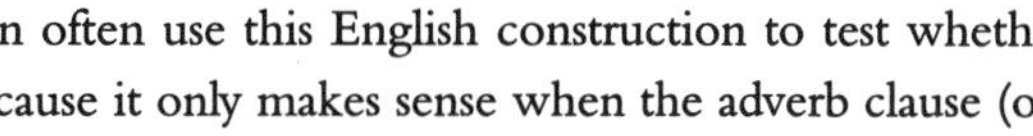

dd.ṯn pꜣ ꜥqw n r(m)ṯ.j, jw.sn ḥr jrt kꜣt
"You should give that salary to my people (only) when they are doing work" or
"It is (only) when are doing work that you should give that salary to my people."

In this case the speaker is instructing his listeners both to "give that salary to my people" and to do this "(only) when they are doing work" (§ 15.9). The use of the emphatic construction here not only emphasizes the adverb clause: it also serves as a way to prioritize the information in the sentence. While both clauses of the sentence are important, the adverb clause is more important than the predicate of the main clause. This is the reverse of a normal sentence, where the main clause is more important. The speaker indicates this reversal of priority by using the relative form *dd.ṯn* in the main clause instead of the normal subjunctive *dj.ṯn* "you should give."

This example is a good illustration of what is going on in a Middle Egyptian emphatic sentence. By using a nonattributive relative form for the predicate instead of a normal verb form or construction, Egyptian shows that the predicate — which is normally the most important part of a clause or sentence — is less important than something else in the sentence. Emphatic sentences, therefore, are actually sentences with a "de-emphasized" predicate. Such de-emphasized predicates serve as a clue to the listener or reader that the real focus of the sentence (the rheme) is something other than the predicate.

25.11 Sentences with initial subordinate clauses

So far we have seen examples of emphatic sentences in which the rheme is an interrogative, a prepositional phrase or adverb, or an adverb clause. In these kinds of sentences the relative form is either the only predicate in the sentence or the predicate of the sentence's main clause. The nonattributive relative forms also appear, however, in sentences where the main clause is **not** the one that contains the relative form. Middle Egyptian uses this construction as a way of subordinating the clause with the relative form to the rest of the sentence. There are four major uses of such clauses in Middle Egyptian:

1. **to express an initial condition**

Middle Egyptian normally uses the construction with initial *jr* plus the subjunctive or prospective to express the first clause (the protasis) of a conditional sentence (§§ 19.7, 21.6). The nonattributive relative forms can also be used for this purpose: for example,

mrr.k mꜣn.j snb.kw, sjhm.k sw ꜥꜣ

"If (or 'As') you wish to see me healthy, you should detain him here.' "[13]

Here the main clause is *sjhm.k sw ꜥꜣ* "you should detain him here," with the subjunctive. By using the imperfective relative *mrr.k* as the predicate of the first clause, the speaker shows that this clause is not a separate statement ("you wish to see me healthy") but rather is subordinate to something that follows. This use is possible because the clause with the nonattributive relative form expresses a statement that is understood as given: in other words, "(given) that you wish to see me healthy, (then) you should detain him here."

In Lesson 19 we saw that the subjunctive can also be used without *jr* in the protasis of a conditional sentence (§ 19.7). Such uses are not emphatic sentences. Instead, they are similar to English conditional sentences with *should* in the protasis, without *if*: for instance,

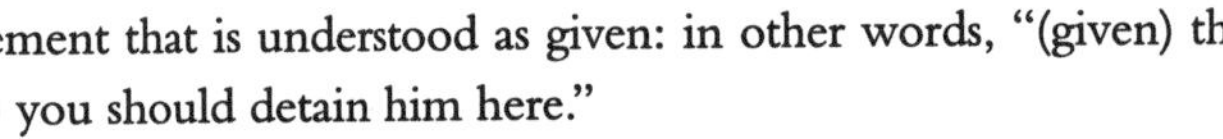

mr.ṯn ꜥnḫ msḏ.ṯn ḫpt, jw.ṯn r drp n.j m ntt m ꜥ.ṯn

"Should you love to live and hate to pass on, you are to offer to me from what you have,"

where *mr.ṯn* and *msḏ.ṯn* are subjunctives (see the last example in § 19.7). To complicate the picture even further, Middle Egyptian sometimes uses the perfective relative — which often looks like the subjunctive — in the same way: for instance,

13 This sentence is a variant of the last example cited in § 25.3.1, above. The two sentences come from different copies of the same text (the story of the Eloquent Peasant).

mr.ṯn ᶜnẖ msḏḏ.ṯ(n) m(wt) … ḏd.ṯn t ḥnqt k3(w) 3pdw ḥtpw ḏf(3)w n nb ᶜb(3) pn

"As you love to live and hate to die … you should say: 'Bread, beer, cattle, fowl, and offerings of food for the owner of this offering-stone!' "

Although the first verb here, *mr.ṯn*, could be the subjunctive, the geminated form *msḏḏ.ṯ(n)* in the second clause can only be the imperfective relative. This second form indicates that the sentence is an emphatic construction, and *mr.ṯn* must therefore be the perfective relative form.

Middle Egyptian thus has three ways of expressing a conditional protasis: with *jr* plus the subjunctive or prospective; with the subjunctive alone; or with an emphatic sentence, using the perfective or imperfective relative form. Although all three can be translated with an "if" (or "as") clause, each construction has a slightly different meaning. Clauses with *jr* are most similar to English "if" or "when" clauses; those with the subjunctive alone are analogous to English conditional clauses beginning with "should"; and the clauses with relative forms mean something like "given that." This may seem overly complicated, but it is no more so than English, which has three comparable ways of expressing conditions.

2. **to express an initial adverb clause**

In Egyptian, unmarked adverb clauses always follow the main clause (§ 12.18). The emphatic construction, however, can be used as a way of expressing an unmarked adverb clause at the beginning of a sentence: for example,

zpp z(j) m ḫt mjnt, rdjw zpw.f r gs.f m ᶜḥᶜw

"When a man survives after dying, his deeds will be placed beside him in heaps."[14]

The main clause of this sentence, with the prospective passive *rdjw*, describes what happens to a man after death. The initial clause is not meant to state that a man survives after death (which was obvious to the Egyptians) but to indicate **when** the main clause is true. It is therefore adverbial in meaning, even though syntactically it is not an adverb clause. Egyptian indicates this relationship by using a nonattributive relative form — here, the imperfective *zpp* — in the initial clause.

This kind of initial clause is especially common with the expression *ḥḏ t3* "the land becomes bright," which is an Egyptian idiom for "at dawn": for instance,

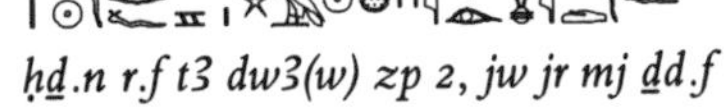

ḥḏ.n r.f t3 dw3(w) zp 2, jw jr mj ḏd.f

"So, after the land became bright the next morning it was done as he said."[15]

In this case the first clause is not meant to report that dawn occurred but simply to provide background for the main clause: the sentence as a whole is a statement of what happened at dawn. In effect, therefore, the initial clause is adverbial. The verb form in this clause is therefore the perfect relative form and not the normal perfect.

14 This sentence was used in Exercise 21, no. 11. *mjnt* "mooring" is a euphemism for "dying."

15 *dw3(w) zp 2* (§ 9.5) is literally "in the morning, in the morning." The main clause contains a passive *sḏm.f* with unexpressed subject (§ 21.9) and a nonattributive relative form used as object of the preposition *mj* (§ 25.3.1).

When the nonattributive relative forms are used to express an initial adverb clause they have the same meaning that the corresponding forms of the suffix conjugation have in normal adverb clauses: the imperfective expresses concomitant action (§ 20.10) and the perfect denotes prior circumstance (§ 18.11). Thus, in the two examples just cited, the action of the imperfective relative *zpp zj* "(when) a man survives" is concomitant with that of the main clause *rdjw zpw.f* "his deeds will be placed," and the perfect relative *ḥḏ.n t3* "(after) the land became bright" expresses an action that happened before that of the main clause *jw jr* "it was done."

3. **to express an initial concession**

Middle Egyptian also uses the nonattributive relative forms to express an initial concession, corresponding to an *although* clause in English: for instance,

jw rʿ jwd.f [sw r] r(m)ṯ, wbn.f wn wnwt, nn rḫ.tw ḫpr mtrt

"The Sun will be separating himself from people. Although he will rise when it is time, one will not know that noon has happened."[16]

These two sentences are part of Neferti's prediction of disastrous times (see Essay 19). Here *wbn.f wn wnwt* cannot be a simple statement that the sun will rise, since this would hardly qualify as a disaster. What is important is the fact that no one will be able to tell that this has happened (because "the Sun is separating himself from people"). The statement that "he will rise when it is time" is a given that Neferti concedes: i.e., "(given) that he will rise when it is time, one will not know that noon has happened."

4. **in oaths**

Oaths are a special use of the sentence with an initial nonattributive relative form. In this construction the initial clause consists of the relative form *w3ḥ* "endures" or *ʿnḫ* "lives," normally with the name of a god or the king as its subject: for example,

 *w3ḥ jmn qn, nn w3ḥ.j tw*

"As Amun the Brave endures, I will not let you be!"

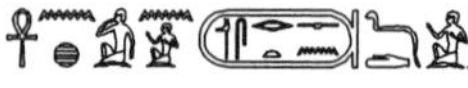 *ʿnḫ n.j Z(J)-N-WSRT, ḏd.j m m3ʿt*

"As SENWOSRET lives for me, I speak in truth!"[17]

In such sentences the statement of the first clause is always a given: it is obvious, for example, that "Amun the brave endures" and that "SENWOSRET lives for me." The main clause follows this initial clause. In the first example the main clause contains a negated subjunctive (§ 19.11.1). In the second example the main clause is itself an emphatic construction, since the important part of this clause is the prepositional phrase *m m3ʿt* and not the predicate *ḏd.j*: "it is in truth that I speak" — i.e., "I am telling the truth."

16 The first clause contains a SUBJECT-imperfective construction, which is tenseless (§ 20.7); the future tense of the translation is indicated by the sentence context (a prophecy). *wn wnwt* is an adverb clause dependent on the relative form: literally, "(when) the hour exists." In the main clause, *ḫpr mtrt* is a nonattributive relative form serving as object of *rḫ* (§ 25.3.3).

17 The "speaking-man" determinative of *ʿnḫ* here reflects the word *ʿnḫ* "oath," which is derived from the use of the relative form *ʿnḫ* in such sentences.

25.12 Balanced sentences

The sentences we examined in the preceding section all consist of an initial nonattributive relative clause followed by a main clause. Middle Egyptian also has sentences consisting of two clauses with a nonattributive relative form in each. Egyptologists call these "balanced" sentences. Syntactically they look like balanced A B nominal sentences (§ 7.8.2), but with two nonattributive relative clauses instead of two nouns: for example,

prr.ṯn r pt m nrwt, prr.j ḥr tpt ḏnḥw.ṯn

"You go up to the sky as vultures and I go up on top of your wings."

In this example both clauses have the imperfective relative *prr* as predicate, with two different subjects and adjuncts.

In sentences where an initial nonattributive relative clause is followed by a main clause, the initial clause is subordinate in meaning to the main clause. In the balanced sentence, however, the two clauses are **mutually dependent**. In the example just cited, the two clauses together make up a sentence in which the action of the first clause is dependent on that of the second, and vice versa. We can express this interdependence in English not only by a neutral translation such as that given above but also by making one or the other of the two clauses a dependent clause: for example, "If/when/whenever you go up to the sky as vultures, I go up on top of your wings" or "You go up to the sky as vultures only if/when I go up on top of your wings."

In balanced sentences the verb form in both clauses must be the same, though not necessarily of the same verb: for example,

 *ẖdd.k, dd.tw n.k z3 t3*

"You go downstream and homage is given to you" or

"Whenever you go downstream, homage is given to you,"[18]

where each clause has an imperfective relative form of a different verb. In the first example of § 25.11.2, however, the predicate in the second clause is a prospective passive, so this cannot be a balanced sentence. The verb form must also be the rheme in each clause of a balanced sentence. For this reason the last example in § 25.11.4 cannot be a balanced sentence, even though both of its clauses contain a nonattributive relative form, since the relative form in the second clause is not the rheme.

Balanced sentences apparently can be made with all three of the nonattributive relative forms, but we can only identify them with certainty when they have a distinctive relative form, such as the geminated forms in the examples above. In the following sentence, for instance, the two verb forms could be either the perfective relative or the subjunctive:

 *pr.f r pt, pr.j ḏs.j ḥnꜥ.f r pt*

"He goes to the sky and I myself go with him to the sky" (balanced sentence) or

"Should he go to the sky, I myself will go with him to the sky" (subjunctive).

18 The term *z3 t3* "homage" literally means "protection of the earth." The expression apparently reflects the image of someone prostrate on the ground, "protecting" it with his body.

The fact that the two clauses have the same verb suggests that this is a balanced sentence with the perfective relative, although a conditional sentence with two subjunctives (see § 25.11.1 above) cannot be ruled out. Similarly, the next example could be a balanced sentence with two perfect relative forms, but the second clause could also be a main clause with the perfect:

 *ḫmᶜ.n.f wj, st.n.j sw*

"He charged me and I shot him" (balanced sentence with two relative forms) or

"Once he charged me I shot him" (emphatic sentence with a relative form and the perfect).

In terms of translation, of course, either analysis of these two examples makes sense. Despite their special syntax, balanced sentences can be translated like other emphatic sentences with an initial subordinate clause.

25.13 The subordination of emphatic sentences

Like most other kinds of Egyptian sentences, emphatic sentences can be used not only as independent statements but also as noun clauses or adverb clauses. Unlike other kinds of sentences, however, the emphatic constructions do not serve as relative clauses, either marked or unmarked.

An emphatic sentence can be subordinated as an unmarked noun clause, just by virtue of the context in which it is used: for example,

wn.jn sḫtj pn snḏ.(w), jb.f jrr.t(w) r ḫsf n.f ḥr mdt tn ḏdt.n.f

"Then this peasant was afraid, thinking it was done in order to punish him because of this speech he had said."[19]

At first glance, the nonattributive imperfective relative *jrr.t(w)* "it was done" (referring to an action mentioned in a previous sentence) might appear to be the object of *jb.f* (§ 25.3.3) in this example. In the noun clause, however, the rheme is the prepositional phrase *r ḫsf n.f* "in order to punish him" and not the verb *jrr.t(w)*: the peasant was not afraid because he thought "it was done" but because he thought "it was done in order to punish him." The object of *jb.f* is therefore an emphatic sentence serving as an unmarked noun clause.

This kind of unmarked subordination of an emphatic sentence is not common. Usually emphatic sentences require a word of some sort to show that they are being used as a dependent clause. Such sentences can be subordinated in marked noun clauses by means of *ntt* or *wnt* "that," which are used to subordinate other kinds of sentences in a noun clause (§§ 16.6.6, 16.6.11): for example,

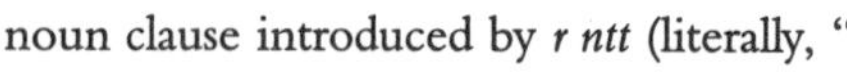 *ḏd.(j) rḫ.k r ntt ḫpr prt spdt m 4 prt 16*

"I speak so that you may learn that the emergence of Sothis will occur on 4 Growing 16."

In the noun clause introduced by *r ntt* (literally, "with respect to the fact that") here, the rheme is clearly the prepositional phrase reporting **when** the Sothic rising (see Essay 9) will take place and not the fact that the rising will occur (which is a given). The clause after *r ntt* is therefore an emphatic sentence used in a marked noun clause, and *ḫpr* is a nonattributive relative form.

19 *jb.f* is an imperfective *sḏm.f* used in an adverb clause (§ 20.10). *ḫsf* "punish" is used with the dative: literally, "in order to punish to him."

Most often, emphatic sentences are subordinated by means of the enclitic particle *js* (§ 16.7.3), placed after the nonattributive relative form. Emphatic sentences marked by *js* can serve both as noun clauses and as adverb clauses: for instance,

 *ḏd.sn n rꜥ ḏsr r(m)n m j3bt pr.n.k js m nṯr*
"They say to Re, who lifts his arm in the east, that you have emerged as a god"

 *ꜥnd j3dr.f, jr.n.f js hrw r nw st*
"His herd is small, but he has spent the day to gather it."

In the first of these examples *js* subordinates an emphatic sentence as the object of *ḏd.sn* "they say." The important part of the clause is not the statement that the listener has emerged but the prepositional phrase describing how he has done so: *m nṯr* is therefore the rheme. In the second example *js* subordinates an emphatic sentence in an adverb clause. The important part of the adverb clause is not the fact that "he has spent the day" but that he has done so in order to gather his herd; the prepositional phrase *r nw st* is therefore the rheme.

Occasionally Middle Egyptian uses both *wnt* or *ntt* and *js* to subordinate an emphatic sentence in a noun clause: for example,

 *nj sḫm rd.k jm.j, n ntt j.n.j js mjn m ṯnw*
"Your foot will not have control over me, because I have come here from This."[20]

Here the emphatic sentence is used in a noun clause after *n ntt*, literally "because of (the fact) that." The important part of the noun clause is not the statement "I have come here today" but the prepositional phrase *m ṯnw* "from This," since it is this origin that gives the speaker the immunity described in the first clause.

Middle Egyptian thus has four ways of subordinating an emphatic sentence: by context alone (as an unmarked noun clause), by *ntt* or *wnt* (in a marked noun clause), by *js* (in a marked noun or adverb clause), and by *ntt* or *wnt* plus *js* (in a marked noun clause). Of these four constructions, the two with *js* are sure signs that the subordinated clause is an emphatic sentence. The other two are also used with subordinated clauses that are not emphatic (§§ 18.13, 20.6, 20.12), so only the context or the form of the verb indicate whether the subordinated clause is emphatic.

25.14 The negation of emphatic sentences

In a nonemphatic sentence, negation of the verb form also negates the rheme, because the verb expresses the rheme. In the English sentence *Jill does not like to sing in the shower*, for example, the negated verb form tells us something negative about Jill. In emphatic sentences, however, negation of the verb form does not negate the rheme, because the rheme is something other than the verb form. This means that emphatic sentences can have two negations:

a. negation of the verb form. This produces an affirmative sentence with a negated verb: for example, *Jill does not like to sing* IN THE SHOWER or *It is in the shower that Jill does not like to sing*. This sentence answers the question *Where does Jill not like to sing?* and says something about the negative statement *Jill does not like to sing*.

20 This sentence comes from an early Middle Egyptian text: *nj sḫm* is a future negation with either the subjunctive or the prospective (see § 21.5). *ṯnw* "This" was the capital of the nome of Abydos.

b. negation of the rheme. This produces a negative sentence with an affirmative verb: for example, *It is not in the shower that Jill likes to sing.* This is one way of answering the question *Where does Jill like to sing?*, by telling us that of all the places Jill may like to sing, the shower is not one of them. Note that the verb form is affirmative, even though the rheme is negated: the sentence tells us that Jill does in fact like to sing, but not in the shower.

Middle Egyptian uses two different negations for the emphatic sentence, depending on whether the predicate or the rheme is being negated.[21]

The **verb form** in emphatic sentences is negated by means of the negative verb *tm* plus the negatival complement, like the relative forms in attributive and nominal uses: for example,

 *tm.k tr sḏm ḥr mj* "Why do you not listen?"

 *tm.f ḫr jm [r] ḥr, rḫ.f rn.f*
"It is because he knows his name that he doesn't fall on (his) face there"

 *tm.k jw r.j, tm.j ḏd r.k*
"If you don't come against me, I won't speak against you."

These examples illustrate how *tm* negates the verb in sentences with an emphasized interrogative (§ 25.8) and an emphasized adverb clause (§ 25.10), and in a balanced sentence (§ 25.12): literally, "You do not listen on account of what?" (for *tr* see § 16.7.11), "He does not fall on the face there when he knows his name," and "You don't come against me, I don't speak against you."

The **rheme** in emphatic sentences is negated by means of the negative particle *nj* before the verb **plus** the enclitic particle *js* after the verb: for instance,

 *šm.n.k ꜥnḫ.t(j), nj šm.n.k js m(w)t.(tj)*
"You have gone away alive: you have not gone away dead."[22]

This example is from a spell of the Coffin Texts spoken to the deceased. It consists of two sentences with an emphasized adverb clause. In each sentence the rheme is the adverb clause, not the predicate *šm.n.k*. The fact that the deceased has "gone away" is a given: what is important is **how** he has "gone away." Note that the negation in the second sentence does not apply to the predicate *šm.n.k* (since the deceased has in fact "gone away"), but to the rheme: i.e., "it is not dead that you have gone away (but alive)."

The use of *js* shows that the negative *nj* does not apply to the verb that follows it but to the rheme: without *js* the sentence would mean "you do not go away, though you are dead." The particle *js* is therefore an important clue to the meaning of a sentence. The construction *nj* VERB *js* is **always** the sign of an emphatic sentence; without *js*, the sentence is a normal, nonemphatic construction with a negated predicate. This use of *js* with the negative particle *nj* is similar to that which we have seen in nominal sentences (§ 11.7). In both constructions *js* serves as a signal to the reader or listener that the negation is not meant to apply to the word that follows *nj*.

21 It is also possible to negate both the verb form *and* the rheme, producing a negative sentence with a negated verb: for instance, *It is not because he's afraid that Jack doesn't fly (but because he doesn't like airplanes).* This kind of doubly negated sentence is not very common in English or Egyptian.

22 For the spelling of the stative *m(w)t.(tj)* see § 17.2 (2S).

General Considerations

25.15 The nonattributive relative forms of *wnn*

In Lesson 24 we saw how the relative forms of the verb *wnn* "exist, be" make it possible for an adverbial predicate to serve as attributive relative clauses (§ 24.11). The relative forms of *wnn* also allow such a predicate to function as a nonattributive relative form, either as a noun clause or as the predicate of an emphatic sentence. An example of the first use has been cited in § 25.3.4 above, where the imperfective relative *wnn* allows an adverbial sentence to serve as the subject of another verb. Another example of nominal use is the following:

ḏd.jn.f n.j, rḫ.n.(j) qd.k tj wj m zšj, m wn.k m šmswt jt(j).j

"Then he said to me: 'I learned of your character when I was still a nestling, while you were in the following of my father.' "[23]

Here the perfective relative of *wnn* allows a sentence with an adverbial predicate to serve as object of the preposition *m* (see § 25.3.1): literally, "in (that) you were in the following of my father."

The relative forms of *wnn* also make it possible for a construction that does not have a relative form of its own to function as the predicate in an emphatic sentence: for instance,

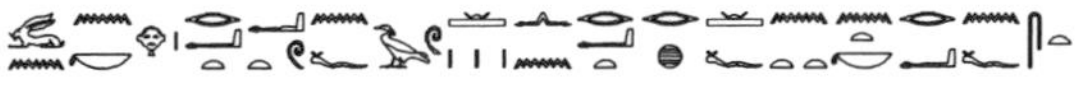

wnn.k ḥr rdjt dj.tw n.f ꜥqw, nn rdjt rḫ.f ntt ntk rdj n.f st

"You shall be having rations given to him without letting him know that you are the one who has given them to him."

In this example the imperfective relative of *wnn* allows a pseudoverbal construction to serve as the predicate in an emphatic sentence. The adverb clause *nn rdjt rḫ.f ntt ntk rdj n.f st* is the rheme of the sentence: compare the last example in § 25.10 and the discussion there.

Of course, the nonattributive relative forms of *wnn* can also be used as verbs in their own right. Common examples of this use are balanced sentences such as the following:

 *wnn pt, wnn.ṯ ḫr.j*

"As long as the sky exists, you will exist with me."

25.16 Identifying nonattributive relative forms

Throughout the discussions in this lesson we have seen that it is often impossible to tell just from its appearance whether a verb form is one of the three nonattributive relatives or a form of the suffix conjugation. The two kinds of forms often look alike: the perfect relative like the perfect, and the perfective and imperfective relatives like one or more of the *sḏm.f* forms of the suffix conjugation. In fact, only the geminated forms of final-weak verbs with active meaning can be identified as nonattributive relatives by their form alone, since this stem is not used for the various *sḏm.f* forms of these verbs in the suffix conjugation (§ 21.15). There are, however, other kinds of clues that can help us identify when a particular verb form is a nonattributive relative:

23 This sentence records the speech of the king to one of his officials. For *tj* see § 12.16.2. The expression "nestling" is an idiom for childhood — i.e., "when I was still a child." Note that the king's speech is an emphatic sentence: the king is not simply telling the official that he learned of his character, but *when* he did so.

1. **the construction in which the verb is used**

The kind of construction a form is used in often helps to identify it. Noun clauses, in particular, normally use one of the three nonattributive relative forms as a verbal predicate, although the subjunctive, prospective, or infinitive can also be used as the predicate in such clauses (§ 25.4). Some emphatic sentences are easy to recognize, especially balanced sentences (§ 25.12) and those in which the verb form is negated by *nj* ... *js* (§ 25.14).

Questions with an adverbial interrogative are also distinctive emphatic constructions (§ 25.8). It is important to note, however, that this is true only for questions in which the interrogative is an adverb, or is used adverbially, or is part of a prepositional phrase (which can function as an adverb: § 8.11). When the interrogative has another function in the sentence Egyptian does not use the nonattributive relative forms: for example,

 *ḏd nḏs ḥrwj, jry.j mj*
"The commoner says: 'How terrible! What shall I do?' "

Here the interrogative *mj* "what?" is the object of the verb. Even though the interrogative is the rheme in this sentence (as it is in all questions), the verb form is not the perfective relative (see § 25.2), but the subjunctive. The sentence is emphatic in **meaning** (since the rheme is not the predicate), but it is not an emphatic construction (see § 25.7).

Questions such as that in the last example are actually fairly unusual. When the interrogative is the object of a verb, Middle Egyptian seems to prefer a nominal sentence with the verb expressed as an **attributive** relative form: for example,

 *ptr jrt.n.k* "What have you done?"

literally, "What is that which you have done?," with the perfect relative *jrt.n.k*. Similarly, when the interrogative is the subject, the participial statement is used: for instance,

 *(j)n mj jn tw zp 2 nḏs*
"Who brought you, who brought you (§ 9.5), commoner?"

literally, "Who is the one who brought you?" (§ 23.13), where the verb is expressed as the perfective active participle *jn*.

2. **the nature of the verb itself**

In Lesson 18 we learned that Middle Egyptian normally uses the perfect to express completed action only with transitive verbs, while the stative is regularly used for the same purpose with intransitive verbs (§ 18.3). This preference has an important corollary: **the *sḏm.n.f* of intransitive verbs is normally a nonattributive relative form.** The only major exception to this rule is when an intransitive *sḏm.n.f* is used after the negative particle *nj* (§ 18.14). In this case the sentence is nonemphatic — unless, of course, the verb form is also followed by *js*. Otherwise, however, sentences in which this form serves as the predicate are normally emphatic sentences.

Since the stative is normally used to express completed action for intransitive verbs, the use of the *sḏm.n.f* of such a verb instead of the stative is usually a good indication that the clause or sentence in which it occurs is emphatic. The difference can be seen in the following example, where both verb forms are used in a single inscription:

ᶜḥᶜ.n.(j) pr.kw m gbtjw … pr.n.(j) m mšᶜ n z 3000

"Then I went up from Coptos … It was with a force of 3000 men that I went up."

The first sentence of this example reports what the speaker did. In this case the predicate is the rheme, expressed by the stative *pr.kw*. The second sentence repeats the predicate of the first statement, but here the predicate is no longer the rheme: it is now a given, and the important part of the sentence is the prepositional phrase telling **how** "I went up." In this case, therefore, the perfect relative *pr.n.(j)* is used instead of the stative.

Of course, the perfect relative of a **transitive** verb can also be used as the predicate in an emphatic sentence (for examples, see §§ 25.10 and 25.12). Since this form looks exactly like the perfect, only the construction or the context of the sentence in which it is used can indicate whether a transitive *sḏm.n.f* is the perfect relative form or the perfect — that is, whether the sentence is emphatic or not. As a rule, the perfect relative form is not used after *jw* or the introductory words *ᶜḥᶜ.n* and *wn.jn*. These typically introduce nonemphatic sentences: a *sḏm.n.f* preceded by one of these words is usually the perfect and not the perfect relative form. The particle *m.k*, however, can introduce not only the perfect (§ 18.7) but also emphatic sentences: for example,

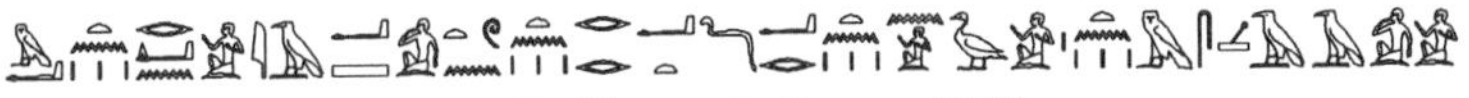

m.tn rdj.n.j j3ᶜš.tw n.tn r rdjt ḏᶜr.tn n.j z3.tn m s33(j)

"Look, I have had you summoned in order to have you seek out for me

a son of yours who is (literally, "as one who is") wise."

The particle *jw* can also introduce the perfect relative form in questions after *jn* (compare the use of the perfect in this construction: § 18.18): for example,

 *jn jw jj.n.t r jtt.f, nn dj.j jt.t sw m ᶜ.j*

"Have you come to take him? I will not let you take him from me."

Here the purpose of the question is not to ask "Have you come?" but "Have you come **to take him**?": the rheme is the prepositional phrase *r jtt.f*.

A *sḏm.n.f* form in a main clause can therefore be either the perfect or the perfect relative form, as the following chart summarizes.

	TRANSITIVE VERBS	INTRANSITIVE VERBS
initial	perfect or relative	relative, rarely perfect
after *jw*, *ᶜḥᶜ.n*, *wn.jn*	perfect	relative or perfect (after *jw*)
after *m.k*	perfect or relative	relative or perfect
negated by *nj* (or *nn*)	perfect	perfect
negated by *nj … js*	relative	relative

As you can see from this chart, both the kind of construction it is used in and the nature of the verb itself are important clues to whether a *sḏm.n.f* is the perfect relative form or the perfect, and therefore whether the sentence or clause in which it occurs is emphatic or not. In general there is little ambiguity except in the case of the *sḏm.n.f* of a transitive verb used after *m.k* or without an introductory word.

3. **the form of the passive**

In Lesson 21 we saw that the passive *sḏm.f* and the stative are the normal passive counterparts of the perfect (§ 21.10). This preference also has an important corollary: **the *sḏm.n.tw.f* is normally a nonattributive relative form.** As with intransitive verbs, the only major exception to this rule is when the *sḏm.n.tw.f* is used after the negative particle *nj* (§ 18.14). In this case the sentence is nonemphatic — unless, of course, the verb form is also followed by *js*. Otherwise, however, sentences in which this form serves as the predicate are normally emphatic sentences.

When the predicate is passive, Middle Egyptian normally uses the passive *sḏm.f* to express completed action, although the stative is preferred for pronominal subjects. When the *sḏm.n.tw.f* is used instead of these forms, the sentence is usually emphatic. The following example, with both the *sḏm.n.tw.f* and the passive, illustrates the difference:

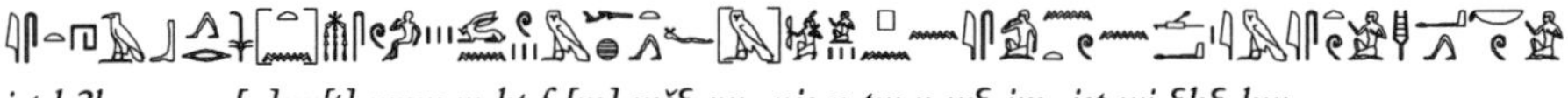

jst h3b r msw-[n]sw[t] wnw m ḫt.f [m] mšꜥ pn, njs.n.tw n wꜥ jm, jst wj ꜥḥꜥ.kw

"although the king's children who were in his following in this force had been sent for. One of them was summoned while I was in attendance."[24]

This passage has two examples of a passive used without an expressed subject. The first of these describes something that was done: here the predicate (*h3b*) is the rheme, and the passive *sḏm.f* is used for the verb. In the second sentence the interest is no longer on the verb — since it merely repeats the action already described in the preceding sentence — but on the adverb clause that describes the circumstances under which "one of them was summoned." Here the adverb clause is the rheme, and the perfect relative *njs.n.tw* is used instead of the passive *njs*: i.e., "it was while I was in attendance (literally, "standing") that one of them was called to."

25.17 Emphatic sentences without nonattributive relative forms

When we began our discussion of emphatic sentences, we saw that a normal Middle Egyptian sentence can have emphatic **meaning** without using an emphatic construction (§ 25.7). As opposed to sentences in which the emphatic meaning is signaled by the use of a nonattributive relative form, such sentences can be called "contextually emphatic." In the example cited in § 25.7 the predicate is a stative; we have also seen an example with the subjunctive used as predicate in an emphatic sentence (§ 25.16.1). The passive *sḏm.f* can also be used in this way, instead of the *sḏm.n.tw.f*: for example,

 *msy.j m ḥsbt 1 n z3 rꜥ JMN-M-Ḥ3T*

"I was born in Year 1 of the Son of Re AMENEMHAT."

This sentence is clearly intended to tell **when** the speaker was born; **that** he was born is a given. It is therefore an emphatic sentence (since the rheme is not the predicate), but it is not an emphatic construction: the emphatic sense comes from the meaning of the sentence itself, not from the verb form that is used as the predicate. The form of the verb itself is thus only one indication of the meaning of a sentence, and not necessarily the most important one. It is also necessary to consider the content and context of the sentence in order to determine the proper translation.

24 The first clause is an adverb clause dependent on a preceding main clause: see § 21.12.

25.18 Emphasized subjects

In the emphatic sentences we have considered above, the rheme has been an adverb, a prepositional phrase, or another clause. It is also possible for the subject of a verb to be the rheme: for example, *JILL sings in the shower*, where the subject *Jill* is the rheme (answers the question *Who sings in the shower?*).

In Middle Egyptian an emphasized subject is normally indicated by means of the particle *jn*, if it is a noun, or by an independent pronoun. The most common use of this construction in verbal sentences is the normal future counterpart of the participial statement, with the subjunctive or prospective (§ 23.13): for instance,

 *jn nmtj ḥz.f sw*
"**Nemti** will bless him" or "It is Nemti who will bless him"

 *ntf sḏm.f st*
"**He** will hear it" or "He is the one who will hear it."

The participial statement itself is the most common example of a nominal sentence with emphasized subject (§§ 23.13–23.14).

In adverbial sentences the adverbial predicate is the normal rheme, but such sentences can also have an emphasized subject: for example,

 *sḫr pn jn n.f jb.k, nn (n)tf m jb.(j) r.k*
"This plan that made off with your mind, **it** was not in my mind for you."[25]

This sentence implies "I had something in mind for you, but this plan wasn't it": in other words, the adverbial predicate *m jb.(j) r.k* is a given, and *ntf* is the rheme. This is the only kind of adverbial sentence in which the independent pronoun can be used as subject (§ 10.5).

One element that verbal, nominal, and adverbial sentences have in common is the use of the independent pronoun to express an emphasized subject. Coptic indicates that this was the only form of the personal pronoun that could be fully stressed as a separate word. In nominal sentences, moreover, Coptic shows two different forms of this pronoun, which correspond to the way it is used in the sentence: when the pronoun is the rheme, it is fully stressed (e.g., **ⲚⲦⲞⲔ**, from *ntk*); when it is the theme, it has a reduced form (e.g., **ⲚⲦⲔ̄**, also from *ntk*). This feature suggests that Egyptian, like English, put the primary stress of a sentence on the rheme. Thus, a sentence such as  *jnk jr pt* "I am the one who made the sky," which can have two different meanings (§ 23.14), was probably ambiguous only in writing. The spoken language probably distinguished between the two meanings by stress, just as English can do for its translation: *JNK jr pt* "**I** am the one who made the sky" (participial statement with *jnk* as rheme) vs. *jnk JR PT* "I am **the one who made the sky**" (nominal sentence with *jr pt* as rheme). It is reasonable to conclude that the rheme was similarly stressed in other kinds of sentences as well.

25 In other words, "this misunderstanding of yours is not what I had in mind for you." The negation can also be read *nj ntf*, with *nj* negating just the pronoun (§ 11.7): "not *it* (i.e., 'something else') was in my mind for you."

ESSAY 25. LETTERS

Of all the kinds of Egyptian texts that have survived, letters bring us closest to the ancient Egyptians as real people. Letters also give us the best example of Egyptian as a spoken language. Like the nonliterary texts discussed in Essay 24, they were concerned with content rather than form. Egyptian letters were composed, like our own, as a substitute for spoken communication. As such they reflect the everyday language of their writers much more closely than literary texts.

Letters have survived from almost all periods of ancient Egyptian history, and from all but the very lowest levels of Egyptian society. We have copies of letters written by Egyptian kings to other rulers and to their own officials, and real letters written by Egyptians to their superiors (including the king), their subordinates, and to their own friends and family.

The earliest preserved letters are copies of messages sent by King Izezi of Dynasty 5 (ca. 2350 BC) to his officials and reproduced in their tomb biographies. A century later the young king Pepi II of Dynasty 6 sent a letter to one of his officials, named Harkhuf, which was later carved into the façade of Harkhuf's tomb at Aswan. In it, the king responds to a letter that Harkhuf had sent with news of an expedition he had led to Nubia for the king:

> You have said in this letter of yours that you are bringing a dwarf of the god's dances from the land of the horizon dwellers, like the dwarf that the god's sealbearer Bawer-djed brought from Punt in the time of Izezi ... Come downstream to the capital at once! Cast off and bring this dwarf with you ... When he boards the boat with you, assign excellent people who will be around him on both sides of the boat and who will keep him from falling in the water. Also assign excellent people who will sleep around him in his cabin. Inspect 10 times a night. My Incarnation wants to see this dwarf more than the products of Sinai or Punt!

The letter is dated to Year 2 of Pepi II's reign, when the king was about eight years old.

Most letters were written on ostraca or on individual sheets of papyrus, cut to about the size of a modern sheet of paper. Very few were dated. Many were dictated to scribes, but quite a few preserved letters were actually written by their senders. As such they are a good indication of the level of literacy among educated Egyptians, including some women. Once a letter on papyrus was completed, it was rolled up from left to right, then folded in half or thirds. The address was written on the outside of the folded letter: for example,

 *dd ḥm k3 ḥq(3)-nḫt.(w) r pr.f n nbsyt*

"What funerary-priest Heqa-nakht sends to his household of Nebsyt."

Official letters on papyrus were regularly tied with a strip of linen and sealed, but other kinds seem to have been posted without sealing. There was no mail service in ancient Egypt, so letters were usually entrusted to travelers for delivery.

The content of Egyptian letters is as varied as those of our own society. Most deal with business or administrative matters, but others were written just to keep in touch. An example of the latter is the following, written by a woman in Thebes to her mother in the Thinite nome, near Abydos, in early Dynasty 12:

> A thousand phrases of greeting you, in lph (§ 17.20.2)! May you be [well], with your heart comforted. May Hathor comfort your heart for me. Don't worry about me. Look, I am healthy ... And greet Gereg in lph. Look, I have had Si-[Hathor] (the letter carrier) come to check on you. Don't let Gereg forget about [what I told] him. And greet the whole house for me in life, soundness, and health.

The purpose of such correspondence is reflected in a common Egyptian idiom for letters or letter writing: *swḏ3 jb* "make sound the heart." This expression is often used as an infinitival phrase in letters, referring to the letter itself: for instance,

> *swḏ3 jb pw n nb.j ꜥnḫ-(w)ḏ3-s(nb) r ntt h3w nb n nb.j ꜥnḫ-(w)ḏ3-s(nb) ꜥḏ.(w) wḏ3.(w)*
> "This is a communication to my lord, lph, to the effect that all the affairs of my lord, lph, are safe and sound" —

literally, "It is making sound the heart of my lord, lph, with respect to (the fact) that all the affairs of my lord, lph, are safe and sound."

Egyptian letters often use stock phrases in the same way that our own use expressions such as "Dear Sir," "Sincerely," and "Yours truly." Many of these occur in letters from individuals to their superiors. As a term of respect, the letter writer often refers to himself as *b3k jm* "your humble servant" or "yours truly" (literally, "the worker therein": § 8.10). In the same way, the superior to whom the letter is directed can be addressed as *nb.j ꜥnḫ-(w)ḏ3-s(nb)* "my lord, lph," as in the passage just cited, or indirectly as *zẖ3.k* "your scribe" — presumably indicating that the letter would be dealt with by the recipient's secretary.

Besides the odd individual letter, a number of important archives have also been found. For Middle Egyptian the most important are the **Heqanakht Papers**, containing four letters and several accounts composed by a funerary priest of early Dynasty 12 in Thebes; the **Semna Dispatches**, copies of administrative letters found in a Nubian fortress; and the **Illahun Papyri**, a series of several dozen business and administrative letters discovered in a Middle Kingdom village near the Fayum. Although most letters exist in only one copy, some model letters were used to train scribes in the New Kingdom and later. Among such letters is a Middle Kingdom composition that was known as *kmyt* "**Kemit**" — literally, "Compendium."

The Egyptians wrote letters not only to the living but also to the dead. From the early Middle Kingdom and later we possess a number of such **Letters to the Dead**, written on objects that were deposited in the tomb to seek the intercession of the deceased. A typical example is the following, written inside an offering bowl and addressed to "Courtier Nefer-sefekh":

> A sister speaking to her brother. My woe is great ... on account of one who is acting against my daughter very wrongly, though there is nothing I did against him. I did not consume his property and he gave nothing to my daughter. Invocation offerings (such as those in the bowl) are given to an akh for intercession on behalf of a survivor. Make litigation against the one who is doing this ill!

Such letters are a poignant reminder of how vividly the ancient Egyptians felt their deceased relatives to be a part of their own daily lives.

EXERCISE 25

Transliterate and translate the following passages; identify the nonattributive relative forms and their function in the clause or sentence. For emphatic sentences, identify the rheme.

1. 
2. 
3. 
4.  — *z(j) n ḥḥ* "a man of a million": i.e., unique
5. 
6. 
7. 
8. 
9. 
10.  — *mj wn* "like"
11. 
12. 
13. 
14. 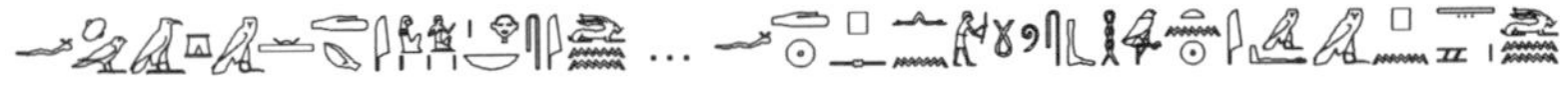
15.  — *ng3w* "Cattle-town" (a place near modern Cairo)
16. 
17. 
18. 
19. 
20. 
21. 
22. 
23. 
24. 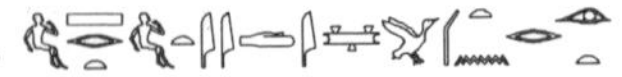
25. 
26. 

 … — *ḥn* is an imperative

26. Middle Egyptian Grammar

26.1 Rules and exceptions

In order to read and understand texts in any foreign language you need two basic tools, a dictionary and a grammar. A dictionary tells you what the words of a language mean and something about how they are used, and a grammar shows you how the words are put together into actual sentences. The purpose of this book has been to give you a solid grounding in the grammar of Middle Egyptian.

Human languages defy neat and orderly classification. Although all languages obey fundamental rules for the formation of words and sentences, they are also notoriously fluid about how those rules are applied. To appreciate this in English, you have only to look at the works of Lewis Carroll, James Joyce, or Dr. Seuss. Middle Egyptian is no different in this respect than any other language. Although we can approach its grammar in an orderly fashion — as the content and arrangement of the lessons in this book have tried to do — we are often puzzled and even frustrated by the continual appearance of exceptions to the rules. Middle Egyptian can be especially difficult in this regard, as you have seen throughout the course of these lessons. There are a number of reasons why this is so.

Like any language, Middle Egyptian has its own unique way of understanding the phenomena of the world and the relationships between them. Every language is different in this respect from every other language, but some are more different than others. It is relatively easy for speakers of English to learn modern languages such as Spanish or German because to a great extent these languages share with English a common civilization and a common experience of the world. Ancient Egypt, however, is separated from us by a much greater gulf of time and culture. The people who spoke and wrote Middle Egyptian understood the world in many ways much differently than we do, and they organized their experience of it differently as well. Even though we may understand the individual words and grammar of an Egyptian sentence, therefore, there are times when the meaning of the sentence as a whole can still elude us.

Of course, we can come up against similar problems with modern languages, but when we do we have the advantage of being able to ask a native speaker for explanation. This luxury is not available for Middle Egyptian. As a result, we cannot always be certain whether the problem lies in our own understanding or in the ancient text itself. Individual languages also vary from region to region and even from speaker to speaker. What is acceptable usage to one group of speakers may not be so to another. Our knowledge of modern languages usually allows us to appreciate the difference between such dialectical variation and a genuinely ungrammatical usage. Here again, we have no such luxury for Middle Egyptian. It is not always possible, therefore, to know whether an unusual construction represents a real exception or simply a scribal error. Because languages are capable of great flexibility, however, we have to give the texts the benefit of the doubt: as a rule Egyptologists are (or should be) wary of labeling something an error rather than an exception.

Languages also change over the course of time. When we learn a modern language, we normally study only one stage of its historical evolution, and the knowledge we acquire of that stage ultimately allows us to recognize a different historical usage when we encounter it. Students who learn modern English as a foreign language, for example, soon come to realize that constructions such as *thou hast* belong to an earlier stage of the language and are used today only in very limited and narrowly defined contexts, such as prayers or archaic dialects. As you have learned in the course of these lessons, Middle Egyptian was a spoken language for several hundreds of years and was written for many centuries more. Our understanding of the language has improved slowly to the point where we are often able to recognize an archaic usage as such, but it is still evolving, and much work remains to be done in this area of Middle Egyptian grammar. Here again, the imperfect state of our knowledge does not always allow us to know whether an unusual construction is a deliberate archaism or simply a less common contemporary usage.

All of these factors mean that our appreciation of what actually constitutes Middle Egyptian is less precise than we might like — and, correspondingly, more difficult to teach and learn. Nonetheless, it is possible to identify and organize the basic core of Middle Egyptian grammar, and this fundamental core is what we have been studying in the lessons of this book. To make it easier for you to appreciate and remember these basics, the following sections present a summary and overview of Middle Egyptian grammar.

26.2 Categories of words

Middle Egyptian words are normally classified into seven basic categories: nouns, pronouns, adjectives, prepositions, adverbs, particles, and verb forms. Each word in a Middle Egyptian sentence belongs to one of these seven categories.

It is important to remember that these are categories of **form**, not **function**. As we have seen throughout these lessons, it is possible for a word of one category to be **used** like that of another: for example, nouns of time can be used as adverbs (§ 8.14), prepositional phrases can be used as adjectives (§ 6.7) or nouns (Exercise 16, no. 21), and verb forms can be used like nouns (for instance, the subjunctive in a noun clause: § 19.9). Despite this flexibility in use, however, the words themselves are still nouns, prepositions, verbs, and so forth.

26.3 Nouns (Lesson 4)

All Egyptian nouns consist of a root and an ending. The root carries the basic meaning of the noun: for example, *sn* "sibling." The ending identifies the noun as belonging to one of two genders, masculine or feminine, and tells whether it is singular, dual, or plural in number. Masculine singular nouns can have no ending (i.e., a "zero" ending), but the other endings consist of one or more consonants: thus, *sn* "brother" (masculine singular), *snt* "sister" (feminine singular), *snwj* "two brothers" (masculine dual), *sntj* "two sisters" (feminine dual), *snw* "brothers" (masculine plural), and *snwt* "sisters" (feminine plural).

When they are used in a sentence, nouns are either defined or undefined. These features are not marked in the form of the noun but by what the noun refers to. Nouns can also be used together in noun phrases of apposition, conjunction ("and"), disjunction ("or"), or possession. These relationships can be expressed simply by putting two nouns together, or by linking them with a separate word such as a preposition or the genitival adjective.

26.4 Pronouns (Lesson 5 and §§ 10.5, 15.5)

There are three kinds of pronouns in Middle Egyptian: interrogative, demonstrative, and personal. Interrogative pronouns have only one form and are used exclusively in questions. Demonstrative pronouns have different forms to distinguish gender and number. They can be used either by themselves or to modify a noun or noun phrase.

Personal pronouns distinguish person as well as gender and number, and have four different forms as well: independent, dependent, suffix, and subject. Independent pronouns are used as the subject or predicate in nominal sentences (§ 7.11), as part of the predicate in adjectival sentences of possession (§ 7.5), to express the agent of the infinitive (§ 14.4), and as emphasized subject (§ 25.18). The subject pronouns are another kind of independent pronoun used as the subject of an adverbial or pseudoverbal predicate (§§ 10.5, 15.4).

The dependent pronouns always follow some other word. They are used as the subject in adjectival sentences (§ 7.3) and in adverbial sentences after certain introductory words (§ 10.4), as the expressed subject of the imperative (§ 16.3), and as the object of verb forms.

The suffix pronouns are always attached as part of a word. There are two sets of suffix pronouns. One is used exclusively with the stative (§ 17.2). The other set has a wider range of use: as the possessor of a noun (§ 5.7), the object of a preposition (§ 8.4), the subject in adverbial sentences after certain introductory words (§ 10.3), the subject or object of the infinitive (§§ 14.4–14.5), and the subject of verb forms; and for the gender and number markings of the prospective participle (§ 23.2).

The impersonal pronoun *tw* (§ 15.5) is used like both a dependent and a suffix pronoun, as the subject of an adverbial or verbal predicate. As a suffix it is also used to make the passive of some verb forms.

26.5 Adjectives (Lesson 6)

The category of adjectives is primarily a functional one. There is only one Egyptian word that can only be used as an adjective: *nb* "all, each, every." All other Middle Egyptian adjectives are words of other categories that are used as adjectives. These include demonstrative pronouns, the nisbes of nouns and prepositions (§§ 6.1, 8.6), ordinal numbers (§ 9.3), the relative clause markers *ntj* and *jwtj* (§§ 12.3, 12.9), and the attributive forms of the verb (participles and relative forms). The ordinal numbers are nouns, and the relative clause markers can be categorized either as nouns or pronouns. Adjectives such as *nfr* "good, perfect" are actually participles of adjective verbs (§ 23.9).

Except for *nb*, adjectives can be used either to modify a preceding noun or noun phrase or as nouns in their own right, without an expressed antecedent. In either case, they are marked for the gender and number of their antecedent, with the same endings used for nouns. Participial adjectives, and some nisbes, can also be used as adjectival predicates (Lesson 7 and § 23.11). The participial adjective *wr* can also be used as an interrogative meaning "how much?" (§§ 6.6, 7.5.4).

26.6 Prepositions and adverbs (Lesson 8)

Middle Egyptian has 17 basic prepositions and a large number of compound prepositions formed from the basic prepositions plus a noun, infinitive, or adverb. The category of adverbs includes three primary adverbs, one interrogative, several adverbs formed from adjectives, and prepositional adverbs. Words of other categories, such as nouns and verb forms, can also be used as adverbs.

26.7 Particles (Lesson 16)

The category of particles includes words that do not fit readily into one of the other categories of Egyptian words. Particles are classified as proclitic or enclitic, depending on whether they can occur at the head of a clause or only after another words. Some particles are interjections.

Egyptian particles other than interjections can also be characterized as converters or statement auxiliaries. Converters have a syntactic function, such as marking a certain kind of clause. Statement auxiliaries have no specific syntactic function, but they do add a nuance of meaning to their clause.

26.8 Verb forms (Lessons 13–25)

Middle Egyptian verbs belong to one of fifteen root classes and are basically transitive or intransitive (Lesson 13). When a verb is used in a clause or sentence it must appear in a particular form. Middle Egyptian uses twenty-four such forms, which Egyptologists divide into six formal categories:

1. **the suffix conjugation** — eleven forms, divided into three subcategories:
   a. six *sḏm.f* forms: the subjunctive (Lesson 19), the perfective and imperfective (Lesson 20), the passive (Lesson 21), and the prospective active and passive (Lesson 21)
   b. four suffixed forms: the perfect (or *sḏm.n.f*: Lesson 18), and the *sḏm.jn.f*, *sḏm.ḫr.f*, and *sḏm.k3.f* (Lesson 22)
   c. the *sḏmt.f* (Lesson 22).
2. **the stative** — a single form, with obligatory pronominal suffixes indicating person, gender, and number (Lesson 17).
3. **the imperative** — a single form (Lesson 16). The spoken language seems to have distinguished between masculine or feminine and singular or plural imperatives, at least for some verbs, but written forms show at most a difference between singular and plural in a few classes.
4. **the participles** — five forms, distinguished by aspect and voice: perfective and imperfective active, perfective and imperfective passive, and prospective (Lesson 23). Each form is marked for gender and number by an ending or, in the prospective participle, a pronominal suffix.
5. **the relative forms** — three forms, distinguished by aspect: perfective, imperfective, and perfect (Lessons 24–25). Each of the three forms also has an ending indicating gender and number.
6. **the infinitival forms** — three forms: the infinitive, the negatival complement, and the complementary infinitive (Lesson 14).

The participles, relatives, and infinitival forms are known collectively as the nominal forms of the verb, because they can function by themselves as nouns.

26.9 Verb forms: formal features

Each of the twenty-four verb forms of Middle Egyptian is composed of one to four formal elements (§ 13.4):

1. **the verb stem** appears in every verb form. There are two such stems in Middle Egyptian, base and geminated. Most forms use one or the other of these stems in each root class, but some can use either: for example, the perfect of 2ae-gem. verbs and the perfective passive participle of 2-lit. verbs (§§ 18.2, 23.7).

2. **endings** are added to the verb stem in some forms. There are two kinds of endings: formal (which distinguish particular forms) and attributive (which mark gender and number). Some verb forms can use both kinds of endings together: for example, in the masculine plural imperfective active participle *rḫyw* "who know," *y* is a formal ending (a sign of the imperfective form) and *w* is an attributive ending (marking the masculine plural). Attributive endings are used in the imperative (plural) and the attributive forms (participles and relative forms). They are the same as the gender and number endings of nouns and adjectives, except in the imperative (§ 16.1) and the prospective participle (§ 23.2). Formal endings are less consistent. The only formal endings that are used for all verbs of all classes are the endings –*t* of the *sḏmt.f* and the complementary infinitive (§§ 22.12, 14.20) and –*tj* of the prospective participle (§ 23.8). Other formal endings are used for some verbs or root classes in the *sḏm.f* (except the perfective: § 21.15), the *sḏmt.f* (–*yt* in some 3ae-inf. forms: § 22.12), the participles (except the perfective: § 23.5), the prospective participle (–*wtj* in some 3ae-inf. forms: § 23.8), the perfective and imperfective relative forms when they are used attributively (§ 24.2), the infinitive and the negatival complement (§§ 14.3, 14.17). Only a few verb forms have no ending in any class: these include the perfective *sḏm.f*, the perfect, the *sḏm.jn.f*, *sḏm.ḫr.f*, and *sḏm.k3.f*, the stative, and the relative forms when they are used nonattributively.

3. **suffixes** are added after any endings to distinguish some verb forms. There are five such suffixes in Middle Egyptian: *n*, used in the perfect and perfect relative (*sḏm.n.f*: §§ 18.2, 24.1); the biliteral suffixes *jn*, *ḫr*, and *k3*, used in the *sḏm.jn.f*, *sḏm.ḫr.f*, and *sḏm.k3.f* (§ 22.1); and the suffix *tw*, which is used to make the passive of some verb forms (see § 26.12 below). The passive suffix is added after the other four suffixes.

4. **the prefix** *j* can be added before the verb stem in some forms. This is a fairly uncommon feature in Middle Egyptian, and may be dialectical in origin. It is used only for some verbs or verb classes, usually as an option, in the imperative (§ 16.2), the imperfective and subjunctive *sḏm.f* (§ 21.15), and the imperfective active participle (§ 23.6).

26.10 Verb forms: action versus state

The normal, or unmarked, meaning of most Middle Egyptian verb forms is that of action. The stative, however, expresses a state of being, either as an existing condition or as the result of some action (Lesson 17). The distinction between action and state is not part of the English verbal system. As a result, the stative often has to be translated by an English verb form or construction implying action rather than state, even though the stative itself does not have this connotation.

26.11 Verb forms: mood

The Middle Egyptian verbal system has two moods, indicative and subjunctive (§ 13.3.3). The indicative is the normal or unmarked mood, denoting the action or state expressed by the verb as a statement of fact; the subjunctive is a marked mood, indicating that the verbal action or state is viewed as contingent, possible, or desirable. The only verb form marked for mood is the subjunctive *sḏm.f* (Lesson 19). The other verb forms are unmarked for mood. As such, some of them can occasionally be used with subjunctive as well as indicative meaning: for example, the stative expressing a wish or command and the perfect denoting an action contrary to fact (§§ 17.17.2, 18.8).

26.12 Verb forms: voice

The Middle Egyptian verbal system has two voices, active and passive (§ 13.3.4). Some verb forms are neutral with regard to voice, and can be used with passive as well as the normal active meaning: these include the stative, the *sḏmt.f*, the prospective participle, and the infinitival forms. Only four verb forms are specifically passive: the passive *sḏm.f*, the prospective passive, and the passive participles (perfective and imperfective). All the other verb forms are active. The imperative and the active participles (perfective and imperfective) can only be used with active meaning. The other active forms can be made passive by means of the suffix *tw*. This option is rare, however, for the prospective *sḏm.f* and the perfect. The normal passive counterpart of the prospective is the prospective passive. The regular passive counterpart of the perfect is the passive *sḏm.f* with nominal subjects and the stative for pronominal subjects (§ 21.10).

26.13 Verb forms: tense

Middle Egyptian verb forms can express both absolute and relative tense: that is, action that is past, present, or future with respect to either the moment of speaking or another action (§ 13.3.1). Most forms are unmarked for tense, and none are marked for absolute tense. A few verb forms, however, are normally associated with a specific relative tense: these include the prospective *sḏm.f* (active and passive) and the prospective participle, denoting action yet to occur with respect to some other action; and the *sḏm.jn.f* and *sḏm.k3.f*, which denote subsequent or consequent action. Other verb forms are often associated with particular tenses because of certain features they possess. The subjunctive, for example, often expresses future tense because actions that are contingent, possible, or desirable are most often seen as lying in the future (§ 19.1).

26.14 Verb forms: aspect

Most Middle Egyptian verb forms are aspectually unmarked. Those that are marked for this feature express two kinds of aspect: completion and repetition (§ 13.3.2). The aspect of completion is expressed by two sets of marked forms and constructions:

- those expressing the **perfect**, or completed action. These include the perfect, the passive *sḏm.f*, the *sḏmt.f*, and the perfect relative form. The stative often expresses completed action, but this is a secondary connotation of its basic meaning of state.
- those expressing the **imperfect**, or incomplete action. These include the imperfective verb forms (*sḏm.f*, participles, and relative), the pseudoverbal construction with *ḥr* plus infinitive (§ 15.2), and the SUBJECT-imperfective construction (§ 20.8).

Forms marked for the aspect of completion are often associated with specific tenses because of this marking: the perfect forms with past action, and the imperfect forms with the present.

The aspect of repetition can be expressed by the imperfective verb forms. The imperfective forms are not marked for this aspect. Instead, they are marked for incomplete action, and this feature allows them to express repeated action as well. There are no verb forms or constructions marked for actions done only once (the opposite of repeated action). Despite their name, the perfective forms (*sḏm.f*, participles, and relative) are aspectually unmarked. Although they can be used to express single actions, they are not specifically marked for this feature, and can therefore express generic action as well.

26.15 Predicates

Middle Egyptian clauses and sentences are classified into four different types, based on the nature of their predicate:

1. **nominal** (Lessons 7 and 11)

Clauses or sentences with nominal predicates basically express the identity of their subject. The predicate can be a noun or noun equivalent (noun phrase, pronoun, noun clause, or nominal form of the verb). Because the same elements are used as the subjects of Egyptian sentences, the predicate can be identified only by the composition of the sentence or its context. There are three basic nominal-sentence patterns: A *pw*, A B, and A *pw* B. The predicate in the first is always A. In the other two patterns it can be either A or B.

2. **adjectival** (Lessons 7 and 11)

Clauses or sentences with adjectival predicates basically express a quality of their subject. The predicate can be a participial adjective or a nisbe. The predicate always precedes its subject and is always masculine singular (or dual: § 7.2), regardless of the gender and number of the subject.

3/ **adverbial** (Lessons 10–11 and 15)

Clauses or sentences with adverbial predicates basically express the location of their subject. The predicate can be an adverb or adverb equivalent, including prepositional phrases and the pseudoverbal construction, and almost always follows the subject.

4. **verbal** (Lessons 16–25)

Clauses or sentences with verbal predicates express an action or state of their subject. The predicate can be any verb form that can have a subject of its own, expressed or unexpressed; this includes all forms except the negatival complement and complementary infinitive.[1] Verbal predicates always precede their subject. Certain verbal constructions — notably, the SUBJECT-stative and SUBJECT-imperfective — require the subject to be expressed before the verb form, but in such cases it is also repeated after the verb in the form of a pronominal suffix. The various elements of a verbal clause follow a specific word order, summarized as **VsdoSOA** (§ 14.6): verb (**V**), pronominal suffix subject (**s**), pronominal dative (**d**), pronominal object (**o**), nominal subject (**S**), nominal object (**O**), and adjuncts (**A**) such as adverbs and prepositional phrases (including nominal datives).

26.16 Clauses

Middle Egyptian sentences have four kinds of clauses (Lesson 12): main clauses, noun clauses, relative clauses, and adverb clauses. Main clauses are those that can stand by themselves as independent sentences; all sentences must have a main clause. Noun clauses serve as nouns: for example, as the object of a preposition or verb or as the subject of another predicate. Relative clauses are those with attributive function, modifying an antecedent (expressed or unexpressed). Adverb clauses have the same function as adverbs and prepositional phrases, describing when, where, why, or how something happens or is true. Main clauses are also known as independent clauses; the other three kinds of clauses are dependent or subordinate.

1 The latter two forms could also have subjects of their own in Old Egyptian. In Middle Egyptian, however, the subject is almost always omitted or transferred to the governing verb.

All four kinds of clauses can be unmarked or marked. Unmarked clauses usually have nothing but the context in which they are used to indicate their function. Marked clauses have a word of some kind, such as particles (Lesson 16), to show how they are being used. The major indicators of this sort are the following:

- main clauses: the introductory words *ꜥḥꜥ.n*, *wn.jn*, and *wn.ḫr*; the proclitic particles *jn*, *jsw*, *m.k*, *nḥmn*, *ḥ3*, and *smwn*
- noun clauses: the proclitic particles *wnt* and *ntt*, and the enclitic particle *js*
- relative clauses: the relative adjectives *ntj* and *jwtj* (Lesson 12)
- adverb clauses: the proclitic particles *jsṯ* and *tj*, and the enclitic particle *js*.

The function of clauses with a verbal predicate can also be indicated by the form of the verb. Four verb forms are used exclusively in main clauses: the *sḏm.jn.f*, *sḏm.ḫr.f*, *sḏm.k3.f*, and the imperative. The participles and relative forms are the normal means Middle Egyptian uses to make relative clauses with a verbal predicate (Lessons 23–24). Noun clauses with a verbal predicate can be expressed with the infinitive or the nonattributive relative forms, and the latter can also be used to express an initial adverb clause (Lesson 25). There are no verb forms specifically marked for use in adverb clauses except perhaps for the complementary infinitive, which serves as complement to another form of the same verb (§ 14.19).

26.17 Noun clauses

Middle Egyptian noun clauses can have all four types of predicate, but adjectival predicates are rarely used in such clauses and adverbial predicates are limited to marked noun clauses. The following table summarizes the normal distribution of the various kinds of predicates in umarked and marked noun clauses:[2]

	UNMARKED	WITH *js*	WITH *ntt/wnt*
NOMINAL PREDICATE	✓	✓	✓
ADJECTIVAL PREDICATE		[✓]	
ADVERBIAL PREDICATE			✓
VERBAL PREDICATE	nominal forms: infinitive, nonattributive relative forms other forms: subjunctive, prospective, perfect(?), *sḏmt.f* SUBJECT-stative SUBJECT-imperfective	nonattributive relative forms (emphatic sentences)	[subjunctive], perfect, passive SUBJECT-stative SUBJECT-imperfective

Marked noun clauses are used primarily as the object of a verb or preposition. Unmarked noun clauses can also serve as the second part of a genitival phrase, as the predicate in a nominal sentence, as the subject of another predicate, and as titles or captions — in other words, in most of the functions that ordinary nouns or noun phrases have in a clause or sentence.

2 In this table and those in the following two sections, square brackets indicate that a form or construction is only rarely attested in a particular kind of use. For nonverbal predicates a check mark (✓) indicates that the predicate is attested in a particular kind of clause.

26.18 Relative clauses

All four types of predicate can also be used in relative clauses, but nominal and adjectival predicates are mostly limited to unmarked relative clauses. The following table summarizes the normal distribution of the various kinds of predicates in unmarked and marked relative clauses:

	UNMARKED	WITH *ntj*	WITH *jwtj*
NOMINAL PREDICATE	✓		
ADJECTIVAL PREDICATE	✓	[✓]	
ADVERBIAL PREDICATE	✓	✓	
VERBAL PREDICATE	attributive forms (participles and relatives) stative, imperfective, perfect, passive SUBJECT-stative	perfect, passive SUBJECT-stative [SUBJECT-imperfective]	perfect, passive, and nonattributive relative forms

The difference between unmarked and marked relative clauses generally corresponds to a difference in the kind of antecedent. Undefined antecedents are normally modified by unmarked relative clauses, rarely by marked ones. Vocatives and proper names can also be modified by unmarked relative clauses (§ 20.14). Defined antecedents are normally modified by marked relative clauses or by the attributive verb forms.

Like adjectives, relative clauses can be used both to modify an expressed antecedent and as nouns by themselves. The latter use is limited to the attributive forms and marked relative clauses, except in nominal sentences of the pattern *jnk mr.f* "I am one who loves" (§ 20.13).

26.19 Adverb clauses

Middle Egyptian adverb clauses can have all four types of predicate. The following table summarizes their normal distribution in unmarked and marked adverb clauses:

	UNMARKED	WITH *js*	WITH *jsṯ/tj*
NOMINAL PREDICATE	✓	✓	✓ (*jsṯ*)
ADJECTIVAL PREDICATE	✓		✓ (*jsṯ*)
ADVERBIAL PREDICATE	✓		✓
VERBAL PREDICATE	imperfective, subjunctive, prospective, perfect, passive, stative nonattributive relative forms SUBJECT-stative SUBJECT-imperfective	nonattributive relative forms (emphatic sentences)	imperfective, perfect, passive SUBJECT-stative SUBJECT-imperfective

Adverb clauses can also be expressed by means of a prepositional phrase consisting of a preposition and a marked noun clause (§§ 12.16, 15.11, 18.13, 21.12, 25.13).

Adverb clauses normally follow the clause on which they are dependent. Marked adverb clauses, however, can precede their governing clause (§§ 12.18, 18.11). Certain kinds of adverb clauses always precede the main clause: these include the protasis of a conditional sentence (§ 19.7) and unmarked adverb clauses expressed with a nonattributive relative form (§ 25.11.2). The particle *ḫr* (§ 16.6.13) can also be used to allow an adverb clause to stand at the head of its sentence.

Syntactically, all adverb clauses are adverbial modifiers of a main or governing clause. Adverb clauses can express a number of different meanings, however, often depending on the nature of their predicate. These are summarized in the following sections.

26.20 Circumstantial clauses

Clauses of circumstance describe a circumstance or situation under which the governing clause happens or is true. Such clauses express three kinds of circumstance:

1. **prior circumstance** — action that happened, or a state or situation that existed, before that of the governing clause. Prior circumstance is expressed by
   - a verb form — the perfect (§ 18.11) and passive (§ 21.12), or the perfect relative form in an initial clause (§ 25.11); the stative or SUBJECT-stative construction often implies previous action, but actually describes a concomitant state
   - a preposition plus a noun clause — *m ḫt* and *r s3* "after" plus the infinitive ( *m ḫt jt* "after returning"), a nonattributive relative form ( *r s3 jr.f jrt.f* "after he does what he should do"), or the SUBJECT-stative construction (§ 17.11); *ḏr* "since" plus the infinitive or the perfective relative form used nonattributively ( *ḏr prt m ḫt* "since emerging from the womb,"  *ḏr wn ḥm.j m jnp* "since (the time) My Incarnation was a child").
2. **concomitant circumstance** — action that happens, or a state or situation that exists, at the same time as that of the governing clause. Concomitant circumstance is expressed by
   - an adverbial predicate (Lesson 12)
   - a verb form or construction — *ḥr* plus infinitive (§ 14.11.1) by itself and as pseudoverbal predicate (§ 15.9), the imperfective or SUBJECT-imperfective construction (§ 20.10), the stative or SUBJECT-stative construction (§ 17.12, 17.19), the imperfective relative form in an initial clause (§ 25.11), or a balanced sentence with a nonattributive relative form (§ 25.12)
   - a preposition plus a noun clause — *ḥr, m,* or *ḫft* "while, when" plus the infinitive (§ 14.11) or a nonattributive relative form (§ 25.15).
3. **future circumstance** — action that happens, or a state or situation that exists, after that of the governing clause. Future circumstance is expressed by the prospective (§ 21.6), but such clauses are quite rare in Middle Egyptian. A kind of future circumstance is also expressed by "until" clauses, with the preposition *r* plus the *sḏmt.f* (§ 22.14) or a nonattributive relative form (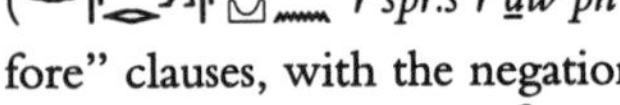 *r spr.s r ḏw pn* "until she arrived at this mountain," also § 22.16); and by "before" clauses, with the negation *nj sḏmt.f* (§ 22.13) or the prepositional phrase *tp ꜥ* plus a nonattributive relative form (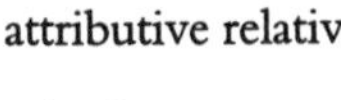 *tp ꜥ s3ḥ.n t3* "before we touched land").

26.21 Result clauses

Clauses of result describe action that happens as a result of some other action. Result is expressed by the subjunctive, for action (§ 19.8.2), and by the stative or SUBJECT-stative construction, for state (§§ 17.13, 17.19). Result can also be expressed by the particles *jḫ* and *ḫr* plus the subjunctive and the particle *k3* plus the subjunctive or SUBJECT-imperfective construction (§§ 19.6, 20.9.2), and in main clauses by the *sḏm.jn.f* and *sḏm.k3.f* (Lesson 22).

26.22 Purpose clauses

Clauses of purpose describe the motivation for the action of the governing clause. Purpose is expressed by means of the preposition *r* plus the infinitive (§ 14.11.3) or by the subjunctive (§ 19.8.1). The subjunctive is used when the verb has a subject, and the infinitival construction when it does not. Purpose can also be expressed by the prepositional phrase *n mrwt* "for the sake of, in order that" plus the infinitive or a nonattributive relative form: for example,  *n mr(w)t swꜥb r-pr pn* "for the sake of cleaning this temple,"  *n mrwt ꜥḥ3.ṯn ḥr.f* "in order that you may fight for it."

26.23 Causal clauses

Clauses of causality are "because," "since," or "for" clauses, describing the reason for the statement of the governing clause. Causality is expressed either by a circumstantial clause or by a preposition or prepositional phrase plus a noun clause. Circumstantial clauses indicating causality often employ the perfect (§18.11), indicating prior circumstance, but clauses of concomitant circumstance can also have causal meaning (§§ 12.17, 25.14 second example).

The preposition *ḥr* can express causality when it is used with the infinitive (§ 14.11.1), and the prepositions *n* and *ḥr* when they govern a nonattributive relative form (for example,  *n njs.k r.n* "because you summoned us,"  *ḥr ꜥẖẖ mw* "because the water evaporates"). The preposition *ḏr* expresses causality with the *sḏmt.f* (§ 22.14) or an imperfective relative form (for instance,  *ḏr ngg 3js* "since the brain is exposed").[3]

More often, prepositional phrases expressing causality govern a noun clause introduced by *ntt* (§§ 12.13.2, 17.11, 18.13, 21.12, 25.13). In older or archaizing texts the preposition *n* can also be used with a noun clause marked by *js*: for example,  *n ṯwt js sb(3) pw ms.n jmnt nfrt* "because you are that star whom the beautiful West has birthed." Causality is also expressed with the compound prepositional phrases  *n jqr n*,  *n ꜥ3t n*, and  *n wr n*, all of which mean "because of how much," plus a nonattributive relative form: for instance,  *n ꜥ3t n mrr.j sw* "because of how much I love him."

26.24 Conditional clauses

Clauses of condition are those that describe a condition under which the main clause is true. The conditional clause, introduced by "if," "when," or "should" in English, is called the protasis, and the main clause is known as the apodosis. A conditional protasis can be expressed by *jr* plus the subjunctive or prospective (§§ 19.7, 21.6), by the subjunctive alone (§ 19.7), by a nonattributive relative form (§ 25.11.1), or by the preposition *m* plus a nonattributive relative form (§ 25.3.1). These constructions have slightly different meanings: see the discussions in §§ 25.3.1 and 25.11.1. Conditional clauses regularly precede the main clause, but those expressed by *m* plus a nonattributive relative form can follow it. Questions introduced by *jn* can sometimes be interpreted as conditional clauses: for example, 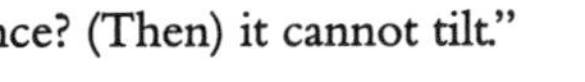 *jn jwsw pw nj gs3.n.f* "If it is a balance, it cannot tilt" or "Is it a balance? (Then) it cannot tilt."

3 Note that *ḏr*, like English "since," can have two meanings, temporal ("since the time of") and causal ("since" = "because"). When *ḏr* has temporal meaning it governs the infinitive or a perfective relative form (§ 26.20.1); when it has causal meaning it is used with the *sḏmt.f* or an imperfective relative form.

26.25 Concessive clauses

Clauses of concession are a kind of condition on which the statement of another clause is based. Such clauses are normally introduced by "as" or "although" in English. In Middle Egyptian they are usually expressed by means of a nonattributive relative form (§§ 25.11.1, 25.11.3–25.11.4) or by the preposition *m* plus a nonattributive relative form (§ 25.3.1). Like the protasis of a conditional sentence, concessive clauses regularly precede the main clause, but those expressed by *m* plus a nonattributive relative form can follow it.

26.26 Other kinds of adverb clauses

The various kinds of clauses summarized in the preceding six sections are the major kinds of adverb clauses found in Middle Egyptian sentences. Adverb clauses of other types are expressed by means of a preposition plus a noun clause, and take their meaning from the preposition: for example, clauses of comparison introduced by *mj* "like," or *ḫft* "according as" (§§ 18.13, 25.3.1).

26.27 Clause relationships

All sentences consist of at least one clause, but they can also contain many clauses. In sentences with more than one clause, one of the clauses must be the main clause. In Middle Egyptian sentences this is normally the first clause, but some sentences have the main clause second. This is particularly true of conditional sentences (§ 26.24) and those with concessive clauses (§ 26.25) or initial clauses with a nonattributive relative form (§ 25.11).

Clauses other than the main clause can be dependent on or subordinate to it, or they can be secondary main clauses. Dependent clauses usually follow or precede the main clause, but they can also be embedded within the main clause. Common examples of embedding are noun clauses or relative clauses serving as subject to the predicate of a main clause, and noun clauses that are the object of a verb in the main clause (for examples, see § 19.9, Exercise 24, no. 18, and § 25.3). Dependent clauses can also be embedded within other dependent clauses (§§ 23.9, 24.5.4).

Secondary main clauses occur in compound sentences (§§ 17.9, 18.5). In English they are usually linked to the main clause by the conjunction *and*. Compound sentences in Middle Egyptian have no such linking word. Often there is no indication whether two clauses belong to a compound sentence or are consecutive independent statements (for examples, see Exercise 17, nos. 11 and 14, Exercise 18, no. 15). The relationship between the two clauses, however, can be signaled overtly by omitting some element in the secondary main clause that is already present in the preceding clause, such as an introductory word or particle or the subject of the verb. This kind of omission, known as "gapping," is often a mark of compound sentences in Egyptian, as it is in English (see the examples in §§ 17.9 and 18.5).

26.28 Kinds of sentences

Sentences in Middle Egyptian can be statements or questions, and nonemphatic or emphatic. Statements and nonemphatic sentences are unmarked constructions: no special features are used to indicate that a sentence is a statement or that it is nonemphatic. Because they are unmarked, statements can sometimes be used as questions (§ 11.11.1), and nonemphatic constructions can occasionally have emphatic meaning (§§ 25.7, 25.16.1, 25.17). Questions and emphatic sentences are marked constructions, with special words or verb forms to indicate their function.

Emphatic sentences are those in which something other than the predicate is the important part, or rheme, of the sentence (Lesson 25). Sentences in which the subject is the rheme normally mark such a subject by using the independent form of the suffix pronoun for pronominal subjects, and by *jn* before other emphasized subjects (§ 25.18). Those in which the rheme is an adverbial adjunct or an adverb clause use a nonattributive relative form as the predicate of the main clause. The nonattributive relative forms can also be used to express an initial subordinate clause before a main clause.

Questions are of two kinds: those in which the predicate is questioned, and those in which some other element of the sentence is questioned (§ 18.18). The first kind, which we have called a predicate question, is marked by the proclitic particle *jn* (§ 16.6.2), sometimes in conjunction with the enclitic particle *tr* (§ 16.7.11). Such questions can have a nonverbal or pseudoverbal predicate (§§ 11.11, 15.12) or a verbal predicate, including a nonattributive relative form (§§ 17.14, 18.18, 19.12, 20.19, 21.14, 25.16.2); the *sḏm.jn.f*, *sḏm.ḫr.f*, *sḏm.k3.f*, and *sḏmt.f* are not used as the predicate in questions. The second kind of question, which we have called an adjunct question, uses an interrogative pronoun (§ 5.11), adjective (§ 6.6), or adverb (§ 8.13). The structure of such questions depends on the function of the interrogative word in the sentence. When it is an adverb, or part of a prepositional phrase, the predicate of the sentence is normally a nonattributive relative form (§ 25.8), although an interrogative adverb or prepositional phrase can serve as the predicate itself (§ 10.10) or as an adverbial adjunct to a nonemphatic predicate (§ 15.12). The interrogative pronouns and adjective can also serve as the subject of an adjectival sentence (§ 7.5.4), the predicate of a nominal sentence (§§ 7.13, 23.13), or the object of a verb (§ 19.12).

26.29 Negations

Middle Egyptian has eight negative words, which are used for the most part with different constructions and meanings:

1. *nj* (§ 16.6.8)

The negative particle *nj* is primarily a negation of words. It is used both by itself and in combination with other words. When used by itself, *nj* is the normal negation of:

- individual words (§ 11.7)
- the perfect (§ 18.14) — negation of action, ability, or necessity, usually present: *nj sḏm.n.f* "he does not hear, he cannot hear"
- the passive (§21.13) — passive counterpart of the negated perfect: *nj sḏm.f* "he is not heard, he cannot be heard"
- the perfective (§ 20.5) — negation of past or completed action: *nj sḏm.f* "he did not hear, he has not heard"; the negated perfective of *p3* "do in the past" plus the infinitive has the meaning "not once, never": *nj p3.f sḏm* "he has not once heard, he never heard"
- the imperfective (§ 20.15), rare and uncertain — negation of generalizations: *nj sḏm.f* "he does not hear"
- the prospective, active and passive (§§ 21.5, 21.7) — negation of future actions: *nj sḏm.f* "he will not hear"
- the *sḏmt.f* (§ 22.13): *nj sḏmt.f* "before he heard/has heard, he has not yet heard"

The particle *nj* can also be used as a negation in the following combinations:

- *nj js* (*nj* followed directly by *js*) — negation of contrastive words or phrases (§ 11.7); *js* serves to subordinate the negative phrase, as it does with words and clauses (§ 16.7.3)
- *nj ... js* (*nj* and *js* separated by a word or phrase) — negation of nominal sentences (including the participial statement), adjectival sentences of possession, and emphatic sentences (§§ 11.5–11.6, 23.13, 25.14); the use of the particle *js* shows that the negation applies to the sentence as a whole rather than just the word that follows *nj*
- *nj zp* plus the subjunctive (§ 20.5): *nj zp sḏm.f* "he never heard"
- *nj wnt* (§ 22.15) — negation of existence, usually in dependent clauses and with nominal subject: *nj wnt X* "X being nonexistent, without X"; *wnt* is the *sḏmt.f* of *wnn*.

In early or nonstandard Middle Egyptian texts the particle *nj* can also be used in place of the negative particle *nn* (§ 16.6.8).

2.  *nn* (§ 16.6.8)

The negative particle *nn* is primarily a negation of clauses and sentences. It is mostly used by itself, as the negation of:

- existence (of a noun, pronoun, or the infinitive), either by itself or with the perfective of *wnn* (*nn wn*: § 20.16.3), in main clauses or adverb clauses (§§ 11.4, 12.17, 14.15.1)
- sentences with adverbial or adjectival predicate (§§ 10.4.2, 11.4, 11.6)
- sentences with nominal predicate, in later Middle Egyptian (§ 11.5)
- sentences with a pseudoverbal predicate, rarely (§ 15.8)
- the SUBJECT-stative construction, rarely (§ 17.15)
- the subjunctive (§ 19.11.1) — negation of the future: *nn sḏm.f* "he will not hear."

The particle *nn* can be used as a spelling of the negative particle *nj* in nonstandard Middle Egyptian (§ 16.6.8). It is also occasionally used in place of *nj*, particularly in texts from the New Kingdom and later: for example, in the negations *nn ... js* (§ 11.5), *nn sḏm.n.f* (§ 18.14), and *nn zp sḏm.f* (§ 19.11.1).

3.  *nfr* (§ 16.6.9)

The negative particle *nfr* is used only in combination with other words. It occurs in Middle Egyptian in three constructions:

- *nfr pw* "not at all, not even" — negation of existence, stronger than *nn* or *nn wn*
- *nfr n* plus the nonattributive imperfective relative form — used almost exclusively in place of *tm* as a negation of the protasis of conditional sentences (compare § 19.11.3): for example, 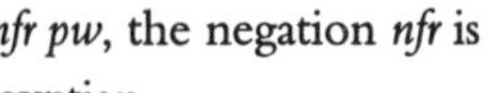 *jr nfr n wnn m ꜥ.ṯn* "if there is nothing at all with you"
- *nfr 3* plus the nonattributive imperfective relative form or as a predicate in its own right — negative counterpart of the subjunctive, in dependent clauses (the latter as variant of *nfr n*) or main clauses: for example, *nfr 3 dd.j wg n.ṯn* "I won't make it be distressful for you at all," *nfr 3 ḫr.k r p3 mn* "Should there be nothing (more) with you than that cloth."

Except for *nfr pw*, the negation *nfr* is limited to older Middle Egyptian texts, where it is a holdover from Old Egyptian.

4.  *w* (§ 16.7.4)

The negative particle *w* is used as an enclitic negation after the subjunctive or prospective in wishes or commands: for example,  *srw.ṯn w mꜥḥꜥt ṯn m st.s tn r nḥḥ* "You shall not remove this stela from this its place forever." This is a rare variant of the more common subjunctive negation *jm.f sḏm* (§ 19.11.2). It is found in older Middle Egyptian texts, as a survival from Old Egyptian.

5.  *jwt*

The negative word *jwt* is the noun-clause counterpart of the negative particle *nj*. In Old Egyptian it was used to allow a number of the constructions negated by *nj* to serve as a noun clause, but in Middle Egyptian it is primarily limited to the construction *jwt wnt*, the noun-clause counterpart of *nj wnt* (§ 22.15).

6.  *jwtj* (§ 12.9)

The negative relative *jwtj* is a nisbe of *jwt*, and serves as the relative-clause counterpart of the negative particles *nj* and *nn* in a few constructions:

- as negation of existence, in the expressions *jwtj-n.f* and *jwtj-sw* "have-not" and with a following noun or infinitive (§ 14.15.2) — relative-clause counterpart of *nn* as a negation of existence
- with the perfect (§ 18.17) — relative-clause counterpart of *nj sḏm.n.f*
- with an imperfective relative form (§ 25.5) — relative-clause counterpart of the negated perfective or imperfective *sḏm.f*.

7.  *jm* and  *m*

The negative words *jm* and *m* are the subjunctive and imperative, respectively, of the negative verb *jmj*, the only two forms in which this defective verb appears (§ 13.7). Both are used with the negatival complement. The subjunctive *jm.f sḏm* is used mainly as the negation of the subjunctive as a wish or command in main clauses, less often in a purpose clause (§ 19.11.2). The imperative *m sḏm* is the negative counterpart of the imperative (§ 16.4).

8. 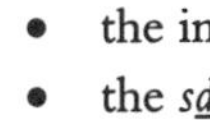 *tm*

The negative *tm* is a 2-lit. verb meaning "cease, fail," but it is used more often as the negative counterpart of various verb forms than as a verb in its own right. As a negation it is followed by the negatival complement or the infinitive (the latter usually in texts later than the Middle Kingdom). The verb *tm* serves as the negative counterpart of:

- the subjunctive in dependent clauses (§ 19.11.3)
- the imperfective in adverb clauses (§ 20.15)
- the *sḏm.k3.f* (§ 22.10)
- the participles (§ 23.18)
- the relative forms, both attributively (§ 24.12) and nonattributively (§§ 25.5, 25.14)
- the infinitive (§ 14.16).

The *sḏm.ḫr.f* and *sḏmt.f* are also negated by *tm*, but examples are quite rare. In each of its uses *tm* takes the same form as that of the verb form it negates.

THEORY

26.30 Gardiner's theory

The first grammars of the Egyptian language were written in the early nineteenth century, not long after the hieroglyphs themselves were deciphered, and our understanding of Egyptian grammar has been evolving ever since. Those original grammars depended greatly on Coptic, since this stage of the language had been known even before the hieroglyphic texts could be read. As the study of Egyptian progressed, scholars began to realize that the earlier stages of the language were quite different from Coptic. We now know that written Egyptian passed through five major stages in its historical evolution, from Old Egyptian to Coptic (§ 1.2).

Middle Egyptian is the second-oldest of these stages, and as you have seen, it retains much of its Old Egyptian ancestor. In fact, it was not until the middle of the twentieth century that the distinction between Old and Middle Egyptian was fully described. Egyptologists are still refining our understanding of Middle Egyptian grammar, particularly in the area of its greatest complexity, the verbal system. In the process there have been historically three major schools of thought about how the verbal system of Middle Egyptian works.

The earliest approach was dominated by the belief that Egyptian was essentially a Semitic language (§ 1.1). There are, in fact, many features that Egyptian shares with Semitic languages: in particular, some of its verb and noun roots and its pronouns; its use of two genders, with the feminine marked by the ending *–t*; its system of number and the endings used to denote plural and dual; and its stative form (§§ 17.1–17.2). Historically, the verbal system of most Semitic languages has a primary aspectual distinction between two kinds of forms, often labeled "perfective" and "imperfective." These labels were adopted for the Egyptian verbal system and applied to three of its categories: the *sḏm.f*, the participles, and the relative forms. Although the labels themselves are in some ways less than ideal, they have proved to be a useful way of analyzing and describing one of the major distinctions between different forms of the participles and relatives, and so have been almost universally accepted for these two categories.

Until about 1960, most Egyptologists analyzed the *sḏm.f* on the basis of the same primary aspectual distinction. The chief proponents of this approach were the German Egyptologist Kurt Sethe and his British pupil, Alan H. Gardiner. In 1927 Gardiner published a monumental study of Middle Egyptian, whose third edition is still in print and remains the primary reference tool for this phase of the language.[4] Gardiner's grammar recognizes only two basic forms of the active *sḏm.f*, "perfective" and "imperfective" (see Lesson 20, n. 1), distinguished largely by the use of the geminated stem in the imperfective *sḏm.f*, as in the attributive forms. In the last edition of his grammar Gardiner conceded that his perfective *sḏm.f* probably concealed more than one form, but he still attempted to explain the uses of the *sḏm.f* primarily on the basis of an aspectual distinction between perfective and imperfective forms like that which exists in the attributive forms. Gardiner even went beyond mere similarity, arguing that his perfective and imperfective *sḏm.f* derived historically from the perfective and imperfective passive participles.

4 Sir Alan Gardiner, *Egyptian Grammar*, 3d ed., revised (Oxford: Griffith Institute, and London: Oxford University Press, 1964). The book remains in print thanks to a subsidy from Gardiner's estate.

Even before the publication of Gardiner's first edition, however, Egyptologists had begun to suspect that there were more than just two kinds of *sḏm.f*. The first to be identified as a distinct form was the subjunctive, and most Egyptologists accepted its existence as a third form of the *sḏm.f* alongside the perfective and imperfective of Sethe and Gardiner. The active prospective was identified as a separate form in the 1950s, though it was not until 1979 that its full paradigm and its relationship to the passive prospective were established (§ 21.16). With the passive and passive prospective, these discoveries have resulted in the six kinds of *sḏm.f* now universally recognized as distinct forms (§ 21.15). Gardiner's perfective *sḏm.f* has been shown to contain two separate forms, the perfective and subjunctive, and part of a third, the prospective, while his imperfective *sḏm.f* contains not only the imperfective form but part of the prospective as well.

26.31 The "Standard Theory"

Along with the discovery of the different forms of the *sḏm.f*, some Egyptologists were becoming uncomfortable with the idea that the primary function of these forms was simply to distinguish different kinds of action. A similar controversy about meaning existed in the realm of Coptic grammar. Coptic has two different forms for many of its verbal categories, generally known as "First Tenses" and "Second Tenses": for example, the First Perfect ⲁϥⲥⲱⲧⲙ̄ and the Second Perfect ⲛ̄ⲧⲁϥⲥⲱⲧⲙ̄, both of which mean "he heard" or "he has heard." The existence of these separate forms was not in question, but the reason for their existence was unknown.

In 1944 another of Sethe's former pupils, Hans Jakob Polotsky, published a groundbreaking study that contained the first coherent explanation for the difference between First and Second Tenses of Coptic. Polotsky discovered that the Second Tenses were consistently used in emphatic sentences while the First Tenses were used in normal, nonemphatic sentences. Since Coptic is simply the latest phase of Egyptian, Polotsky reasoned that similar uses might underlie some of the formal distinctions that could be observed in earlier stages of the language. In the same study he was able to show that the imperfective *sḏm.f* of Sethe and Gardiner was in fact used in many of the same kinds of sentences as the Coptic Second Tenses. Polotsky argued that this verb form was not simply an imperfective form of the *sḏm.f* but a special use of the imperfective relative form.

In a number of subsequent publications between 1944 and 1976 Polotsky refined his discovery into a new understanding of the verbal system of Middle Egyptian and that of the language's other phases. The basis of Polotsky's theory is the structure of the adverbial sentence. In this view the predicate in an emphatic sentence is not the verb form but the emphasized adverb, prepositional phrase, or adverb clause; the verb form itself is a noun clause serving as subject of this adverbial predicate. The two constructions can be compared in the following two hypothetical sentences:

	SUBJECT		ADVERBIAL PREDICATE
ADVERBIAL	𓇳𓏤𓁛 *rꜥ*		𓅓𓊪𓏏𓇯 *m pt*
SENTENCE	Re	(is)	in the sky
EMPHATIC	𓈍𓂝𓂝𓇳𓏤𓁛 *ḫꜥꜥ rꜥ*		𓅓𓊪𓏏𓇯 *m pt*
SENTENCE	that Re appears	(is)	in the sky = It is in the sky that Re appears.

Similarly, the balanced sentence (§ 25.12) is analyzed as an A B nominal sentence with two noun clauses instead of two nouns: for example,

	SUBJECT		NOMINAL PREDICATE
NOMINAL SENTENCE	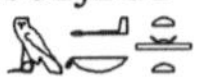 *mkt.t* your protection	(is)	 *mkt rʿ* the protection of Re (§ 7.8.2)
EMPHATIC SENTENCE	 *mrr.f* that he likes	(is)	 *jrr.f* that he acts = When he likes, he acts.

Although Polotsky retained the analysis of the verb forms in such emphatic sentences as special uses of the relative forms, other Egyptologists identified them as special nominal forms of the *sḏm.f* because they are also found in noun clauses (§ 25.3). Gardiner's imperfective *sḏm.f* thus became the "nominal" or "emphatic" *sḏm.f*, and the perfect was divided into two forms, the "nominal" or "emphatic" *sḏm.n.f* and the "nonemphatic" *sḏm.n.f*; the perfective relative form was not generally recognized as a nominal or emphatic form.

Polotsky also proposed a new understanding of nonemphatic constructions. Based again on the structure of the adverbial sentence, he analyzed the verb forms in the SUBJECT-stative and SUBJECT-imperfective constructions as adverbial predicates. The comparison can be illustrated by the following hypothetical examples:

	SUBJECT		ADVERBIAL PREDICATE
ADVERBIAL SENTENCE	 *jw rʿ* Re	(is)	 *m pt* in the sky
SUBJECT-STATIVE	 *jw rʿ* Re	(is)	 *ḫʿ.(w)* appeared = Re has appeared (§ 17.9)
SUBJECT-IMPERFECTIVE	 *jw rʿ* Re	(is)	 *ḫʿ.f* appearing (§ 20.8).

As a result of this analysis, the verb forms used in such constructions, as well as those used in adverb clauses, were identified as adverbial (or "circumstantial") forms of the verb. Particles such as *jw* and introductory words such as *ʿḥʿ.n* and *wn.jn* were seen as converters allowing such adverbial forms to function as the predicate of a main clause. Forms appearing without such converters were analyzed as either adverbial or nominal. Thus, for example, the *sḏm.n.f* after *jw*, *ʿḥʿ.n*, or *wn.jn* was understood as an adverbial or "circumstantial" form serving as the predicate of a main clause, while the *sḏm.n.f* standing at the head of its clause without such introductory words was seen as either adverbial (the predicate of a circumstantial clause) or a nominal/emphatic form.

By the mid 1970s Polotsky's analysis of the verbal system and the structure of Egyptian sentences had won widespread acceptance, so much so that it came to be recognized as the "standard theory" of Egyptian grammar. In this theory, the *sḏm.n.f* and the forms of the *sḏm.f* are understood to have different forms corresponding to how they are used in a sentence. The *sḏm.n.f* and its passive counterpart, the passive *sḏm.f*, are both divided into two forms, nominal and circumstantial (adverbial). The *sḏm.f* is divided into four forms, usually called indicative, circumstantial, nominal, and prospective. The last is identical with the form we have been calling the subjunctive. In the "Standard Theory" it is generally analyzed as a nonemphatic nominal form (because it is often used in noun clauses) that can also be used adverbially, and the form we have called the prospective is usually understood as its emphatic counterpart.

26.32 Current theory

The following table shows the forms you have learned in this book and how they are identified in Gardiner's system and that of the "Standard Theory."

	GARDINER	STANDARD THEORY
perfective *sḏm.f*	perfective *sḏm.f*	indicative *sḏm.f*
imperfective *sḏm.f*	perfective/imperfective *sḏm.f*	circumstantial *sḏm.f*
subjunctive *sḏm.f*	perfective *sḏm.f*	prospective *sḏm.f*
prospective *sḏm.f*	perfective/imperfective *sḏm.f*	*sḏmw.f* (emphatic prospective)
passive *sḏm.f*	passive *sḏm.f*	nominal/circumstantial passive *sḏm.f*
perfect	*sḏm.n.f*	circumstantial *sḏm.n.f*
perfective relative (na)[5]	perfective *sḏm.f*	—
imperfective relative (na)	imperfective *sḏm.f*	nominal *sḏm.f*
perfect relative (na)	*sḏm.n.f*	nominal *sḏm.n.f*

As you can see, the grammatical approach used in this book is neither Gardiner's nor that of the "Standard Theory." It is based instead on more recent advances in our understanding of how the grammar of Middle Egyptian works.

Although most Egyptologists had accepted the "Standard Theory" by the mid 1970s, they also realized that it did not solve every problem of Middle Egyptian grammar, and in fact created a few new ones. In the 1980s a number of scholars began to question two basic tenets of the "Standard Theory": the analysis of the emphatic sentence as a sentence with adverbial predicate, and the notion that verb forms in other constructions are actually adverbial predicates. Both ideas confuse the roles of form and function.

As we have seen, the rheme of a sentence is not necessarily identical with the sentence's predicate (§ 25.6). In the emphatic sentence, therefore, the fact that an emphasized element is the **rheme** does not mean that it is also the **predicate**. Polotsky's analysis often does seem to work in sentences with an emphasized adverb, prepositional phrase, or adverb clause, but it is not uniformly applicable. For example, in an emphatic sentence such as 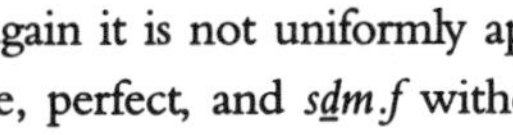 *prr n.f n3 n gmḥwt* "It is to him that those wicks go," the adverbial predicate *n.f* "to him" would occur inside the nominal subject *prr n3 n gmḥwt* "that those wicks go" — a construction that is impossible for other adverbial sentences (and odd in any language). In emphatic sentences where the verb form precedes a main clause (§ 25.11), moreover, the main clause cannot be an adverbial predicate. Polotsky's analysis of verb forms as adverbial predicates in other constructions also seems to work in some cases, such as those illustrated in the preceding section, but again it is not uniformly applicable. Middle Egyptian texts contain numerous examples of the stative, perfect, and *sḏm.f* without introductory words in clauses that cannot be analyzed as adverb clauses or emphatic sentences.

These inconsistencies have led many Egyptologists to reconsider Polotsky's explanation of the "nominal" and "circumstantial" forms, and to return to the notion that these verb forms express primarily differences in meaning rather than syntactic function. This is the approach that has been used in this book.

5 Used nonattributively.

The "circumstantial" forms are simply verb forms expressing state (the stative) or the aspects of completed or incomplete action (the perfect and passive, and the imperfective). When they are used as predicates in adverb clauses they have adverbial **function**, but they are not adverbial **forms**. The verb forms in such functions are the same ones used as predicate in other syntactic functions, such as main clauses, unmarked noun clauses, and sentences with emphatic meaning. Just as with other categories (§ 26.2), we should not confuse function with form. A good example of the difference is the subjunctive. As we have seen, this verb form can be used as the predicate in noun clauses and adverb clauses as well as main clauses. Such uses do not mean that the subjunctive has nominal and adverbial forms (although Polotsky once suggested that it does). The subjunctive is simply a single verb form expressing a particular meaning (subjunctive mood), which can be **used** in a number of different syntactic functions — just as nouns, for example, can be used as adverbs, or prepositional phrases as nouns.

While Polotsky's theory of adverbial verb forms has been rejected, his analysis of the verb forms in emphatic sentences as nominal remains an essential part of the current theory of Middle Egyptian grammar. Although the "Standard Theory" identifies them as nominal forms of the *sḏm.f* and *sḏm.n.f*, this book has retained Polotsky's original idea that they are special uses of the relative forms. The reasons for doing so are partly synchronic (from within Middle Egyptian itself) and partly diachronic (from parallels in later stages of the language). Since the emphatic forms of Middle Egyptian are identical to the relative forms except for their lack of gender and number endings, there is no reason to ignore this clear formal equivalence and identify them instead as additional forms of the suffix conjugation, especially since the suffix conjugation does not have other forms marked for specific syntactic functions. The same formal similarity between emphatic and relative forms exists in later phases of Egyptian as well. In Late Egyptian, for example, the construction  *j.jr.f sḏm* is used to express the predicate both in emphatic sentences and in relative clauses, and in Coptic the emphatic perfect ⲛ̄ⲧⲁϥⲥⲱⲧⲙ̄ is derived from the perfect relative ⲉⲛⲧⲁϥⲥⲱⲧⲙ̄ (from *ntj jr.f sḏm*, literally, "who did hearing").

Since the Middle Egyptian emphatic forms are simply special uses of the relative forms, they are nominal forms (§ 26.8). This does not mean, however, that they function as the subject of the emphatic sentence, as we have already seen. The fact that Middle Egyptian uses such forms as the predicate of an emphatic sentence is simply a feature of the language. The reason it does so has been explained on the basis of the nominal nature of these forms. In normal sentences with a verbal predicate the sentence's theme is naturally associated with the subject of the verb, which is either a noun or noun equivalent (pronoun or noun clause), and the rheme with the verb itself. By using a nominal form of the verb in emphatic sentences, Egyptian indicates that the verb is meant to be understood as part of the theme rather than the rheme, and that the hearer or reader is to look for the rheme elsewhere in the sentence.

The current theory of Egyptian grammar is still in the process of formation. It does not even have a name, though one Egyptologist has called it the "Not-so-standard Theory." Many Egyptologists still adhere to the "Standard Theory," however, and you should be aware of this when you read other grammatical studies. This discussion and the lessons in this book should give you enough information to allow you to make up your own mind on the question.

WHERE TO GO FROM HERE

26.33 Other grammars

This book was written to give you a fundamental understanding of the essentials of Middle Egyptian grammar based on the most recent advances in grammatical theory. It was also written because there are very few such grammars in English specifically intended for the serious beginner.

The basic reference book for Middle Egyptian grammar remains Gardiner's *Egyptian Grammar* (see n. 4, above). This book is still in print, and if you intend to continue working with Middle Egyptian texts you owe it to yourself to have your own copy. Its grammatical theory is now outdated but it is still unmatched in depth and detail. James E. Hoch's *Middle Egyptian Grammar* (Society for the Study of Egyptian Antiquities Publications, 15; Mississauga: Benben Publications, 1996) is a good grammar for the beginning student, and Gertie Englund's *Middle Egyptian, an Introduction*, 2d ed. (Uppsala: Uppsala University, Department of Egyptology, 1995) gives a handy summary of the main points of Middle Egyptian. Both these books follow the Standard Theory; an excellent, though abbreviated, nonstandard approach is presented by Mark Collier and Bill Manley, *How to Read Egyptian Hieroglyphs* (London: British Museum Press, 1998).

One thing you will learn if you continue studying Egyptian is that many Egyptological studies are written in French and German. In fact, universities require a reading knowledge of both these languages in their Egyptological curricula. If you read French, a good counterpart to Gardiner is Gustave Lefebvre's *Grammaire de l'Égyptien classique*, 2d ed. (Bibliothèque d'étude, 12; Cairo: Institut français d'archéologie orientale, 1955). Although this book is as outdated as Gardiner's in theory and is not as detailed, it is much better organized and easier to use. For German readers, an excellent introductory grammar is Erhart Graefe's *Mittelägyptisch: Grammatik für Anfänger*, in its 5th edition at the time this book was written (Wiesbaden: Harrassowitz, 1997).

26.34 Dictionaries

The fundamental dictionary of Egyptian is the *Wörterbuch der Aegyptischen Sprache*, by Adolf Erman and Hermann Grapow (Berlin: Akademie-Verlag, 1971), in seven volumes with five volumes of references. As you may imagine, this work can be found only in specialized Egyptological libraries and those of professional Egyptologists. Fortunately there is a smaller one-volume dictionary, in English, that is based specifically on Middle Egyptian texts and is still in print: Raymond O. Faulkner, *A Concise Dictionary of Middle Egyptian* (Oxford: Griffith Institute, 1988). For German readers there is also Rainer Hannig's *Großes Handwörterbuch Ägyptisch-Deutsch* (Kulturgeschichte der Antiken Welt, 64; Mainz: Verlag Philipp von Zabern, 1995). Also in one volume, this is much more comprehensive than Faulkner's dictionary, including special lists of the names of gods, kings, and places. Many grammars also include limited dictionaries, such as the one in the present book.

26.35 Texts

Generally available collections of hieroglyphic texts are as scarce as grammars and dictionaries. Two of the best are Adrian de Buck's *Egyptian readingbook*, 2d ed. (Leiden: Nederlands Instituut voor het Nabije Oosten, 1963), and Kurt Sethe's *Ägyptische Lesestücke*, 3d ed. (Hildesheim: Georg Olms Verlagsbuchhandlung, 1959). A number of individual texts are also available in hieroglyphic transcription: A.M. Blackman, *The Story of King Kheops and the Magicians*, ed. by W.V. Davies

(Reading: J.V. Books, 1988); Roland Koch, *Die Erzählung des Sinuhe* (Bibliotheca Aegyptiaca, 17; Brussels: Éditions de la Fondation Égyptologique Reine Élisabeth, 1990); R.B. Parkinson, *The Tale of the Eloquent Peasant* (Oxford: Griffith Institute, 1991). A number of wisdom texts have been edited by Wolfgang Helck in the series "Kleine Ägyptische Texte" (Wiesbaden: Otto Harrassowitz), including the Instruction of Amenemhat, the Instruction for King Merikare, the Satire of the Trades, the Prophecy of Neferti, and the Admonitions of Ipuwer.

These publications only include the texts themselves. Several good English translations of Egyptian literature are readily available, however, including William Kelly Simpson, ed., *The Literature of Ancient Egypt* (New Haven: Yale University Press, 1973); Miriam Lichtheim, *Ancient Egyptian Literature*, Vol. 1: *The Old and Middle Kingdoms* (Berkeley: University of California Press, 1973); and R.B. Parkinson, *The Tale of Sinuhe and Other Ancient Egyptian Poems 1940–1640 BC* (Oxford: Clarendon Press, 1997). It is a good idea to use a number of such translations when you work with Middle Egyptian texts, to see how different Egyptologists have understood them.

26.36 Resources

As you have probably already discovered, the only books on Egyptian language or texts that can be found in most bookstores are reprints of works by E.A.W. Budge, which were not too reliable when they first appeared and are now woefully outdated. The bookstore of the Metropolitan Museum of Art, New York, however, consistently carries the most recent publications for a general audience, including Gardiner's *Grammar* and Faulkner's *Dictionary*. Many Egyptologists rely on book dealers specializing in current Egyptological publications, especially Blackwell's (Oxford, UK) and Harrassowitz (Wiesbaden, Germany).

If you have access to the Internet, there are a number of excellent sites on that provide information and links to other reputable Egyptological resources, including the web sites of the Oriental Institute (www-oi.uchicago.edu/OI/DEPT/RA/ABZU/ABZU.HTML), the International Association of Egyptologists (http://www.fak12.uni-muenchen.de/aegyp/IAEPage.html), the Centre for Computer-aided Egyptological Research (www.ccer.ggl.ruu.nl/ccer), and a site maintained at Cambridge University (www.newton.cam.ac.uk/egypt/index.html).

The best way to find other resources and to keep in touch with what is happening in Egyptian studies is through the national Egyptological societies, such as the American Research Center in Egypt, the Society for the Study of Egyptian Antiquities, and the Egypt Exploration Society. All of these publish a newsletter and an annual journal of Egyptological studies, and all of them welcome individual members, professional or amateur. Their addresses can be found through the Internet sites mentioned above.

26.37 A final word

If you have made it through all of these lessons, congratulations! The course has not always been easy, and sometimes was probably frustrating, but in the end it is worth the time and effort you put into it. With the foundation you have gained here, you can now go on to begin reading the ancient texts for yourself. No matter how much grammar you study, reading texts is ultimately the best way to learn Egyptian. The more you read, the easier you will find it. And the reward is discovering for yourself the thoughts of people who lived thousands of years ago, but whose hopes and dreams were not all that different from our own.

References

Listed below are the sources of the examples and quotations used in the discussions, essays, and exercises of this book, arranged by lesson and section number. Citations of references use the standard abbreviations of Egyptological literature and are intended primarily as aids to teaching or further research. Where no references are given, it is either because the example is so common that a reference is unnecessary (as in particular verb forms) or because it has been created on the basis of other examples for the sake of illustration.

1.6	Offering table after Gauthier and Jéquier, *Fouilles de Licht*, 54 fig. 53; Scene after *Meir* V, pl. 18.
1.9	CT IV 255b–257a (T1Be: Lepsius, *Aelteste Texte*, pl. 2, 28); Ptahhotep 277–78 (Möller, *HL* I, no. 2B, 2).
1.10	Erichsen, *Demotische Lesestücke* I, 73.
Exercise 1	(1a) Piankoff, *Shrines*, Fig. 28. (1b) *TPPI* 20, 4 (omitting *n ḏt.f*). (1c) Hornung, *The Tomb of Pharaoh Seti I*, pl. 16, col 210. (1d) *TPPI* 17, 5. (2a) *Urk.* VII, 2, 9. (2b) numerous examples. (2c) ShS. 149. (2d) Westcar 11, 10–11. (2e) Siut IV, 23.
2.6	Sethe, *Lesestücke*, 79, 18–19.
Exercise 2	Sethe, *Lesestücke*, 83–84.
3.7	Kamose CT 7 and Stela 1, 9 plus CT 8 (Helck, *HBT*, 86, 87).
4.12	Siut I, 289; Ebers 99, 13; Westcar 11, 14; Hearst med. 12, 1; Hearst med. 9, 11.
4.13	(1) Sin. B 195; Westcar 9, 9; Peas. R 6, 5; CT IV, 237b (M1C); *Urk.* IV, 59, 16; Merikare 3, 10–11. (2) Neferti 61; Sin. R 17; CT IV, 237b (T3Be); Ebers 71, 15; *Urk.* IV, 185, 8; CT I, 271a (omitting *jptntj*); Peas. B1, 21; CT IV, 236b (Sq1C); Neferhotep Stela 36 (Helck, *HBT*, 28).
4.15	Examples from the *Wb.* and Ranke, *PN* I; Peas. B1, 20.
5.10	(5) Kamose Stela 2, 22 (Helck, *HBT*, 94).
Essay 5	Merikare 11, 10–12, 8.
Exercise 5	(1a) ShS 128. (1b) Kamose CT 6 (Helck, *HBT*, 85). (1d) Peas R 1, 2. (1e) Peas R 7, 2–3. (1f) Peas, R 9, 4. (1g) Peas. B1, 47. (1h) Peas. R 18, 1 plus B1, 112. (ii) ShS. 152. (1j) ShS. 8. (1k) ShS. 77–78. (1l) Neferhotep Stela 6 (Helck, *HBT*, 22). (1m) ShS. 154. (1n) ShS. 170. (1r) Kamose Stela 2, 5–6 (Helck, *HBT*, 92). (1s) Siut I, 295. (1t) Siut I, 269.
6.3	Sin B 44 and 106.
6.5	Sethe, *Lesestücke*, 79, 21–22; Westcar 5, 10; Neferti 10.
6.7	CT III, 184a; CT III, 97f; *Urk.* IV, 330, 4; Peas. Bt 30–31; *Urk.* IV, 55, 9; Adm. 7, 3; Peas. B1, 79; Westcar 9, 11; Petrie, *Koptos*, pl. 8, 2.
6.8	Siut 2, 6; Peas. B1, 84; *Urk.* VII, 39, 6.
Essay 6	Composite from various sources in Gauthier, *LdR* I, 319–36; *Urk.* IV, 161, 2.
Exercise 6	(2) Peas. B1, 15. (3) Westcar 5, 1 (restored). (4) Westcar 5, 3. (5) CT IV 30h. (6) *Urk.* IV, 862, 5. (7) Sin. R 73. (8) Neferhotep Stela 36 (Helck, *HBT*, 28). (9) pRam IV D, 2, 2. (10) Westcar 12, 8 (stative). (11) after *Urk.* IV, 618, 15. (12) Siut I, 269. (13) *Kahun*, pl. 36, 25. (14) *Urk.* IV, 6, 9. (15) Neferhotep Stela 6 (Helck, *HBT*, 22). (16) Ebers 19, 11. (17) Sin. B 92. (18) Sin. B 155.

7.4 *Bersheh* I, pl. 14, 1; ShS. 134; *Paheri*, pl. 3.

7.5 Ebers 1, 7–8; Ranke, *PN* I, 176, 14; CT I, 254f; *Urk.* IV, 96, 6; CT VI, 240f; Ranke, *PN* I, 171, 11; Ranke, *PN* I, 172, 22; Rhind Problem 45.

7.7 *Hatnub* 14, 9; Sin. B 23; Leb. 37.

7.8 BD 69 (Ca); Newberry, *Scarabs*, pl. 32.3; MuK. vo. 4, 7.

7.9 Sethe, *Lesestücke*, 84, 13; BD 17 (Da); Westcar 9, 9; Sethe, *Lesestücke*, 84, 8; Sin. B 267–68; Rhind Problem 60; Peas. R 1, 1; Sin. B 81; CT IV 231a.

7.10 Leb. 20–21; CT II, 22b (B1Bo); Stewart, *Egyptian Stelae* II, pl. 18, 16; Peas. B2, 48–49.

7.13 (1) CT III, 59b; BD 122 (Nu); ShS. 69; CT V, 102a. (2) BD 125; Westcar 9, 8–9. (3) Westcar 6, 25 (*pw* restored). (4) BD 122 (Nu); CT IV, 287a.

7.13 end Rhind Problem 73.

7.15 Peas. B1, 25.

Exercise 7 (1) *Kahun*, pl. 2, 11. (2) ShS. 89. (3) *Beni Hasan* I, pl. 26, 166–67. (4) CT IV, 200b. (5) Siut I, 288. (6) Sin. B 155. (7) *Urk.* IV, 1741, 12. (8–9) Neferhotep Stela 36 (Helck, *HBT*, 28). (10) Kamose Stela 2, 9–10. (11) Ahmose Bad Weather Stela ro. 10 (Helck, *HBT*, 107, *r b3w n nṯr ꜥ3* omitted). (12) Urk. IV, 410, 11. (13) Leb. 20. (14) Leb. 38. (15) ShS. 182. (16) ShS. 12–13. (17) ShS. 29–30. (18) ShS. 58–59. (19) ShS. 61. (20) ShS. 62–63. (21) ShS. 63–64. (22) ShS. 66. (23) ShS. 134. (24) ShS. 152. (25) CT IV, 37f. (26) Sethe, *Lesestücke*, 71, 11. (27) *Bersheh* I, pl. 15. (28) Ranke, *PN* I, 172, 22. (29) CT VII, 49m. (30) Peas. R 1, 2. (31) Peas. R 8, 6. (32) Peas. B1, 51–52. (33) Peas. B1, 148–49. (34) Peas. B1, 171. (35) Peas. B1, 298. (36) Peas. B2, 39. (37) Peas. B2, 49. (38) Peas. B1, 320. (39) Peas. B1, 351–52. (40) Peas. B2, 92–93. (41) BD 1. (42) Adm. 5, 14.

8.2 Examples from Gardiner, *EG*, §§ 162–78, and the *Wb.*, plus the following: (8.2.1) *jmjtw šzpw* Sin. B 249. (8.2.3) *ḫꜥj m nswt* *Urk.* IV, 2027, 2; *jnj m zš3* ShS. 129. (8.2.4) *mj sḫr nṯr* Sin. B 43. (8.2.5) *mm ꜥnḫw* Neferhotep Stela 37 (Helck, *HBT*, 29); *mm mw* *Urk.* IV, 616, 9; for adverbial *mm* see Merikare 8, 7 and 12, 7. (8.2.6) *rdj j3w n wsjr* Sethe, *Lesestücke*, 63, 4; *šmj n ky* Peas. R 13, 6; *dg3 n qꜥḥwj.k* Smith 7, 16. (8.2.7) *šmj r nn-nswt* Peas. B1, 63–64; *r tr pn* *Sinai* 90, 3; *r jnt ꜥqw* Peas. R 1, 3; *rḫ wḫ3 r rḫ* *Urk.* IV, 970, 1; *fḫ r kpnj* Sin. R 53; *jr sf wsjr pw* CT IV, 193b. (8.2.8) *z3 ḥ3 ẖrd* MMA 08.200.19 (unpublished). (8.2.9) *ḥnꜥ snw.j* ShS. 126. (8.2.10) Amenemhat 1, 3; Ebers 19, 2; Siut I, 273; *Urk.* IV, 965, 4. (8.2.15) Leb. 133; Peas. R 7, 6. (8.2.17) Merikare 9, 1.

8.4 Peas. B1, 314.

8.5 *Urk.* IV, 123, 4; Adm. 6, 8.

8.10 *Urk.* IV, 1068, 10; 650, 5; 666, 17. CT III, 259g.

8.14 Horemkhauef 9 (Helck, *HBT*, 49); Westcar 6, 24.

Essay 8 *Paheri*, pl. 9, 5, 6, 17–19.

Exercise 8 (1) Sin. B 31. (2) Sin. B 194. (3) Sin. R 63. (4) Sin. B 193. (5) Sin. B 45. (6) Sin. B 57–58. (7) *Urk.* IV, 1021, 5. (8) Sin. R 44–45. (9) Adm. 4, 12. (10) Sin. B 182–83. (11) Sin. B 113. (12) Pyr. 122b (Q1Q). (13) Sin. B 205. (14) Sin. B 82. (15) Sin. B 267–68. (16) BM 574, 15. (17) Sin. B 43. (18) Sin. R 55. (19) Sin. AO 8–9. (20) Sin. AO 25. (21) Sin. B 252. (22) Sin. B 105–106 (omitting *m nmtwt.j*). (23) Sin. B 244. (24) Sin. AO 41. (25) Sin. B 213–14. (26) Peas. B1, 350 = B2, 83–84. (27) Amenemhat 3, 8. (28) Merikare 13, 4.

9.1 *Urk.* IV, 630 (restored); *Kahun*, pl. 16, 32; *Kahun*, pl. 8, 19; Harris I 73, 5 (partial).

9.4 Peas. B1, 182; Siut IV, 25; Merikare 6, 2; *Urk.* IV, 689, 5; Siut III, 20; *Urk.* IV, 741, 4; Merikare 6, 1; Westcar 4, 13; Hearst med. 11, 14; Rhind Problems 76 and 65; *Urk.* IV, 1070, 3; CG 20003, 4; BD 72; Peas. B1, 40; Siut I, 288; *Urk.* IV, 1069, 5; *Urk.* IV, 650, 9; Westcar 8, 3.

9.5 Ebers 40, 18; *Urk.* IV, 729, 16.

9.6 Siut I, 285; Rhind Problem 34.

9.7	(4) *Urk.* IV, 429, 12; Heqanakht V, 35; Rhind Problem 82 (partial).
9.8	Sin. R 5; *Urk.* IV, 649, 3; *Urk.* IV, 836, 2; Siut I, 305; Naville, *Deir el Bahari*, pls. 114 and 116.
9.9	*Hamm.* 43, 1; *Urk.* IV, 836, 2.
Exercise 9	(1) *Urk.* IV, 702, 9–14 (first line restored). (2a) *Kahun*, pl. 9, 1. (2b) Peas. B2, 91. (2c) Peas. R 7, 5–6. (2d) Peas. B1, 112–13. (2e) *JEA* 31 (1945), pl. 2A, 12. (2f) BD 108 = *ZÄS* 59 (1924), 47*. (2g) *Urk.* IV, 836, 2–3. (2h) Sin. B 298. (2i) *Hamm.* 114, 12. (2j) Siut I, 300. (2k) *Urk.* IV, 716, 13. (2l) Westcar 7, 23. (2m) *Urk.* IV, 483, 6. (2n) ShS. 42. (4) *Kahun*, pl. 16, 13–20 (restored).
10.2	Peas. B1, 124; *Bersheh* I, pl. 20; Sin. R 10–11; *Urk.* IV, 221, 13; pBerlin 9010, 5 (*HP* III, pl. 1); Ptahhotep 128 (L2).
10.3	Leb. 132; *Urk.* IV, 1090, 3; Westcar 11, 24; *Theban Tomb Series* III, pl. 26, 15.
10.4	(1) ShS. 108; Kamose Stela 2, 23 (Helck, *HBT*, 94); Adm. 7, 10. (2) MuK. vo. 2, 3; Sin. B 223–24. (3) Sin. B 117–18. (4) CT IV, 48d.
10.5	Kamose CT 7 (Helck, *HBT*, 86, restored).
10.6	Peas. B1, 208.
10.7	Sethe, *Lesestücke*, 79, 20–21; *Urk.* IV, 123, 10; CG 20538 IIc, 19; *Kahun*, pl. 12, 4; *Urk.* IV, 561, 2; Peas. Bt 25.
10.8	Heqanakht II, 41; CT VI, 196t; Peas. B1, 58; Neferhotep Stela 32 (Helck, *HBT*, 28).
10.9	Sin. B 43; *Urk.* IV, 101, 12.
10.10	Westcar 9, 4; *Urk.* IV, 649, 15.
Essay 10	Ptahhotep 88–98 (L2); CT VII, 463f–464b; Adm. 8, 2; both sentences in Hannover 11, 4–5: R. Drenkhahn, *Ägyptische Reliefs im Kestner-Museum Hannover* (Hannover, 1989), 73.
Exercise 10	(1) Sin. B 50. (2) Neferhotep Stela 37 (Helck, *HBT*, 29). (3) Adm. 2, 10. (4) ShS. 131. (5) *Theban Tomb Series* II, pl. 11. (6) Gardiner, *EG*, § 124. (7) Peas. B1, 102. (8) Ptahhotep 588. (9) CG 20538 IIc, 19. (10) Peet, *Cemeteries of Abydos* II, pl. 23, no. 20, 5. (11) *Urk.* IV, 2, 10. (12) *Urk.* IV, 59, 5. (13) Ebers 101, 15. (14) Ebers 69, 3. (15) Siut III, 69. (16) Heqanakht I, 12–13. (17) Sin. R 8. (18) Siut I, 227. (19) Sin. B 77. (20–21) Sin. B 193. (22) Sin. B 194. (23) Sin. B 215. (24) Sin. B 217–18. (25) Sin. B 222. (26) Sin. B 233. (27) Sin. B 239–40. (28) Sin. B 240. (29) Sin. B 290. (30) Sin. B 263. (31) Westcar 6, 10–11. (32) Westcar 7, 1–2. (33) CT II, 292a. (34) Neferti 21. (35) ShS. 52. (36) ShS. 7–8. (37) *Urk.* IV, 561, 2. (38) ShS. 67–68. (39) CT II, 354b. (40) Peas. R 16, 7–8. (41) Peas. B1, 323. (42) *Kahun*, pl. 11, 21–22.
11.4	Leb. 122; Peas. B2, 100; Sin. R 38; Smith 16, 15; MuK. vo. 2, 3.
11.5	Leb. 31; Peas. R 7, 4; Peas. B1, 196; Sethe, *Lesestücke*, 84, 16; Ptahhotep 213 (L2); CG 20530, 7.
11.6	Siut I, 295; CT III, 390e.
11.7	Smith 15, 15; Siut I, 301; Ptahhotep 75; *Hatnub* 49, 8; Ebers 104, 8.
11.9	Sethe, *Lesestücke*, 79, 20–21; Sin. B 154–55; Ebers 1, 7–8; CT VI, 240f; CG 20538 IIc, 19; Sin. B 222; *Urk.* IV, 123, 10; Kamose CT 7 (Helck, *HBT*, 86, restored).
11.11	(2) Peas. B2, 77; Peas. B1, 50; CT I, 227c; Peas. R 8, 7–8; Leb. 20; ShS. 150; Sin. B 114.
Essay 11	Sethe, *Amun*, pl. 4.
Exercise 11	(1) ShS. 100–101. (2) Siut III, 69. (3) Sin. B 230. (4) Sin. R 71–72 (restored). (5) Heqanakht I, 14. (6) *Urk.* IV, 835, 14. (7) Kamose Stela 2, 33 (Helck, *HBT*, 96). (8) Adm. 7, 12. (9) Peas. B2, 55. (10) *Urk.* IV, 123, 7. (11) Peas. B1, 126–27. (12) Ebers 108, 20. (13) Adm. 12, 1. (14) MuK. 2, 8–9 (with a phrase omitted). (15) Ptahhotep 435. (16) Peas. B1, 220–21. (17) Peas. B2, 100–101. (18) Sethe, *Lesestücke*, 84, 7–8. (19) Peas. B2, 109 (restored). (20) Peas. B1, 342–43. (21) BD 110, 19. (22) Amenemhat 2, 4. (23) Peas. B2, 110. (24) *Urk.* IV, 1071, 8. (25) Siut I, 284. (26) Peas. B2, 110–11. (27) Kagemni 1, 3. (28) Peas. B1, 333. (29) Adm. 14, 13. (30) Sin. B 267.
12.4	Siut I, 290; Sin. B 166; Sin. B 33–34.

12.5	Westcar 8, 5; CG 20485, B4; Ebers 13, 20–21; BD 17 (= CT IV, 315a-b).
12.6	CT V, 91c; CT VII, 96p–q (restored); Westcar 9, 3–4.
12.7	Leb. 41–42; Ebers 14, 6; *Kahun*, pl. 11, 23; Leiden V 103; Pyr. 1102a.
12.8	ShS. 51–52.
12.9	Ebers 30, 7.
12.10	CT VI, 273d; CT V, 373b.
12.11	Leb. 42; Westcar 8, 5; BD 17 (= CT IV, 315a–b); Rhind Problem 62; Ebers 88, 4; Westcar 6, 26–7, 1 (restored); Neferti 10; Sin. R 38.
12.13	(1) CT III, 181b–c; CT IV, 84i. (2) BD 148; Peas. B1, 93; *Kahun*, pl. 28, 21 (restored); CT III, 49e; BD 131. (3) CT II, 70c and 77a (B3L).
12.14	ShS. 61–62.
12.16	BD 148.
12.16	(1) *Urk.* IV, 219, 3–4 (omitting phrase in apposition to *jty*); *Bersheh* I, 14, 1; Louvre C15, 7. (2) *Urk.* IV, 890, 11–12. (3) CT VII, 470a–b. (4) CT VII, 321a–b.
12.17	Kamose Stela 2, 2 (Helck, *HBT*, 91); ShS. 32–33 = 101–102; Kamose Stela 2, 17 (Helck, *HBT*, 93).
Essay 12	CT Spell 76 (CT II, 2c–e).
Exercise 12	(1) Sin. B 173–74. (2) Caminos, *Lit. Frag.*, pl. 2, B2, 6–7. (3) Peas. B1, 351–52 = B2, 85–86. (4) Sin. B 145. (5) ShS. 84–86. (6) ShS. 15–16. (7) CG 583, 3. (8) CG 20543, 17 (omitting relative *jr.n.j*). (9) *Urk.* IV, 897, 11–12. (10) Peas. B1, 221–22. (11) Peas. R 13, 5. (12) Peas. B1, 310. (13) Neferhotep Stela 11 (Helck, *HBT*, 23, restored). (14) Peas. B2, 131–32. (15) ShS. 156. (16) Siut I, 288. (17) CG 20543, 7–9 (omitting epithets). (18) Adm. 9, 3–4 (omitting superfluous *m* after *nb*). (19) Sin. B 81. (20) Ebers 51, 19–20. (21) CT V, 49b–c. (22) CT I, 106b–c. (23) Peas. B1, 207 (with *m* added from R 31, 6). (24) Adm. 8, 3. (25) ShS. 67–68. (26) ShS. 41–42. (27) ShS. 131. (28) Peas. R 6, 5–6. (29) Siut I, 307. (30) CT II, 214a–b. (31) CG 20057 s. (32) Peas. B1, 160. (33) Peas. B1, 94–95 = R 13, 5. (34) *Urk.* IV, 657, 12–13. (35) ShS. 51–52.
Essay 13	CT 714 (CT VI, 344b–d); Siut III, 4; CG 20539 II b 5; Merikare 12, 6–7; *KRI* II, 356, 9–11; Bremner-Rhind 26, 24 and 28, 22; CT 320 (CT IV, 145b–c); CT 261 (CT III, 382e–383a, 383d, 384c); CT 647 (CT VI, 268o).
14.3	(2a) Westcar 10, 5; Siut IV, 20; Westcar 12, 1; Ahmose Bad Weather Stela ro. 18 = vo. 20 (Helck, *HBT*, 109). (2b) CT II, 344b (*m wnn ḥrw* ~ *m wn.f*). (2c) references in *EG* § 299.
14.4	(1) *Urk.* IV, 9, 3; Siut I, 307; Leiden 88, 10 (*EG*, p. 309). (2) *Beni Hasan* I, pl. 24, 3; Siut I, 298: *Kêmi* 3 (1930), 61 (restored).
14.5	(1) Siut I, 126; *Urk.* IV, 6, 2. (2) CT IV, 336d (T1Be); Sin. B 23; Sin. B 107–108 (superfluous seated man after *ḥ3t* omitted); Ebers 59, 7–8.
14.6	Pyr. 1808a; Siut I, 290; *Urk.* IV, 367, 8; Turin 1447 (*EG*, § 301).
14.8	Kamose Stela 2, 30–31 (Helck, *HBT*, 96); Heqanakht I, vo. 16; CG 20057 d 1–2.
14.9	*Deir el Gebrâwi* I, pl. 13; BD 17 = CT IV, 174a; Hearst med. 12, 13; Ebers 1, 10.
14.10	CT IV, 232b (M4C); CT III, 327a; Ebers 68, 8; *Bersheh* II, pl. 21, 4–5; *Hamm.* 12, 3.
14.11	(1) *Leb.* 12; *Urk.* IV, 745, 12; Sin. B 201; Peas. B1, 65–66. (2) Peas. R 12, 6–7. (3) *Beni Hasan* I, pl. 8, 11. (4) Ebers 2, 6; *Urk.* IV, 745, 12.
14.12	*Urk.* IV, 834, 1; Sin. B 112; *Urk.* IV, 618, 16; *Urk.* IV, 893, 5.
14.13	ShS. 182; *Leb.* 77; Smith 2, 8–9.
14.14	(1) Neferhotep Stela 1–2 (Helck, *HBT*, 21). (2) Sin. B 107–108 (superfluous seated man after *ḥ3t* omitted). (3) Westcar 7, 14; Sin. B 236.
14.15	(1) *Urk.* IV, 147, 2–3. (2) CT IV, 189a–191b (T3Be).
14.16	CT III, 396g.

14.18 CT V, 8b; *Urk.* IV, 693, 13; Smith 4, 2–3; CT V, 38a (restored).

14.19 CT III, 334a.

Essay 14 BM 498, 2, 53–56, 59–60: *ZÄS* 39 (1902), pls. 1–2.

Exercise 14 (1) *Urk.* VII, 14, 20. (2) CT V, 16f. (3) Sin. R 27–28. (4) Sin. B 6–7. (5) Sin. B 15–16. (6) Sin. R 142 (restored). (7) Sin. R 156. (8) Sin. R 163. (9) Sin. B 190–91. (10) Sin. B 215–16. (11) ShS. 16–17. (12) ShS. 20–21. (13) ShS. 172. (14) Westcar 2, 9. (15) Westcar 3, 7–8. (16) Westcar 4, 6–7. (17) Westcar 7, 4. (18) Westcar 7, 15–16. (19) Westcar 7, 20–21. (20) Westcar 8, 2. (21) Westcar 12, 1. (22) Westcar 12, 6–7. (23) Westcar 12, 17–18. (24) Westcar 12, 19–20. (25) CT II, 291l–m. (26) Peas. B1, 79–80. (27) CT VI, 144a. (28) Peas. R 17, 6. (29) Peas. B1, 177. (30) Peas. B1, 263–65.

15.3 Peas. B1, 123–24; Neferti 35–36; Peas. B1, 332–33; Peas. R 1, 2–3; Peas. B1, 42.

15.4 Kamose CT 4 (Helck, *HBT*, 84).

15.5 Dunham, *Second Cataract Forts* II, pl. 25, 3; *Kahun*, pl. 28, 36; *Urk.* IV, 656, 14; *Paheri*, pl. 3, reg. 4 (with superfluous dual strokes in *tw.tw* omitted); *Urk.* IV, 2031, 15.

15.6 ShS. 170–71; Neferhotep Stela 7 (Helck, *HBT*, 22); *Urk.* IV, 4, 3; *Urk.* IV, 3, 5; Kagemni 2, 6.

15.7 *Urk.* IV, 17, 10–11.

15.8 ShS. 74–75 (with  emended from ); Moalla 5 (II α 2); *Paheri*, pl. 7.

15.9 (a) CT VI, 172n–o. (b) Sin. B 1–2 = C 4; *Lit.Frag.*, pl. 1.2, B1.

15.10 (a) Westcar 10, 4; *Urk.* IV, 120, 13; Adm. 4, 6–7. (b) Westcar 7, 1–2; ShS. 61–62; Neferti 58–59 (*nẖn* and *ḥḏ* restored); Ebers 40, 5.

15.11 CT VI, 328g; CT VI, 278b; *Urk.* IV, 656, 2–3.

15.12 *Meir* I, pl. 5; Adm. 14, 14.

Essay 15 Selections from Pap. Leiden I 350: 4, 17–19; 3, 26 and 4, 1–15 (excerpts); 4, 21–22.

Exercise 15 (1) ShS. 59–60. (2) Neferti 27. (3) Neferti 40. (4) Neferti 63–65 (pPet. 63–64 plus C 25224, 8). (5) Peas. R 9, 5–6. (6) Peas. B1, 129. (7) Peas. B1, 179–80. (8) Peas. B1, 314. (9) Peas. B2, 113–14. (10) *Urk.* IV, 4, 10–13. (11) Adm. 6, 13. (12) *Hatnub* 25, 19–20. (13) Möller, *HL* I, no. 7A, 1. (14) Merikare 9, 1. (15) CT II, 340a.

16.1 Peas. B1, 351; Peas. B1, 278; ShS. 179; ShS. 12; Peas. B1, 351; Peas. R 7, 7; Ptahhotep 54; Merikare 1, 2; Merikare 3, 2 (emended from *sẖr*); Peas. B1, 272; Merikare 4, 7; Merikare 6, 3; Peas. B1, 98; Sethe, *Lesestücke* 71, 1; Sethe, *Dramatische Texte*, pl. 4/15, 52; Rhind Problem 41; Sin. B 282; Siut III, 43: *Kêmi* 3 (1930), 95; BD 112; *Urk.* IV, 1023, 16.

16.2 (1) Peas. R 7, 6 = Bt 32; *Meir* I, pl. 10. (2) *Meir* I, pl. 10; *Urk.* IV, 255, 12; Sin. B 160; CT II, 213c. (3) *Urk.* IV, 651, 7; *Urk.* IV, 20, 11; *KRI* IV, 16, 10. (4) Erman, *Hymnen*, 13, 4–5; Sethe, *Dramatische Texte*, pl. 2/13, 19.

16.3 ShS. 13–14; Peas. R 7, 6–7; Westcar 8, 9; Merikare 12, 11; Sin. B 275; Peas. B2, 133; Sin. B 282; *Theban Tomb Series* II, pls. 22 and 7.

16.4 MuK. 3,6; Peas. B1, 123; Ptahhotep 52.

16.6 (4) *Kahun*, pl. 2, 19. (7) Sin. B 232. (8) Peas. B1, 230–31. (9) *Urk.* IV, 772, 6. (13) Hymn to Hapi (Helck, *Nilhymnus*, 20, after oGol. 4470, 7; *ẖr* restored from other copies); Westcar 13, 10–11. (14) Peas. R 13, 5.

16.7 (1) Peas. B1, 255. (2) Adm. 12, 5 (original *nj* for *nn*, as often in this MS); Leb. 67; Westcar 6, 10–11. (3) Smith 15, 15; Siut I, 301; Ptahhotep 75. (5) CG 20543, 16. (6) Khakheperre-seneb vo. 1. (7) Adm. 2, 8. (8) Peas. R 9, 5–6.

16.8 (1) CG 20530, 1. (2) CT I, 27c. (4) CG 405.

Exercise 16 (1) CT IV, 128i–129b S1C. (2) Peas. R 1, 3–4. (3) Peas. B1, 57 = R 11, 6. (4) Peas. R 16, 1–3 (restored from B1, 98). (5) Peas. R 25, 4. (6) Peas. B1, 194–95. (7) Leb. 67–68. (8) Sin. B 275 (*n ntj* emended from B2). (9) Merikare 1, 2. (10) Merikare 4, 2. (11) Merikare 11, 7–8 (*jrt* emended from other copies).

(12) Neferti 4 (restored from other copies). (13) Neferti 12–13. (14) Heqanakht II, 34. (15) *Rekhmire*, pl. 96, 1, 11 (omitting titles and name). (16) Ptahhotep 316. (17) Ptahhotep 372. (18) Peas. B1, 182–83. (19) ShS. 111–12. (20) *Paheri*, pl. 7. (21) Siut III, 43: *Kêmi* 3 (1930), 95. (22) *Kahun*, pl. 2, 17. (23) Peas. R 7, 3. (24) Westcar 11, 23. (25) Admonitions 2, 8–9. (26) Westcar 5, 7. (27) *Urk.* IV, 7, 3/7 (omitting intervening clauses). (28) CT IV, 176e–g. (29) CT IV, 345a–c. (30) CT IV, 68b. (31) CT VII, 358d–359b (B2P). (32) CT I, 119d (S1C). (33) BD 27. (34) *Urk.* IV, 20, 9–16.

17.2 Verb forms: Sin. B 182; Peas. B1, 147; ShS. 130; *Hamm.* 191, 4; ShS. 38; *Urk.* IV, 758, 16.

17.3 ShS. 116; Ebers 37, 3; Ebers 105, 2; ShS. 158; ShS. 130; Ebers 39, 2; Ebers 38, 3; Smith 4, 14; BM 614, 11; Leb. 75; *Bersheh* II, 25; Ebers 36, 17; Peas. B1, 229; CG 20001, b 6; *Urk.* VII, 2, 11; Ebers 76, 8; *Urk.* VII, 2, 11; ShS. 4; Sin. B 193; Sin. B 257; ShS. 7; *Urk.* IV, 84, 7.

17.4 Neferti 23; Neferti 26, *jtrw* partly restored; ShS. 116; Peas. R 26, 4–5; Kamose CT 4 (Helck, *HBT*, 85).

17.5 BM 562, 9.

17.6 ShS. 101–102; Westcar 8, 12; ShS. 169; Westcar 8, 21; *Rekhmire*, pl. 11, 11–12 = Gardiner, *ZÄS* 60 (1925), 67; ShS. 39–41.

17.7 Westcar 12, 7–8; Peas. B2, 131–32.

17.8 CT V, 223d/i.

17.9 Sin. R 70 (final determinative restored); Westcar 4, 1; Adm. 2, 5; CT III, 4e–f G1T; CT V, 223d–e.

17.10 Ebers 1, 11; BD 108 = *ZÄS* 59 (1924), 44*, 8; Merikare 5, 4; Westcar 7, 2 and 4.

17.11 CT III, 48h–49a; Louvre C 10, 9–10 (Lefebvre, *GEC*, § 701); CG 20001, b 6; CT I, 269i; Westcar 8, 12–13.

17.12 Neferhotep Stela 16–17 (partly restored; Helck, *HBT*, 24); *Urk.* IV, 5, 12–13; *Urk.* IV, 894, 1.

17.13 Sin. B 138–39.

17.14 Adm. 12, 5.

17.15 Leb. 126–27.

17.17 (1) *Beni Hasan* I, pl. 8, 15; *Urk.* IV, 59, 13–14; ShS. 23–24; Sin. B 286; CT III, 342b; Sethe, *Lesestücke*, 75, 17–18. (2) Hornung, *Himmelskuh*, 13, 37–38; CT VI, 275t (partly restored); ShS. 158; Merikare 5, 2.

17.18 Ebers 49, 1–2.

17.19 ShS. 41–44; *Kahun*, pl. 5, 33–34; Adm. 7, 10–11; Peas. R 6, 4–5; Westcar 6, 10.

17.20 (1) Neferhotep Stela 11 (final sign restored; Helck, *HBT*, 23); *Bersheh* I, pl. 14, 4; *ASAE* 23 (1923), 6. (2) Sethe, *Lesestücke*, 79, 2; Westcar 8, 14; *Kahun*, pl. 31, 6–7.

Essay 17 *jzwt.ṯn* ShS. 7; *jntw.f* Westcar 8, 3. Middle Kingdom examples of group writing (except *ḫnḏr*): Sethe, *Ächtung feindlicher Fürsten*, f 9; *Beni Hasan* I, pl. 30; Posener, *Princes et Pays*, 70, 66, 71. New Kingdom examples of group writing: *LES* 74, 5; *LES* 76, 12; *HO* 75 vs. 6; KRI II, 249, 13; KRI I, 12, 10; KRI IV, 19, 3; *LEM* 22, 3. The vocalizations are from James Hoch, *Semitic Words in Egyptian Texts of the New Kingdom and Third Intermediate Period* (Princeton, 1994).

Exercise 17 (1) ShS. 7–8. (2) ShS. 10–11. (3) ShS. 57–59. (4) ShS. 109–110. (5) ShS. 174. (6) Sin. R 11–14 (omitting *nṯr nfr Z-N-WSRT*). (7) Sin. B 21. (8) Sin. B 45. (9) Sin B 75–76 (*n ntt.s* emended). (10) Sin. R 156. (11) Sin. B 131–33. (12) Sin. B 254–55. (13) Sin. B 264–65. (14) Sin. B 292–94. (15) Peas. B1, 46–47. (16) Peas. B1, 155–56. (17) Peas. B1, 190. (18) Peas. B1, 337. (19) Peas. B2, 117. (20) Westcar 5, 16–17. (21) Westcar 6, 9–10. (22) Westcar 7, 14–15. (23) Westcar 9, 9–10. (24) Westcar 10, 5. (25) Westcar 11, 19–20. (26) Westcar 12, 25–26 (partly restored). (27) Adm. 8, 2. (28) Kamose Stela 2, 5 (Helck, *HBT*, 92). (29) Kamose Stela 2, 23 (Helck, *HBT*, 94, partly restored). (30) Kamose Stela 2, 32–33 (Helck, *HBT*, 9). (31) Leb. 5. (32) Merikare 3, 11. (33) Merikare 4, 9. (34) *Urk.* IV, 611, 15–17. (35) CG 20537, 4–5.

18.2 Westcar 9, 10; *Urk.* IV, 17, 8; Ebers 108, 6; Westcar 6, 21; MuK. 13, 3; *Hatnub* 24, 7; *Hatnub* 14, 5; CG 20512 b 4; Peas. B1, 348–49; *JEA* 47 (1961), 7, 5; Neferhotep Stela 22 (Helck, *HBT*, 25); CT VI, 224r; Hatnub 24, 9; *TPPI* § 20, 4; Westcar 11, 4; *Hatnub* 16, 10; Amenemhat 1, 6; Chassinat, *Fouilles d'Assiout*

(MIFAO 24), 192 (3), 4–5 and 234 (1), 1; Adm. 3, 8; *Urk.* IV, 566, 10; Peas. Bt 29 = B1, 25 (the latter with *n.f* restored); Amenemhat 3, 2 (Mill. with one *n*, other copies with two); CT I, 275f T1C and T2C.

18.3 *Hatnub* 14, 6; *JEA* 47 (1961), 7, 5.

18.4 Sin. B 141–42; Sin. R 50; ShS. 175; Siut I, 293; Westcar 8, 1; Neferti 62–63; Sin. B 168–69 (spelling of *wgg* emended); Kamose Stela 2, 15 (Helck, *HBT*, 93); *JNES* 19 (1960), fig. 1 opp. p. 258, 8–9.

18.5 ShS. 161; Peas. B1, 225–26; ShS. 130; ShS. 130–31

18.6 CT IV, 134c; CT II, 389b; Sethe, *Lesestücke* 87, 2.

18.7 *Urk.* IV, 303, 16–17; *Urk.* IV, 822, 4–6; Westcar 8, 8; ShS. 2–3; Amenemhat 1, 11–12.

18.8 Adm. 6, 5; Amenemhat 2, 3.

18.9 ShS. 157; ShS. 81–82; Westcar 12, 25–26 (partly restored); Peas. Bt 34–35; C 20003 a 6.

18.10 CT I, 160b–c.

18.11 Peas. R 1, 7; CT VII, 271c–272a; *TPPI* § 20, 6; *Urk.* IV, 83, 1–2; ShS. 131–32; ShS. 157.

18.12 Siut I, 295 (omitting a relative clause between *ḥnqt* and *ntj*); Hearst med. 4, 13; Ebers 102, 1–2.

18.13 *JEA* 16 (1930), 19, 1; CT VI, 283k; Ebers 40, 19; CT I, 267b; BD 18 (Nu).

18.14 Merikare 4, 8; Peas. B2, 113–14; Ptahhotep 382–83; Peas. B1, 356–57 (omitting dittograph *r*); Adm. 2, 4; Leb. 104; Westcar 12, 3.

18.15 Merikare 9, 1; Ptahhotep 13; Westcar 5, 17.

18.16 Siut I, 280–81.

18.17 *Urk.* IV, 616, 9–10; Ebers 97, 2; Ebers 12, 16; CT IV, 66f; BD 149e.

18.18 CT V, 102g; CT V, 115c; Westcar 5, 19 (*ḫn.n.tn* emended from *ḫnn.n.tn*); *JEA* 31 (1945), pl. 3a, 14; CT V, 96b (M2C).

Essay 18 Neferti 7–8 and Ptahhotep 58; Peas. B1, 106; Ptahhotep 58–59; Merikare 4, 9; Sin. B 57–58; pCB IV (BM 10684) vo. 2, 5–3, 11 (excerpts).

Exercise 18 (1) Peas. B1, 105–107. (2) *Kahun*, pl. 31, 19–20. (3) *JEA* 33 (1947), pl. 2, 7–8 (final *wj* emended). (4) *Kahun*, pl. 30, 41. (5) Neferhotep Stela 2 (Helck, *HBT*, 21). (6) Sin. B 32–34. (7) Sin. B 34–35. (8) Peas. B1, 40–41. (9) Peas. R 11, 2–3. (10) Ebers 102, 2–3. (11) BD 149b (Nu). (12) *Urk.* IV, 1279, 8–16. (13) ShS. 154–56. (14) Sin. R 19–20. (15) Sin. R 41–42 (partly restored). (16) Sin. B 143–46 (omitting a clause). (17) Sin. B 257. (18) Peas. B1, 347 (*tw* emended). (19) Westcar 6, 23–24 (partly restored). (20) Merikare 6, 11. (21) Sin. R 70–71 (partly restored). (22) Sethe, *Lesestücke*, 70, 22–23. (23) Leb. 83–84. (24) Amenemhat 2, 7. (25) *HTBM* I, pl. 47, 11–12. (26) *Urk.* IV, 819, 1–3. (27) *Urk.* IV, 882, 10–14. (28) *LD* III, 72.

19.2 Ebers 30, 16; Louvre C 10, 9 (Helck, *HBT*, 5); BD 7 (Nu); Peas. B1, 91 = R 15, 1; Ebers 30, 16; *Kahun*, pl. 6, 17; Adm. 12, 2; Westcar 8, 3; *Urk.* IV, 559, 11; *Paheri*, pl. 9, 14; Siut I, 270; *Kahun*, pl. 6, 15; Sin. B 167–68; Brunner, *Hieroglyphische Chrestomathie*, pl. 11, 10; *Urk.* IV, 1165, 16; Sethe, *Lesestücke*, 76, 7; CT IV, 69a B6C and T1C; CT IV, 167e; Westcar 7, 24; Peas. B1, 60; *Urk.* IV, 1077, 9; Peas. B1, 88.

19.4 *Paheri*, pl. 9, 8 (first sign restored); *Paheri*, pl. 9, 18; Helck, *Lehre des Dw3-Ḫtjj* II, 86; Westcar 5, 11; Merikare 10, 5 (C).

19.5 (1) CT IV, 311c–312c; Peas. R 26, 5–6; Adm. 1, 1; Neferhotep Stela 6 (Helck, *HBT*, 22). (2) ShS. 119–22; Peas. B1, 42–43; Kamose CT 4–5 (Helck, *HBT*, 84).

19.6 Kamose Stela 2, 11 (Helck, *HBT*, p. 93); Westcar 2, 7; BD 154 (Nu). (1) Ptahhotep 37–39. (2) pCB V, 4, 8 (Helck, *Nilhymnus*, 71; partly restored). (3) *Urk.* IV, 1074, 14–15.

19.7 CT IV, 4b–c; CG 20003 a 1–3.

19.8 (1) Merikare 12, 1–2 (pCarlsberg VI 5, 4–5). (2) Neferti 26–27 (P 38, beginning restored from pPet. 1116B). (3) Merikare 3, 11–4, 1; Merikare 11, 9.

19.9 pBerlin 3029, 2, 4 (*Studia Aegyptiaca* I, 50); Louvre C 14, 13–14; Adm. 4, 2 (*ḥr* restored); Heqanakht I, 10–11; Peas. B1, 268–69; *Urk.* IV, 807, 2–3; Sin. B 111 .

19.10 Neferti 6; Sethe, *Lesestücke*, 70, 16–17; Neferhotep Stela 10 (Helck, *HBT*, 23); Sin. B 73–74; Westcar 4, 13.

19.11 (1) MuK. 2, 3; Sin. B 71–72 (spelling of *t3w šmꜥw* emended); Herdsman 6. (2) Ptahhotep 204–205; BD 27 (Nu); Peas. B1, 162. (3) Leb. 45–46; pBerlin 3038, vo. 2, 4–5 (*msy.s* emended from *msyt.st*); Peas. B1, 245–46; Sin. B 74–75.

19.12 Peas. B1, 49; Peas. B1, 39–40; Adm. 2, 9.

19.13 CT I, 393b (T3C); Neferhotep Stela 28 (Helck, *HBT*, 27); CT VII, 31i; Neferhotep Stela 29–30 (Helck, *HBT*, 27); *Urk.* IV, 2030, 9.

19.14 Merikare 10, 9–10; Ptahhotep 315 (L1).

Exercise 19 (1) *Paheri*, pl. 9, 12–19. (2) Peas. Bt 25–27. (3) Peas. R 8, 5. (4) Peas. B1, 85–91. (5) Peas. B1, 240–41. (6) Peas. B1, 252–53. (7) Kamose Stela 2, 2–4 (Helck, *HBT*, 91). (8) Leb. 7. (9) Merikare 3, 6 (partly restored). (10) Merikare 4, 7–8. (11) Neferhotep Stela 6 (Helck, *HBT*, 22). (12) ShS. 132–34. (13) ShS. 139–40. (14) ShS. 146–47. (15) *Urk.* IV, 368, 13–14. (16) Ptahhotep 374. (17) Ptahhotep 28–29 (L2). (18) Ptahhotep 175–76. (19) Ptahhotep 197–213 (L2). (20) Khakheperre-seneb vo. 1. (21) Khakheperre-seneb ro. 13–14. (22) Ptahhotep 298–99. (23) Ptahhotep 350. (24) Ptahhotep 481. (25) CT I, 312i. (26) Westcar 7, 4–5. (27) Leb. 150–54. (28) Helck, *Djedefhor*, 66. (29) CG 28085 (B3C). (30) Helck, *Dw3-Ḫtjj* I, 28–29 (S 148, emended from other copies).

20.2 (1) Sin. B 7; Peas. R 1, 2; ShS. 73; Amenemhat 1, 10; *Beni Hasan* I, pl. 8, 21; Amenemhat 2, 6; BM 828, 8; *Kahun*, pl. 28, 30; CG 20001 b 8; CT I, 20b. (2) Sethe, *Lesestücke*, 79, 4; Leiden V 89, 1 and Horemkhauef 5 (Helck, *HBT*, 49); Sin. B 59; Sin. B 262; Sethe, *Dramatische Texte*, pl. 6/17, 72; Leb. 78; Ptahhotep 349; Horemkhauef 4 (Helck, *HBT*, 49); ShS. 19; Ebers 40, 1; Peas. B2, 122; Sin. R 15.

20.3 Ptahhotep 349; ShS. 73.

20.4 BM 828, 8–9; ShS. 76–77; Kagemni 2, 7; pRam VI, 105–106.

20.5 Sin. R 29–30 (partly restored); *Meir* III, pl. 23; Sin. B 114; *Sinai* 90, 11; Ptahhotep 93; CG 20729 a 3.

20.6 Amenemhat 2, 6; ShS. 73; ShS. 148.

20.7 Sin. B 66; Ptahhotep 349; *Urk.* IV, 489, 2; *Urk.* IV, 3, 7.

20.8 Sin. B 94–95; Peas B2, 98; Leb. 69–70 (spelling of *3(t)p.f* emended).

20.9 Peas. B1, 128–29; Sethe, *Lesestücke*, 75, 5. (1) Ebers 87, 9–10. (2) *Urk.* IV, 768, 16–18.

20.10 *Urk.* IV, 658, 10–13; *Theban Tomb Series* I, 40 and pl. 5; Sin. B 52–53; Sin. R 25; Sin. B 1–2 (in n. 17); CT V, 99b–d.

20.11 Lacau and Chevrier, *Une chapelle d'Hatshepsout*, 291 and pl. 14 (55).

20.12 CT VI, 408o–408q.

20.13 CT VII, 177f–g; Ebers 51, 15–16; BM 159, 11 (Gunn, *Studies*, 60).

20.14 Peas. B1, 271–72; Sethe, *Lesestücke*, 79, 3–5 (collated); Sethe, *Dramatische Texte*, pl. 6/17, 72.

20.15 CT VII, 365g–366c; Ebers 49, 8; Ptahhotep 348–49.

20.16 (1) *Hatnub* 14, 4; *Hatnub* 22, 2–3; *Sinai* 90, 8. (2) *Urk.* IV, 2028, 14 and 16. (3) CT II, 377c (B17C); Merikare 10, 9–10; Ptahhotep 315; Peas. B2, 69–70; *Urk.* IV, 138, 13 and 139, 2–3; Sin. R 34.

20.17 *Urk.* IV, 2027, 11 (sim. Khakheperre-seneb ro. 11); *Kahun*, pl. 34, 19–21; CT IV, 184b–186a (M4C).

20.18 ShS. 41; CT IV, 187a (M57C, partly restored; sim. L3Li); CT IV, 187a (T3L[a]).

20.19 Peas. R 26, 2 = B1, 166; Peas. B1, 353–54; Amenemhat 2, 7–8; Sin. B 123; Sin. B 133–34.

Exercise 20 (1) Sin. R 5–22. (2) Sin. B 58–59. (3) Sin. B 96. (4) Sin. B 109–10; (5) Sin. B 174–76. (6) Sin. B 183–84. (7) Sin. B 226–28. (8) Sin. B 233–34. (9) Westcar 3, 1–4. (10) Petrie, *Dendereh 1898*, pl. 8C/25B. (11) *Urk.* IV, 57, 11. (12) CG 20729 a 1–3. (13) Leb. 120–21. (14) Sin. B 35–36. (15) Helck, *Djedefhor*, 39 (collated from various copies). (16) Neferti 51. (17) Peas. R 1, 1–2. (18) Westcar 6, 26–7, 1. (19) ShS. 126. (20) ShS. 18–19. (21) CT II, 375c–376a. (22) Herdsman 4–5. (23) Herdsman 23–24. (24) Herdsman 24–25. (25) Helck, *Dw3-Ḫtjj* I, 60 (DeM 1023, restored and emended). (26) Ebers 48, 3–4. (27) pRam. III B 10–11. (28) Adm. 3, 2.

21.2 (1) CT VI, 74n; CT V, 324c; CT VII, 390b; CT VI, 380m; CT VII, 413d; CT I, 189b; CT III, 77f; CT IV, 324a; CT VI, 134i; CT V, 238c; CT I, 281a; Westcar 9, 17; CT I, 196i; Heqanakht I vo. 11; Heqanakht II 38. (2) CT V, 312h; CT I, 398b; CT II, 62c; CT I, 212e (two variants); CT V, 312g; CT III, 197a; CT III, 142d (two variants); CT I, 71g; CT V, 41d.

21.3 CT VI, 46g; CT V, 312g.

21.5 CT VI, 41c–d; CT II, 112e; CT VI, 46g.

21.6 Ebers 75, 12; Peas. B1, 67–68; Westcar 9, 17–18; *Urk.* IV, 1070, 1–4 (partly restored: cf. Lacau, *Stèle juridique*, 18); Sin. B 280–81.

21.7 CT IV, 180f; Horemkhauef 10 (Helck, *HBT*, 49); Hornung, *Himmelskuh*, 29; Sin. B 125; Heqanakht II, 35–36; *Beni Hasan* I, pl. 25, 96–99.

21.8 Adm. 6, 7; *Hamm.* 110, 6; Louvre C 11, 2; ShS. 3; Khakheperre-seneb 3; Sin. B 87; Merikare 8, 6; *Urk.* IV, 605, 16; Adm. 3, 5; Peas. B1, 107; Sin. B 300; Westcar 8, 25; Kagemni 2, 8; Neferhotep stela 18 (Helck, *HBT*, 25); Neferhotep stela 18 (Helck, *HBT*, 25); Louvre C11, 6; *Urk.* IV, 1297, 13/14; Neferhotep stela 18 (Helck, *HBT*, 25); *Urk.* IV, 897, 7; Khakheperre-seneb 12; Spiegelberg, *Ägyptische Grabsteine und Denksteine aus süd-deutschen Sammlungen* II, 3, 23; Sethe, *Lesestücke*, 75, 7; *Urk.* IV, 652, 9.

21.9 Herdsman 23; Sin. B 291.

21.10 CT IV, 91j (partly restored).

21.11 ShS. 3–4; Sethe, *Lesestücke*, 75, 7; Sin. B 300; Westcar 11, 5–6; *Hamm.* 110, 6; *Kemit*, pl. 17.

21.12 Sin. R 21–23; Khakheperre-seneb 3; Westcar 10, 11–12; Merikare 5, 3; *Urk.* IV, 1107, 14 = *Rekhmire*, pl. 119, 10 (restored with W and A).

21.13 CT V, 62c (M22C); *Urk.* IV, 484, 9–10; Heqanakht 18, 10; *Urk.* IV, 795, 9–10; CT VI, 167a–b (S10C).

Essay 21 Sethe, *Lesestücke*, 79, 19–23; *Hamm.* 114, 15–16; Sethe, *Lesestücke*, 82, 12; *Urk.* IV, 689–90.

Exercise 21 (1) Westcar 8, 17–22. (2) Westcar 8, 15–16. (3) Westcar 5, 13. (4) Adm. 6, 7–8. (5) Adm. 11, 13. (6) CT VII, 168b. (7) CT VII, 411c–412c. (8) CT I, 188a–189a (B12C, suffix of *wnn.k* emended). (9) Peas. B2, 5–6. (10) Merikare 5, 10. (11) Merikare 5, 9–10 (emended with M). (12) Ptahhotep 84–86 (L2). (13) Helck, *Dw3-Ḥtjj* II, 130 (collated). (14) Neferti 53 (determinative restored). (15) Helck, *HBT*, 18. (16) Sethe, *Lesestücke*, 71, 6–7. (17) Louvre C12, 5–7. (18) Louvre C12, 16–17. (19) Neferti 47. (20) Neferhotep Stela 18–19 (Helck, *HBT*, 25).

22.2 ShS. 111; CT II, 334–335d; Westcar 2, 11; CT IV, 287d; Westcar 10, 11; *Kahun*, pl. 7, 68 (first sign restored: cf. *Wb. med.*, 564); Peas. B2, 130; Westcar 11, 13; *Urk.* IV, 158, 17; Peas. R 14, 1; BD 175, 31.

22.3 Neferhotep Stela 16 (Helck, *HBT*, 24); Peas. R 7, 7.

22.4 Neferti 11–12; Westcar 8, 17–22; Ebers 40, 18–19.

22.5 Ebers 36, 8; Ebers 36, 7; CT V, 200b; BD 99 (Nu); Peas. B1, 219; Ebers 36, 9; Smith 21, 11–12; Smith 8, 19; Smith 22, 2; Ebers 54, 20; Ebers 107, 1; Ebers 36, 19; *Urk.* IV, 246, 14.

22.6 CT V, 184c–d; *Kahun*, pl. 7, 39–40.

22.7 Ebers 52, 6–7; Smith 9, 19–20; CT II, 379b–380a; Sinai 90, 8–10; Hornung, *Himmelskuh*, 28–29; CT V, 209i–j.

22.8 CT III, 148c; Lacau and Chevrier, *Une chapelle d'Hatshepsout*, 248 and pl. 11 (141); CT IV, 379b; CT II, 97c; CT IV, 83b; CT VII, 467f; CT IV, 357a; CT II, 197c; CT VII, 212o; CT V, 179b; CT VI, 247l.

22.9 CT II, 190a.

22.10 CT I, 273f–g; CT IV, 359a–b; CT II, 174f–i (emended); CT II, 166b.

22.12 *Beni Hasan* I, pl. 41 c; CT II, 401a; CG 46048; CT II, 25b; Amenemhat 2, 5; *Urk.* IV, 2, 15; CT II, 401b; CT V, 207c; Amenemhat 2, 5; CT I, 17b; CT I, 167f; CT I, 176k; CT II, 58c (two variants); ShS. 98; Westcar 11, 16; Hornung, *Himmelskuh*, 4; pRam. X, 1, 5; Naville, *Iouiya*, pl. 22.

22.13 CT II, 400a; CT IV, 76a–c; Peas. B2, 27; CT IV, 343i.

22.14 ShS. 117–19; CT V, 186f–g; MuK. 2, 10.

22.15 Ptahhotep 315 (L2); Smith 9, 14–15; *Bersheh* II, pl. 21 top, 14; CT II, 125f; Ptahhotep 86–87 (L2); CT I, 141d–e.

22.16 Siut V, 29 = *Kêmi* 3 (1930), 110, 36.

22.18 CT I, 76i; CT I, 107b; CT I, 121b; CT III, 48g; CT III, 86h; CT II, 159e; CT I, 92b; *Urk.* IV, 1075, 10; *Kahun*, pl. 29, 42; *JEA* 31 (1945), pl. 3A, 13; BD 52 (Nu); CT IV, 94q; *Kahun*, pl. 31, 16; Peas. B1, 160.

22.19 *Kahun*, pl. 29, 41–42; *Kahun*, pl. 31, 13–16.

Essay 22 PT 142; CT VI, 323g.

Exercise 22 (1) Neferhotep Stela 12–13 (Helck, *HBT*, 23–24. (2) ShS. 97–98. (3) Kamose Stela 2, 23 (Helck, *HBT*, 94). (4) Kamose Stela 2, 26 (Helck, *HBT*, 95). (5) Hornung, *Himmelskuh*, 3–4. (6) CT V, 354–55. (7) CT I, 242f (omitting *N pn*). (8) Peas. B2, 27–28. (9) Smith 7, 7–10. (10) CT V, 199g–200b (restored). (11) Hornung, *Himmelskuh*, 25. (12) Hornung, *Himmelskuh*, 27 (collated text). (13) CT II, 359c–360a. (14) *JEA* 31 (1945), pl. 5A, 9–10. (15) CT IV, 363a–c (emended). (16) CT VII, 418c–419c (restored). (17) CT I, 145b–d. (18) BD 6 (Nu). (19) CT III, 86f–i. (20) Peas. B1, 214.

23.3 Sin. B 94.

23.5 Ptahhotep 588; MuK. 1, 4; Adm. 12, 14; *Urk.* IV, 506, 3; Ebers 42, 15.

23.6 Neferti 24; Siut I, 286b; Hornung, *Himmelskuh*, 20; BM 101 c 7; Leb. 79; Sin. B 80; Peas. B1, 247; CT VI, 412g; *Urk.* IV, 894, 1; Peas. B2, 93; Merikare 6, 2; Neferti 4; Peas. B1, 350; *Urk.* IV, 85, 14; CT IV, 383e (T3Be); *Beni Hasan* I, pl. 8, 4; Leiden V 38 b 3; Sin. B 94; Hornung, *Himmelskuh*, 29; Hornung, *Himmelskuh*, 26; Ebers 1, 6; Sin. R 79; Helck, *Nilhymnus*, 13; CT I, 383a (M23C); CT I, 382a–383a; CG 20539 I, b 10; CT VII, 377c; CT VI, 218d; Peas. B1, 115; Leiden V 4, 7; *Urk.* IV, 1094, 17; Helck, *Nilhymnus*, 4 (3 variants); Siut I, 310; Peas. R 18, 6; Peas. B1, 117; CT VI, 370t.

23.7 Rhind Problem 66; *Kahun*, pl. 13, 24; Ptahhotep 568; Ptahhotep 557; Smith 5, 1; CT II, 381e; Leb. 103; CG 20538 II, c 12; *Hamm.* 114, 16; Westcar 8, 11; Sethe, *Lesestücke*, 79, 6; Sin. B 276; Sin. B 254; Sin. R 43; Neferti 22; Leiden V 4, 12; Peas. R 10, 5; Ebers 67, 5; Sethe, *Lesestücke*, 83, 22–23; Sin. B 97; CT VI, 11a; Siut I, 339; *Hamm.* 43, 6; Siut I, 233; CG 20089 d 5; *Urk.* IV, 7, 6; Siut I, 302; Ebers 56, 18.

23.8 Siut I, 225; Siut I, 226; Sin. B 75; Ptahhotep 602; Siut I, 226; Louvre C5, 3; Khakheperre-seneb 6; Siut I, 282; Heqanakht III, 8; Neferti 18; Neferti 20.

23.9 Peas. R 18, 6; Posener, *Enseignement loyaliste*, 83; Heqanakht I, 9; Adm. 2, 13; Heqanakht I, vo. 14; Hornung, *Himmelskuh*, 2; Merikare 11, 3; Heqanakht II, 37; Heqanakht II, 42.

23.10 Neferti 17–18 (*jw* restored); Leb. 78–80; CT V, 389g–h; Sin. B 278; *TPPI*, § 20, 5; ShS. 147; Heqanakht II, 42; Sin. R 76–79; Helck, *Nilhymnus*, 13; Hornung, *Himmelskuh*, 26; Adm. 9, 1–2; *Urk.* IV, 2028, 13; Merikare 11, 10 (pCarlsberg VI); ShS. 147; Sin. B 94–95.

23.11 Sin. B 66–67; ShS. 65; CG 20538 II c 12–13.

23.12 Adm. 2, 3; *Urk.* IV, 2026, 13; Sin. B 71; Peas. B2, 48–49; BM 558, 4.

23.13 CT II, 1g; Ptahhotep 184; CT VI, 249q; Peas. B1, 116–17; Hornung, *Himmelskuh*, 20; Ebers 1, 8; *Urk.* IV, 815, 1–2; Westcar 9, 6–7; CT II, 232a; CT VII, 241k.

23.14 Hornung, *Himmelskuh*, 26; Sin. R 74 (partly restored); Sin. B 71; *Urk.* I, 229, 16; Siut I, 230 = *Kêmi* 3 (1930), 49; Peas. R 11, 1.

23.15 Ebers 2, 12–13; *Urk.* IV, 2028, 13; Leb. 114–15; *Kahun*, pl. 35, 28; *Kahun*, pl. 13, 1; *Kahun*, pl. 11, 18; *Kahun*, pl. 12, 8; CG 20538 I c 10; MuK. 3, 5–6 (partly restored); Siut I, 296; *Urk.* IV, 78, 8; Leb. 98–99; Westcar 12, 3; CT I, 248e; BD 52 (Nu).

23.16 Rifeh IV, 56–57; Ptahhotep 581; CG 20538 II c 12.

23.17 *Urk.* IV, 758, 6–7; Neferti 69–70 (CG 25224); Sin. R 50.

23.18 Adm. 9, 4; CT II, 272a; Sethe, *Lesestücke*, 84, 15–16.

23.19 Sin. B 94; Ebers 2, 12–13; CT V, 99b–c; Westcar 6, 9–10.

Essay 23 Sethe, *Lesestücke*, 63, 12 and 4; pBoulaq 17, 10–11, 1; BD 15A I (La); pHarris 500, 7, 2–3.

Exercise 23 (1) *Kahun*, pl. 1. (2) Merikare 11, 6. (3) Neferhotep Stela 36 (Helck, *HBT*, 28). (4) Adm. 9, 4–5 (final *t* omitted). (5) Adm. 7, 13–14. (6) CG 20538 II c 12. (7) CG 20538 II c 15–16. (8) Heqanakht II, 28. (9) Kamose Stela 2, 16 (Helck, *HBT*, 93). (10) Louvre C 12, 13–14. (11) Ptahhotep 557. (12) Sethe, *Lesestücke*, 70, 24–71, 1. (13) Brunner, *Hieroglyphische Chrestomathie*, pl. 11, 16–18. (14) Peas. B1, 114–15. (15) Peas. B1, 246–48. (16) Peas. B2, 123–24. (17) Hornung, *Amduat* III, 15. (18) Leiden V 88, 10–11. (19) Ebers 103, 2–3. (20) CT I, 312e–f. (21) Westcar 9, 5–8. (22) ShS. 83–86. (23) Ebers 58, 10–11. (24) Sin. B 35–36. (25) Sin. B 62–63. (26) Sin. B 309. (27) Hatnub 49, 10–11. (28) Siut III, 62–64 (Edel, *Siut-Gräber*, 27).

24.2 Brunner, *Hieroglyphische Chrestomathie*, pl. 11, 17; *Urk.* IV, 202, 8; *Urk.* IV, 1195, 8.

24.3.1 Westcar 4, 17; Peas. R 10, 6; CT IV, 385e; Tylor, *Sebeknekht*, pl. 3; Helck, *Djedefhor*, 6; CT V, 324d; Helck, *Djedefhor*, 6; Sin. B 44; Adm. 15, 1; Sin. B 158; BD 125 (Nu); Siut I, 272; *Kahun*, pl. 12, 10; Sin. B 237; Ebers 98, 14; Peas. B1, 267; Merikare 11, 8; Hamm. 192, 5; Neferhotep Stela 32 (Helck, *HBT*, 27); Hamm. 114, 5; Sethe, *Lesestücke*, 79, 13; Peas. B1, 52; Hamm. 113, 6; Helck, *Djedefhor*, 36; Adm. 12, 13; Siut I, 306; ShS. 46; Turin 1534, 5; Siut I, 289; Smith 5, 5; Helck, *Dw3-Ḫtjj* II, 89; Siut I, 234; *Urk.* IV, 17, 1; CG 20539 I b 15.

24.3.2 Peas. B2, 118; ShS. 143; CT VI, 343o; Peas. B1, 318; *Beni Hasan* I, pl. 25, 38–39; Merikare 11, 2 (MC); CT II, 158e; Merikare 11, 2; Peas. B2, 46; BM 566, 2; Rifeh I, 4; Siut I, 287 and 270; Sethe, *Lesestücke*, 70, 18; *Bersheh* I, pl. 14, 1; Westcar 11, 10.

24.4 Hornung, *Amduat* III, 4 (2 examples); *Kemit*, pl. 5 (emended); *JEA* 74 (1988), 7, 9; *Urk.* IV, 618, 11; Heqanakht I, vo. 9.

24.5 ShS. 129; Neferhotep Stela 8 (Helck, *HBT*, 22); Sin. B 188; Hornung, *Himmelskuh*, 28; Sin. B 164; Brunner, *Hieroglyphische Chrestomathie*, pl. 11, 2–3; Sin. B 44–45; *Urk.* IV, 2026, 14; Peas. B1, 316; Sin. B 144–45; Sethe, *Lesestücke*, 70, 18; Neferhotep Stela 35 (Helck, *HBT*, 28).

24.6 Erman, *Hymnen*, 1, 1–2; CT III, 324g–h: Pyr. 1645b.

24.7 Adm. 3, 7; CG 20538 I c 10; MuK. 3, 5–6 (partly restored).

24.8 *Kemit*, pl. 8; Louvre C11, 1–2; Westcar 12, 2; Merikare 11, 7 (C); pBerlin 3029, 1, 7 (*Studia Aegyptiaca* I, 49); Helck, *Nilhymnus*, 68; Siut I, 272; Kagemni 1, 3–4; Hornung, *Himmeslkuh*, 3; Ebers 98, 14b; *Bersheh* I, pl. 15; CG 20133 e; CG 20162 a 1; CG 20358 b 1.

24.9 Ranke, *PN* I, 160, 23; Ranke, *PN* I, 403, 7; Peas. R 1, 1; Brunner, *Hieroglyphische Chrestomathie*, pl. 11, 4–5; BM 574, 1; *Urk.* IV, 2031, 4; *Urk.* I, 197, 6.

24.10 Vienna ÄS 168, 8–12; Gauthier and Jéquier, *Fouilles de Licht*, 85 fig. 102.

24.11 CT VI, 403n; *Beni Hasan* I, pl. 25, 110–13.

24.12 *Urk.* IV, 1074, 5 (partly restored).

Exercise 24 (1) Hersdman 6. (2) Louvre C15, 3. (3) Hornung, *Amduat* III, 17. (4) CT IV, 182n. (5) Adm. 3, 13. (6) Hornung, *Amduat* III, 13. (7) Hornung, *Amduat* III, 23. (8) pBerlin 3029, 1, 5–6 (*Studia Aegyptiaca* I, 49). (9) pBerlin 3029, 2, 8–9 (*Studia Aegyptiaca* I, 51). (10) Hornung, *Himmelskuh*, 10. (11) Hornung, *Himmelskuh*, 30. (12) Peas. R 10, 6. (13) Peas. R 13, 6. (14) Peas. B1, 99–100. (15) Peas. B1, 227–28. (16) Peas. B1, 318. (17) Helck, *Djedefhor*, 29. (18) Amenemhat 1, 7. (19) Lacau, *Stèle juridique*, 19. (20) Kagemni 2, 2. (21) Kamose Stela 2, 20–21 (Helck, *HBT*, 94). (22) Kamose Stela 2, 37–38 (Helck, *HBT*, 97). (23) Helck, *Lehre des Dw3-Ḫtjj* II, 90. (24) Leb. 50–51. (25) Merikare 11, 8. (26) Neferhotep Stela 6 (Helck, *HBT*, 22). (27) Neferhotep Stela 9 (Helck, *HBT*, 23). (28) Sethe, *Lesestücke*, 71, 1. (29) ShS. 45–46. (30) ShS. 124. (31) ShS. 152. (32) Sin. B 183. (33) Sin. B 159–60. (34) Sin. B 237–38. (35) Sin. B 261. (36) Westcar 4, 7. (37) Westcar 11, 9–10. (38) Westcar 11, 6–7. (39) *Urk.* IV, 1090, 5. (40) CG 20720, 1–6.

25.3 (1) *Kemit*, pl. 2; pBerlin 3029, 2, 13 (*Studia Aegyptiaca* I, 51); Siut I, 298; CG 20606 b 3; Peas. B1, 109–10. (2) Hornung, *Himmelskuh*, 25; Sin. B 187. (3) *Urk.* IV, 363, 6; Westcar 5, 3–4. (4) Westcar 10, 4; Neferti 1. (5) Ebers 102, 15–16; Hornung, *Himmelskuh*, 23–24; ShS. 186–87. (6) CT III, 204a.

25.4 CT VI, 336k; *Hamm.* 113, 10.

25.5 Siut I, 229; Smith 14, 13–15 (omitting dittograph *ntt ḥr*); BM 334, 6–8; CT VII, 190b.

25.7 Westcar 3, 6–8 (partly restored).

25.8 Westcar 9, 15; Adm. 5, 9; *JEA* 31 (1945), pl. 3A, 13–14.

25.9 Peas. B1, 298–99; Westcar 9, 15; *JEA* 31 (1945), pl. 3A, 14; Sin. B 165.

25.10 Sethe, *Lesestücke*, 70, 22–23.

25.11 Heqanakht II, 29–30; Peas. R 17, 6–7; CG 20003 a 2–3; Sethe, *Lesestücke*, 80, 4–7; Merikare 5, 9–10 (emended with M); Herdsman 22–23; Neferti 51–52 (C 25224, 8–9); Kamose Stela 2, 10 (Helck, *HBT*, 92); Hatnub 49, 5.

25.12 CT III, 61f–g; Naville, *Deir el Bahari* IV, pl. 114; CT VI, 338c–d; Sin. B 137–38.

25.13 Peas. B2, 117–18; Sethe, *Lesestücke*, 96, 23–97, 1; CT I, 278d–f; Adm. 12, 1; CT VI, 332p–q.

25.14 Peas. B1, 211; CT VII, 110; CT I, 287e.

25.15 *Urk.* IV, 897, 10–13; Peas. B1, 114–15; *Urk.* IV, 348, 9.

25.16 Adm. 2, 9; Sin. B 183; ShS. 83–84; *Hamm.* 114, 10–12; Neferti 6; MuK. 2, 3; Sin. R 22–24.

25.17 CG 20518 a 1.

25.18 Hatnub 49, 11; Ptahhotep 519; Sin. B 185; Hornung, *Himmelskuh*, 26.

Essay 25 *Urk.* I, 128, 14–130, 15; Heqanakht I, vo. 18–19; Heqanakht IV; *Kahun*, pl. 29, 2–4; Gardiner and Sethe, *Letters to the Dead*, pl. 4.

Exercise 25 (1) CT V, 323h–i. (2) CT VI, 401n–o. (3) Merikare 11, 14–12, 1 (C, emended). (4) CT VII, 494f. (5) Hornung, *Himmelskuh*, 2. (6) Heqanakht I, vo. 7. (7) Heqanakht I, vo. 9. (8) Heqanakht I, vo. 11–12. (9) Heqanakht II, 3–4. (10) Kamose CT 14 (Helck, *HBT*, 90). (11) Khakheperre-seneb 6. (12) Leb. 116–18 (det. of *ḏrḏrw* emended). (13) MuK. 1, 7. (14) Neferti 24–26 (emended). (15) Sin. B 11–13. (16) Sin. B 70. (17) Sin. B 72–73. (18) Sin. B 199–200. (19) Sin. B 202. (20) Sin. B 236. (21) Westcar 6, 4–5. (22) Westcar 7, 20–21. (23) Westcar 11, 21–22. (24) Westcar 12, 14–15. (25) *Urk.* IV, 324, 6–11. (26) Merikare 11, 10–12, 8 (P and C).

26.20 (1) *Urk.* IV, 916, 3; Siut I, 298; *Urk.* IV, 1198, 16; *Urk.* IV, 157, 7. (3) Hamm. 110, 4; ShS. 103.

26.22 *Urk.* IV, 835, 7; Sethe, *Lesestücke*, 84, 18.

26.23 Smith 21, 17; *Urk.* IV, 566, 12; CT I, 30d–31a (B6C); Neferhotep Stela 40 (Helck, *HBT*, 29).

26.24 Peas. B1, 342–43 (spelling of *gs3* emended).

26.29 (3) CG 20003 a 3–4; Heqanakht II, 31; Heqanakht I, 5–6. (4) CG 20539 I b 20–21.

26.32 Siut I, 301.

Sign List

Listed below are the hieroglyphic signs most often found in Middle Egyptian texts, arranged into 27 groups on the basis of what they depict. The selection and order are those most commonly used by Egyptologists, based on the list in Gardiner's *Egyptian Grammar*, with some additional signs.[1] Each sign is identified as to what it depicts (as far as possible) and its uses, whether phonogram, ideogram, or determinative, arranged in order of frequency; words in SMALL CAPITALS indicate the class of words with which a sign is used as determinative. At the end of the sign list is a supplemental list of signs arranged by shape.

A. Human Beings, Male

1	𓀀	seated man	Phonogram *j* (1s suffix pronoun). Determinative MAN; also in 1s pronouns *jnk*, *wj*, *.kw/kj*. Ideogram for *zj* "man" or *rḫw* "companion." With B1 and plural strokes, determinative PEOPLE and ideogram for *rmṯ* "people."
2	𓀁	man with hand to mouth	Variants (A68), (A84). Determinative SPEAK, THINK, EAT, DRINK, and for emotions such as LOVE and HATE.
3	𓀂	man sitting on heel	Determinative SIT.
4	𓀃	man with hands raised	Determinative WORSHIP; also HIDE (for A5).
5	𓀄	man hiding behind wall	Determinative HIDE.
6	𓀆	A1 + W54	Variant of D60.
7	𓀉	fatigued man	Determinative WEARY, WEAK, SOFT.
8	𓀊	man performing *hnw*	Determinative in *hnw* "jubilation."
9	𓀋	man with basket on head	Variant (A119) in *f3j*. Determinative LOAD, CARRY, WORK. Ideogram for *3tp* "load," *f3j* "carry, lift," *k3t* "work."
10	𓀌	man with oar	Determinative SAIL, ROW.
11	𓀍	man with scepter and crook	Determinative FRIEND.
12	𓀎	soldier	Determinative SOLDIER. Ideogram with plural strokes for *mšꜥ* "expeditionary force, army."
13	𓀏	prisoner	Determinative ENEMY.

1 A number of signs that Gardiner placed in category Aa ("Unclassified") have since been identified. The sign R13 is included as a separate entry in G. The supplemental sign R61 is listed under I as well as R, and Y10 under M as well as Y. Additional signs are numbered, where possible, after the list in N. Grimal, J. Hallof, and D. van der Plas, eds., *Hieroglyphica* (Publications interuniversitaires de recherches égyptologiques informatisées, 1: Utrecht, Centre for Computer-aided Egyptological Research, Utrecht University, 1993). Such signs are placed where they belong in each group rather than in their numerical position: thus, for example, A359 after A28.

14	wounded man	Variant (A14a). Determinative DIE, ENEMY.
15	man falling	Variant (A97). Determinative FALL, DIE. Ideogram for *ḫr* "fall."
16	man bowing	Determinative BOW.
17	child	Variant (A17a). Determinative CHILD, YOUNG; in hieratic also SIT (for A3), DIGNITARY (for A21). Ideogram for *ẖrd* "child." Phonogram *nnj* "child" in *nnj-nswt* "Herakleopolis."
18	child with Red Crown	Determinative CHILD-KING.
19	old man with staff	Determinative OLD, DISTINGUISHED. Ideogram for *j3w* "old," *smsw* "eldest," *wr* "great, chief." Phonogram *jk* in *jky* "miner" (from *j3k* "age"). In hieratic sometimes for A25.
20	old man with forked staff	Variant of last. Determinative in *smsw* "elder," also ideogram for same.
21	dignitary	Determinative DIGNITARY. Ideogram for *srj* "official." Also as variant of A11 and A22. In hieroglyphic not always distinguishable from A19–20.
22	statue on base	Determinative STATUE. The form often varies.
23	king	Determinative KING.
24	man striking	Determinative FORCE, EFFORT. Ideogram for *nḫt* "victory."
25	man striking	Determinative in *ḥwj* "hit," often (striking the phonogram).
59	man threatening	Determinative DRIVE OFF.
26	man beckoning	Variant (A366). Determinative CALL. Ideogram for *j* "oh!" and *ꜥš* "call."
27	man running	Phonogram *jn* in *jn* "by" (from *jn* "messenger").
28	excited man	Determinative HIGH, JOY, MOURN, FRUSTRATION.
359	man with arms clasped	Determinative in *ḥsj* "freeze." Also rare variant of A1 (man pointing to himself).
29	man upside down	Determinative INVERT.
30	man worshipping	Determinative WORSHIP, RESPECT.
31	man shunning	Determinative TURN AWAY.
32	man dancing	Determinative DANCE.
33	man with stick and bundle	Variant (A166). Determinative in *mnjw* "herdsman," also ideogram for same. Determinative WANDER, STRANGER.
34	man pounding	Determinative in *ḫwsj* "pound, construct."
35	man building a wall	Determinative in *qd* "build," also ideogram for same.
37	man in vat	Variant (A36). Determinative in *ꜥftj* "brewer," also ideogram for same.
38	man with two animals	Variant (A39, with two giraffes). Ideogram for *qjs/qsj* "Qus" (town).

40	seated god	Determinative GOD, KING. Variant of A1 for 1s pronouns when the speaker is a god or the king.
41	seated king	Variant (A42). Determinative KING. Variant of A1 for 1s pronouns when the speaker is the king.
43	king with White Crown	Variant (A44). Determinative of *nswt* "king," also ideogram for same. Determinative of *wsjr* "Osiris."
45	king with Red Crown	Variant (A46). Determinative of *bjtj* "king of Lower Egypt," also ideogram for same.
47	shepherd seated	Determinative in *z3w* "guard," also ideogram for same. Ideogram for *mnjw* "herdsman." Sometimes variant of A48.
48	seated man with knife	Phonogram *jr* in the nisbe *jrj* "pertaining to."
49	foreigner with stick	Determinative FOREIGNER.
50	noble on chair	Determinative DIGNITARY, DECEASED. Variant of A1 for 1s pronouns when the speaker is deceased. Also variant of A51.
51	noble on chair, with flail	Determinative in *špsj/špss* "noble," also ideogram for same. Determinative DIGNITARY, DECEASED.
52	seated noble with flail	Determinative DIGNITARY, DECEASED.
53	mummy standing	Determinative MUMMY, STATUE, LIKENESS, FORM. Ideogram for *twt* "likeness, statue."
54	mummy recumbent	Determinative DEAD.
55	mummy on bed	Determinative LIE, DEAD. Ideogram for *sḏr* "lie down." The mummy is sometimes replaced by a man when used in/for *sḏr* "lie down."

B. Human Beings, Female

1	seated woman	Variant (B24). Determinative FEMALE. Rarely variant of A1 when the speaker is female.
2	pregnant woman	Determinative PREGNANT.
3	woman giving birth	Variant (B4). Determinative in *msj* "give birth," also ideogram for same.
5	woman nursing	Determinative in *mnꜥt* "nurse."
6	nurse with child	Determinative in *rnn* "rear, foster."
7	seated queen	Determinative in queens' names.

C. Anthropomorphic Gods

1	god with sun-disk	Variant (falcon-headed, C2). Determinative in *rꜥ* "Re," also ideogram for same.
3	ibis-headed	Determinative in *ḏḥwtj* "Thoth," also ideogram for same.
4	ram-headed	Variant (C5). Determinative in *ẖnmw* "Khnum," also ideogram for same.

6	jackal-headed	Determinative in *jnpw* "Anubis" and *wp-w3wt* "Wepwawet," also ideogram for same.
7	Seth-animal-headed	Determinative in *stẖ/stš* "Seth," also ideogram for same.
8	Min figure	Determinative in *mnw* "Min," also ideogram for same.
9	goddess with horned disk	Determinative in *ḥwt-ḥrw* "Hathor," also ideogram for same.
10	goddess with feather	Variants (C10a), (C175a). Determinative in *m3ʿt* "Maat" (as goddess), also ideogram for same.
11	*ḥḥ*-figure	Ideogram for *ḥḥ* "million (§ 9.1)" and "Heh" (god supporting the sky).
12	Amun figure	Determinative in *jnmw* "Amun," also ideogram for same.
17	Montu figure	Determinative in *mnṯw* "Montu," also ideogram for same.
18	Tatjenen figure	Determinative in *t3-ṯnnj* "Ta-tjenen," also ideogram for same.
19	Ptah figure	Variant (C20). Determinative in *ptḥ* "Ptah," also ideogram for same.

D. Parts of the Human Body

1	head	Ideogram for *tp* and *ḏ3ḏ3* "head." Phonogram *tp* in *tpj* "first." Determinative HEAD.
2	face	Ideogram for *ḥr* "face." Phonogram *ḥr*.
3	hair	Determinative HAIR, SKIN, COLOR; also words associated with hair: BALD, MOURN, WIDOW. Ideogram for *wš* "missing."
4	eye	Phonogram *jr*. Determinative for actions associated with the eye. Ideogram for *jrt* "eye."
5	eye with paint	Variants (D6) and (D7a). Determinative for actions associated with the eye.
140	two eyes	Determinative in *ptr* "see, look," also ideogram for same.
7	eye with paint	Determinative ADORN. Also determinative in *ʿn* "beautiful" and *ʿnw* "Tura" (quarry near Cairo), from the Semitic root *ʿjn* "eye."
8	eye enclosed	Variant of D7 as determinative in *ʿn* "beautiful" and *ʿnw* "Tura."
9	eye weeping	Determinative in *rmj* "weep," also ideogram for same.
10	eye with falcon markings	Determinative in *wḏ3t* "Sound Eye (of Horus)," also ideogram for same.
11	part of D10	Ideogram for ½ heqat (§ 9.7.3).
12	part of D10	Ideogram for ¼ heqat (§ 9.7.3). Also determinative in *ḏfḏ* "pupil" and *m33* "see," the latter as variant of D4.
13	part of D10	Ideogram for ⅛ heqat (§ 9.7.3). Also determinative EYEBROW.
14	part of D10	Ideogram for 1/16 heqat (§ 9.7.3).
15	part of D10	Ideogram for 1/32 heqat (§ 9.7.3).
16	part of D10	Ideogram for 1/64 heqat (§ 9.7.3).
17	D15 + D16	Determinative of *tjt* "image," also ideogram for same.
18	ear	Determinative in *msḏr* "ear," also ideogram for same.
19	face in profile	Variant (D20). Determinative NOSE, FACE, and associated actions. Ideogram for *fnḏ* "nose." Phonogram *ḫnt*. In hieratic not always distinguishable from U31 or Aa32.

21	mouth	Phonogram *r*. Ideogram for *r* "mouth."
154	mouth plus water	Determinative in *jꜥw-r* "breakfast," also ideogram for same.
22	mouth plus 2 strokes	Ideogram for *rwj* $\frac{2}{3}$ (§ 9.6).
23	mouth plus 3 strokes	Ideogram for *ẖmt-rw* $\frac{3}{4}$ (§ 9.6).
24	lip with teeth	Variant (D24a). Determinative in *spt* "lip," also ideogram for same. Sometimes in error for F42.
25	two lips and teeth	Determinative in *sptj* "lips," also ideogram for same.
26	lips and water	Determinative SPIT, SPEW.
27	breast	Variant (D27a). Determinative BREAST, NURSE. Ideogram for *mnḏ* "breast."
28	two arms	Phonogram *k3*. Ideogram for *k3* "ka" (variant D29).
30	two arms and tail	Determinative in *nḥb-k3w* "Assigner of Kas" (a god).
32	two arms embracing	Variant in hieratic. Determinative EMBRACE, OPEN.
31	D32 plus U36	Variant . Ideogram for *ḥm-k3* "ka-servant" (mortuary priest).
33	arms and oar	Phonogram *ẖn* (from *ẖnj* "row").
34a	arms with shield and mace	Variant (D34). Ideogram for *ꜥḥ3* "fight."
35	gesture of negation	Ideogram for *nj* "not" and phonogram *nj* or *n* (§ 8.2.6), especially in *nn* "not"; *jw* or *jwt* in *jwt* "that not" and *jwtj* "which not" (§§ 12.9, 26.29.5). Determinative NEGATION.
36	forearm	Phonogram ꜥ. Ideogram for ꜥ "arm, hand." Often variant for D37–44.
36a	forearm	Ideogram for *ꜥwj* "arms, hands."
212a	forearm with water	Determinative in *jꜥj* "wash," also ideogram for same.
37	forearm with X8	Phonogram *dj* in forms of *rdj* "give." Also variant of D38.
38	forearm with bread	Phonogram *mj* or *m*. Determinative in *jmj* "give!" (§ 16.2.3).
39	forearm with pot	Determinative OFFER. Sometimes variant of D37–38.
218a	O43 + D36	Ideogram for *šzp* "receive."
40	forearm with stick	Determinative FORCE, EFFORT. Ideogram for *ḫ3j* "measure, evaluate." Rarely variant of D37.
41	forearm with palm down	Determinative ARM and actions associated with the arm or hand. Ideogram *rmn* "shoulder." Phonogram *nj*.
42	forearm with palm down	Determinative in *mḥ* "cubit" (§ 9.7.1), also ideogram for same.
43	forearm with flail	Phonogram *ḫw*.
44	forearm with scepter	Determinative in *ḫrp* "manage," also ideogram for same.
45	forearm with brush	Variant (D251). Determinative in *ḏsr* "sacred, clear away, raise the arm," also ideogram for same.
46	hand	Phonogram *d*. Ideogram for *ḏrt* "hand."
46a	hand with water	Ideogram for *jdt* "fragrance."
47	hand	Determinative of *ḏrt* "hand" when spelled with phonograms.
48	hand without thumb	Ideogram for *šzp* "palm" (§ 9.7.1).
49	fist	Determinative GRASP.
50	finger	Ideogram for *ḏbꜥ* "finger" and *ḏbꜥ* "10,000" (§ 9.1). When doubled, determinative ACCURATE.

51	finger	Determinative for actions associated with the finger: *ḫ3j* "measure," *ṯ3j* "take," *dqr* "press." Determinative in *ᶜnt* "fingernail," also ideogram for same. Determinative FRUIT, FLOWER, also ideogram for *dqrw* "fruit," *q3w* "flour."
52	penis	Determinative MALE. Phonogram *mt*. With E1, ideogram for *k3* "bull."
53	penis with fluid	Determinative PENIS and associated actions, also MALE. Determinative of *b3ḥ* in *m b3ḥ* "in the presence of," *ḏr b3ḥ* "since," *r b3ḥ* "before," also ideogram for same.
279	testicles	Determinative in *ẖrwj* "testicles," also ideogram for same.
280a	pelvis and vulva	Phonogram *ḥm*. Ideogram for *jdt* "vulva, cow."
54	walking legs	Determinative MOTION. Phonogram *jw* in forms of the verb *jwj* "come." Ideogram for *nmtt* "step."
55	legs walking backwards	Determinative REVERSE.
56	leg	Determinative FOOT and associated actions. Ideogram for *rd* "foot." Phonogram *pd* (from *p3d* "knee"). Ideogram for *wᶜrt* "district" (from *wᶜrt* "shin"), *sbq* "excellent" (from *sbq* "leg"), *gḥs* "gazelle."
57	leg with knife	Determinative MUTILATE. Ideogram for *j3ṯw* "place of execution" and *sj3tj* "cheater" (from *j3ṯ* "short").
58	foot	Phonogram *b*. Ideogram for *bw* "place, thing."
59	D36 + D58	Phonogram *ᶜb*.
60	D58 + W54	Ideogram for *wᶜb* "clean, pure."
61	stylized toes	Variants (D62) and (D63). Determinative in *s3ḥ* "toe; kick, touch with the foot," also ideogram for same.

E. Mammals

1	bull	Determinative CATTLE. Ideogram for *k3* "bull, ox" *jḥw* "cattle."
166	bulls	Plural of E1.
177	two bulls joined	Determinative in *ḫns* "go back and forth."
176	bull tied for slaughter	Determinative *rḫs* "slaughter," also ideogram for same. Ideogram for *k3* "bull" as offering.
2	bull charging	Determinative in *sm3* "wild bull." Ideogram for *k3* in *k3 nḫt* "victorious bull" (epithet of the king).
3	calf	Determinative in *bḥz* "calf" and *wnḏw* "short-horned cattle."
4	sacred cow	Determinative in *ḥz3t* "sacred cow."
5	cow and calf	Determinative in *3ms* "solicitous."
6	horse	Determinative HORSE. Ideogram for *ssmt* "horse."
7	donkey	Determinative in *ᶜ3* (originally *jᶜ3*) "donkey."
8	kid	Variant (E8a). Phonogram *jb*. Determinative GOAT.
9	newborn bubalis	Phonogram *jw*.
10	ram	Variant (E11). Determinative SHEEP. Ideogram for *b3* "ram," *ḫnmw* "Khnum."
12	pig	Determinative PIG.
13	cat	Determinative in *mjw/mjt* "cat."

14	dog (saluki)	Determinative DOG.
15	jackal recumbent	Variant (D16). Determinative in *jnpw* "Anubis," also ideogram for same. Ideogram (D15) for title *ḥrj-sšt3* "master of secrets."
17	jackal	Determinative in *z3b* "jackal; dignitary," also ideogram for same.
18	jackal on standard	Variant (E19). Determinative in *wp-w3wt* "Parter of the Ways (Wepwawet)," also ideogram for same.
20	Seth animal	Variant (E21). Ideogram for *stẖ/stš* "Seth." Determinative TURMOIL, CHAOS. In hieratic often for E7 and E27.
22	lion	Determinative in *m3j* "lion," also ideogram for same.
23	lion recumbent	Phonogram *rw* (from *rw* "lion"). In hieratic often for U13.
128	two lions joined	Determinative in *3kr* "Horizon (god)," also ideogram for same.
24	panther or leopard	Determinative in *3by* "panther, leopard," also ideogram for same.
25	hippopotamus	Determinative HIPPOPOTAMUS.
26	elephant	Determinative in *3bw* "elephant." Ideogram for *3bw* "Elephantine" (in modern Aswan).
27	giraffe	Determinative in *sr* "foretell." Determinative in *mmj* "giraffe," also ideogram for same.
28	oryx	Determinative in *m3ḥḏ* "oryx."
29	gazelle	Determinative in *gḥs* "gazelle."
30	ibex	Determinative in *nj3w*, *nr3w*, *n3w* "ibex."
31	goat with collar	Determinative in *sꜥḥ* "privilege," also ideogram for same.
32	baboon	Determinative BABOON, MONKEY, FURIOUS.
33	monkey	Determinative in *gjf* "monkey."
34	hare	Phonogram *wn*.

F. Parts of Mammals

1	head of ox	Variant (F63). Ideogram for *k3* "cattle" (in offering formulas).
2	head of charging bull	Determinative in *ḏnd* "rage."
3	head of hippopotamus	Determinative in *3t* "power," and *3t* "moment," also ideogram for latter.
4	forepart of lion	Ideogram for *ḥ3t* "front" and related words.
5	head of bubalis	Variant (F6). Determinative in *šs3* "skilled," and related words, also ideogram for same. Determinative in *sš3* "prayer" and *bẖnt* "pylon."
7	head of ram	Variant (F8). Determinative in *šfyt* "worth" (from *šft* "ram's head"), also ideogram for same.
9	head of leopard	Determinative in *pḥtj* "strength," also ideogram for same (often doubled).
11	head and neck of animal	Variant (F10). Determinative NECK, THROAT and related actions.
12	head and neck of jackal	Phonogram *wsr*.
13	horns	Phonogram *wp*. Ideogram for *wpt* "brow." For see O44.

14	F13 + M4	Variant (F15). Ideogram for *wpt-rnpt* "Opening of the Year" (New Year's Day).
16	horn	Phonogram *ʿb*. Determinative HORN, also ideogram for same.
17	F16 + W54	Determinative in *ʿbw* "purification," also ideogram for same.
18	tusk	Determinative TOOTH and associated actions. Phonograms *bḥ* and *ḥw*. Determinative in words with root *bj3*.
19	jawbone of ox	Determinative in *ʿrt* "jaw."
20	tongue	Phonogram *ns*. Determinative for actions associated with the tongue. Ideogram for *ns* "tongue" and *jmj-r* "overseer" (§ 8.9). Sometimes for Z6.
21	ear of bovine	Phonograms *sḏm* and *jdn*. Determinative EAR and associated actions. Ideogram for *msḏr* "ear" and *ḏrḏ* "leaf."
22	hindquarters of feline	Phonogram *pḥ*. Determinative END, BOTTOM. Ideogram for *pḥwj* "end" and *kf3* "discreet" (from *kf3* "bottom").
23	foreleg of ox	Variant (F24). Determinative in *ḫpš* "strong arm; foreleg," also ideogram for same. Determinative in *msḫtjw* "Foreleg" (Ursa Major).
25	leg and hoof of ox	Phonogram *wḥm*. Ideogram for *wḥm/wḥmt* "hoof."
26	goatskin	Phonogram *ẖn*. Ideogram for *ẖnt* "hide, skin."
27	cowskin	Determinative HIDE, MAMMAL. Sometimes for N2.
28	cowskin	Phonogram *s3b* in *s3b* "dappled." Sometimes for U23.
29	cowskin with arrow	Determinative of *stj* "shoot," also ideogram for same. Phonogram *st*.
30	water-skin	Phonogram *šd*.
31	three fox-skins	Phonogram *ms*.
32	animal's belly and udder	Phonogram *ẖ*. Ideogram in *ẖt* "belly, body."
33	tail	Determinative in *sd* "tail," also ideogram for same.
34	heart	Ideogram for *jb* "heart." Determinative in *ḥ3tj* "heart."
35	heart and windpipe	Phonogram *nfr*.
36	lung and windpipe	Phonogram *zm3*.
37	spine and ribs	Variants (F38), (F37b). Determinative BACK. Ideogram for *j3t* "back." Sometimes for M21.
39	spine and spinal cord	Determinative in *jm3ḫ* "honor" (Essay 21), also ideogram for same. Determinative in *jm3ḫ* "spinal cord," also ideogram for same. Occasionally for F37 as determinative.
40	spine and spinal cord	Phonogram *3w*.
41	vertebrae	Variant of Y10. Determinative in *psḏ* "back."
42	rib	Phonogram *spr*. Determinative in *spr* "rib," also ideogram for same.
43	ribs	Determinative in *spḥt* "ribs."
44	joint of meat	Determinative in *jwʿ* "inherit" and related words, also ideogram for same. Phonogram *jsw*. Determinative in *jwʿ* "femur," *swt* "tibia."
45	cow uterus	Determinative in *jdt* "vulva, cow," also ideogram for same.
46	intestine	Variants (F47), (F48), (F49). Determinative MIDST, TURN, INTESTINE. Determinative in *wḏb* "shore" (from *wḏb* "turn").
50	S29 + F46	Phonogram *spẖr*.

51	piece of meat	Also , , . Determinative FLESH. Ideogram for *kns* "vagina" and (tripled) *ḥꜥw* "body." Phonogram *js* in *jst* "Isis" and *ws* in *wsjr* "Osiris" in some Coffin Texts.
52	excrement	Determinative in *ḥs* "excrement."

G. Birds

1	Egyptian vulture	Phonogram *ȝ*. Often distinguishable from G4 only by flatter head.
2	two vultures	Phonogram *ȝȝ*.
3	U1 + G1	Phonogram *mȝ*.
4	buzzard	Variant (G4a). Phonogram *tjw*. G4 often distinguishable from G1 only by rounder head.
5	falcon	Ideogram for *ḥrw* "Horus."
6	falcon with flail	Determinative in *bjk* "falcon."
7	falcon on standard	Determinative DIVINE. Also variant of A1 when the speaker is a god or the king.
R13	falcon on standard	Ideogram for *jmnt* "West" (older form of R14).
7b	falcon in boat	Variant (G7a). Ideogram for *nmtj* "Nemti" (a god).
8	G5 + S12	Ideogram for *bjk nbw* "Gold Falçon" (title of the king: Essay 6).
9	falcon with sundisk	Ideogram in *rꜥ-ḥrw-(ȝḫtj)* "Re-Harakhti" (Essays 4, 12, 16).
10	falcon in Sokar bark	Determinative in *zkr* "Sokar" (a god) and *ḥnw* "Sokar-bark."
11	falcon image	Variant (G12). Determinative in *ꜥẖm/ꜥšm/ꜥḫm* "idol" and *šnbt* "breast."
13	falcon image with plumes	Determinative in *spdw* "Sopdu" (a god). Ideogram for *ḥrw nḫnj* "Horus of Hierakonpolis."
14	vulture	Phonogram *mjwt/mjt/mwt/mt*, most common in *mwt* (*mjwt*) "mother." Determinative in *nrt* "vulture" and words with root *nr*.
14a	vulture on basket	Determinative in *nḫbt* "Nekhbet" (goddess).
15	vulture with flail	Determinative in *mwt* (*mjwt*) "Mut" (goddess), also ideogram for same.
16	G14a + I13	Ideogram for *nbtj* "Two Ladies" (title of the king: Essay 6).
17	owl	Phonogram *m*.
18	two owls	Phonogram *mm*.
20	G17 + D36	Variant (G19 = G17 + D37). Phonogram *mj*, *m*.
21	guinea-fowl	Phonogram *nḥ*. Ideogram for *nḥ* "guinea-fowl." Often with body like G1 or G43, but with "horns" and lappet of G21.
22	hoopoe	Phonogram *ḏb/db* in *ḏbt/dbt* "brick."
23	lapwing	Variant (G24). Determinative in *rḫwt/rḫyt* "subjects," also ideogram for same.
25	crested ibis	Phonogram *ȝḫ*.

26	ibis on standard	Variant (G26a). Ideogram for *ḏḥwtj* "Thoth." Determinative in *hbj* "ibis."
27	flamingo	Phonogram *dšr* "red." Determinative in *dšr* "flamingo."
28	black ibis	Phonogram *gm*.
29	jabiru	Phonogram *b3*.
30	three jabirus	Ideogram for *b3w* "impressiveness."
31	heron	Determinative HERON.
32	heron on a perch	Determinative in *bꜥḥj* "inundate," also ideogram for same.
33	egret	Determinative in *sd3/sd3d3* "tremble."
34	ostrich	Determinative in *njw* "ostrich."
35	cormorant	Phonogram *ꜥq*.
36	forktailed swallow	Phonogram *wr*. Determinative in *mnt* "swallow."
37	sparrow	Determinative SMALL, BAD. Distinguished from G36 by the rounded tail.
38	goose	Phonogram *gb* in *gbb*, *gbw* "Geb." Determinative BIRD, INSECT. Variant of G39 as phonogram *z3*. Determinative in *wf3* "discuss," *wzf* "idle," *wdfj* "delay," *ḥtm* "perish, destroy."
39	pintail duck	Phonogram *z3*. Determinative in *zr/zrt/zj/zjt* "pintail duck." Often distinguishable from G38 only by more pointed tail.
40	pintail duck flying	Phonogram *p3*. Occasional variant of G41.
41	pintail duck landing	Phonogram *p3*, especially in hieratic. Determinative in *ḫnj* "land, alight" and other words with *ḫn*. Determinative in *sḥwj* "gather" and *qmyt* "gum." In combination with T14, determinative in *qm3* "throw," *qm3j* "create," and words with *ṯn/tn*.
42	fattened bird	Determinative in *wš3* "fatten," also ideogram in same. Determinative in *ḏf3w* "food."
43	quail chick	Phonogram *w*. Ideogram for *w* "chick."
44	two quail chicks	Phonogram *ww*.
45	G43 + D36	Phonogram *wꜥ*.
46	G43 + U1	Phonogram *m3w*.
47	duckling	Phonogram *ṯ3*. Ideogram *ṯ3* "duckling."
48	ducklings in nest	Variants (G48a), (G49). Determinative in *zš* "nest," also ideogram for same.
50	two plovers	Ideogram for *rḫtj* "washerman."
51	bird and fish	Determinative in *ḥ3m/ḥjm* "catch fish."
52	bird picking up grain	Determinative in *snm* "feed."
53	human-headed bird	Ideogram for *b3* "ba."
54	plucked bird	Phonogram *snḏ/snd*. Determinative in *wšn* "wring the neck of birds."

H. Parts of Birds

1	head of duck	Ideogram for *ꜣpd* "bird" (in offering formulas). Determinative in *wšn* "wring the neck of birds." Variant of H2.
2	head of a crested bird	Determinative in *mꜣꜥ* "temple (of the head)," occasionally also *mꜣꜥ* "correct, true, real." Phonograms *pꜣq* (variant of H3), *wšm*.
3	head of spoonbill	Phonogram *pꜣq*.
4	head of vulture (G14)	For G14 as determinative in *nrt* "vulture" and words with root *nr*. Ideogram for *rmṯ* "people."
5	wing	Determinative WING and associated actions.
6	feather	Variants (H6a), (H6b). Phonogram *šw*. Ideogram for *šwt* "feather." Determinative in *mꜣꜥt* "Maat" (Essay 10), also ideogram for same.
7	claw	Phonogram *šꜣ* in *šꜣt* "Shat" (a place). Determinative in *jꜣft* "claw."
8	egg	Ideogram for *zꜣ* "son" in proper names. Determinative in *swḥt* "egg." Determinative in *pꜥt* "the elite."

I. Reptiles, Amphibians, and their Parts

1	gecko	Phonogram *ꜥšꜣ*. Determinative LIZARD.
2	turtle	Determinative in *štjw* "turtle," also ideogram for same.
3	crocodile	Determinative CROCODILE, AGGRESSION. When doubled, ideogram for *jty* "sovereign."
4	crocodile on shrine	Variant (I5a, crocodile image). Determinative in *sbkw* "Sobek," also ideogram for same.
5	crocodile with curved tail	Determinative in *sꜣq* "collect," also ideogram for same.
6	crocodile scales	Phonogram *km*.
7	frog	Determinative FROG. Ideogram for *wḥm ꜥnḫ* "repeating life" (epithet of deceased).
8	tadpole	Ideogram for *ḥfn* "100,000" (§ 9.2). Determinative TADPOLE.
9	horned viper	Phonogram *f*. Determinative in *jtj* "father."
10	cobra	Phonogram *ḏ*.
R61	emblematic cobra	Determinative in *ṯnjw* "desert border," also ideogram for same.
11	two cobras	Phonogram *ḏḏ*.
12	erect cobra	Variant (I64). Determinative in *jꜥrt* "uraeus" and names of goddesses.
13	cobra on basket	Determinative in *wꜣḏt* "Wadjet" (a goddess) and name of goddesses.
14	snake	Variant (I15). Determinative SNAKE, WORM.

K. Fish and Parts of Fish

1	bulti	Phonogram *jn*. Determinative in *jnt* "bulti."
2	barbel	Determinative in *bwt* "abomination."
3	mullet	Phonogram *ꜥḏ* in *ꜥḏ-mr* "district administrator." Determinative in *ꜥdw* "mullet."

4	oxyrhynchus	Phonogram *ḫ3*. Ideogram in *ḫ3t* "oxyrhynchus."
5	pike	Determinative in *bzj* "introduce." Determinative FISH, FISHY.
6	fish scale	Variant . Determinative in *nšmt* "fish scale," also ideogram for same.
7	blowfish	Determinative in *špt* "angry."

L. Insects and Invertebrates

1	scarab beetle	Phonogram *ḫpr*. Determinative in *ḫprr* "scarab beetle," also ideogram for same.
2	bee or wasp	Ideogram for *bjt* "bee; honey," and *bjtj* "King of Lower Egypt."
3	fly	Determinative in *ꜥff* "fly."
4	locust	Determinative in *znḥm* "locust."
5	centipede	Ideogram in *sp3* "Sepa" (place near Heliopolis). Determinative in *zp3* "centipede."
6	shell	Phonogram *ḫ3* in *ḫ3wt* "offering table."
7	emblematic scorpion	Variant (L7a). Determinative in *srqt* "Selket" (a goddess), also ideogram for same.

M. Vegetation

1	tree	Variant (M1a, with M3). Determinative TREE; also in *mꜥr* "fortunate." Phonogram *jm3*, often with only G17 *m* as complement = *jm(3)*.
2	plant	Determinative PLANT. Phonogram *ḥn*. Determinative in *jzj* "light," *jz* "tomb," *js* "old" (from *jzw* "reeds"). Rarely for A1 as determinative or in 1s pronouns (from *j* "reed"). Occasional variant of T24.
3	stick	Phonogram *ḫt*. Determinative WOOD. Ideogram for *ḫt* "wood, stick, tree, mast." Also vertically as determinative of *ḏꜥr* "seek."
4	rib of palm branch	Ideogram for *rnpt* "year" and *ḥsbt* "regnal year" (§ 9.9). Determinative in *rnpj* "young." Determinative TIME in *tr* "time, season." When doubled, ideogram for *snf* "last year."
5	M4 + X1	Determinative TIME in *tr* "time, season," also ideogram for same. Variant of M6.
6	M4 + D21	Determinative TIME in *tr* "time, season," also ideogram for same. Determinative of some roots ending in *tr* and *rj*.
7	M4 + Q3	Determinative in *rnpj* "young," also ideogram for same.
8	pool with lilies	Phonogram *š3*. Ideogram for *3ḫt* "Inundation (season)" (§ 9.8). Ideogram for *š3* "pool, marsh."
9	lily (lotus)	Determinative in *zššnj* "lily (lotus)," also ideogram for same.
10	lily (lotus) bud	Determinative in *nḥbt* "lily (lotus) bud."
11	flower on stem	Determinative in *wdn* "dedicate, offer," also ideogram for same. Occasional variant of F46 as determinative in *wḏb* "shore."
12	lily (lotus) plant	Phonogram *ḫ3*. Ideogram for *ḫ3* "1,000" (§ 9.1) and "lily (lotus)."
13	papyrus	Variant (M14, with I10). Phonogram *w3ḏ/w3d*, also *wḏ/wd*. Ideogram for *w3ḏ* "papyrus column."

15	clump of papyrus with buds	Determinative for *mḥw* "Delta," also ideogram for same. Determinative PAPYRUS, SWAMP. Phonogram *3ẖ* in *3ẖ-bjt* "Chemmis" (Delta town).
16	clump of papyrus	Phonogram *ḥ3*. Variant of M15 in *mḥw* "Delta."
17	reed	Phonogram *j*. When doubled, phonogram *y*. Occasional variant of A1. Ideogram for *j* "reed."
18	M17 + D54	Variant . Phonogram *j* in forms of *jj* "come."
19	emblem for offerings	Determinative in *ᶜ3b* "offer," also ideogram for same.
20	field of reeds	Determinative in *sẖt* "field" and *sẖtj* "peasant," also ideogram for same. Occasional variant of M21.
21	reeds with root	Determinative in *sm* "grass" and *sm* "help."
22	rush	Phonogram *nẖb*. When doubled, phonogram *nn*.
23	sedge	Phonogram *sw*. Ideogram for *nswt* "king." Ideogram for *swt* "sedge." Occasional variant of M24 and M26.
163	M23 + Aa1	Ideogram for *rẖ-nswt* "king's acquaintance."
24	M23 + D21	Variant (M25). Ideogram for *rsw* "south."
26	flowering sedge	Variant (M27, with D36). Phonogram *šmᶜ*. Ideogram for *šmᶜw* "Nile Valley" (Upper Egypt).
28	M26 + V20	Ideogram in title *wr mḏw-šmᶜw* "chief of the tens of the Nile Valley."
29	pod	Phonogram *nḏm* "pleasant."
30	root	Determinative in *bnr* "sweet," also ideogram for same.
31	rhizome	Variant (M32). Determinative in *rd* "grow," also in *rwḏ* "firm."
33	grain	Variants , . Ideogram for *jtj* "grain." Determinative GRAIN.
34	sheaf of emmer	Ideogram for *btj* (originally *bdt*) "emmer," also determinative for same.
35	heap of grain	Determinative HEAP.
36	bundle of flax	Variant (M37). Phonogram *ḏr*. Determinative in *dm3* "bundle."
38	bundle of flax	Determinative in *mḥᶜw* "flax" and *dm3* "bundle."
Y10	bundle of stems	Determinative in *šᶜt* "murderousness" (from *šᶜ* "cut").
39	basket of fruit or grain	Determinative VEGETABLES.
40	bundle of reeds	Phonogram *jz*.
41	piece of wood	Determinative WOOD.
42	rosette	Phonogram *wn*. In hieratic indistinguishable from Z11.
43	grapes on trellis	Variant (M43a). Determinative VINE, WINE, GARDENER, FRUIT. Ideogram for *jrp* "wine" and *k3ny* "gardener."
43b	wine or olive press	Determinative in *šzmw* "Shesmu" (god of the wine or olive press), also ideogram for same.
44	thorn	Determinative in *spd* "sharp," also ideogram for same. Determinative in *srt* "thorn." Determinative in *t-ḥḏ* "white-bread" (as bread of this form).

N. Sky, Earth, Water

1	sky	Determinative SKY, ABOVE. Ideogram for *ḥrj* "upper" (§ 8.6.7). Determinative in *rwt* "gate" and *h3yt* "ceiling, portal," also ideogram for latter.
2	sky with scepter	Variants (N3, with oar), (N46b, with star). Determinative NIGHT. Ideogram for *grḥ* "night."
4	sky with rain	Determinative DEW, RAIN. Ideogram for *j3dt* "dew."
5	sun	Determinative SUN, DAY, TIME. Ideogram for *rᶜ* "sun, Re," *hrw* "day," and *sw* "day" (in dates: § 9.8).
5a	sun with two strokes	Variant (N5 + N23). Determinative TIME.
6	sun with uraeus	Determinative in *rᶜ* "Re," also ideogram for same.
7	N5 + T28	Ideogram for *ẖrt-hrw* "daytime, course of the day."
8	sun with rays	Determinative SUNLIGHT. Phonogram *wbn* (from *wbn* "rise"). Ideogram for *ḥnmmt* "human beings."
9	moon	Variant (N10). Phonogram *psḏ* in *psḏt* "Ennead" and *psḏntjw* "new-moon festival." Variant of X6 in *p3t* "origin."
11	crescent moon	Variant as determinative. Determinative in *jᶜḥ* "moon," also ideogram for same. Ideogram for "month"(*3bd*) in dates (§ 9.8). Occasional variant of F42. Determinative in *wᶜḥ* "carob bean," also ideogram for same. Determinative in *šzp* "palm" (measure: § 9.7.1), also ideogram for same.
12	crescent moon	Variant as determinative. Determinative in *jᶜḥ* "moon," also ideogram for same. Occasional variant of F42.
64	N11 + N14	Ideogram for *3bd* "month."
13	half N11 + N14	Ideogram for *mḏdjwnt* "15th-day festival."
14	star	Determinative STAR, TIME. Phonogram *sb3* (from *sb3* "star"). Phonogram *dw3* (from *dw3* "morning"). Ideogram for *wnwt* "hour."
15	star in circle	Ideogram for *dw3t* "Duat" (Essay 2).
16	strip of land with sand	Variants (N16d), (N17). Ideogram for *t3* "land, earth, world." Phonogram *t3*. Determinative in *ḏt* "estate" and *ḏt* "eternity."
18	strip of sand	Ideogram for *jw* "island." Determinative DESERT, FOREIGN LAND. Ideogram for *st3t* "aroura" (§ 9.7.2).
19	two strips of sand	Ideogram for *3ḫt* "Akhet" (Essay 2) in *ḥrw-3ḫtj* "Harakhti" (Essay 12).
20	tongue of land	Variant (N22). Phonogram *wḏb/wdb* in *wḏb* "turn." Determinative LAND, especially in *wḏb* "shore." Determinative in *ḥ3b-sd* "Sed Festival."
21	tongue of land	Determinative LAND. Ideogram for *jdb* "bank," when doubled *jdbwj* "Two Banks" (a term for Egypt).
23	irrigation canal	Variants , . Determinative LAND, especially IRRIGATED LAND. Also used in variant of N5a. Ideogram for *gbb/gbw* "Geb."
24	irrigation canal system	Determinative of *sp3t* "nome," also ideogram for same. Determinative in names of nomes and divisions of Egypt, also in *ḥzp* "garden." Ideogram for *ḏ3tt* "estate, farm."
25	mountain range	Ideogram for *ḫ3st* "desert cliffs, foreign land." Determinative DESERT, FOREIGN LAND.
76	N25 on standard	Ideogram for *ḥ3* "Ha" (desert god).

26	mountain	Phonogram *ḏw*. Ideogram for *ḏw* "mountain."
27	sun rising above mountain	Ideogram for *3ḫt* "Akhet" (Essay 2).
28	sun's rays above hill	Phonogram *ḫꜥ*, especially in *ḫꜥj* "appear."
29	sandy slope	Phonogram *q*.
30	hill with shrubs	Determinative in *j3t* "mound," also ideogram for same.
31	path with shrubs	Variant (N31e). Determinative for *w3t* "road," also ideogram for same. Determinative ROAD, DISTANCE, POSITION. Ideogram for *w3j* "tend, start" (from *w3t* "road"). Phonogram *ḥr* in *jn-ḥrt* "Onuris" (a god), *ḥrw* "Horus," and *ḥrw r* "except" (from *ḥrj* "go far away").
32	lump of clay	Variant of Aa2 and F52.
33	grain of sand	Variants ○○○ (N33a), ○̥, ○̥○, ○̥○̥. Determinative SAND, MINERAL, PELLET. When single, occasional substitute for signs with bad connotations, such as A14 and Z6. When triple, occasional substitute for plural strokes. Determinative in words with *qd* (from *qdj* "go around").
34	ingot of metal	Variant (N34a). Ideogram for *ḥmt* "copper, bronze." Determinative COPPER, BRONZE.
35	ripple of water	Phonogram *n*.
35a	three ripples of water	Ideogram for *mw* "water." Determinative WATER. Phonogram *mw*.
36	canal	Determinative BODY OF WATER. Phonogram *mr* and *mj*. Ideogram for *mr* "canal."
37	basin	Variants (N37a), (N38), (N39), etc. Phonogram *š*. Ideogram for *šj* "basin, pool, lake." Determinative of *st3t* "aroura" (§ 9.7.2), also ideogram for same. Variant of X4 as determinative of *zn* "open" and *znj* "pass." Variant of O36.
40	N37 + D54	Phonogram *šm* in forms of *šmj* "go."
41	well with water	Variants (N42), (D280a). Determinative WELL. Determinative in *bj3* "cauldron, copper" and words with root *bj3*. Determinative in *pḥww* "outer limits," also ideogram for same (tripled). Often for D280a.

O. Structures and Parts of Structures

1	schematic house plan	Proportions vary. Ideogram for *pr* "house." Phonogram *pr*. Determinative BUILDING, PLACE.
2	O1 + T3	Ideogram for *pr-ḥḏ* "treasury."
3	O1 + P8 + X3 + W22	Ideogram for *prt-ḫrw* "invocation offering."
4	reed shelter	Phonogram *h*. Ideogram for *h*(?) "courtyard."
5	winding wall	Phonogram *nm*. Determinative in *mrrt* "street." Phonogram *mr* in *mr-wr* "Mnevis" (sacred bull of Heliopolis).
6	plan of enclosure	Variant (O7). Ideogram for *ḥwt* "enclosure."
8	O7 + O29	Ideogram for *ḥwt-ꜥ3t* "Great Enclosure" (temple of Heliopolis).
9	V30 + O6	Ideogram for *nbt-ḥwt* "Nephthys."
10	O6 + G5	Ideogram for *ḥwt-ḥrw* "Hathor."
11	palace plan with battlements	Variant (O12). Ideogram for *ꜥḥ* "palace."
104	O11 + T3	Ideogram for *ꜥḥ-ḥḏ* "White Palace" or "Palace of the Mace" (a shrine).

13	enclosure with battlements	Variant (O14). Determinative in *sbḫ* "wall in" and related words.
15	enclosure + W10 + X1	Variant (O15a). Ideogram for *wsḫt* "broad hall."
16	cornice with cobras	Variant (O17). Determinative for *t3yt* "curtain," also ideogram for same and *t3jtj* "he of the curtain" (title of the vizier). O17 variant of S22 in *t3-wr* "port."
18	shrine in profile	Determinative in *k3r* "shrine," also ideogram for same.
19	shrine with poles	Determinative in *pr-wr* "Great House" (original shrine of Upper Egypt at Hierakonpolis), also in *jtrt šmꜥt* "Nile Valley Shrine" (same).
20	shrine	Determinative SHRINE.
21	shrine façade	Determinative in *zḥ* "booth," also ideogram for same.
22	booth with pole	Determinative in *zḥ* "counsel, advice" and *zḥ* "tent, booth," also ideogram for latter.
23	double platform	Determinative in *ḥ3b-sd* "Sed Festival," also ideogram for same.
24	pyramid and enclosure wall	Determinative PYRAMID.
25	obelisk	Determinative in *tḫn* "obelisk," also ideogram for same.
26	stela	Determinative STELA, also ideogram for *wḏ* "stela."
27	columned hall	Determinative HALL. Determinative of *ḫ3wj* "dusk" (from *ḫ3* "office"), also ideogram for same.
28	column with tenon	Phonogram *j(w)n*. Ideogram for *jwn* "column."
29	wood column	Variant . Phonogram *ꜥ3*.
30	support	Determinative SUPPORT, also ideogram for *zḫnt* "support."
31	door leaf	Variant (O31a). Variant in *ꜥ3wj* "door" (two door leaves). Determinative OPEN. Determinative in *ꜥ3* "door," also ideogram for same.
32	gateway	Determinative DOORWAY, also ideogram for *sb3* "doorway."
33	palace façade	Determinative in *srḫ* "serekh" (Essay 6).
34	doorbolt	Phonogram *z*. Ideogram for *z* "doorbolt." Variant of R22.
35	O34 + D54	Phonogram *z* in *zj* "go away, perish," *zy* "which?" (§ 5.11), *zbj* "send away, go away," and *mz* "bring."
36	wall	Determinative WALL. Ideogram for *jnb* "wall."
37	wall falling	Determinative TOPPLE, TILT.
38	corner	Determinative CORNER. Ideogram for *qnbt* "council." Determinative or ideogram for *tm* in the administrative title *ḥrj (n) tm* "chief of the *tm*."
39	stone block or brick	Determinative STONE, BRICK.
40	stairs	Determinative STAIRWAY, TERRACE. Ideogram for *rwd* "stairs" and *ḫtjw* "terrace."
41	double stairs	Determinative STAIRWAY, ASCEND.
43	fence	Variant (O42). Phonogram *šzp*, *sšp*.
44	emblem of Min	Variant (O44a) Determinative in *j3t* "office," also ideogram for same.

45	domed structure	Variant (O46). Determinative in *jpꜣt* "private quarters," also ideogram for same.
47	enclosed mound	Variant (O48). Ideogram for *nḫn* "Hierakonpolis" and *mḫnt* "jasper."
49	area with intersection	Variant (O49a). Ideogram for *nwt* "town." Determinative TOWN, SETTLEMENT.
50	threshing floor with grain	Phonogram *zp* in *zp* "occasion, event," *zpj* "be left over," and related words. Determinative in *zpt* "threshing floor."
51	pile of grain	Variant (O51b). Determinative in *šnwt* "granary," also ideogram for same.

P. Ships and Parts of Ships

1	boat on water	Variants (P1c), (P26). Determinative BOAT. Ideogram for "boat" (various readings: *dpt, ḥꜥw, jmw, qꜣqꜣw*).
1a	boat capsized	Determinative in *pnꜥ* "capsize."
2	boat under sail	Determinative in *ḫntj* "sail upstream."
3	sacred boat	Variants (P30), (P34). Determinative GOD'S BOAT. Ideogram for *wjꜣ* "sacred bark."
3a	P3 + M23	Ideogram for *wjꜣ-nswt* "king's bark."
4	boat with net	Variant (P4a). Phonogram *wḥꜥ*.
5	mast with sail	Determinative WIND, AIR. Ideogram for *ṯꜣw* "air" and *nfw* "sailor."
5f	sail	Determinative in *ḥtꜣw* "sail."
6	mast	Variant (P7). Phonogram *ꜥḥꜥ*.
8	oar	Variant in *mꜣꜥ ḫrw* "justified" (Essay 8). Phonogram *ḫrw*. Determinative OAR. Ideogram for *ḥjpt* "oar."
9	P8 + I9	Ideogram for *ḫr.fj* "says, said" (§ 22.18).
10	steering oar with rope	Determinative in *ḥmw* "rudder" and *ḥmy* "steerer."
11	mooring stake	Determinative in *mjnj* "moor, die" and related words. In hieratic often identical with T14.

Q. Domestic and Funerary Furniture

1	seat	Ideogram for *st* "seat, place." Phonogram *st*. Phonogram *ws* in *wsjr* "Osiris." Phonogram *ḥtm*.
2	portable seat	Phonogram *ws* in *wsjr* "Osiris." Ideogram for *st* "seat."
3	stool	Phonogram *p*.
4	headrest	Determinative in *wrsw* "headrest."
5	chest	Determinative CHEST, BOX.
6	coffin	Determinative in *qrs* "bury" and related words, also ideogram for same.
7	brazier with flame	Determinative FIRE. Ideogram for *srf* "temperature." When doubled, ideogram for *nsrsr* "flame" in *jw-nsrsr* "Island of Flame" (locality of creation and in the Duat).

R. Temple Furniture and Sacred Emblems

1	table with offerings	Variants (R2), (R36a). Determinative in *ḫ3wt/ḫ3yt* "altar," also ideogram for same.
3	low table with offerings	Determinative in *wdḥw* "offering table," also ideogram for same.
4	bread loaf on mat	Phonogram *ḥtp*. Ideogram for *ḥtp* "offering slab."
5	censer	Variant (R6). Phonogram *k(3)p*. Determinative in *k3p* "fumigate," also ideogram for same.
7	bowl with smoke	Determinative of *snṯr* "incense," also ideogram for same. Variant of W10a/Aa4.
8	cloth wound on pole	Ideogram for *nṯr* "god." Phonogram *nṯr*. Determinative GOD.
9	R8 + V33	Determinative for *bd* "incense," also ideogram for same.
10	R8 + T28 + N29	Variants (R10e), (R50). Ideogram for *ẖrj-nṯr/ẖrt-nṯr* "necropolis."
11	reed column	Phonogram *ḏd*, also doubled with the same value. Ideogram for *ḏd* "*djed*-column/amulet."
12	carrying standard	Determinative in *j3t* "standard." Usually part of other signs.
14	feather on standard	Variant (R13). Ideogram for *jmnt* "West" and *wnmj* "right."
15	spear emblem	Variant (R15b). Ideogram for *j3b* "East, left." Variant of U23.
16	scepter with feathers	Determinative in *wḫ* (emblem of Qus), also ideogram for same.
17	wig with feathers on pole	Variants (R17b), (R18). Determinative in *t3-wr* "This" (nome of Abydos), also ideogram for same.
19	S40 with feather	Ideogram for *w3st* "Thebes" (town and nome).
20	Seshat emblem	Variant (R21). Ideogram for *sš3t* "Seshat" (a goddess).
22	Min emblem	Variants (R22a), (R23), (R23a). Ideogram for *mnw* "Min" (a god). Without standard, phonogram *ḫm* in *ḫm* "shrine" and *ḫm* "Letopolis" (town in the Delta).
24	Neith emblem	Variants , (R24a), (R24b), (R24c), (R25), (R25a), (R25b). Determinative in *njt* (originally *nrt*) "Neith," also ideogram for same.
61	emblematic cobra	Determinative in *ṯnjw* "desert border," also ideogram for same.

S. Regalia and Clothing

1	White Crown	Variant (S2). Determinative WHITE CROWN. Ideogram for *ḥḏt* "White Crown."
47a	S1 on standard with flail	Determinative in *b3b3y* "Babay" (a god), also ideogram for same.
3	Red Crown	Variant (S4). Determinative RED CROWN. Phonogram *n*. S3 variant of L2 as emblem of King of Lower Egypt.
5	Double Crown	Variant (S6). Determinative in *sḫmtj* "Double Crown," also ideogram for same. Determinative CROWN.

7	Blue Crown	Determinative in *ḫprš* "Blue (War) Crown," also ideogram for same.
8	Atef Crown	Determinative in *3tf* "Atef Crown," also ideogram for same.
9	double plumes	Determinative in *šwtj* "double plumes," also ideogram for same.
10	headband	Phonogram *mḏḥ*. Determinative in *w3ḥw* "wreath" and *mḏḥ* "headband," also ideogram for latter.
11	broad collar	Determinative in *wsḫ* "broad collar," also ideogram for same. Phonogram *wsḫ*.
12	bead collar	Variant (S12a). Ideogram for *nbw* "gold" and related words. Determinative PRECIOUS METAL.
13	S12 + D58	Phonogram *nb*.
14	S12 + T3	Ideogram for *ḥḏ* "silver."
14a	S12 + S40	Ideogram for *ḏᶜm* "electrum."
15	faience pectoral	Variants (S16), (S17), (S17a). Determinative in *ṯḥn* "sparkle" and related words, also ideogram for same. Ideogram for *šzmt* "malachite" and related words.
18	bead necklace	Determinative in *mnjt* "bead necklace, counterweight," also ideogram for same.
19	seal on necklace	Ideogram for *ḫtm* "seal" and related words.
20	seal on necklace	Determinative SEAL. Ideogram for *ḫtm* "seal" and *š(n)ᶜtj* "ring" (§ 9.7.3). Variant of E31.
21	ring	Determinative RING.
22	shoulder knot	Phonogram *s(3)ṯ*. Determinative in *t3-wr* "port (of ship)," also ideogram for same.
23	knotted cloth	Phonogram *dmḏ/dmd*. Different from Aa6.
24	knotted belt	Phonogram *ṯ3z*. Ideogram for *ṯ3zt* "knot, vertebra."
25	garment with ties	Ideogram for *jᶜ3w* "guide, dragoman, interpreter."
26	kilt	Determinative in *šndyt* (originally *šnḏwt*) "kilt," also ideogram for same.
130a	strip of cloth	Determinative in *d3jw* "cloak," also ideogram for same.
27	cloth with two fringes	Determinative in *mnḫt* "cloth," also ideogram for same.
116	cloth with four fringes	Determinative in *jfdj* "four-ply linen," also ideogram for same.
118	cloth with six fringes	Determinative in *sjsj* "six-weave linen," also ideogram for same.
28	cloth with fringe + S29	Variant (V48). Determinative CLOTH.
29	folded cloth	Phonogram *s*. Abbreviation for *snb* in *ᶜnḫ.(w)-(w)ḏ3.(w)-s(nb.w)* (§ 17.20.2).
30	S29 + I9	Phonogram in *sf* "yesterday."
31	S29 + U2	Phonogram *sm3*.
32	cloth with fringe	Phonogram *sj3*. Ideogram for *sj3t* "fringed cloth."
33	sandal	Determinative SANDAL. Ideogram for *ṯbt* "sandal," *ṯbw* "sandalmaker."
34	sandal strap	Phonogram *ᶜnḫ*. Ideogram for *ᶜnḫ* "sandal strap" and "mirror."

35	sunshade or fan	Variant (S36). Ideogram for *šwt* "shadow, shade." Determinative in *sryt* "fan," also ideogram for same. Doubled (S36), ideogram for *ḫjpwj* "Hepwi" (a god).
37	fan	Determinative in *ḫw* "fan," also ideogram for same.
38	crook	Phonogram *ḥq3*. Determinative in *ḥq3t* "scepter," also ideogram for same. Variant of S39.
39	shepherd's crook	Phonogram *ꜥwt* in *ꜥwt* "flock" (from *ꜥwt* "crook").
40	animal-headed staff	Phonogram *w3s*. Ideogram for *w3s* "staff" of this shape. Ideogram for *j3tt* "milk, cream" and "Iatet" (milk goddess). Doubled, phonogram *w3b* in *w3bwj* "Wabwi" (name of a nome) and *w3bwt* "Wabut" (a town). Variant of S41 and R19.
40a	S40 on standard	Variant of S40 as ideogram for *j3tt* "milk, cream" and "Iatet."
41	animal-headed staff	Phonogram *ḏꜥm* in *ḏꜥmw* "fine gold" (from *ḏꜥm* "staff" of this shape).
42	scepter	Phonogram *sḫm*. Determinative in *ḫrp* "manage," also ideogram for same, especially in titles. Phonogram *ꜥb3*. Ideogram for *ꜥb3* "scepter" and "stela." Ideogram for *sḫm* "sistrum."
42a	lotus-bud scepter	Determinative in *nḥbt* "lotus-bud scepter," also ideogram for same.
43	staff	Phonogram *md*. Ideogram for *mdw* "staff."
44	staff with flail	Determinative for *3ms* "staff," also ideogram for same.
45	flail	Determinative in *nḫ3ḫ3w* "flail," also ideogram for same.

T. Warfare, Hunting, and Slaughter

1	mace with flat head	Phonogram *mn*.
2	T3 tilted	Determinative SMITE.
3	mace with round head	Variant (T4). Phonogram *ḥḏ*. Ideogram for *ḥḏ* "mace" of this shape.
5	T3 + I10	Phonogram *ḥḏ*.
6	T3 + I10 + I10	Phonogram *ḥḏḏ*.
7	axe	Determinative AXE and related words.
7a	axe	Determinative in *3qḥw* "axe" of this shape.
8	dagger	Phonogram *tp*. Determinative in *mṯpnt* "dagger" of this shape.
8a	dagger	Determinative in *b3gsw* "dagger" of this shape.
9	bow	Variants (T9a), (T10). Phonogram *pḏ/pd*. Determinative in *pḏt* "bow," also ideogram for same and words of the same root.
11	arrow	Phonogram *zwn*. Determinative ARROW.
12	bowstring	Phonogram *rwḏ/rwd*. Determinative in words with *3r* (*3j*, *3jr*, from *3r* "restrain"). Ideogram for *d3r* "subdue." Determinative for *rwḏ* "bowstring," also ideogram for same.
13	pieces of wood tied	Phonogram *rs* in *rs* "wake" and related words.

14	throw-stick	Variant (T15). Determinative with G41 in words with *ṯn/tn*. Determinative FOREIGN. Determinative in *qm3* "throw" and *qm3j* "create," also ideogram for same. Ideogram for *ꜥ3m* "Asiatic," *ṯḥnw* "Libya." Ideogram for *ḥq3t* "heqat" (§ 9.7.4). Variant of D50 as determinative ACCURATE; of M3 as determinative in *ḏꜥr* "seek"; of P11 as determinative in *mjnj* "moor, die"; of S39 as phonogram in *ꜥwt* "flock"; and of T13 and Aa6.
16	scimitar	Determinative in *ḫpš* "scimitar."
17	chariot	Determinative in *wrrt* "chariot," also ideogram for same.
18	crook with package attached	Phonogram *šms*.
19	bone harpoon head	Variant (T20). Phonogram *qs*. Determinative BONE, TUBE. Determinative in *qrs* "bury," *twr* "pure" (from *twr* "tube"). Ideogram for *gnwt* "annals" and *gnwtj* "sculptor" (often double in the latter).
21	harpoon	Variant. Phonogram *wꜥ* in *wꜥ* "one" and related words.
22	arrowhead	Variant (T23). Phonogram *sn*.
24	fishing net	Phonogram *ꜥḥ/jḥ*. Determinative NET.
25	reed float	Phonogram *ḏb3/db3*.
27	bird trap	Variant (T26). Determinative in *sẖt* "trap," also ideogram for same.
28	butcher's block	Phonogram *ẖr*.
29	T30 + T28	Determinative in *nmt* "slaughtering place," also ideogram for same.
30	knife or saw	Determinative KNIFE, SHARP. Ideogram for *dmt* "knife."
31	knife sharpener	Variants (T32), (T33). Phonogram *sšm* in *sšm* "guide" and related words.
35	butcher knife	Variant (T34). Phonogram *nm*. Determinative in *nm* "butcher knife."

U. Agriculture, Crafts, and Professions

1	sickle	Variant (U2). Phonogram *m3*. Determinative REAP, CROOKED.
3	U1 + D4	Phonogram *m3* in *m3* "see."
4	U1 + Aa11	Variant (U5). Phonogram *m3ꜥ* in *m3ꜥ* "true, correct," and related words.
6	hoe	Variants (U7), (U6a), (U7a). Phonogram *mr*. Determinative HACK. Variant of U8.
8	hoe	Phonogram *ḥn* (from *ḥnn* "hoe").
9	grain-measure with grain	Determinative GRAIN. Ideogram for *ḥq3t* "heqat" and *jpt* "oipe" (§ 9.7.4).
10	M33 + U9	Ideogram for *jtj* "barley, grain." Variant of U9 as determinative.
11	S38 + U9	Variant (U12). Ideogram for *ḥq3t* "heqat" (§ 9.7.4).
109	pitchfork	Variant (U109a). Determinative (U109) in *sḏb* "obstacle," also ideogram for same. Determinative in *ꜥbj* "collect" and *ꜥbt* "pitchfork."
13	plow	Variant (U14). Phonogram *šnꜥ*. Phonogram *hb*. Determinative PLOW. Ideogram for *prt* "seed."
15	sled	Phonogram *tm*.

16	loaded sled with jackal's head	Determinative in *bjꜣ* "wonder" and related words, also ideogram for same. Determinative SLED.
17	pick and basin	Variant (U18). Phonogram *grg*.
19	adze	Variant (U20). Phonogram *nw*.
21	adze and block of wood	Phonogram *stp/sṯp*.
22	chisel	Determinative in *mnḫ* "functional." Determinative CARVE.
23	chisel	Phonograms *ꜣb* and *mr*.
25	drill for stone	Variant (U24). Ideogram for *ḥmwt* "craft" and related words.
26	drill for beads	Variant (U27). Ideogram for *wbꜣ* and related words. Occasional variant of U24–25.
29	fire-drill	Variant (U28). Phonogram *ḏꜣ*. Abbreviation for *wḏꜣ* in *ꜥnḫ.(w)-(w)ḏꜣ.(w)-s(nb.w)* (§ 17.20.2).
30	kiln	Phonogram *tꜣ*.
31	baker's rake	Determinative in *ḫnr* "restrain" and related words, also ideogram for same. Determinative in *rtḥ/jtḥ* "restrain." Determinative in *rtḥtj* "baker," also ideogram for same. Variant of D19–20.
32	pestle and mortar	Determinative in *smn* "set, fix" (from *smn* "flatten dough"). Determinative POUND, HEAVY. Determinative in *ḥzmn* "natron; bronze," also ideogram for same.
33	pestle	Phonogram *tj/t*.
34	spindle	Variant (U35). Phonogram *ḫsf*. Determinative in *ḫsf* "spin."
36	launderer's club	Phonogram *ḥm*.
37	razor	Determinative in *ẖꜥq* "shave."
38	scale	Determinative in *mḫꜣt* "scale," also ideogram for same.
39	upright of scale	Variants (U40), (U40a). Determinative in *wṯz* "hold up, carry, wear" and *ṯzj* "pick up."
41	plumb bob	Determinative in *tḫ* "plumb bob."

V. Rope, Baskets, and Cloth

1	coil of rope	Variant (V1a). Determinative ROPE, TIE, COIL. Ideogram for *št* "100" (§ 9.1). Phonogram *šn* in *šnt* "dispute." Different from Z7.
2	V1 + O34	Determinative in *sṯꜣ* "pull" and *ꜣš* "hasten." Ideogram for *sṯꜣt* "aroura" (§ 9.7.2).
3	three V1 + O34	Ideogram *sṯꜣw* in *r-sṯꜣw* "necropolis" (of Giza).
4	lasso	Phonogram *wꜣ*.
5	looped rope	Determinative in *sntj* "lay out," also ideogram for same.
6	cord with ends up	Phonogram *šs* and *šsr*. Ideogram for *šsrw/šs* "linen." Variant of V33.
7	cord with ends down	Variant (V8). Phonogram *šn*.
9	round cartouche	Determinative in *šnw* "circuit" (of the sun), also ideogram for same. Determinative in *šnw* "cartouche."

10	cartouche	Surrounding names of kings, queens, and some gods. Determinative in *šnw* "cartouche" and *rn* "name."
11	end of cartouche	Determinative in *dnj* "dam" and *pẖ3* "split." Ideogram for *pẖ3*, a kind of grain. Ideogram for *djwt/dyt* "shriek."
12	string	Determinative in *fẖ* "loosen," *ʿrq* "bind," *šfdw* "papyrus scroll," and other words associated with STRING. Determinative in *ʿrq* "swear" and *ʿrqy* "last day of the month" (§ 9.8) (from *ʿrq* "bind"), also ideogram for latter. Ideogram for *fẖ* "loosen." Determinative in *fnḫw* "Phoenicians."
13	hobble	Variant (V14). Phonogram *ṯ/t*.
15	V13 + D54	Phonogram *jṯ* in forms of *jṯj* "take possession."
16	hobble for cattle	Variants (V16a), (V17, rolled-up tent), (V18). Phonogram *z3* in *z3* "protection" and related words.
19	hobble for cattle	Determinative SHRINE in *k3r* "shrine," *qnj* "palanquin" (also *qnj* "sheaf"), *šṯyt* "Sokar shrine." Determinative in *tm3* "mat" and *ṯm3* "cadaster," also ideogram for latter. Determinative in *ẖ3r* "sack" (§ 9.7.4), also ideogram for latter. Determinative in *mḏt* "stable, stall," also ideogram for latter.
20	V19 without horizontal	Ideogram for *mḏw* "10" (§ 9.7.1).
21	V20 + I10	Phonogram *mḏ*.
23	whip	Variant (V22). Phonogram *mḥ*.
24	cord wound on stick	Variant (V25). Phonogram *wḏ/wd*.
26	spool with thread	Variant (V25, without thread). Phonogram *ʿḏ/ʿd*. Determinative in *ʿḏ* "reel," also ideogram for same.
28	wick	Phonogram *ḥ*.
29	swab	Phonograms *w3ḥ* and *sk*. Determinative in *ẖsr* "ward off." Variant of M1 in *mʿr* "fortunate."
30	basket	Phonogram *nb*.
31	basket with handle	Variant (V31a) in hieroglyphic transcriptions of hieratic texts, where the handle always faces the front. Phonogram *k*.
32	wicker satchel	Variant (V96). Determinative in *g3wt* "bundle," hence also in *g3w* "absence, lack," hence also in *ḏ3rw* "need." Determinative in *msnw* "harpooner." Phonogram *msn* in *msn* "Mesen" (a Delta town).
33	bag	Variants (V34), (V35). Determinative in *ʿrf* "pack, envelop," *stj* "perfume," and *šs(r)* "fine linen." Phonogram *g* in a few words. Ideogram for *sšrw* "grain." Determinative LINEN.
36	receptacle of cloth	Phonogram *ḥn*.
37	bandage	Determinative in *jdr* "herd," also ideogram for same. Determinative in *jdr* "bandage."
38	bandage	Determinative in *wt* "wrapping."
39	tie	Ideogram for *tjt* "Isis-knot" (amulet).

W. Stone and Ceramic Vessels

1	oil-jar	Determinative OIL. Ideogram for *mrḥt* "oil."

2	W1 without ties	Phonogram *b3s* in *b3stt* "Bastet" (goddess). Determinative in *b3s* "oil jar." Variant of W1.
3	alabaster basin	Variant (W4). Determinative FEAST. Ideogram for *ḥ3b* "feast."
5	T28 + W3	Ideogram for *ẖrj-ḥ3bt* "lector priest."
6	metal vessel	Determinative in *wḥ3t* "cauldron."
7	granite bowl	Variant (W8). Determinative in *m3ṯ* "granite" and *m3ṯ* "proclaim." Determinative in *3bw* "Elephantine," also ideogram for same. Determinative in *3bt* "family."
9	stone jug	Phonogram *ẖnm*.
10	cup	Determinative in words with *ꜥb*. Determinative in *wsḫ* "wide" and related words, also ideogram for same. Phonogram *ḥnw* in *ḥnwt* "mistress" (from *ḥnt* "cup"). Determinative CUP. Variant of N41 in words with *bj3*.
10a	pot	Variant (Aa4). Phonogram *b3* in conjunction with E10 or G29.
12	jar stand	Variant (W11). Phonogram *g* Determinative in *nst* "seat," also ideogram for same. Variant of W13 and O45.
13	pot	Determinative in *dšrt* "red-ware," also ideogram for same.
14	water jar	Phonogram *ḥz/ḥs*. Determinative in *ḥzt* "water jar" and *snbt* "jar," also ideogram for former.
15	water jar with water	Variant (W16). Determinative in *qbb* "cool" and *qbḥ* "cool, water," also ideogram for latter.
18	water jars in a rack	Variants (W17), (W18a), (W17a). Phonogram *ẖnt*. Ideogram for *ẖntw* "jar-rack."
19	milk jug with handle	Phonogram *mj* (originally *mr*). Determinative in *mhr* "milk jug."
20	milk jug with cover	Variant (W59). Determinative in *jrṯt* "milk."
21	wine jars	Determinative in *jrp* "wine."
22	beer jug	Variant (W23). Determinative POT. Ideogram for *ḥnqt* "beer" in offering formulas. Ideogram for *wdpw* "waiter."
24	pot	Phonogram *nw*. Phonogram *jn* in *jnk* (1s pronoun). Variant of N33 in words with *qd*. Determinative in *ḏ3ḏ3t* "council" and *nẖbt* "Nekhbet" (goddess), for unknown reasons. Often combined with Aa27 as phonogram *nḏ*. Variant of W22–23 as determinative.
24a	W24 + N35a	Ideogram for *m-ẖnw* "inside" = *m(w)-ẖ(r)-nw*.
25	W24 with legs	Phonogram *jn* in forms of *jnj* "get, fetch, bring."
54	pot pouring water	Variant of D60 and A6.

X. Bread

1	flat loaf of bread	Phonogram *t*. Ideogram for *t* "bread." Often phonogram for *(j)t(j)* "father," alone or in conjunction with I9.
2	tall loaf of bread	Variant (X3). Determinative BREAD, FOOD. Ideogram for *t* "bread" in offering formulas. Ideogram for *ḏḥwtj* "Thoth." Variant of X1 as phonogram for *(j)t(j)* "father."

4 bread roll		Variants , (X4a), and (X5). Determinative BREAD, FOOD. Determinative in words with *zn* (from *znw* "food offerings"). Variant of W3.
6 round loaf of bread		Determinative in *p3t* "origin" and related words; and in *p3t* "loaf."
7 half-loaf of bread		Determinative BREAD. Doubled, ideogram for *wnm* "eat."
8 bread mold		Phonogram *dj/d* (originally *ḏj*) in forms of *rdj* "give," rarely in other words.

Y. Writing, Games, and Music

1 papyrus scroll	Variants , (Y2), (Y1a). Determinative WRITING, ABSTRACT CONCEPTS. Ideogram for *dmḏ* "total." Ideogram for *mḏ3t* "scroll" and *mḏ3t* "chisel."
3 scribe's kit	Variant (Y4). Ideogram for *zẖ3* "write" and related words. Determinative in *nᶜᶜ* "smooth" and *ṯms* "ruddy" and related words, also ideogram for same. Determinative in *mnhd* "scribe's kit."
5 game board and pieces	Phonogram *mn*.
6 game piece	Determinative in *jb3* "game piece," also ideogram for same. Determinative in *jb3* "dance," also ideogram for same.
7 harp	Determinative in *bjnt* "harp."
8 sistrum	Determinative in *zššt* "sistrum." Variant of S42.
10 bundle of stems	Determinative in *šᶜt* "murderousness" (from *šᶜ* "cut").

Z. Strokes and Figures

1 stroke	Used as ideogram of signs meant to be read as ideograms rather than phonograms (§ 3.3). Occasionally transferred to phonograms: for example, *ḥr* "face" but also preposition *ḥr* "upon." Determinative in *wᶜ* "one," also ideogram for same. Written one to nine times as ideogram for numerals 1 to 9 (§ 9.1). Substitute for A1.
5 diagonal stroke	Replacement for complex or dangerous signs.
4 two strokes	Variant (Z49). Phonogram *j* as ending. Determinative DUAL.
2 three strokes	Variants , (Z2c), (Z3a), , (Z3), and (Z2a-b), , (N33a). Determinative PLURAL. Also used with words that are plural in meaning, such as collectives, food, and minerals, and with singular words ending in *w* or *wt* ("false plurals"): § 4.6. Determinative in *ḫmt* "think" (from *ḫmtw* "three").
6 hieratic variant of A13–14	Determinative DIE, ENEMY. Sometimes similar to F20.
7 from hieratic variant of G43	Phonogram *w*. Different from V1.
8 oval	Determinative ROUND, OVAL.
9 crossed sticks	Variant (Z10). Determinative BREAK, CROSS, NUMBER. Phonograms *sw3/zw3* in *sw3j* "pass" and *zw3* "cut off," *sḏ* in *sḏt* "flame," *šbn* in *šbn* "mix" and related words, *ḫbs* in *ḫbsw* "cultivation," *wp* in *wp-st* "detail, breakdown," and *wr* in a few words.
11 crossed planks	Phonogram *jm*. Variant of M42.

Aa. Unclassified

1	placenta?	Variant ○. Phoneme *ḫ*.
2	pustule or gland	Determinative SWELLING, UNHEALTHY. Variant of a number of older signs: F52 and N32 as determinative EXCREMENT, CLAY; M41 as determinative in *ʿš* "cedar"; V32 as determinative in *g3w* "absence, lack" and *g3wt* "bundle"; V38 as determinative in *wt* "bandage" and related words, and *srwḫ* "treat," also ideogram for former; W6 as determinative in *wḥ3t* "cauldron," also phonogram *wḥ3* in same and in *wḥ3t* "oasis"; W7 as determinative in *m3ṯ* "granite" and *3bw* "Elephantine"; Z10 as determinative in *ḥsb* "count," also ideogram for same.
3	Aa2 with liquid emerging	Variant of Aa2 as determinative SWELLING, UNHEALTHY.
4	pot	Variant of W10a.
5	part of a ship	Variant (Aa5a). Phonogram *ḥ(j)p*. Ideogram for *ḥjpt* "oar."
6	unknown	Determinative in *ṯm3* "cadaster" and *tm3* "mat." Different from S23.
7	unknown	Variant . Determinative in *sqr* "smash."
8	irrigation channel?	Phonogram *qn*. Determinative of *sp3t* "estate, farm," also ideogram for same. Determinative of *ḏ3ḏ3t* "council." Variant of N24 as ideogram in *sp3t* "nome"; O34 as phonogram *z* in *zmjt* "desert"; V26 as phonogram *ʿḏ*.
9	unknown	Determinative in *ḫwd* "rich."
10	unknown	Determinative in *drf* "writing."
11	platform	Variants , , (Aa12). Phonogram *m3ʿ*. Determinative in *ṯnt3t* "platform."
13	unknown	Variants (Aa14), (Aa15, with horizontals parallel). Phonograms *jm* and *m*. Variant of Aa16.
16	front half of Aa13	Ideogram for *gs* "side, half," phonogram *gs*.
17	lid	Variant (Aa18). Phonogram *s3*. Ideogram for *s3* "back."
19	unknown	Determinative in *ḥr* "prepare" and *ḥrj* "terrified" and related words. Determinative in *ṯ3r* "secure."
20	bag for clothing	Phonogram *ʿpr*.
21	unknown	Variant (Aa22). Phonogram *wḏʿ*. Ideogram for *wḏʿw* "judged one" (term used in place of *stḫ/stš* "Seth").
24	warp between stakes	Variant (Aa23). Determinative in *mḏd* "puncture, press, adhere" and related words, also ideogram for same.
25	unknown	Ideogram in *zm3* "stolist" (priest's title).
26	unknown	Determinative in *sbj* "rebel."
27	spindle	Phonogram *nḏ*. Often used in conjunction with W24.
28	builder's level	Variant (Aa29). Phonogram *qd*.
31	frieze element	Variant (Aa30). Determinative in *ḫkr* "adorn" and related words, also ideogram for same.
32	bow	Variant . Phonogram *sṯj/stj* in *t3-stj* "Nubia" and *stj* "ocher."

Signs Arranged by Shape

Often the group to which a particular hieroglyph belongs is not immediately evident from the sign itself. To make it easier to find such signs in the preceding list, they are arranged below in four groups according to their shape. Signs that are readily identifiable, such as figures of people and animals, are not included. Signs that have no separate entry in the preceding list, such as variant forms, are identified by the number of the primary sign with which they are listed, plus an asterisk, rather than by their own number: N10, for example, is numbered N9*, because it will be found under N9 in the preceding list.

The size and proportions of the signs in the four groups below are those most often found in hieroglyphic inscriptions. Because hieroglyphs can vary in size and proportion depending on the surrounding signs, however, you may need to look in more than one group before you find a particular sign: , for example, appears under "Small Signs" (, its usual shape) rather than in "Horizontal Signs."

Small Signs

N33 D12 S21 Aa1* N5 N9 N9* O47* X6 Aa1 O50 O49 O49*
N15 N5a N5a* N7 N8 N27 V9 W24 S10 N6 S11 H8 Aa2
Aa3 Z8 O47 N20* N21 X1 X2* X2 M35 Y6 U22 O45* O45
N28 X7 N29 N26 V20 V19 Aa19 V7 V7* S20 V6 N41 N41*
D280a V37 D27 D27* V33 V33* N32 F52 V33* F51 F21 F43 F41
N34 U30 D279 N34* W13 W12* W12 T28 W10 W10a W10a* R7 M39
M36 M36* M38 U9 U10 F34 W6 W7 W22 W22* W20* W20 W21
U41 W9 M31 I6 D11 D14 K6 K6* L6 M41 Q3 O39 Aa17
Aa17* O38 Aa5* Aa5 O1 O4 O5 Aa16 N23 N23* Z9 V1 V1*
Z7 T12 V11 T24 F22 F37* F37* N33* N33* M33*

Horizontal Signs

N35	O34	R22	R22*	S24	W7*	O35	V2	V3	V26*	Aa8	Aa10	T11
T21	M3	U31	Y10	N24	N16*	N16	N16*	N18	S130a	X4*	X4	X4*
X4*	N19	N20	V26	R24	V10	D48	M8	Aa11*	Aa11	N37	N37*	N37*
N37*	Y1*	Y1	R4	Y5	N36	Aa9	S32	N40	U17	U17*	T27*	T27
O43	O43*	N31*	N31	O31	O31*	N1	N4	T9	T9*	Q5	Q6	Q2
O16	O16*	O37	D21	D154	D22	D23	D25	N11	N12	F42	D24	D24*
V30	V31	W3	V32*	W5	S12	S12*	S15*	S25	N30	P4	P4*	N25
Aa24	Aa24*	Aa32*	T9*	V32	V23	V23*	F30	F32	O29	P8*	T1	R5
R5*	F44	I4*	T30	T31	T31*	T31*	T29	T16	U37	F16	F17	F18
Aa7	D51	F23	F33	T2	T7	U19*	U19	U20	F37	F39	F40	D61*
D61	D61*	U2	U4*	U6*	U8	U13	U13*	U15	U16	Aa13	Aa13*	Aa13*
V13	V13*	V14	D13	Z6	D3	D15	D17	F46	F46*	M11	V12	V16*
V16	S23	Aa6	S23	S22	Q4	Z9*	R12	M33	N33*			

Vertical Signs

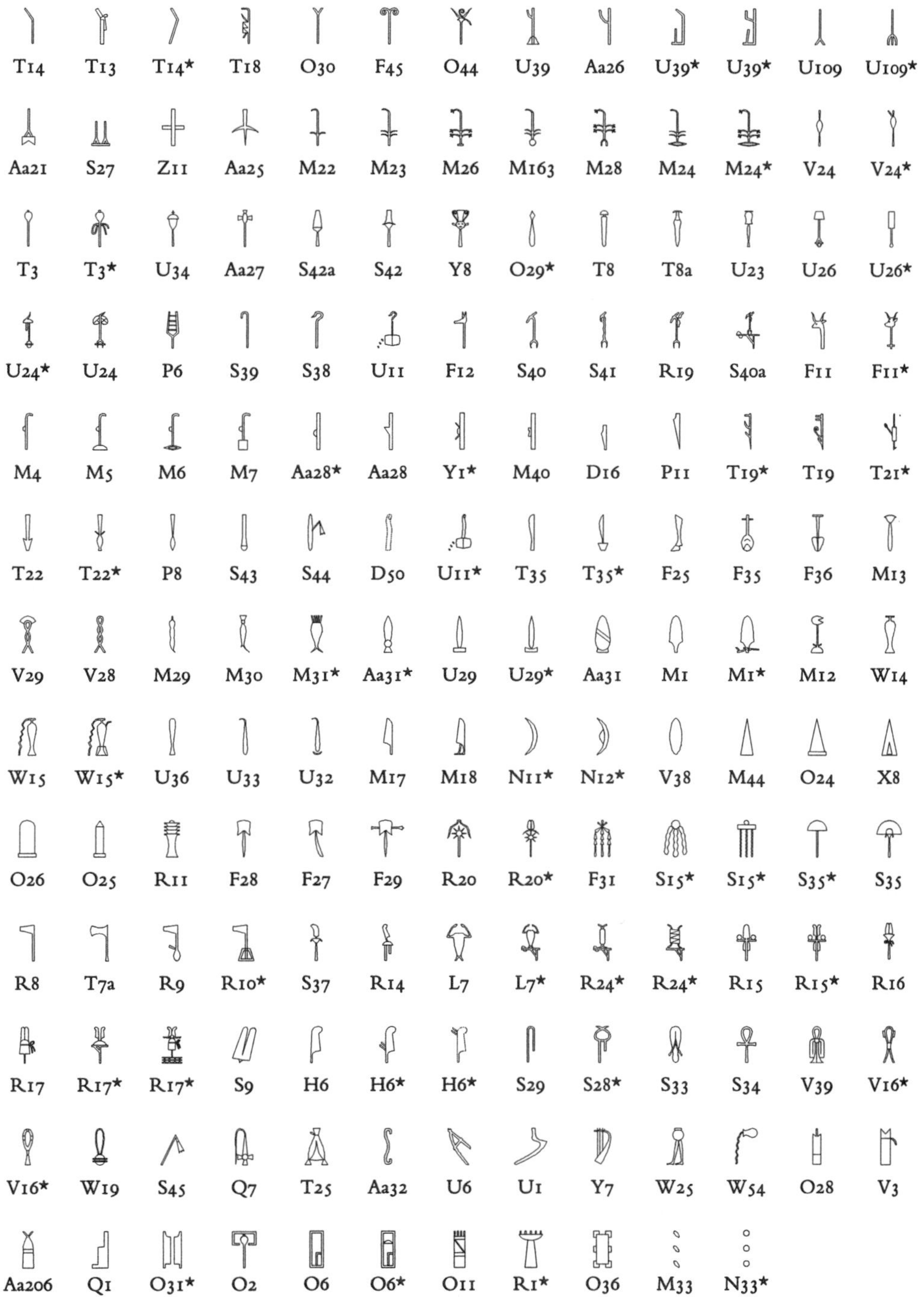
T14 T13 T14* T18 O30 F45 O44 U39 Aa26 U39* U39* U109 U109*
Aa21 S27 Z11 Aa25 M22 M23 M26 M163 M28 M24 M24* V24 V24*
T3 T3* U34 Aa27 S42a S42 Y8 O29* T8 T8a U23 U26 U26*
U24* U24 P6 S39 S38 U11 F12 S40 S41 R19 S40a F11 F11*
M4 M5 M6 M7 Aa28* Aa28 Y1* M40 D16 P11 T19* T19 T21*
T22 T22* P8 S43 S44 D50 U11* T35 T35* F25 F35 F36 M13
V29 V28 M29 M30 M31* Aa31* U29 U29* Aa31 M1 M1* M12 W14
W15 W15* U36 U33 U32 M17 M18 N11* N12* V38 M44 O24 X8
O26 O25 R11 F28 F27 F29 R20 R20* F31 S15* S15* S35* S35
R8 T7a R9 R10* S37 R14 L7 L7* R24* R24* R15 R15* R16
R17 R17* R17* S9 H6 H6* H6* S29 S28* S33 S34 V39 V16*
V16* W19 S45 Q7 T25 Aa32 U6 U1 Y7 W25 W54 O28 V3
Aa206 Q1 O31* O2 O6 O6* O11 R1* O36 M33 N33*

Large Signs and Combinations

F20 V4 V5 M42 F50 S31 S30 P9 U34* T5 T6 M13* V21

O8 O11* P6* Aa21* S13 S14 S14a O22 W3* U38 W18* W18* W18*

W18* S28 P5 N2 N2* N2* S15 M43 M43* M43b O33 S113 S116

S118 O3 O9 O10 O104 O13 O13* O15 O15* O51 O51* R10 R10*

N76 R22* R22* R24* R24* R24* R1 R1* R2 P3a F14 F14* U3

U4 P10 S18 Y3 M19 M20 M21 N35a W24a

Dictionary

This dictionary lists the words that appear in hieroglyphs in Exercises 1–25, in alphabetical order (see § 2.3). Words that share a common root are normally grouped together, with the root word first and related words in indented entries beneath; causatives, however, are listed alphabetically (under *s*) rather than under the root verb. Feminine endings are disregarded in alphabetizing: for example, *sḫt* "field" (root *sḫ*) is listed before *sḫ3j* "recall" rather than after *sḫt* "strike" (root *sḫt*). When a word appears in more than one exercise, usually only the most representative spelling is listed. Additions to a main or indented entry are given in transliteration only, unless their spelling differs significantly from that of the first entry.

3t (noun) "moment; moment of rage"

3wj (adjective-verb 3ae-inf.) "long; extend"; *3wj jb* "be happy" (literally, "long of heart")

  3w (noun) "length"; *r 3w* "complete, entire" (§ 6.7)

  3wt "offering-gifts"; *3wt ˁ* "gift" (literally, "extending of the arm"); *3wt-jb* "happiness"

3b (verb 2-lit.) "stop"

3bj (verb 3ae-inf.) "desire, wish"

3bḫ (verb 3-lit.) "mix, mingle"

3bd (noun) "month"

3bḏw (noun) "Abydos" (see map)

3pd (noun) "bird"

3m (verb 2-lit.) "burn up"

3hw (noun) "needy person"

3ḥt (noun) "field, plot of (cultivated) land"

3ḫ (adjective-verb 2-lit.) "effective"

3ḫt (noun) "Akhet" (see Essay 2)

3ḫt (noun) "Inundation (season)" (§ 9.8)

  3ḫtj (nisbe) "of the Inundation season"

3tp (verb 3-lit., originally *3ṯp*) "load"

3d (adjective-verb 2-lit.) "angry, aggressive"

3d (adjective-verb 2-lit.) "weak, listless"

j (interjection: § 16.8.1) "oh"

j "say" (§ 22.18)

j33t (noun) "branch"

j3jw (noun) "praise"

j3wt (noun) "office, function, profession"

j3wj (noun) "old age"

j3bt (noun) "East"

  j3btj (nisbe) "eastern"; *j3btt* (nisbe) "East"

j3dr — see *jdr*

jj (verb anom.) "come, return"; *jj.tj* (stative) "welcome!"; *jjwj* (participle) "welcome!"

jyt (noun) "wrong"

jˁb (verb 3-lit.) "join together, unite"

jˁrt, *ˁrˁt* (noun) "uraeus" (protective serpent)

jˁḥ (noun) "moon" (also as a god, identified with Thoth)

jw (particle: §§ 10.3, 16.6.1)

jw (noun) "island"

jw (noun) "complaint, error, wrong"

jw3 (noun) "ox"

jwj (verb anom.) "come, return"

jwꜥ (verb 3-lit.) "inherit"

jwꜥt (noun) "inheritance"

jwꜥw (noun) "heir"

jwf — see *jf*

jwms (noun) "exaggeration" — from the phrase *jw ms*: § 16.7.7

jwntj (noun) "desert Nubian"

jwr (verb 3-lit.) "conceive"

jwsw (noun) "balance" (a scale with two pans:)

, , *jwtj* (negative relative adjective) "who/which not"; *jwtt* "that which does not exist"

jwd (verb 3-lit.) "push off" (*r* "from")

jb (noun) "heart, mind"; *jmj-jb* "confidante"; *ḥr jb* "in the midst of"; *ḥrj jb* "middle"

jb (verb 2-lit.) "think, suppose"

jbj (verb 3ae-inf.) "thirst"

jp (verb 2-lit.) "allot, assign"; *jp ḏt* "collect (one)self"

jpt-swt (noun) "Karnak" (temple: see map) (literally, "(Most) Select of Places"); also singular *jpt-st*

jf (noun) "meat" — often written *jwf*

jm (preposition, prepositional adverb) — see *m*

jmy — see § 8.10

jmj (prepositional nisbe) — see *m*

jm3 (noun) "tent" (the writing shows the loss of final *3* in pronunciation)

jmj (imperative: § 16.2.3) "give, put, cause"

jm (negative subjunctive: § 19.11.2)

, *jm3ẖ* (noun) "honor" (see Essay 21)

jm3ẖy (participle/noun) "honored" (*ẖr* "by")

jmw (noun) "boat"

jmw (noun) "mourning"

jmn "hide"

jmn(w) (noun) "Amun" (see Essay 15)

jmnt (noun) "West"

jmntj (nisbe) "western"; *jmntt* (nisbe) "West"

jmḫt (noun) "Cavern" (a place in the Duat)

jn (preposition: § 8.2.2) "by"; (particle: § 16.6.2)

jn "say" (§ 22.18)

jnj (verb 3ae-inf.) "fetch, get, use"; *jnj m* "turn to, have recourse to"

jnw (noun) "produce, products"

jnb (noun) "wall"

jnpw (proper noun) "Anubis" (god of the cemetery)

jnm (noun) "skin"

jnr (noun) "stone"

jnq (verb 3-lit.) "embrace"

jnk (1s independent pronoun) — see § 5.5

j.nḏ ḥr (interjection: § 16.8.1) "hail to"

jr, *r* (preposition: § 8.2.7) "with respect to, toward"

jrj (prepositional adverb) "thereunto, with respect to it/them"

jrj (nisbe) "he who is at, who pertains to"

jrj, *jrt* (noun) "duty"

jrt (noun) "eye"

— see *wsjr* "Osiris"

jrj (verb 3ae-inf.) "make, do"; "pass" (time); "act as" (a function); "beget" (children); "work" (a field); *jrj r* "act against (someone), make for (a place)," *jrj n* "act/do for"; *jrj ḥnꜥ* "deal/act with"

jrw (noun) "form"

jrp (noun) "wine"

jhm (verb 3-lit.) "stall"

jḫw (noun) "cattle"

jḫ (particle: § 16.6.3) "then"

— see *zj*

jz (noun) "tomb"

jzwt (noun) "crew"

jzr (noun) "tamarisk"

js (particle: § 16.7.3)

jsw (particle: § 16.6.4) "look, behold"

, *jsṯ*, *jst* (particle: § 16.6.5)

jšwt — see *ḫt* "thing"

, *jšst* (interrogative pronoun: § 5.11) "what?"; *ḥr zj jšst* "how?, why?"

jqr (adjective-verb 3-lit.) "excellent, successful"

jkmw (noun) "shield"

jkn (verb 3-lit. and noun) "scoop"

, , *jtj* (noun) "father"

, *jty* or *jtjj* (noun) "sovereign" (Essay 6)

jtj (noun) "barley, grain"

jtj-mḥj "Lower Egyptian barley"

jtmw (noun) "suffocation"

jtn (noun) "sundisk"

jtn (verb 3-lit.) "contradict"

jtnw (noun) "ashes"

, *jtrw* (noun) "river"; measurement "river" (§ 9.7.1)

jṯḥ (verb 3-lit.) "draw, pull"

jṯj, *jṯj*(verb 3ae-inf.) "take possession of"

jdj (adjective verb 3ae-inf.) "senseless, deaf, dumb"

jdyt (noun) "girl"

jdw (noun) "pestilence"

, , *jdr* (noun) "herd"

ꜥ (noun) "hand, arm"; *m ꜥ* "with, from"

3wt ꜥ "gift" (see *3wj*)

nt-ꜥ "custom, practice, procedure" (literally, "what belongs to the hand")

ꜥt (noun) "limb"

ꜥt (noun) "room"

ꜥ3 (adverb) "here"

ꜥ3 (noun) "doorleaf"; often dual , *ꜥ3wj* "door"

ꜥ3 (noun) "donkey"

ꜥ3j (verb 3ae-inf.) " big, important"; *ꜥ3* (adjective) "big, important"

ꜥ3 (noun) "greatness"

ꜥ3wt (noun) "lump"

ꜥ3ppj (noun) "Apophis" (giant snake who inhabits the Duat and tries to prevent the sun's nightly journey through it)

, *ꜥ3m* (noun) "Asiatic"

ꜥ3g (verb 3-lit.) "pound, thrash"

ꜥjꜥj (verb 4-lit.) "wail"

ꜥꜥft (noun) "rate of payment"

ꜥwt (noun) "flock; sheep and goats"

ꜥw3j (verb 4ae-inf.) "rob, steal"

ꜥw3y (noun) "robber"

ꜥwn (adjective-verb 3-lit.) "greedy"

ꜥb (noun) "horn, flank"

ꜥb (noun) "horned crocodile"

ꜥbj (verb 3ae-inf.) "collect"; *ꜥbj m t3* "inter" (literally "collect in the ground")

ꜥpj (verb 3ae-inf.) "pass" (*ḥr* "by")

ꜥpr (verb 3-lit.) "equip"; *ꜥpr* (adjective) "experienced"

ꜥf3y (noun) "camp"

ꜥm (verb 2-lit.) "swallow"

ꜥmꜥm (verb 4-lit.) "give a massage"

ʿnḫ (verb 3-lit.) "live" (*m* "on"); *ʿnḫ.(w)-(w)ḏ3.(w)-s(nb.w)* "lph" (see § 17.20.2)

ʿnḫ (noun) "living person"

ʿnḫw (noun) "life"

ʿr (verb 2-lit.) "ascend, penetrate"

ʿrʿt — see *jʿrt*

ʿrryt (noun) "gate"

ʿrq (verb 3-lit.) "bend"

ʿrqy (noun) "last day of the month" (§ 9.8)

ʿḥ (noun) "palace, cabin"

ʿḥ3 (verb 3-lit.) "fight"

ʿḥ3 (noun) "arrow, weapon"

ʿḥʿ (noun) "(masted) boat"

ʿḥʿ (verb 3-lit.) "stand up, go on duty; "steadfast" (adjective)"; *ʿḥʿ n* "wait for, expect"

ʿḥʿ.n (introductory word) "then"

ʿḥʿ (noun) "heap, pile" (often, of riches)

ʿḥʿw (noun) "lifetime"

ʿḫm (verb 3-lit.) "quench, douse"

ʿḫḫw (noun) "nightfall"

ʿḫj (verb 3ae-inf.) "fly off"

ʿẖnwtj (noun) "chamber"

ʿš3 (adjective-verb 3-lit.) "many"

ʿš3t (noun) "multitude"

ʿq (verb 2-lit.) "enter" (*r* "into," *ḫr* "before, into the presence of")

ʿqw (noun) "rations, salary"

ʿq3 (adjective-verb 3-lit.) "straight, accurate"

ʿd (adjective-verb 2-lit., originally *ʿḏ*) "safe"

w3t (noun) "road, path, way"; *rdj ḥr w3t* "show the way" (literally, "put on the way"), *rdj w3t n* "let go" (literally, "give the road to")

w3j (verb 3ae-inf.) "fall, go off" (into a state or condition)

w3w (noun) "wave"

w3ḥ (verb 3-lit.) "set, place; add; stop; remain, last"; *w3ḥ* (adjective) "lasting"; *w3ḥ jb* "be patient" (literally, "lasting/set of heart")

w3ḥyt (noun) "abundance (of grain)"

w3ḫj (noun) "columned hall" (literally, "marsh" of papyrus and lotus columns)

w3s (noun) "dominion"

w3st (noun) "Thebes" (nome and city)

w3s (noun) "ruin" (infinitive of 4ae-inf. verb *w3sj* "fall into ruin")

w3gj (verb 4ae-inf.) "make festival"

w3ḏ (adjective-verb 3-lit.) "green, blue-green, fresh; fortunate"

w3ḏ-wr (noun) "sea" (literally, "great blue-green")

w3ḏyt "Wadjyet" (cobra goddess of Lower Egypt)

— see *wḏ*

wj (1s dependent pronoun) — see § 5.4

wj (noun) "mummiform coffin"

wj3 (noun) "bark"

wjn (verb 3-lit.) "reject, put aside"

wʿ (number) "one"; (adjective) "unique, sole"

wʿj (adjective-verb 3ae-inf.) "alone"

wʿ3 (verb 3-lit.) "blaspheme"

wʿw (noun) "soldier"

wʿb (adjective-verb 3-lit.) "clean, pure"

wʿb (noun) "laypriest" (see Essay 5)

wʿbt (noun) "cleansing"

wʿrt (noun) "flight"

wʿrt (noun) "district"

wb3yt (noun) "maid"

wbn (verb 3-lit.) "rise, swell"

wbnw (noun) "wound"

wpj (verb 3ae-inf.) "part, split, open"

wp-w3wt "Wepwawet" ("Parter of the Ways," jackal god of Abydos)

wpw ḥr "except"

wpt (noun) "land-register"

wpwt (noun) "assignment, mission, message"

wpwtj (noun) "messenger"

wmwt (noun) "niche"

wmt (adjective-verb 3-lit.) "thick"

wn (verb 2-lit.) "open"

wnwt (noun) "hour"

wnwt (noun) "hourly staff"

wnm (verb 3-lit.) "eat"

wnmw (noun) "food"

wnn (verb 2ae-gem.) "exist, be"

wn m3ʿ (noun) "reality"; *n wn m3ʿ* "truly"

wn.jn (introductory word) "then"

wnn-nfr.w "Wenen-nefer, Onnophris," epithet of Osiris ("He who is continually young")

wnnt (particle: § 16.7.5) "really, indeed"

wndw (noun) "short-horned cattle"

wndwt (noun) "tenants"

wr (adjective) "great, elder, important" (from 2ae-gem. adjective-verb *wrr*)

wrt (adverb) "greatly, much"

wrrt (noun) "crown"

wrš (verb 3-lit.) "spend the day"

wršy (noun) "watchman"

wrd (verb 3-lit., originally *wrḏ*) "tire" (intransitive); also a euphemism for "die"

wḥyt, wḥwt, wḥyw (noun) "tribe"

wḥm (verb 3-lit.) "repeat"

wḥmw (noun) "herald"

wḫ3 (noun) "fool"

wḫdw (noun) "forbearance, tolerance"

wzfw (noun) "forgetter"

wsjr (noun, originally perhaps *js-jrt*) "Osiris," literally "seat of the Eye (of the sun)" (see Essays 8 and 12)

wsḫ (adjective-verb 3-lit.) "broad, wide"

wsḫt (noun) "broad hall"; *wsḫt nt m3ʿtj* "the Two Maats" (name of the Hall of Judgment in the Netherworld, so called because the judges sit in two rows on either side of it)

wsḫt (noun) "barge (broad boat)"

wstn/wsṯn (verb 4-lit.) "stride"

wšb (verb 3-lit.) "answer"

wšʿ (verb 3-lit.) "chew"

wšd (verb 3-lit.) "address, question"

wt (verb 2-lit.) "bandage"

wt (noun) "bandage, mummy-wrappings"

jmj wt "he who is in the mummy-wrappings" (epithet of Anubis)

wtt (verb 3-lit., originally *wtṯ*) "beget"

wdj (verb 3ae-inf.) "put, set, push"

wdpw (noun) "waiter"

wdfj (verb 4ae-inf.) "be late, dawdle"

wḏ (verb 2-lit.) "command"; *wḏ tp* "give orders" (literally, "command head")

wḏ (noun) "stela"

wḏ (noun) "decree"

wḏt (noun) "command"

wḏ3 (verb 3-lit.) "proceed"

wḏyt (noun) "(military) campaign"

wḏʿ (verb 3-lit.) "sever, separate"

wḏb (noun) "bank (of a canal or river)"

b3 (noun) "ba" (see Essay 7)

b3w (noun) "impressiveness"

b3t (noun) "bush, sprig"

b3ḥ (noun) "presence"; *m b3ḥ* "in the presence of"

b3ḥj (nisbe) "ancestor, predecessor"

b3ḫw (noun) "Bakhu" (a western mountain range on the horizon of the Akhet: see Essay 2)

b3k (noun) "worker, servant"; *b3k jm* "your humble servant"

b3kw (noun) "tribute"

b3gj (adjective-verb 4ae-inf.) "lazy"

bjn (adjective-verb 3-lit.) "bad"

bjn (noun) "badness, evil"

bjnt (noun) "harp"

bjk (noun) "falcon"; *bjk nbw* Gold Falcon" (royal title)

bw (noun) "thing, place"; also, with adjectives, a means of forming abstract nouns:

bw-nb "everyone"

bw-nfr "goodness"

bw-ḏw "evil"

— see *bjnt*

bnr (adjective-verb 3-lit.) "sweet"

btj (noun, feminine: originally *bdt*) "emmer" (a kind of wheat)

pt (noun) "sky"

p3 (demonstrative pronoun) — see § 5.8

p3y — see §§ 5.10.4–5.10.5

p3 (verb 2-lit.) "do in the past"

p3wt (noun) "original time, creation"

p3qt (noun) "fine linen"

p3qyt (noun) "sherd"

p3ḏ (noun) "ball"

pꜥt (noun) "loaf of bread"

pꜥt (noun) "the elite"

pw (demonstrative pronoun) — see § 5.8

pwy (demonstrative pronoun) — see § 5.10.1

— see *ptr*

pf (demonstrative pronoun) — see § 5.8

pn (demonstrative pronoun) — see § 5.8

pr (noun) "house"; *pr-nswt* "king's house, palace"

prj (verb 3ae-inf.) "go up, emerge, issue"

prt (noun) "Growing (season)" (§ 9.8)

prt (noun) "seed"

prt-ḫrw "invocation offering" (literally, "sending forth of the voice")

pḥ (verb 2-lit.) "reach, catch, attack"

pḥ (noun) "result, end"

pḥtj (noun) "(physical) strength"

pḥrr (verb 3ae-gem.) "run"

pẖr (verb 3-lit.) "go around"; *pẖr n* "serve"

pẖrt (noun) "prescription, remedy"

pzšt (noun) "division"

psḏt (noun) "Ennead" (see Essay 12)

psdj (verb 4ae-inf., originally *psḏj*) "shine"

pšš (verb 2ae-gem.) "spread out"

ptpt (verb 4-lit.) "trample"

ptr, ptj, pw-trj (interrogative pronoun) — see § 5.11

pḏt (noun) "bow"

pḏtj/pdtj (nisbe) "bowman"

f3j (verb 3ae-inf.) "carry, lift"

fnd (noun, originally *fnḏ*) "nose"

fḫ (verb 2-lit.) "lose, loosen"

, *m, jm* (preposition: § 8.2.3) "in"

jm (prepositional adverb) "there, thereby, therewith, therein"

jmj (prepositional nisbe) "who/which is in"

jmj-jb "confidant" (literally, "one who is in the heart")

, *jmj-r* "overseer" (§ 8.9)

jmj-r pr "steward"

jmj-r šj "quarry-overseer"

m-n.k (imperative: § 16.2.4) "take!"

m (imperative: § 16.4) "don't!"

mj (interrogative pronoun) — see § 5.11

mj (particle: § 16.7.6) "now, please"

m.k (particle: § 16.6.7) "look" (2ms); *m.ṯ* 2fs, *m.ṯn* 2pl

, *mj, my* (imperative: § 16.2.2) "come!"

m3j (noun) "lion"

, *m33* (verb 2ae-gem.) "see, regard"; *m33 n* "look at"

m3ᶜ (verb 3-lit.) "guide, direct"

, *m3ᶜt* (noun) "Maat" (Essay 10)

wn m3ᶜ — see *wnn*

, *m3ᶜ* (adjective) "true, proper, correct" (i.e. "Maat-like")

, , *m3ᶜ ḫrw* (adjective phrase) "justified" (see Essay 8); also "justification" (noun phrase)

m3ᶜw (noun) "proper wind"

m3wj (adjective-verb 4ae-inf.) "new"

m3r/m3j (adjective-verb 3-lit.) "poor, needy"

m3ẖ (verb 3-lit.) "smolder"

m3st (noun) "lap"

mj (preposition: § 8.2.4) "like"; *mj rᶜ* "like Re" (honorific transposition)

mj n3 "here" (literally "like this")

mjtj, mjtw (noun) "one like, equal"

mjtt (noun) "likeness"; *m mjtt* "likewise"

mjn (noun) "today"; *m mjn* "today" (adverb)

mjnj (verb 4ae-inf.) "moor" (often, a euphemism for "die")

mjk3 (adjective) "brave"

mjṯn/mjtn (noun) "path"

mw (noun) "water"

mwt (noun) "mother" (actually, *mjwt*)

mwt (verb 3-lit.) "die"

m-bj3 (interjection: § 16.8.3) "no"

mfk3t/mf3kt (noun) "turquoise"

mm (preposition: § 8.2.5) "among"

mn "be set, be fixed, remain"

— see *mjnj*

, *mnjw* (noun) "herder"

mnw (noun) "Min" (god)

, *mnw* (noun) "monument, monuments"

mnmn (verb 4-lit.) "quake"

mnmnt (noun) "herd (of cattle)"

mnḥ (noun) "wax"

mnḫ (adjective-verb 3-lit.) "functional, worthwhile, beneficent"

mnḫt (noun) "clothing"

mntw (noun, originally *mnṯw*) "Montu" (patron god of Thebes)

mnḏ (noun) "breast"

(j)m(j)-r — see *m* (preposition)

mr (noun) "pyramid"

mr (adjective-verb 2-lit.) "sick, painful"

mryt (noun) "riverbank"

mrwt (noun) "serfs, dependents"

mrj (verb 3ae-inf.) "desire, want, like"

mrwt (noun) "love," *n mrwt* "for the sake of"

mrt (noun) "Meret" (goddess of song)

mrḥt (noun) "oil, ointment"

mḥ (verb 2-lit.) "fill"

mḥ with numerals: see § 9.3

mḥ (noun) "cubit" (§ 9.7.1)

mḥj (verb 3ae-inf.) "be in water, flood, swim"

mḥj (verb 3-lit.) "care, worry" (spelling influenced by *mḥ* "cubit")

mḥtj (nisbe) "northern"

mḥyt (noun) "northwind"

, *mḫ3t* (noun) "scale"

mḫr (noun) "storehouse"

ms (particle: § 16.7.7) "truly"

msj (verb 3ae-inf.) "give birth, bear"

ms (noun) "child, offspring"

mswt (noun) "birth"

msyt (noun) "supper"

msyt (noun) "waterfowl"

msnḥ (verb 4-lit.) "spin around"

msḥ (noun) "crocodile"

mskj (noun) "gossip"; *mskj n mdt* "gossip" (literally, "gossip of speech")

msḏj/msdj (verb 4ae-inf.) "hate"

msḏr (noun) "ear"

mšꜥ (noun) "expeditionary force, army"

mšrw (noun) "evening"

mkj (verb 3ae-inf.) "protect"

mkwt (noun) "protection"

mktj (noun) "protector"

— see *mwt*

mt (noun) "vessel" (of the body)

, *mtr/mtj* (verb 3-lit.) "testify, bear witness"; (adjective) "straightforward"; *mt(r)t nt jb* "advice"

mṯ3 (verb 3-lit.) "taunt"

mdw (noun) "staff"; *mdw j3wj* "staff of old age" (a son who cares for his father)

mdwj (verb 4ae-inf.) "speak"; *mdwj m* "contest"

mdt (noun) "word"

mdw (noun) "speech"; *mdw-nṯr* "hieroglyphs"

n (preposition: § 8.2.6) "to, for"

n(j) (prepositional nisbe: § 4.13.2) "belonging to, of"

n (1pl dependent pronoun) — see § 5.4

n3 (demonstrative pronoun) — see § 5.8

mj n3 "here" (literally, "like this")

n3y — see §§ 5.10.4–5.10.5

nj (particle: § 16.6.8) "not, no"

njs (verb 3-lit.) "call, summon" (with *r* "to")

njtjt (verb 5-lit.) "stammer"

nꜥj (verb 3ae-inf.) "sail, travel by boat"

n(j)w (plural nisbe) — see *n*

nw (demonstrative pronoun) — see § 5.8

nw (noun) "time"

nw (verb 2-lit.) "look after, see to"

nwj (verb 3ae-inf.) "bring back"

nwt (noun) "town" (often transcribed *njwt*)

nwt (noun) "Nut" (the sky: see Essay 2)

nwy (noun) "waters"

nwt (noun) "wave"

nb (adjective) "all, each, every, any"

nb (noun) "lord, master, owner"

nbt (noun) "lady, mistress, owner"

nbtj "Two Ladies" (royal title: see Essay 6)

nbw (noun) "gold"

nfꜣ (demonstrative pronoun) — see § 5.8

nfꜥ (verb 3-lit.) "remove, take away"

nfr (adjective-verb 3-lit.) "perfect, good, beautiful"

nfr (particle: §§ 16.6.9, 26.29.3) "not at all"

nfrw (noun) "beauty, perfection"

nfryt (noun) "tiller-rope"

nftft (verb 5-lit.) "leap"

nmtj (noun) "Nemti" (a god)

nmj (verb 3ae-inf.) "travel (by foot)"; *nmj-šꜥ* "Nomad" (literally, "sand traveler")

nmtwt (noun) "steps"

nn "this, here" (demonstrative pronoun) — see § 5.8

nn (particle: § 16.6.8) "not, no"

nnm (verb 3-lit.) "transgress"

nnk — for *n(j)-(j)nk* (§ 7.5.2)

nht (noun) "sycamore"

nhj (noun) "little, few"

nhw (noun) "loss, need"

nḥ (noun) "prayer"

nḥbt (noun) "neck"

nḥp (noun) "potter's wheel"

nḥm (verb 3-lit.) "take away, save"

nḥmn (particle: § 16.6.10) "surely"

nḥḥ (noun) "eternal repetition, continuity, eternity, forever" (Essay 9)

nḥsj (noun) "Nubian" (see map)

nẖ (adjective-verb 2-lit.) "pitiful"

nẖꜣw (noun) "pendant" (shaped like a fish)

nḫt (adjective-verb 3-lit.) "successful, victorious"

nḫt (noun) "victory"

nḫt (participle/noun) "champion"

ns (noun) "tongue"

nswt (noun) "(tongue of) flame"

ns — for *n(j)-sj* (§ 7.5.1)

nsw — for *n(j)-sw* (§ 7.5.1)

nswt (noun, originally *nj-swt*: § 4.15) "king"

nswt bjtj (noun phrase) "King of Upper and Lower Egypt" (royal title)

nswyt "kingship"

nšnj (noun) "tempest, rainstorm"

nkn (noun) "harm, punishment"

ngꜣw (noun) "steer"

nt-ꜥ — see *ꜥ*

ntj (relative adjective) "who, which"; *ntt* "that, that which exists"

ntf (3ms independent pronoun) — see § 5.5

ntk (2ms independent pronoun) — see § 5.5

ntt (2fs independent pronoun) — see § 5.5

nṯr (noun) "god"

nṯrj (nisbe) "divine"

— see *snṯr*

nṯrt/ntrt (noun) "goddess"

ndb (written *nḏb*; verb 3-lit.) "sip"

ndbyt (noun) "reefs (of a sail)"

nḏtj (noun) "savior"

nḏm (adjective-verb 3-lit.) "sweet"

nḏrj (verb 4ae-inf.) "seize"

nḏs (adjective-verb 3-lit.) "little"

nḏs (noun) "commoner" (literally, "little man")

r (preposition) — see *jr*

r with numerals: see § 9.6

r (noun) "mouth, speech, spell"

r-ʿwj "activity"

r-pw "or, either" (§ 4.12)

r-pr "temple, chapel"

r-ẖt "stomach, belly" (literally, "mouth of the belly")

rʿ (noun) "sun"; *rʿ nb* "every day"

rʿ "Re, Sun" (god); see *mj*

— see *r*

rwt (noun) "gate"

rwtj (nisbe) "outside"

rwj (verb 3ae-inf.) "go away, escape; drive off"

rwd (noun, originally *rwḏ*) "bowstring"

rwḏ/rwd (adjective-verb 3-lit.) "firm"

— see *r*

rm (noun) "fish"

rmj (verb 3ae-inf.) "weep, weep for"

rmyt (noun) "tears"

rmṯ (noun) "people"

rn (noun) "identity, name"

rnpw (adjective-verb 4ae-inf.) "young"

rnpt (noun) "year"

— see *ḥsbt*

rhnj (verb 4ae-inf.) "rest, rely, depend"

rḫ (verb 2-lit.) "learn, know"

rḫ "wise (man), knowledgeable"

rḫ-nswt "king's acquaintance" (court title)

rḫwt, rḫyt (noun) "subjects"

rḫs (verb 3-lit.) "butcher, slaughter"

rswt (noun) "dream"

ršj, ršw (verb 3ae-inf.) "delight, rejoice"; *rš* (adjective) "joyful"

rqj (verb 3ae-inf.) "oppose, revolt"

rk (noun) "time, age, era"

rtḥ (verb 3-lit.) "restrain"

— see *rmṯ*

rṯnw/(r)tnw (noun) "Retjenu" (the area of modern Lebanon)

rd (noun) "foot"

rd (noun) "stairway, terrace"

rd (verb 2-lit.) "grow, flourish" (spelling influenced by *rwḏ* "firm")

rdj (verb anom., originally *rḏj*) "give, put, cause"; "appoint" (*r* or *m* "to" office); *rdj m ḥr* "assign" (literally, "put in the face"); *rdj ḥr gs* "lean to the side, be partial"

rḏw (noun) "fluid"

h (noun) "courtyard"

h3 (interjection: § 16.8.4) "oh!"

h3j (verb 3ae-inf.) "go down, head" (*r* "for")

h3w (noun) "time, vicinity, area, affairs"

h3b (verb 3-lit.) "send, send word"

hbj (verb 3ae-inf.) "plow"

hp (noun) "law, custom"

hn (noun) "jar; hin" (§ 9.7.4)

hrw (noun) "day, daytime, (day's) duty"; *hrw nfr* "holiday"

hh (noun) "blast (of fire)"

ḥ3 (preposition: § 8.2.8) "behind, around"; *r ḥ3* "out, outside"

ḥ3j (nisbe) "one who is behind, around"

ḥ3 (particle: § 16.6.12) "would that, if only"

ḥ3t (noun) "front, beginning"; *rdj ḥ3t n* "head toward" (literally, "give front to"); *ḫr ḥ3t* "before, preceding"

ḥ3tj ʿ "high official" (literally, "one whose hand is in front")

ḥ3tj (noun) "heart"

, *ḥ3j* (adjective-verb 3ae-inf.) "naked, undressed"; transitive "make naked, undress, reveal"

ḥ3w (noun) "excess, more"; *ḥ3w ḥr* "more than" (literally, "excess over")

ḥ3b (noun) "festival"

ḥ3p (verb 3-lit.) "conceal"; *ḥ3pw ẖt* "discreet" (literally, "concealed of belly")

ḥ3q (verb 3-lit.) "loot, plunder"

ḥ3qt (noun) "plunder"

ḥjḥj (verb 4-lit.) "seek"

ḥʿ (noun) "ship"

ḥʿ (noun) "body"; usually plural *ḥʿw* "body" (see Essay 7)

ḥʿj (verb 3ae-inf.) "become aroused, excited"

, *ḥʿpj* (noun, originally *ḥʿpr*) "inundation" (also as a god)

ḥwt (noun) "enclosure"

ḥwt-wʿrt "Avaris" (capital of the Hyksos, in the eastern Delta: see map)

— *ḥwt-nbw* "Enclosure of Gold" (a shrine)

ḥwt-nṯr "temple" (literally, "god's enclosure")

ḥwt-ḥrw "Hathor" (goddess: § 3.6)

ḥwj (verb 3ae-inf.) "hit, strike, smite"; with object of place, "visit"

ḥwn (noun) "youth"

ḥwr (adjective, noun) "poor, wretched"

ḥwtf (verb 4-lit.) "plunder"

ḥb3b3 (verb 5-lit.) "waddle"

ḥbs (verb 3-lit.) "cover, clothe, get dressed"

ḥbsw (noun) "clothing, clothes"

ḥf3w (noun) "snake"

ḥf3t (noun) "snake"

ḥm "incarnation"

ḥmw (noun) "servant"

ḥm-nṯr (noun) "priest" (literally, "god's servant")

ḥmt (noun) "servant"

, *ḥm* (particle: § 16.7.8) "and, also"

ḥmt (noun) "woman, wife" (actually, *ḥjmt*)

ḥmt (noun) "bronze, copper"

ḥmw (noun) "rudder"

ḥmw (noun) "craftsman"

ḥmwtj (noun) "craftsman" (nisbe from *ḥmwt* "craft")

ḥmsj (verb 4ae-inf.) "sit down; reside"

ḥms (noun) "seat"

ḥn (verb 2-lit.) "rush, hurry, attack"

ḥn (verb 2-lit.) "commend, command; take care of"

ḥnʿ (preposition: § 8.2.9) "with"

, *ḥnw* (noun) "property"

ḥnwt (noun) "mistress"

ḥnmmt (noun) "humanity"

ḥnḥn (verb 4-lit.) "hinder"

ḥns (adjective-verb 3-lit.) "narrow"

, *ḥnqt* (noun) "beer"

ḥnkyt (noun) "bed"

ḥr (noun) "face"; *rdj m ḥr* "assign" (literally, "put in the face")

ḥr-nb "everyone"

ḥr (preposition: § 8.2.10) "upon"

, *ḥrj* (prepositional nisbe) "who/which is over, upper, chief"

ḥrj jb (noun) "middle"

ḥr ḫw (prepositional phrase) "except"

— see *šj*

ḥrj tp (preposition nisbe) "chief" (also "nomarch," the governor or ruler of a nome)

ḥrj-ḏbʿ (noun) "hornless cattle" (literally, "one upon the finger")

ḥrt "sky, upland"

, *ḥrj* (verb 3ae-inf.) "go far away"

ḥrw (noun) "Horus" (god of kingship, royal title)

ḥrw (noun) "plot, plotting"

ḥḥ (noun) "million" (§ 9.2)

— see *nḥḥ*

— see *hjhj*

ḥzj (verb 3ae-inf.) "bless"

ḥzwt (noun) "blessing"

ḥz3 (adjective-verb 3-lit.) "wild"

ḥsj (verb 3ae-inf.) "sing"

ḥsb (verb 3-lit.) "count"

ḥsbt (noun) "(regnal) year" (§ 9.9)

ḥsq (verb 3-lit.) "sever"

— see *ḥnqt*

, *ḥq3* (noun) "ruler"

ḥq3-ḥwt (noun) "mayor" ("ruler of the enclosure")

ḥq3t "heqat" (§ 9.7.4)

ḥqr (verb 3-lit.) "hunger"

ḥqrw (noun) "hunger"

ḥk3w (noun) "magic"

ḥknw (noun) "oil"

ḥt3 (noun) "sail"

ḥtp (adjective-verb 3-lit.) "calm, content; occupy (a seat)"; *m ḥtp* "in peace, safely"

ḥtp-dj-nswt "royal offering" (see § 24.10)

ḥtpt "offerings"

ḥtm (verb 3-lit.) "equip"

ḥtm (verb 3-lit.) "perish"

ḥtr (noun) "team"

ḥtrj (noun) "team-ox"

ḥḏ (adjective-verb 2-lit.) "bright, white"; *ḥḏ ḥr* "cheerful" (literally "bright of face"); *ḥḏ t3* "dawn" (literally, "the land becomes bright")

ḥḏt (noun) "(white) hippopotamus"

ḥḏwt (noun) "chapel"

ḫt (noun) "thing, property" (often written as plural)

jšwt, "things, property" (variant plural)

ḫt (noun) "fire"

ḫ3 (noun) "office"

, *ḫ3j* (verb 3ae-inf.) "measure, weigh, examine"

ḫ3ʿ (verb 3-lit.) "throw"

ḫ3wj (noun) "dusk"

ḫ3st (noun) "desert hills, foreign land"

ḫʿj (verb 3ae-inf.) "appear"

ḫʿw "appearance"

ḫwsj (verb 4ae-inf.) "pound, build"

ḫwd (adjective-verb 3-lit.) "rich"

ḫb3 (verb 3-lit.) "hoe, hack up; subtract, diminish"

ḫbj (verb 3ae-inf.) "dance"

ḫbzwt (noun) "beard"

ḫpj (verb 3ae-inf.) "walk; meet"

ḫpr (verb 3-lit.) "evolve, happen, occur; grow up"; *ḫpr m* "become (something/someone)" (literally, "evolve into")

ḫprw (noun) "evolution, development"

ḫpš (noun) "strong arm"

ḫft (preposition: § 8.2.11) "opposite, according"

ḫftj (nisbe) "opponent, enemy"

ḫm (verb 2-lit.) "ignore, not learn, not know"

ḫmt (verb 3-lit.) "think" (spellings influenced by *ḫmtw* "three" and *ḫm* "ignore")

ḫnj (verb 3ae-inf.) "land, alight"

ḫnm (verb 3-lit.) "breathe"

ḫnms (noun) "friend"

ḫnms (verb 4-lit.) "befriend, associate with"

ḫnrj (nisbe) "prisoner"

ḫnt (preposition: § 8.2.12) "at the head of"; *ḫntj* (nisbe) "foremost of, he who is at the head of"

ḫnt (noun) "brow, front"

ḫntj (verb 4ae-inf.) "go forward/upstream/south"; *m ḫntyt* "upstream, south"

ḫnt (noun) "Upstream" (a term for Nubia)

ḫnd (verb 3-lit.) "step on"

ḫr (preposition: § 8.2.13) "by, near, during"

ḫr (particle: § 16.6.13)

ḫr (verb 2-lit.) "fall"

ḫrwj (noun) "enemy"

ḫrw (noun) "voice, sound, noise"

ḫrw "say" (§ 22.18)

ḫrp (verb 3-lit.) "manage"

ḫsbd (noun) "lapis-lazuli"

ḫsf (verb 3-lit.) "bar, punish"

ḫsfj (verb 4ae-inf.) "meet, oppose"

ḫsfw (noun) "opponent"

ḫt (noun, masculine) "wood, tree, stick, mast"

ḫt (noun) "wake, train, aftermath"; *m ḫt* "after," (as a noun) "future"

ḫtm (verb 3-lit.) "seal, shut"

ḫdj (verb 3ae-inf.) "go/sail downstream/north"; *m ḫd* "downstream, north"

ẖt (noun) "belly, womb"

ẖ3t (noun) "corpse"

ẖ3rt (noun) "widow"

ẖ3k (verb 3-lit.) "truncate"

ẖ3k-jb "estranged" ("truncated of heart")

ẖnj (verb 3ae-inf.) "row; transport by boat"

ẖnt "excursion" (in a rowboat)

ẖnyt (noun) "crew"

ẖnw (noun) "interior, home, capital (city)"; *m ẖnw* "inside"

ẖnm (verb 3-lit.) "join, unite"

ẖnmw (noun) "Khnum" (god who forms peoples' bodies on a potter's wheel)

ẖntj (noun) "statue, picture"

ẖr (preposition: § 8.2.15) "under"

ẖrj (nisbe) "lower, underlying, having" (§ 8.6.11)

ẖrj-nṯr, ẖrt-nṯr "necropolis"

ẖrd (noun) "child, boy"

ẖzj (adjective-verb 3ae-inf.) "wretched, miserable, vile"

z(j) (noun) "man"

zt ḥmt "woman"

z3 (noun) "son"

z3 zj (noun phrase) "gentry" (a man of standing in the community: literally, "son of a man")

z3t (noun) "daughter"

z3, z3w (noun) "protection, safeguard"

z3 (noun) "phyle" (shift of priests or workers)

zj (verb 2-lit.) "go"

j.zj (imperative) "go!" (§ 16.2.1)

zy (interrogative pronoun) — see § 5.11; *ḥr zj jšst* "how?, why?"

zjn (verb 3-lit.) "rub"

 *zbj* (verb 3ae-inf.) "send "

 *zp* (noun) "time, occasion, event, deed"; *n zp* "together"; *zp tpj* "First Occasion" (the creation)

 *zp 2* "twice": see § 9.5

 *zp* (verb 2-lit.) "happen"; *nj zp*, *nn zp* "never" (§§ 19.11.1, 20.5)

 *zpj* (verb 3ae-inf.) "be left, remain, survive"

 *zm3* (verb 3-lit.) "join"; *zm3 t3* "land" (verb), "landing" (noun)"

 *zn* (verb 2-lit.) "pull back"

 *znj* (verb 3ae-inf.) "pass" (*ḥr* "by")

 *zḥ* (noun) "tent"

 *zḥ* (noun) "advice"

,  *zḫz* (verb 3-lit.) "run"

 *zḫ* (verb 2-lit.) "be deaf to" (transitive)

 *zẖ3* (verb 3-lit.) "write"

 *zẖ3w* (noun) "writing"

 *zẖ3w* (noun) "scribe"

 *zẖ3-qdwt* "outline-scribe" (artist who draws the first draft for an inscription or painting)

 *zšj* (noun) "nestling"

 — see *zn*

 *st* (dependent pronoun) — see § 5.4

 *st* (noun) "place, throne"

 — see *wsjr* "Osiris"

 *s3* (noun) "back"; *m s3* "in back of, in charge of"; *r s3* "after"; *ḥr s3* "behind"

 *s3j* (verb 3ae-inf.) "become sated"

 *s3wj* (verb caus. 3ae-inf.) "extend, lengthen"; *s3wj jb* "make happy" (see *3wj*)

 *s3ḥ* (verb 3-lit.) "touch (with the toe), kick, set foot"; *s3ḥ t3* "touch land" = "be buried"

 *s3ḥ* (noun) "Orion"

 *s3ḫ* (verb caus. 2-lit.) "make effective"

,  *s3s3* (verb 4-lit.) "attack headlong, push back"

 *sj* (3fs dependent pronoun) — see § 5.4

 *sj3* (verb 3-lit.) "recognize"

 *sjm3* (noun) "pleasure"

 *sjqr* (verb 3-lit.) "make excellent, successful"

 *sꜥ3j* (verb caus. 3ae-inf.) "make great"

 (verb caus. 3-lit.) "make live, nourish"

 *sꜥnḫw* (noun) "life-giver"

 *sꜥḥ* (noun) "noble, privileged person"

 *sꜥḥꜥ* (verb caus. 3-lit.) "erect"

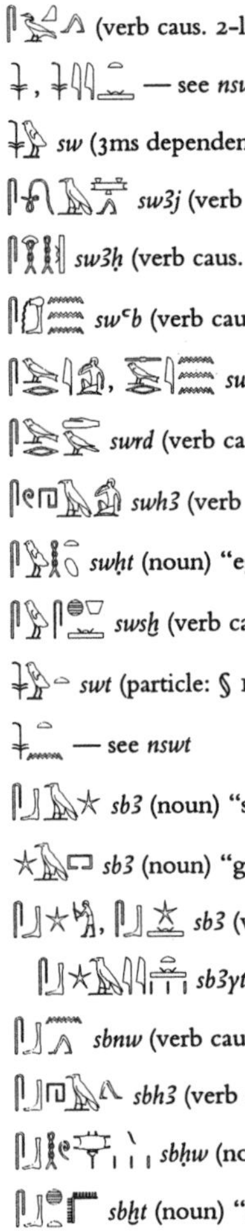 (verb caus. 2-lit.) "introduce, bring in"

— see *nswt*

sw (3ms dependent pronoun) — see § 5.4

sw3j (verb 4ae-inf.) "pass" (*ḥr* "by")

sw3ḥ (verb caus. 3-lit.) "set, make endure"

swꜥb (verb caus. 3-lit.) "clean, purify"

swr/swj (verb 3-lit.) "drink"

swrd (verb caus. 3-lit.) "tire"

swh3 (verb caus. 3-lit.) "extol"

swḥt (noun) "egg"

swsḫ (verb caus. 3-lit.) "broaden"

swt (particle: § 16.7.9) "but"

— see *nswt*

sb3 (noun) "star"

sb3 (noun) "gate, doorway"

sb3 (verb 3-lit.) "teach"

sb3yt (noun) "teaching, instruction"

sbnw (verb caus. 3ae-inf.) "go off course"

sbh3 (verb caus. 3-lit.) "cause to flee"

sbḥw (noun) "howling wind"

sbḫt (noun) "barrier"

sbkw (noun) "Sobek" (crocodile god)

sbt (verb 3-lit., originally *sbṯ*) "laugh"

sp3t (noun) "nome"; *sp3t* "estate, farm"

spr (verb 3-lit.) "arrive" (*r* "at")

spr "petition"

sprw (noun) "petitioner"

spdd (verb 4-lit., originally *spdḏ*) "prepare"

sf (noun) "yesterday"

sfn (verb caus. 2-lit.) "be mild, merciful"

sfḫḫ (verb caus. 2ae-gem.) "loosen"

sfṯ (verb 3-lit.) "cut up, butcher"

sm3 (verb 3-lit.) "kill"

sm3^c (verb caus. 3-lit.) "make correct"

smj (verb caus. 2-lit.) "report"

smn (verb caus. 2-lit.) "set, fix"

smn (noun) "goose"

smnḫ (verb caus. 3-lit.) "make functional, useful"; *smnḫ* (adjective) "useful"

smr (noun) "courtier"

smḥj (verb caus. 3ae-inf.) "flood, irrigate, cause to be in water"

smḫ (verb caus. 2-lit.) "forget" (simplex *ḫm*)

smsj (verb caus. 3ae-inf.) "cause to give birth"

smsw (adjective/noun) "eldest"

sn (verb 2-lit.) "smell, kiss"

sn (noun) "brother, sibling"

snt (noun) "sister" (also a term for "wife")

snw (noun) "companion, equal" (= *snnw* "second": § 9.3)

snb (adjective-verb 3-lit.) "healthy," (noun) "health"

snf (noun) "blood"

snf3 (verb caus. 3-lit.) "vent"

snm (verb caus. 2-lit., simplex *wnm*) "feed"

snn (noun) "likeness"

snq (verb caus. 2-lit.) "suck; suckle, nurse"

sntr (noun, originally *snṯr*) "incense"

snḏ (verb 3-lit.) "become afraid"

snḏw (noun) "fearful (person)"

snḏw (noun) "fear"

snḏm (verb caus. 3-lit.) "sweeten, reside"

sr (verb 2-lit.) "predict"

srj (noun) "official"

srwj (verb caus. 3ae-inf.) "remove"

srd (verb caus. 2-lit.) "plant, cause to grow"

sh3j (verb caus. 3ae-inf.) "bring down"

shrj (verb caus. 3ae-inf.) "pacify"

sḥtm (verb caus. 3-lit.) "annihilate"

sḥrj (verb caus. 3ae-inf.) "distance, distance oneself, go above"

sḥḏ (verb caus. 2-lit.) "brighten"

sḫt (noun) "field"

sḫt j3rw "Field of Reeds" (a place in the netherworld)

sḫt ḥm3t "Field of Salt" (modern Wadi Natrun, NW of Cairo)

sḫtj (noun) "peasant, farmer"

sḫ3j (verb caus. 3ae-inf.) "bring to mind, recall"

sḫ^c*j* (verb caus. 3ae-inf.) "cause to appear"

sḫw (noun) "width" (see *wsḫ*)

sḫpr (verb caus. 3-lit.) "bring about, make become, create"

sḫm (verb 3-lit.) "gain/have control" (*m* "of"); *sḫm jb* "violent"

sḫmt (noun) "Sekhmet" (goddess of violence)

sḫnj (verb caus. 3ae-inf.) "cause to land, land"

sḫr (verb caus. 2-lit.) "fell, overthrow"

sẖr (noun) "plan, method, advice, conduct, position"; plural often with singular meaning

sẖry (noun) "pilot"

— see *zẖz*

sẖt (verb 3-lit.) "strike"

sspd (verb caus. 3-lit.) "prepare"

sš3 (adjective-verb 3-lit., originally *šs3*) "aware, wise"

sšmj (verb caus. 3ae-inf.) "lead"

sšmw (noun) "situation, procedure, conduct"

sšmw (noun) "leader, guide, pilot"

, *sqr* (verb 3-lit.) "flatten, strike down"

sqr-ᶜnḫ "prisoner of war" (literally, "one struck down alive")

sqdj (verb caus. 3ae-inf.) "sail, voyage"

sqd (noun) "voyager"

sk (verb 2-lit.) "wipe"

skjw (noun) "troops"

, , *sk3* (verb 3-lit.) "plow"

sgr (verb caus. 2-lit.) "cause to be still/silent"

sgr (noun) "stillness, silence"

st3 (verb caus. 2-lit.) "light (a wick)"

stj (noun, originally *sṯj*) "smell, odor"

stj-r "breakfast"

stj (verb 3ae-inf.) "shoot"

stt (noun) "boil"

sttjw (noun, plural) "Beduin"

, *stwt* (noun) "rays"

stp-z3 "palace"

stš, *stẖ* (noun) "Seth" (god of disorder)

sṯ (particle) — see *jsṯ*

sd (verb 2-lit.) "get dressed (in a kilt)"

sdg3 (verb caus. 3-lit.) "conceal"

sḏm (verb 3-lit.) "hear"; *sḏm n* "listen to"

sḏmw (noun) "hearer, obedient one"

sḏr (verb 3-lit.) "lie down, spend the night, sleep"

sḏd (verb caus. 2-lit.) "relate"

š3 (noun) "marsh, field"; *jmj-š3* "marsh-dweller"

š3 (noun) "boar, wild pig"

š3w3btj (noun) "shawabti" (a small mummiform statue representing the deceased)

š3s (verb 3-lit.) "go off, proceed"

šj (noun) "lake, precinct; basin-land"

ḥrj-šj.f "Harsaphes" (a god — literally, "He who is on his lake")

šᶜ (noun) "sand"

šᶜt (noun) "slaughter"

šw (noun) "sunlight"

šwt (noun) "shade, shadow"

šw3w (noun) "outcast, renegade"

šwj (adjective-verb 3ae-inf.) "empty, free" (*m* "of")

špss (adjective-verb 3ae-gem.), *špsj* (adjective-verb 4ae-inf.) "fine, special, noble"

špst (noun) "noblewoman"

špssw (noun) "finery, fine things"

špt (verb 3-lit.) "get angry"

šfj (verb 3ae-inf.) "respect"

, *šmj* (verb 3ae-inf.) "go, walk"

šmᶜ (verb 3-lit.) "chant"

šmᶜ (noun) "singer, chanter"

šmᶜw (noun) "Nile Valley"

šmᶜj (noun) "southern barley"

šmw (noun) "harvest"

šmw "Harvest (season)" (§ 9.8)

, *šmsj* (verb 4ae-inf.) "follow"

šmsw (noun) "following"

šmsw (noun) "follower"

šnyt (noun) "circle, court"

šnʿ (verb 3-lit.) "refuse, bar"

šnʿw (noun) "ban"

, *šnw*, *šnwy* (noun) "hair"

, *šnwt* (noun) "granary"

šndyt (noun) "kilt"

šrj (adjective) "little" (from 2ae-gem. adjective-verb *šrr*)

šzp (verb 3-lit.) "receive, accept"

šzp (noun) measurement "palm" (§ 9.7.1)

šzp (noun) "image (of a god)"

šzp (noun, originally *sšp*) "dawn"

šs or *šst* (noun) "alabaster"

šs3j (verb caus. 3ae-inf., originally *sš3j*) "plead, pray"

šs3 (noun) "wisdom" (see *sš3*)

ššr (noun) "arrow"

šsrw (noun, originally *sšrw*) "linen"

, *št3* (adjective-verb 3-lit.) "inaccessible, secret"

šdj (verb 3ae-inf.) "take, pull, rescue"

šd (noun) "plot (of land)"

, *šdj* (verb 3ae-inf.) "recite, read"

, *q3j* (adjective-verb 3ae-inf.) "high"; *q3 s3* "arrogant" (literally, "high of back")

q33 (noun) "hill"

qbb (verb 2ae-gem.) "cool, calm"

qbt (noun) "coolness, cool place"

qbw (noun) "cool breeze"

qm3 (verb 3-lit.) "throw"

qm3j (verb 4ae-inf.) "create"

qnj (adjective-verb 3ae-inf.) "diligent, brave, persevering"

qn (noun) "audacity"

qnyt (noun) "braves"

qnj (noun) "embrace"

, *qnbt* (noun) "council"

qrt (noun) "doorbolt"

qrrt (noun) "cavern"

, *qrs* (verb 3-lit.) "bury"

qs (noun) "bone"

qsn (adjective-verb 3-lit.) "difficult"

, , *qd* (verb 2-lit.) "build"

qdw (noun) "form, manner, character"; *mj qd* "all, entire, whole" (§ 6.7)

qdt (noun) measurement "deben" (§ 9.7.3)

qdd (verb 2ae-gem.) "sleep"

qddw (noun) "sleep"

kt — see *ky*

kt-ḫj — see *ky*

k3 (particle: § 16.6.15) "then"

k3 "say" (§ 22.18)

k3 (noun) "ka" (see Essay 7)

, *k3* (noun) "bull"

k3j (verb 3ae-inf.) "think, plan"

k3w (noun) "fruit, fruits"

k3wt (noun) "work, works"

k3r (noun) "shrine"

ky (adjective/noun: § 6.7) "other, another"; feminine *kt*; plural *kjwj*, *kt-ḫj*

kfj (verb 3ae-inf.) "strip, unravel"

kft (noun) "gash"

km (verb 2-lit.) "complete"

km (adjective) "black" (from 2ae-gem. adjective-verb *kmm*)

km-wr "Great Black" (the region of the Bitter Lakes, in the area of the modern Suez Canal: see map)

kmt (noun) "Egypt" (literally "The Black," referring to the cultivated soil along the Nile)

kš (noun) "Kush" (northern Sudan: see map)

ktkt (verb 4-lit.) "sneak, be surreptitious"

g3w (noun) "absence, lack"

gb3 (noun) "side"

gbb (noun) "Geb" (god of the earth)

gp (verb 2-lit.) "cloud up"

gm3 (noun) "cheekbone"

gmj (verb 3ae-inf.) "find"

gmw (noun) "grief"

gmḥ (verb 3-lit.) "glimpse, look at, see"

gmgm (verb 4-lit.) "smash, crack"

gr (adjective-verb 2-lit.) "still, silent"

grt (particle: § 16.7.10) "moreover"

grḥ (noun) "night"

grḥ (noun) "end"

grg (verb 3-lit.) "set up, found, establish"

grg (verb 3-lit.) "lie"

grg (noun) "lie"

grgw (noun) "lying"

gs (noun) "side, half"; *rdj ḥr gs* "lean to the side, be partial"

gs (verb 2-lit.) "get anointed, anoint"

gs3 (verb 3-lit.) "tilt"

t (noun) "bread"

t-ḥḏ "white-bread"

t3 (demonstrative pronoun) — see § 5.8

t3 (noun) "land"; *r t3* "down"

t3-wr "This" (the nome of Abydos: see map)

t3-zm3 "landing stage"

t3 ḏsr "Sacred Land" (the necropolis)

t3wj "Two Lands" (Egypt)

t3š (noun) "border"

tj (particle: § 16.6.16)

tjw (interjection: § 16.8.5) "yes"

tjmḥj (noun) "Libyan"

tjsw (noun) "staff"

tw (2ms dependent pronoun) — see § 5.4

tw (impersonal pronoun) — see § 15.5

(subject pronoun) — see § 10.5

twt (noun) "image"

twr/twj (verb 3-lit.) "show respect" (*ḥr* "for")

tp (noun) "head, top"

tpj (nisbe) "first, headman"

tpt (noun) "first-class oil"

tp (preposition: § 8.2.16) "upon"

tpj (prepositional nisbe) "who/which is upon"

tpj-t3 (noun) "survivor, one who is on earth"

tf (demonstrative pronoun) — see § 5.8

— see *jtj* "father"

tm (verb 2-lit.) "not do"

tm3 (noun) "mat" (the writing shows the loss of final *3* in pronunciation) *tmm* (verb 2ae-gem.) "close, shut"

tn (demonstrative pronoun) — see § 5.8

— see *ṯnj*

tnj (verb 3ae-inf., originally *ṯnj*) "distinguish"

— see *ṯnw*

tr (particle: § 16.7.11)

tr (noun) "time, season"

thj (verb 3ae-inf.) "violate"

tẖ (verb 2-lit.) "get drunk"

tẖtẖ (verb 4-lit.) "mess up, disorder"

tk3 (noun) "wick, taper"

ṯ3j (verb 3ae-inf.) "take"

ṯ3w/ṯ3y (noun) "man, male"

ṯ3w (noun) "air, wind, breath"

ṯ3bt (noun) "loan of grain"

ṯ3m (verb 3-lit.) "veil"; *ṯ3m ḥr* "lenience" (literally, "veiling of the face")

ṯ3z (verb 3-lit.) "tie, knot"; *ṯ3z skjw* "raise troops"

ṯ3z (noun) "sentence (of speech)"

ṯw (2ms dependent pronoun) — see § 5.4

ṯbwt (noun) "sandal"

ṯnj/tnj (interrogative adverb: § 8.13) "where?"

ṯnw/tnw (noun) "each, every" (§ 6.7)

ṯḥnw (noun) "the Libyan desert"

ṯzj (verb 3ae-inf.) "pick up, lift"

d3 (verb 2-lit.) "shake"

d3jw (noun) "cloak"

d3r (verb 3-lit.) "subdue" (the spelling represents the change of original *d3j* to *d3r*)

dj (verb anom.) — see *rdj*

dw3 (verb 3-lit.) "worship"

dw3w (noun) "morning, tomorrow"

dw3t (noun) "Duat" (see Essay 2)

dwn (verb 3-lit.) "stretch"

db3 — see *ḏb3*

dbb (verb 2ae-gem.) "stop up, block"

dbn (noun) measurement "deben" (§ 9.7.3)

dp (verb 2-lit.) "taste"

dpwt (noun) "boat, ship"

dmj (verb 3-lit.) "reach, touch"

dmj (noun) "harbor"; "town" (in later texts)

dmḏj/dmdj (verb 4ae-inf.) "unite, total, sum"

dmḏ/dmd (noun) "total"

dr (verb 2-lit.) "remove, repulse"

dḥj (verb 3-lit.) "become humiliated"

ds (noun) "flint, flint knife"

dgj (verb 3ae-inf.) "look" (*r* "at")

dgj (verb 3ae-inf.) "hide"

ḏt (noun) "body, self"

ḏt (noun) "estate"; *rmṯ-ḏt* "serfs" (literally, "people of the estate")

ḏt (noun) "eternal sameness, eternity, forever" (Essay 9)

ḏ3j (verb 3ae-inf.) "cross (the river), ferry"

ḏ3mw (noun) "recruits"

ḏ3rw (noun) "need"

ḏ3ḏ3 (noun) "head"

ḏ3ḏ3t (noun) "lyre"

ḏ^{c} (noun) "windstorm"

ḏ^{c}*m* (noun) "electrum"

ḏ^{c}*r* (verb 3-lit.) "probe, seek out"

ḏw (noun) "mountain"

, *ḏwj* (adjective-verb 3ae-inf.) "evil"

ḏwt (noun) "evil"

ḏb3/db3 (verb 3-lit.) "replace"

(noun) *ḏf3w* "food"

, *ḏr* (noun) "limit"; *r ḏr* "all, whole, entire" (§ 6.7)

ḏr (verb 2-lit.) "end up"

ḏr (preposition: § 8.2.17) "since"

ḏrt (noun) "hand"

ḏrt (noun) "calf"

ḏrḏr (noun) "stranger"

ḏḥwtj (noun) "Thoth" (god of wisdom, counting, and writing)

ḏs (noun) "self, own" (see § 8.14)

ḏsr (adjective-verb 3-lit.) "sacred, holy"

ḏsrt (noun) "sacred area"

ḏd (verb 2-lit.) "say, tell, speak"

ḏd-mdw "recitation" (§ 14.9)

ḏdwt "sayings"

ḏdj (adjective-verb 3ae-inf.) "stable, steady"

ḏdw (noun) "Busiris" (a town in the Delta: see map)

ḏdf (verb 3-lit.) "have goose-bumps (of skin), stand on end (of hair)"

Answers to the Exercises

Exercise 1.

1\. a. 

b. 

c. 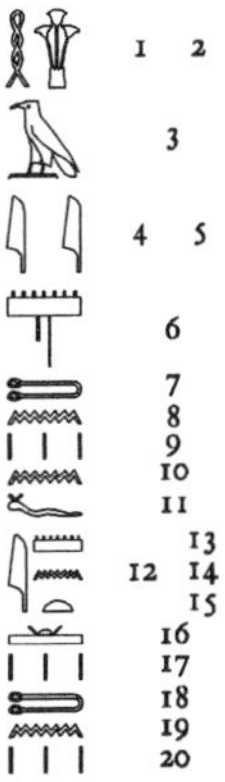

d. 

2\. a. 

b. 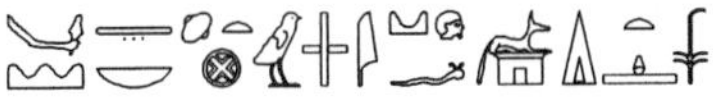

c. 

d. 

e. 

Exercise 2

1. a. EE-nek NES-oot JED-oo EE-rer-oo
   b. eer ger em khet peh, se-SEKH-em eeb poo en KHER-oo-ee
   c. KEN-et poo ahd, KHYEZ-et poo HEM-khet
   d. nee REM-ech ees net SHEF-et set, HOO-roo poo SEJ-oo EE-boo
   e. se-ROOD tahsh en WET-et soo
   f. en MER-oot ah-HAH-chen HER-ef
   g. er tem RED-ee zen soo NEH-see neb em khed em HER-et
2. (a) I-em-hetep (more commonly, Imhotep), (b) Mentju-weser, (c) Ni-maat-ra, (d) Kha-em-waset, (e) Qen-em khepesh, (f) Djehuti-em-hat
3. (a) *wsr-ḥ3t*, (b) *mrt-mwt*, (c) *jmn-m-ḥ3t*, (d) *jmn-ḥtp*, (e) *snḏm-jb*, (f) *ṯntj*

4. *3w, jʿj, jnm, jrj, jz, ʿ3, ʿb, w3ḫ, wj3, b3q, b3k, pn, fsj, fdt, mnmnt, mrj, nḥḥ, nḫ3, nḫt, nḫ, rw, rn, hrw, ḥd, ḫd, ẖzj, zḥ, sw, sqr, sk, sgr, šw, šft, q3j, k3, gr, t3, ṯ3, ṯzj, dpt, dšr, ḏd*

Exercise 3

1. *jmn*	13. *nbt*	25. *mry*	37. *msḏr*	49. *mw*	61. *ns*	73. *ḫws*
2. *ḥzt*	14. *snw*	26. *m3wj*	38. *ḏd*	50. *p3ḏ*	62. *mḥ*	74. *nḥḥ*
3. *tp*	15. *mjtt*	27. *msst*	39. *tjsw*	51. *jrt*	63. *jnm*	75. *wḏ*
4. *št3*	16. *wr*	28. *mtr*	40. *sk3*	52. *jb*	64. *ḫ3rt*	76. *ḫb3*
5. *qd*	17. *wnn*	29. *ḫnw*	41. *šsr*	53. *ḏ3t*	65. *ḏj* or *dj*	77. *pḥtj*
6. *šm*	18. *ʿq*	30. *nḫt*	42. *ḥz3*	54. *ḥ3y*	66. *sw3*	78. *jrrt* (see § 3.2)
7. *sw*	19. *ʿ3*	31. *sk*	43. *sḥḏ*	55. *jwr*	67. *pḏt*	
8. *ḫr*	20. *jw*	32. *st*	44. *sḫ3*	56. *ḥns*	68. *jrw*	
9. *ḫʿ*	21. *3b*	33. *šnw*	45. *nḥm*	57. *z3*	69. *ḥtm*	
10. *ḥr*	22. *mr*	34. *šd*	46. *snḏw*	58. *z3t*	70. *km*	
11. *ḥrt*	23. *s3ḫ*	35. *rdj*	47. *rwt*	59. *ḫf3w*	71. *šw*	
12. *snm*	24. *jnt*	36. *rdw*	48. *prt*	60. *jz*	72. *z3*	

Exercise 4

1. a. *z3w, z3wj*
   b. *ḥmwt, ḥmtj*
   c. *jtjw, jtjwj*
   d. *mwwt, mwtj*
   e. *mjww, mjwwj*
   f. *zḫ3ww, zḫ3wwj*
   g. *mnjww, mnjwwj*
   h. *nbwt, nbtj*
   i. *šmʿywt, šmʿytj*
   j. *swt, stj*
   k. *prw, prwj*
   l. *nwwt, nwtj*
   m. *ḥwwt-nṯr, ḥwtj-nṯr*
   n. *z3w-nswt, z3wj-nswt*
   o. *sḫtjw, sḫtjwj*
   p. *ḏrwt, ḏrtj*

2. a. *rdwj* "two feet"
   b. *ẖwt* "bellies"
   c. *msḏrwj* "two ears"
   d. *sprww* "petitioners"
   e. *ḫwt* "things"
   f. *jʿrtj* "two uraei"
   g. *msw* "children"
   h. *ʿwj* "two arms"
   i. *z3wt* "daughters"
   j. *msyt* "waterfowl" ("false" plural!)

3. a. *nbt pt* "mistress of the sky"
   b. *ḥwwt-nṯr* "temples" ("enclosures of the god")
   c. *st nt ʿnḫw* "place of the living"
   d. *rmw ḥnʿ 3pdw* "fish and birds"
   e. *pt t3* "sky and land," "sky or land"
   f. *rmw nw jtrw* "fish of the river"
   g. *sb3w pt* "stars of the sky"
   h. *z3-nswt* "king's son"
   i. *nswt nṯrw* "king of the gods"
   j. *nṯrw nṯrwt* "gods and goddesses"
   k. *nb t3wj* "Lord of the Two Lands"
   l. *r n kmt* "speech of Egypt" (Egyptian)
   m. *t mw* "bread and/or water"
   n. *ṯ3w ʿnḫ* "breath of life"

4. a. 
   b. 
   c. 
   d. 
   e. 
   f.  (*ḫt* is masculine!)

Exercise 5

1. a. *msw.j ḥnʿ snw.j* "my offspring and my siblings"
   b. *3ḥwt.sn* "their fields"
   c. *ḥmt.k pr.k* "your wife and your house"
   d. *ḥmt.f tn* "this his wife" or "that wife of his"
   e. *ḫnw n sḫtj pn* "the property of this peasant"
   f. *n3 n ʿ3* "these donkeys" or "those donkeys" — literally, "this of donkey"
   g. *nb n sp3t tn* "lord of this estate"
   h. *ḥmt sḫtj pn ḥnʿ ẖrdw.f* "the wife of this peasant and his children"
   i. *ḥknw pf* "that oil"
   j. *nhw n mšʿ.n* "the loss of our army"
   k. *st.f nt snḏm* "his place of residence"
   l. *nn n smrw* "these courtiers" or "those courtiers"
   m. *dpt tf* "that boat"
   n. *h3w dpt tn* "the vicinity of this boat"
   o. *pr.ṯn pn* "this house of yours (2pl)" or "that house of yours"
   p. *ḥr.ṯn* "your (2pl) face" — not *ḥr tn* "this face" because *ḥr* is masculine!
   q. *mwt.ṯ tn* "this your (2fs) mother"

r. *n3y.j n qnyt* "my braves"
s. *t3 qnbt nt ḥwt-nṯr* "that council of the temple" or "the council of the temple"
t. *nn n ḫwt* "these things" or "those things"

2. d.  *nn n ḥmwt.f* "these his wives" or "those wives of his"
m. 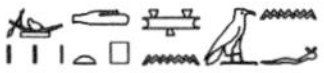 *nf3 n dpwt* "those boats"
o.  *nn n prw.ṯn* "these houses of yours" or "those houses of yours"
q.  *nn n mwwt.ṯn* "these your mothers"

3. f.  *ᶜ3 pn* "this donkey" or "that donkey"
l.  *smr pn* "this courtier" or "that courtier"
t. 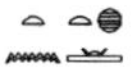 *ḫt tn* "this thing" or "that thing"

4. b.  *n3y.sn n 3ḥwt* or  *n3y.sn 3ḥwt* "their fields"
c.  *t3y.k ḥmt p3y.k pr* "your wife and your house"

Exercise 6

1. *sḫr nb n nb t3wj* "every plan of the lord of the Two Lands"
2. *jnw nb nfr n sḫt-ḥm3t* "every good product of the Wadi Natrun"
3. *ᶜt nbt nt pr-nswt* "every room of the king's house" — honorific transposition!
4. *nfrwt nbt nt ẖnw ᶜḥ.k* "all the beautiful women of the interior of your palace"
5. *3ḫt j3btt nt pt* "the eastern Akhet of the sky"
6. *pr.k pn nfr* "this your beautiful house"
7. *jqr sḫrw* "one who has excellent plans" — literally, "excellent of plans"
8. *nswt ᶜ3 pḥtj* "a king of great strength" — literally, "a king, one great of strength"
9. *ky.s mnd* "her other breast" — for *mnḏ* > *mnd*, see § 2.8.3
10. *nfr r ḫt nbt* "better than anything" — or, "better than all things"
11. *wr mnw r nswt nb* "one who has more monuments than any king" — literally, "greater of monuments than any king"
12. *nn n ḫwt r ḏr* "all these things" — literally, "these things to the limit"
13. *ṯnw zp* "each time"
14. *t3 ẖnyt r 3w.s* "this entire crew" — literally, "this crew to its length"
15. *jty nb.j* "the sovereign, my lord"
16. *kt pẖrt 3ḫt* "another effective prescription"
17. *rnpwt ᶜš3t* "many years" (see § 6.2)
18. *ᶜš3 mrwt* "one who has many serfs" — literally, "many of serfs" (see § 6.5)

Exercise 7 (predicate in boldface)

1. *wrwj nb* "**How great** is the lord."
2. *jnk pw* "It is **I**."
3. *z3 pw mnḫ* "He is **a beneficent son**."
4. *ptr sw* "**Who** is he?"
5. *ḫt.j pw* "It is **my property**."
6. *nfr pr.j, wsḫ st.j* "My house was **good**, my place was **broad**" — two sentences!
7. *rn n mwt.s ṯwj3* "The name of her mother is **Tjuia**."
8. *jnk z3.f* "I am his son" — either *jnk* or *z3.f* can be the predicate.
9. *jnk nswt ᶜ3 pḥtj* "I am **a king of great strength**" — either *jnk* or *nswt ᶜ3 pḥtj* can be the predicate, but the latter is more likely; *ᶜ3 pḥtj* is a *nfr ḥr* construction: § 6.5.
10. *ḥn pw* "It is **an attack**."
11. *wrwj n3 r sḫrw nṯrw* "**How (much) greater** is this than the plans of the gods" — for *wrwj*, see p. 79 n. 4.
12. *jnk wr wrw* "I am **the greatest of the great**" — either *jnk* or *wr wrw* can be the predicate, but the latter is more likely; for *wr wrw*, see § 6.8.
13. *qsnt pw* "It is **a difficult one**" (see § 7.15).
14. *dmj pw jmnt* "The West is **a harbor**" — either *dmj* or *jmnt* can be the predicate, but the sentence is more likely to say what the West is than what a harbor is.

15. *nfr sḏm n r(m)ṯ* "Listening is **good** for people."
16. *jnk šw ḥ3w* "I am **(one) free of excess**" — either *jnk* or *šw ḥ3w* can be the predicate, but the sentence probably says something about *jnk*, which is therefore the subject.
17. *mjk3 jb.sn r m3w* "Their heart(s) are **braver** than lions."
18. *w3w pw n w3ḏ-wr* "It is **a wave of the sea.**"
19. *ḥf3w pw* "It was **a snake.**"
20. *n(j)-sw mḥ 30* "He **belonged to 30 cubits**" — i.e., "He was 30 cubits long."
21. *ḫbzwt.f wr s(j) r mḥ 2* "His beard, it was **greater** than 2 cubits."
22. *ᶜrq sw* "He was **bent.**"
23. *nfr st r ḫwt nbt* "It is **better** than all things" (§ 7.4.2).
24. *bw pw wr n jw pn* "It is **the chief product of this island.**"
25. *ntf z3 wsjr* "**He** is the son of Osiris" (§ 7.12.1).
26. *jnk wᶜb ᶜ* "I am (one) clean of hand(s)" (see no. 16, above).
27. *pr.f pr jt(j).f* "His house is **his father's house**" (§ 7.12.2).
28. *nnk sw* "He belongs to **me**" or "He is **mine**" (§ 7.5.4).
29. *n(j)-s(j) ḏt.k* "She **belongs to (you) yourself.**"
30. *mrt rn.s* "Her name was **Meret.**"
31. *nfr mjtn.j* "My way is **good.**"
32. *jnk pw mdw* "**I** am the speaker" (§ 7.12.3).
33. *nḫwj m3jr* "**How pitiful** is the poor man."
34. *ntk rᶜ nb pt* "You are Re, lord of the sky" — either *ntk* or *rᶜ nb pt* can be the predicate, depending on the context.
35. *ntk ḥmw n t3 r ḏr.f* "You are the rudder of the entire land" — a metaphorical statement; either *ntk* or *ḥmw n t3 r ḏr.f* can be the predicate, depending on the context; for *r ḏr.f*, see § 6.7.
36. *ptr ḏ3rw.k* "**What** is your need?" — i.e., "What do you need?"
37. *nbw bw-nfr pw* "They are **lords of goodness.**"
38. *ḥmwt(j)w pw* "They are **craftsmen.**"
39. *wr s(j), ᶜ3 s(j), w3ḥ s(j)* "It is **great**, it is **big**, it is **lasting**" — three sentences!
40. *mḫ3t pw nt r(m)ṯ ns.sn* "The measure of people's worth is **their tongues**" — literally, "The scale of people is their tongues": either *mḫ3t nt rmṯ* or *ns.sn* can be the predicate, but the sentence clearly identifies what "the measure of people's worth" is and not what "their tongues" are.
41. *n(j) wj wnḏwt.k* "I **belong to your tenants**" — i.e., "I am one of your tenants."
42. *grḥ pw* "It is **the end.**"

Exercise 8

1. *nfr tw ḥnᶜ.j* "You are well with me."
2. *šmᶜw ḫr ḥ3t.k* "chanters in front of you" — literally, "under your front"
3. *ḥr w3t nt wᶜrt* "on the path of flight"
4. *pt ḥr.k* "the sky above you"
5. *mj sḫmt rnpt jdw* "like Sekhmet in a year of pestilence" (see § 8.14 end)
6. *ᶜḥᶜ jb pw m 3t s3s3* "He is steadfast of heart in the moment of headlong attack."
7. *m ḫt j3w n.k jmy* "after your own old age" — literally, "in the wake of the old age of yours"
8. *wršy tp(j) jnb jmj hrw.f* "the watchman on duty on the wall" — literally, "who is on the wall and in his day"
9. *pḫrt jrj* "the remedy for it"
10. *ḫr zḫ n jb.k* "with (literally, 'under') the advice of your heart"
11. *ḫr zḫ n wḥyw.f* "under the tent of his tribe"
12. *nfr n.f m hrw pn r sf* "It is better for him today than yesterday."
13. *m ḥtp nfr wrt* "in very good peace"
14. *wr n.f jrp r mw* "He has more wine than water" — literally, "Wine is great to him with respect to water."
15. *ntf pw m m3ᶜt* "It is he, in truth" — i.e., "It is really he."
16. *r bw ḫr(j) nṯr* "to the place where the god is" (§ 8.8)
17. *mj sḫr nṯr* "like the plan of a god"
18. *ḥq3 pw n rṯnw ḥrt* "He is the ruler of Upper Retjenu."
19. *m qdnw r rṯnw* "from Qatna to Retenu"
20. *ḥrw ḥrj tp ḫ3swt* "Horus, chief (literally, 'who is over the head') of foreign lands"
21. *ḥr st wrt m wmwt nt ḏᶜm* "on the great throne in a recess of electrum"
22. *m ḫpš.j m pḏt.j m sḫrw.j jqrw* "by my strong arm, by my bow, by my excellent plans"

23. *(j)m(j)-r sḫtjw mnḫ n pr-nswt* "an efficient overseer of peasants of the king's house"
24. *ḥm nb ẖrj jrjw.f* "every servant who is at (literally, 'under') his tasks" — literally, "those which pertain to him"
25. *nḥ pw n b3k jm n nb.f* "It is the prayer of your humble servant to his lord."
26. *m r n rʿ ḏs.f* "in (or 'from') the mouth of Re himself"
27. *jb.j ḏs.j* "my own heart"
28. *n.f ḏs.f* "for him himself"

Exercise 9

1.

b3kw n kš ẖzt m rnpt tn	Tribute of wretched Kush in this year:
nbw dbn 155 qdt 2	Gold, 155 deben and 2 qite (= 31.14 lb)
ḥmw ḥmwt 134	Male and female servants, 134
jw3w wnḏw 114	Oxen and short-horned cattle, 114
k3w jdr 305	Herd bulls, 305
dmd jḥw 419	Total cattle, 419

2. a. *ḥsbt 3 4 3ḫt 25 ẖr ḥm n (n)sw(t) bjt(j) SḪM-K3-Rʿ* "Year 3, 4 Inundation 25, during the incarnation of the King of Upper and Lower Egypt SEKHEM-KA-RE"
   b. *9nw zp* "the ninth time"
   c. *w3t.f wʿt ẖr mw kt ẖr jtj* "its one path under water, the other under grain"
   d. *wʿ m n3 n sḫtj* "one of these peasants"
   e. *ky nḥs(j) 6* "another 6 Nubians"
   f. *mḥ 1 šzp 3 m mw* "1 cubit 3 palms in water" (= 2.46 feet of water)
   g. *m ḥsbt 24 2 prt ʿrqy hrw-ḥ3b mḥ-10 n jmn m jpt-swt* "in Year 24, 2 Growing last day, the 10th festival-day of Amun in Karnak"
   h. *zp 3 zp 4 n hrw* "3 or 4 times a day" — literally, "3 times, 4 times for a day"
   i. *m mšʿ n z(j) 3000* "in an expeditionary force of 3,000 men"
   j. *jr hrw ḥwt-nṯr r-360 pw n rnpt* "As for a day of the temple, it is 1/360th of the year."
   k. *m wḏyt mḥt-13 nt nḫt* "in the 13th campaign of victory"
   l. *m ḥtp zp 2* "in peace, in peace"
   m. *ḥm-nṯr tp(j) n jmn* "first priest of Amun" (title of the High Priest of Amun)
   n. *jb.j m snw.j* "my heart as my second" — i.e., "my companion"

3. a.  or  *tpt* "first"
   b.  *mḥ-437* "437th"
   c.  *8nw* "8th"
   d.  *2nw* "second"
   e.  *mḥ-10* "10th"
   f.  *mḥ-60* "60th"
   g.  *6nw* "6th"
   h.  *mḥ-3009* "3,009th"

4. The two tables below show the transliteration of the account first and its translation second. In both, the right-to-left order of the example has been flipped to normal English left-to-right orientation. The fractions have been added together in the translation.

jdr-mnjw	*wpt nn (n)g(3)w*	*ḥr(j)-ḏbʿ*	*ḏrt*	*dmd*	*ḥtr*
2212 1/3 1/4					
156 1/3 1/15	41 1/4 1/45	41 1/4 1/45	41 1/4 1/45	123 2/3 1/10 1/20	32 1/2 1/12
36	9 1/2	9 1/2	9 1/2	28 1/2	7 1/2
20 2/3	5 1/3 1/12	5 1/3 1/12	5 1/2 1/36	16 1/4 1/9	5 1/3 1/18
360					
2785 1/2	56 1/6 1/45	56 1/6 1/45	56 1/5 1/10	168 2/3 1/90	45 1/3 1/12 1/18

tended herd	the splitting of these steer	hornless cattle	calf	total	team ox
2212 7/12					
156 6/15	41 49/180	41 49/180	41 49/180	123 49/60	32 7/12
36	9 1/2	9 1/2	9 1/2	28 1/2	7 1/2
20 2/3	5 5/12	5 5/12	5 19/36	16 13/36	5 7/18
360					
2785 1/2	56 17/90	56 17/90	56 3/10	168 61/90	45 17/36

The last row in each column is the sum of the column. Columns 2–4 break the amount in column 1 into 3 categories ("the splitting of these"). Column 5 totals the amounts in columns 2–4. Column 6 is the difference between columns 1 and 5. The fractions seem to be divisions of 360: this suggests that the amounts have to do with the 12-month apportionment of something related to a large herd of cattle (compare the sentence in 2j of this exercise).

Exercise 10

1. *jw jt(j).f m ḫnw ꜥḥ.f* "His father is inside his palace."
2. *nn m.f mm ꜥnḫw* "His name will not be among the living."
3. *jw ms jtrw m snf* "Indeed, the river is blood."
4. *nn wj m ḫr(j) jb.sn* "I was not in their midst."
5. *m.ṯ sw r wnmw* "Look (fem.), it is for food."
6. *sj m ḥr.f mj t3 pt* "It is in his face like the sky" (§ 10.5).
7. *m.k wj m nhw* "Look, I am in need."
8. *z3 sḏmw m šms(w) ḥrw* "An obedient son is a follower of Horus."
9. *jw ẖ3t.f m qm3 n mw* "His corpse is one that is thrown in the water."
10. *jw n.k ṯ3w nḏm n mḥyt* "You will have the sweet air of the northwind."
11. *jw jt(j).j m wꜥw* "My father was a soldier."
12. *jw.j m ḥzwt ḥm.f* "I am in His Incarnation's blessing."
13. *nn sw m st.f* "It is not in its place."
14. *mw jm, nn mw jm* "Is water there, or is water not there?"
15. *nn sḫ3.f ḫr tp(j)w-t3* "His memory will not be with those who are on earth."
16. *m.k nn s(j) m ꜥꜥft qsnt* "Look, it is not a difficult rate of payment."
17. *jw ḫnw m sgr* "The capital was in stillness."
18. *jw.f r j3w n nwt.f* "He is to be an old man of his town."
19. *m.k tw ꜥ3* "You are here" (§ 8.12).
20. *wj m nbw, tp m ḫsbd* "The coffin is of gold, the head is of lapis-lazuli."
21. *pt ḥr.k* (§ 8.2.10) "The sky is above you."
22. *šmꜥw ḫr ḥ3t.k* "Chanters are in front of you."
23. *jw mj ḫt ꜥ3* "It is like something big" — subject unexpressed (§ 10.9).
24. *jw ḥm.k m ḥrw* "Your Incarnation is Horus."
25. *n.k jm s(j)* "It is yours."
26. *mw m jtrw* "Water is in the river."
27. *z3.j smsw.j m s3 wḥyt.j* "My eldest son (literally, 'my son, my eldest': § 4.11) is in charge of my tribe."
28. *ḫwt.j nbt m ꜥ.f* "He has all my things" — "All my things are in his hand": § 10.7.
29. *wdpw nb ḥr jrt.f* "Every waiter was at his duty" — *jrt.f* "that which pertains to him."
30. *m.k wj m b3ḥ.k* "Here I am before you" — literally, "Behold, I am in your presence."
31. *jr p3 mw jw.f m mḥ 12* "As for that water, it was 12 cubits (deep)."
32. *jw.f m nḏs n mpt 110* "He is a commoner of 110 years (in age)."
33. *ṯn(j) sw* "Where is he?"
34. *m.k st ḫft ḥr.k* "Look, it is in front of your face."
35. *nn st m ḫnw.f* "It is not inside it."
36. *nn nhw n mšꜥ.n* "Our expedition has no loss(es)" — literally, "No loss is for our expeditionary force."
37. *jw n.k ꜥnḫ* "Life is yours."
38. *jw.j ḥr ḫt.j m b3ḥ.f* "I was on my belly in his presence."
39. *jw tr rmw n sbk r mj* "Why does Sobek have fish?" — literally, "Fish are for Sobek with respect to what?"
40. *m.k wj m 3hw* "Look, I am a needy person" — adjective as noun: note the determinative.
41. *nn n.k st* "It is not yours."
42. *jw.f n n3y.j n ẖrdw* "It is for my children" (§ 5.10.5).

Exercise 11

1. *nn wḫ3 m ḫr jb.sn* "There was no fool in their midst."
2. *nn sḫ3.f ḫr tpjw-t3* "His memory will not be with those on earth."
3. *nj jnk js q3 s3* "I am not an arrogant person" — literally, "I am not one high of back."
4. *nṯr pw grt nn 2nw.f* "Moreover, he is a god without equal" — or "who has no equal": literally, "his second not."
5. *nj mpt js n3 nt b3g* "This is not the year for (literally, 'of') being lazy" — a negated A *pw* B nominal sentence; *n3* is a demonstrative pronoun (§ 5.8); *b3g* is the infinitive (§ 14.3.1).

6. *nn ṯ3z n jwms mm* "There is no sentence of exaggeration among them."
7. *nn ḥr ẖr rmyt* "No face was in (literally, 'under') tears."
8. *nn st m ꜥ.f* "He does not have it" — literally, "It is not in his hand."
9. *nn 3ḫ n.k* "It is not effective for you."
10. *nn jww n nṯr r.j* "There are no complaints of a god against me."
11. *nj jw js pw jwsw gs3w* "Is not a balance that tilts an error?" — a negated A *pw* B sentence.
12. *nn sj mj nf3 n ꜥ3wt* "It is not like those lumps."
13. *mnjw pw n.bw-nb nn bjn m jb.f* "He is a shepherd for everyone, with no bad in his heart."
14. *jn jw ntt ḥmt jn jw ntt špst* "Are you (2fs) a servant, (or) are you a noblewoman?"
15. *nn tw ḥ3 ky mjtw.k* "You will not be behind another (who is) your equal."
16. *m.k tw m nwt nn ḥq3-ḥwt.s* "Look, you are a town without mayor" — a metaphor: literally, "you are in a town, its mayor not."
17. *nn msw.f nn jwꜥww.f tp t3* "He has no children, he has no heirs on earth."
18. *nj r(m)ṯ js nt šft st* "They are not a people (worthy) of respect" — a negated A *pw* nominal sentence, with *pw* omitted: literally, "(They) are not a people of respecting them."
19. *nn sf n wzfw* "There is no yesterday for the one who forgets" or "The one who forgets has no yesterday."
20. *jn jwsw pw* "Is it a balance?"
21. *nn ḫwt nbt ḏwt jm.s* "There aren't any evil things in it."
22. *nn swt qn grḥ* "But there is no brave man at night" — i.e., "no one is brave at night"; *qn* is used as a noun, hence its determinative.
23. *nn ḫnms n zḫ m3ꜥt* "The one who cannot heat Maat has no friend" or "There is no friend for the one who is deaf to Maat."
24. *nn sbḫt n nṯr r.f* "There is no barrier of a god against him."
25. *m ḫwt.f nw pr (j)t(j).f nj js m ḫwt pr ḥ3t(j)-ꜥ* "from his things of his father's house and not from the things of the high official's house."
26. *nn hrw nfr n ꜥwn-jb* "There is no holiday for the greedy man."
27. *nn ḥn nj js ḥr zp.f* "There is no hurrying except at (literally, 'on') its proper time" — i.e., there is no use hurrying until the proper time.
28. *jn jw.k m ꜥw3y* "Are you a robber?"
29. *jn jw.s m tjmḥjw* "Is it Libyans?"
30. *(j)n ntf pw m m3ꜥt* "Is it really he?" — literally, "Is it he in truth?" — *not* a negative sentence: see § 11.11.2.

Exercise 12

1. *sšmw pn ntj wj ẖr.f* "this situation that I was in (literally, 'under')"
2. *jw.j n qbw, rmw.j n šw* "I am in the cool breeze, while my fish are in the sunlight" (spoken by a fisherman).
3. *ḏr ntt wr s(j) ꜥ3 s(j)* "since it is great and it is big"
4. *jt.n.j ntt m jm3m.f* "I took what was in his tent."
5. *jw pn n w3ḏ-wr ntj gs(wj).fj m nwy* "this island of the Great Blue-Green, whose two sides are in the waters"
6. *mdw.k n nswt, jb.k m ꜥ.k* "You shall speak to the king with your heart with you" — literally, "in your hand."
7. *wjn.sn tp t3, nn tw jm.f* "They don't want to be on earth without you in it."
8. *jr.n.(j) nn mj qd, jsṯ w(j) m jmj-jb nbt.f* "I did all this while I was a confidant of his lady."
9. *rḫ.n.(j) qd.k, tj wj m zšj* "I learned of your character while I was (still) a nestling."
10. *mj dpt nn sḫry jm.s* "like a boat with no pilot in it" — literally, "a pilot not in it."
11. *srjw ntj r gs.f* "the officials who were at his side"
12. *snf(3).n.j ntt m ẖt.j* "I have vented what was in my belly" — said by someone complaining of an injustice.
13. *jnk jmj-jb n (j)t(j.j) rꜥ nb ntt jwtt* "I am a confidant of my father Re, lord of what is and what is not."
14. *nfr st ḥr jb.f r ḫt nbt ntt m t3 pn r ḏr.f* "It was better on (i.e., 'in') his heart than anything that is in this entire land."
15. *sj3.n.j ntjw m ẖnw.s* "I recognized those who were inside it."
16. *ḥr ntt jnk z3 wꜥb mj wꜥ jm.ṯn nb* "because I am a priest's son like every one of you" (see § 9.4).
17. *jw jr.n.(j) ꜥḥꜥw ꜥ3 m rnpwt ẖr ḥnwt.(j), jsṯ s(j) m z3t nswt* "I spent a lifetime of many years (literally, 'great in years') near my mistress, while she was a princess."
18. *m.tn jwtj ḥtrj.f m nb j3drw* "Look (§ 10.4.1), he who had no plow-team is (now) an owner of herds."
19. *t3 pw nfr, j33 rn.f* "It was a good land (see § 7.9), whose name was Iaa."
20. *z(j) stwt m nḥbt.f* "a man with boils on his neck"
21. *ḏd.k n h3b ṯw 3ḫ js r.j r ds.f* "You shall say to the one who sent you that my mouth is effective against his knife."
22. *mr.ṯ sw, z3.k js pw* "You should love him, for he is your son."

23. *m.k tw m wdpw rš.f pw rḫs* "Look, you are a waiter whose joy is butchering."
24. *m.tn jwtj pꜥt.f m nb mḫr* "Look, he who had no loaf of bread is (now) the owner of a food-storehouse."
25. *jw wp.n.f r.f r.j, jw.j ẖr ẖt.j m b3ḥ.f* "He opened his mouth to me, while I was on my belly in his presence."
26. *jr.n.j hrw 3 wꜥ.kw, jb.j m snw.j* "I spent 3 days alone, with my heart my (only) companion."
27. *3m.nj, nn wj m ḥr(j) jb.sn* "They burnt up while I was not in their midst."
28. *z3 z(j) pw, jsry m.f* "He was the son of a man whose name was Isry."
29. *ẖnt(j).f ntj m rd ẖr(j) n jz.f* "his statue that is on (literally, 'in') the lower (§ 8.6.11) stairway of his tomb"
30. *rḫ m jb.ṯn nb.ṯn js pw nṯr pn jm(j) swḥt.f* "Know in your heart(s) that this god who is in his egg is your lord" — an A *pw* B nominal sentence as a noun clause.
31. *n ntj nb ḥr wḏ pn* "for everyone who is on this stela"
32. *jšst pw ntj jm* "What is the one who is there?" — for *jšst* see §§ 5.11, 7.13.3.
33. *šndyt nt jwt(j) mwt.f* "the kilt of the motherless" — literally, "of the one who his mother is not"
34. *p3 ꜥb mḥtj r mḥtj-jmntj mjktj, jw ḥm.f m ḥr(j) jb.sn* "The northern flank was at the northwest of Megiddo, and His Incarnation was in their midst."
35. *nn ntt nn st m ḫnw.f* "There was nothing that was not inside it" — i.e., everything was inside it: a *nn* A sentence (§ 11.4) in which A is the relative clause *ntt nn st m ḫnw.f* "that which was not inside it" (§ 12.8).

Exercise 13

1. *3ḫ* 2-lit., intrans.
2. *jp* 2-lit., trans.
3. *jnj* 3ae-inf., trans.
4. *jrj* 3ae-inf., trans.
5. *jṯj* 3ae-inf., trans.
6. *ꜥnḫ* 3-lit., intrans.
7. *ꜥḥ3* 3-lit., trans.
8. *ꜥḥꜥ* 3-lit., intrans.
9. *w3ḥ* 3-lit., trans.
10. *wꜥb* 3-lit., intrans.
11. *wnn* 2ae-gem., intrans.
12. *wḥm* 3-lit., trans.
13. *wdfj* 4ae-inf., intrans.
14. *wḏ* 2-lit., trans.
15. *b3gj* 4ae-inf., intrans.
16. *prj* 3ae-inf., intrans.
17. *pḫrr* 3ae-gem., intrans.
18. *psḏj* 4ae-inf., intrans.
19. *ptpt* 4-lit., trans.
20. *f3j* 3ae-inf., trans.
21. *m33* 2ae-gem., trans.
22. *mwt* 3-lit., intrans.
23. *mrj* 3ae-inf., trans.
24. *msḏj* 4ae-inf., trans.
25. *mdwj* 4ae-inf., intrans.
26. *njtjt* 5-lit., intrans.
27. *nḥm* 3-lit., trans.
28. *rwj* 3ae-inf., intrans.
29. *h3j* 3ae-inf., intrans.
30. *h3b* 3-lit., trans.
31. *ḥjḥj* 4-lit., trans.
32. *ḥwj* 3ae-inf., trans.
33. *ḥmsj* 4ae-inf., intrans.
34. *ḥqr* 3-lit., intrans.
35. *ḥtp* 3-lit., intrans.
36. *ḫꜥj* 3ae-inf., intrans.
37. *ḫpr* 3-lit., intrans.
38. *ḫntj* 4ae-inf., intrans.
39. *ḫr* 2-lit., intrans.
40. *ḫdj* 3ae-inf., intrans.
41. *s3ḫ* caus. 2-lit., trans.
42. *sꜥnḫ* caus. 3-lit., trans.
43. *sꜥḥꜥ* caus. 3-lit., trans.
44. *sꜥq* caus. 2-lit., trans.
45. *spdḏ* 4-lit., trans.
46. *sfḫḫ* caus. 2ae-gem., trans.
47. *smn* caus. 2-lit., trans.
48. *smnḫ* caus. 3-lit., trans.
49. *sn* 2-lit., trans.
50. *snḏ* 3-lit., intrans.
51. *snḏm* caus. 3-lit., trans.
52. *srwj* caus. 3ae-inf. trans.
53. *sh3j* caus. 3ae-inf. trans.
54. *sḫpr* caus. 3-lit., trans.
55. *sḫm* 3-lit., intrans.
56. *sḫr* caus. 2-lit., trans.
57. *sšmj* caus. 3ae-inf. trans.
58. *stj* 3ae-inf., trans.
59. *sḏr* 3-lit., intrans.
60. *šmj* 3ae-inf., intrans.
61. *šmsj* 4ae-inf., trans.
62. *šzp* 3-lit., trans.
63. *šdj* 3ae-inf., trans.
64. *qm3* 3-lit., trans.
65. *qd* 2-lit., trans.
66. *qdd* 2ae-gem., intrans.
67. *gmj* 3ae-inf., trans.
68. *gmgm* 4-lit., trans.
69. *gr* 2-lit., intrans.
70. *tmm* 2ae-gem., trans.
71. *ṯzj* 3ae-inf., trans.
72. *dr* 2-lit., trans.
73. *ḏ3j* 3ae-inf., trans.
74. *ḏd* 2-lit., trans.

Exercise 14

1. *jj.n.j ḥr šms.f* "I returned following him" — 4ae-inf. *šms(j)*.
2. *tm jṯ ḥ3tj n z(j) m ꜥ.f m jmnt* "Not taking the heart of a man from him in the West" — 2-lit. *tm*; 3ae-inf. *jṯ* is the negatival complement.
3. *nfꜥ.n.j wj m nftft r ḥ(j)ḥ(j) n.j st dg* "I took myself off, leaping, in order to seek for myself a place of hiding" — 4-lit. *ḥjḥj*; 5-lit. *nftft* and 3ae-inf. *dg* are verbal nouns: see §§ 14.3.1 and 14.11.2.
4. *nj k3.(j) spr r ḫnw pn* "I did not plan to arrive at this capital city" — 3-lit. *spr*.
5. *rdjt.j w3t n rdy.j m ḫd* "I gave a path to my feet northwards" — anom. *rdjt*; 3ae-inf. *ḫd* is a verbal noun (see § 14.11.2); *rdy.j* is a variant form of the dual *rdwj.j*.
6. *m33.f wj ḥr jrt wpwt.k* "He sees me doing your assignment" — 3ae-inf. *jrt*.
7. *jwt pw jr.n.f n.j* "What he did was to come to me" — anom. *jwt*.
8. *ḫmt.n.f ḥwtf.j* "He thought to plunder me" — 4-lit. *ḥwtf*.

9. *sḫ3.n.k hrw n qrs* "You have remembered the day of burial" — 3-lit. *qrs*.
10. *jw mj ḫt* ˤ*3 wḥm st* "It is like something big to repeat it" — i.e., "Repeating it is something major"; 3-lit. *wḥm*.
11. *wšb.k nn njtjt* "You should answer without stammering" — 5-lit. *njtjt*.
12. *swrd pw ḏd n.k* "Speaking to you is tiring" — an A *pw* B nominal sentence with caus. 3-lit. *swrd* and 2-lit. *ḏd*.
13. *n*ˤ*t pw jr.n.n m ḫd r ḫnw n jtj* "What we did was to sail northward to the capital of the sovereign" — 3ae-inf. *n*ˤ*t*.
14. *wrš.n.s jm ḥr swrj* "She spent the day there drinking" — 3-lit. *swj*, originally *swr*.
15. *m.k wj jj.kw r ḥmst jm.s* "Look, I have come in order to sit in it" — 4ae-inf. *ḥmst*.
16. *h3t pw jr.n p3 msḥ* "What that crocodile did was to go down" — 3ae-inf. *h3t*.
17. *jw.f rḫ ṯ3z tp ḥsq* "He knows how to tie on a severed head" — 3-lit. *ṯ3z*.
18. *ḥmw ḫr tp.f ḥr* ˤ*m*ˤ*m n.f* "A servant was at (literally, 'under') his head, giving him a masssage" — 4-lit. ˤ*m*ˤ*m*.
19. *jj.n.j* ˤ*3 r njs r.k m wpwt nt jt(j).j* "I have come here to summon (literally, 'call to') you on an assignment of my father" — 3-lit. *njs*.
20. *wḏ3 pw jr.n.f ḥn*ˤ*.f r mryt ḥr rdjt n.f* ˤ*.f* "What he did was to proceed with him to the riverbank, giving him his arm" — 3-lit. *wḏ3*, anom. *rdjt*.
21. ˤ*ḥ*ˤ*.n sḏm.n.s ḫrw ḥzj šm*ˤ *ḫbt w3g* "Then she heard the sound of singing, chanting, dancing, and festival-making" — 3ae-inf. *ḥzj* (see § 14.3.2a), 3-lit. *šm*ˤ, 3ae-inf. *ḫbt*, 4ae-inf. *w3g*.
22. *jwt pw jr.n r*ˤ*-wsr m jj m š3* "What Re-weser did was to come, returning from the field" — anom. *jwt*; anom. *jj* is a verbal noun (see § 14.11.2).
23. *š3s pw jr.n t3 wb3yt r jnt n.s jkn n mw* "What that maid did was to go off to get herself a scoop of water" — 3-lit. *š3s*, 3ae-inf. *jnt*.
24. *š3s pw jry r ḏd st n r(w)d-ḏdt jn p3y.s sn* "What was done was the coming to tell it to Rud-djedet by her brother" — 3-lit. *š3s*, 2-lit. *ḏd*.
25. *tm m(w)t ky zp m ḫr(j)-nṯr jn b3* "Not dying another time in the necropolis by a ba" — 2-lit. *tm*; 3-lit. *m(w)t* is the negatival complement.
26. *wḏ.tw n.f db3 st* "Let him be commanded to replace it" — 3-lit. *db3*.
27. *tm ḏ3 z(j) r j3bt* "A man's not crossing to the East" — 2-lit. *tm*; 3ae-inf. *ḏ3* is the negatival complement.
28. *mrr.k m3n.j* "You wish to see me" — 2ae-gem. *m3n* (see § 14.3.2c).
29. *ṯ3w pw n fnd jrt m3*ˤ*t* "Doing Maat is air for the nose" — an A *pw* B nominal sentence with 3ae-inf. *jrt m3*ˤ*t* as B.
30. *ṯ3w pw n m3jr ḫwt.f, dbb fnd.f pw nḥm st* "The air of a needy man is his things: to take them away is to stop up his nose" — two A *pw* B nominal sentences; in the second, 2ae-gem. *dbb fnd.f* is A and 3-lit. *nḥm st* is B.

Exercise 15

1. *ḫtw ḥr gmgm t3 ḥr mnmn* "Trees were cracking, the earth was quaking."
2. *tw r ḥ(j)ḥj mw n* ˤ*ḥ*ˤ*w* "One will have to look for water for the masted boats."
3. *jw.tw r jrt* ˤ*ḥ3w m ḥmt* "Weapons of bronze are to be made" — literally, "one is to make."
4. *jw* ˤ*3mw r ḫr n š*ˤ*t.f, tjmḥ(j)w r ḫr n nswt.f, jw* ˤ*r*ˤ*t jmt ḫnt.f ḥr shrt n.f ḫ3kw-jb* "The Asiatics are to fall to his slaughter and the Libyans are to fall to his flame. The uraeus on his brow will be pacifying the estranged for him" — the second sentence is an adverb clause; the future tense of the third sentence is indicated by the context.
5. *m.k ḥm* ˤ*3.k ḥr wn(m) jtj.j, m.k sw r hbt ḥr qn.f* "And look, your donkey is eating my grain. Look, he has to plow (i.e., be yoked to a plow) because of his audacity."
6. *sr(j)w ḥr jrt jyt* "The officials are doing wrong."
7. *jn jw mḫ3t ḥr rdjt ḥr gs* "Is the scale leaning to the side?"
8. *jn jw.k swt r gmt ky sḫtj mjtw.j* "But are you to find another peasant like me?" — literally, "… the likeness of me," in apposition to *sḫtj*.
9. *m.k wj ḥr spr n.k* "Look, I am petitioning to you."
10. *wn.jn.tw ḥr ḥ3q ḥwt-w*ˤ*rt, wn.jn.j ḥr jnt ḥ3qt jm z(j) 1 zt-ḥmt 3 dmḏ r tp 4, wn.jn ḥm.f ḥr rdjt st n.j r ḥmw* "Then Avaris was being plundered. Then I was getting plunder there: 1 man and 3 women, totalling to 4 head. Then His Incarnation was giving them to me for servants" — the word-order of *ḥr rdjt st n.j* is an exception to the rule discussed in § 14.6: here the dependent pronoun *st* is treated like a suffix pronoun and so comes before the dative *n.j*.
11. *rḫ ḥr tjw, wḫ3 ḥr m-bj3* "The wise man is saying 'Yes' and the foolish man is saying 'No.'"
12. *jn zḫ3w* ˤ*ryt z3-nḫt* ˤ*ḥ3-nḫt jrr nn n ḫntjw jw.f ḥr jwt r jnt šs ḥn*ˤ *(j)m(j)-r š(j) sbk-m-ḥ3t* "It is scribe of the gate Nakht's son Aha-nakht who makes these pictures as he is coming to get alabaster with quarry-overseer Sebek-em-hat."
13. *smj z3 tp(j) n wnwt ḥwt-nṯr tn ntj m* ˤ*ḥ*ˤ *m 3bd* "Report of the first phyle of the hourly staff of this temple, which is going on duty in the month."
14. *jw.f ḥr* ˤ*ḥ3 ḏr rk ḥrw* "He has been fighting since the time of Horus."
15. ˤ*ḥ*ˤ*.n ḥrw ḥr dgt r š3 pf km* "Then Horus was looking at that black pig."

Exercise 16

1. *m3 wj r.tn ntrw, my m šms.j, jmj n.j j3(jw)* "See me, gods! Come, following me (§ 14.11.2)! Give me praise!"
2. *šm swt, h3 n.j n3 n jtj ntj m p3 mhr* "But go, measure for me the (§§ 5.9, 5.10.3) barley that is in the (§ 5.10.3) storehouse."
3. *m q3 hrw.k shtj* "Don't raise your voice, peasant!" — literally, "Don't let your voice get high."
4. *shtm grgw, shpr m3ˁt, jmj bw-dw r t3* "Annihilate lying, bring about Maat, put evil down" — literally, "to the ground."
5. *m dd grgw* "Don't tell lies."
6. *m sbn, jr r.k hmw, šd hr nfryt* "Don't go off course! Work (literally, 'do') the rudder, pull on the tiller-rope!"
7. *sdm r.k n.j, m.k nfr sdm n r(m)t, šms hrw nfr, smh mh* "So listen to me. Look, listening is good for people. Follow a holiday, forget worrying" — *mh* is an infinitive.
8. *jmj t3w n ntj m jtmw* "Give air to the one who is suffocating" — literally, "who is in suffocation."
9. *m sfn hr zp, ndr n.k hsf(w).k* "Don't be mild about a matter: seize for yourself your opponent!"
10. *sw3h mnw.k m mrwt.k* "Make your monuments endure through love of you."
11. *sjqr hwt.k nt jmnt smnh st.k nt hr(j)-ntr m ˁq3 m jrt m3ˁt* "Make excellent your enclosure of the West and make functional your place of the necropolis by being straight and by doing Maat" — *ˁq3* and *jrt* are infinitives.
12. *j.zj jn n.j qnbt nt hnw* "Go, get me the council of the capital."
13. *mj mj nfrtj hnms.j* "Come now, Neferti, my friend."
14. *jr grt hnw nb n jnp(w) nt(j) m ˁ.k dj mj n.f sw* "Now, as for any property of Anubis that you have (§ 10.7), please give it to him."
15. *h3 wsjr m-n.k jrt hrw, htm hr.k jm.s* "Oh, Osiris! Take to you the Eye of Horus: equip your face with it."
16. *m ˁwn jb.k hr pzšt* "Don't let your heart be greedy about a division."
17. *m wd tp nj js r sšmw* "Don't give orders except (§ 11.7) according to procedure."
18. *m wšb nfrt m bjnt, m rdj kt m st kt* "Don't answer what is good by what is bad: don't put one in place of the other."
19. *m snd m snd nds* "Don't be afraid, don't be afraid, little one!"
20. *swrj, m jr ndb, nn jw.j r w3h.t* "Drink, don't sip! I'm not going to stop you!" (see §§ 16.4, 15.8).
21. *dgy n.tn n m ht* "Look for yourselves to the future."
22. *jsw šwt pw 3htt qbt m šmw* "Behold, he is an Inundation-season shade (literally, 'he is a shade, an Inundation-season one'), a cool place in Harvest-season."
23. *jst r.f pr nmtj-nht pn hr zm3 t3* "Now, the house of this Nemti-nakht was at the landing."
24. *nfr pw smnh ˁ3 wpw hr p3 jtj* "There is nothing at all usable here (§ 8.12) except that barley."
25. *jw ms t3 hr msnh mj jrt nhp, ˁw3y m nb ˁhˁw* "Surely, the land is spinning around like the action (literally, 'doing': infinitive) of a potter's wheel: the robber is an owner (§ 6.9) of heaps of riches."
26. *jw.j hm r jrt hnt.j* "And I am to do my rowing excursion."
27. *wn.jn hm.f hr sq(r) jwnt(j) pf m hr(j) jb mšˁ.f, jst wj m tp(j) n mšˁ.n* "Then His Incarnation was flattening that desert Nubian in the middle of his (the Nubian's: note the determinative) army, while I was the headman of our army."
28. *jnk pw, jnk w3dyt, jnk wnnt nbt t3wj* "It is I: I am Wadjyet; I am indeed the mistress of the Two Lands."
29. *jr(j)w hmww hr h3(t) r t3, sšmww hr md(w)t n m3ˁt, jw hm st.j m hnw ˁh* "Those at the rudders are heading toward land, the pilots are talking to Maat (Essay 10), and my place is inside the cabin."
30. *j hrw m(j) r.k r ddw* "Oh, Horus, come to Busiris!"
31. *j.nd hr.k wsjr, tz tw, shm jr.k* "Hail to you, Osiris! Lift yourself, take control!"
32. *j.nd hr.t jmnt nfrt, m(j) m šmsw wsjr* "Hail to you, beautiful West! Come in the following of Osiris!"
33. *j.nd hr.tn nbw (n)hh gr(g)w dt, m jtw jb.j m ˁ.j* "Hail to you, lords of eternal repetition, founders of eternal sameness! Don't take my heart from me."
34. *sdm pˁt hnmmt rhwt hr-nb šmsw (n)swt r nmtwt.f, jmj b3w.f n kt-hj, wˁb hr rn.f, twrj hr ˁnh(w).f, m.tn ntr pw m t3, jmj n.f j3(j)w mj rˁ, dw3 sw mj jˁh* "Listen, elite, humanity, subjects, and all people who follow the king in his footsteps! Give his impressiveness to others. Be pure about his name, be respectful about his life. Look, he is a god in the land. Give him praise like the Sun, worship him like the Moon."

Exercise 17

1. *jzwt.tn jj.t(j) ˁd.t(j), nn nhw n mšˁ.n* "Our crew has returned intact, without the loss of our expeditionary force" — the spelling *jzwt.tn* is for *jzwt.n*: see Essay 17.
2. *m.k r.f n jj.n(w) m htp* "So (§ 16.7.2) look, we have returned in peace" — for the 1pl stative ending see § 17.2.
3. *jb.kw w3w pw n w3d-wr* "I thought it was a wave of the sea" — the clause *w3w pw n w3d-wr* is an A *pw* sentence used as an unmarked noun clause, object of *jb.kw* (§ 12.14).
4. *ˁhˁ.n.(j) jn.kw r jw pn jn w3w n w3d-wr* "Then I was brought to this island by a wave of the sea."

5. *ꜥḥꜥ.n.(j) ꜥq.kw ḥr jtj* "Then I entered before the sovereign."
6. *jst r.f zb.n ḥm.f mšꜥ r tꜣ tjmḥjw, zꜣ.f smsw m ḥrj jrj, tj sw hꜣb.(w) r ḥ(w)t ḫꜣswt* "Meanwhile, His Incarnation had sent an expedition to the land of the Libyans, his eldest son as the one over it, he having been sent to smite foreign lands" — for *jst r.f* see § 16.7.2; *ḥrj* is a nisbe and *jrj* is a prepositional adverb (literally, "the one above thereto": §§ 8.6, 8.15); *tj* introduces a marked adverb clause (§ 16.6.16).
7. *ḫn.kw r jw n km-wr* "I landed at an island of the Great Black."
8. *ḏd.k(w) r.j n.f* "So I spoke to him."
9. *ḫr ḥm kmt nfr.t(j) n ntt.s rḫ.t(j) rd.f* "And then Egypt must be happy, because it knows he flourishes" — for *ḫr ḥm* see §§ 16.6.13 and 16.7.8: the sense of inevitability conveyed by *ḫr* is the reason for the translation "must be happy" instead of "is happy" (though the latter is also acceptable); for *n ntt.s* see § 12.13.2.
10. *jwt pw jr.n.f n.j ꜥḥꜥ.kw* "What he did was to come to me as I waited."
11. *ḥꜣtj nb mꜣḫ.(w) n.j, ḥmwt ṯꜣyw ḥr ꜥ(j)ꜥj, jb nb mr.(w) n.j* "Every chest smoldered for me, women and men were wailing, and every heart was sick for me."
12. *jw.j mj z(j) jtw m ꜥḫḫw, bꜣ.j zj.w, ḥꜥw.j ꜣd.w* "I was like a man overtaken by nightfall, my ba gone, my body listless."
13. *m.t zꜣ-nht jw.(w) m ꜥꜣm(w)* "Look, Sinuhe has come back as an Asiatic."
14. *sd.kw m pꜣqt, gs.kw m tpt, sḏr.kw ḥr ḥnkyt* "I was dressed in fine linen, I was anointed with first-class oil, I slept on a bed."
15. *jw.j grt rḫ.kw nb n spꜣt tn* "Moreover, I know the owner of this estate."
16. *jw.k swt sꜣ.t(j) m t.k tḫ.t(j) m ḥ(n)qt.k* "But you are sated on your bread and drunk on your beer."
17. *m ḏd grg, jw.k wr.t(j)* "Don't tell a lie when you have become great."
18. *ḥr.t(j) r jrt jyt* "Keep away from doing wrong" — literally, "Be far from doing wrong."
19. *wn.jn sḫtj pn snḏ.(w)* "Then this peasant became afraid" or "Then this peasant was afraid."
20. *ꜥḥꜥ.n nḫꜣw n mfꜣkt mꜣt ḫr.(w) ḥr mw* "Then a fish-pendant of new turquoise fell in the water."
21. *gm.n.f pꜣ nḫꜣw wꜣḥ.(w) ḥr pꜣqyt* "He found that fish-pendant set on a sherd."
22. *gm.n.f sw sḏr.(w) ḥr tmꜣm* "He found him lying on a mat" — *tmꜣm* is a spelling of *tmꜣ*: the final *m* is meant to show the loss of the original final *ꜣ* (see Essay 17).
23. *ḥmt wꜥb pw n rꜥ nb sꜣḫbw, jwr.tj m ḫrdw 3* "She is the wife of a laypriest of Re, lord of Sakhbu, who is pregnant with 3 boys."
24. *m.k n rḫ.wjn smsj* "Look, we know midwifery" — literally, "we know causing to give birth."
25. *jn jw pꜣ pr sspd.(w)* "Is that house prepared?"
26. *ꜥḥꜥ.n.s šm.tj r jkn n.s nhj n mw* "Then she went to scoop up for herself a little water" — for *nhj* see § 6.7.
27. *m.tn šwꜣww nw tꜣ ḫpr.(w) m ḫwdw* "Look, the outcasts of the land have become rich men" — literally, "have evolved into rich ones"; the position of the seated man determinative after the plural strokes is unusual.
28. *tw.j ḏꜣ.kw n.sn r wšd st* "I crossed over to them in order to address it."
29. *nn ntj ꜥḥꜥ.(w) n.k ḥr tꜣ kmt* "There is no one expecting you in this part of Egypt" — literally, "there is not (one) who stands (still) for you."
30. *ḥmwt ṯꜣww jw.w r mꜣ n.j* "Women and men came to look at me."
31. *jw nꜣ wr.(w) r.j m mjn* "This has become (too) great for me today."
32. *m.k mdwt.sn mn.(w) m zḫꜣw* "Look, their words are fixed in writing."
33. *wr wr wrw.f wr.(w)* "Great is a great one whose great ones are great" — *wr wr* is an adjectival sentence, with the first *wr* as adjectival predicate and the second *wr* (written differently) an adjective used as nominal subject; *wrw.f wr.(w)* is a SUBJECT–stative sentence used as an unmarked relative clause, with *wrw.f* "his great ones" as subject and *wr.(w)* as predicate (literally, "his great ones have become great"). This sentence is a good example of the kind of wordplay the Egyptians enjoyed. It means "A king whose high officials are great is truly great himself." If you succeeded in figuring it out, congratulations! If not, don't be discouraged: it took Egyptologists themselves some time to understand in the first place.
34. *jj.tj n.j, ḥꜥ.tj n mꜣ nfr(w).j, zꜣ.j nḏtj.j MN-ḪPR-Rꜥ ꜥnḫ.(w) ḏt* "Welcome to me! Be aroused at seeing my beauty, my son and my savior, MEN-KHEPER-RE, alive forever!"
35. *dj.n.j t n ntj ḥqr.(w) ḥbsw n ntj ḥꜣ.w ṯbwwt n jwtj sw* "I have given bread to the one who was hungry, clothes to the one who was naked, and sandals to the one who had none."

Exercise 18

1. *nb.j jw gm.n.j wꜥ m nn n sḫtj nfr mdw n wn mꜣꜥ* "My lord, I have found one of those peasants who is truly beautiful of speech" — *wꜥ m* § 9.4; *nn n* § 5.9.

2. *m.k h3b.n.j ḥr ḥn.k n (j)m(j)-r pr ḥtw* "Look, I have sent (word) commending you to the steward Hetu" — *ḥr ḥn.k* is an infinitival construction: § 14.11.1.
3. *rdj.n.f wj m ḥrj jm(w) jzwt, jsṯ grt rḫ.n.f wj m sr(j) mnḫ n ḥwt-nṯr.f* "He put me as the chief of a boat and crew, for he also knew me as an efficient official of his temple" — *ḥrj* is a nisbe: literally, "one over."
4. *m.k grt ḏd.n n.j z3-rn.f-snb z3-nb jw rdj.n.j n.f jtj-mḥ(j) ḥq(3)t 2 btj ḥq(3)t ¼ 5* "Moreover look, Renef-seneb's son Za-neb said to me: 'I have given him 20 heqat of northern barley and 30 heqat of emmer.' "
5. *jw 3b.n jb.j m33 zḫ3w p3(w)t tpt* "My heart has desired to see the writings of the first original time" — *m33* is the infinitive: § 14.12.
6. *ḏd.n.f nn, rḫ.n.f qd(w).j, sḏm.n.f šs3.j, mt(r).n wj r(m)ṯ kmt ntjw jm ḥnᶜ.f* "He said this because he had learned of my character and had heard of my wisdom, people of Egypt who were there with him having testified about me" — note the logical sequence of events: first "people testified," then "he learned ... and ... heard," and then "he said."
7. *ᶜḥᶜ.n ḏd.n.f n.j pḥ.n.k nn ḥr mj* "Then he said to me: 'Why have you reached this situation?' " — *ḥr mj* literally, "on account of what?"
8. *ᶜḥᶜ.n mḥ.n wᶜ m n3 n ᶜ3 r.f m b3t nt šmᶜ(j)* "Then one of those donkeys filled his mouth with a sprig of southern barley."
9. *ᶜḥᶜ.n ṯ3.n.f j33t nt jsr w3ḏ r.f, ᶜḥᶜ.n ᶜ3g.n.f ḥr ᶜt.f nbt jm.s* "Then he took a branch of green tamarisk-wood to him; then he pounded on each of his limbs with it" — *ᶜt.f nbt* literally, "his every limb."
10. *jw jb.f gp.(w) mj z(j) wnm.n.f k3w nw nht* "His mind is clouded, like a man who has eaten fruits of the sycamore."
11. *jnk ḫnn nj wrd.n.f m wj3 n rᶜ* "I am a rower who does not tire in the bark of Re."
12. *jst grt ḫᶜ.n ḥm.f m (n)swt m ḥwn nfr, jp.n.f ḏt.f, km.n.f mpt 18 ... nj pḥ.n.tw.f m sḫs* "Now, when His Incarnation appeared as king, as a fine youth, having collected himself and completed 18 years (of age) ... he could not be caught when running."
13. *ᶜḥᶜ.n dpt tf jj.t(j) ... ᶜḥᶜ.n.j šm.kw, rdj.n.(j) wj ḥr ḫt q3, sj3.n.j ntjw m ḫnw.s* "Then that ship came .... Then I went and put myself on a high tree, and recognized those who were inside it."
14. *gm.n sw wpwtjw ḥr w3t, pḥ.n.sn sw r tr n ḫ3wj* "The messengers found him on the road; they reached him at the time of dusk."
15. *rdj.n.j w3t n rdwj.j m ḫd, dmj.n.j jnbw-ḥq3* "I gave the road to my feet downstream and reached Walls of the Ruler."
16. *ᶜḥᶜ.n jn.n.j ḫwt.f, ḥ3q.n.j mnmnt.f, jt.n.j ntt m jm3m.f, kf.n.j ᶜf3y.f* "Then I got his things, plundered his cattle, took what was in his tent, and stripped his camp" — the spelling *jm3m* shows that the word *jm3* had lost its final *3*.
17. *m.k tw jw.t(j), ḥ(w).n.k ḫ3swt* "Look, you have returned after visiting foreign lands."
18. *m pḥ ntj nj pḥ.n.f tw* "Don't attack one who doesn't attack you."
19. *nj rḫ.n.tw m3ᶜt r grgw* "One cannot know truth from lying" — literally, "cannot learn truth with respect to lying."
20. *nj qbb.n ḫrwy m ḫnw kmt* "An enemy cannot become calm in the capital of Egypt."
21. *nḥmn z3.f ᶜq.(w) r ᶜḥ, jt.n.f jwᶜt nt jt(j).f* "His son has surely entered the palace, having taken the inheritance of his father" — or "and taken the inheritance of his father"; for the first clause see § 17.9.
22. *jw dj.n ṯw ḥm.j r smr, jw.k m ḥwn n mpt 26, jr.n ḥm.(j) nw, m3.n.j ṯw m jqr sḫr* "My Incarnation has appointed you as courtier, although you are (only) a youth of 26 years: My Incarnation has done this because I have seen you as one who is excellent of conduct" — *jw dj.n ṯw ḥm.j r smr* is literally "My Incarnation has given you to courtier"; *jqr sḫr* is a *nfr ḥr* construction (§ 6.5).
23. *ḥmt.f ḥr šs3 n.f, nj sḏm.n.f n.s* "His wife was pleading to him, but he couldn't listen to her" — for the first clause, see § 15.3).
24. *jn jw p3.n ḥmwt ṯ3z sk(j)w* "Have women done the raising of troops in the past?" — i.e., "ever raised troops."
25. *jnk ᶜ3 m nwt.f šps m pr.f ... jwt(j) sḏr.n r(m)ṯ špt.(w) r.f* "I am one great in his town and noble in his house ... one at whom people do not go to bed angry" — literally, "one who people do not go to bed angered at him"; *špt.(w)* is the stative.
26. *[jr.n].f m mnw.f n (j)t(j).f ḥrw nb bhn jrt n.f wsḫt ḥ(3)bt ... [jr.f] dj ᶜnḫ [ḏt]* "He [has made], as his monument to his father Horus, lord of Buhen, the creation for him of a festival broad-hall ... [that he might achieve] given-life [forever]."
27. *jr.n.f m mnw.f n (j)t(j).f jmn nb nswt t3wj ḫnt(j) ḏsrt jmntt sᶜḥᶜ n.f st.f ḏsrt nt zp tpj smnḫ sj m k3wt nt (n)ḥḥ, jst gm.n (sw) ḥm.f w3.(w) r w3s, jr.f dj ᶜnḫ mj rᶜ ḏt* "He has made, as his monument to his father Amun, lord of the thrones of the Two Lands, foremost of the western sacred area, the erection for him of his sacred place of the First Occasion and the making of it functional with work of eternity, since His Incarnation had found (it) fallen to ruin, so that he might achieve given-life like Re forever" — both *sᶜḥᶜ* and *smnḫ* are infinitives (§ 14.5.2); *jst* introduces an adverb clause (§ 18.11); *w3.(w)* is the stative (§ 17.19), with its subject (*sw*) left unexpressed because it is obvious from the context.

28. Right: *(n)swt-bjt(j) nb t3wj nb ḫ*ᶜ*w NB-M3*ᶜ*T-R*ᶜ*, z3 r*ᶜ *n ẖt.f mr.f JMN-ḤTP ḤQ3-W3ST* "King of Upper and Lower Egypt, lord of the Two Lands, lord of appearance, NEB-MAAT-RE, bodily son of Re, his beloved, AMEN-HOTEP RULER OF THEBES."
Middle: *dj.n.(j) n.k* ᶜ*nḫ w3s nb 3wt-jb nb r*ᶜ *nb* "I have given you all life and dominion, and all happiness, every day."
Left: *jmn-r*ᶜ "Amun-Re"; *ḏd-mdw dj.n.(j) n.k (n)swyt r*ᶜ *ḥtpt nb ḏf(3)w nb snb nb mj r*ᶜ *ḏt* "Recitation: I have given you the kingship of Re, all offerings, all food, and all health like Re forever" — *mj r*ᶜ is written with the god's name in honorific transposition.

Exercise 19

1. *ḫnms.k šmsww ḥrw*
*pr.k h3.k nn ḫnḫ(n).k nn šn*ᶜ*.k ḥr sb3 dw3t*
wn.tw n.k ᶜ*3wj 3ḫt, zn n.k qrwt ḏsw.sn*
*ḫnm.k wsḫt nt m3*ᶜ*tj, wšd tw nṯr jm(j).s*
*jr.k ḥms m ḫnw jmḥt, wstn.k m nwt nt ḥ*ᶜ*pj*
3w jb.k m sk3.k m šd.k n sḫt j3rw, jwt n.k šmw m w3ḫyt …
pr.k r ḥ3 tnw dw3w, nw.k tw tnw mšrw, st3.tw n.k tk3 m grḥ …
ḏd.tw n.k jjwj zp 2 m pr.k pn n ᶜ*nḫw*
"May you be friendly with the followers of Horus. May you go up and go down without your being hindered and without your being refused at the gate of the Duat; may the door of the Akhet be opened to you; may the doorbolts pull back for you themselves. May you join the broad hall of the Two Maats; may the god in it question you. May you make a seat inside the Cavern; may you stride in the town of the Inundation. May your heart be happy (literally, 'wide') in your plowing in your plot of the Field of Reeds; may the harvest come to you with abundance of grain … May you go out each morning and return (literally, 'bring yourself back') each evening. May a taper be lit for you in the night … may there be said to you 'Welcome, welcome, in this your house of the living' " — *ḫnḫn.k* and *šn*ᶜ*.k* are infinitives: literally, "without the hindering of you, without the refusing of you" (§ 14.15.1); *sk3.k* is also an infinitive.
2. *ḥ3 n.j šzp nb mnḫ,* ᶜ*w3y.j ḫnw n sḫtj pn jm.f* "I wish I had any effective image of a god (§ 10.7), so that I might steal the goods of this peasant from him" — or *jm.f* "with it," referring to the image.
3. *jn ḫnd.k ḥr ḥbsw.j* "Do you intend to step on my clothes?"
4. *jr h3.k r š(j) n m3*ᶜ*t sqd.k jm.f m m3*ᶜ*w, nn kf nbdyt ḥt3.k, nn jhm dpwt.k, nn jwt jyt m ḫt.k … nn jt tw nwt, nn dp.k ḏwt nt jtrw, nn m3.k ḥr snḏ* "If you go down to the lake of Maat and sail in it with a right wind, the reefs of your sail will not unravel, your boat will not stall, misfortune will not come in your mast … a wave will not take you, you will not taste the evil of the river, you will not see the face of fear."
5. *w3ḥ jb.k, rḫ.k m3*ᶜ*t* "Be patient, that you may learn Maat" or "and you will learn Maat."
6. *s*ᶜ*nḫw m rdj m(w)t.tw* "Life-giver, don't make one die!"
7. *m3 s3.k bjn, mš*ᶜ*.j m s3.k, nn jwr ḥmwt ḥwt-w*ᶜ*rt … dj.j m3 jppj 3t ḥwrt* "Your back will see evil, since my army is in back of you (§ 12.17). The women of Avaris will not conceive … I will make Apophis see a wretched time."
8. *jm šm b3.j,* ᶜ*ḥ*ᶜ*.f n.j* "My ba should not go: he should wait for me."
9. *sm3*ᶜ *ḫrw.k r gs nṯr, jḫ ḏd r(m)ṯ ḫft ḫmt.k* "Make right your voice beside the god: then people will speak according to your thinking" — *ḫmt* is an infinitive.
10. *s*ᶜ*3 srjw.k, jr.sn hpw.k* "Make great your officials, and they will do your laws" or "that they may do your laws."
11. *wḏ3 ḥm.k r prw nw zḫ3w, m3 ḥm.k mdw-nṯr nbw* "Your Incarnation should proceed to the houses of writings, that Your Incarnation might see all the hieroglyphs" or "and Your Incarnation will see all the hieroglyphs."
12. *jr qn.n.k, rwḏ jb.k, mḥ.k qnj.k m ẖrdw.k, sn.k ḥmt.k, m3.k pr.k* "If you have persevered and your heart has been firm, you will fill your embrace with your children, you will kiss your wife, you will see your house."
13. *sḏd.j b3w.k n jtj, dj.j sš3.f m* ᶜ*3.k* "I will relate your impressiveness to the sovereign; I will make him become aware of your greatness."
14. *dj.j jn.t(w) n.k ḥ*ᶜ*w 3tp.w ḫr špssw nb n kmt* "I will send you ships loaded with all the fine things of Egypt" — *rdj jn.tw* "have one fetch" = "send"; *3tp.w* is a stative.
15. *m3*ᶜ*.n.f n.(j) wnt ḫr.f, rḫ.n.f ḫrp.j n.f st* "He has directed to me what he had, knowing (§ 18.11) I would manage it for him."
16. *m q3 jb.k, tm.f dḥj* "Don't let your heart become exalted (§ 16.4), and it won't become humiliated."
17. *jmj wḏ.tw n b3k-jm jrt mdw j3wj dj.tw* ᶜ*ḥ*ᶜ *z3.j m st.j* "Let it be commanded to your humble servant to make a 'staff of old age' and to have my son stand in my place" — *wḏ.tw* and *dj.tw* are both subjunctives, objects of *jmj*; *jrt* is an infinitive serving as object of *wḏ.tw*; ᶜ*ḥ*ᶜ *z3.j* is a subjunctive serving as object of *dj.tw*: literally, "Give that one command to the servant therein to make a staff of old age and that one give that my son stand in my place."

18. *jr ẖz.k, šms z(j) jqr, nfr sšmw.k nb ḫr nṯr* "If you are lowly, follow a successful man, and let all your conduct be good before the god."
19. *jr jqr.k, grg pr, jr.k z3 n sjm(3) nṯr*
   jr mtj.f, pẖr.f n qdw.k, sḏm.f n sb3yt.k, sjqr sḫrw.f m ẖnw pr.k, nw.f jšwt.k r st jrj
   ḥ(j)ḥj n.f zp nb jqr, z3.k pw … jm.k jwd jb.k r.f
   jr nnm.f, th.f sḫrw.k, tm.f jrt sb3yt.k
   ẖzj sḫrw.f m ẖnw pr.k … rwj.k sw, nn z3.k js pw
   "When you become successful, found a house and beget (literally, 'make') a son at the pleasure of the god. If he is straightforward, serves your character, and listens to your teachings, make excellent his position inside your house, so that he might look after your property at the place pertaining to it. Seek out for him every excellent opportunity. He is your son … you should not separate your heart from him. If he transgresses, violates your advice, and does not do your teachings, let his position be miserable inside your house … You should expel him: he is not your son."
20. *mj mj jb.j, mdw.j n.k, wšb.k n.j t̠3zw.j* "Come now (§ 16.7.6), my heart, that I might speak to you and you might answer for me my sentences."
21. *ḫ3 n.j jb m rḫ wḫdw, k3 jry.j sḫnj ḥr.f* "Would that I had a heart that knew (literally, 'as one that knew') how to bear up: then I would make landing on it."
22. *jr mr.k nfr sšmw.k, nḥm tw m ᶜ ḏwt nbt* "If you want your conduct to be good, take yourself away from all that is evil" — *mr.k* and *nfr* are both subjunctives.
23. *jm.k wḥm mskj n mdt* "You should not repeat gossip."
24. *ḥḏ ḥr.k tr n wnn.k* "Let your face be bright in the time of your existing" — i.e., "You should be cheerful as long as you exist"; *wnn.k* is an infinitive.
25. *wp.k w3wt n nṯrw, wn.k n.sn m wp-w3wt* "You shall part the ways for the gods and be Wepwawet for them" — literally, "you shall be for them as Wepwawet."
26. *jw.f rḫ.(w) rdjt šm m3j ḥr s3.f* "He knows (how) to make a lion walk at his back" — *rdjt* is an infinitive: see § 14.12.
27. *mr wj ᶜ3, wjn n.k jmnt*
   mr ḥm pḥ.k jmnt, s3ḥ ḥᶜw.k t3, ḫny.j r s3 wrd.k
   jḫ jr.n dmj n zp
   "Desire me here, put aside for yourself the West, (but) also (§ 16.7.8) desire that you reach the West, that your body 'touch land', and that I alight after your 'weariness': then we will make harbor together."
28. *jr gr.k, ḫpr n.k pḥw* "If you are silent (or 'still'), results will happen for you."
29. *pšš.n s(j) mwt.ṯ nwt ḥr.ṯ, dj.s wn.ṯ m nṯr nn ḫft(j)w.ṯ m ẖr(j)-nṯr* "Your mother Nut has spread herself over you, that she might cause you to be a god, with no enemies of yours in the necropolis" — for Nut see Essay 2; *nn ḫftjw.ṯ m ẖrj-nṯr* is an adverb clause (see § 12.17); *ḫftjw* and *ẖrj-nṯr* are nisbes (see §§ 8.6, 8.8).
30. *dj.j mr.k zḫ3w r mwt.k*
   dj.j ᶜq nfrw.f m ḥr.k
   wr sw grt r j3wt nbt
   "I will make you love writing more than your mother; I will make its perfection enter your face. Moreover, it is greater than any office."

Exercise 20

1. *ḥsbt 30 3 3ḫt 7, ᶜr nṯr r 3ḫt.f (n)swt bjt(j) SḤTP-JB-Rᶜ, sḥr.f r pt, ẖnm.(w) m jtn, ḥᶜ-nṯr 3bḫ.(w) m jr sw*
   jw ẖnw m sgr, jbw m gmw, rwtj wrtj ḫtm.(w), šnyt m tp ḥr m3st, pᶜt m jmw
   jst r.f zb.n ḥm.f mšᶜ r t3 tjmḥjw, z3.f smsw m ḥrj jrj nṯr nfr Z(J)-N-WSRT,
   tj sw h3b.(w) r ḥ(w)t ḫ3swt r sqr jm(j)w-ṯḥnw
   tj sw ḥm jy.f, jn.n.f sqrw-ᶜnḫ.(w) mnmnt nbt nn ḏrw.s
   smrw nw stp-z3 h3b.sn r gs jmntj r rdjt rḫ z3-nswt sšmw ḫpr m ᶜḥnwtj
   gm.n sw wpwtjw ḥr w3t, pḥ.n.sn sw r tr n ḫ3wj …
   bjk ᶜḥ.f ḥnᶜ šmsww.f, nn rdjt rḫ st mšᶜ.f
   "Regnal year 30, 3 Inundation 7. Ascent (§ 14.14.1) of the god to his Akhet, the King of Upper and Lower Egypt SEHETEP-IB-RE, going above to the sky, united (§ 17.19) with the sun-disk, the god's body mixed with the one who made it. The capital was in stillness, hearts in grief, the great double gates shut, the court with head on lap, the nobility in mourning. Now (§ 16.7.2), His Incarnation had sent an expedition to the land of the Libyans, his eldest son as the one over it, the perfect god SENWOSRET, he having been sent (§ 17.12) to smite foreign lands and to strike down those in the Libyan desert. And (§ 16.7.8) while he was returning, having gotten (§ 18.11) prisoners of

war and all kinds of herds without limit, the courtiers of the palace were sending (word) to the western side to let the king's son know (§ 19.10) the events that had happened in the (royal) chamber. The messengers found him on the way (home); they reached him at the time of dusk … The falcon was flying off with his followers, without letting (§ 14.15.1) his army know it" — The first sentence describes the death of Amenemhat I; *sḫr.f* is an imperfective in an adverb clause; *tj sw ḥm jy.f* is the SUBJECT-imperfective construction in a marked adverb clause; *smrw nw stp-zꜣ hꜣb.sn* and *bjk ꜥẖ.f* are the SUBJECT-imperfective construction in main clauses.

2. *wmt jb pw, mꜣꜣ.f ꜥšꜣt* "He is one thick of heart (§ 6.5) when he sees a multitude (of enemies)."
3. *jw.j dj.j mw n jb* "I used to give water to the thirsty."
4. *jwt nḫt n ⟨r⟩tnw, mtꜣ.f wj m jmꜣm.j* "There came a champion of Retjenu, taunting me in my tent."
5. *wn.jn ḥm.f hꜣb.f n.j ḫr ꜣwt-ꜥ nt ḫr-nswt, sꜣw.f jb n bꜣk jm mj ḥqꜣ n ḫꜣst nbt* "Then His Incarnation was sending to me with (literally, 'under') gifts of the king's possession, gladdening the heart of (this) humble servant like the ruler of any foreign land" — i.e., the king sent me the same kinds of gifts he sent to foreign rulers.
6. *ptr jrt.n.k, jr.tw r.k*
   nj wꜥꜣ.k, ḫsf.tw mdw.k
   nj mdw.k m zḥ n sr(j)w, jtn.tw ṯꜣzw.k
   "What (§ 5.11) have you done (literally, 'what is that which you have done'), so that one should act against you? You did not blaspheme, so that one should bar you from speaking (§ 19.9). You did not contest the advice of officials, so that your sentences should be contradicted."
7. *nj zḫz.t(w) m sꜣ.j, nj sḏm.j ṯꜣz ḥwrw, nj sḏm.tw rn.j m r wḥmw* "No one ran after me, I did not hear a hue and cry (after me), my name was not heard in the mouth of the herald" — i.e., no one put out an order for my arrest.
8. *mw m jtrw swrj.t(w).f mr.k, ṯꜣw m pt ḫnm.t(w).f ḏd.k* "The water in the river is drunk when you wish; the air in the sky is breathed when you say."
9. *ḏd.n.f n.f j[r m] ḫt hꜣw nḏs r pꜣ š(j) mj nt-ꜥ.f nt rꜥ nb*
   kꜣ.k ḫꜣꜥ.k [pꜣ m]sḥ [n mnḥ] r sꜣ.f
   "He said to him: 'After the commoner goes down to the lake like his custom of every day, then you will throw the crocodile of wax after him.' "
10. *jnk msḏ.f ḫt bjn* "I am one who hates something bad."
11. *kꜣwt pw nj jr.t(w).s ḏr bꜣḥ(j)w* "It is a work that has not been done since the ancestors."
12. *ḥtp-dj-(n)swt … n kꜣ n jmꜣḫy … (j)m(j) r pr nḫt-sbkw nb jmꜣḫ ḏd.f, nj zp jry.j ḫt nbt ḏwj r r(m)ṯ nb* "A royal offering … for the ka of the honored … steward Nakht-Sobek, possessor of honor, who says: I have never done anything badly against any men" — see n. 5 in this lesson.
13. *jbw ꜥwn.(w), nn wn jb n z(j) rhn.tw ḥr.f* "Hearts are greedy (§ 17.7); there is no heart of a man one can rely on" — *rhn.tw ḥr.f* is an unmarked adverb clause after an undefined antecedent (*jb n zj* "a heart of a man"): literally, "there is not a heart of a man (that) one relies on it."
14. *jn jw wn ḫprt m ḫnw* "Is there something that has happened at home?"
15. *jn jw wꜣḥ.tw hrw n ꜥḥꜥ(w), jn jw ḫbꜣ.tw jm.f r pw* "Can one add a day to a lifetime? Can one subtract from it either?"
16. *wbn.f wn wnwt* "He will rise when it is time" — literally, "when the hour exists"; *wbn.f* is subjunctive.
17. *z(j) pw wn.(w), ḫw.n-jnpw rn.f, sḫtj pw n sḫt ḥmꜣt, jst wn ḥmt.f, mrt rn.s* "There was a man named Khuen-inpu. He was a peasant of the Wadi Natrun, and he had a wife named Meret" — literally, "his wife (also) existing."
18. *jw wn nḏs, ḏdj rn.f, ḥms.f m ḏd-SNFRW* "There is a commoner named Djedi, who resides in Snefru-Endures."
19. *wn.j jm.f ḥnꜥ snw.j* "I used to be in it with my siblings" or "I was in it with my siblings."
20. *jw r n z(j) nḥm.f sw, jw mdw.f dj.f tꜣm n.f ḥr* "The mouth of a man saves him; his speech makes one lenient to him" — literally, "his speech causes the face to be veiled to him."
21. *jw.j rḫ.kw ḏw pf n bꜣḫw nt(j) pt tn rhn.s ḥr.f* "I know that mountain of Bakhu on which this sky rests" — literally, "which this sky rests on it."
22. *šnwy.j ḏdf.(w), mꜣꜣ.j st* "My hair stood on end (§ 17.6) when I saw it."
23. *ḫp r.f sw ntrt tn, jw.f dj.f ḥꜣt n š(j)* "So this goddess met (§ 20.4) him as he was heading to the lake."
24. *jj.n.s, ḫꜣ.s m ḥbsw.s, ṯḥṯḥ.s šnw.s* "She came undressing from her clothes and messing up her hair."
25. *wnn.f m rwtj n sbḫw, j.qd.f nn dꜣjw* "He is constantly out in the howling wind, building without a cloak."
26. *jr dꜣ tp n z(j), ḥr.k wꜣḥ.k ḏrt.k ḥr tp.f* "If the head of the man shakes, you have to put your hand on his head."
27. *rdjt šzp ḫrd, tm.f snqw* "(How) to make (§ 14.9) a boy accept (the breast) when he doesn't nurse" or "(How) to make a boy who doesn't nurse accept (the breast)."
28. *nn ms wn r(m)ṯ m st nb* "Surely (§ 16.7.7) there are no people anyplace" — literally, "Surely, people do not exist in any place."

Exercise 21

1. *ꜥḥꜥ.n jn n.f smn, wḏꜥ ḏꜣḏꜣ.f*
   ꜥḥꜥ.n rdj pꜣ smn r gbꜣ jmntj n wꜣḫj ḏꜣḏꜣ.f r gbꜣ jꜣbtj n wꜣḫj
   ꜥḥꜥ.n ḏd.n ḏdj ḏdwt.f m ḥkꜣw
   wn.jn pꜣ smn ꜥḥꜥ.(w) ḥr ḥbꜣbꜣ, ḏꜣḏꜣ.f m mjtt
   "Then a goose whose head had been severed was fetched for him. Then the goose was put on the west side of the columned hall and its head on the east side of the columned hall. Then Djedi said his sayings of magic, and the goose stood up waddling, and its head likewise." — the first sentence can also be translated "Then a goose was brought to him, after its head had been severed"; the first clause can be read *ꜥḥꜥ.n jn.n.f smn* "Then he fetched a goose," but this is less likely in the context of the story from which this excerpt comes; the reading *ḏꜣḏꜣ.f* in the first sentence is indicated by the following sentences, where the word is spelled out.
2. *jmj jn.tw n.j ḫnrj wd nkn.f* "Have fetched for me a prisoner whose punishment has been set."
3. *ꜥḥꜥ.n jr mj wḏt nbt ḥm.f* "Then it was done like all that His Incarnation commanded."
4. *jw ms wn ḫꜣ, šd wpwt, sḫpr r(m)ṯ-ḏt m nb ḏt* "Surely, the office has been opened, the land-registers have been taken, and serfs have been made to become landowners" — i.e., the theft of written land records has allowed false land claims.
5. *nj tnj snḏw r sḫm-jb* "The fearful cannot be distinguished from the violent."
6. *jr hꜣb.ṯn wp(w)t(j)w.ṯn r.j, nj jw.j n.ṯn* "If you send your messengers for me, I will not come to you."
7. *nj ḫsff.j, nj jṯ wj hh n ꜣt.k, nj pr šnꜥw m r.k r.j, nj šm.j ḥr wꜣt jꜣdw* "I will not be barred, the blast of your moment of rage will not take me, a ban will not come out of your mouth against me, I will not walk on the road of Iadu" — the verb in the first clause is a prospective passive; those in the remaining clauses are prospective active forms rather than the perfective, since the first clause is future rather than past.
8. *nn ṯw mm.sn, nj wnn.k mm.sn* "You are not among them; you will not be among them."
9. *jr jn.k, jmj n sn.k* "When you get, give to your brother" — i.e., share your wealth.
10. *jr pḥ st, nn jrt jw, wnn.f jm mj nṯr* "As for he who reaches it without doing wrong, he will be like a god there."
11. *zpp z(j) m ḫt mjnt, rdjw zpw.f r gs.f m ꜥḥꜥw* "When a man survives after dying, his deeds will be placed beside him in heaps" — *rdjw* is probably the prospective passive rather than the passive.
12. *jr wnn.k m sšm(w) ḥr wḏ sḫrw n ꜥšꜣt, ḥ(j)ḥj n.k zp nb mnḫ* "If you are a leader who is commanding the conduct of a multitude, seek out for yourself every worthwhile deed."
13. *jw ḥꜣpw ẖt jr n.f jkmw* "The one who is discreet, a shield has been made for him" — *ḥꜣpw ẖt* is a preposed noun phrase (object of the preposition *n*).
14. *wnn.f m pt mj jꜥḥ* "He will be in the sky like the moon."
15. *ꜥḥꜥ.n mdw r.s m ḫꜣ n wḥm(w) n wꜥrt mḥtt* "Then it was spoken about in the office of the herald of the northern district" — literally, "Then was spoken about it."
16. *dj.n.j [sbꜣ.t(w)] wnwt-ḥwt-nṯr r jrt jrwt.sn, dj rḫ.sn nt-ꜥ nt rꜥ nb* "I had the hourly temple-staff taught to do their duties, and they were made to know the procedure of every day" — literally, "that they know ... was made."
17. *ꜥḥꜥ.n rdj.n sr(j) pn wḏt m ḥr.j m ḏd, m.k wḏ swꜥb.k pꜣ r-pr n ꜣbḏw*
    rdj n.k ḥmww r nt-ꜥ.f ḥnꜥ wnwt-ḥwt-nṯr nt tꜣ spꜣt
    "Then that official assigned me a command, saying: 'It has been commanded that you clean the temple of Abydos. You have been given craftsmen for its procedure as well as the hourly temple-staff of that nome' " — literally, "that you clean the temple has been commanded" and "craftsmen have been given to you."
18. *ꜥḥꜥ.n mꜣ nꜣ n kꜣwt, ꜥḥꜥ.n.tw ḥꜥ.w jm wr r ḫt nbt* "Then those works were seen. Then there was excitement over it more than anything" — literally, "then one was excited."
19. *nḥm ḫwt z(j) r.f, rdj.w n ntj m rwtj* "A man's things have been taken from him and given to the one who is outside" — *rdj.w* is the stative (§ 21.9).
20. *ꜥḥꜥ.n sḫꜥw ḥm n nṯr pn, psḏt.f jꜥb.tj [m ḫt.f] ...*
    ꜥḥꜥ.n rdj wḏꜣ ḥm n nṯr pn r ḥdwt, ḥtp.f st.f m ḥwt-nbw
    "Then the incarnation of this god was made to appear, with his Ennead united in his wake .... Then the incarnation of this god was made to proceed to the chapel, so that he might occupy his place in the enclosure of gold."

Exercise 22

1. *rdj.jn ḥm.f njs.tw n.f rḫ-(n)swt ntj m ḫt ḥm.f, ḏd.jn n.f ḥm.f*
   šꜣs jr.k m ḫntyt ḥnꜥ jzwt ꜥprw
   m sḏr grḥ mj hrw r sprt.k r ꜣbḏw

"Then His Incarnation had a king's-acquaintance who was in His Incarnation's following called to him, and His Incarnation said to him: 'Go upstream with a crew of experienced (sailors). Don't lie down by night or (literally, 'like') day until you have arrived at Abydos.' "

2. *sr.sn ḏᶜ nj jjt.f nšnj nj ḫprt.f* "They could predict a windstorm before it came, a rainstorm before it happened."
3. *m.k nn dj.j n.f w3t r sprt.k* "Look, I won't let him leave (literally, 'give him the road') until you have arrived."
4. *snḏ.n.f n.j, jw.j m ḫd, nj ᶜḥ3t.n* "He became afraid of me as I was (still) sailing downstream, before we had (even) fought" — *ᶜḥ3t.n* for *ᶜḥ3t.n* (see § 2.8.3).
5. *nj sm3.n.j st r sḏmtw.j ḏdtj.tn r.s* "I cannot kill them until I have heard what you might say about it" — *sḏmtw.j* for *sḏmt.j* (§ 22.12).
6. *šj n ḥḏt jtrw 1000 pw m 3w.f, nj ḏd sḫ(w).f, nj wnt rm ḥf3w nb jm.f* "The Lake of the White Hippopotamus: it is 1000 rivers (§ 9.7.1) in its length, its width cannot be told (§ 21.13), and there is not any fish or snake in it" — retrograde text!
7. *m(j) mj, rm.n wsjr, ḏr ḥrt.f r.n* "Come now (§ 16.7.6), let us weep for Osiris, since he has gone far away from us."
8. *m ḥᶜw n ntt nj ḫprt* "Don't get excited because of what has not yet happened."
9. *jr ḫ3.k z(j) n wbnw m gm3.f, nj wnt kft.f, jst wbnw pf ᶜr.(w) n qs*
dᶜr.ḫr.k wbnw.f ... wt.ḫr.k sw ḥr jwf w3ḏ
"If you examine a man with (literally, 'of') a wound in his cheekbone, which has no gash (literally, 'its gash not existing'), although that wound has penetrated to the bone, you have to probe his wound ... you have to bandage it with fresh meat" — the man in question has a flesh wound above his cheekbone, which has reached to the bone but has not cut the bone itself.
10. *wšᶜ.ḫr.f nn n jtj-mḥj nn n btj, zjn.ḫr.f jf.f jm, wn.ḫr ḥᶜw.f w3ḏ.(w) mj nn n nṯrw* "He has to chew this northern barley and this emmer, he has to rub his flesh with it, and his body is inevitably freshened like those gods."
11. *jr wnn jb n ḏḥwtj r šd(t) st ḥr rᶜ, wᶜb.ḫr.f m wᶜbt 9 hrww* "If the mind of Thoth will be toward reciting it (§ 21.7) over Re, he has to become clean in a cleansing for 9 days" — *šd(t)* is an infinitive (object of the preposition *r*); since *šdj* is 3ae-inf., the infinitive should be *šdt* (§ 14.3).
12. *ḏd.ḫr z(j), jr.f mkwt.f m ḥk3w, jnk ḥk3w pwy wᶜb jmj r-ḫt rᶜ, nṯrw ḥrj.tjwnj r.j* "A man has to say, so that he may make (§ 19.8.1) his protection by magic: 'I am that (§ 5.10.1) pure Magic that is in the belly of Re: gods, be far (§ 17.17.2) from me!' "
13. *jw.sn ḥnᶜ.j, k3.k, ḏr.k3.sn ḥnᶜ.k r rḫt stš wnt.sn ḥnᶜ.k* " 'They are with me,' you shall say, 'and they will end up with you, until Seth has learned that they are with you.' "
14. *wšd ḥr sḫr ḫ3st, ᶜḥᶜ.n ḏd.n.sn nj sḏm.n ḫt nbt, jw t3 ḫ3st ḥr m(w)t m ᶜ ḥqrw, ḫr.fj st* "They were questioned about the condition of the desert. Then they said: 'We have not heard anything. The desert is dying from hunger,' they said."
15. *zm3.k t3 r t3-sm3 n t3-wr, pr.k3.k r.k r tp q33 q3* "You will land (literally, 'join land') at the landing-stage of This, and then you will go up to the top of a high hill."
16. *jr jwt.k r.j m ḥf3t, m(w)t.k3 rᶜ, sft.k3.t(w) ᶜ3pp* "If you come against me as a snake, Re will die and Apophis will be butchered."
17. *ḫp m ḥtp, ḫnm.j tw, j.t(j) jn jmnt nfrt* " 'Walk in peace and I will join you,' says the beautiful West" — mutilated hieroglyphs.
18. *r n rdjt jry š3w3btj k3wt m ḫrt-nṯr*
ḏd-mdw ... j š3w3btj jpn jr jp.tw wsjr N r jrt k3(w)t nb(t) jrrwt jm m ḫrt-nṯr ...
r srd sḫwt, r smḥt wḏbw, r ḫnt šᶜ n jmntt n j3btt,
jry.j, m.k wj, k3.k
"Spell for making a shawabti do (§ 19.10) works in the necropolis. Recitation ... Oh, this shawabti! If Osiris N is allotted to do any works that are done in the necropolis ... to plant fields, to flood the banks (of irrigation canals), to transport sand for the west or for the east (bank), 'I will do (it): here I am!,' you shall say."
19. *ᶜnḫ.k jr.f m jšst, j.n.sn nṯrw, ᶜnḫ.j m ḫt pw bnr jm(j) k3r nṯr* " 'So, on what (§ 5.11) will you live?,' say they, the gods. I will live on that sweet wood that is in the shrine of the god."
20. *m grg dw3(w) nj jjt.f* "Don't set up tomorrow before it has come."

Exercise 23

1. *ḥrw nṯrj ḫprw, nbtj nṯrj mswt, bjk-nbw ḫpr, (n)swt-bjt(j) Ḫᶜ-K3W-Rᶜ, z3-rᶜ Z(J)-N-WSRT, jt.f t3wj m m3ᶜ ḫrw, (2) j.nḏ-ḥr.k Ḫᶜ-K3W-Rᶜ ḥrw.n nṯrj ḫprw, mk t3, swsḫ t3šw.f, (3) d3jr ḫ3swt m wrr(j)t.f, jnq t3wj m r-ᶜw ᶜwj.f, (4) [rww] ḫ3swt m r-ᶜwj.f, sm3m pdt(j)w nn sḫt ḫt, st šsr (5) n(n) jtḥ rwd ..., (7) [st] šsr mj jrr sḫmt sḫr.f ḫ3w m ḫ[mw] b3w.f, ns n ḥm.f (8) rtḥ ḫnt, ṯ3zw.f sbh3 sttjw, wᶜ mpw (9) [ᶜḥ3] ḥr t3š.f, tm rdj wrd mrwt.f, rdj sḏr (10) pᶜt r šsp ḏ3mw.f n qddw.sn, ḥ3tj.f m mktj.sn*

"Horus Divine of Evolution, Two Ladies Divine of Birth, Gold Falcon Who Has Evolved, King of Upper and Lower Egypt KHA-KAU-RE ('Apparent One of Re's Life Force'), Son of Re SENWOSRET ('Man of the Powerful Goddess'), as he takes possession of the Two Lands in justification. (2) Hail to you, KHA-KAU-RE, our Horus divine of birth, who protects the land, who broadens its borders, (3) who subdues foreign lands with his crown, who embraces the Two Lands with the activity of his arms, (4) who drives off foreign lands with his activity, who kills bowmen without the blow of a stick, who shoots the arrow (5) without drawing the bowstring ... (7) who shoots the arrow as Sekhmet does when he fells (§ 20.10) thousands of those who do not know his impressiveness, the tongue of His Incarnation (8) being that which restrains the Upstream, his sentences being that which makes the Beduin flee, unique youngster (9) who fights for his border, who does not let his dependents get weary, who lets (10) the elite sleep until dawn (by keeping them free of worry) and (gives) his recruits to their sleep, with his heart as their protector" — *mk, swsḫ, d3jr (d3r), jnq, sm3m (sm3), st, rtḥ, sbh3, ᶜḥ3, tm,* and *rdj* are all perfective active participles, and *nww* is an imperfective active participle; *rdj* after *tm* is the negatival complement.

2. *nn jtrw rdj sdg3.f* "There is no river that lets itself be hidden" — *rdj* perfective active participle.
3. *nn ᶜnḫ rqtj.f wj* "He who will oppose me will not live" — *rqtj.f* prospective participle; *ᶜnḫ* is the subjunctive.
4. *m.tn jwtj prt.f m nb šnwt, jn n.f ṯ3bt m dd(j) pr.s* "Look, he who had no seed-grain is (now) owner of a granary, and he who got for himself a grain-loan is (now) one who issues it" — *jn* perfective active participle; *dd(j)* imperfective active participle.
5. *m.tn ḫm ḏ3ḏ3t m nb b(j)nt, tm ḥsjw n.f ḥr swh3 mrt* "Look, he who did not know the lyre is (now) owner of a harp, and he who did not sing for himself is (now) extolling Meret" — *ḫm* and *tm* are perfective active participles; *ḥsjw* is the negatival complement.
6. *rᶜ pw m33w m stwt.f, sḥḏw(j) sw t3wj r jtn* "He is the sun, by whose rays one sees. How much more illuminating of the Two Lands is he than the sundisk!" — *m33w* imperfective passive participle (§ 23.16), *sḥḏw(j)* perfective active participle.
7. *ẖnmw pw n ẖᶜw nb, wttw sḫpr rḫyt* "He is Khnum for every body, the begetter who creates the subjects" — *wttw* is a noun of agent; *sḫpr* is an active participle, probably imperfective.
8. *m.ṯn nj ddw n.sn p3 ᶜqw m st nbt* "Look, there are none to whom such rations are given anywhere" — literally, "there are not those given to them such rations in any place"; *ddw* imperfective passive participle.
9. *ᶜ3m ḫz wn ḥr ḏd jnk nb* "the vile Asiatic who was saying 'I am the lord' " — *wn* perfective active participle.
10. *w3ḏwj jr n3 n nṯr.f* "How fortunate is he who has done this for his god!" — *jr* perfective active participle.
11. *ršwj ḏddj n.f nn* "How joyful is he to whom this has been said!" — literally, "the one said to him this"; *ḏddj* perfective passive participle.
12. *[h3]b ṯw ḥm.j r jrt nn sj3.n ḥm.j wnt nn jrt(j).f st nb ḥr ḫw.k* "My Incarnation sends you to do this because My Incarnation has recognized that there is none who will do it except you" — literally, "there is not any one-who-will-do it": *jrt(j).f* prospective participle; *sj3.n* is the perfect in an adverb clause (§ 18.11), with the suffix *.n* placed before the determinative.
13. *jr jrtj.f nn ḏdwy.j, wnn.j m z3 snb.f m mktj n ẖrdw.f* "As for the one who shall do this which I say, I will be the safeguard of his health and protector of his children" — *jrtj.f* prospective participle.
14. *wnn.k ḥr rdjt dj.tw n.f ᶜqw, nn rdjt rḫ.f ntt ntk rdj n.f st* "You shall be having rations given to him, without letting him know that you are the one who has given it to him" — *rdj* perfective active participle; for *wnn.k ḥr rdjt*, see § 21.17.
15. *jn wnm dp(j), jw wšdw wšb.f, jn sḏrw m33(j) rswt* "The one who eats is the one who tastes, the one questioned answers, the sleeper is the one who sees the dream" — *wnm* is an active participle; *dp(j)* and *m33(j)* are parallel imperfective active participles (§ 23.10 end); *wšdw* is a passive participle, subject of a SUBJECT-imperfective construction (§ 20.8); *sḏrw* is a noun of agent (§ 23.5 end).
16. *m.k jr r.k r jrt ḥnᶜ.j* "Look, the one who acted against you is to deal with me" — *jr* perfective active participle.
17. *jw 3ḫ n jrrw n.f st* "It is effective for him for whom it is done" — *jrrw* imperfective passive participle: literally, "the one done it for him"; *3ḫ* is a subjectless adjectival predicate (§ 8.5).
18. *j.k(w) m ḥtp r šmᶜw, jr.n.(j) h3bt wj r.s* "I returned (§ 17.17.1) in peace to the Nile Valley, having done (§ 18.11) that for which I was sent" — *h3bt* perfective passive participle: literally, "having done that sent me for it."
19. *jr z(j) jw mt 12 jm.f n ḥ3tj.f, ntsn dd(j) n ᶜt.f nbt* "As for a man, there are 12 vessels in him for the heart: they are the ones that give to his every part" — *dd(j)* imperfective active participle.
20. *nj jnk js ḏd n.k nw, jn gbb ḏd n.k nw ḥnᶜ wsjr* "I am not the one who says (or 'said') this to you: Geb is the one who says (or 'said') this to you, along with Osiris" — *ḏd* active participle.
21. *ḏd.jn ḏdj jty ᶜnḫ.(w)-(w)ḏ3.(w)-s(nb.w) nb.j nn jnk js jnn(j) n.k sj*
ḏd.jn ḥm.f jn mj r.f jn.f n.j sj
ḏd.jn ḏdj jn smsw n p3 ẖrdw 3 ntj m ẖt n r(w)d-ḏdt jn.f n.k sj

"Said Djedi: 'Sovereign, lph, my lord, I am not the one who can get (literally, 'gets') it for you.' Said His Incarnation: 'So, who will get it for me?' Said Djedi: 'The eldest of the 3 boys who are in the womb of Rud-djedet is the one who will get it for you' " — *jnn(j)* imperfective active participle; *jn.f* is the prospective *sḏm.f* (§ 23.13): the subjunctive would be *jnt.f* (§ 19.2).

22. *ꜥḥꜥ.n ḏd.n.f n.j (j)n mj jn tw zp 2 nḏs, (j)n mj jn tw r jw pn n w3ḏ-wr* "Then he said to me: 'Who brought you, who brought you (§ 9.5), commoner? Who brought you to this island of the sea?' " — *jn* perfective active participle.
23. *jn mj jr.f jn.f sw gm.f sw, jnk jn.j sw, jnk gm.j sw* "So who will get him and find him? I will get him, I will find him."
24. *jn jw wn ḫprt m ḫnw* "Is there something that has happened at home?" — see Exercise 20, no. 14; *ḫprt* perfective active participle.
25. *nn wn rwj ꜥḥ3w.f, nn jtḥ pḏt.f* "There is no one who can escape his arrow, no one who can draw his bow" — *rwj* and *jtḥ* perfective active participles.
26. *nn šw3w jry n.f mjtt* "There is no outcast for whom the like has been done" — literally, "there is not an outcast (false plural!) done for him the like"; *jry* perfective passive participle.
27. *jr ḥmwtj nb sqd nb r(m)ṯ nbt f(3)wt(j).sn ꜥ.sn n twt pn, jn nmtj ḥz.f sw* "As for any craftsman, any voyager, or any people who shall lift their hand to this image, Nemti is the one who will bless him" — *f(3)wt(j).sn* prospective participle.
28. *jr ḥr(j)-tp nb z3-z(j) nb sꜥḥ nb nḏs nb tmt(j).f mk jz pn ḥnꜥ ntt jm.f, nn šzp nṯr.f t-ḥḏ.f, nn qrs.t(w).f m jmnt* "As for any nomarch, any gentry, any noble, or any commoner who will not protect this tomb and that which is in it, his god will not accept his white-bread and he will not be buried in the West" — *tmt(j).f* prospective participle (*mk* is the negatival complement); *šzp* and *qrs.t(w).f* are subjunctives (§§ 19.4, 19.11.1).

Exercise 24

1. *nn zp jry.j ḏdt.n.s* "I would never do (§ 19.11.1) what she said" — *ḏdt.n.s* perfect relative.
2. *nn st nbt tmt.n.(j) jr mnw jm.s* "There is not any place in which I did not make a monument" — *tmt.n.(j)* perfect relative; the coreferent is the suffix pronoun of *jm.s*.
3. *jw rḫ st m tmw ꜥb ꜥm b3.f* "He who knows it is one whose ba the horned crocodile does not swallow" — *tmw* imperfective relative; the coreferent is the suffix pronoun of *b3.f*; *rḫ* is an active participle.
4. *jw.j m ḥ(j)ḥ(j) bw wn.n.j jm* "I am seeking (§ 15.2) the place in which I was" — *wn.n.j* perfect relative.
5. *pw-trj jrt.n r.s* "What can we do about it?" — literally, "What is that which we can do about it?"; *jrt.n* perfective relative; the coreferent is the suffix pronoun of *r.s*.
6. *3wt.sn ḫpr.sn m wḏt n.sn nṯr pn ꜥ3* "Their offering-gifts come about (§ 20.8) from what this great god commands for them" — *wḏt* perfective or imperfective relative.
7. *qrrt št3t nt dw3t ꜥppt nṯr pn ꜥ3 ḥr.s* "the secret cavern of the Duat, by which this great god passes" — *ꜥppt* imperfective relative; the coreferent is the suffix pronoun of *ḥr.s*.
8. *ms.n.f wj [m] jrr(j) jrt.n.f* "He has given me birth as one who does what he did" — *jrt.n.f* perfect relative; *jrr(j)* is an imperfective active participle.
9. *jr.tw k3wt [ḫft] mrt.n ḥm.j ḫpr.s* "Let the works be done (§ 19.5.1) according to that which My Incarnation has wanted to happen" — *mrt.n* perfect relative; the coreferent is the suffix pronoun of *ḫpr.s* (a subjunctive dependent on *mrt.n*: literally, "which My Incarnation has wanted that it happen").
10. *jw.k sḫm.tj m mrrt.k* "You have control (2ms stative) of what you like" — *mrrt.k* imperfective relative.
11. *nj ḥsb.n.tw ꜥw3t nb jr.n.f tp t3* "Any robbing he did on earth is not counted" — *jr.n.f* perfect relative; *ꜥw3t* is an infinitive, which is masculine (§ 14.8).
12. *jn p3 pw ḏdw r(m)ṯ* "Is this what people say?" — *ḏdw* imperfective relative.
13. *m.k jrrt.sn pw r sḫtjw.sn šmw r kt-ḫj* "Look, it is what they do to their peasants who go to others (§ 6.7)" — an A *pw* nominal sentence: *jrrt.sn* imperfective relative; *šmw* is an imperfective active participle.
14. *jr m3ꜥt ḥzy ḥzz ḥzyw* "Do Maat, you blessed one whom the blessed bless!" — *ḥzz* imperfective relative; *ḥzy* and *ḥzyw* are perfective active participles.
15. *ḥz tw ḥr(j)-š(j).f jj.n.k m pr.f* "May Harsaphes, from whose house you have come, bless you" — *jj.n.k* perfect relative; the coreferent is the suffix pronoun of *pr.f* (literally, "who you have come from his house").
16. *nn ḫm rdj.n.k rḫ.f, nn wḫ3 sb(3).n.k* "There is no one ignorant whom you have made learn; there is no fool whom you have instructed" — *rdj.n.k* and *sb(3).n.k* perfect relatives; the coreferent in the first sentence is the suffix pronoun of *rḫ.f* (a subjunctive dependent on *rdj.n.k*: literally, "who you have given that he learn").
17. *m fḫ jb.k ḥr ḏdtj.j n.k* "Don't lose heart (literally, 'your heart') over what I will say to you" — *ḏdtj.j* perfective relative.
18. *rdj.n.j n.f ꜥwj.j ḥr sḫpr ḫrww* "He to whom I gave my arms was creating plots" — *rdj.n.j* perfect relative; the coreferent is the suffix pronoun of *n.f* (literally, "he who I gave my arms to him").

19. *ḏdt.n.f pw* "It is what he said" — *ḏdt.n.f* perfect relative.
20. *nj rḫ.n.tw ḫprt jrrt nṯr ḫft ḫsf.f* "No one knows what may happen, or what the god does when he punishes" — *jrrt* imperfective relative; *ḫprt* is an active participle.
21. *jn jw gmḥ.k jrt.n kmt r.j* "Do you see what Egypt has done to me?" — *jrt.n* perfect relative.
22. *jmj jr.tw jrt.n nbt ḥm.j m nḫt ḥr w3ḏ ḥtp st.f m jpt-st m w3st r nḥḥ ḥnᶜ ḏt* "Have all that My Incarnation has done in victory put on a stela whose place shall rest in Karnak in Thebes continually forever" — *jrt.n* perfect relative; *ḥtp* perfective relative; the coreferent of the second relative clause is the suffix pronoun of *st.f* (referring to *w3ḏ* "stela": literally, "which its place shall rest in Karnak"); for *jmj jr.tw* see § 19.10.
23. *wr ddyt.f n jmjw-š3 ddy sw ḥr w3t* "What he gives to the marsh-dwellers who put him on the way is great" — an adjectival sentence: *ddyt.f* imperfective relative; *ddy* is an imperfective active participle.
24. *nn gm.k ḫnt.k ḥr.s m jmnt* "You will not find that which you can land on in the West" — *ḫnt.k* perfective relative; the coreferent is the suffix pronoun of *ḥr.s* (literally, "what you can land on it").
25. *rhnt jb.sn pw ḥr.s* "It is something that their heart can depend on" — an A *pw* nominal sentence: *rhnt* perfective relative; the coreferent is the suffix pronoun of *ḥr.s* (literally, "It is what their heart can depend on it").
26. *wḏt.n k3.k pw ḫpr[t] jty nb.j* "What happens is what your ka has commanded, sovereign my lord" — an A *pw* B nominal sentence: *wḏt.n* perfect relative; *ḫpr[t]* is an active participle.
27. *jw.j m z3.f ... rdj.n n.f gbb jwᶜt.f* "I am his son ... to whom Geb has given his inheritance" — *rdj.n* perfect relative; the coreferent is the suffix pronoun of *n.f* (literally, "who Geb has given him his inheritance").
28. *j.zj, jw, jr.n.k mj wḏt.n nbt ḥm.j* "Go (§ 16.2.1), and return when you have done (§ 18.11) like all that My Incarnation has commanded" — *wḏt.n* perfect relative.
29. *ᶜḥᶜ.n dwn.n.j rdwj.j r rḫ djt.j m r.j* "Then I stretched my legs to learn what I might put in my mouth" — *djt.j* perfective relative.
30. *ršwj sḏd dpt.n.f, zn ḫt mr* "How joyful is he who relates what he has experienced after (§ 21.12) a painful thing has been passed" — an adjectival sentence (§ 23.11): *dpt.n.f* perfect relative; *ršwj* and *sḏd* are active participles.
31. *ḥknw pf ḏd.n.k jn.t(w).f bw pw wr n jw pn* "That oil you said would be brought, it is the chief thing of this island" — an A *pw* nominal sentence; *ḏd.n.k* perfect relative; the coreferent is the suffix pronoun of *jn.t(w).f* (a passive subjunctive dependent on *ḏd.n.k*: literally, "which you said it would be brought").
32. *ptr jrt.n.k* "What have you done?" — literally, "What is that which you have done?"; *jrt.n.k* perfect relative.
33. *ptr wrt r ᶜbt ḫ3t.j m t3 ms.k wj jm.f* "What is more important than interring my corpse in the land in which you gave me birth?" — literally, "What is that which is great with respect to interring my corpse in the land which you birthed me in it?"; *ms.k* perfective relative; the coreferent is the suffix pronoun of *jm.f.*
34. *mr rᶜ ḥrw ḥwt-ḥr(w) fnd.k pw špss mrrw mntw nb w3st ᶜnḫ.f ḏt* "May Re, Horus, and Hathor love that noble nose of yours, which Montu, lord of Thebes, wishes to live forever" — *mrrw* imperfective relative; the coreferent is the suffix pronoun of *ᶜnḫ.f* (subjunctive dependent on *mrrw*: literally, "which Montu, lord of Thebes, wants that it live forever").
35. *ptr ḏdt n.j nb.j* "What is my lord saying to me?" — literally, "What is that which my lord says to me?"; *ḏdt* imperfective relative.
36. *nj rḫ.tw bw šm.n.f jm* "No one knew the place where he went" — *šm.n.f* perfect relative.
37. *wḏ3 pw jr.n.sn r bw jj.n.sn jm* "What they did was proceed to the place they came from" — *jr.n.sn* and *jj.n.sn* perfect relatives.
38. *ᶜḥᶜ.n ḏd.n.f n.sn ḥnwt.j ptj jrt.j n.tn* "Then he said to them: 'My mistresses, what can I do for you?' " — literally, "What is that which I can do for you?"; *jrt.j* perfective relative.
39. *m3.k rḫ.n.k mj ḫm.n.k* "You should regard him whom you know like him whom you do not know" — *rḫ.n.k* and *ḫm.n.k* perfect relatives (§ 24.8).
40. *ḥtp-dj-(n)swt wsjr nb 3bḏw nṯr ᶜ3 wnn-nfr.(w) wp-w3wt mnw nṯrw jm(j)w 3bḏw*
dj.sn prt-ḫrw t ḥnqt k3w 3pdw šsr mnḫt sntr mrḥt ḫt nbt nfrt wᶜbt ᶜnḫt-nṯr jm ddt pt q(m)3t t3
n k3 n zḫ3 qdwt sbkw-nḫt.(w) jr.n m3t m3ᶜ ḫrw nb jm3ḫ
n k3 n ḥmt.f mrt.f jnj jrt.n z3t-sty(t) m3ᶜ ḫrw
"A royal offering of Osiris, lord of Abydos, Wenennefer; Wepwawet; Min; and the gods who are in Abydos, giving an invocation offering of bread and beer, cattle and fowl, linen and clothing, incense and oil, every good and pure thing on which a god lives, which the sky gives and the earth creates, for the ka of the outline-scribe Sebek-nakht, begotten of Mat, justified, possessor of honor; and for the ka of his wife, whom he loves, Ini, begotten of Sit-Satis, justified" — *dj* perfective relative; *ᶜnḫt, ddt, q(m)3t* imperfective relatives (the subject of *ᶜnḫt* in honorary transposition); *jr.n* and *jrt.n* perfect relatives; *mrt.f* perfective relative.

Exercise 25

1. *jw.k r.j ḏd.j r.k, tm.k jw r.j nn ḏd.j r.k* "If you come against me I will speak against you. If you don't come against me, I won't speak against you" — two sentences: the first is a balanced sentence with two imperfective relatives; in the second sentence *tm.k* is an imperfective relative serving as an initial conditional clause (the rheme is the main clause *nn ḏd.j r.k*).
2. *nj j.n.f js ḏs.f, jn wp(w)t jt r.f* "It is not by himself that he has come: it is a message that came for him" — the rheme in the first sentence is the noun phrase *ḏs.f* used adverbially (§ 8.14); the predicate *j.n.f* is a perfect relative. The second sentence is a participial statement; its rheme is the emphasized subject *wpt.*
3. *m.k zp ḫzj ḫpr.(w) m h3w.j ... ḫpr.n nj js m jrt.n.j, rḫ.n.j st r s3 jr.tw* "Look, a vile event happened in my time ... It happened, but not from what I did: I learned of it after it was done" — the *ḫpr.n* and *rḫ.n.j* sentences are both emphatic, with perfect relative forms as predicates. In the first, the rheme is the negated adverbial phrase *nj js m jrt.n.j* (§ 11.7). In the second, the rheme is the prepositional phrase *r s3 jr.tw*. Both *ḫpr.n* and *jr.tw* have unexpressed subjects; *jr.tw* is a perfective relative used as object of the preposition *m*.
4. *jnk z(j) n ḥḥ jwt(j) m33.t(w).f jn ḥ3(j)w.f* "I am a man of a million, who is not seen by those around him" — *m33.t(w).f* is an imperfective relative after *jwt(j)*; *ḥ3(j)w.f* is a masculine plural nisbe from the preposition *ḥ3*.
5. *jnn.k st m ktkt, jm m33 r(m)ṯ* "You should bring them surreptitiously, so that the people don't see" — *jnn.k* is an imperfective relative; the rheme is the prepositional phrase *m ktkt*. For the last clause, see § 19.11.2.
6. *zbb.k n.j sw r s3 sk3* "You should send him to me after the plowing" — *zbb.k* is an imperfective relative; the rheme is the prepositional phrase *r s3 sk3*.
7. *m.k rnpt n3 nt jrr z(j) n nb.f* "Look, this is the year for a man to act for his master" — literally, "the year of a man acts for his master"; *jrr* is an imperfective relative serving as the second noun of an indirect genitive.
8. *jrr.k grt p3 šj m jtj-mḥ(j), m jr btj jm; jr grt jw.f m ḥ*ᶜ*p(j)* ᶜ*3, jrr.k sw m btj* "Now, you should do that basin-land in northern barley: don't do emmer there. But if it comes as a big inundation, you should do it in emmer" — *jrr.k* in both cases is an imperfective relative; the rheme is the prepositional phrase *m jtj-mḥ(j)* in the first clause and *m btj* in the second.
9. *[m].ṯn j.n.j mj n3 m ḫntyt, jr.n.j* ᶜ*qw.ṯn r nfr* "Look, before I came upstream here, I made your rations to perfection" or "it was (only) after I made your rations to perfection that I came upstream here" — *j.n.j* is a perfect relative serving as an initial adverb clause; the rheme is the main clause *jr.n.j* ᶜ*qw.ṯn r nfr*.
10. *ḥḏ.n t3 jw.j ḥr.f mj wn bjk, ḫpr.n nw n stj-r s3s3.j sw* "At dawn I was on him like a falcon; by the time breakfast had come I was driving him back" — literally, "When the land became bright I was on him like a falcon; it was as I was driving him back that the time of breakfast happened"; *ḥḏ.n* and *ḫpr.n* are both perfect relative forms serving as initial adverb clauses; the rhemes are the main clauses *jw.j ḥr.f mj wn bjk* and *s3s3.j sw* (the latter an imperfective); *wn* is a perfective relative form (literally, "like (it) was a falcon").
11. *ḏd.n.j nn ḫft m3.n.j* "I have said this according as I have seen" or "It is according as I have seen that I have said this" — both *ḏd.n.j* and *m3.n.j* are perfect relative forms, the latter serving as object of the preposition *ḫft*; the rheme is the prepositional phrase.
12. *ḏd.j n mj mjn, snw bjn.(w), jnn.tw m ḏrḏrw r mt(r)t nt jb* "To whom can I speak today? Brothers have become bad: one turns to strangers for advice" — in the first sentence *ḏd.j* is a relative form serving as theme to the interrogative prepositional phrase *n mj*; in the last sentence *jnn.tw* is an imperfective relative form serving as theme to the prepositional phrase *r mt(r)t nt jb*.
13. *m.tn ḫt pr.tj,* ᶜ*ḫm.tw.s jr.f m mj,* ᶜ*ḫm.tw.s m jtnw n h* "Look, a fire has emerged. So, with what is it doused? It is doused with the ashes of the courtyard" — ᶜ*ḫm.tw.s* is a relative form in both clauses: in the first, the rheme is the interrogative prepositional phrase *m mj*; in the second, the prepositional phrase *m jtnw n h*.
14. *wnn t3 pn m mj, jtn ḥbs.w, nn psd.f ... wnn js ḥr-nb jd.(w) m g3(w).f* "What will this land be when the sun-disk is covered and will not shine ... since it is in his absence that everyone is senseless?" — *wnn* is an imperfective relative form in both clauses. In the first, the rheme is the interrogative prepositional phrase *m mj* "as what?"; in the second, the rheme is the prepositional phrase *m g3(w).f*. In the last clause, *wnn* makes it possible for the SUBJECT-stative construction *ḥr-nb jd.(w)* to function as a nonattributive relative form. The particle *js* indicates that this clause is subordinated: in this case, as an adverb clause.
15. *ḫpr.n tr n msyt s3ḥ.n.j r dmj ng3w, ḏ3.n.j m wsḫt nn ḥm(w).s* "When suppertime came I set foot at the harbor of Cattle-town. It was in a barge without a rudder that I crossed (the river)" — in the first sentence *ḫpr.n* is a perfect relative form serving as an initial adverb clause; the rheme is the main clause *s3ḥ.n.j r dmj ng3w*. In the second sentence *ḏ3.n.j* is also a perfect relative form; the rheme is the prepositional phrase *m wsḫt nn ḥm(w).s* (for *nn ḥm(w).s* see § 11.4).

16. *wꜤ pw n dd nṯr* "He is a unique one of the god's giving" — *dd nṯr* is an imperfective relative form serving as the second noun of an indirect genitive.
17. *jr.n.t(w).f r ḥ(w)t stjw r ptpt nmjw-šꜤ* "It is to strike the Beduin and to trample the Nomads that he has been made" — *jr.n.t(w).f* is a perfect relative; the prepositional phrases are the rheme.
18. *spr.n wḏ pn r.j ꜤḥꜤ.kw m ḥr(j) jb wḥwt.j, šd.n.t(w).f n.j dj.n.(j) wj ḥr ẖt.j* "This decree reached me as I was standing in the middle of my tribe. When it was read to me, I put myself on my belly" — in the first sentence, *spr.n* is a perfect relative form; the rheme is the adverb clause *ꜤḥꜤ.kw m ḥr(j) jb wḥwt.j*. In the second sentence *šd.n.t(w).f* is a perfect relative form serving as an initial adverb clause; the rheme is the main clause *dj.n.(j) wj ḥr ẖt.j*.
19. *jr.tw nn mj mj* "How was this done?" — *jr.tw* is a perfective relative form; the rheme is the interrogative prepositional phrase *mj mj* "like what?"
20. *jrr ḥm.k m mrr.f, Ꜥnḫ.tw m ṯ3w n dd.k* "Your Incarnation does as he wishes. It is from the air of your giving that one lives" — all four verb forms are imperfective relatives: *jrr* and *Ꜥnḫ.tw* serve as the predicate of emphatic sentences; the rhemes are the prepositional phrases; *mrr.f* serves as the object of the preposition *m*; *dd.k* is the second noun of an indirect genitive.
21. *ꜤḥꜤ.n ḏd.n.j n.s tm.t ẖn ḥr mj* "Then I said to her: 'Why do you not row?' " — *tm.t* is a nonattributive relative form serving as predicate of an emphatic sentence; the rheme is the interrogative prepositional phrase *ḥr mj* "on account of what?"
22. *jj.n.j Ꜥ3 r njs r.k m wpwt nt jt(j).j* "I have come here to summon you on a mission of my father" — *jj.n.j* is a perfect relative form; the rheme is the prepositional phrase *r njs r.k m wpwt nt jt(j).j*.
23. *tm.tw ms jn hnw ḥr mj* "Why indeed were the jars not brought?" — literally, "The jars were indeed not brought on account of what?" *tm.tw* is a perfective relative form; the rheme is the interrogative prepositional phrase *ḥr mj*.
24. *jr.t r tn(j) jdyt šrt* "Where were you making for, little girl?" — *jr.t* is a perfective relative form; the rheme is the interrogative prepositional phrase *r tn(j)* "to where?"
25. *pḥ.[n].ṯn nn ḥr zj jšst r ḫ3st ṯn ḫmt.n r(m)ṯ, jn jw h(3).n.ṯn ḥr w3wt ḥrt* "How have you reached here, to this foreign land that people have not known? Have you come down on roads of the sky?" — in the first sentence *pḥ.[n].ṯn* is a perfect relative serving as the predicate of a emphatic sentence; the rheme is the interrogative prepositional phrase *ḥr zj jšst* (literally, "upon which what?"). The second sentence is also emphatic, with the perfect relative *h(3).n.ṯn* as predicate; the rheme is the prepositional phrase *ḥr w3wt ḥrt*.
26. *ḥn r(m)ṯ Ꜥwt nt nṯr, jr.n.f pt t3 n jb.sn ... jr.n.f ṯ3w n jb Ꜥnḫ fnḏw.sn*
snnw.f pw prw m ḥꜤw.f, wbn.f m pt n jbw.sn ...
rmm.sn jw.f ḥr sḏm ... jw nṯr rḫ.w rn nb
"Take care of people, the flock of the god. It is for their heart that he has made the earth and the sky ... He has made air for the heart (just) so that their noses might live.
They are his likenesses, that came from his body. It is for their hearts that he rises in the sky ...
When they weep, he is listening ... For the god knows every name."
This text was quoted more extensively in Essay 5. Both instances of *jr.n.f* are perfect relative forms serving as the predicate of emphatic sentences. The rheme in the first is the prepositional phrase *n jb.sn*; in the second, it is the purpose clause *Ꜥnḫ fnḏw.sn* (§ 19.8.1). *wbn.f* is an imperfective relative form serving as predicate of an emphatic sentence; the rheme is the prepositional phrase *n jbw.sn*. *rmm.sn* is an imperfective relative form serving as an initial adverb clause; the rheme is the main clause *jw.f ḥr sḏm*.

Index

This index is divided into two parts, English terms (A) and Egyptian terms in transliteration (B). Single numbers refer to the Essays: for example, 8 = Essay 8. Compound numbers refer to the sections of each lesson: for instance, 4.6 = § 4.6. References to footnotes are cited by lesson and footnote number: for example, 9 n. 4 = Lesson 9, note 4. The slash (/) is used as an abbreviation for "and": for instance, 12.16.1/4 = § 12.16.1 and § 12.16.4.

A. English Terms

▨ indicating loss 24 n. 15
* (hypothetical mark) 3.1
2-lit. (verb class) 13.5.1
2ae-gem. (verb class) 13.5.2
3-lit. (verb class) 13.5.3
3ae-gem. (verb class) 13.5.5
3ae-inf. (verb class) 13.5.4
4-lit. (verb class) 13.5.6
4ae-inf. (verb class) 13.5.7
5-lit. (verb class) 13.5.8

Ability 18.14, 21.13
Abstract nouns 4.6
Abydos 14.14.1, 21
Action 26.10
Active (voice) 13.3.4, 26.12
Active participle 23.1, 23.6, 26.12
Address on letters 25
Adjectival predicate 7.2–5, 7.14–17, 8.5, 11.2, 11.6, 11.11.2, 15.6, 23.11, 25.3.4, 26.5, 26.15.2, 26.17–19
  participles as 23.11
Adjective 6.1, 23.9, 26.2, 26.5
  apparent 6.7
  as modifier 6.2–3, 6.5, 26.5
  as noun 6.4–5, 26.5
  comparative and superlative 6.8, 7.4
  interrogative 6.6, 7.5.4, 7.13, 26.5
  participles as 23.3, 23.9, 26.5
  relative forms as 24.4, 26.5
  stative as 17.20.1
  verb 13.2, 16.4, 17.7, 18.3, 26.5
Adjunct 14.6, 25.6
Administrative texts 24
Admonitions 19
Adverb 8.1, 8.11–17, 26.2, 26.6
  as rheme, in emphatic sentence 25.9
  comparative and superlative 8.17
Adverb clause 12.15, 23.19, 26.16, 26.19–27
  as rheme, in emphatic sentence 25.10, 26.28
  initial 25.11.2
  marked 12.16, 12.18, 18.11, 20.10, 20.16.3, 21.12, 22.13, 25.13
  markers 26.16
  of concomitant circumstance 14.11.1–2, 17.12, 20.10, 20.16.3, 25.11.2, 26.20, 26.23
  of future circumstance 21.6, 26.20
  of prior circumstance 18.11, 21.12, 25.11.2, 26.20, 26.23
  unmarked 12.17, 15.9, 17.12, 17.19, 18.11, 18.15, 19.8, 20.10, 20.14, 20.16.3, 20.17, 21.12–13, 22.13, 22.15, 25.11.2
  with adjectival predicate 12.16.1, 12.17
  with adverbial predicate 12.16.1–2, 12.17, 15.9, 26.20
  with imperfective 20.10–11, 26.20
  with *jw* 12.17, 15.9
  with *js* 12.16.3–4, 25.13
  with *jsṯ* 12.16.1/4, 15.9, 17.12, 21.12, 22.13
  with negated passive 21.13
  with negated perfect 18.15
  with *nj wnt* 22.15
  with *nj sḏmt.f* 22.13
  with *nn* 12.17, 18.15
  with nominal predicate 12.16.1/3, 12.17
  with nonattributive relative form 25.11.2, 26.20
  with passive 21.12, 26.20
  with perfect 18.11, 26.20
  with prospective *sḏm.f* 21.6, 26.20
  with pseudoverbal predicate 15.9, 26.20
  with stative 17.19, 17.20.1, 26.20
  with SUBJECT-stative construction 17.12, 26.20
  with subjunctive 19.8
  with *ṯj* 12.16.2
Adverbial forms of verb 26.31
Adverbial phrase 8.11

B. Egyptian Terms (in transliteration)